Communications
in Computer and Information Science 960

Commenced Publication in 2007
Founding and Former Series Editors:
Phoebe Chen, Alfredo Cuzzocrea, Xiaoyong Du, Orhun Kara, Ting Liu,
Dominik Ślęzak, and Xiaokang Yang

More information about this series at http://www.springer.com/series/7899

Huanguo Zhang · Bo Zhao
Fei Yan (Eds.)

Trusted Computing and Information Security

12th Chinese Conference, CTCIS 2018
Wuhan, China, October 18, 2018
Revised Selected Papers

 Springer

Editors
Huanguo Zhang
School of Cyber Science and Engineering
Wuhan University
Wuhan, China

Fei Yan
School of Cyber Science and Engineering
Wuhan University
Wuhan, China

Bo Zhao
School of Cyber Science and Engineering
Wuhan University
Wuhan, China

ISSN 1865-0929   ISSN 1865-0937 (electronic)
Communications in Computer and Information Science
ISBN 978-981-13-5912-5   ISBN 978-981-13-5913-2   (eBook)
https://doi.org/10.1007/978-981-13-5913-2

Library of Congress Control Number: 2018966820

This Springer imprint is published by the registered company Springer Nature Singapore Pte Ltd.
The registered company address is: 152 Beach Road, #21-01/04 Gateway East, Singapore 189721, Singapore

Preface

The 12th Chinese Conference on Trusted Computing and Information Security (CTCIS 2018) continued the series of events dedicated to trusted computing and information security, focusing on new theories, mechanisms, infrastructures, services, tools, and benchmarks. CTCIS provides a forum for researchers and developers in academia, industry, and government to share their excellent ideas and experiences in the areas of trusted computing and information security in the broad context of cloud computing, big data, Internet of Things, etc.

This year, CTCIS received 242 submissions. After a thorough reviewing process, 39 English papers and 34 Chinese papers were selected for presentation as full papers, with an acceptance rate of 30.2%. Furthermore, this year's CTCIS also included ten English papers and 16 Chinese papers as posters, with an acceptance rate of 10.7%. This volume contains the 24 English full papers presented at CTCIS 2018.

The high-quality program would not have been possible without the authors who chose CTCIS 2018 as a venue for their publications. We are also very grateful to the Program Committee members and Organizing Committee members, who put a tremendous amount of effort into soliciting and selecting research papers with a balance of high quality and new ideas and new applications.

We hope that you enjoy reading and benefit from the proceedings of CTCIS 2018.

October 2018

Huanguo Zhang
Bo Zhao
Fei Yan

Organization

CTCIS 2018 was organized by the China Computer Federation, and Wuhan University.

Organizing Committee

Conference Chair

Changxiang Shen Chinese Academy of Engineering, China

Conference Associate Chair

Huanguo Zhang Wuhan University, China

Program Chair

Bo Zhao Wuhan University, China

Program Associate Chair

Fei Yan Wuhan University, China

Steering Committee

Changxiang Shen	Chinese Academy of Engineering, China
Huanguo Zhang	Wuhan University, China
Zhong Chen	Peking University, China
Kefei Chen	Hangzhou Normal University, China
Dengguo Feng	Beijing Academy of Information Science and Technology, China
Zhen Han	Beijing Jiaotong University, China
Yeping He	Institute of Software Chinese Academy of Sciences, China
Jiwu Huang	Shenzhen University, China
Jiwu Jing	Institute of Information Engineering, Chinese Academy of Sciences, China
Jianhua Li	Shanghai Jiao Tong University, China
Jianwei Liu	Beihang University, China
Zhoujun Li	Beihang University, China
Jianfeng Ma	Xidian University, China
Zhiguang Qin	University of Electronic Science and Technology of China, China
Jinshu Su	National University of Defense Technology, China
Wenchang Shi	Renmin University of China, China
Qingxian Wang	Information Engineering University, China
Xiaoyun Wang	Tsinghua University, China

Zhiying Wang	National University of Defense Technology, China
Xiaoyao Xie	Guizhou Normal University, China
Xiaoyuan Yang	Engineering University of PAP, China
Yixian Yang	Beijing University of Posts and Telecommunications, China
Zhiqiang Zhu	Information Engineering University, China

Program Committee

Bo Zhao	Wuhan University, China
Fei Yan	Wuhan University, China
Zuling Chang	Zhengzhou University, China
Fei Chen	Shenzhen University, China
Kai Chen	Institute of Information Engineering, Chinese Academy of Sciences, China
Qingfeng Cheng	Information Engineering University, China
Ruizhong Du	Hebei University, China
Xiutao Feng	The System Science Institute of China Science Academy, China
Shaojing Fu	National University of Defense Technology, China
Wei Fu	Naval University of Engineering, China
Jianming Fu	Wuhan University, China
Shanqing Guo	Shandong University, China
Yuanbo Guo	Information Engineering University, China
Weili Han	Fudan University, China
Debiao He	Wuhan University, China
Wei Hu	Naval University of Engineering, China
Yupeng Hu	Hunan University, China
Qiong Huang	South China Agricultural University, China
Li Lin	Beijing University of Technology, China
Weizhong Qiang	Huazhong University of Science and Technology, China
Yu Qin	Institute of Software, Chinese Academy of Sciences, China
Longjiang Qu	National University of Defense Technology, China
Jun Shao	Zhejiang Gongshang University, China
Lei Sun	Information Engineering University, China
Ming Tang	Wuhan University, China
Shaohua Teng	Guangdong University of Technology, China
Donghai Tian	Beijing Institute of Technology, China
Yan Tong	Huazhong Agricultural University, China
Wei Wang	Beijing Jiaotong University, China
Wenxian Wang	Sichuan University, China
Zhibo Wang	Wuhan University, China
Qianhong Wu	Beihang University, China
Ming Xian	National University of Defense Technology, China
Liang Xiao	Xiamen University, China
Mingdi Xu	China Shipbuilding Industry Corporation, China
Peng Xu	Huazhong University of Science and Technology, China

Contents

Ciphertext-Policy Attribute-Based Encryption for Circuits from Lattices Under Weak Security Model

Jian Zhao$^{(\boxtimes)}$, Haiying Gao, and Bin Hu

Zhengzhou Information Science and Technology Institute, Zhengzhou 450001, China
back_zj@126.com

Abstract. The existing Ciphertext-Policy Attribute-Based Encryption (CP-ABE) scheme from lattices can only support a simple threshold access structure, resulting in its limited application scenario. In order to improve the flexibility and expressiveness of the CP-ABE scheme, we present a CP-ABE for circuits from lattices in this paper. The new scheme generates secret key for each attribute of the attribute set by invoking the sampling algorithm from lattices and embeds the attribute set into the secret keys. Meanwhile, to associate the ciphertext with a circuit, we design a Secret Matrix Distribution Mechanism (SMDM) for circuits, which distributes a matrix with specific form to each node of the circuit, and the scheme can generate the ciphertexts by combining the matrices of the leaf nodes. In the decryption phase, the SMDM guarantees the user who satisfies the access structure can decrypt the ciphertexts correctly. Finally, we prove that our scheme is secure against chosen plaintext attack in the selective weak security model under the Learning with Errors (LWE) assumptions.

Keywords: Ciphertext-policy · Attribute-Based Encryption (ABE)
Learning with Errors (LWE) · Lattices · Circuits

1 Introduction

Cloud storage synthesizes a large number of storage devices in the network by some softwares, and then provides data storage and access services. In consideration of security, the data is encrypted before uploading to the cloud. However, it is very cumbersome and uncontrollable for users to access cloud data by traditional encryption methods. In the existing cryptography methods, Attribute-Based Encryption (ABE) gets many researchers attention for its fine-grained access control ability.

In 2005, Sahai et al. [1] introduced the notion of ABE. Through the introduction of attribute set and access structure the ABE gives us unprecedented flexibility and expressiveness with which recipients can be designated in a wholesale manner. In 2006, Goyal et al. [2] divided ABE into two variants: Key-Policy

© Springer Nature Singapore Pte Ltd. 2019
H. Zhang et al. (Eds.): CTCIS 2018, CCIS 960, pp. 1–15, 2019.
https://doi.org/10.1007/978-981-13-5913-2_1

Attribute-Based Encryption (KP-ABE) and Ciphertext-Policy Attribute-Based Encryption (CP-ABE). A KP-ABE means that the secret key of a user is labeled with an access structure while the ciphertext is labeled with a set of descriptive attributes. A CP-ABE, by contrast, means that the ciphertext is associated with an access structure and the secret key is associated with a set of descriptive attributes. A particular user can decrypt the ciphertexts only if his attribute set satisfies the access structure.

Generally speaking, CP-ABE schemes are more difficult to design and be proved secure than KP-ABE schemes. In practical application, KP-ABE schemes are suitable for situations when access specific static data, and have advantages when the system adds new users or elevates some users access permissions. CP-ABE schemes are suitable for dynamic access control of arbitrary data, and the senders can directly control the decryption permissions of the message, which is closer to the actual situation in real life [3].

The existing ABE schemes are mainly based on the machinery of bilinear maps or lattices and the lattice-based cryptosystem is considered as an important post-quantum cryptography for its quantum attack resistance. Moreover, the lattice-based cryptosystem has other advantages, e.g. worst-case hardness, high efficiency and rich mathematical structure.

In 2012, Shweta Agrawal constructed an efficient Fuzzy Identity-Based Encryption (FIBE) scheme and an insecure KP-ABE scheme based on the standard learning with errors (LWE) problem in [4]. Jiang Zhang proposed a CP-ABE scheme from lattices, which supports flexible threshold access policy on literal (or Boolean) attributes in [5] at the same year. Xavier Boyen developed the idea further by introducing linear secret sharing scheme (LSSS) into access policy in [6] in 2013.

The ABE scheme of [7] supports a subclass of circuits called OR-restricted circuits. OR-restricted circuits are those that for any input x, if $f(x) = 0$, then for all the OR gates in circuit f, at least one of its incoming wires will evaluate to 0. Although this scheme supports a very limited subclass of circuits, it has accumulated rich experience in constructing an ABE scheme for circuits from lattices.

The ABE scheme of [8] presents a type of recoding mechanism called Two-to-One Recoding (TOR). The authors successfully construct the relationships between TOR and circuits, TOR and ABE, and TOR and LWE, then propose an ABE scheme for general circuits of any arbitrary polynomial size.

The key-homomorphism ABE scheme of [9] provides two advantages over previous ones. First, its secret keys are much shorter. Second, it supports general circuits with arbitrary fan-in (and fan-out) gates. Compared with a Boolean circuit with gates of fan-in two, a circuit with gates of arbitrary fan-in has shallower depth and smaller size; the parameters and ciphertexts are subsequently smaller than those of previous schemes, thus rendering this scheme more efficient. However, this scheme is only suited for environments where access policies are expressed as arithmetic circuits, or capture statistical properties of the data or depend on arithmetic transformations of the data. This scheme would not be appropriate when access policies are expressed as circuits with AND gates and OR gates.

In 2014, Yongtao Wang presented a CP-ABE scheme for AND-gates in [10]. In 2015, Boyen [11] proposed a KP-ABE scheme for deterministic finite automata and their scheme is simpler and more efficient than previous schemes.

Table 1. Development of ABE from lattices.

Scheme	Access policy	Access structure
[10]	Ciphertext-Policy	AND gate
[5]	Ciphertext-Policy	(t, n) threshold
[6]	Key-Policy	LSSS
[7]	Key-Policy	Subclass of circuits
[8]	Key-Policy	General circuits
[9]	Key-Policy	Arithmetic circuits
[11]	Key-Policy	Deterministic finite automata

From the development of ABE from lattices in Table 1, we found that the KP-ABE schemes occupy most of the ABE schemes, and the CP-ABE schemes are few. The CP-ABE scheme, which has the best results, can only support the threshold access structure, and the expressiveness and flexibility of the scheme are poor. In this case, an ABE scheme with advantages of ciphertext policy for flexible circuit access structure from lattices is proposed in this paper.

1.1 Our Work

In the existing KP-ABE schemes for circuits from lattice like [7,8], generating corresponding secret key for each node of a circuit by the public matrices and the master key is a usual method when the scheme tries to embed the information of the circuit into secret keys. However, the circuit is associated with ciphertext in a CP-ABE scheme. Some public matrices and randomly selected vector are the only information the sender can get when generating the ciphertext, so how to embed a circuit into the ciphertext in a CP-ABE scheme is a difficult problem.

To solve the problem in constructing a CP-ABE scheme for circuits from lattices, we design a Secret Matrix Distribution Mechanism (SMDM) for circuits. From the root node of the circuit, this mechanism distributes a matrix calculated by a random vector and other matrices containing random information to each node layer by layer. At the same time, the matrices assigned to the child nodes can reconstruct the matrix of their parent node, which ensures that the users who satisfy the ac-cess structure can decrypt ciphertexts correctly. Finally, the SMDM can distribute a matrix to each leaf node of the circuit, and the scheme can generate the ciphertexts by combining these matrices. It is important to note that all these matrices have a unified form, which is calculated by a random vector multiplied by a selected vector and multiple matrices from specific distributions. The unified form ensures that the challenger can effectively return challenge ciphertexts from the LWE samples when prove security of the scheme.

In conclusion, we present a CP-ABE for circuits from lattices and prove that the new scheme is secure against chosen plaintext attack in the selective weak security model under the LWE assumptions in this paper.

2 Preliminaries

2.1 Symbol Description and Basic Definitions

We use uppercase boldface alphabet for matrices, as in $\mathbf{A}$, lowercase boldface characters for vectors, as in $\mathbf{e}$, swash letter for attribute set, as in $\mathcal{S}$, and lowercase regular characters for scalars, as in l. For any integer $q \geq 2$, we let $\mathbb{Z}_q$ denote the ring of integers module q and we represent $\mathbb{Z}_q$ as integers in $(-q/2, q/2]$. We let $\mathbb{Z}_q^{n \times m}$ denote the set of $n \times m$ matrices with entries in $\mathbb{Z}_q$. The notation $\mathbf{A}^{\mathrm{T}}$ denotes the transpose of matrix $\mathbf{A}$. $[\mathbf{A}_1 | \mathbf{A}_2]$ denotes the $n \times (m + m')$ matrix formed by concatenating $\mathbf{A}_1$ and $\mathbf{A}_2$, where $\mathbf{A}_1$ is an $n \times m$ matrix and $\mathbf{A}_2$ is an $n \times m'$ matrix. $\lfloor q/2 \rfloor$ denotes the maximum integer less than q/2. $\lceil q/2 \rceil$ denotes the minimum integer greater than q/2. Here are some common definitions of lattices.

Integer Lattices [9]: Find an $m \times m$ matrix $\mathbf{B}$ whose columns are linearly independent vectors $\mathbf{b}_1, \cdots, \mathbf{b}_m \in \mathbb{Z}^m$. Then the m-dimensional integer lattice $\Lambda \in \mathbb{Z}^m$ generated by $\mathbf{B}$ is the following set ($\mathbf{B}$ can be called a basis of lattice Λ):

$$\Lambda = \mathcal{L}(\mathbf{B}) = \left\{ \mathbf{y} \in \mathbb{Z}^m \quad s.t. \quad \begin{array}{l} \exists \mathbf{s} = (s_1, \cdots, s_m) \in \mathbb{Z}^m, \\ \mathbf{y} = \mathbf{Bs} = \sum_{i=1}^{m} s_i \mathbf{b}_i \end{array} \right\}$$

For prime q, $\mathbf{A} \in \mathbb{Z}_q^{n \times m}$, and $\mathbf{u} \in \mathbb{Z}_q^n$, we can also define integer lattices as

$$\Lambda_q(\mathbf{A}) = \left\{ \mathbf{e} \in \mathbb{Z}^m \quad s.t. \quad \exists \mathbf{s} \in \mathbb{Z}_q^n, \mathbf{A}^{\mathrm{T}} \mathbf{s} = \mathbf{e} \,(\mathrm{mod}q) \right\}$$
$$\Lambda_q^{\perp}(\mathbf{A}) = \{ \mathbf{e} \in \mathbb{Z}^m \quad s.t. \quad \mathbf{Ae} = \mathbf{0} \,(\mathrm{mod}q) \}$$
$$\Lambda_q^{\mathbf{u}}(\mathbf{A}) = \{ \mathbf{e} \in \mathbb{Z}^m \quad s.t. \quad \mathbf{Ae} = \mathbf{u} \,(\mathrm{mod}q) \}$$

Matrix Norms [9,12]: Let matrix $\mathbf{R} = \{\mathbf{r}_1, \cdots, \mathbf{r}_k\} \in \mathbb{Z}^{m \times k}$, where $\mathbf{r}_i = (r_{i,1}, \ldots, r_{i,m})^{\mathrm{T}} (1 \leq i \leq k)$ is a column vector. We use the following notations.

$||\mathbf{r}_i||$: $||\mathbf{r}_i|| = \sqrt{\sum_{j=1}^{m} (r_{i,j})^2}$ denotes the l_2 length of $\mathbf{r}_i$.

$||\mathbf{r}_i||_1$: $||\mathbf{r}_i||_1 = \sum_{j=1}^{m} |r_{i,j}|$ denotes the sum of the absolute values of all elements in $\mathbf{r}_i$.

$||\mathbf{r}_i||_\infty$: $||\mathbf{r}_i||_\infty = \max_j |r_{i,j}|$ denotes the maximum of all the absolute values of the elements in $\mathbf{r}_i$.

$||\mathbf{R}||$: $||\mathbf{R}|| = \max||\mathbf{r}_i||$ ($1 \leq i \leq k$) denotes the length of the longest vector in $\mathbf{R}$.

$||\mathbf{R}||_1$: $||\mathbf{R}||_1 = \max_i ||\mathbf{r}_i||_1$ denotes the maximum of $||\mathbf{r}_i||_1$ in $\mathbf{R}$.

$||\mathbf{R}||_2$: $||\mathbf{R}||_2 = \sup_{||x||=1} ||\mathbf{R}x||$ is the operator norm of $\mathbf{R}$.

Note that always $||\mathbf{R}|| \leq ||\mathbf{R}||_2 \leq \sqrt{k}||\mathbf{R}||$.

Discrete Gaussians [13]: Let m be a positive integer and $\Lambda \in \mathbb{R}^m$ an m-dimensional lattice. For any vector $\mathbf{c} \in \mathbb{R}^m$ and any positive parameter $\sigma \in \mathbb{R}$, we define:

$\rho_{\sigma,c}(x) = \exp\left(-\pi\frac{||x-c||^2}{\sigma^2}\right)$ denotes a Gaussian-shaped function on with center $\mathbf{c}$ and parameter σ.

$\rho_{\sigma,c}(\Lambda) = \sum_{x \in \Lambda} \rho_{\sigma,c}(x)$ denotes a (always converging) discrete integral of $\rho_{\sigma,c}$ over the lattice Λ.

$D_{\Lambda,\sigma,c}$ denotes a discrete Gaussian distribution over Λ with center $\mathbf{c}$ and parameter σ,

$$\forall y \in \Lambda, D_{\Lambda,\sigma,c}(y) = \frac{\rho_{\sigma,c}(y)}{\rho_{\sigma,c}(\Lambda)}$$

For notational convenience, $D_{\Lambda,\sigma,0}$ are abbreviated as $D_{\Lambda,\sigma}$ or $D_\sigma(\Lambda)$.

2.2   Circuits

We describe a circuit f based on the definition of circuits in [14]. According to the discussion of [15], we can transform any Boolean circuit to a monotonic circuit with the same depth. Therefore, the circuits mentioned in this article are all monotonic, i.e. only have AND and OR gates.

The whole circuit consists of nodes and wires. The nodes are divided into two classes: leaf nodes and non-leaf nodes. The leaf nodes which are associated with attributes are the inputs of a circuit. A leaf node will input 1 if a user gets this attribute, otherwise input 0. We call the interior nodes of a circuit which are AND gates or OR gates as non-leaf nodes. Besides, the root node, one of the non-leaf nodes, gives us the final output of a circuit.

The wires linking up two neighboring layers of a circuit pass the output of a node in lower layer to a node in higher layer and do not change the value of the output. For two nodes been linked up, we call the node in lower layer the child node and regard another node as its parent node.

A circuit starting with the inputs of leaf nodes which are associated with attributes, through the connection of wires and interior non-leaf nodes which are AND gates and OR gates, ends with the output of root node which is also a gate.

$Gatetype : Gates \rightarrow \{\text{AND}, \text{OR}\}$ is a function that identifies a gate is either an AND gate or an OR gate. We have

$$Gatetype(\omega) = \text{AND} : g(x_0, x_1) = x_0 x_1$$

$$Gatetype(\omega) = \text{OR} : g(x_0, x_1) = 1 - (1 - x_0)(1 - x_1)$$

where x_0 and x_1 are the inputs of node ω.

2.3   LWE and Relevant Algorithms

For a positive integer n, a prime $q = q(n) > 2$, and a secret vector $\mathbf{s} \in \mathbb{Z}_q^n$, A $(\mathbb{Z}_q, n, \mathcal{X}) - \text{LWE}$ problem instance consists of access to an unspecified challenge oracle O. It is either from a noisy pseudo-random sampler $O_{\mathbf{s}}$ of the form $(\mathbf{w}_i, v_i) = (\mathbf{w}_i, \mathbf{w}_i^T \mathbf{s} + e_i) \in \mathbb{Z}_q^n \times \mathbb{Z}_q$ carrying some constant uniformly chosen $\mathbf{s} \in \mathbb{Z}_q^n$, where $e_i \in \mathbb{Z}_q$ is a fresh noise component in distribution $\mathcal{X}$, and $\mathbf{w}_i \in \mathbb{Z}_q^n$ is a fresh uniformly distributed vector, or from a truly random sampler $O_{\tilde{\mathbf{s}}}$ of the form $(\mathbf{w}_i, v_i)$ [16].

The LWE problem is: given a $poly(n)$ number of samples, output 0 if they are from O_s or 1 if they are from $O_{\tilde{s}}$.

An algorithm $\mathcal{A}$ can decide the LWE problem if $\rho = |\Pr[\mathcal{A}^{O_{\mathbf{s}}} = 1] - \Pr[\mathcal{A}^{O_{\tilde{\mathbf{s}}}} = 1]|$ is non-negligible for a random $\mathbf{s} \in \mathbb{Z}_q^n$ after it makes a number of queries to the challenge oracle.

Notably, the $\mathcal{X}_{\max}$-bounded distribution $\mathcal{X}$ means that there is always $||\mathbf{e}_i|| \leq \mathcal{X}_{\max}$ for any noise vector $\mathbf{e}_i$ sampled from distribution $\mathcal{X}$ in problem. The difficulty of the LWE problem is measured by the ratio $q/\mathcal{X}_{\max} > 1$. The problem remains hard when $q/\mathcal{X}_{\max} < 2^{n^{\varepsilon}}$ for some fixed $\varepsilon \in (0, 1/2)$ and the smaller the ratio is the harder the problem [17].

Let n, m, $q > 0$ be integers with q prime. There are polynomial time algorithms Algorithm 1–3 as follows:

Algorithm 1. TrapGen$(1^n, 1^m, q) \rightarrow (\mathbf{A}, \mathbf{T_A})$ [13]: A randomized algorithm that, when $m = \Theta(n \log q)$, outputs a full-rank matrix and basis for $\Lambda_q^{\perp}(A)$ such that $\mathbf{A}$ is $\text{negl}(n)$-close to uniform and $||\tilde{T}_A|| = O(\sqrt{n \log q})$, with all but negligible probability in n.

Algorithm 2. RightSample$(\mathbf{A}, \mathbf{T_A}, \mathbf{B}, \mathbf{P}, \sigma) \rightarrow \mathbf{K}$ [17]: An algorithm that given full-rank matrices $\mathbf{A}, \mathbf{B} \in \mathbb{Z}_q^{n \times m}$, a basis $\mathbf{T_A} \in \mathbb{Z}^{m \times m}$ of $\Lambda_q^{\perp}(\mathbf{A})$, a randomly selected matrix $\mathbf{P} \in \mathbb{Z}_q^{n \times (h+n)}$, when $\sigma = ||\tilde{\mathbf{T}}_\mathbf{A}|| \cdot \omega(\sqrt{\log 2m})$ outputs a matrix $\mathbf{K} \in \mathbb{Z}_q^{2m \times (h+n)}$ whose distribution is statistically close to $D_{\Lambda_q^{\mathbf{P}}(\mathbf{A}|\mathbf{B}), \sigma}$ and satisfies $(\mathbf{A}|\mathbf{B})\mathbf{K} = \mathbf{P}$.

Algorithm 3. LeftSample$(\mathbf{A}, \mathbf{B}, \mathbf{R}, \mathbf{T_B}, \mathbf{P}, \sigma) \rightarrow \mathbf{K}$ [9,17,18]: An algorithm that given full-rank matrices $\mathbf{A}, \mathbf{B} \in \mathbb{Z}_q^{n \times m}$, a basis $\mathbf{T_B} \in \mathbb{Z}^{m \times m}$ of $\Lambda_q^{\perp}(\mathbf{B})$, a low-norm matrix $\mathbf{R} \in \mathbb{Z}_q^{m \times m}$, a randomly selected matrix $\mathbf{P} \in \mathbb{Z}_q^{n \times (h+n)}$, when $\sigma = O(||\mathbf{R}||_2)$ outputs a matrix $\mathbf{K} \in \mathbb{Z}_q^{2m \times (h+n)}$ whose distribution is statistically close to $D_{\Lambda_q^{\mathbf{P}}(\mathbf{A}|\mathbf{AR}+\mathbf{B}), \sigma}$ and satisfies $(\mathbf{A}|\mathbf{AR} + \mathbf{B})\mathbf{K} = \mathbf{P}$.

Here are two Lemmas that we will use in our schemes.

Lemma 1 [9]: For integers n, m, k, q, $\sigma > 0$, matrices $\mathbf{A} \in \mathbb{Z}_q^{n \times m}$ and $\mathbf{U} \in \mathbb{Z}_q^{n \times k}$, if $\mathbf{K} \in \mathbb{Z}_q^{m \times k}$ is sampled from $D_{\sigma}(\Lambda_q^{\mathbf{U}}(\mathbf{A}))$ and $\mathbf{R}$ is sampled uniformly in $\{\pm 1\}^{m \times m}$, then

$$||\mathbf{K}|| \leq \sigma\sqrt{m}, \quad ||\mathbf{K}^{\mathrm{T}}||_2 \leq \sqrt{k} \cdot ||\mathbf{K}|| \leq \sigma\sqrt{mk}$$

$$||\mathbf{K}||_2 \le \sigma\sqrt{mk}, \quad ||\mathbf{R}||_2 \le 20\sqrt{m}$$

Lemma 2 [17]: Suppose that $m > (n+1)\log q + \omega(\log n)$. Choose $\mathbf{A} \in \mathbb{Z}_q^{n \times m}$, $\mathbf{B} \in \mathbb{Z}_q^{n \times k}$ and $\mathbf{R} \in \{-1,1\}^{m \times k}$. Then, for all vectors $\mathbf{w} \in \mathbb{Z}^m$, the distribution $(\mathbf{A}, \mathbf{AR}, \mathbf{R}^T\mathbf{w})$ is statistically close to the distribution $(\mathbf{A}, \mathbf{B}, \mathbf{R}^T\mathbf{w})$.

2.4 Definition and Weak Security Model of CP-ABE

Take an encrypted communication system of a company, for example of CP-ABE. The CEO wants some staffs to write some investigation reports about sports goods and he will send an encrypted message embedded with access policy of circuit (Fig. 1) to all staffs. Suppose node 1 is associated with the attribute of age 20–25, node 2 with the attribute of age 25–30, node 3 with the attribute of age 30–35, node 4 with the attribute of male, node 5 with the attribute of working at planning division. Every employee in this company can be described in a three tuple (age, gender, office). For instance, here are several staffs Alice (25, female, sales division), Abel (25, male, sales division), Alina (25, female, planning division) and Adam (45, male, planning division). After receiving the message, only Abel and Alina can decrypt the message while Alice is a lady but not in planning division and Adam is too old. So we can see that the CEO wants some young men or some young planning experts to write these investigation reports about sports goods. Maybe, he thinks that young men are very close to sports and staffs in planning division are better at investigating.

Compared with the traditional public key encryption scheme, the above example shows us the flexibility and expressiveness of an ABE scheme.

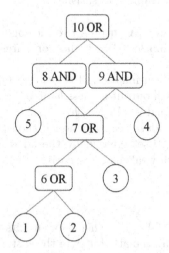

Fig. 1. Circuit access structure

Definition 1 (CP-ABE for circuits). A CP-ABE for circuit f consists of the following four algorithms:

Setup $(1^\lambda, \mathcal{W}, l) \rightarrow (\text{PP}, \text{MSK})$. This is a randomized algorithm that takes a security parameter λ, an attribute set $\mathcal{W}$ including all the attributes in the system and the number of inputs of the circuit l. It outputs a public key PP and a master key MSK.

Enc $(\text{PP}, f, \mathbf{H}) \rightarrow \text{CT}$. This is a randomized algorithm that takes as input a public key PP, a message matrix $\mathbf{H}$, and a description of a circuit f. It outputs a ciphertext CT.

KeyGen $(\text{PP}, \text{MSK}, \mathcal{S}) \rightarrow \text{SK}$. This is a randomized algorithm that takes as input the public key PP, the master secret key MSK and the attribute set of user $\mathcal{S}$. It outputs a decryption key SK.

Dec $(\text{SK}, \text{CT}) \rightarrow \mathbf{H}$. This algorithm takes a decryption key SK, and a ciphertext CT. It outputs $\mathbf{H}$ or a special symbol $\bot$.

Definition 2 (Weak Security Model of CP-ABE for Circuits) [19]: A CP-ABE scheme is said to be weak secure against selective chosen plaintext attack (CPA) if the advantage of adversary is negligible in the following game between a challenger B and an adversary A:

Target. The adversary A announces a target circuit f^* to be challenged upon.

Setup. The challenger B runs the Setup algorithm, then he gives the PP to the adversary A and keeps MSK to himself.

Queries. The adversary A can adaptively make a number of key generation queries on attribute set $\mathcal{S}^*$ with constraint that any attribute in $\mathcal{S}^*$ is not an input of circuit f^* (and certainly $\mathcal{S}^*$ satisfies $f^*(\mathcal{S}^*) = 0$). The challenger B returns the secret key SK.

Challenge. At some time, A outputs two messages $\mathbf{H}_0$ and $\mathbf{H}_1$. The challenger B flips a random coin $b \in \{0, 1\}$ and computes CT from message $\mathbf{H}_b$. Then B gives CT to A.

Continuation. This a continuation of the earlier Queries phase.

Decision. Finally, A will output a guess b' of b. The advantage of an adversary A in this game is defined as $|\Pr[b' = b] - 1/2|$.

Compared with the standard security model, the weak model requires more restrictions on the attribute set queried by the adversary in the Queries and Continuation phases, which weakens the security of the model to some extent.

3   Construction

In this section, we present a CP-ABE scheme for circuits from lattices. $\mathcal{W}$ denotes an attribute set including all the attributes in the system and $\mathcal{S} \subseteq \mathcal{W}$ is a user's attribute set. Moreover, all the inputs in circuit f compose an attribute set $\mathcal{L} \subseteq \mathcal{W}$, where $|\mathcal{L}| = l$. The scheme is made up of the following four algorithms.

Setup $(1^\lambda, \mathcal{W}, l) \rightarrow (\text{PP}, \text{MSK})$. Given a security parameter λ, an attribute set $\mathcal{W}$, and the number of circuits inputs l.

1. The algorithm first generates integers $n = n(\lambda, l)$, $q = q(n)$, $m = \Theta(n \log q)$.
2. Generate a uniformly random matrix $\mathbf{A}_0 \in \mathbb{Z}_q^{n \times m}$ with a full-rank m-vector sets $\mathbf{T}_{\mathbf{A}_0} \subseteq \Lambda_q^{\perp}(\mathbf{A}_0)$ that satisfies a low-norm condition through invoking $\mathbf{TrapGen}(1^n, 1^m, q)$.
3. Choose two uniform random matrices $\mathbf{B}, \mathbf{U} \in \mathbb{Z}_q^{n \times m}$; for $i \in \mathcal{W}$, choose a uniform random matrix $\mathbf{A}_i \in \mathbb{Z}_q^{n \times m}$.
4. Finally, return the public parameters PP and master key MSK:

$$\text{PP} = \{\mathbf{A}_0, \mathbf{B}, \{\mathbf{A}_i\}_{i \in \mathcal{W}}, \mathbf{U}\} \qquad \text{MSK} = \{\mathbf{T}_{\mathbf{A}_0}\}$$

KeyGen (MSK, $\mathcal{S}$) $\rightarrow$ SK. This algorithm takes as input the master key MSK and a user's attribute set $\mathcal{S}$.

1. For $i \in \mathcal{S}$, compute

$$\mathbf{K}_i \leftarrow \mathbf{RightSample}(\mathbf{A}_0, \mathbf{T}_{\mathbf{A}_0}, \mathbf{A}_i + \mathbf{B}, \mathbf{U}, \sigma)$$

where $\mathbf{K}_i$ satisfies $(\mathbf{A}_0 | (\mathbf{A}_i + \mathbf{B})) \mathbf{K}_i = \mathbf{U}$.
2. Output

$$\text{SK} = \{\mathbf{K}_i \in \mathbb{Z}^{2m \times m}\}_{i \in \mathcal{S}}$$

Enc (PP, f, $\mathbf{H} \in \{0,1\}^{m \times n}$) $\rightarrow$ CT. This algorithm takes as input the public parameters PP, a circuit f and a message matrix $\mathbf{H} \in \{0,1\}^{m \times n}$.

1. Choose a uniform random vector $\mathbf{s} \in \mathbb{Z}_q^n$ and $\mathbf{e}_0$, $\mathbf{e} \leftarrow \mathcal{X}^m$, where $\mathcal{X}$ is a $\mathcal{X}_{\max}$-bounded noise distribution in $(\mathbb{Z}_q, n, \mathcal{X}) - \text{LWE}$.
2. The SMDM assigns a random matrix to each node of the circuit f. In particular, node ω corresponds to a matrix $\mathbf{S}^{\omega} = \mathbf{s}\mathbf{d}^{\mathrm{T}}\mathbf{D}^{\omega} \in \mathbb{Z}_q^{n \times n}$, where $\mathbf{d}$ is an n-vector chosen from a specific distribution and $\mathbf{D}^{\omega}$ is an $n \times n$-matrix determined by the following SMDM and the circuit, and the child nodes ω_0 and ω_1 respectively correspond to matrices $\mathbf{S}^{\omega_0} \in \mathbb{Z}_q^{n \times n}$ and $\mathbf{S}^{\omega_1} \in \mathbb{Z}_q^{n \times n}$, where both matrices have specific forms similar to matrix $\mathbf{S}^{\omega}$. Now, we introduce how SMDM works as follows.

First define a matrix $\mathbf{S}^{\omega} = \mathbf{s}\bar{\mathbf{d}}^{\mathrm{T}}\mathbf{I}$ corresponding to the root node, where $\bar{\mathbf{d}}$ is chosen from $\{0, \pm 1\}^n$ and $\mathbf{I}$ denotes an $n \times n$ identity matrix, and here $\mathbf{D}^{\omega} = \mathbf{I}$, so the root node owns a matrix with the specific form $\mathbf{S}^{\omega} = \mathbf{s}\bar{\mathbf{d}}^{\mathrm{T}}\mathbf{D}^{\omega}$. Then construct the sharing matrix for other nodes from top to bottom.

(1) If $Gatetype(\omega) = OR$, let $\mathbf{S}^{\omega_0} = \mathbf{S}^{\omega_1} = \mathbf{S}^{\omega}$.
(2) If $Gatetype(\omega) = AND$, there are two situations as follows.
  (a) If node ω is a root node, or it links to the root node only through some OR gates, we have $\mathbf{S}^{\omega} = \mathbf{s}\bar{\mathbf{d}}^{\mathrm{T}}\mathbf{I}$. Then compute $\mathbf{S}^{\omega_0} = \mathbf{S}^{r_0} = \mathbf{s}\mathbf{d}_0^{\mathrm{T}}\mathbf{I}$, where $\mathbf{d}_0$ is chosen from $\{0, \pm 1\}^n$, and compute $\mathbf{S}^{\omega_1} = \mathbf{S}^{r_1} = \mathbf{s}\mathbf{d}_1^{\mathrm{T}}\mathbf{I}$, where $\mathbf{d}_1 = \bar{\mathbf{d}} - \mathbf{d}_0$. Here $\mathbf{D}^{\omega_0} = \mathbf{D}^{\omega_1} = \mathbf{I}$, $\mathbf{S}^{\omega} = \mathbf{S}^{\omega_0} + \mathbf{S}^{\omega_1}$ and both child nodes own matrices with specific form.

(b) If node ω links to the root node through k $(1 \leq k \leq \log l)$ AND gates and some (maybe 0) OR gates, we have $\mathbf{S}^{r_i}(i \in \{0,1\})$ and $\mathbf{D}^\omega$ from $\mathbf{S}^\omega = \mathbf{sd}_i^T \mathbf{D}^\omega$. Compute $\mathbf{S}^{\omega_0} = \mathbf{S}^{r_i} \mathbf{D}^{\omega_0} = \mathbf{sd}_i^T \mathbf{D}^{\omega_0}$, where $\mathbf{D}^{\omega_0}$ is randomly chosen from $\{\pm 1\}^{n \times n}$; Let $\mathbf{D}^{\omega_1} = \mathbf{D}^\omega - \mathbf{D}^{\omega_0}$, and compute $\mathbf{S}^{\omega_1} = \mathbf{S}^{r_i} \mathbf{D}^{\omega_1} = \mathbf{sd}_i^T \mathbf{D}^{\omega_1}$. In fact, matrix $\mathbf{D}^{\omega_1}$ may be constructed from k matrices from $\{\pm 1\}^{n \times n}$. Concretely, $\mathbf{D}^{\omega_1} = \mathbf{I} - (\mathbf{D}^{\omega_0})_1 - \ldots - (\mathbf{D}^{\omega_0})_k$, where $(\mathbf{D}^{\omega_0})_i$ $(i \in [k])$ denotes the $\mathbf{D}$ matrix corresponding to the child node ω_0 of node ω that links to the root node through i AND gates. Here $\mathbf{S}^\omega = \mathbf{S}^{\omega_0} + \mathbf{S}^{\omega_1}$.

Note that we define $\mathbf{S} = \mathbf{s\bar{d}}^T \mathbf{I} \in \mathbb{Z}_q^{n \times n}$ in the special circuit consisting only OR gates, where $\mathbf{\bar{d}}$ is chosen from $\{0, \pm 1\}^n$, and all nodes correspond to matrix $\mathbf{S}$.

Finally, each leaf node i $(i \in [l])$ of circuit f corresponds to a matrix $\mathbf{S}_i$ according to the SMDM described above. Concretely, $\mathbf{S}_i = \mathbf{sd}_{i_1}^T \mathbf{D}^i$ $(i_1 \in \{0,1\})$, where $\mathbf{D}^i$ is determined by SMDM and the circuit f.

3. For $i \in \mathcal{L}$, choose a uniform random matrix $\mathbf{R}_i \in \{-1,1\}^{m \times m}(i \in \{0,1\})$ and compute $\mathbf{E}_i = \mathbf{ed}_{i_1}^T \mathbf{D}^i$ $(i_1 \in \{0,1\})$. Then compute

$$\mathbf{C}_0 = \mathbf{U}^T \mathbf{s\bar{d}}^T + \mathbf{H} \lfloor q/2 \rfloor + \mathbf{e}_0 \mathbf{\bar{d}}^T$$

$$\mathbf{C'}_i = \mathbf{A}_0^T \mathbf{S}_i + \mathbf{E}_i$$

$$\mathbf{C}_i = (\mathbf{A}_i + \mathbf{B})^T \mathbf{S}_i + \mathbf{R}_i \mathbf{E}_i$$

4. Finally, output

$$\mathrm{CT} = \{\mathbf{C}_0 \in \mathbb{Z}_q^{m \times n}, \{(\mathbf{C'}_i, \mathbf{C}_i) \in (\mathbb{Z}_q^{m \times n}, \mathbb{Z}_q^{m \times n})\}_{i \in \mathcal{L}}\}$$

Dec $(\mathrm{SK}, \mathrm{CT}) \to \mathbf{H}$. This algorithm takes as input the secret key SK and a ciphertext CT. We attach a matrix $\mathbf{O}_\omega$ to each node ω. Suppose the user's attribute set is $\mathcal{S}$, then we show the decryption process as follows.

1. For a leaf node $i \in \mathcal{S}$, compute $\mathbf{O}_i = \mathbf{K}_i^T \left(\frac{\mathbf{C'}_i}{\mathbf{C}_i} \right)$.
2. The algorithm computes the corresponding matrix $\mathbf{O}$ of each node in the circuit by the known matrices $\mathbf{O}_i$ $(i \in \mathcal{S})$ of leaf nodes from the bottom to the top. For a non-leaf node ω (with matrix $\mathbf{O}_\omega$ and output x_ω), it has two child nodes ω_0 (with matrix $\mathbf{O}_{\omega_0}$ and output x_{ω_0}) and ω_1 (with matrix $\mathbf{O}_{\omega_1}$ and output x_{ω_1}).

If $x_\omega = 0$, the algorithm cannot compute $\mathbf{O}_\omega$ for node ω due to the lack of the required matrix $\mathbf{O}$ of its child nodes.

If $x_\omega = 1$ and $Gatetype(\omega) = \mathrm{OR}$, let $\mathbf{O}_\omega = \mathbf{O}_{\omega_i}$ $(x_{\omega_i} = 1, i \in \{0,1\})$; or $Gatetype(\omega) = \mathrm{AND}$, let $\mathbf{O}_\omega = \mathbf{O}_{\omega_0} + \mathbf{O}_{\omega_1}$.

Finally, we can get the matrix $\mathbf{O}_r$ for root node r.

3. Compute $\mathbf{O'} = \mathbf{C}_0 - \mathbf{O}_r$. $o'_{i,j}$ is the (i,j)th component of matrix $\mathbf{O'}$, then for $i \in [m], j \in [n]$, return

$$h_{i,j} = \begin{cases} 1 \ if \ |o'_{i,j}| > q/4 \\ 0 \ if \ |o'_{i,j}| \leq q/4 \end{cases}$$

Output the message matrix $\mathbf{H}$.

4 Correctness

We analyze the correctness and the parameters in this section. According to the decryption method of the new scheme, we discuss as follows.

1. For $i \in \mathcal{S}$, compute

$$\begin{aligned}
\mathbf{O}_i &= \mathbf{K}_i^\mathrm{T}\left(\frac{\mathbf{C}_i'}{\mathbf{C}_i}\right) = \mathbf{K}_i^\mathrm{T}\left(\frac{\mathbf{A}_0^\mathrm{T}\mathbf{S}_i + \mathbf{E}_i}{(\mathbf{A}_i + \mathbf{B})^\mathrm{T}\mathbf{S}_i + \mathbf{R}_i\mathbf{E}_i}\right) \\
&= \mathbf{K}_i^\mathrm{T}(\mathbf{A}_0|(\mathbf{A}_i + \mathbf{B}))^\mathrm{T}\mathbf{S}_i + \mathbf{K}_i^\mathrm{T}\left(\begin{matrix}\mathbf{E}_i \\ \mathbf{R}_i\mathbf{E}_i\end{matrix}\right) \\
&= \mathbf{U}^\mathrm{T}\mathbf{S}_i + \mathbf{K}_i^\mathrm{T}\left(\begin{matrix}\mathbf{E}_i \\ \mathbf{R}_i\mathbf{E}_i\end{matrix}\right)
\end{aligned}$$

We first discuss the norm of $\mathbf{E}_i = \mathbf{e}\mathbf{d}_{i_1}^\mathrm{T}\mathbf{D}^i$ ($i_1 \in \{0,1\}$) before considering the norm of $\mathbf{K}_i^\mathrm{T}\left(\begin{matrix}\mathbf{E}_i \\ \mathbf{R}_i\mathbf{E}_i\end{matrix}\right)$. $\|\mathbf{e}\| \le \mathcal{X}_{\max}$ because of $\mathbf{e} \leftarrow \mathcal{X}^m$. $\mathbf{D}^i = \mathbf{I} - (\mathbf{D}^i)_1 - \dots$
$- (\mathbf{D}^i)_k$ when $\mathbf{D}^i$ has the maximum norm, where $k \le \log l$ and $(\mathbf{D}^i)_j$ ($j \in [k]$) is chosen from $\{\pm 1\}^{n \times n}$, so $\|\mathbf{D}^i\|_1 \le nk + 1$. And $\mathbf{d}_0 \leftarrow \{0, \pm 1\}^n$, $\mathbf{d}_1 \leftarrow \{0, \pm 1, \pm 2\}^n$, so $\|\mathbf{d}_{i_1}^\mathrm{T}\mathbf{D}^i\|_\infty \le 2(nk + 1)$. Then we have $\|\mathbf{E}_i\| = \|\mathbf{e} \cdot \mathbf{d}_{i_1}^\mathrm{T}\mathbf{D}^i\| \le 2(nk + 1)\mathcal{X}_{\max}$. According to the properties of matrix norm and Lemma 1, we have $\|\mathbf{K}_i^\mathrm{T}\| \le \|\mathbf{K}_i^\mathrm{T}\|_2 \le \sigma\sqrt{2m \cdot m} = \sqrt{2}\sigma m$ and $\|\mathbf{R}_i\| \le 20\sqrt{m}$, so

$$\begin{aligned}
\left\|\mathbf{K}_i^\mathrm{T}\left(\begin{matrix}\mathbf{E}_i \\ \mathbf{R}_i\mathbf{E}_i\end{matrix}\right)\right\| &\le \|\mathbf{K}_i^\mathrm{T}\|(\|\mathbf{E}_i\| + \|\mathbf{R}_i\mathbf{E}_i\|) \\
&\le \|\mathbf{K}_i^\mathrm{T}\|(\|\mathbf{E}_i\| + \|\mathbf{R}_i\| \cdot \|\mathbf{E}_i\|) \\
&\le 2\sqrt{2}\sigma m(1 + 20\sqrt{m})(nk + 1)\mathcal{X}_{\max}
\end{aligned}$$

Define $\beta = 2\sqrt{2}\sigma m(1 + 20\sqrt{m})(nk + 1)\mathcal{X}_{\max}$.

2. The algorithm computes the corresponding matrix $\mathbf{O}$ of each node in the circuit by the known matrices $\mathbf{O}_i$ ($i \in \mathcal{S}$) of leaf nodes from the bottom to the top. For a non-leaf node ω, if $Gatetype(\omega) = $ OR, let $\mathbf{O}_\omega = \mathbf{O}_{\omega_i}$ ($x_{\omega_i} = 1$, $i \in \{0, 1\}$); if $Gatetype(\omega) = $ AND, let

$$\begin{aligned}
\mathbf{O}_\omega &= \mathbf{O}_{\omega_0} + \mathbf{O}_{\omega_1} \\
&= \mathbf{U}^\mathrm{T}\mathbf{S}_{\omega_0} + \mathbf{E}_{\omega_0} + \mathbf{U}^\mathrm{T}\mathbf{S}_{\omega_1} + \mathbf{E}_{\omega_1} \\
&= \mathbf{U}^\mathrm{T}(\mathbf{S}_{\omega_0} + \mathbf{S}_{\omega_1}) + (\mathbf{E}_{\omega_0} + \mathbf{E}_{\omega_1})
\end{aligned}$$

According to the SMDM described in the **Enc** algorithm, $\mathbf{S}_{\omega_0} + \mathbf{S}_{\omega_1} = \mathbf{S}_\omega$, so $\mathbf{O}_\omega = \mathbf{U}^\mathrm{T}\mathbf{S}_\omega + \mathbf{E}_\omega$, where $\mathbf{E}_\omega = \mathbf{E}_{\omega_0} + \mathbf{E}_{\omega_1}$. It also means that the noise in $\mathbf{O}$ will increase after an addition on the AND gate. Finally, we can get

$$\mathbf{O}_r = \mathbf{U}^\mathrm{T}\mathbf{s}(\mathbf{d}_0^\mathrm{T} + \mathbf{d}_1^\mathrm{T}) + \mathbf{E}_{r_0} + \mathbf{E}_{r_1} = \mathbf{U}^\mathrm{T}\mathbf{s}\bar{\mathbf{d}}^\mathrm{T} + \mathbf{E}_r$$

where $\mathbf{E}_r < l \cdot \beta$ (the number of AND gates is less than l).

3. Compute

$$\begin{aligned}
\mathbf{O}' &= \mathbf{C}_0 - \mathbf{O}_r \\
&= \mathbf{U}^{\mathrm{T}}\mathbf{s}\bar{\mathbf{d}}^{\mathrm{T}} + \mathbf{H}\lfloor q/2 \rfloor + \mathbf{e}_0\bar{\mathbf{d}}^{\mathrm{T}} - (\mathbf{U}^{\mathrm{T}}\mathbf{s}\bar{\mathbf{d}}^{\mathrm{T}} + \mathbf{E}_r) \\
&= \mathbf{H}\lfloor q/2 \rfloor + \mathbf{e}_0\bar{\mathbf{d}}^{\mathrm{T}} - \mathbf{E}_r
\end{aligned}$$

where $||\mathbf{e}_0\bar{\mathbf{d}}^{\mathrm{T}}|| \leq ||\mathbf{e}_0|| \cdot ||\bar{\mathbf{d}}^{\mathrm{T}}||_\infty = \mathcal{X}_{\max}$. If we can ensure $||\mathbf{e}_0\bar{\mathbf{d}}^{\mathrm{T}} - \mathbf{E}_r|| \leq q/4$, the decryption algorithm will get the right message. We have

$$\begin{aligned}
||\mathbf{e}_0\bar{\mathbf{d}}^{\mathrm{T}} - \mathbf{E}_r|| &\leq ||\mathbf{e}_0\bar{\mathbf{d}}^{\mathrm{T}}|| + ||\mathbf{E}_r|| \\
&< \mathcal{X}_{\max} + l \cdot 2\sqrt{2}\sigma m(1 + 20\sqrt{m})(nk+1)\mathcal{X}_{\max} \\
&= (1 + l \cdot 2\sqrt{2}\sigma m(1 + 20\sqrt{m})(nk+1))\mathcal{X}_{\max}
\end{aligned}$$

Therefore, if we define

$$1 + l \cdot 2\sqrt{2}\sigma m(1 + 20\sqrt{m})(nk+1) \leq q/4\mathcal{X}_{\max}$$

in **Setup** phase, the user can decrypt the ciphertexts correctly.

5   Security

Theorem 1. *For any circuit f, if there exists an adversary A can attack against above scheme with non-ignorable advantage in the selective weak security model, then there exists a simulator B that can decide the $(\mathbb{Z}_q, n, \mathcal{X}) - $ LWE problem with non-ignorable advantage.*

Proof. B requests from oracle and obtains some LWE samples that we denote as,

$$[(\mathbf{w}_0^1, v_0^1), \ldots, (\mathbf{w}_0^m, v_0^m)] \in (\mathbb{Z}_q^n \times \mathbb{Z}_q)^m$$
$$[(\mathbf{w}_1^1, v_1^1), \ldots, (\mathbf{w}_1^m, v_1^m)] \in (\mathbb{Z}_q^n \times \mathbb{Z}_q)^m$$
$$\vdots$$
$$[(\mathbf{w}_{l+1}^1, v_{l+1}^1), \ldots, (\mathbf{w}_{l+1}^m, v_{l+1}^m)] \in (\mathbb{Z}_q^n \times \mathbb{Z}_q)^m$$

Target. A announces a target challenge circuit f^*.

Setup. B prepares the public parameters according to the target circuit f^* as follows. The attribute set $\mathcal{L}^*$ contains the attributes that corresponding to the leaf nodes of f^*.

1. B chooses the parameters n, m, q as the real game.
2. B sets $\mathbf{A}_0 = [(\mathbf{w}_0^1)^{\mathrm{T}} | \cdots | (\mathbf{w}_0^m)^{\mathrm{T}}]$ from the LWE samples.
3. B generates $\mathbf{TrapGen}(1^n, 1^m, q) \rightarrow (\mathbf{B}, \mathbf{T_B})$ and sets $\mathbf{U} = [(\mathbf{w}_{l+1}^1)^{\mathrm{T}} | \cdots | (\mathbf{w}_{l+1}^m)^{\mathrm{T}}]$. For $i \in \mathcal{W}$, choose $\mathbf{R}_i^* \leftarrow \{\pm 1\}^{m \times m}$. If $i \in \mathcal{L}^*$, let $\mathbf{A}_i = \mathbf{A}_0\mathbf{R}_i^* - \mathbf{B}$; if $i \in \mathcal{W}\backslash\mathcal{L}^*$, let $\mathbf{A}_i = \mathbf{A}_0\mathbf{R}_i^*$.

   Note that, the matrix $\mathbf{A}_i$ here is indistinguishable with the matrix in the real scheme according to Lemma 2.

4. Finally, B returns the public parameters

$$\text{PP} = \{\mathbf{A}_0, \mathbf{B}, \{\mathbf{A}_i\}_{i \in \mathcal{W}}, \mathbf{U}\}$$

Queries. The adversary A can adaptively make a number of key generation queries on attribute set with a constraint that $\mathcal{S}^* \subseteq \mathcal{W} \backslash \mathcal{L}^*$ and $f^*(\mathcal{S}^*) = 0$. B generates a private key as follows.

1. For $i \in \mathcal{S}^*$, we already know $\mathbf{A}_i = \mathbf{A}_0 \mathbf{R}_i^*$, and then compute

$$\mathbf{K}_i \leftarrow \textbf{LeftSample}(\mathbf{A}_0, \mathbf{B}, \mathbf{R}_i^*, \mathbf{T}_\mathbf{B}, \mathbf{U}, \sigma)$$

where $\mathbf{K}_i$ satisfies

$$(\mathbf{A}_0|(\mathbf{A}_0 \mathbf{R}_i^* + \mathbf{B}))\mathbf{K}_i = (\mathbf{A}_0|(\mathbf{A}_i + \mathbf{B}))\mathbf{K}_i = \mathbf{U}$$

2. Finally, B outputs the secret key

$$\text{SK} = \{\mathbf{K}_i \in \mathbb{Z}^{2m \times m}\}_{i \in \mathcal{S}^*}$$

Challenge. A submits two message matrices $\mathbf{H}_0, \mathbf{H}_1 \in \{0,1\}^{m \times n}$. B randomly chooses $b \in \{0,1\}$ and encrypts $\mathbf{H}_b$.

1. B gets $\mathbf{d}$ vectors and $\mathbf{D}$ matrices according to the SMDM for f^* as in the real scheme.
2. In a real scheme, $\mathbf{C}_0 = \mathbf{U}^\mathrm{T} \mathbf{s} \bar{\mathbf{d}}^\mathrm{T} + \mathbf{H} \lfloor q/2 \rfloor + \mathbf{e}_0 \bar{\mathbf{d}}^\mathrm{T}$. When set

$$\mathbf{U} = [(\mathbf{w}_{l+1}^1)^\mathrm{T} | \cdots | (\mathbf{w}_{l+1}^m)^\mathrm{T}]$$

B can output
$$\mathbf{C}_0 = (v_{l+1}^1, \ldots, v_{l+1}^m)^\mathrm{T} \bar{\mathbf{d}}^\mathrm{T} + \mathbf{H}_b \lfloor q/2 \rfloor$$

from the LWE samples.
For $i \in \mathcal{L}^*$, $\mathbf{C}'_i = \mathbf{A}_0^\mathrm{T} \mathbf{S}_i + \mathbf{E}_i$ in the real scheme. When set

$$\mathbf{A}_0 = [(\mathbf{w}_0^1)^\mathrm{T} | \cdots | (\mathbf{w}_0^m)^\mathrm{T}]$$

B can output
$$\mathbf{C}'_i = (v_0^1, \ldots, v_0^m)^\mathrm{T} \mathbf{d}_{i_1}^\mathrm{T} \mathbf{D}^i \quad (i_1 \in \{0,1\})$$

from the LWE samples, where $\mathbf{d}_{i_1}$ and $\mathbf{D}^i$ are decided by the SMDM and circuit f^*.

$\mathbf{C}_i = (\mathbf{A}_i + \mathbf{B})^\mathrm{T} \mathbf{S}_i + \mathbf{R}_i^\mathrm{T} \mathbf{E}_i$ in the real scheme so we have $\mathbf{C}_i = (\mathbf{A}_0 \mathbf{R}_i^*)^\mathrm{T} \mathbf{S}_i + (\mathbf{R}_i^*)^\mathrm{T} \mathbf{E}_i$ when set $\mathbf{A}_i = \mathbf{A}_0 \mathbf{R}_i^* - \mathbf{B}$, and then B can output

$$\mathbf{C}_i = (\mathbf{R}_i^*)^\mathrm{T}(v_0^1, \ldots, v_0^m)^\mathrm{T} \mathbf{d}_{i_1}^\mathrm{T} \mathbf{D}^i \quad (i_1 \in \{0,1\})$$

according to $\mathbf{C}'_i$.

3. Finally, output

$$CT = \{\mathbf{C}_0, \{\mathbf{C'}_i, \mathbf{C}_i\}_{i \in \mathcal{L}^*}\}$$

Continuation. This a continuation of the earlier query phase.

Decision. Finally, A will output a guess b' of b. If $b = b'$, B guesses that the samples are $O_{\mathbf{s}}$ samples; otherwise, it guesses that they are $O_{\bar{\mathbf{s}}}$ samples.

Suppose the advantage of adversary A is $\Pr[b' = b] \geq 1/2 + \varepsilon$ in the above game, then the simulator B can decide the $(\mathbb{Z}_q, n, \mathcal{X}) - \text{LWE}$ problem with the advantage of

$$\frac{1}{2}\Pr[b' = b|O_{\mathbf{s}}] + \frac{1}{2}\Pr[b' = b|O_{\bar{\mathbf{s}}}] = \frac{1}{2} \times (\frac{1}{2} + \varepsilon) + \frac{1}{2} \times \frac{1}{2} = \frac{1}{2} + \frac{\varepsilon}{2}$$

The new scheme is secure according to Theorem 1 and the security of $(\mathbb{Z}_q, n, \mathcal{X}) - \text{LWE}$ problem.

6   Conclusion

We present a CP-ABE scheme for circuits from lattices in this paper. Compared with the existing CP-ABE schemes from lattices, our scheme is the first one that can support the most flexible access structure of circuits. However, there are also some shortcomings in our scheme. First, the SMDM would increase the magnitude of the noise in some degree. Second, the new scheme can only be proved secure in the selective weak security model, which need to be further improved to the standard security model.

References

1. Sahai, A., Waters, B.: Fuzzy identity-based encryption. In: Cramer, R. (ed.) EURO-CRYPT 2005. LNCS, vol. 3494, pp. 457–473. Springer, Heidelberg (2005). https://doi.org/10.1007/11426639_27
2. Goyal, V., Pandey, O., Sahai, A., et al.: Attribute-based encryption for fine grained access control of encrypted data. In: Proceedings of the ACM Conference on Computer and Communications Security (CCS 2006), pp. 89–98. ACM, New York (2006). https://doi.org/10.1145/1180405.1180418
3. Yinan, S.: Attribute-based encryption algorithm. M.S. dissertation, Shanghai Jiao Tong University, pp. 32–33 (2010)
4. Agrawal, S., Boyen, X., Vaikuntanathan, V., Voulgaris, P., Wee, H.: Functional encryption for threshold functions (or Fuzzy IBE) from lattices. In: Fischlin, M., Buchmann, J., Manulis, M. (eds.) PKC 2012. LNCS, vol. 7293, pp. 280–297. Springer, Heidelberg (2012). https://doi.org/10.1007/978-3-642-30057-8_17
5. Jiang, Z, Zhenfeng, Z, Aijun, G.: Ciphertext policy attribute-based encryption from lattices. In: Proceedings of the 7th ACM Symposium on Information, Computer and Communications Security (ASIACCS 2012), pp. 16–17. ACM, New York (2012). https://doi.org/10.1145/2414456.2414464

6. Boyen, X.: Attribute-based functional encryption on lattices. In: Sahai, A. (ed.) TCC 2013. LNCS, vol. 7785, pp. 122–142. Springer, Heidelberg (2013). https://doi.org/10.1007/978-3-642-36594-2_8

7. Xiang, X., Rui, X.: Attribute-Based Encryption for a Subclass of Circuits with Bounded Depth from Lattices. IACR Cryptology ePrint Archive, http://eprint.iacr.org/2013/342. Accessed 2013

8. Gorbunov, S., Vaikuntanathan, V., Wee, H.: Attribute-based Encryption for Circuits. IACR Cryptology ePrint Archive, http://eprint.iacr.org/2013/337. Accessed 2013

9. Boneh, D, Nikolaenko, V, Segev, G.: Attribute-based Encryption for Arithmetic Circuits. IACR Cryptology ePrint Archive, http://eprint.iacr.org/2013/669. Accessed 2013

10. Yongtao, W.: Lattice ciphertext policy attribute-based encryption in the standard model. Int. J. Netw. Secur. **16**(6), 444–451 (2014)

11. Boyen, X., Li, Q.: Attribute-based encryption for finite automata from LWE. In: Au, M.-H., Miyaji, A. (eds.) ProvSec 2015. LNCS, vol. 9451, pp. 247–267. Springer, Cham (2015). https://doi.org/10.1007/978-3-319-26059-4_14

12. Fang, B.R.: Matrix Theory. Tsing University Press, Beijing (2013)

13. Alwen, J., Peikert, C.: Generating shorter bases for hard random lattices. Theory Comput. Syst. **48**(535), 75–86 (2011)

14. Zhao, J.: Research on attribute-based encryption from lattices. M.S. dissertation, Zhengzhou Information Science and Technology Institute, 4–7 2015

15. Garg, S., Gentry, C., Halevi, S., Sahai, A., Waters, B.: Attribute-based encryption for circuits from multilinear maps. In: Canetti, R., Garay, J.A. (eds.) CRYPTO 2013. LNCS, vol. 8043, pp. 479–499. Springer, Heidelberg (2013). https://doi.org/10.1007/978-3-642-40084-1_27

16. Oded, R.: On lattices, learning with errors, random linear codes, and cryptography. J. ACM STOC **56**(34), 1–40 (2005)

17. Agrawal, S., Boneh, D., Boyen, X.: Efficient lattice (H)IBE in the standard model. In: Gilbert, H. (ed.) EUROCRYPT 2010. LNCS, vol. 6110, pp. 553–572. Springer, Heidelberg (2010). https://doi.org/10.1007/978-3-642-13190-5_28

18. Gay, R., Méaux, P., Wee, H.: Predicate encryption for multi-dimensional range queries from lattices. In: Katz, J. (ed.) PKC 2015. LNCS, vol. 9020, pp. 752–776. Springer, Heidelberg (2015). https://doi.org/10.1007/978-3-662-46447-2_34

19. Ibraimi, L., Tang, Q., Hartel, P., Jonker, W.: Efficient and provable secure ciphertext-policy attribute-based encryption schemes. In: Bao, F., Li, H., Wang, G. (eds.) ISPEC 2009. LNCS, vol. 5451, pp. 1–12. Springer, Heidelberg (2009). https://doi.org/10.1007/978-3-642-00843-6_1

Impossible Differential Cryptanalysis of SPECK

Mingming Li, Jiansheng Guo$^{(\boxtimes)}$, Jingyi Cui, and Linhong Xu

Information Science and Technology Institute, Zhengzhou, China
tsg31@126.com

Abstract. The security of SPECK under impossible differential cryptanalysis is studied. Based on multiple 6-round impossible differential distinguishers and combined with the divide-and-conquer attack and time-and-memory tradeoff, the improved 10-round impossible differential cryptanalysis of SPECK32/64 and SPECK48/96 is presented by adding one round forward and three rounds backward. In addition, by further analyzing the properties of the differential diffusion of addition, many 7-round impossible differential distinguishers of SPECK families of block ciphers are constructed. And the 11-round impossible differential cryptanalysis of SPECK32/64 and SPECK48/96 is presented by adding one round forward and three rounds backward.

Keywords: Lightweight block cipher · SPECK
Impossible differential cryptanalysis
Impossible differential distinguisher · Addition

1 Introduction

SPECK [1] is a family of lightweight block ciphers published by National Security Agency (NSA) in 2013. The algorithms with outstanding software performance adopt a modified Feistel structure that applies a combination of addition (module 2^n), rotation and XOR (the so-called ARX structure). Since SPECK was put forward, it has been widely concerned by cryptography. And there are several security analysis results for SPECK so far [2–10].

Impossible differential cryptanalysis, as a variant of differential cryptanalysis, proposed by Knudsen [11] and Biham [12] respectively, is one of the most common cryptanalysis methods. Miss-in-the-middle is one of the most useful ways to find an impossible differential distinguisher. From the encryption direction, let the probability of the difference $\alpha \rightarrow \gamma_1$ be 1, and from the decryption direction, let the probability of the difference $\gamma_2 \leftarrow \beta$ be 1 too. If $\gamma_1 \neq \gamma_2$, then $\alpha \nrightarrow \beta$ is an impossible differential distinguisher.

For the impossible differential cryptanalysis of SPECK, the following research results are available so far. Due to the limitation of computing power, Lee et al. [13] only searched for input and output with only one bit difference value by using Mixed Integer Linear Programming (MILP), and found some 6-round impossible differential distinguishers. Xu et al. [14] found some new 6-round impossible differential distinguishers of SPECK32/64 and SPECK48/96 by analyzing differential diffusion property

© Springer Nature Singapore Pte Ltd. 2019
H. Zhang et al. (Eds.): CTCIS 2018, CCIS 960, pp. 16–31, 2019.
https://doi.org/10.1007/978-981-13-5913-2_2

of addition, and the 10-round impossible differential cryptanalysis of these two ciphers was presented with a time complexity of $2^{62.24}$ 10-round encryptions, a data complexity of 2^{32} chosen-plaintexts and a time complexity of $2^{93.28}$ 10-round encryptions, a data complexity of 2^{48} chosen-plaintexts respectively. Besides, Li et al. [15] used the differential diffusion property of addition given by Xu et al. to analyze the differential diffusion properties of SPECK in encryption and decryption direction, and got many new 6-round impossible differential distinguishers of SPECK.

In this article, based on those 6-round impossible differential distinguishers of SPECK given by Li et al. and combined with the divide-and-conquer attack and time-and-memory tradeoff, the improved 10-round impossible differential cryptanalysis of SPECK32/64 and SPECK48/96 are presented by adding one round forward and three rounds backward. In addition, by further analyzing the properties of the differential diffusion of addition, 7-round impossible differential distinguishers of SPECK are constructed and the 11-round impossible differential cryptanalysis of SPECK32/64 and SPECK48/96 is presented by adding one round forward and three rounds backward. Table 1 shows the comparison of impossible differential attacks on SPECK.

Table 1. Comparison of impossible differential attacks on SPECK

Algorithm	Round	Time Comp.	Data Comp.	Mem Comp.	Ref.
SPECK32/64	10	$2^{62.24}$	2^{32}	–	[14]
	10	$2^{61.65}$	$2^{30.58}$	$2^{57.58}$	Sect. 3
	11	$2^{63.34}$	2^{32}	2^{55}	Sect. 4
SPECK48/96	10	$2^{93.28}$	2^{48}	–	[14]
	10	$2^{92.91}$	$2^{39.88}$	$2^{87.88}$	Sect. 5.2
	11	$2^{93.77}$	2^{48}	$2^{86.81}$	Sect. 5.2

2 Preliminaries

2.1 Notations

Here are some notations used in the following paper.

x_i	The left word of input state of i-round of SPECK
y_i	The right word of input state of i-round of SPECK
Δx_i	The XOR difference of two input x_i' and x_i''
Δy_i	The XOR difference of two input y_i' and y_i''
$\Delta x_i[j]$	The j-th bit of Δx_i
$\Delta y_i[j]$	The j-th bit of Δy_i
$+$	Addition module 2^n
$\ggg \alpha$	Right circular shifts by α bits
$\lll \beta$	Left circular shifts by β bits

K_n The n-th round key

K_n^{j-i} The i-th to the j-th bits of K_n

*   The uncertain differential bit, differential value may be 0 or 1.

2.2   SPECK Family Block Ciphers

SPECK is a family of lightweight block ciphers published by NSA in 2013. The algorithms adopt a modified Feistel structure that applies ARX structure composed of addition (module 2^n), rotation and XOR. The shape of the round function is shown in Fig. 1.

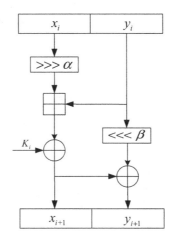

Fig. 1. Round function of SPECK

We will write SPECK $2n/mn$ to mean the SPECK block cipher with a $2n$-bit block and mn-bit key, where $n \in \{16, 24, 32, 48, 64\}$, the number of key words $m \in \{2, 3, 4\}$. SPECK's key schedule is as follows.

Key Schedule. We write master key as $K = (L_{m-2}, L_{m-3}, \cdots, L_0, K_0)$, where $K_0, L_i \in \{0, 1\}^n$. Two sequences K_i and L_i are then generated by

$$\begin{cases} L_{i+m-1} = (K_i + (L_i \ggg \alpha)) \oplus i \\ K_{i+1} = (K_i \lll \beta) \oplus L_{i+m-1} \end{cases}$$

The value K_i is the i-th round key, for $i \geq 0$. Master key can be derived when m adjacency round key $K_i, \cdots, K_{i-m+1}$ is known. The versions of SPECK and related parameters are shown in Table 2.

Table 2. All versions of SPECK families of block ciphers

Block size	Key size	Rounds	n	m	α	β
32	64	22	16	4	7	2
48	72	22	24	3	8	3
	96	23		4		
64	96	26	32	3		
	128	27		4		
96	96	28	48	2		
	144	29		3		
128	128	32	64	2		
	192	33		3		
	256	34		4		

2.3 Differential Diffusion Properties of Addition

Xu et al. [14] gave the differential diffusion property of addition, see Property 1.

Property 1. [14] $z = x + y \pmod{2^n}$ is addition module 2^n. Let $\Delta x = x' \oplus x'' = (\Delta x[n-1], \Delta x[n-2], \cdots, \Delta x[0])$, $\quad \Delta y = y' \oplus y'' = (\Delta y[n-1], \Delta y[n-2], \cdots, \Delta y[0])$ be the difference of input x, y respectively, and let $\Delta z = z' \oplus z'' = (x'+y') \bmod 2^n \oplus (x''+y'') \bmod 2^n = (\Delta z[n-1], \Delta z[n-2], \cdots, \Delta z[0])$ be the difference of output z. Note $l_1 = \min\{k | \Delta x[k] = 1\}$, $l_2 = \min\{k | \Delta y[k] = 1\}$, $l = \min\{l_1, l_2\}$, it follows that

(1) If $l_1 = l_2 = l$, then $\Delta z[l] = \Delta z[l-1] = \cdots = \Delta z[0] = 0$ and $\Delta z[i] = *$, for $l+1 \le i \le n-1$.

(2) If $l_1 \ne l_2$, then $\Delta z[l] = 1, \Delta z[l-1] = \cdots = \Delta z[0] = 0$ and $\Delta z[i] = *$, for $l+1 \le i \le n-1$.

Property 2. $z = x + y \pmod{2^n}$ is addition module 2^n. If $\Delta x = \Delta y = (\overset{n-1}{0} \cdots 0 \overset{l}{1} 0 \cdots \overset{0}{0})$, then $\Delta z = (\overset{n-1}{0} 0 \cdots \overset{1}{0})$ if and only if $x'[l] \ne y'[l]$ or $x''[l] \ne y''[l]$. In addition, the probability of $x'[l] \ne y'[l]$ or $x''[l] \ne y''[l]$ is 1/2.

Proof. Note $x = (x[n-1], x[n-2], \cdots, x[0]), y = (y[n-1], y[n-2], \cdots, y[0]), z = (z[n-1], z[n-2], \cdots, z[0])$. Let $c = (c[n-1], c[n-2], \cdots, c[0])$ be the carry of $x+y$, then $z[i] = x[i] \oplus y[i] \oplus c[i-1]$, $\quad c[i] = x[i]y[i] \oplus x[i]c[i-1] \oplus y[i]c[i-1]$, for $1 \le i \le n-1$, where $z[0] = x[0] \oplus y[0], c[0] = x[0]y[0]$. Thus the output difference satisfies $\Delta z[i] = \Delta x[i] \oplus \Delta y[i] \oplus \Delta c[i-1]$.

If $\Delta z = (\overset{n-1}{0} 0 \cdots 0)$, then, by $\Delta x = \Delta y = (\overset{n-1}{0} \cdots 0 \overset{l}{1} 0 \cdots \overset{0}{0})$, we have $\Delta c[i] = 0$. Thus $\Delta c[l] = x'[l]y'[l] \oplus x''[l]y''[l] = 0$. And since $\Delta x[l] = \Delta y[l] = 1$, we might as well suppose that $x'[l] = 0, x''[l] = 1$, clearly $\Delta c[l] = x''[l]y''[l] = 0$. Thus $y'[l] = 1, y''[l] = 0$, i.e. $x'[l] \ne y'[l]$ or $x''[l] \ne y''[l]$.

Conversely, suppose $x'[l] \ne y'[l]$ or $x''[l] \ne y''[l]$. Since $\Delta x = \Delta y = (\overset{n-1}{0} \cdots 0 \overset{l}{1} 0 \cdots \overset{0}{0})$, we can obtain $\Delta z[i] = 0, i \le l$ from Property 1. Might as well suppose $x'[l] = 0, x''[l] = 1$ due to $x'[l] \ne y'[l]$ or $x''[l] \ne y''[l]$, it is clear that $y'[l] = 1, y''[l] = 0$. Then $\Delta c[l] = x'[l]y'[l] \oplus$

$x''[l]y''[l] = 0$. And since $\Delta x[l+1] = \Delta y[l+1] = 0$, it follows $\Delta x[l+1]y[l+1] = x'[l+1]y'[l+1] \oplus x''[l+1]y''[l+1] = 0, \Delta x[l+1]c[l] = \Delta y[l+1]c[l] = 0$. Hence $\Delta c[l+1] = \Delta x[l+1]y[l+1] \oplus \Delta x[l+1]c[l] \oplus \Delta y[l+1]c[l] = 0$. Similar reasoning shows $\Delta c[i] = 0, i > l+1$ due to $\Delta x[i] = \Delta y[i] = 0, i > l+1$. From $\Delta z[i] = \Delta x[i] \oplus \Delta y[i] \oplus \Delta c[i-1]$, it can be seen $\Delta z[i] = 0, i > l$. To sum up, we have $\Delta z = (\overset{n-1}{0} 0 \cdots \overset{1}{0})$.

In addition, for any state whose difference satisfies $\Delta x = \Delta y = (\overset{n-1}{0} \cdots 0 \overset{l}{1} 0 \cdots \overset{0}{0})$, the probability of $x'[l] \neq y'[l]$ or $x''[l] \neq y''[l]$ is 1/2. QED

3 Improved Impossible Differential Attack on 10-Round SPECK 32/64

Li et al. [15] used the Property 1 to analyze the differential diffusion properties of SPECK32 in encryption and decryption direction and got 41 6-round impossible differential distinguishers of SPECK shown in Table 3.

Table 3. 6-round impossible differential correspondences of SPECK32

Input difference in encryption direction		Output difference in decryption direction
$\Delta x_i = (00\cdots 0 \overset{6\;5\;4\;3}{***1}000)$		
$\Delta x_i = (00\cdots 0 \overset{6\;5\;4\;3}{**1}0000)$	$\Delta y_i = (00\cdots 0)$	$(\Delta x_{i+6}, \Delta y_{i+6}) = (10\cdots 0, 100\cdots 010)$
$\Delta x_i = (00\cdots 0 \overset{6\;5\;4\;3}{1}000000)$		
$\Delta x_i = (00\cdots 0 \overset{6\;5\;4\;3}{***}0000)$	$\Delta y_i = (00 \overset{13\;12}{*}\;10\cdots 0)$	
$\Delta x_i = (00\cdots 0 \overset{6\;5\;4\;3}{***1}000)$	$\Delta y_i = (00 \overset{13\;12}{1}\;00\cdots 0)$	
$\Delta x_i = (00\cdots 0 \overset{6\;5\;4\;3}{**}000)$		

We select 16 6-round impossible differential distinguishers of SPECK from Table 3. The details are as Fig. 2 shows. Based on these distinguishers, the impossible differential attack on 10-round SPECK32/64 can be given.

By using the distinguisher shown in Fig. 2, we add 1 round forward and 3 rounds backward to give a 10-round impossible differential trail of SPECK32/64. The details are as Fig. 3 shows. Combined with the divide-and-conquer attack and time-and-memory tradeoff, the improved 10-round impossible differential cryptanalysis is presented as follows.

1. Choose 2^n plaintext structures where $x_0[7,8]$ and $y_0[0,1,5,6,7,8,9,10,12, 13,14,15]$ are fixed and the other bits take all possible values, then each structure consists of 2^{18} plaintexts and 2^{35} plaintext pairs. So we can get 2^{n+18} chosen plaintexts and 2^{n+35} plaintext pairs.

2. Consider the first round encryption which needn't guess round key. Filter the pairs such that $(\Delta x_1, \Delta y_1) = (0000\ 0000\ 0***\ 0000, 00*10000\ 00000000)$, i.e. $\Delta s_0[i] = 0, i \neq \{4,5,6\}$ and $\Delta x_1[4,5,6] \oplus \Delta t_0[4,5,6] = (000)$. Since $\Delta s_0 = ((x_0' \ggg 7) + y_0') \oplus ((x_0'' \ggg 7) + y_0'')$, $t_0 = y_0 \lll 2$, there are an average of $2^{n+35} \times 2^{-11} \times 2^{-3} = 2^{n+21}$ pairs left after this step, and the time complexity is approximately $2^{n+35} \times 2 = 2^{n+36}$ additions.

3. Guess K_9. Filter the pairs such that $\Delta t_8[2,3] = (00)$, where $\Delta t_8 = \Delta x_9 \oplus \Delta y_9, y_9 = (x_{10} \oplus y_{10}) \ggg 2, x_9 = ((x_{10} \oplus K_9) + y_9) \lll 7$. There are an average of $2^{n+21} \times 2^{-2} = 2^{n+19}$ pairs left after this step, and the time complexity is approximately $2^{n+21} \times 2^{16} \times 2 = 2^{n+38}$ additions. Store $2^{n+19}(x_9', y_9'), (x_9'', y_9'')$ in Table Ω_1 with the index of 2^{16} possible K_9.

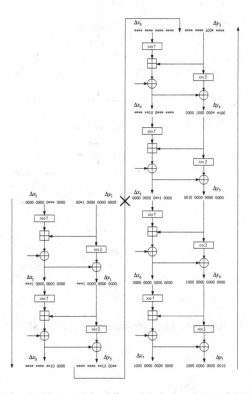

Fig. 2. 6-round impossible differential distinguisher of SPECK32

4. Guess K_8^{10-0}. For the remaining pairs (x_9', y_9'), (x_9'', y_9'') in Table Ω_1, filter the pairs such that $\Delta r_8[10, 9] = (10)$, i.e. $\Delta x_8[1, 0] = (10)$, where $y_8 = (x_9 \oplus y_9) \ggg 2$, $r_8 = (x_9 \oplus K_8) + y_8$. There are an average of $2^{n+19} \times 2^{-2} = 2^{n+17}$ pairs left after this step, and the time complexity is approximately $2^{n+19} \times 2^{16} \times 2^{11} \times 2 = 2^{n+47}$ additions. Store 2^{n+17}, (x_9', y_9'), (x_9'', y_9'') in Table Ω_2 with the index of 2^{11} possible K_8^{10-0}.

5. Guess K_8^{15-11}. For the remaining pairs (x_9', y_9'), (x_9'', y_9''), in Table Ω_2, filter the pairs such that $\Delta t_7 = (0000\ 0000\ 0000\ 1010)$, where $\Delta t_7 = \Delta x_8 \oplus \Delta y_8$, $y_8 = (x_9 \oplus y_9) \ggg 2$, $x_8 = ((x_9 \oplus K_8) + y_8) \lll 7$. There are an average of $2^{n+17} \times 2^{-14} = 2^{n+3}$ pairs left after this step, and the time complexity is approximately $2^{n+17} \times 2^{16} \times 2^{11} \times 2^5 \times 2 = 2^{n+50}$ additions. Store $2^{n+3}(x_8', y_8')$, (x_8'', y_8'') in Table Ω_3 with the index of 2^5 possible K_8^{15-11}.

6. Guess K_7. For the remaining pairs (x_8', y_8'), (x_8'', y_8'') in Ω_3, filter the pairs such that $\Delta x_7 = (1000\ 0000\ 0000\ 0000)$, where $y_7 = (x_8 \oplus y_8) \ggg 2$, $x_7 = ((x_8 \oplus K_7) + y_7) \lll 7$. The time complexity is approximately $2^{n+3} \times 2^{16} \times 2^{11} \times 2^5 \times 2^{16} \times 2 = 2^{n+52}$ additions in this step. After the round decryption, we obtain the output of impossible differential distinguishers with the probability of 2^{-14}.

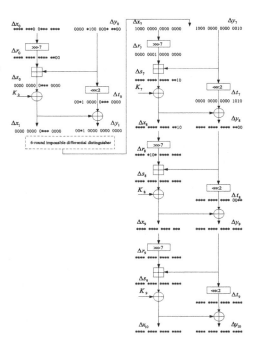

Fig. 3. 10-round impossible differential trail of SPECK32

The time complexity is mainly determined by Step 6 during the above attack. Known approximately $\varepsilon = 2^{48} \times (1 - 2^{-14})^{2^{n+3}}$ key candidates after excluding wrong key at Step 6, exhaust the candidate key and the rest 16 bits key with a time complexity of $\varepsilon \times 2^{16}$. When $n = 12.58$, the time complexity of the attack is $2^{n+52}/10 + \varepsilon \times 2^{16} = 2^{n+52}/10 + 2^{48} \times (1 - 2^{-14})^{2^{n+3}} \times 2^{16} \approx 2^{61.65}$ 10-round SPECK32 encryptions, the data complexity is $2^{30.58}$ chosen plaintexts. In addition, the memory complexity is mainly determined by Step 4, which is $2^{16} \times 2^{11} \times 2^{n+17} \times 2 \approx 2^{57.58}$ SPECK32 states.

4   Impossible Differential Attack on 11-Round SPECK 32/64

Based on Properties 1 and 2, we give 7-round impossible differential distinguishers of SPECK32 as follows.

Theorem 1. When the input difference satisfies $(\Delta x_1, \Delta y_1) = (0000\ 0000\ 0000\ 0010,\ 0000\ 0100\ 0000\ 0000)$ and $x_1[1] \neq y_1[10]$, it is impossible that the output difference satisfies $(\Delta x_8, \Delta y_8) = (1000\ 0000\ 0000\ 0000,\ 1000\ 0000\ 0000\ 0010)$ after 7-round SPECK32 encryption. The details are as Fig. 4 shows.

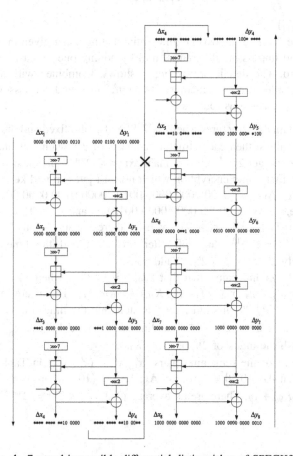

Fig. 4. 7-round impossible differential distinguisher of SPECK32

Proof. Note $r_1 = x_1 \ggg 7$. Since $x_1[1] \neq y_1[10]$, it follows $r_1[10] \neq y_1[10]$. And since $x_2 = ((x_1 \ggg 7) + y_1) \oplus K_1$, it's clearly that $x_2 = (r_1 + y_1) \oplus K_1$. From Property 2, we can obtain the output difference $\Delta x_2 = (0000\ 0000\ 0000\ 0000)$ after 1-round SPECK32 encryption, then $\Delta y_2 = \Delta x_2 \oplus (\Delta y_1 \lll 2) = (0001\ 0000\ 0000\ 0000)$. In addition, the output difference satisfies $\Delta z_4[5] = 1$ after 2-round SPECK32 encryption for (x_2, y_2) from Property 1.

Nevertheless, the output difference satisfies $\Delta z_4[5] = 0$ after 4-round SPECK32 decryption for (x_8, y_8) from Property 1. That is a contradiction. QED

We can also proof Theorem 1 based on the known 6-round impossible differential distinguishers from Table 3. We have known output difference $(\Delta x_2, \Delta y_2) = (0000\ 0000\ 0000\ 0000, 0001\ 0000\ 0000\ 0000)$ after 1-round SPECK32 encryption in Theorem 1. Besides, $(\Delta x_2, \Delta y_2) \nrightarrow (\Delta x_8, \Delta y_8)$ is a 6-round impossible differential distinguisher which can be seen from Table 3, so $(\Delta x_1, \Delta y_1) \nrightarrow (\Delta x_8, \Delta y_8)$ is a 7-round impossible differential distinguisher when $x_1[1] \neq y_1[10]$.

Expect the 7-round impossible differential distinguisher given in Theorem 1, the similar method gets the following 7-round impossible differential distinguisher of SPECK.

$$(0000\ 0000\ 0000\ 0100, 0000\ 1000\ 0000\ 0000) \nrightarrow (10 \cdots 0,\ 100 \cdots 010)$$

where $x_1[2] \neq y_1[11]$.

Based on the 7-round impossible differential distinguisher given in Theorem 1, we give an 11-round impossible differential trail by adding one round forward and three rounds backward. The details are as Fig. 5 shows. Combined with the divide-and-conquer attack and time-and-memory tradeoff, 11-round impossible differential cryptanalysis is presented as follows

1. Choose 2^n plaintext structures where $x_0[7, 8]$ and y_0 are fixed and the other bits take all possible values, then each structure consists of 2^{14} plaintexts and 2^{27} plaintext pairs. So we can get 2^{n+14} chosen plaintexts and 2^{n+27} plaintext pairs.

2. Consider the first round encryption which needn't guess round key. Filter the pairs such that $(\Delta x_1, \Delta y_1) = (0000\ 0000\ 0000\ 0010,\ 0000\ 0100\ 0000\ 0000)$ and $x_1[1] \neq y_1[10]$, i.e. $\Delta s_0 = (0000\ 0000\ 0000\ 0010)$ and $x_1[1] \neq y_1[10]$. Since $\Delta s_0 = ((x'_0 \ggg 7) + y'_0) \oplus ((x''_0 \ggg 7) + y''_0)$, there are an average of $2^{n+27} \times 2^{-14}/2 = 2^{n+12}$ pairs left after this step, and the time complexity is approximately $2^{n+27} \times 2 = 2^{n+28}$ additions.

3. Guess K_{10}. Filter the pairs such that $\Delta t_9[2, 3] = (00)$, where $\Delta t_9 = \Delta x_{10} \oplus \Delta y_{10}$, $y_{10} = (x_{11} \oplus y_{11}) \ggg 2$, $x_{10} = ((x_{11} \oplus K_{10}) + y_{10}) \lll 7$. There are an average of $2^{n+12} \times 2^{-2} = 2^{n+10}$ pairs left after this step, and the time complexity is approximately $2^{n+12} \times 2^{16} \times 2 = 2^{n+29}$ additions. Store $2^{n+10}(x'_{10}, y'_{10}), (x''_{10}, y''_{10})$ in Table Ω_1 with the index of 2^{16} possible K_{10}.

4. Guess K_9^{10-0}. For the remaining pairs $(x'_{10}, y'_{10}), (x''_{10}, y''_{10})$ in Table Ω_1, filter the pairs such that $\Delta r_9[10, 9] = (10)$, i.e. $\Delta x_9[1, 0] = (10)$, where $y_9 = (x_{10} \oplus y_{10}) \ggg 2$, $r_9 = (x_{10} \oplus K_9) + y_9$. There are an average of $2^{n+10} \times 2^{-2} = 2^{n+8}$ pairs left after

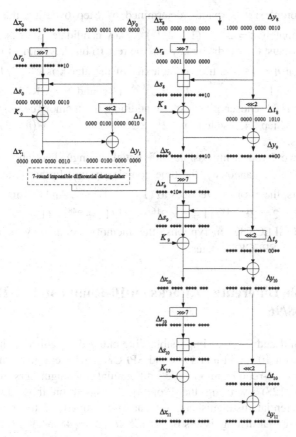

Fig. 5. 11-round impossible differential trail of SPECK32

this step, and the time complexity is approximately $2^{n+10} \times 2^{16} \times 2^{11} \times 2 = 2^{n+38}$ additions. Store $2^{n+8}(x'_{10}, y'_{10})(x''_{10}, y''_{10})$ in Table Ω_2 with the index of 2^{11} possible K_9^{10-0}.

5. Guess K_9^{15-11}. For the remaining pairs (x'_{10}, y'_{10}), (x''_{10}, y''_{10}) in Table Ω_2, filter the pairs such that $\Delta t_8 = (0000\ 0000\ 0000\ 1010)$, where $\Delta t_8 = \Delta x_9 \oplus \Delta y_9$, $y_9 = (x_{10} \oplus y_{10}) \ggg 2$, $x_9 = ((x_{10} \oplus K_9) + y_9) \lll 7$. There are an average of $2^{n+8} \times 2^{-14} = 2^{n-6}$ pairs left after this step, and the time complexity is approximately $2^{n+8} \times 2^{16} \times 2^{11} \times 2^5 \times 2 = 2^{n+41}$ additions. Store 2^{n-6} (x'_9, y'_9), (x''_9, y''_9) in Table Ω_3 with the index of 2^5 possible K_9^{15-11}.

6. Guess K_8. For the remaining pairs (x'_9, y'_9), (x''_9, y''_9) in Table Ω_3, filter the pairs such that $\Delta x_8 = (1000\ 0000\ 0000\ 0000)$, where $y_8 = (x_9 \oplus y_9) \ggg 2$, $x_8 = ((x_9 \oplus K_8) + y_8) \lll 7$. The time complexity is approximately $2^{n-6} \times 2^{16} \times 2^{11} \times 2^5 \times 2^{16} \times 2 = 2^{n+43}$ additions in this step. After the round decryption, we obtain the output of impossible differential distinguishers with the probability of 2^{-14}.

The time complexity is mainly determined by Step 6 during the above attack. Known approximately $\varepsilon = 2^{48} \times (1 - 2^{-14})^{2^{n-6}}$ key candidates after excluding wrong key at Step 6, exhaust the candidate key and the rest 16 bits key with a time complexity of $\varepsilon \times 2^{16}$. When $n = 18$, the time complexity of the attack is $2^{n+43}/11 + \varepsilon \times 2^{16} = 2^{n+43}/11 + 2^{48} \times (1 - 2^{-14})^{2^{n-6}} \times 2^{16} \approx 2^{63.66}$ 11-round SPECK32 encryptions, the data complexity is 2^{32} chosen plaintexts. In addition, the memory complexity is mainly determined by Step 4, which is $2^{16} \times 2^{11} \times 2^{n+8} \times (2 + (n+27)/32) \approx 2^{54.77}$ SPECK32 states.

If we use two 7-round impossible differential distinguishers above to attack 11-round SPECK32 simultaneously, the time complexity will further reduce. Utilize 2^{32} chosen plaintexts, the error rate reduces to $(1 - 2^{-14})^{2^{12} \times 2}$. And the time complexity is approximately $2 \times 2^{18+43}/11 + \varepsilon \times 2^{16} = 2^{61}/11 + 2^{48} \times (1 - 2^{-14})^{2^{12} \times 2} \times 2^{16} \approx 2^{63.34}$ 11-round SPECK32 encryptions, the memory complexity is approximately $2^{54.77} \times 2 = 2^{55.77}$ SPECK32 states.

5   Impossible Differential Attacks on 10-Round and 11-Round SPECK48/96

Based on 6-round and 7-round impossible differential distinguishers, impossible differential attacks on 10-round and 11-round SPECK32/64 were given above. Li et al. [15] got many 6-round impossible differential distinguishers of SPECK2n ($2n = 48, 64, 96, 128$) by using the Property 1. Based on those known 6-round impossible differential distinguishers, we can use Property 2 to construct 7-round impossible differential distinguishers of SPECK2n ($2n = 48, 64, 96, 128$).

5.1   6-Round and 7-Round Impossible Differential Distinguishers of SPECK2n

Li et al. [15] used the Property 1 to analyze the differential diffusion properties of SPECK2n ($2n = 48, 64, 96, 128$) in encryption and decryption direction and got those 6-round impossible differential distinguishers shown in the following.

$$(\ast\ast\cdots\ast\overset{21}{1}00\cdots0\ast\ast\cdots\ast,\ 000\ast\ast\cdots\ast\overset{14}{0}0\cdots0) \nrightarrow (10\cdots0,\ 100\cdots0100) \tag{1}$$

$$(\ast\ast\cdots\ast\overset{21}{0}00\cdots0\ast\ast\cdots\ast,\ 000\ast\ast\cdots\ast\overset{14}{1}0\cdots0) \nrightarrow (10\cdots0,\ 100\cdots0100) \tag{2}$$

$$(\ast\ast\cdots\ast\overset{22}{0}00\cdots0\ast\ast\cdots\ast,\ 000\ast\ast\cdots\ast\overset{15}{0}0\cdots0) \nrightarrow (10\cdots0,\ 100\cdots0100) \tag{3}$$

$$(\ast\ast\cdots\ast\overset{22}{1}00\cdots0\ast\ast\cdots\ast,\ 000\ast\ast\cdots\ast\overset{15}{1}0\cdots0) \nrightarrow (10\cdots0,\ 100\cdots0100) \tag{4}$$

We can select part of these 6-round impossible differential distinguishers of SPECK2n($2n = 48, 64, 96, 128$) to attack corresponding algorithms. For example, we select such 6-round impossible differential distinguishers of SPECK48 as Fig. 6 shows.

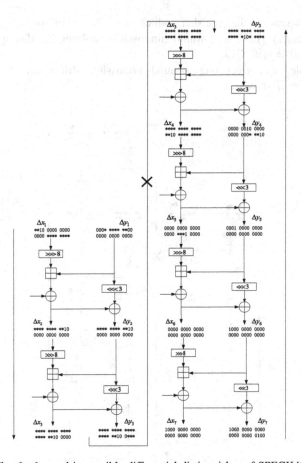

Fig. 6. 6-round impossible differential distinguisher of SPECK48

Besides, based on those known 6-round impossible differential distinguishers, we further use Property 2 to construct 7-round impossible differential distinguishers of SPECK2n(2n = 48, 64, 96, 128).

Theorem 2. When the input difference satisfies $(\Delta x_1, \Delta y_1) = (00\cdots0\ \overset{(i+8)\bmod n}{1}\ 00\cdots0,\ 00\cdots0\overset{i}{1}00\cdots0)$, where $i \in \{10\} \cup [12, n-7]$, and $x_1[(i+8) \bmod n] \neq y_1[i]$, it is impossible that the output difference satisfies $(\Delta x_8, \Delta y_8) = (100\cdots0,\ 100\cdots0100)$ after 7-round SPECK2n (2n = 48, 64, 96, 128) encryptions.

Proof. Note $r_1 = x_1 \ggg 8$. Since $x_1[(i+8) \bmod n] \neq y_1[i]$, it follows $r_1[i] \neq y_1[i]$. And since $x_2 = ((x_1 \ggg 8) + y_1) \oplus K_1$, it's clearly that $x_2 = (r_1 + y_1) \oplus K_1$. From Property 2, we can obtain the output difference $\Delta x_2 = (00\cdots0)$ after 1-round SPECK2n encryption, then $\Delta y_2 = \Delta x_2 \oplus (\Delta y_1 \lll 3) = (00\cdots0\overset{i+3}{1}00\cdots0)$. Thus $(\Delta x_2, \Delta y_2) = (00\cdots0,\ 00\cdots0\overset{i}{1}00\cdots0)$, where $i \in \{13\} \cup [15, n-4]$. In addition, $(\Delta x_2, \Delta y_2) \nrightarrow (\Delta x_8, \Delta y_8)$ is a 6-round impossible differential distinguisher which can be seen in (2) and (3), so $(\Delta x_1, \Delta y_1) \nrightarrow (\Delta x_8, \Delta y_8)$ is a 7-round impossible differential distinguisher when $x_1[(i+8) \bmod n] \neq y_1[i]$. QED

For example, we select one 7-round impossible differential distinguisher of SPECK48 as Fig. 7 shows.

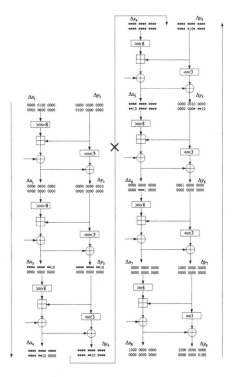

Fig. 7. 7-round impossible differential distinguisher of SPECK48

5.2 Impossible Differential Attacks on 10-Round and 11-Round SPECK 48/96

By using the distinguisher shown in Fig. 6, we add 1 round forward and 3 rounds backward to obtain a 10-round impossible differential trail of SPECK48/96.The details are as Fig. 8 shows. Combined with the divide-and-conquer attack and time-and-memory tradeoff, a 10-round impossible differential cryptanalysis of SPECK48/96 is presented with a time complexity of $2^{92.91}$ 10-round encryptions, a data complexity of $2^{39.88}$ chosen-plaintexts, a memory complexity of $2^{87.88}$ SPECK48 states. The process of impossible differential attacks on SPECK48/96 is similar with SPECK32/64's, so omitting.

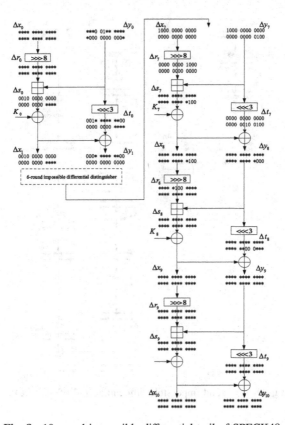

Fig. 8. 10-round impossible differential trail of SPECK48

Further, by using the distinguisher shown in Fig. 7, we add 1 round forward and 3 rounds backward to give an 11-round impossible differential attack on SPECK48/96. The details are as Fig. 9 shows. Combined with the divide-and-conquer attack and time-and-memory tradeoff, the time complexity of the attack is approximately $2^{95.65}$ 11-round encryptions, the data complexity is 2^{48} chosen-plaintexts, the memory complexity is 2^{84} SPECK48 states.

If we use all seven 7-round impossible differential distinguishers in Theorem 2 to attack 11-round SPECK48 simultaneously, the time complexity will further reduce. Utilize 2^{48} chosen plaintexts, the error rate reduces to $(1 - 2^{-21})^{2^{19} \times 7}$. And the time complexity is approximately $7 \times 2^{92}/11 + 2^{96} \times (1 - 2^{-21})^{2^{19} \times 7} \approx 2^{93.77}$ 11-round SPECK48 encryptions, the memory complexity is approximately $2^{76} \times 7 = 2^{86.81}$ SPECK48 states.

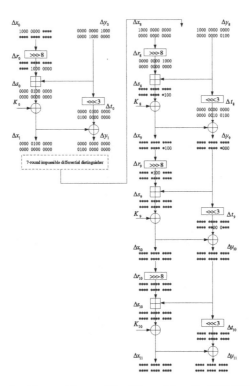

Fig. 9. 11-round impossible differential trail of SPECK48

6 Conclusion

In this article, we concentrate on the security of lightweight block cipher SPECK under impossible differential attack in the single key setting. This article utilizes multiple 6-round impossible differential distinguishers of SPECK32/64 and SPECK48/96 and combined with the divide-and-conquer attack and time-and-memory tradeoff, impossible differential attacks on these two ciphers are improved. In addition, by further analyzing the properties of the differential diffusion of addition, multiple 7-round impossible differential distinguishers of SPECK families of block ciphers are constructed. And the 11-round impossible differential cryptanalysis of SPECK32/64 and SPECK48/96 is presented by adding one round forward and three rounds backward. For other block ciphers of SPECK, based on multiple 7-round impossible differential distinguishers presented in this paper, the corresponding impossible differential cryptanalysis results can be given with the similar method.

Acknowledgments. Supported by the Foundation of Science and Technology on Information Assurance Laboratory (No. KJ-17-003).

References

1. Beaulieu, R., Shors, D., Smith, J., et al.: The SIMON and SPECK Families of Lightweight Block Ciphers. http://eprint.iacr.org/2013/404.pdf
2. Abed, F., List, E., Lucks, S.: Cryptanalysis of the SPECK Family of Block Ciphers. https://eprint.iacr.org/2013/568.pdf
3. Abed, F., List, E., Lucks, S., Wenzel, J.: Differential cryptanalysis of round-reduced SIMON and SPECK. In: Cid, C., Rechberger, C. (eds.) FSE 2014. LNCS, vol. 8540, pp. 525–545. Springer, Heidelberg (2015). https://doi.org/10.1007/978-3-662-46706-0_27
4. Biryukov, A., Roy, A., Velichkov, V.: Differential analysis of block ciphers SIMON and SPECK. In: Cid, C., Rechberger, C. (eds.) FSE 2014. LNCS, vol. 8540, pp. 546–570. Springer, Heidelberg (2015). https://doi.org/10.1007/978-3-662-46706-0_28
5. Dinur, I.: Improved differential cryptanalysis of round-reduced SPECK. In: Joux, A., Youssef, A. (eds.) SAC 2014. LNCS, vol. 8781, pp. 147–164. Springer, Cham (2014). https://doi.org/10.1007/978-3-319-13051-4_9
6. Yao, Y., Zhang, B., Wu, W.: Automatic search for linear trails of the SPECK family. In: Lopez, J., Mitchell, Chris J. (eds.) ISC 2015. LNCS, vol. 9290, pp. 158–176. Springer, Cham (2015). https://doi.org/10.1007/978-3-319-23318-5_9
7. Chen, Y.Q.: Zero correlation cryptanalysis of block cipher SPECK. Master thesis, Shandong University (2015)
8. Cui, T.T., Jia, K.T., Fu, K., Chen, S.Y., Wang M.Q.: New Automatic Search Tool for Impossible Differentials and Zero-Correlation Linear Approximations. http://eprint.iacr.org/2016/689.pdf
9. Biryukov, A., Velichkov, V., Le Corre, Y.: Automatic search for the best trails in ARX: application to block cipher SPECK. In: Peyrin, T. (ed.) FSE 2016. LNCS, vol. 9783, pp. 289–310. Springer, Heidelberg (2016). https://doi.org/10.1007/978-3-662-52993-5_15
10. Fu, K., Wang, M.Q., Guo, Y.: MILP-based automatic search algorithms for differential and linear trails for SPECK. In: Peyrin, T. (ed.) Fast Software Encryption. LNCS, vol. 1267, pp. 268–288. Springer, Heidelberg (2016)
11. Knudsen, L.R.: DEAL A 128-bit block cipher. Department of Informatics, Complexity (1998)
12. Biham, E., Biryukov, A., Shamir, A.: Cryptanalysis of skipjack reduced to 31 rounds using impossible differentials. J. Cryptol. 18(4), 291–311 (2005)
13. Lee, H.C., Kang, H.C., Hong, D., Sung, J., Hong, S.: New Impossible Differential Characteristic of SPECK64 Using MILP. https://eprint.iacr.org/2016/1137.pdf
14. Xu, H., Su, P.H., Qi, W.F.: Impossible differential cryptanalysis of reduced-round SPECK. J. Electron. Inf. Technol. 39(10), 2479–2486 (2017)
15. Li, M.M., Guo, J.S., C, J.Y., Xu, L.H.: Analysis of impossible differential characteristic for SPECK family of block ciphers. J. Cryptol. Res. 5(6), 631–640 (2018)

Detect Peer-to-Peer Botnet with Permutation Entropy and Adaptive Information Fusion

Yuanzhang Song[1]([✉]), Junting He[2], and Hongyu Li[1]

[1] Changchun Institute of Optics, Fine Mechanics and Physics,
Chinese Academy of Sciences, Changchun 130033, China
songyuanzhang@163.com
[2] Jiefang Business Division, China FAW Corporation Limited,
Changchun 130011, China

Abstract. Aim to improve the detection accuracy, a novel peer-to-peer botnet detection method based on permutation entropy and adaptive information fusion algorithm was proposed. Permutation entropy was utilized to characterize the complexity measure of network traffic, which did not vary with the structure of peer-to-peer network, peer-to-peer protocol and attack type. Kalman filter was utilized to detect the abnormalities of the complexity measure. Furthermore, the features of TCP packets were utilized to reduce the negative impact of web applications on botnet detection, especially the web applications that were based on peer-to-peer protocols. To get more accurate information fusion result, an adaptive information fusion algorithm was proposed to fuse the above detection results to get the final detection result, which combined Dempster-Shafer theory and Dezert-Smarandache theory by using their superiorities and overcoming their disadvantages. The experiment results show that the proposed method is able to detect peer-to-peer botnet with higher accuracy and stronger robustness.

Keywords: Peer-to-peer botnet · Permutation entropy
Adaptive information fusion

1 Introduction

The botnet is one type of malicious host group, and botmaster can use the secondary injection process to modify and regenerate the payload of the bot nodes, so as to easily launch many types of attacks, including DDoS attack, spam attack and so on. As the representative of the new emerging botnet, Storm builds and maintains the C&C mechanism with Overnet/eDonkey in order to overcome the single point fault of the traditional network structure, which is one classic kind of peer-to-peer network. Changing the former centralized structure to the peer-to-peer structure can allow the botnet continue to effectively propagate and launch attacks after many bot nodes have been eliminated. Therefore, how to detect the new botnet equipped with the peer-to-peer structure has come to the center of network security area.

A novel detection method based on permutation entropy and adaptive information fusion algorithm was proposed based on analyzing the lifecycle of Storm, and it focused on the complexity measure of network traffic, which did not vary with the

H. Zhang et al. (Eds.): CTCIS 2018, CCIS 960, pp. 32–50, 2019.
https://doi.org/10.1007/978-981-13-5913-2_3

structure of peer-to-peer network, peer-to-peer protocol and attack type. Permutation entropy was used to characterize the complexity measure of network traffic, and Kalman filter was used to detect the abnormalities of it. Moreover, considering that the traffic flow of web applications was likely to affect the detection result, the features of TCP packets were used to solve the problem. To get the more accurate information fusion result on the decision level, an adaptive information fusion algorithm based on Dempster-Shafer theory (DST) and Dezert-Smarandache theory (DSmT) was proposed. Depending on the conflict factor of evidences, DST and DSmT were adaptively utilized to get the final detection result by fusing the above detection results. The experiment results show that the proposed method is able to detect peer-to-peer botnet with higher accuracy and stronger robustness.

2 Related Work

Porras et al. [1] incisively analyzed on Storm's logic, and discussed the mechanism that how botnets avoided the detections, and put forward a peer-to-peer botnet detection method based on dialog, which detected peer-to-peer botnet by processing the dialog with the help of the pattern matching theory.

Wang et al. [2] proposed an approach to infer botnet C&C protocol using some inherent patterns in the bot execution trace coverage of basis blocks. The coverage analysis approach is evaluated on Zeus, Sdbot and Agobot, and the result shows that the approach an accurately and efficiently extract the botnet control commands.

Yahyazadeh et al. [3] proposed a general botnet detection system (named as Bot-Grab) that considers both malicious activities and the history of coordinated group activities in the network. A suspected host will be identified as being bot-infected if it has a high negative reputation score or performs some malicious activities.

Wang et al. [4] proposed a detection method focusing on the periodic communication, and introduced quantum computing into accelerating the periodic communication detection based on the existing algorithm.

Chen et al. [5] proposed a lightweight real-time botnet detection framework called Bot-Guard, which uses the global landscape and flexible configurability of software defined network (SDN) to identify botnets promptly. A convex lens imaging graph (CLI-graph) was given to depict the topology characteristics of botnet, which allows SDN controller to locate attacks separately and mitigate the burden of network devices.

References [6–8] gave an comprehensive introduction of the working mechanisms of botnet in terms of its definition, transmission, lifecycle, malicious behaviors and command and control channels, and divided the botnet development into two stages, namely, attacks to traditional PC and extensive attacks, with the technological features, behavioral characteristics, case studies and evolutionary patterns of each stage elaborated in a detailed manner. After a summary of existing work on the defense of botnet with the limitations of each approach discussed, possible future attempts were presented.

Although some detection methods of peer-to-peer botnet were proposed, there are still many problems as follows:

1. Many detection methods mainly focus on some unique abnormalities of peer-to-peer botnet. The methods will no longer effectively work when a new botnet emerges.
2. Most detection methods do not consider the negative impact of web applications on botnet detection, especially the web applications that are based on peer-to-peer protocols. Essentially, the peer-to-peer botnet is an illegal peer-to-peer network for launching many malicious attacks. Their network features are so similar that it results in a larger false-positive rate.
3. Many detection methods require a great quantity of historical data, which result in the fact that they are not able to be used in the real-time detection scenarios.

Based on the above analysis, a novel peer-to-peer botnet detection method based on permutation entropy and adaptive information fusion algorithm is proposed. The possible creative works are concluded are as follows:

1. The essential features of network traffic of peer-to-peer botnet are focused. Permutation entropy is used to characterize the complexity measure of network traffic, which does not vary with the structure of peer-to-peer network, peer-to-peer protocol and the attack type of peer-to-peer botnet. Therefore, the proposed detection method will be able to detect the new emerging peer-to-peer botnet with stronger robustness.
2. It utilizes the features of TCP packets to reduce the negative impact of web applications on botnet detection, especially the web applications that were based on peer-to-peer protocols.
3. With the help of focusing on the complexity measure of network traffic, the prior knowledge is not required in the adaptive information fusion algorithm, so it is able to be used in the real-time detection scenarios.

3 Detect Peer-to-Peer Botnet with Permutation Entropy and Adaptive Information Fusion

3.1 Overview of Detection Method

As the representative of the new emerging botnet, the lifecycle process of Storm is shown as Fig. 1. The following network features deserve more attention:

1. The number of UDP packets is sharply increasing, because UDP packets are used to build and maintain the C&C mechanism, including publishing itself, keeping alive, peer discovery and so forth.
2. To implement the bootstrap process so as to connect to other peers, the bot nodes send many requests randomly, which leads to such a large number of ICMP destination unreachable packets rarely observed in normal network scenarios.

3. The number of SMTP packets is in an increasing trend when the bot nodes are launch the spam attack.

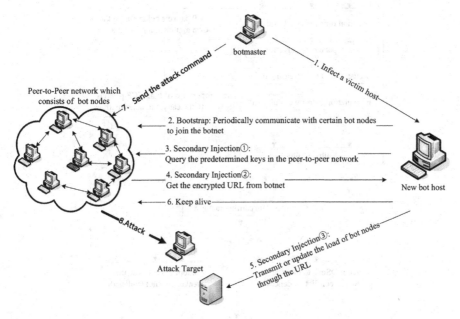

Fig. 1. Lifecycle of peer-to-peer botnet.

After analyzing on the lifecycle process and network features, the process of proposed detection method is described as follows (see Fig. 2):

1. Use permutation entropy to characterize the complexity measure of ICMP, UDP and SMTP packets, and use Kalman filter to detect the abnormalities of the complexity measure.
2. The proportion of long TCP packets is used to identify the objects responsible for the above abnormalities, which are peer-to-peer botnets or web applications, so as to reduce the negative impact of web applications on botnet detection, especially the web applications that were based on peer-to-peer protocols.
3. To get more accurate information fusion result, an adaptive information fusion algorithm was proposed to fuse the above detection results to get the final detection result, which combined DST and DSmT by using their superiorities and overcoming their disadvantages.
4. Make the final detection decision based on the final detection result.

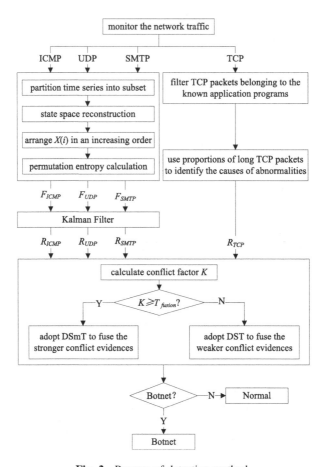

Fig. 2. Process of detection method.

3.2   Permutation Entropy

The complexity measure of network traffic is focused in the paper, which does not vary with the structure of peer-to-peer network, peer-to-peer protocol and the attack. Permutation entropy is a parameter of average entropy to characterize the complexity of a time series, and reflects and magnifies the subtle transformation of the time series [9]. Compared with Approximate Entropy and Lempel-Ziv Complexity and so on, permutation entropy makes only use of the order of the values of the time series, so that it can not only compare the variable length time series, but also resist the noise in the signal, which are very common in the network data acquisition. Therefore, permutation entropy is selected to characterize the complexity measure of network traffic.

Given a time series $\{x(i), i = 1, 2, \ldots, N\}$, with the help of Takens-Maine theorem, it will be reconstructed to be

$$\begin{cases} X(1) = \{x(1), x(1+\tau), \ldots, x(1+(m-1)\tau)\} \\ \cdots \\ X(i) = \{x(i), x(i+\tau), \ldots, x(i+(m-1)\tau)\} \\ \cdots \\ X(N-(m-1)\tau) = \{x(N-(m-1)\tau), x(N-(m-2)\tau), \ldots, x(N)\} \end{cases} \quad (1)$$

where m is the embedded dimension and τ is the time delay [10]. The m number of real values contained in each $X(i)$ can be arranged to be an non-descending order as

$$\{x(i+(j_1-1)\tau) \leq x(i+(j_2-1)\tau) \leq \ldots \leq x(i+(j_m-1)\tau)\} \quad (2)$$

If there exist such cases such as $x(i+(j_1-1)\tau) = x(i+(j_2-1)\tau)$ and $j_1 \leq j_2$, then $x(i+(j_1-1)\tau) \leq x(i+(j_2-1)\tau)$. Therefore, map $X(i)$ to a group of symbols

$$S(l) = (j_1, j_2, \ldots, j_m) \quad (3)$$

where $l = 1, 2, \ldots, k$ and $k \leq m!$. $S(l)$ is one of the $m!$ symbol permutations, which is mapped to be the $j_1, j_2, \ldots, j_m$ number symbols m in m-dimensional embedding space. The permutation entropy of order $\{x(i), i = 1, 2, \ldots, N\}$ for named as $H_p(m)$ can be defined as the Shannon information entropy for the k symbol sequences.

$$H_p(m) = -\sum_{l=1}^{k} (P_l \ln P_l) \quad (4)$$

where $P_1, P_2, \ldots, P_k$ are the probability distribution of each symbol sequences, $\sum_{l=1}^{k} P_l = 1$. When all the above symbol sequences have the same probability, $H_p(m)$ will take the maximum value as $\ln(m!)$, therefore, the permutation entropy of order m can be normalized as

$$0 \leq H_p = \frac{-\sum_{l=1}^{k} (P_l \ln P_l)}{-\sum_{l=1}^{l=m!} \left(\frac{1}{m!} \ln\left(\frac{1}{m!}\right)\right)} = \frac{-\sum_{l=1}^{k} (P_l \ln P_l)}{\ln(m!)} \leq 1 \quad (5)$$

The permutation entropy H_p characterizes the local order structure of $\{x(i), i = 1, 2, \ldots, N\}$, which reflects and magnifies the subtle transformation of $\{x(i), i = 1, 2, \ldots, N\}$. The smaller the value of H_p is, the more regular the time series is. When all permutations have the same probability, $H_p(m)$ will take the maximum value as 1.

As mentioned above, botnet will lead to the increasement of UDP packets, ICMP packets and SMTP packets, which will lead to the decreasement of H_p, and thus the abnormalities of the complexity measure of network traffic are able to be caught with the help of H_p. To improve the detection sensitivity, H_p is input to Kalman filter to earlier detect the above abnormalities. To fuse the results with the proposed adaptive information fusion algorithm, the detection variable of permutation entropy for a time series $\{x(i), i = 1, 2, \ldots, N\}$ is defined as

$$F_t = 1 - H_p \tag{6}$$

where t is the current time step.

3.3　Kalman Filter

The discrete Kalman filter estimates a process by using a form of feedback control. It estimates the process state at some certain time step and then obtains feedback in the form of measurement [11–16] (see Fig. 3).

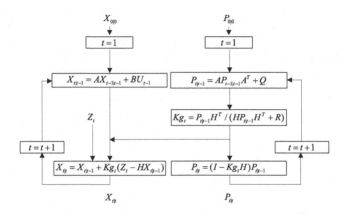

Fig. 3. Kalman filter.

3.3.1　Time Update Equations

The priori estimate $(X_{t|t-1})$ is calculated on the basis of the process prior to step t.

$$X_{t|t-1} = AX_{t-1|t-1} + BU_{t-1} \tag{7}$$

where $X_{t-1|t-1}$ is the posteriori estimate at step $t - 1$, U_{t-1} represents the control input, A and B are system parameters.

The priori estimate error covariance is

$$P_{t|t-1} = AP_{t-1|t-1}A^T + Q \tag{8}$$

where $P_{t-1|t-1}$ is the posteriori estimate error covariance of $X_{t-1|t-1}$, and Q is the process noise covariance.

The time update equations project forward the current state and error covariance estimates to obtain a priori estimate for the next time step.

3.3.2   Measurement Update Equations

The posteriori estimate $(X_{t|t})$ is calculated on the basis of the measurement Z_t and $X_{t|t-1}$.

$$X_{t|t} = X_{t|t-1} + \frac{P_{t|t-1}H^T}{HP_{t|t-1}H^T + R}(Z_t - HX_{t|t-1}) \tag{9}$$

where H is the system parameter for measurement, and R is the measurement noise covariance.

The posteriori estimate error covariance is

$$P_{t|t} = \left(I - \frac{P_{t|t-1}H^T}{HP_{t|t-1}H^T + R}H\right)P_{t|t-1} \tag{10}$$

where I is an identity matrix.

The measurement update equations are responsible for incorporating a new measurement into the priori estimate to obtain an improved posteriori estimate.

After each time and measurement update pair, the process is repeater with the previous posteriori estimates used to project or predict the new priori estimates. As known, Storm causes abnormities of the complexity measure of network traffic, which are represented by F_{ICMP}, F_{UDP} and F_{SMTP}. After input F_{ICMP}, F_{UDP} and F_{SMTP} separately into Kalman filter, the posteriori estimate of them are obtain as R_{ICMP}, R_{UDP} and R_{SMTP}.

3.4   Identify Objects Responsible for Abnormalities

Essentially, the peer-to-peer botnet is an illegal peer-to-peer network for launching many malicious attacks. Their network features are so similar that it results in a larger false-positive rate. Therefore, features of TCP packets were utilized to reduce the negative impact of web applications on botnet detection, especially the web applications that were based on peer-to-peer protocols.

In general, Web applications typically use long TCP packets to transmit the payload, which are longer than 1300 bytes. However, the short TCP packets are mainly used to implement the secondary injection process to modify and regenerate the payload of the bot nodes, the botmaster update the payload with HTTP protocol. Therefore, the proportion of the long TCP packets is used to identify the objects responsible for the above abnormalities, which are peer-to-peer botnets or web applications, so as to reduce the negative impact of web applications on botnet detection, especially the web applications that were based on peer-to-peer protocols. It is important to note that TCP packets of the known web applications must be filtered firstly. Given that Pr denotes the proportion of TCP packets longer than 1300 bytes, the smaller Pr, the larger the probability of the hypothesis that the objects responsible for the above abnormalities are peer-to-peer botnets, and the process of dealing with TCP packets is shown in Fig. 4. PKT_i is the current TCP packet, N is the total number of TCP packets, and N_L is the number of long TCP packets.

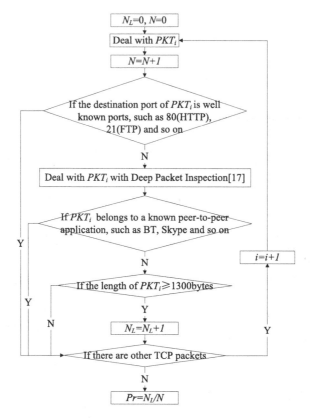

Fig. 4. Process of dealing with TCP packets.

Define the decision function as follows.

$$R_{TCP_t} = \begin{cases} 1 & Pr < T_{TCP} \\ 0 & Pr \geq T_{TCP} \end{cases} \tag{11}$$

If $Pr < T_{TCP}$, the network abnormalities mentioned above are possibly caused by peer-to-peer botnet, and use the Kaufman algorithm [18] to adjust T_{TCP} dynamically.

3.5 Adaptive Information Fusion

The network features of peer-to-peer botnet are uncertain and changeable. Therefore, using a single network feature to describe the details of the network changes to detect peer-to-peer botnet will be very likely to result in the higher false-negative and false-positive rate. The proposed adaptive information fusion algorithm on the decision level is adopted in order to dispose of the problem.

Bayesian theory and DST are the most widely used decision-level information fusion algorithms. As the classical generalization of Bayesian theory, DST has no use for the conditional probability and priori probability, and the hypothesis set is reduced with combining evidences gradually. While, DST exhibits many limitations, for example, DST will draw a paradoxical paradox when the amount of conflict between the evidences is large. DSmT is a new emerging static and dynamic fusion algorithm, which overcomes some limitations of DST, but the calculation of DSmT is oversized. An adaptive fusion algorithm based on DST and DSmT is proposed to fuse R_{ICMP}, R_{UDP}, R_{SMTP} and R_{TCP} to get the fusion detection result RF_k.

3.5.1 Dempster-Shafer Theory

Let U denote the universal set, which represents all possible values of a random variable X, and the elements of U are inconsistent, then $U = \{\theta_1, \theta_2, \ldots, \theta_n\}$ is called the discernment frame. The power set 2^U is the set of all subsets of U. If a function $m : 2^U \rightarrow [0, 1]$ exhibits the two follow properties:

$$m(\varnothing) = 0 \tag{12}$$

$$\sum_{A \in 2^U} m(A) = 1 \tag{13}$$

then $m(A)$ is called the basic belief assignment of set A. Let BEL_1 and BEL_2 denote the two belief functions of U, the corresponding focus elements of them are $A_1, \ldots, A_k$ and $B_1, \ldots, B_r$, the corresponding basic belief assignments are m_1 and m_2, and the combination of m_1 and m_2 is calculated with Dempster's rule of combination shown as Eq. (14), and K is used to measure the degree of conflict of the two evidences.

$$m(X) = \begin{cases} \dfrac{\displaystyle\sum_{\substack{A_i, B_j \in 2^U \\ A_i \cap B_j = X}} m_1(A_i)m_2(B_j)}{1-K} & X \neq \varnothing \\ 0 & X = \varnothing \end{cases} \tag{14}$$

where

$$K = \sum_{\substack{A_i, B_j \in 2^U \\ A_i \cap B_j = \varnothing}} m_1(A_i)m_2(B_j) \tag{15}$$

Dempster's rule of combination can be directly extended for the combination of $n \geq 2$ independent sources of evidence and its major interest comes from its commutativity and associativity properties [19].

3.5.2 Dezert-Smarandache Theory

Although very appealing, DST presents some limitations, for example, DST will draw a paradoxical paradox when the amount of conflict between the evidences is large ($K \rightarrow 1$), which lead to lower confidence to trust the fusion result [20–23]. There are two categories of approaches to overcome the above problems. From the perspective of modifying the Dempster's combination rule, the first one is to propose new rules of combination in the DST framework, such as Murphy's rule of combination, Yager's rule of combination, Smets' rule of combination and Dubois & Prade's rule of combination. From the perspective of modifying the evidence source, the second one is to propose totally new alternative rules, and DSmT falls into this category. DSmT can be considered to be an extension of DST, but they are fundamentally different. Classically, DSmT focuses on fusing the imprecise, uncertain and highly conflicting sources of evidence. It is able to formally combine any types of independent sources of information which are represented in term of the belief functions.

The foundation of DSmT is based on the definition of Dedekind's lattice D^U also called hyper power set of frame U in the sequel. In the DSmT framework, U is first considered as only a set $\{\theta_1, \theta_2, \ldots, \theta_n\}$ of n exhaustive elements (closed world assumption) without introducing other constraint (exclusivity or non-existential constraints). If a function $m : D^U \to [0, 1]$ exhibits the two follow properties.

$$m(\varnothing) = 0 \tag{16}$$

$$\sum_{A \in D^U} m(A) = 1 \tag{17}$$

Then $m(A)$ is called generalized basic belief assignment of set A. Because some subsets of U can contain elements known to be truly exclusive but also truly non existing at all at a given time, taken into account some known integrity constraints, one has to work with a proper hybrid DSm model. In such case, the hybrid DSm rule of combination based on the chosen hybrid DSm model for $n \geq 2$ independent sources of information is defined for all $A \in D^U$ as Eq. (18).

$$m(X) = \delta(A)[S_1(A) + S_2(A) + S_3(A)] \tag{18}$$

$$\delta(A) = \begin{cases} 0 & A \in \varnothing_m \\ 1 & A \notin \varnothing_m \end{cases} \tag{19}$$

$$S_1(A) = \sum_{\substack{X_1, X_2, \ldots, X_n \in D^U \\ X_1 \cap X_2 \cap \ldots \cap X_n = A}} \prod_{i=1}^{n} m_i(X_i) \tag{20}$$

$$S_2(A) = \sum_{\substack{X_1, X_2, \ldots, X_n \in \varnothing \\ [u(X_1) \cup \ldots \cup u(X_n) = A] \vee [(u(X_1) \cup \ldots \cup u(X_n) \in \varnothing) \wedge (A = \theta_1 \cup \theta_2 \cup \ldots \cup \theta_n)]}} \prod_{i=1}^{n} m_i(X_i) \tag{21}$$

$$S_3(A) = \sum_{\substack{X_1, X_2, \ldots, X_n \in D^U \\ (X_1 \cup X_2 \cup \ldots \cup X_n) = A \\ X_1 \cap X_2 \cap \ldots \cap X_n = \varnothing}} \prod_{i=1}^{n} m_i(X_i) \tag{22}$$

$\emptyset_m$ is the set of all elements of D^U which have been forced to be empty within the constraints of the model, and $\emptyset$ is the classical empty set. $u(X)$ is the union of all singletons θ_i that compose X. $S_1(A)$ corresponds to the classic DSm rule of combination for n independent sources based on the free DSm model, $S_2(A)$ represents the mass of all relatively and absolutely empty sets which is transferred to the total or relative ignorances, $S_3(A)$ transfers the sum of relatively empty sets to the non-empty sets.

3.5.3 Adaptive Information Fusion Algorithm

DST is an efficient fusion algorithm to fuse the lowlier conflict sources of evidence. Meanwhile, DSmT focuses on fusing the imprecise, uncertain and highly conflicting sources of evidence, but DSmT is very computationally intensive. So DST and DSmT are combined by using their superiorities and overcoming their disadvantages. Given the frame $U = \{\theta_1, \theta_2, \ldots, \theta_n\}$, the adaptive information fusion algorithm is as follows (see Fig. 5):

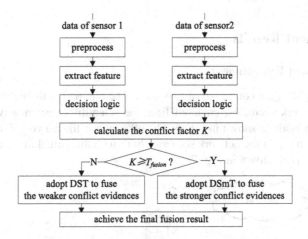

Fig. 5. Adaptive information fusion algorithm.

1. Calculate conflict factor K by Eq. (15), and set the judgment threshold T_{fusion}.
2. If $K \geq T_{fusion}$, fuse the evidences with DSmT by Eq. (18). Otherwise, fuse the evidences with DST by Eq. (14).

Based on the analysis of evidences, the judgment threshold T_{fusion} should be different for different types of evidences, perhaps even be several point or range. According to above mentioned the problem, in-depth discussion will not be taken in the paper. To simplify the calculation, $T_{fusion} = 0.7$ [24].

4   Process of Detection Method

Given the current time step t, detecting the peer-to-peer botnet based on permutation entropy and adaptive information fusion algorithm is described as follows:

1. Get the number of ICMP, UDP and SMTP packets of network traffic captured with the monitoring devices.
2. Detect the abnormity of the complexity measure of network traffic: calculate permutation entropy of network traffic, and get F_{ICMP}, F_{UDP} and F_{SMTP}; get the output R_{ICMP}, R_{UDP} and R_{SMTP} after input F_{ICMP}, F_{UDP} and F_{SMTP} into Kalman filter.
3. Get R_{TCP} of TCP packets to identify the objects responsible for the above abnormalities, which are peer-to-peer botnets or web applications, so as to reduce the negative impact of web applications on botnet detection, especially the web applications that were based on peer-to-peer protocols.
4. Get the final detection result R_t with adaptive fusion algorithm based on DST and DSmT to fuse R_{ICMP}, R_{UDP}, R_{SMTP} and R_{TCP}.
5. Make the decision. If $R \geq T$, the current network traffic is judged to be abnormal, the botnet is considered to appear in the current network, otherwise not, otherwise not. Use the Kaufman algorithm [18] to adjust the threshold T dynamically to adapt to the different network scenarios.

5   Experiment Results

5.1   Experiment Environment

The experiment data are composed of two parts. The one part is the network traffic of the normal network scenarios, captured from the scientific research network from a certain research institute shown in Fig. 6. The other part is the network data of peer-to-peer botnet, captured in the network scenarios built with the virtual machine (VM) and referred to Ref. [25] shown in Fig. 7.

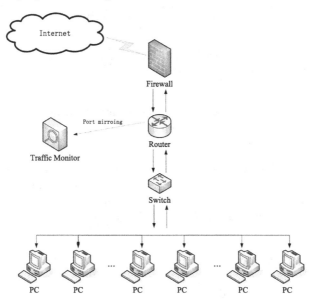

Fig. 6. Real network structure.

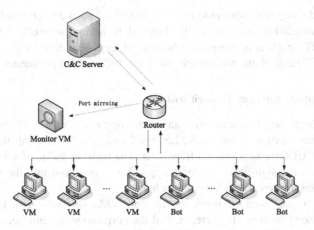

Fig. 7. Simulated botnet.

To simulate a great quantity of hosts, many VMs are set up with the help of Virtualbox, and a VM (called Monitor VM) is selected to work as the router of the local experiment network. Wireshark is chosen to be the packet analyzer installed on the Monitor VM, and capture the sample packets every 10 s. Inject Storm bots to some VMs after the experiment has run normally for a period of time.

5.2   Network Traffic Experiment

In the experiment, the change of network traffic is discussed. From Fig. 8, when bot nodes start to communicate with each other, the number of UDP packets dramatically increases to nearly 21 times lager. The number of the ICMP packets also exhibits a skyrocketing trend when bot nodes are beginning to publish itself, keep alive and discover peers. To implement the bootstrap process so as to connect to other peers, the

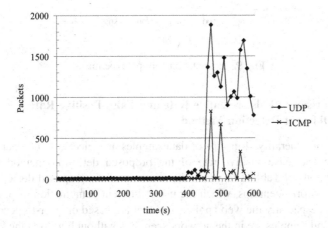

Fig. 8. Network traffic experiment.

bot nodes send many requests randomly, which leads to such a large number of ICMP destination unreachable packets rarely observed in normal network scenarios. The number of SMTP packets is almost zero because of the time delays for the spam attack, and thus SMTP packets are not considered in the following experiments.

5.3   Permutation Entropy Experiment

In the experiment, the change of permutation entropy is discussed, which reflects the complexity measure of network traffic. Let $\tau = 2$ and $m = 5$ when calculate permutation entropy of UDP packets and ICMP packets. The network traffic of normal network scenarios shows the significant randomicity, and it is observed that the value of the permutation entropy remains relatively stable.

From Fig. 9, after bots are injected into some VMs, the number of UDP packets and ICMP packets continue to increase, and the corresponding time series show significant regularity, which make the permutation entropy start to decrease. With the increasing number of the bot nodes and the growing size of the peer-to-peer botnet, the network traffic exhibits a sick new kind of randomicity that is abnormal in the normal scenarios.

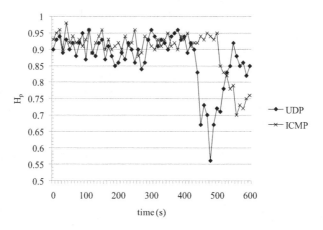

Fig. 9. Permutation entropy experiment.

5.4   Comparison of False-Negative Rate and False-Positive Rate with Different Detection Methods

Without loss of generality, 4 groups of data samples are selected to compare the false-negative rate and false-positive rate of the proposed detection method with other detection methods of Table 1 to verify the accuracy of the proposed detection method in different network scenarios, which are using different combination of protocols and net flow rates, especially the web applications that are based on peer-to-peer protocols. The 1st and 2nd samples are in the network scenarios without bots, and the 2nd and 4th samples contain a great quantity of packets from peer-to-peer applications and other web applications. With the help of the method proposed in Ref. [26], the 3rd sample is acquired by merging the 1st sample with the bot traffic captured from the network scenarios (see Fig. 7), and the 4th sample is acquired by merging the 2nd sample with the bot traffic captured from experiment environment (see Fig. 7).

Table 1. Overview of detection method of compare.

Detection method	Description of method
Multi-chart CUSUM [27]	Use the extended nonparametric CUSUM algorithm to detect the abnormalities of several types of packets
KCFM [28]	Based on multi-observed sequence, use Kalman filter to detect abnormalities, and improve detection precision by Multi-chart CUSUM as an amplifier
DMFIF [29]	Use the fractal theory to describe the macroscopic characteristics of network traffic in the different time scales, use the nonparametric CUSUM algorithm to detect the abnormalities, and use Dempster-Shafer theory to fuse the above detection results to achieve the final detection result
Proposed Method	Focus on the complexity measure of network traffic, which does not vary with the structure of peer-to-peer network, the peer-to-peer protocol and the attack, and consider the negative impact of web applications on botnet detection, and use an adaptive fusion algorithm based on DST and DSmT to fuse the several detection results to acquire the final detection result

Table 2. Detection results of different detection methods.

Sample No.	Description of sample	Real situation	Detection result			
			Multi-chart CUSUM	KCFM	DMFIF	Proposed method
1	Normal	0	23	10	11	4
2	Normal + peer-to-peer	0	121	73	23	10
3	Normal + bot	1000	762	757	882	875
4	Normal + peer-to-peer + bot	1000	1268(784)	1245 (823)	1021 (783)	1023 (862)

Table 3. False-negative rate and false-positive rate of different detection methods.

Detection method	Accuracy rate	False-negative rate	False-positive rate
Multi-chart CUSUM	0.64	0.24	0.23
KCFM	0.75	0.13	0.20
DMFIF	0.83	0.10	0.13
Proposed method	0.89	0.07	0.19

From Tables 2 and 3, the detecting accuracy rate of the proposed method is satisfactory, and the false-positive rate and false-negative rate of the 1st and 3rd sample are very close to the real situation. All detection methods show error detection results for the 2nd and 4th sample, in which the network traffic consists of a great quantity of packets from web applications generate, especially the web applications that are based on peer-to-peer protocols. While, the proposed method utilizes the features of TCP packets to identify the objects responsible for the above abnormalities, which are peer-to-peer botnets or web applications, so as to reduce the negative impact of web applications on botnet detection, especially the web applications that were based on peer-to-peer protocols. Even in such extreme case as the 4th sample, the proposed method stands out in the relatively lowest false-positive rate and false-negative rate than the other detection methods. The network features of peer-to-peer botnet are uncertain and changeable, so using a single network feature to describe the details of the network changes to detect peer-to-peer botnet will be very likely to result in the higher false-negative rate and false-positive rate. Therefore, the proposed method is equipped with the adaptive fusion algorithm based on DST and Dezert-Smarandache theory to overcome the problem. "1023(862)" of Table 2 represents that the method proposed in the paper detects 1023 times attack and 862 times of 1023 times are correct.

6   Conclusion

A novel peer-to-peer botnet detection method based on permutation entropy and adaptive information fusion algorithm was proposed. The paper mainly focused on the complexity measure of network traffic, which did not vary with the structure of peer-to-peer network, the peer-to-peer protocol and the attack. Permutation entropy was used to characterize the complexity measure of network traffic, and Kalman filter was used to detect the abnormalities of it. Considering that the network traffic of web applications was likely to affect the detection result, the features of TCP packets were utilized to dispose of the problem. Then use the adaptive information fusion algorithm to get the more accurate information fusion result. The experiment results show that the proposed method is able to detect peer-to-peer botnet with higher accuracy and stronger robustness. In the future, further reduce the negative impact of web applications on botnet detection should be discussed.

Acknowledgements. This work was supported by the National High Technology Re-search and Development Program of China ("863" Program) (Grant No. 2011AA7031024G) and the National Natural Science Foundation of China (Grant No. 61373053, 61472161).

References

1. Porras, P., Saidi, H., Yegneswaran, V.: A multi-perspective analysis of the storm (Peacomm) Worm. Computer Science Laboratory, SRI International, CA (2007)
2. Wang, Z., Cai, Y.Y., Liu, L., et al.: Using coverage analysis to extract Botnet command-and-control protocol. J. Commun. **35**(1), 156–166 (2014)

3. Yahyazadeh, M., Abadi, M.: BotGrab: a negative reputation system for Botnet detection. Comput. Electr. Eng. **41**, 68–85 (2015)
4. Wang, X., Yang, Q., Jin, X.: Periodic communication detection algorithm of Botnet based on quantum computing. Chin. J. Quant. Electron. **33**(2), 182–187 (2016)
5. Chen, J., Cheng, X., Ruiying, D., et al.: BotGuard: lightweight real-time Botnet detection in software defined networks. Wuhan Univ. J. Nat. Sci. **22**(2), 103–113 (2017)
6. Karim, A., Salleh, R.B., Shiraz, M., et al.: Review: botnet detection techniques: review, future trends, and issues. J. Zhejiang Univ.-Sci. C (Comput. Electron.) **15**(11), 943–983 (2014)
7. Mahmoud, M., Nir, M., Matrawy, A.: A survey on botnet architectures, detection and defences. Int. J. Netw. Secur. **17**(3), 272–289 (2015)
8. Li, K., Fang, B., Cui, X., et al.: Study of Botnets trends. J. Comput. Res. Dev. **53**(10), 2189–2206 (2016)
9. Yan, R., Liu, Y., Gao, R.X.: Permutation entropy: a nonlinear statistical measure for status characterization of rotary machines. Mech. Syst. Sig. Process. **29**(5), 474–484 (2012)
10. Cao, L.Y.: Practical method for determining the minimum embedding dimension of a scalar series. Phys. D Nonlinear Phenom. **110**(1/2), 43–50 (1997)
11. Wang, L., Wenqi, W., Wei, G., et al.: Online performance evaluation of RLG INS based on joint rotation and modulation. Opt. Precis. Eng. **26**(3), 578–587 (2018)
12. Zongming Liu, Yu., Zhang, S.L., et al.: Closed-loop detection and pose optimization of non-cooperation rotating target. Opt. Precis. Eng. **25**(4), 504–511 (2017)
13. Cheng, L., Chen, J., Chen, M.: Fast acquisition of time optimal sliding model control technology for photoelectric tracking system. Opt. Precis. Eng. **25**(1), 148–154 (2017)
14. Li, Z., Li, X., Liu, Q., et al.: Adaptive fast initial attitude estimation for inflight loitering munition. Opt. Precis. Eng. **25**(2), 493–501 (2017)
15. Min, W., Shi, J., Han, Q., et al.: A distributed face recognition approach and performance optimization. Opt. Precis. Eng. **25**(3), 780–785 (2017)
16. Zhou, J., Chen, J., Li, Y., et al.: Research on target prediction algorithm of shipboard photoelectric tracking equipment. Opt. Precis. Eng. **25**(2), 519–528 (2017)
17. Sen, S., Spatscheck, O., Wang, D.: Accurate, scalable in-network identification of P2P traffic using application signatures. In: 13th International Conference on World Wide Web, pp. 512–521. ACM (2004)
18. Kasera, S., Pinheiro, J., Loader, C.: Fast and robust signaling overload control. In: 9th International Conference on Network Protocols, pp. 323–331. IEEE, Riverside (2001)
19. Yager, R.R., Liu, L.: Classic Works of the Dempster-Shafer Theory of Belief Functions. Springer, Berlin (2008). https://doi.org/10.1007/978-3-540-44792-4
20. Mruphy, C.K.: Combing belief function when evidence conflicts. Decis. Support Syst. **29**(1), 1–9 (2000)
21. Voorbraak, F.: On the justification of Dempster's rule of combination. Artif. Intell. **48**, 171–197 (1991)
22. Zadeh, L.: A simple view of the Dempster-Shafer theory of evidence and its implication for the rule of combination. AI Mag. **7**(2), 85–90 (1986)
23. Mathon, B.R., Ozbek, M.M., Pinder, G.F.: Dempster-shafer theory applied to uncertainty surrounding permeability. Math. Geosci. **42**, 293–307 (2010)
24. Smarandache, F., Dezert, J.: Advances and Applications of DSmT for Information Fusion, vol. 2. American Research Press, Rehoboth (2006)
25. Detection of Peer-to-Peer Botnets. http://staff.science.uva.nl/~delaat/sne-2007-2008/p22/report.pdf. Accessed 13 Aug 2017
26. Zhaoa, D., Traorea, I., Sayed, B., et al.: Botnet detection based on traffic behavior analysis and flow intervals. Comput. Secur. **39**, 2–16 (2013)

27. Kang, J., Zhang, J.-Y., Li, Q., et al.: Detecting New P2P botnet with multi-chart CUSUM. In: International Conference on Networks Security, Wireless Communications and Trusted Computing, pp. 688–691. IEEE, Wuhan (2009)

28. Kang, J., Song, Y.: Application KCFM to detect new P2P botnet based on multi-observed sequence. In: Geomatics and Information Science of Wuhan University, vol. 35, no. 5, pp. 520–523 (2010)

29. Song, Y.: Detecting P2P botnet by analyzing macroscopic characteristics with fractal and information fusion. China Commun. **12**(2), 107–117 (2015)

Research of Snort Rule Extension and APT Detection Based on APT Network Behavior Analysis

Yan Cui[✉], Jingfeng Xue, Yong Wang, Zhenyan Liu, and Ji Zhang

School of Computer Science and Technology,
Beijing Institute of Technology, Beijing, China
`cuiyan_72@163.com`

Abstract. At present, APT attack detection has become the focus of the network security protection field. APT attacks are one of the most difficult attacks in cyber attacks. The complexity and variability of APT attack behavior greatly increases the difficulty of attack detection. In order to cope with APT attack, some well-known network security companies at home and abroad have developed a commercial APT intrusion detection system. This highly targeted attack can not be identified by the traditional intrusion detection system. Therefore, in order to deal with this new type of cyber attack. The paper proposes a new method to detect APT attack from different organizations. Data mining algorithm is used to analyze every organization's APT network attack behavior and obtain association rules, so as to customize the design of the Snort rules and apply them to intrusion detection system. Experiments have shown that the evaluation index of the intrusion detection system using the extended Snort rule is significantly better than the traditional Snort intrusion detection system when detecting the same test data. The precision of the extended Snort intrusion detection system is as high as 98.3%, and the false alarm rate is almost 0, which ultimately achieves the purpose of APT detection.

Keywords: APT · Snort rule · Network behavior · Data mining

1 Introduction

Since 2007, APT has attracted importance to attention at home and broad. APT is a behavior that an organization or individual aims to steal information or destroy the target system, and use advanced technologies to invade or attack the target system. The attacker who initiates this malicious activity must have a profound knowledge of computer network, and collects target information, conducts detailed research before attack. Attackers use social engineering to infiltrate the target system, and evade the protection procedures to ensure the concealment and continuity of the attack, and stay in the system after the attack is successful, retaining the possibility of continuing attack. APT attacks have

© Springer Nature Singapore Pte Ltd. 2019
H. Zhang et al. (Eds.): CTCIS 2018, CCIS 960, pp. 51–64, 2019.
https://doi.org/10.1007/978-981-13-5913-2_4

caused serious damage to countries and groups around the world. Hence, how to build a secure and powerful network system to ensure the safety of important information, and real-time defense and detection of malicious attacks by APT attacks has become a research hot topic nowadays [5,6].

Kelai, a network security company, developed an APT attack detection system for the characteristics of APT attacks.It conducts deep dynamic behavior analysis of various mail attachments and files, according to system vulnerabilities, the malicious files constructed by advanced technologies, to discover and confirm APT attacks. Kaspersky Anti-attack platform uses a multi-layered approach to detect threats, builds cores around machine learning, and uses static, behavioral, cloud reputation, sandbox, and pattern-based detection engines in conjunction with targeted attack analysis programs, automatic defense and response of high level threat. Although the APT attack detection systems are perfect, it can not be universally applicable because of their commercial nature. In order to solve this problem, this paper uses the open source network security tool Snort IDS to detect APT attacks.

Snort rules based intrusion detection system(IDS), which is an open source network security tool that can customize the detection rules and adaptive network attacks. According to this characteristic, data mining can be applied to the field of intrusion detection [27], and useful data information can be found from intercepted network packets, and Snort rules can be constructed, so that the intrusion of APT organizations can be more targeted to achieve the purpose of APT detection.

Through analyzing several APT reports, we get different APT organizations' malicious samples, taking FP-Growth association analysis algorithm to mine their network behavior [7]. Finally we compile Snort rules. The proposed method helps to better understand the network access characteristics of every APT organization, and applies effective Snort rules to intrusion detection system, aiming at targeted network protection.

We get different APT organizations' malicious samples from several APT reports, and take FP-Growth association analysis algorithm to mine their network behavior, and design Snort rules. The method, in this paper, helps to better understand the network access characteristics of each APT organization, targeted network protection and detection of APT attacks. Rest of this paper is organized as follows: Sect. 2, We summarize APT development and some relevant researches about using association algorithm to analyze its network behaviors. Snort IDS are described in Sect. 3. A brief introduction to the FP-Growth algorithm is given in Sect. 4. Detailed description of how to use association rule algorithms to build the Snort rules in Sect. 5. Experiments and conclusions are discussed in Sects. 6 and 7.

2   Related Work

In recent years, for the detection and protection of APT attacks, a large number of research work has been done by scholars at home and abroad. For instance, log audit, dynamic behavior analysis, and big data processing. Meicong Li, Communication University of China, analyzed a lot of APT attack cases, and discussed the purpose and the characteristics of APT attack, while put forward the concept of APT attack model [1]. For a APT attack activity, it usually does not use only one virus file. Therefore, if the file features of new variants are not found, it is difficult to detect in virus files [12].

In contrast, the mode of malware communication with the server is same. Therefore, a more general detection index can be obtained by studying the known malicious network behavior [14]. Using data mining algorithm to analyze network behavior is a commonly used method [16]. To analysis the network behavior of malicious code, Apriori algorithms can be used to analysis access time, source address, destination address and DNS request content and so on. According to the rules generated, the user's access mode is obtained [3]. It can also filter network traffic data, to find out IP whose flows more than the threshold, and use FP-Growth algorithm to dig out the correlation between IP [13]. The analysis of a single protocol allows us to understand the special network behavior of a malicious sample [7], but it can not be applied to the detection system.

Intrusion detection system plays an important role in maintaining network security. It detects and monitors network traffic data on the network system and notifies the user when a malicious attack occurs [4]. Among them, Snort IDS is a popular open source network intrusion detection system.

Reviewing several papers that discuss Snort IDS through data mining we find the explanation and implementation of intrusion detection systems utilizing a Snort-based IDS within the Linux operation system [17]. Within this operating system alerts were generated based on the results of Snort IDS through the utilization of the Basic Analysis and Security Engine (BASE) [18]. This effort assists the administrator in the analysis of the network's internet connection. The intrusion detection system was further implemented with Snort and WinPcap, within the Windows operating system [19] and a firewall was configured, based on the Windows operating environment. The Snort IDS rules, however, were not improved.

What's more, DNS and HTTP are popular protocols used by most malware samples, so as to further analyze the use of these protocols, finally, the analysis results can be used in network level malware detection [10]. In 2015, Li H proposed a method to design Snort rules for DNP3 data exception detection [2].

Further utilization of Snort IDS involved monitoring web content in real-time for any abnormal behavior patterns within a campus network [20]. The results generated in the alert analysis of the Snort IDS, in high-speed networks within a campus network [21] demonstrated the highest detection of ICMP PING attacks. In designing a Snort IDS model to analyze and pattern match the protocol (in order to improve the speed and accuracy of the intrusion detections system in the campus network), ACID (Analysis Center Intrusion Detection) was chosen to display alarm information [22]. The Snort IDS rules, however, were not improved.

In the same year, Khamphakdee N proposed an application of association rule algorithm in the intrusion detection system based on Snort rules [15]. Data mining techniques and data mining algorithms involved in the intrusion detection system and the architecture of the data mining have also been proposed [23].

A model of an intrusion detection system based on data mining is presented and described further in [24]. The authors also proposed modules consisting of a data collection module, preprocessing module, detection module, and response module. Thus, the design and implementation of an intrusion detection system based on data mining utilizing the Apriori algorithm [25] were executed. The experiment resulted in the efficient detection of new types of attacks. Additionally, an intrusion detection system based on data mining technique on database was further introduced [26]. The application of the Apriori algorithm extracted user behavior patterns and generated a greater efficiency of the Snort IDS Rules.

3   Snort IDS

3.1   Overview

Snort is a system for detecting network intrusions, which is a free, open source, and lightweight system based on libpcap. Snort are widely used worldwide. The system is easy to use and easy to manage, and has excellent performance. Snort IDS can analyze data traffic timely and effectively, and can detect network attacks by matching feature patterns and take corresponding measures.

Snort is a libpcap-based packet sniffer and logger that can be used as a lightweight network intrusion detection system (NIDS). The sniffer mode reads packets transmitted over the network and displays them as data streams on the console. The packet log mode is to specify a log directory, and snort IDS will automatically log all packets to the log file for analysis.

NIDS features rules based logging to perform content pattern matching and detect a variety of attacks and probes, such as buffer overflows, stealth port scans, CGI attacks, SMB probes, and much more. Snort has real-time alerting capability, with alerts being sent to syslog, Server Message Block (SMB) Win-Popup messages, or a separate alert file. Snort is configured using command line switches and optional Berkeley Packet Filter commands. The detection engine is programmed using a simple language that describes per packet tests and actions. Ease of use simplifies and expedites the development of new exploit detection rules.

3.2   Snort Rules

Snort intrusion detection system is based on rules, rules are the core of the detection engine. Because the most illegal intrusion activities have certain characteristic types, the method proposed to this paper is to find out the network behavior characteristics of APT organization using association analysis algorithm, and transform the generated association rules into Snort rules that can be applied to intrusion detection system.

3.3   Snort Rule Syntax

Snort uses a simple, lightweight rule description language to formulate a series of rules, then matches the intercepted packet of the existing rule set and takes corresponding actions based on the matching results. A rule instance is given below, which detects the PHF service that attempts to access the WEB server of the local network.

e.g. alert tcp any any → 10.1.1.0/24 80 (content: "/cgi-bin/phf"; msg: "PHF probe!";)

The Snort rule is divided into two parts: the rule head and the rule options, as shown in Fig. 1. Each part of a rule must be met at the same time to be executed, equivalent to "AND" operation. There is an "OR" operation between all the rules for the same regular database file.

Fig. 1. Structure of the snort rule.

(1) Rule Header

The part of the Snort rule in front of the parenthesis is the rule head. The rule header contains information that defines where packets come from, where to go, what to do, and what to do when it finds a packet that satisfies all conditions of the rules. The rule header contains the matched behavior, protocol type, source IP, source port, packet direction, target IP, target port. The structure of the rules head is shown in Fig. 2.

(1) The commonly used behavior includes the following three types:
   - alert The alarm is generated in a pre defined way and the data packet is recorded in the log.
   - log Log packets into logs
   - pass Ignore the packet
(2) Protocol: What kind of protocol is used to attack.
(3) IP address and port: the keyword "ANY" can be used to define any IP address. Port numbers can be specified in several ways: "ANY", number, range, and "!". "ANY" specifies an arbitrary port. The static value specifies a single port, such as 80 for HTTP, 23 for TELNET, and so on. The specified port range is ":" and it can specify all ports within range.
(4) Direction operator → It specifies the direction of data flows applied by the rule. The left IP address are the starting point of the data flow, and the right side are the end point. The bidirectional operator is "<>", which tells SNORT to focus on the data flow in any direction.

Action	Protocol	Source Address	Source Port	Direction	Destination Address	Destination Port

Fig. 2. Structure of snort rule header.

(2) Rule Options

The rule options form the core of the detection system, with ease of use, strong function and flexibility. It includes alarm information, index information and pattern information that needs to be detected. There may be more than one option on a rule's rule options. Use ";" to separate the different options. The relationship between them is "AND". The options consist of keywords and parameters, each of which is separated by a colon ":". Some of the keywords mentioned in this article are explained as follows:

(1) msg - Print messages in alarms and recorded data

(2) content - Search for a specific pattern string in the packet's payload

(3) dsize - Check if the payload of the packet equals a specific value

Content is one of the most important keywords in Snort, namely content matching keywords. The data feature information in the attack packet is defined in Content. When the Content option is used, the Snort system uses a matching algorithm to search the content in the packet. If an exact match is found, the test is successful and the rest of the test is continued [15].

4   Association Rule Algorithm

The association rule algorithm is one of the main research patterns of data mining at present, focusing on the discovery of the relationship between different attributes. The relationship between intrusion behavior can be found by using association rules in intrusion detection.

This algorithm is different from the "generate-test" paradigm of the Apriori algorithm. Instead, it uses a compact data structure called FP-tree to organize data and extract frequent item sets directly from the structure. The FP-tree is a compressed representation of the input data that is constructed by reading transactions one by one and mapping each transaction to a path of the FP-tree. Since different transactions may have several identical items, their paths may partially overlap. The more paths overlap each other, the better the compression results are obtained by using the FP tree structure. If FP-tree is small enough to be stored in memory, it can extract frequent item sets directly from the result of memory, instead of repeatedly scanning data stored on hard disk [9]. Since this paper focuses on APT attacks, it needs to record a large amount of network behavior and analyze it deeply. Therefore, FP-Growth algorithm is chosen for data mining.

4.1 Related Concepts of the Algorithm

Definition 1. *Association Rules*

$R : X \Rightarrow Y, X \subseteq I, Y \subseteq I, X \cap Y = \varnothing$. *It means that if the item set X appears in a particular transaction, it will inevitably cause the item set Y to appear in the same transaction. X is a prerequisite for a rule, and Y is the result of the rule.*

Definition 2. *Confidence of association rules For association rules, $R : X \Rightarrow Y, X \subseteq I, Y \subseteq I, X \cap Y = \varnothing$. The confidence of rule(R) is defined as:*

$$Confidence(R) = \frac{Support(X \cup Y)}{Support(X)} \tag{1}$$

Confidence describes the reliability of the rule.

Definition 3. *Support: The ratio of transactions containing X and Y to total transactions $|D|$.*

$$Support(X \Rightarrow Y) = \frac{count(X \cup Y)}{|D|} \tag{2}$$

The support degree reacts the probability of X and Y at the same time. The minimum support indicates that association rules require the minimum support threshold that data items must meet, that is to say, min-sup, which represents the minimum importance of data items in statistical.

Definition 4. *Confidence It contains the ratio of the number of transactions X and Y to the number of transactions X.*

$$Confidence(X \Rightarrow Y) = \frac{support(X \Rightarrow Y)}{support(X)} = \frac{count(X \cup Y)}{count(X)} \tag{3}$$

Confidence reacts to the probability that the transaction contains the Y if X is included in the transaction. Minimum confidence is the minimum credibility that the association rules must be satisfied, and it is recorded as min-conf.

Definition 5. *Frequent Itemsets*

The set of items is called an item set. The item set containing the K items is called the K- item set. The occurrence frequency of an item set is the number of transactions containing an item set, referred to as the frequency or the support rate of the item set. If the occurrence frequency of the item set is greater than or equal to the product of the total number of transactions in D and min-sup, it is called the item set to meet the min-sup. If the item set satisfies the min-sup, it is called a frequent itemsets.

4.2 The Core Idea of the Algorithm

(1) Build FP-Tree. Specific structure is described as follows:

    (1) Get frequent itemsets L Calculate support for each item, remove items below the minimum support, and sort in reverse order of support.

    (2) Build FP-Tree The root node is null, traversing every transaction, adding items in the transaction to the tree one by one. If the current item appears, the node support is added one, otherwise the new node will be the child node of the current node and update the header pointer table.

(2) Mining frequent itemsets. Specific structure is described as follows:

    (1) Obtain conditional pattern base Mining the items of L in reverse, to find out the path suffix to the item, remove the suffix, modify the support for suffix support, several paths are conditional model base.

    (2) Construct conditional pattern Tree Construct conditional pattern base as conditional FP-Tree

    (3) Recursion mining frequent item sets A recursive way is used to extract nodes from the tree continuously as a suffix, and then find out the nodes whose support meets min-sup, and merge suffix as frequent item sets.

5 Designing Snort Rules Based on Association Rules

This paper deeply explores the network behavior of APT organization's, to get the association rules for each APT organizations network behavior. Finally, it can be converted to the Snort rule that can be applied to intrusion detection system.

5.1 Data Preprocessing

The quality of data preprocessing will directly affect the results of the association rules and the accuracy of the final detection. The preprocessing methods used in this article are shown as follows. When running a malicious sample in a sandbox, a large number of pcap network data packets will be generated [11]. This paper analyzes the network behavior of these packets [28]. First of all, using the command line version of the Wireshark network traffic analyzer Tshark, the data packet is processed into sample records. Each record includes five information parts, Protocol, Length, udp.dstport, tcp.dstport and info. Because most of the extracted features are numeric. In the association analysis, if we only use numerical type features, we will get confusion on the results. Hence, the hierarchical feature storage method is used to store the feature values. The data preprocessing flow is shown in Fig. 3.

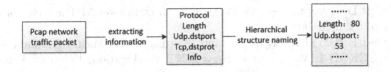

Fig. 3. Data preprocessing flow.

5.2 Data Mining

During the experiment, it was that each APT organization produces some similar association rules. For instance, ('length:60'), ('length:77'), these are obviously meaningless. In order to reduce false positives, they should be removed before converting to Snort rules. Some of the association rules are as follows:

(1) ('BROWSER', 'Domain/Workgroup Announcement WORKGROUP, NT Workstation, Domain Enum', 'length:245') → ('The Sin Digoo Affair')
(2) ('TCP', 'tcp.dstport1151') → ('The Sin Digoo Affair')
(3) ('DNS', 'Standard query 0xf8e9 A ieupdate.mailru-pro.com', 'dstport:53', 'length:83') → ('The Sin Digoo Affair')
(4) ('BROWSER', 'Get Backup List Request', 'dstport:138', 'length:216') → ('Darkhotel')
(5) ('ARP', 'Who has 192.168.56.101? Tell 192.168.56.1', 'length:42') → ('Darkhotel')
(6) ('DNS', 'Standard query 0xd0f2 A microjonjokoss.jumpingcrab.com', 'dstport:53') → ('Darkhotel')

When Protocol is Browser, length is 245, info is Domain/Workgroup Announcement WORKGROUP, NT Workstation, Domain Enum in Rule 1, it is possible to determine that the network behavior characteristics is the "The Sin Digoo Affair". It is possible to judge the network behavior characteristics of the "The Sin Digoo Affair". In the same way, it can be seen that the TCP and the destination port number 1151 are often used by the APT organization from rule2.

5.3 Designing Snort Rules Based on Association Rules

The final rules can describe the network behavior of the APT organization, and these rules can also be used in intrusion detection system. The snort rules extended in this paper are as follows:

(1) The SinDigoo Affair
   • alert DNS any any → any 1032 (msg: From SinDigoo APT ATTACK, Standard query response 0xf8e9 No such name, content: 0xf8e9)
(2) Darkhotel
   • alert DNS any any → any 53 (msg: From Darkhotel APT attack, content: 0xc8e0, dsize: 91)

- alert DNS any any → any 53 (msg: From Darkhotel APT attack, content: 0xd0f2, dsize:90)
- alert BROWSER any any → any 138 (msg: Local Master Announcement CUCKOO-1, Workstation, Server, NT Workstation, Potential Browser, Master Browser, dsize:243)
- alert BROWSER any any → any 138 (msg: Get Backup List Request, dsize:216)
- alert NBNS any any → any 137 (msg: Registration NB <01><02>_ MSBRO WSE_<02><01>, dsize:110)

There are many rules files for Snort intrusion detection. If the rule file is not well understood, when customizing the rule, all rules or inappropriate rules may be blindly loaded, resulting in system detection performance and waste of resources. For the convenience of use, according to the function of different rule files in the /etc/snort/rules directory, the corresponding description message is given, and the rule file is numbered and recorded as class_id. Users can select rules according to their actual needs and formulate a rule template. The background program combines the rules in the local.rules file according to the class_id from the corresponding rule file in the rules directory, and numbers them in turn, and records them as rule_id. When the Snort intrusion detection system starts, you only need to load the local.rules file.

6 Experiment

In order to test whether the Snort rule designed based on association rules has practical application value two different Snort intrusion detection systems were built in the experiment. One is a traditional Snort intrusion detection system, the other is an intrusion detection system based on Snort rules designed by association rules. After selecting the evaluation indicators, the performance of the two intrusion detection systems was tested using the same test data. This chapter mainly describes the data set, the evaluation method of intrusion detection system and the experimental results.

6.1 Experimental Data and Environment

This experiment used malicious samples involved in the 2008–2016 APT report as experimental data. Acquisition process is as follows: First, multiple APT reports are parsed and five pieces of important information are extracted, MD5, IPV4, URL, DOMAIN, EMAIL. Then, we use Python crawler technology to download malicious samples from the Virus Share website and put malicious samples into the Cuckoo Sandbox to generate a large number of network packets.

We divide experimental data into training sets and test sets according to the ratio of 7:3. The training set is used to generate the Snort rules, and the test set is used to verify that the designed Snort rules are valid. The data set is shown in Table 1.

Table 1. Experimental data

APT organization name	Number
Darkhotel	903
The Sin Digoo Affair	196

The test set is shown in Table 2.

Table 2. Test set data

APT organization name	Number
Darkhotel	271
The Sin Digoo Affair	59

The experimental environment is shown as follows: the host operating system is Windows10, and a virtual machine with an operating system of Ubuntu16.04 is deployed through VMware. The sandbox is Cuckoo Sandbox, and the simulation environment for the sandbox is Windows XP. The Snort intrusion detection system uses Snort 2.9.11.

6.2 Evaluation Indicators

After FP-growth mines the network behavior of the APT organization and converts the association rules into Snort rules, the system is tested using the test set. Accuracy, Precision, Recall, False alarm rate and F-measure are the evaluation indicators used in the experiment. The formulas are as follows:

$$Recall = \frac{TP}{TP + FN} \tag{4}$$

$$Precision = \frac{TP}{TP + FP} \tag{5}$$

$$Accuracy = \frac{TP + TN}{TP + TN + FP + FN} \tag{6}$$

$$False\ Alarm\ Rate = \frac{FP}{FP + TN} \tag{7}$$

$$F - measure = 2 \times \frac{Recall \times Precision}{Recall + Precision} = \frac{2TP}{2TP + FP + FN} \tag{8}$$

The TP, TN, FP and FN usually are defined in the binary classification. In this paper, for the family Dark Hotel(D), the definition of TP, TN, FP and FN in the formulas are shown as follows:

- TP (True Positive) is the number of samples that are labeled as family D and do belong to family D.

- TN (True Negative) is the number of samples that are not labeled as family D and do not belong to family D.
- FP (False Positive) is the number of samples that are labeled as family D but do not belong to family D.
- FN (False Negative) is the number of samples that are not labeled as family D but do belong to the family D.

6.3 Experimental Result

Experiments with the DarkHotel and The Sin Digoo Affair to detect two Snort intrusion detection systems, and then to count the data detected by the two systems. The evaluation results are calculated according to the formula. After repeating the experiment several times, the calculation result of the corresponding evaluation is obtained. The evaluation results are shown in Table 3.

Table 3. Evaluation results

IDS type	APT organization name	Recall	Precision	False alarm rate	Accuracy	F-measure
Traditional IDS	Dark Hotel	86.7%	89.3%	1.07%	85.3%	87.9%
	The Sin Digoo Affair	89.2%	91.1%	0.73%	88.4%	87.5%
Promotional IDS	Dark Hotel	90.9%	94.6%	0.53%	92.8%	92.7%
	The Sin Digoo Affair	95.2%	98.3%	0.05%	96.4%	96.9%

We analyze the experimental results in Table 3 and can draw conclusions. When detecting the same test data, the evaluation results of the intrusion detection system that extends the Snort rule are significantly better than the traditional Snort intrusion detection system. The Sin Digoo Affair organization has the most obvious performance. The Precision of the improved intrusion detection system was 98.3%, and the false positive rate was 0.05%. This shows that the Snort rule designed in this paper has practical application value.

7 Conclusion

The APT network attack and defense strategy involves different areas of cyber security. The methods of attack and defense are different from those in the past. Cyber attacks and defenses were launched against a single vulnerability. However, there are few cyber attacks that use comprehensive technology, as with APT cyber attacks, and the corresponding defense research is scarce. Nowadays, the commercial APT intrusion detection system has no universality.

To solve this problem, this paper applies Snort IDS, an open source network security tool, to detect APT attack. It is an intrusion detection system that uses rules to search and match network traffic data. Then, through data mining and rule extension, the system has a certain ability to detect APT attack. This method can not only dig deeper into the network behavior of APT organizations, but also apply data mining algorithms to the expansion of Snort rules, which reduces the difficulty of defense of APT attacks and improves the detection rate of intrusion detection systems based on Snort rules. The experimental evaluation results show that the Snort rules extended in this paper can be applied to the APT intrusion detection system, which has certain practical value.

Acknowledgments. This work was supported in part by the National Key Research and Development Program of China under Grant 2016YFB0801304.

References

1. Li, M., Huang, W., Wang, Y., Fan, W., Li, J.: The study of APT attack stage model. In: IEEE/ACIS, International Conference on Computer and Information Science, pp. 1–5. IEEE (2016)
2. Li, H., Liu, G., Jiang, W., Dai, Y.: Designing snort rules to detect abnormal DNP3 network data. In: International Conference on Control, Automation and Information Sciences, pp. 343–348. IEEE (2015)
3. Kang, Y., Wei, Z.: Research on Apriori algorithm based on DNS visit records mining. Netinfo Security (2012)
4. Rossow, C., Dietrich, C.J., Bos, H., Cavallaro, L., et al.: Sandnet: network traffic analysis of malicious software. In: ACM Eurosys Badgers, pp. 78–88 (2011)
5. Ju, A., Guo, Y., Zhu, T.: Big data network security situation awareness and early warning architecture based on open source toolset. Comput. Sci. **44**(5), 125–131 (2017)
6. Xu, W., Wang, Y., Xue, Z.: Attack indicator automatic generation for threat intelligence. Commun. Technol. **50**(1), 116–123 (2017)
7. Zeng, Y., Yin, S., Liu, J., et al.: Research of improved FP-Growth algorithm in association rules mining. Sci. Program. **2015**, 6 (2015)
8. Bilge, L., Kirda, E., Kruegel, C., Balduzzi, M.: EXPOSURE: finding malicious domains using passive DNS analysis. In: NDSS (2011)
9. Borgelt, C.: An implementation of the FP-growth algorithm, pp. 1–5 (2005)
10. Perdisci, R., Lee, W., Feamster, N.: Behavioral clustering of HTTP-based malware and signature generation using malicious network traces. In: Usenix Conference on Networked Systems Design and Implementation, p. 26. USENIX Association (2010)
11. Xu, Y., Zhang, A.: Network packet analysis software design based on PCAP format. Mod. Electron. Technol. **36**(10), 49–51 (2013)
12. Dai, Z., Cheng, G.: APT attack detection method based on communication features. Comput. Eng. Appl. **53**(18), 77–83 (2017)
13. Qin, L., Shi, Z.: Mining network traffic association rules mining based on iceberg query. Comput. Eng. **31**(7), 354–368 (2005)
14. Li, M., Fan, M.: Research and implementation of unknown malicious code detection system based on network behavior analysis. University of Electronic Science and technology, Chengdu (2009)
15. Khamphakdee, N., Benjamas, N., Saiyod, S.: Improving intrusion detection system based on snort rules for network probe attacks detection with association rules technique of data mining. J. ICT Res. Appl. **8**(3), 234–250 (2015)
16. Wang, J.J., Luo, K., Zhao, Z.X.: Snort network intrusion detection based on data mining techniques. Comput. Eng. Appl. **45**(1), 121–123 (2009)

17. Zhou, Z., Zhongwen, C., Tiecheng, Z., Xiaohui, G.: The study on network intrusion detection system of Snort. In: 2010 2nd International Conference on Networking and Digital Society (ICNDS), vol. 2, pp. 194–196. IEEE (2010)
18. Kumar, V., Sangwan, O.P.: Signature based intrusion detection system using SNORT. Int. J. Comput. Appl. Inf. Technol. **1**(3), 35–41 (2012)
19. Shah, S.N., Singh, M.P.: Signature-based network intrusion detection system using SNORT and WINPCAP. Int. J. Eng. Res. Technol. (IJERT) **1**(10), 1–7 (2012)
20. Geng, X., Liu, B., Huang, X.: Investigation on security system for snort-based campus network. In: 2009 1st International Conference on Information Science and Engineering (ICISE), pp. 1756–1758. IEEE (2009)
21. Rani, S., Singh, V.: SNORT: an open source network security tool for intrusion detection in campus network environment. Int. J. Comput. Technol. Electron. Eng. **2**(1), 137–142 (2012)
22. Huang, C., Xiong, J., Peng, Z.: Applied research on snort intrusion detection model in the campus network. In: 2012 IEEE Symposium on Robotics and Applications (ISRA), pp. 596–599. IEEE (2012)
23. Naiping, S., Genyuan, Z.: A study on intrusion detection based on data mining. In: 2010 International Conference of Information Science and Management Engineering (ISME), vol. 1, pp. 135–138. IEEE (2010)
24. Haixia, G.: Research of the intrusion detection system based on data mining. In: Proceeding of the International Conference on e-Education, Entertainment and e-Management, pp. 190–192. IEEE (2011)
25. Miao, C., Chen, W.: A study of intrusion detection system based on data mining. In: 2010 IEEE International Conference on Information Theory and Information Security (ICITIS), pp. 186–189. IEEE (2010)
26. Gongxing, W., Yimin, H.: Design of a new Intrusion detection system based on database. In: 2009 International Conference on Signal Processing Systems, pp. 814–817. IEEE (2009)
27. Uday, B.P., Visakh, R.: A dynamic system for intrusion detection accomplished with enhanced SVM through apt integration of data mining techniques with improved heuristic rules: performance evaluation with NSL KDD. In: Proceedings of the 2014 International Conference on Information and Communication Technology for Competitive Strategies, p. 46. ACM (2014)
28. Trabelsi, Z., Alketbi, L.: Using network packet generators and snort rules for teaching denial of service attacks. In: Proceedings of the 18th ACM Conference on Innovation and Technology in Computer Science Education, pp. 285–290. ACM (2013)

Network Risk Assessment Method Based on Asset Correlation Graph

Chun Shan[✉], Jie Gao, Changzhen Hu, Fang Guan,
and Xiaolin Zhao

Beijing Key Laboratory of Software Security Engineering Technique,
School of Computer Science and Technology, Beijing Institute of Technology,
5 South Zhong guan cun Street, Haidian District, Beijing 100081, China
sherryshan@bit.edu.en

Abstract. In order to enhance the security of network operations, establish effective security measures, prevent the destruction of security incidents, and reduce or eliminate the losses caused by threats through network risk assessment is of important practical significance. However, most risk assessment methods focus on the research of threats and vulnerabilities. There are relatively few researches on risk based on network assets and there is a lack of accuracy in risk assessment. Therefore, this paper proposes a network risk assessment method based on asset association graphs. The method first describes the network from the perspective of asset interconnection and builds an asset association graph; secondly, it builds a threat scenario based on the asset association graph, identifies a threat event, and uses the probability of a threat event and the loss caused by the asset to obtain a quantitative description of the risk assessment; Different network risk levels and make decisions. Experiments show that the method of network risk assessment based on asset association proposed in this paper can realize the risk assessment of all assets, hosts and entire network system in the network, and provide effective guidance for network security protection.

Keywords: Network security · Risk assessment · Asset association diagram
Vulnerability · Probabilistic risk analysis

1 Introduction

In today's Internet age, the threats and attacks facing the Internet are becoming more and more complex and complicated, making the development of network risk assessment technologies challenging. A series of network security problems and cyber threats make the network systems more and more serious. To enhance the security of network operations, it is of great practical significance to reduce or eliminate the losses caused by threats through network risk assessment.

At present, there are many methods for cyber risk assessment. From the evaluation results can be divided into qualitative assessment methods [1] and quantitative assessment methods [2]. As the scale and structure of networks become more and more complex, more scholars have begun to turn to the research of model-based risk assessment methods. The well-known attack graph-based evaluation method has a high

© Springer Nature Singapore Pte Ltd. 2019
H. Zhang et al. (Eds.): CTCIS 2018, CCIS 960, pp. 65–83, 2019.
https://doi.org/10.1007/978-981-13-5913-2_5

time complexity, and its complexity increases exponentially with the increase in the number of hosts and vulnerable points. The network risk assessment method based on asset association graph proposed in this paper can realize quantitative network risk assessment, reduce time complexity, and have high accuracy.

This article starts from the perspective of the basic unit of risk assessment, that is, assets, and establishes an asset-centric asset association graph model. The specific content includes the completion of network modeling, the formation of a formal description of the various security elements, and the completion of the asset association graph generation algorithm. In the network risk analysis, the probabilistic risk analysis general processes and methods are used to obtain a quantitative algorithm for risk assessment.

The rest of this article is as follows. The second part reviews relevant work and introduces domestic and international research on risk assessment methods. The third part gives the specific introduction of the algorithm of generating asset association graph and the method of network risk assessment. The fourth part is the verification of the assessment method proposed in this paper. The fifth part is the conclusion and future work.

2   Related Work

In model-based risk assessment methods, it is clear that the selection and design of risk assessment models play a key role. This article studies the existing risk assessment model. The attack tree model was first proposed by Schnerier [3]. The model provides a formal and well-organized method to describe the threats faced by the system and the various attacks that the system may be subjected to; the attack graph model was first proposed by Phillips and Swiler [4]. The attack map portrays the attacker's use of the vulnerable points in the system to gradually implement attacks, break them, gradually increase permissions, acquire more resources, and achieve the purpose of attack. Later, Sheyner et al. [5] proposed an attack graph generation algorithm. In the experiment, they found that the attack graph model generation process has a high time complexity, and the time complexity increases exponentially with the increase in the number of hosts and vulnerable points. In order to solve the problem of attack graph state explosion and high time complexity, Ammann et al. [6] proposed a host-centric access graph model. In this model, each node represents a host in the network, and each edge represents the highest level of access that can be achieved between two hosts. In addition, Ammann also proposed the security monotonicity assumption that the attacker would not repeat the same attack action once he obtained the corresponding host authority.

In terms of risk calculation, various scholars also have in-depth studies. One of the more well-known quantitative assessment methods is the probabilistic risk analysis method [7]. Specific probabilistic risk assessment methods include event trees and fault trees. In addition, it is very famous in the quantitative calculation method of risk that the famous analytics expert Saaty put forward the analytic hierarchy process in the late 1970s [8]. Analytic Hierarchy Process (AHP) quantifies the decision-making experience of the decision-makers. The system is hierarchically, quantitatively, and standardized so as to provide decision-makers with quantitative forms of decision-making basis.

3 Network Risk Assessment Method Based on Asset Correlation Graph

3.1 Method Overview

The three elements of cyber-risk sources are assets, threats, and vulnerabilities [9]. Due to the vulnerability of network systems, human or natural threats lead to the occurrence of security incidents that cause the value of assets to be lost, thus creating a risk. The method proposed in this paper starts from the perspective of assets, considers the impact of the relevance of assets on the risk, builds an asset association graph model, adopts probabilistic risk analysis methods and general processes in the risk assessment stage, and builds the threat based on the asset association graph model first. Scenario: A quantitative algorithm for obtaining risk assessment based on the relationship between the risk of threat events and the loss of assets caused by threats and network risks. The overall scheme diagram is shown in Fig. 1.

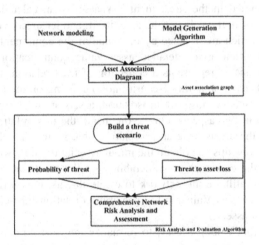

Fig. 1. Overall plan

The first step is network modeling [10], which is a formal description of the entire network system composition and risk elements. Specifically, it includes network assets such as systems and services, network topology, trust relationships among assets, and vulnerabilities are the indication of security vulnerabilities and the penetration of vulnerabilities. The second important step is to study the model generation algorithm. This requires that the algorithm has low time and space complexity. At the same time, the vulnerability of the vulnerability to the overall risk due to network interconnection should also be considered. This paper is divided into three steps in the design of the model generation algorithm. They are the model initialization algorithm based on the trust relationship, the direct edge generation algorithm based on the penetration relationship of the vulnerability point and the transitive closure algorithm considering the highly interconnected network.

With the previously acquired asset association graph model, the next step is to assess and analyze cyber risk based on the asset association graph. At this stage of the network risk assessment, this paper first builds a threat scenario based on the generated asset association graph, and then uses the principles and general processes of probabilistic risk analysis to design the network risk assessment based on probabilistic risk analysis in this paper. The specific method flow is to identify the set of threat events in the network from the threat scenario constructed using the asset association graph model, and to use the relationship between the risk of the threat event and the loss of the threat to the assets and the risk of the network to obtain a risk assessment. The quantitative description algorithm, and obtains the network's risk calculation value at different levels, and then make corresponding security protection decisions.

3.2   Network Modeling

We use a four-tuple to formalize the asset. The quad is A = (Risk, Value, T, Vul), where Risk $\in$ (0, +∞) is used to store the risk value of the asset, initialized When it is zero, it will be assigned in the subsequent risk assessment calculation; Value $\in$ (0, +∞) is used to represent the value of the asset itself, and its specific quantification has different standards, which are affected by the value of the equipment and the value of its own CIA. This article gives detailed asset value quantification methods in the chapter on risk analysis. T represents a collection of trust relationships related to the asset; Vul represents a vulnerability (security hole) existing on the asset.

Since different assets do not exist in isolation, assets are related to each other and are mainly reflected in two aspects: On the one hand, the trust relationship existing in the network makes the assets have an association, that is, the use of assets related to The set of trust relationships can obtain the initial association of network assets. On the other hand, due to the existence of vulnerability on the assets, attackers can use the vulnerable points to infiltrate the network to create threats, thus forming cyber risks. Therefore, the use of assets Vulnerability penetration relationships can also obtain the relationship between assets.

We use a triad (haci, hbcj, access) to formalize the trust relationship (there is an access between the asset haci and the asset hbcj as an access trust). For each infiltration relationship, use the following four-tuple description: exp = (ID, preConditions, access, weight) (ID: represents the unique identifier of the attack rule. preConditions: on behalf of the atomic attack on the source asset The condition that should be possessed: access: represents the impact of the atomic attack on the target component, and specifically refers to the increase of the permission in this article. Weight: The weight value reflects the difficulty of the attack, and the greater the value, the easier the attack.

In obtaining the association relationship of assets, an important measure is the level and quantization of access rights. This article is based on the classification results of Ammann and Dr. Changyong Zhang [11]. The access rights are divided into eight levels, represented by W0 to W7 respectively. The access right from None to Admin is a gradual increase of the authority, and the specific rights Values range from 0.0 to 1.0.

3.3   Algorithm for Generating Asset Association Diagram Model

In order to more intuitively understand the asset association diagram and the need for subsequent algorithm design, this article presents a formal representation of the asset association graph, as shown in Fig. 2.

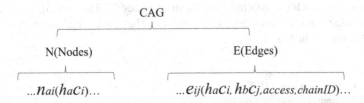

Fig. 2. Formal structure diagram of asset association diagram

The asset association graph CAG = (N, E) consists of asset node N and edge E, where node N represents a set of assets on all hosts in the network N = {nai | nai = haci}, and a specific nai = haci indicates host device Asset i on a; where edge E = {eaibj | eaibj = (haci, hbcj, access, chainID)} represents a collection of all asset associations in the network, with specific eaibj = (haci, hbcj, access, chainID) representing assets The relationship between node haci and node hbcj, where access denotes the highest access right that can be obtained, and chainID denotes the set of trust relationships or vulnerabilities used in forming the combined attack chain, representing a series of basic attacks through an ordered sequence. action. This definition facilitates the identification of threat events in subsequent risk assessments.

Different from the traditional attack graph model, the asset association graph in this paper is not centered on network state transition or vulnerability attack, but is organized around the assets on the network equipment. The nodes in the asset association graph model are assets on each network host. The directed edge from node n1 to node n2 in the generated asset association graph represents the association relationship from asset n1 to asset n2, which is embodied in the highest available access authority obtained by using the trust relationship and the penetration of vulnerability points. The specific flow of the model generation algorithm is shown in Fig. 3.

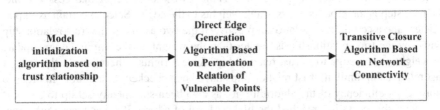

Fig. 3. Model generation algorithm flowchart

Step 1 Model initialization algorithm based on trust relationship.

In the generation algorithm of the asset association graph, the trust relationship between assets is first obtained through a security access policy set based on the network, so that a direct initial relationship between two assets is obtained. Because there may be multiple ways of communication between every two assets in the network, our model will only retain the highest access rights that can be achieved between assets, rather than adding multiple edges in the model. This article uses the InitialFuction algorithm to complete initialization. The code implementation of this algorithm is shown in Fig. 4.

```
1    InitialFuction（H, T, G）
2    Input: A set of host nodes, H
3    Input: A set of trust relationships, T
4    Input: A Asset Correlation graph G, each e_aibj ∈ G is initialized to none
5    Output: Asset Correlation graph with nodes and edges
6
7    for each h_i ∈ H do
8       for each c_j ∈ h_i.C do
9          add h_i.c_j into N
10
11 for each h_a.c_i ∈ N do
12    for each h_b.c_j ∈ N do
13       for each Ti ∈ T & Ti.（h_ac_i,h_bc_j）=（h_ac_i,h_bc_j）do
14          if Ti.access > e_aibj.access   Then
15             /* Update eaibj ∈ E */
16             e_aibj.access = Ti.access   e_aibj.chainID = Ti
17             if e_aibj.access == admin   Then
18                Stop, move to next asset-pair
```

Fig. 4. InitialFuction initialization algorithm

Based on the formal representation of the asset association diagram above, we mainly initialize the node as an asset. The edges in the figure are initialized as access rights between the assets. The initial value is the lowest level, i.e. eaibj.access = None. The next step is the process of assigning weights to the edges. Select a certain asset pair to determine a certain trust relationship between the two assets. If the trust relationship owned by the trust relationship is greater than the weight on the original edge, update the weight on the edge to a trust relationship. Access rights, otherwise check the next trust relationship until all trust relationships have been checked. In addition, in order to improve the efficiency of the algorithm, it has also been specifically set up to check if the edge eaibj.access has reached the highest level of admin. If it has reached the end, the trust relationship is checked and the next asset pair is updated directly.

Step 2 direct Edge Generation Algorithm Based on Permeation Relation.

After the initial set of edges is completed, the second step introduces the penetration of vulnerability points into the model. Source assets can increase access to vulnerable assets by using vulnerability infiltration on the target assets. This step uses the direct penetration edge algorithm, which is a direct edge generation algorithm based on the penetration relationship of vulnerability points. The method code is implemented as shown in Fig. 5.

```
1   directExploitsFuction  (N, E, X)
2   Input: A set of asset nodes, N
3   Input: A set of access edges, E
4   Input: A set of network exploits, X
5   Output: Asset Correlation graph with nodes and edges
6
7   for each ha.ci ∈ N do
8     for each hb.cj ∈ N do
9       for each vk ∈ hb.cj.Vul do
10        for each exp ∈ X against vk
11          if  ha.ci  meets exp.preConditions and vk.access > eaibj.access
Then
12            /* Update eaibj ∈ E */
13            eaibj.access = vk.access   eaibj.chainID = vk
14            if eaibj.access == admin  Then
15              Stop, move to next asset-pair
```

Fig. 5. directExploitsFuction direct penetration edge algorithm

The algorithm DirectExploitsFuction implements the use of the penetration of vulnerability points to obtain the direct edge of the asset association graph based on the network initialization state. Lines 7 through 15 attempt to have each asset node perform a penetration attack on the vulnerable points on each of its neighboring asset nodes to obtain the best direct edge. In some cases, attackers may attack their own assets. These attacks are often referred to as "self-elevated privileges." For example, on multiple platforms including Solaris 2.5 to 2.6, due to incorrect ownership checks, an attacker could use the vulnerability of "dtappgather symbolic link" to overwrite any file existing on the file system regardless of the file's ownership. By. With this vulnerability, attackers can change files and access to gain more access rights on the affected assets. Therefore, the directExploitsFuction algorithm contains (ha.ci, ha.ci) as a valid asset node pair.

Step 3 Transfer Closure Algorithm Based on Internet Connectivity.

This paper designed the indirectExploitsFuction algorithm to calculate the transitive closure of the asset association graph. The specific algorithm of this method is shown in Fig. 6.

```
1    transitiveClosureFuction（N, E）
2    Input: A set of asset nodes, N
3    Input: A set of access edges, E
5    Output: Asset Correlation graph with nodes and edges
6
7    for each hx.ck ∈ N do
8      for each ha.ci ∈ N do
9        if eaixk.access > none Then
10         for each hb.cj ∈ N do
11           if eaibj.access == admin   Then
12             Stop, move to next asset-pair
13           if exkbj.access > eaibj.access and exkbj.access meets
exkbj.preconditons
14             /* Update eaibj ∈ E */
15             eaibj.access = exkbj.access
16             eaibj.chainId = eaixk.chainId+ exkbj.chainId
```

Fig. 6. transitiveClosureFuction transitive closure algorithm

The transitiveClosureFuction algorithm is completed by trying to use other holes that have already been executed to improve their access to another host. In order to improve the performance of the algorithm, line 9 is used to test if the edge eaixk has higher access than none. Since the values of i and k do not change with j, the test of the eaixk edge moves out of the innermost loop. Note that the monotonic assumption ensures that the process will converge and does not involve backtracking, so it is computationally feasible. To help minimize computational costs, the three algorithms have similar breakpoints, and if the edge already has the highest level of access, the algorithm will stop checking for new levels of access. In addition, in this algorithm, if asset node hx.ck successfully updates the weight of edge eaibj as a media asset, in addition to updating eaibj.access, a combinatorial attack chain parameter chainId is also set, and the information of the intermediate node will be recorded here. This approach can facilitate better identification of threat events during the risk analysis phase.

The calculation cost of generating our asset association graph can be roughly analyzed as follows. First, the algorithm InitialFuction uses the trust relationship T to calculate the expected access level of the network. In this algorithm, the number of nodes with assets in the network is n, and the number of pairs of asset nodes formed is at most n^2, so the highest complexity is Tn^2. Next is the algorithm directExploitsFuction, which uses vulnerability infiltration attacks to determine the highest access rights, so its computational cost is slightly higher. In the worst case scenario, the required number of calculations is $XV n^2$, where X is the total number of infiltration relationships across all Vulnerability Points, V is a summary of vulnerabilities across all assets, and n is the total number of assets. The last is the algorithm transitiveClosureFuction, which iterates through the inspection of existing edges and exploits to check the chain until all possible paths are checked. In the densest asset association graph, all access levels are higher than none, and we can calculate the transitive closure in proportion to n3 in time.

Based on the previous algorithm analysis, we can know that the complexity of the algorithm presented in this paper is a polynomial level, which is superior to most attack graph-based research methods.

3.4 Probabilistic Risk Analysis Based Network Risk Assessment Methodology Process

This paper builds a threat scenario based on the previously generated asset association graph in the network risk assessment module, adopts the principles of probabilistic risk analysis and general processes, and designs the process of network risk assessment based on probabilistic risk analysis in this paper, as shown in Fig. 7.

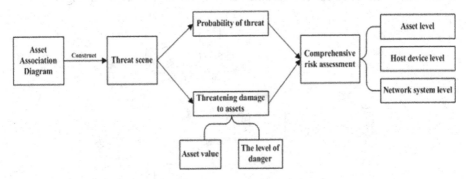

Fig. 7. Probabilistic risk analysis based risk assessment method flow chart

Firstly, the threat scene is constructed based on the asset association graph model, the threat events in the network are identified, and a quantitative description algorithm for risk assessment is derived from the relationship between the risk of occurrence of the threat event and the loss caused to the assets and the network risk, and at different levels. Get network risk levels and make appropriate decisions.

In the module for calculating the probability of occurrence of threats, a set of threat events is first acquired, and then the principle of probabilistic risk analysis is used to decompose the threat events as top events into respective initial events. Specifically, the probability of occurrence of threat events based on trust relationships and the probability of occurrence of threat events based on vulnerability points are decomposed from the combined attack chain of threat events, and then the probability of occurrence of threat events is calculated by calculating the joint probability on the combined attack chain. In the calculation of the damage caused by threats to assets, the module needs to be evaluated from two perspectives. One is to quantify the value of assets; the other is to quantify the degree of damage of threats. This paper considers the importance of the assets and equipment of the system where the assets are located and the valuation of the assets themselves on the three measurement attributes CIA (integrity, availability, confidentiality). Based on the previous quantification of threats and the risk of damage to assets, a comprehensive risk assessment of the network can be achieved. This paper presents risk assessment quantification methods from the asset level, system level and network level.

4 Experimental Verification

4.1 Experimental Environment to Build

In order to better verify the effectiveness and superiority of the network risk assessment method based on the asset association graph proposed in this paper in the actual network, this paper refers to the universally representative network system, and the server sets up a small network system through the virtual machine. In addition, corresponding security policies were configured on the network. On this basis, verification experiments was conducted. The specific network topology is shown in Fig. 8.

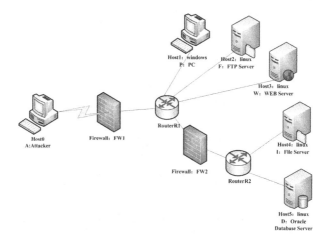

Fig. 8. Network topology

Specific network equipment information is shown in Table 1.

Table 1. Network equipment information table

CPU name	Type	Weights	Information
Host1	PC		Windows7
Host2	FTP server		Linux
Host3	WEB server		Linux
Host4	File server		Linux
Host5	Database server		Linux oracle database
FW1	Firewall		Embedded special system
FW2	Firewall		Embedded special system
R1	Router		Routing and Forwarding Protocol
R2	Router		Routing and Forwarding

4.2 Acquisition of Experimental Data

(1) Asset Association Chart Data

Before getting the asset association graph model, relevant data needed for the network modeling stage needs to be obtained, including the identification of assets, the identification of vulnerable points, the acquisition of trust relationships, and the acquisition of vulnerability infiltration relationships.

Identification of assets. According to the network deployment host device and related information, obtain the asset information to form a network asset list, as shown in Table 2.

Table 2. Asset information table

ID	Assets	Description
1	H1.wos	Windows7 operating system on Host1 personal PC
2	H2.los	Linux operating system on Host2
3	H2.ftp	Host2's ftp service
4	H3.los	Linux operating system on Host3
5	H3.web	Web services on Host3
6	H4.los	Linux operating system on Host4
7	H4.file	File service on Host4
8	H5.los	Linux operating system on Host5
9	H5.orl	Host5 on the oracle database
10	F1.fos	Dedicated system on FW1
11	F2.fos	Dedicated system on FW2
12	R1.fos	R1 routing protocol
13	R2.fos	FR2 routing protocol

Identification of vulnerable points. The Nessus [10] vulnerability scanning tool was used for scanning and identification, and the vulnerability information table was given, as shown in Table 3.

Access to trust. According to the topology structure of the network system built by the experiment and the security access policy set by the firewall rules, the trust relationship set in the network can be obtained, as shown in Table 4.

On the basis of Table 4, this paper obtains the following set of trust relationships in the entire network according to the formal representation method of the network modeling section as follows.

H1.wos.T = $\{Ti|i = 5\}$ = {(H0.os, H1.wos,access), (H4.los, H1.wos,access), (H5.los, H1.wos,access), (H2.los, H1.wos,user), (H3.los, H1.wos,user)}

H2.los. T = $\{Ti|i = 3\}$ = {(H0.os, H2.los,access), (H4.los, H2.los,access), (H5.los, H2.los,access)} (H3.los, H2.ftp,user), (H2.los, H2.ftp,user)}

H2.ftp. T = $\{Ti|i = 2\}$ = {(H3.los, H2.ftp,user), (H2.los, H2.ftp,user)}

Table 3. Vulnerability information table

Number	Assets	CVE number	Vulnerability description
v1	H1.wos	CVE-2018-1003	Microsoft JET Database Engine Remote Code Execution Vulnerability
v2	H2.ftp	CVE-2015-7603	Directory traversal vulnerability
v3	H3.web	CVE-2002-1941	Host Field Header Buffer Overflow Vulnerability
v4	H3.web	CVE-2002-0392	Apache WebServer Block Coding Remote Overflow Vulnerabilities
v5	H4.file	CVE-1999-0017	Multiple Vendor FTP Bounce Attack Vulnerabilities
v6	H5.orl	CVE-2002-0567	Oracle TNS Listener Any Library Call Execution Vulnerability
v7	H5.orl	CVE-2000-1180	Oracle cmctl buffer overflow

Table 4. List of trust relationships between assets

Number	ID(hbcj.ti)	Trust relationship (haci,hbcj.ti,access)
t1	H1.wos.t1	(H0.os, H1.wos,access)
t2	H1.wos.t2	(H4.los, H1.wos,access)
t3	H1.wos.t3	(H5.los, H1.wos,access)
t4	H1.wos.t4	(H2.los, H1.wos,user)
t5	H1.wos.t5	(H3.los, H1.wos,user)
t6	H2.los.t1	(H0.os, H2.los,access)
t7	H2.los.t2	(H4.los, H2.los,access)
t8	H2.los.t3	(H5.los, H2.los,access)
t9	H2.ftp.t1	(H1.wos, H2.ftp,user)
t10	H2.ftp.t2	(H3.los, H2.ftp,user)
t11	H2.ftp.t3	(H2.los, H2.ftp,user)
t12	H3.los.t1	(H0.os, H3.los,access)
t13	H3.los.t2	(H4.los, H3.los,access)
t14	H3.los.t3	(H5.los, H3.los,access)
t15	H3.web.t1	(H1.wos, H3.web,user)
t16	H3.web.t2	(H2.los, H3.web,user)
t17	H3.web.t3	(H3.los, H3.web,user)
t18	H4.file.t1	(H2.ftp, H4.file,subuser)
t19	H4.file.t2	(H4.los, H4.file,user)
t20	H5.orl.t1	(H1.wos, H5.orl,subuser)
t21	H5.orl.t2	(H5.los, H5.orl,user)

H3.los. T = {Ti|i = 3} = {(H0.os, H3.los,access), (H4.los, H3.los,access), (H5.los, H3.los,access)}

H3.web. T = {Ti|i = 3} = {(H1.wos, H3.web,user), (H2.los, H3.web,user), (H3.los, H3.web,user)}

H4.file. T = {Ti|i = 2} = {(H2.ftp, H4.file,subuser), (H4.los, H4.file,user)}

H5.orl. T = {Ti|i = 2} = {(H1.wos, H5.orl,subuser), (H5.los, H5.orl,user)}

Access to the vulnerability of the vulnerability. On the basis of obtaining the vulnerability point information in the network in Table 3, this paper combines the CVE vulnerability database and the CAPEC attack pattern database to obtain a list of vulnerable penetration relationships in the network. As shown in Table 5.

Table 5. Vulnerability infiltration relationship information table

Number	InfiltrationID	Vulnerability	Prerequisites	Authority
e1	v1.exp1	H1.wos.v1	H0.os, remote	H1.wos.admin
e2	v2.exp1	H2.ftp.v1	H1.wos, ftp connection	H2.los.admin
e3	v2.exp2	H2.ftp.v1	H4.los, ftp connection	H2.los.admin
e4	v3.exp1	H3.web.v2	H1.wos, http connection	H3.los.admin
e5	v4.exp1	H3.web.v3	H1.wos, apache connection	H3.los.admin
e6	v4.exp2	H3.web.v3	H5.los, apache connection	H3.los.admin
e7	v5.exp1	H4.file.v4	H2.los	H4.los.subadmin
e8	v6.exp1	H5.orl.v5	H2.los	H5.los.admin
e9	v6.exp2	H5.orl.v5	H3.los	H5.los.admin
e10	v7.exp1	H5.orl.v6	h5.los	h5.orl.subadmin

On the basis of Table 5, this paper obtains the following set of vulnerability trust relationships in the entire network according to the formal representation method of the network modeling section as follows:

v1.EXP = {(e1, H0.os, remote, H1.wos.admin)}

v2.EXP = {(e2, H1.wos, ftp, H2.los.admin), (e3, H4.los, ftp, H2.los.admin)}

v3.EXP = {(e4, H1.wos, http, H3.los.admin)}

v4.EXP = {(e5, H1.wos, apache, H3.los.admin), (e6, H5.los, apache, H3.los.admin) }

v5.EXP = {(e7, H2.los, none, H4.los.admin)}

v6.EXP = {(e8, H2.los, none, H5.los.admin), (e9, H3.los, none, H5.los.admin)}

(2) **Build Asset Association Chart**

After using the algorithm to obtain the relevance of the asset, this experiment uses the graphviz tool to draw the resulting asset association graph, as shown in Fig. 9.

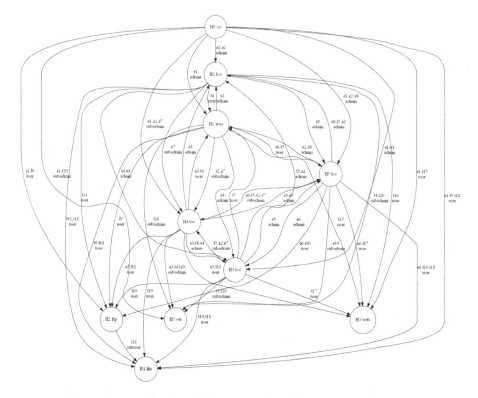

Fig. 9. Final asset association diagram

(3) **Probabilistic Risk Calculation**

(a) *Get a collection of threat events*

In order to calculate the subsequent probability risk, this paper simplifies the final asset association graph and preserves the edges related to security events, that is, the edges that contain vulnerability penetration attacks, as shown in Fig. 10.

The set of threat events is available from the figure, as shown in Table 6.

(b) *Probability of threat*

Based on the evaluation method of the probability of occurrence of threat events p_v in the penetration relationship of vulnerable points [11], and the analysis of vulnerable points, we obtain the following p_v assignment table (Table 7).

(c) *Damage to assets caused by threats*

For a certain threat event, use damage = hbcj.Value × effect to obtain the value of each asset, as shown in Table 8.

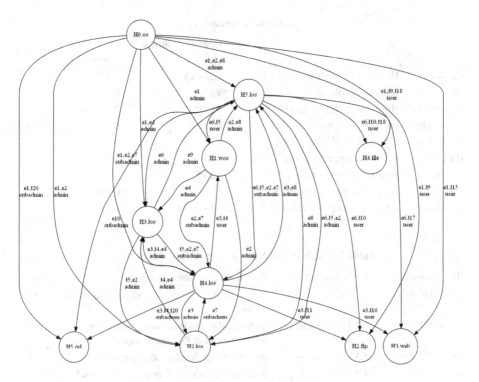

Fig. 10. Simplified asset association diagram

Table 6. Threat event information table

ID	Side	Combined attack chain	Occurrence probability
H1.wos.te1	(H0.os,H1.wos,admin,e1)	v1	0.1
H1.wos.te2	(h4.los,H1.wos,user,e3,t4)	v2,t4	0.3
H2.los.te1	(H0.os,H2.los,admin,e1,e2)	v1,v2	0.03
H2.los.te2	(H1.wos,H2.los,admin,e2)	v2	0.3
H2.los.te3	(H3.los,H2.los,admin,t5,e2)	t5,v2	0.3
H2.los.te4	(H4.los,H2.los,admin,e3)	v2	0.3
H2.los.te5	(H5.los,H2.los,admin,e6,t5,e2)	v4,v2	0.21
H2.ftp.te1	H0.os,H2.ftp,e1,t9,user	v1	0.1
H2.ftp.te2	H4.los,H2.ftp,e3,t11,user	v2,t11	0.3
H2.ftp.te3	H5.los,H2.ftp,e6,t10,user	v4,t10	0.7
H3.los.te1	H0.os,H3.los,e1,e4,admin	v1,v3	0.05
H3.los.te2	H1.wos,H3.los,admin,e4	v3	0.5
H3.los.te3	H2.los,H3.los,admin,t4,e4	t4,v3	0.5

(continued)

Table 6. (*continued*)

ID	Side	Combined attack chain	Occurrence probability
H3.los.te4	H2.los,H3.los,admin,e3,t4,e4	v2,t4,v3	0.15
H3.los.te5	H5.los, H3.ols,admin,e6	v4	0.7
H3.web.te1	H0.os,H3.web,user,e1,t15	v1,t15	0.1
H3.web.te2	H4.los,H3.web,user,e3,t11	v2,t11	0.3
H3.web.te3	H5.los,H3.web,user,e6,t11	v4,t11	0.7
H4.los.te1	H0.os,H4.los,subadmin,e1,e2,e7	v1,v2,v5	0.015
H4.los.te2	H1.wos,H4.los.subadmin,e2,e7	v2,v5	0.15
H4.los.te3	H3.los,H4.los,subadmin,t5,e2,e7	t5,v2,v5	0.15
H4.los.te4	H5.los,H4.los,subadmin,e6,t5,e2,e7	v4,t5,v2,v5	0.105

Table 7. Each vulnerability point p_v assignment table

ID	Assets	CVE number	Attack success rate description	p_v
v1	H1.wos	CVE-2018-1003	Vulnerability information release, no attack method	0.1
v2	H2.ftp	CVE-2015-7603	Vulnerability information is published to roughly explain the attack method	0.3
v3	H3.web	CVE-2002-1941	No attack but detailed attack method	0.5
v4	H3.web	CVE-2002-0392	Available attack tools and detailed attack methods	0.7
v5	H4.file	CVE-1999-0017	No attack but detailed attack method	0.5
v6	H5.orl	CVE-2002-0567	No attack but detailed attack method	0.5
v7	H5.orl	CVE-2000-1180	Vulnerability information is published to roughly explain the attack method	0.3

Table 8. Asset value table

Assets	System equipment value Hv	Own CIA value	Total asset value
H1.wos	PC (H1)0.1	Low (0.4)	0.04
H2.los	FTP server (H2)0.6	Interm ediate (0.6)	0.36
H2.ftp	FTP server (H2)0.6	Interm ediate (0.6)	0.36
H3.los	WEB server (H3)0.5	Interm ediate (0.6)	0.3
H3.web	WEB server (H3)0.5	Interm ediate (0.6)	0.3
H4.los	File server (H4)0.8	High (0.8)	0.64
H4.file	File server (H4)0.8	High (0.8)	0.64
H5.los	Database server (H5)0.9	Top (1.0)	0.9
H5.orl	Database server (H5)0.9	Top (1.0)	0.9

(d) *Final risk value*

According to the comprehensive assessment method of network risk, the risk values of asset level, host equipment level and network system level are shown in Table 9.
Asset-level risk calculations:

$$h_b c_j.risk = \sum_{a,i} p(e_{aibj}) \times (h_b c_j.value \times effect)$$

Host device level risk calculation:

$$h_b.risk = \sum_j h_b c_j.risk$$

Network-level risk calculation:

$$risk = \sum_b h_b \cdot risk \times h_b \cdot h_v$$

Table 9. System risk table

Asset level	Risk value	Host device level	Risk value	Network system level risk
H1.wos	0.016	H1	0.016	4.3103
H2.los	0.4104	H2	0.8	
H2.ftp	0.396			
H3.los	0.57	H3	0.9	
H3.web	0.33			
H4.los	0.2688	H4	0.7808	
H4.file	0.512			
H5.los	1.1835	H5	1.8135	
H5.orl	0.63			

(4) Analysis of experimental results

According to the three levels of the risk value table obtained in the previous section, which gives the value of the risk faced by each asset, the value of the asset H5.los is found to be the largest, which means that the operating system of the Oracle database server is facing The biggest risk is the assets that need to be protected. At the host device level, the risk values faced by each host are given, with the Oracle database server facing the greatest risk. In addition, statistics on the use of vulnerable points in the combined attack chain of threat events show that vulnerability V2 is the most frequently used, so V2 (CVE-2015-7603) needs to be remedied.

5 Conclusion

This paper analyzes the elements of cyber risk and considers the impact of the relationship between assets on cyber risks. This paper analyzes the relevance of assets from aspects such as trust relationships, penetration of vulnerable points on assets, and network connectivity. Thus constructed a new risk assessment model. From the perspective of the risk assessment unit, the model can accurately describe the network system risk status and can achieve quantitative network risk assessment under the highly interconnected network conditions.

The network risk assessment method based on the asset association graph model proposed in this paper still has many deficiencies. This paper adopts a comparative scientific probabilistic risk analysis method and uses risk probabilities and threats to make risk assessments on the losses caused by assets. However, the measurement of various indicators of vulnerable points needs further analysis. Another limitation is that due to the relatively small number of data sets exposed by the experimental network, the experimental data in this paper is relatively small, and the experimental deployment is relatively simple, resulting in relatively simple method verification results. In addition to the need to find or build more comprehensive experimental network datasets, the following tasks need to implement a scientific hierarchical management of network risks in a large number of practical applications, and further advance the work of network risk assessment and safety guidance.

Acknowledgments. This article is supported by National Key R&D Program of China (Grant no. 2016YFB0800700) and National Natural Science Foundation of China (Grant no. U1636115).

References

1. Dai, F.: Research on Network Security Risk Assessment Technology Based on Attack Graph Theory. Beijing University of Posts and Telecommunications, Beijing (2015)
2. He, Y., Di, G., Wang, B., Yang, G.: Quantitative evaluation method of grade protection based on Delphi method assignment. In: National Information Security Level Protection Technology Conference (2014)
3. Schnerier, B.: Attack trees-modeling security threats. Dr Dobb'S J. **12**(24), 21–29 (1999)
4. Phillips, C., Swiler, L.P.: A graph-based system for network vulnerability analysis. Sandia National Laboratories Albuquerque, NM, pp. 71–79 (1998)
5. Sheyner, O., Haines, J., Jha, J., Lippmann, R., Wing, J.M.: Automated generation and analysis of attack graphs. In: Proceedings of the 2002 IEEE Symposium on Security and Privacy, CA, vol. 5, pp. 254–265 (2002)
6. Ammann, P., Pamula, J., Ritchey, R., Street, J.: A host-based approach to network attack chaining analysis. In: Computer Security Applications Conference, pp. 72–84 (2005)
7. Hirschberg, S.: Human reliability analysis in probabilistic safety assessment for nuclear power plants. Saf. Reliab. **25**(2), 13–20 (2005)

8. Saaty, T.L.: The Analytic Hierarchy Process: Planning, Priority Setting. Resource Allocation. McGraw-Hill, New York (1980)
9. Shi, C.: Research on cyber risk assessment methods. Comput. Appl. **10**(10), 2471–2477 (2008)
10. Xiao, X.: Research on Cybersecurity Risk Assessment Based on Model. Fudan University, Shanghai (2008)
11. Thacker, B.H., Riha, D.S., Fitch, S.H.K.: Probabilistic engineering analysis using the NESSUS software. Struct. Saf. **28**(1), 83–107 (2006)
12. Di, W., et al.: Evaluation model of security measures effectiveness in a given vulnerability environment. J. Softw. **23**(7), 1880–1898 (2012)

Password Guessing Based on Semantic Analysis and Neural Networks

Yong Fang[1], Kai Liu[2], Fan Jing[3], and Zheng Zuo[2(✉)]

[1] College of Cybersecurity, Sichuan University, Chengdu 610065, China
[2] College of Electronic and Information Engineering,
Sichuan University, Chengdu 610065, China
leftzheng@gmail.com
[3] International Liaison Office, People's Government of Chongqing,
Chongqing 400065, China

Abstract. Passwords remain the dominant method in data encryption and identity authentication, but they are vulnerable to guessing attack. Most users incline to choose meaningful words to make up passwords. Lots of these words are human-memorable. In this paper, we propose a hierarchical semantic model that combines LSTM with semantic analysis to implement password guessing. With our model, the potential probability relationship between words can be mined. After training the model with 4.5 million passwords from leaked Chinese passwords, we generate lots of passwords guesses ordered by probability. 0.5 million passwords are reserved for model testing. In addition, we also pick up CSDN passwords, the Rockyou passwords, and Facebook passwords as model-testing sets. Each dataset contains 0.5 million passwords. LSTM-based model, PCFG, and Markov-based model are selected for comparison. Experiments show that our model has a higher coverage rate than the other models of the reserved dataset and CSDN dataset. Besides, our model can hit more passwords for the Rockyou dataset and Facebook dataset than PCFG.

Keywords: Password guessing · Semantic · LSTM · HSM

1 Introduction

Recent years, more and more attention has been paid to the personal information security for the reason of frequent cyber-attacks and privacy leaks. As a branch of information security, passwords are the most common method in data encryption and authentication [1]. Unfortunately, most users still use easy-to-guess passwords that are made up of names, birthdays or common strings (e.g. *123456*, *password*). In order to mitigate the threat of password guessing attacks, many Internet providers force users to adopt complex passwords. But for most users, even if the pattern of passwords turns complex, the components of passwords are still easy to remember.

Password guessing provides a valuable way to evaluate a password's strength [2]. Brute-force and dictionary attacks are the most common technologies of password guessing. However, brute-force attack does not work well for passwords longer than 8

© Springer Nature Singapore Pte Ltd. 2019
H. Zhang et al. (Eds.): CTCIS 2018, CCIS 960, pp. 84–98, 2019.
https://doi.org/10.1007/978-981-13-5913-2_6

characters. So, the main task of password guessing is to build an efficient dictionary which covers as many passwords as possible.

In this paper, we propose a hierarchical semantic model (HSM) which is based on semantic analysis and Long Short-Term Memory (LSTM) [3]. We analyze patterns and semantics of leaked Chinese passwords dataset, which is a collection of leaked passwords from several websites, excluding CSDN passwords [4]. The CSDN passwords are reserved for model testing. Then we segment passwords into meaningful words and meaningless strings. Our neural network is trained with these segmented passwords. The contribution of our paper lies on the combination of semantic analysis and LSTM. Compared with password guessing model merely based on LSTM, our model can avoid generating many meaningless substrings and has a higher coverage rate of Chinese passwords with the same size of guesses. Experiments show that our model is also more effective than the template-based model and Markov-based model for Chinese passwords.

Besides, random strings (such as cell phone-numbers) in passwords is marked by special symbols and can be restored with some extra information. We can guess more such passwords than the other models.

The rest of this paper is organized as follows. Section 2 gives a brief overview of related works. In Sect. 3, we discuss the architecture of the hierarchical semantic model. Section 4 introduces the implementation of our model. Section 5 shows experiment results and comparisons with other methods. Sections 6 discuss shortcomings of our model and opportunities for future work. Finally, we conclude in Sect. 7.

2 Related Works

The popular methods of password guessing can be contributed to three types: template-based, Markov-based, and neural networks-based. Probabilistic Context-Free Grammars which analyzes templates of passwords and pads these templates with character sequence are proposed by Weir et al. [5]. The probability of each password can be estimated by the frequency of templates and character sequences. Houshmand et al. apply keyboard patterns and multiword patterns to PCFG and improve its efficiency [6]. Besides, zxcvbn [7] gives accurate strength estimations.

Narayanman et al. apply Markov model to password guessing [8]. Using Markov modeling techniques from natural language processing, they dramatically reduce the size of the password space. Castelluccia et al. apply Markov model to passwords strength measurement [9]. Based on Markov Model, Durmuth et al. use Ordered Markov Enumerator (OMEN) to generate passwords [10]. What the Markov chain does is show us the probability of a character after a n-gram. There are two popular password cracking tools, John the Ripper [11] and Hashcat [12], which implement both template-based model and Markov-based model.

Melicher et al. first model passwords guessing with Long Short-Term Memory Recurrent Neural Networks [13, 14]. They train their neural network with leaked the Rockyou [15] and Yahoo! passwords. When given a sequence of characters, the trained neural network can get the probability of the next character. The probability of each password can be calculated by the probability multi-plication formula. According to their experiments, this model is more accurate than the other models. In addition, they compress the neural network into hundreds of kilobytes, which is small enough in an app for mobile devices, bundled with encryption software or used in a web page [14]. The source code can be obtained from the website https://github.com/cupslab/neural_network_cracking.

In 2017, Hitaj et al. propose a password guessing model named as PassGAN [16] based on Generative Adversarial Networks (GANs) [17]. A GAN is composed of a generative neural network (G) and a distinguish neural network (D). PassGAN randomly samples from the latent password space as the input of G. Then D takes the output of G or real passwords as input. D distinguish the output of G from the real passwords and feedback to G. By the interaction with each other, the output of G can get closer and closer to the real passwords [16]. As their experiments show, PassGAN doesn't work well itself. However, PassGAN can generate more novel passwords, not in the training set. That means, PassGAN is less dependent on the training data and can be combined with other models.

3 Architecture

3.1 Hierarchical Semantic Model

The password guessing model based on LSTM is at the character level. By the hierarchical semantic model, passwords can be processed on the word level. HSM is a top-down model with three layers, as shown in Fig. 1.

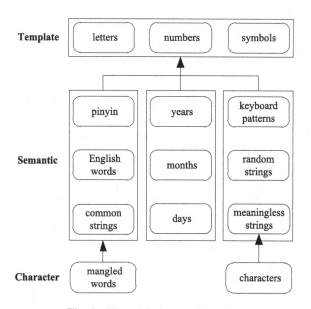

Fig. 1. Hierarchical semantic model

The top layer is template layer, in which passwords can be expressed as templates. Templates contain L, D and S, representing letters strings, numbers strings and symbols strings. We use several ordered instances to describe a template. An Instance in Formula (1) is represented by a tuple with two attributes.

$$Ins = \{T, n\} \tag{1}$$

T is the type of characters in a string. Consecutive characters of the same type make up an instance. So, n represents the length of these consecutive characters. For example, password123 can be expressed as [{L, 8}, {D, 3}].

The middle layer is the semantic layer. The role of the semantic layer is segmenting passwords into words, which is similar to the word segmentation task in Nature Language Process (NLP). In Chinese language processing, there are no separators between words, so it is necessary to manually segment words. There are three common types of segmentation algorithms: string matching, understanding-based and statistics-based.

The key of Understanding-based algorithm is the analysis of syntax, grammar, and semantics. It delimits words by context. But compared with natural language, passwords don't follow fixed syntax rules. Therefore, this algorithm is ruled out.

Statistics-based algorithm counts the frequency of any two Chinese characters appearing at the same time. The higher the frequency, the more likely they are to be a word. Obviously, the method is not suitable for passwords. So, we take string matching, regular matching, and keyboard matching as passwords segmentation strategy.

Table 1 shows seven types of meaningful words we defined. We use three matching algorithms to recognize different kinds of words. String matching requires a predefined dictionary. The dictionary includes pinyin, English words and common strings. We build the dictionary according to some previous researches on passwords and statistics on the training set.

Table 1. Types of words

Pinyin	Years
English words	Months
Common strings	Days
Keyboard patterns	

Years, months and days are extracted by regular matching. And we use the method which Schweitzer et al. proposed to recognize keyboard patterns [18]. It provides a visualizing perspective for keyboard patterns. They counted the most common shapes in keyboard patterns as Fig. 2 [18] shows. We pick *Threes*, *Grouped*, *Snakes*, and *Split Snakes* to recognized keyboard patterns. And long keyboard patterns are segmented into words, according to the turning of the shapes.

The total number of all the recognized words is 1367.

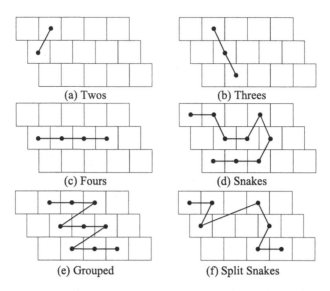

Fig. 2. Visualizing keyboard patterns

The bottom layer is the character layer. It is impossible to express all the passwords with ordered words unless we build an infinite dictionary. So, we consider the unrecognized substrings as meaningless strings and process them at the character level. Even so, the dictionary is still too huge for our model because a word may have several mangled forms. To this end, we transfer some mangled words to their prototypes before training our model and restore them when we generate passwords.

In addition, we put all random strings in two categories, marked by special symbols. Random Strings in this paper merely represent cell-phone numbers and QQ numbers. Since their probability obeys uniform distribution, some random strings can be restored when we get some privacy about a user. Random strings are abandoned when generating passwords. We restore them individually after generating.

3.2   Neural Network

When reading a document, we can understand a word based on the memory of previous words. However, the traditional neural networks can't keep memories like humans. Recurrent neural networks solve this issue. RNN could be regarded as multiple replicates of a neural network, connected in sequence. In theory, RNN can memorize arbitrarily long sequences, but due to the gradient vanishing, RNN can only handle short sequences. Long Short-Term Memory (LSTM), was designed for processing long-term dependencies. It is an improvement of RNN.

Compared with RNN, LSTM adds gate functions to determine information whether to pass or block. As Fig. 3 [19] shows, gates are composed of a sigmoid neural net layer σ and a pointwise multiplication operation. The output of σ ranges from 0 to 1. When the gate is opened (the gradient is close to 1), the gradient will not vanish. And sigmoid does not exceed 1, so the gradient will not explode either.

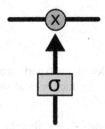

Fig. 3. LSTM gate

Our neural network is organized as Fig. 4. It has an input layer, several LSTM layers, a softmax layer and an output layer. The number of LSTM neurons in each LSTM layer is marked as n. We take the neural network as password generating model. When given a *len*-length training data, $x^{(1)} = L(p_1)$, $x^{(2)} = L(p_2), \ldots, x^{(len)} = L(p_{len})$, $x^{(len+1)} = L(end)$, the supervised learning label is a sequence, $y^{(1)} = x^{(2)}$, $y^{(2)} = x^{(3)}, \ldots, y^{(len)} = x^{(len+1)}$ [20]. After training, the probability of $x^{(t)}$ can be predicted based on the previous input sequence. In addition, when $x^{(1)}$ is given, the probability distribution of output in each time step can be predicted.

$$\text{input} \longrightarrow \begin{matrix} \text{LSTM}(n) \\ \text{layers} \end{matrix} \longrightarrow \text{softmax} \longrightarrow \text{output}$$

Fig. 4. LSTM recurrent neural network

With a set of training data, the neural network can learn the patterns of the pass-words sequences and even generate new patterns. So, the significance of the model is the ability to generate novel passwords [21] guesses and sort all guesses by probability while the training data is limited and unordered. For example, *zhangsan19800101* is an existing password, the model may generate a novel guess *zhangsan19800102* that hit someone's password. But this phenomenon has both advantages and disadvantages.

For model at the character level, when we give a sequence of characters, the model can get the probability of the next character. If we consider the sequence [a, c, t, i, o], the probability of the next character being n is higher than a, because *tion* is often used as the end of a word. But for *actionactionaction*, it is difficult to predict such a password by the model. In addition, the model may generate a meaningless string like *maction*. In order to solve these problems, we combine semantic analysis with LSTM and train our neural network with words rather than characters.

4   Implementation

4.1   Data Processing

Leaked Chinese passwords are divided into two parts: a training set and a test set. Then, we need to process the training set by the hierarchical semantic model. The steps are as follows:

- Set up a mapping between passwords and templates.
- Segment all passwords into words, containing both meaningful words and meaningless strings. The latter will be split into characters.
- Transfer all the mangled words to their prototypes and record their positions in passwords.
- Replace random strings with special symbols.

LSTM can't process text data, so we encode them with one-hot encoding. All characters and words correspond to an index. Based on this, our training data is transformed into a three-dimensional array. The three dimensions represent the size of the index dictionary, the length of a password, and the number of passwords.

4.2   Training and Generating

We train our network with Tensorflow. The neural network contains two LSTM layers with 256 nodes. Considering memory cost, we divide the training data into 45 batches and set the parameter epoch as 5.

We implemented Algorithm 1 as the generating function. When an end flag is got, the current password has ended. Through frequency statistics, it's easy to get the probability of the first element in a password. Since we are able to get the possibility of the next element, the possibility of a string being a password can be calculated by probability multiplication formula.

Algorithm 1. Generate passwords

```
Input: the map of first words to their frequencies P, the
trained neural network L, the index dictionary D and the
threshold T
Output: the list of passwords guesses O
Extends stack S with key of P;
While(S not empty) do begin
    c= S.pop();
    H = L.GetProbability(c);
    for e in D do
        if P[c]*H[e] > T
            if c is end
                O.push(c);
            else
                S.push(c+e);
                P[c+e] = P[c]* H[e];
    end
```

So far, password generating has not been finished. The possibilities of word mangling forms need to be estimated. We take templates, frequencies of their forms and their positions in passwords as features, using softmax regression to get the probability distribution [22]. Softmax regression is often used for multi-classification tasks.

For a given input x, we can estimate the probability value $p = (y = j| x)$ for each class using the hypothesis function. For our model, the probability of each mangled forms can be calculated. The function will output a k-dimensional vector to represent the probability values of the k mangled forms. $h_\theta(x)$ in Formula (2) [22] represents the hypothesis function

$$h_\theta(x^i) = \begin{bmatrix} p(y^i = 1|x^i; \theta) \\ p(y^i = 2|x^i; \theta) \\ \dots \\ p(y^i = k|x^i; \theta) \end{bmatrix} = \frac{1}{\sum_{j=1}^{k} e^{\theta_j^T x}} \begin{bmatrix} e^{\theta_1^T x} \\ e^{\theta_2^T x} \\ \dots \\ e^{\theta_{|C|}^T x} \end{bmatrix} \tag{2}$$

$\theta_1, \theta_2, \dots, \theta_k$ are parameters of the model. $\sum_{j=1}^{k} e^{\theta_j^T x}$ normalizes the probability distribution, so that the sum of probabilities of all classes is 1.

When implementing softmax regression, it is convenient to represent θ in terms of a $k \times (n + 1)$ matrix that lists $\theta_1, \theta_2, \dots, \theta_k$ in rows, as Formula (3) [22] shows:

$$\theta = \begin{bmatrix} -\theta_1^T - \\ -\theta_1^T - \\ \dots \\ -\theta_k^T - \end{bmatrix} \tag{3}$$

Word mangling rules come from John the Ripper. We pick up four rules from the popular mangling rules as Table 2 shows. These rules conform to the preferences of Chinese users when setting passwords.

Table 2. Mangling rules

Uppercase	Capital
Plural	With "1" as tail

4.3 Threshold Estimation

The number of guesses depends on a threshold. When given the number of guesses, we can sample from the outputs of the neural network to estimate the threshold. The relationship is described as Formula (4).

$$N = \frac{\int\limits_{T}^{+\infty} S(p)dp \times |C|^L}{M} \qquad (4)$$

The number of guesses is marked as N. M represents the number of sampled strings. Obviously, the ratio of N to all possible strings is approximately equal to the ratio of the strings with probability greater than the threshold to the sampled strings. C is the character set while L represents the max length of passwords. The probability-number curve is described by $S(p)$. We use Polynomial Curve Fitting to get the function $S(p)$. Using dichotomy, threshold T can be estimated.

5 Experiment

5.1 Sampling

We sample from the probability distribution over all the strings that the neural network may generate. As Fig. 5 shows, the abscissa is the logarithm of possibilities of a string being a password while the ordinate represents the number of strings after normalization. By Formula (2), it is effortless to get the threshold.

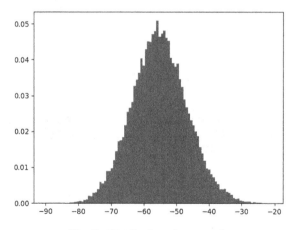

Fig. 5. Distribution of passwords

5.2 Comparison with Other Models

HSM is trained with 4.5 million passwords from leaked Chinese passwords. We generate 10^{15} guesses ordered by probability. The test set contains passwords from reserved leaked Chinese passwords, CSDN dataset, the Rockyou dataset, and Facebook dataset. Each dataset has 0.5 million passwords. We compared our model with PCFG, OMEN, and LSTM.

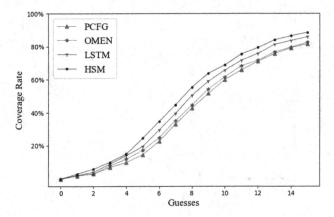

Fig. 6. Coverage rate of the reserved dataset

Figures 6, 7, 8 and 9 shows the coverage rate of the four testing datasets. We take the logarithm of guesses as the abscissa. The ordinate represents the coverage rate of each dataset. For the reserved passwords, HSM always has a higher coverage rate than the other models. For the CSDN dataset, the guess effect of PCFG is much worse than the other models. Most of the time, HSM can hit on more passwords compared with OMEN and LSTM. When the number of guesses reaches 10^{14}, they have almost the same coverage rate.

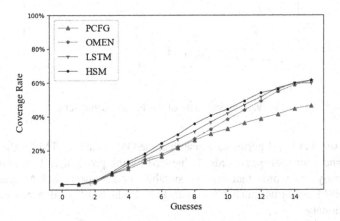

Fig. 7. Coverage rate of the CSDN dataset

Figures 8 and 9 shows the coverage rate of the Rockyou passwords and Facebook passwords. These two datasets are mainly composed of passwords from European and American users while CSDN dataset and the training set come from Chinese users. Lots of Chinese users prefer to use pinyin instead of English words in passwords. HSM and PCFG depends on the predefined word dictionary. Many words rarely appear in English passwords.

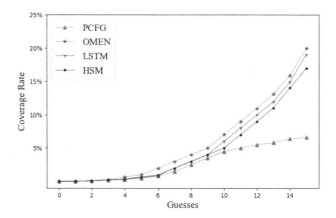

Fig. 8. Coverage rate of the Rockyou dataset

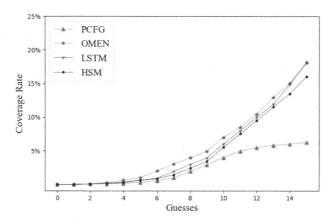

Fig. 9. Coverage rate of the Facebook dataset

We can see that HSM performs worse than the OMEN and LSTM for the Rockyou passwords and Facebook passwords. Influenced by the predefined dictionaries, HSM generates many passwords that are not suitable for European and American users. However, HSM performs much better than PCFG which totally depends on the predefined dictionary.

We further compare HSM and LSTM with 10^{12} generated passwords. The following types of passwords in Table 3 were guessed by HSM, while LSTM didn't hit on them. It is worth raising that they are not original passwords. They only represent the patterns of the original passwords.

Table 3. Typical passwords guessing by HSM

Passwords	Type
zhangsanfeng19900101	Long passwords
zhangsan@163.com	With common strings
ZhangSan0906	Mangled words

As Table 3 shows, with the growth of length of passwords, it becomes much more difficult to predict every character. For HSM, the length of *zhangsanfeng19940101* is 7, much shorter than that for LSTM. Considering *zhangsan@163.com, zhang, san, 163, com* have been recognized as words, so the length is reduced to 6.

For LSTM, it is not difficult to generate strings such as *zhangsan0906* or *Zhangsan0906*. But predicting which letter is uppercase in the middle of a string is not easy. By predefined words and mangled rules in our model, we can find the first letter of a word and transform it to uppercase.

Table 4. Time cost

Model	Training	Generating (10^{15})
PCFG	——	47 h
OMEN	1 min	33 h
LSTM	12 h	38 h
HSM without Mangled words	33 h	15 h
HSM	40 h	23 h

Table 4 shows the time cost of HSM and the other models.

We can generate the same size of guesses in a shorter time than the other models. However, we need to spend more time for training our neural network. Besides, restoring all mangled words takes extra time.

5.3 Restore Random Strings

There are some passwords containing predefined special symbols in the generated dataset. We call them marked passwords. The predefined special symbols represent random strings. When some privacy is given, we can restore these marked passwords. We pick up 20000 passwords from the leaked Chinese passwords dataset. Some privacies related to these passwords are also leaked. Regions and QQ number can be extracted from the privacies. According to the Region-information, we can get all possible cell-phone numbers in a limited range. Replacing all the special symbols strings with the extra information, we generate about 10^7 passwords.

Besides, we add special symbols strings in the predefined dictionary of PCFG. These strings are replaced with cell-phone numbers and QQ numbers after generating. Unfortunately, this method is not effective for LSTM and OMEN.

Table 5. Coverage rate of passwords with random strings

Model	Coverage Rate of Passwords		Guesses
	All	With Random Strings	
PCFG with random strings	16.7%	30.8%	2×10^7
OMEN	17.1%	0.4%	10^7
LSTM	17.8%	1.3%	10
HSM	20.3%	0	10^7
HSM with random strings	20.8%	37.6%	2×10^7

There are 237 passwords with random strings in the test set. Through Table 5, we can see that LSTM and OMEN can't work well for such passwords. With Restoring random strings, HSM can hit 37.6% of all them, much more than the other models.

Password guessing attacking for some specific users have been a long history. From the perspective of such attackers, *zhangsan13912345678* is a simple password once they know something about a target user. But it is too long for LSTM and OMEN to hit on. Therefore, the strength of a user's password should be measured not only by the password itself, but also features of the user.

6   Future Work

Before training the neural network, we transform text data into a sparse matrix with one-hot encoding. The sparse matrix has a high dimension, which leads to a great time and space cost of training. In Natural Language Processing, word2vec model can reduce the dimension of the matrix. Because of the difference between natural language and passwords, word2vec model cannot be applied to password encoding. But drawing on the idea of word2vec model, we may establish similar models.

Michael et al. use transference learning to improve the effectiveness of guessing [14]. They use all passwords to train their neural network. The passwords are classified according to different policies. Then the neural network is retrained for each class. And the effectiveness of their model is improved. Based on this, transfer learning may work well for different data sets. For example, we train our neural network with CSDN dataset and dictionary for Chinese. Then the lower layers of the neural network are frozen. Finally, we can retrain it with the Rockyou dataset and dictionary for Americans.

7   Conclusion

LSTM has achieved good results for password guessing. In order to improve the model's effectiveness further, we add semantic analysis based on LSTM. The experiment results show that our model performs better than LSTM and other models for Chinese passwords. Furthermore, combined with some privacies of users, we can guess much more passwords with random strings than the other models.

Of course, we need to adjust our model to get better results on different datasets. How to make the model have a better adaptability to different data sets and languages will be the focus of our research in the future.

Acknowledgements. This work was supported in part by the National Key R&D Program of China (Grant No. 2017YFB0802900).

References

1. Herley, C., Van Oorschot, P.: A research agenda acknowledging the persistence of passwords. IEEE Secur. Priv. Mag. **10**(1), 28–36 (2012)
2. Kelley, P., et al.: Guess again (and again and again): measuring password strength by simulating password-cracking algorithms. In: 2012 IEEE Symposium on Security and Privacy (2012)
3. Hochreiter, S., Schmidhuber, J.: Long short-term memory. Neural Comput. **9**(8), 1735–1780 (1997)
4. Leaked password lists and dictionaries. http://thepasswordproject.com/leaked_password_lists_and_dictionaries
5. Weir, M., Aggarwal, S., Medeiros, B., Glodek, B.: Password cracking using probabilistic context-free grammars. In: 2009 30th IEEE Symposium on Security and Privacy (2009)
6. Houshmand, S., Aggarwal, S., Flood, R.: Next gen PCFG password cracking. IEEE Trans. Inf. Forensics Secur. **10**, 1776–1791 (2015)
7. Wheeler, DL.: zxcvbn: low-budget password strength estimation. In: USENIX Security Symposium, pp. 157–173 (2016)
8. Narayanan, A., Shmatikov, V.: Fast dictionary attacks on passwords using time-space tradeoff. In: Proceedings of the 12th ACM Conference on Computer and Communications Security - CCS 2005 (2005)
9. Castelluccia, C., Dürmuth, M., Perito D.: Adaptive password-strength meters from Markov models. In: NDSS 2012 (2012)
10. Dürmuth, M., Angelstorf, F., Castelluccia, C., Perito, D., Chaabane, A.: OMEN: faster password guessing using an ordered Markov enumerator. In: Piessens, F., Caballero, J., Bielova, N. (eds.) ESSoS 2015. LNCS, vol. 8978, pp. 119–132. Springer, Cham (2015). https://doi.org/10.1007/978-3-319-15618-7_10
11. John the Ripper password cracker. http://www.openwall.com/john/
12. Hashcat. https://hashcat.net
13. Jozefowicz, R., Zaremba, W., Sutskever I.: An empirical exploration of recurrent network architectures. In: International Conference on Machine Learning, pp. 2342–2350 (2015)
14. Melicher, W., et al.: Fast, lean, and accurate: modeling password guessability using neural networks. In: USENIX Security Symposium, pp. 175–191 (2016)
15. RockYou. http://downloads.skullsecurity.org/passwords/rockyou.txt.bz2
16. Hitaj, B., Gasti, P., Ateniese, G., Perez-Cruz, F.: PassGAN: a deep learning approach for password guessing. arXiv preprint arXiv:1709.00440 (2017)
17. Goodfellow, I., et al.: Generative adversarial nets. In: Advances in Neural Information Processing Systems, pp. 2672–2680 (2014)
18. Schweitzer, D., Boleng, J., Hughes, C., Murphy, L.: Visualizing keyboard pattern passwords. In: 2009 6th International Workshop on Visualization for Cyber Security (2009)
19. Understanding LSTM Networks. https://colah.github.io/posts/2015-08-Understanding-LSTMs/

20. Xu, L., et al.: Password guessing based on LSTM recurrent neural networks. In: 2017 IEEE International Conference on Computational Science and Engineering (CSE) and IEEE International Conference on Embedded and Ubiquitous Computing (EUC) (2017)
21. de Castro, L., Hunter, L., Stephanie, L., Cristina, M.: Modeling password guessing with neural networks
22. Softmax. http://ufldl.stanford.edu/wiki/index.php/Softmax_Regressiony

An Approach of Implementing SW-TPM in Real-Time Operating System

Mingdi Xu[1], Xueyuan Gao[1(✉)], and Fan Zhang[2]

[1] Wuhan Digital Engineering Institute, Wuhan 430205, Hubei, China
xfgxy0@163.com
[2] School of Mathematics and Computing Science, Wuhan 430072, Hubei, China

Abstract. Virus, trojan and malware on embedded systems have brought significant effect for the information security of the industrial control systems (ICS). ICS as the national core infrastructure, the security affects the national economy and livelihood of all people. Trusted computing technology (TCT) is a technology developed and promoted by the trusted computing group (TCG). At present, TCT has been applied to the general systems, such as multitasking and distributed systems. However, it is necessary to verify the feasibility of applying TCT to the specific systems with high real-time requirements. This paper implements a trusted real-time operating system (tRTOS) based on Preempt-rt, which turns the original linux kernel into a fully pre-emptible kernel. The software trusted platform module (SW-TPM) is built in the kernel mode to provide trusted computing services. After that, the schedule policy and priority of tpmd, which is the daemon of SW-TPM, have been adjusted. In this approach, tpmd may not be pre-empted while running. It means that, SW-TPM can provide services of encryption, attestation at real-time, which can meet the requirements of RTOS in embedded systems. This paper has measured the execution time of several TPM commands in the tRTOS and a contrast system. A comparative test is carried out between tRTOS and a non-real-time system. The result shows that, the average execution time of TPM commands in the tRTOS is reduced by 15.3% without system interference, and 32.7% with system interference.

Keywords: Industrial control system · Trusted computing technology Trusted RTOS · SW-TPM · Performance testing

1 Introduction

Industrial control systems (ICS) are widely used in various areas, such as electrical, petroleum, petrochemical, aviation and nuclear facilities. They are the brain of those critical national infrastructures. In recent years, the 'WannaCry' ransomware [1], the 'BlackEnergy' malware [2] and the 'Havex' [3] remote access trojan have indicated the seriousness of the ICS security. As embedded systems are widely used in ICS, protecting the embedded systems from malicious code and attacks is a way to improve the security of ICS.

The widespread use of embedded systems may lead to various security issues, such as remote access trojan and malware which are targeted on ICS. Trusted computing provides an effective method for solving terminal security threats, which is achieved by

H. Zhang et al. (Eds.): CTCIS 2018, CCIS 960, pp. 99–112, 2019.
https://doi.org/10.1007/978-981-13-5913-2_7

providing a new computing platform to ensure security related architectures. Trusted platform module (TPM) is an international standard for a secure crypto processor, a dedicated microcontroller designed to secure hardware through integrated cryptographic keys. However, TPM have several limitations, such as sacrificing system performance and transplant inefficiency [4]. Reference [5] implements trusted boot for embedded systems, especially focuses on security of startup process. With security boot, the bootstrap time overhead of the system is increased by 25% compared to an original linux system. Moreover, the hardware TPM may increase system latency or lead to power consumption, which is not suitable for embedded systems with limited resources. This paper has replaced hardware TPM with SW-TPM to provide trusted computing services in a more flexible way.

As RTOS is an operating system, on which the maximum response time can be calculated or measured. The original linux kernel does not meet the real-time feature. Preempt-rt is an approach to turn a general-purpose linux system into a RTOS. This paper has built a tRTOS based on Preempt-rt, which turns the original linux kernel into a fully pre-emptible kernel. The SW-TPM is built in the kernel mode to provide trusted computing services. After that, the schedule policy and priority of tpmd have been adjusted. Tpmd is the daemon of SW-TPM. With this method, tpmd may not be preempted while running. It means that, SW-TPM could provide services of attestation and encryption at real-time, which can meet the requirements of RTOS in embedded systems.

The remainder of this paper is organized as follows, Sect. 2 summarizes the development of trusted embedded systems, Sect. 3 outlines the implementation and performance testing, performance testing and analysis are arranged in Sect. 4, Sect. 5 sums up conclusions.

2 Background

Research on TCT for embedded system is plentiful and substantial. Intel, IBM and other companies have developed products that support TCT, such as processors supporting trusted execute technology (TXT), the firmware TPM embedded into the chipset, the software trusted platform module (SW-TPM) corresponding to the TPM chip. At the same time, trusted computing organization (TCG) has released the white paper [6] for security embedded platform in June 2012, which provides a solution for the security of embedded devices.

In building trusted computing base (TCB) for embedded devices, the Johannes of the IAIK institute of the Graz institute of industry in Austria combines the TCT with TrustZone technology, and has built an embedded trusted computing platform based on linux [7]. TrustZone enhances system security by opening up a trusted area in the embedded kernel. Lucas and Christoph [8] have proposed a trusted virtual domain construction method for embedded system based on OKL4 micro kernel. This approach can isolate different types of data and applications from the security domain and automate the security configuration. For resource constrained embedded systems, the use of TPM chips will lead to time overhead and power consumption. To solve the time overhead and power consumption in embedded systems, reference [9] points out that independent TPM chips are not suitable for resource constrained embedded systems. Placing SW-TPM on protected execution area is a better choice. In view of how to implement trusted computing and access control in VxWorks, reference [10] puts forward an approach of implementing the embedded trusted platform module and trusted software stack in the wind kernel, which could meet the requirements of embedded system for real-time and low power consumption.

The Linux kernel provides preemptive scheduling under certain conditions. Prior to kernel version 2.4, only the user process was preemptive. Except for the expiration of the time range, if the higher dynamic priority process enters the TASK_RUNNING state, the execution of the current process in user mode will be interrupted. For the 2.6 series of Linux kernels, the ability to interrupt the execution of kernel code is added, although not all parts of the kernel code can be preempted [16].

There are several approach of enhancing the real-time performance for Linux, such as Preempt-rt, RTLinux and dual-kernal (Xenomai and RTAI). Preempt-rt patch is a Linux real-time patch maintained by Ingo Molnar and Thomas Gleixner. It allows almost the whole kernel to be preempted, except for a few very small regions of code ("raw_spinlock critical regions"). And this is done by replacing most kernel spinlocks with mutexes that support priority inheritance and are preemptive, as well as moving all interrupts to kernel threads [15]. At the same time, new operating system enrichments are provided to reduce both maximum and average response time of Linux kernel. In addition, the most important improvements of original Linux kernel are listed below: High resolution timers complete kernel preemption, interrupts management as threads, hard and soft IRQ as threads, and priority inheritance mechanism. High resolution timers is a patch set maintained by Thomas Gliexner, it allows precise timed scheduling and removes the dependency of timers on the periodic scheduler tick.

RTLinux is a hard real-time RTOS microkernel that runs the entire Linux operating system as a fully preemptive process. RTAI and Xenomai originated from a same project, the former is a real-time extension of Linux kernel which lets you write applications with strict timing constrains for Linux; the latter is a powerful real-time extension of the Linux kernel with a double kernel mechanism.

Compare with those dual kernel approaches, Preempt-rt approach is implemented by modifying the original kernel, and POSIX API was retained. As a result, there is no need to recompile original applications. Besides, the RT related project in Linux community is quite active, almost all the kernels have the corresponding patch, while other approaches update slowly. Finally, with high performance and stability, real-time Linux base on Preempt-rt is more and more extensive.

Support for full preemption of critical parts, interrupt handlers, and "interrupt disabled" code sequences can be supported by using the real-time Linux kernel patch PREEMPT_RT. Part of the mainline integration of real-time Linux kernel patches has brought some features to the kernel mainline. Preemption can increase latency, improve responsiveness, and make Linux more suitable for desktop and real-time applications.

3 Implementing and Testing

3.1 System Implementation

As linux is a general-purpose operating system (GPOS), whose complexity does not guarantee for hard real-time property for robot control, data acquisition systems in ICS. To enhance the real-time performance of linux, there are two different approaches. One is Preempt-rt, maintained by Ingo Molnar and Thomas Gleixner [12]; another is based on dual kernel architecture, such as RTLinux, RTAI and Xenomai.

Experiment conducted by Hasan [11] has measured the time needed to switch between threads of the same priority. The test runs on an open source RTOS, which is Linux 3.6.6-rt17, and two commercial RTOS, which are QNX Neurtino 6.5 and Windows CE7. In Table 1, as the number of threads increased, the latency created by thread switch has raised. The real-time performance of Linux 3.6.6-rt17, based on Preempt-rt, is between QNX Neurtino 6.5 and Windows CE7. Preempt-rt is an excellent method to trans-form an original linux kernel into a real-time linux kernel.

Table 1. Average thread switch latency comparison [11].

RTOS	2 threads	10 threads	18 threads	10^3 threads
QNX Neurtino 6.5	0.4	0.4	0.6	0.8
Linux 3.6.6-rt17	1.3	1.4	2.2	3.4
Windows CE7	2.1	2.3	3.7	4.4

The Linux kernel provides preemptive scheduling under certain conditions. Until kernel version 2.4, an execution of current process in user mode would be interrupted if higher dynamic priority processes entered TASK-RUNNING state. Preempt-rt allows almost the whole kernel to be preempted. Support for full preemption of critical sections, interrupt handlers, and 'interrupt disable' code sequences can be supported. Preemption reduces latency, improves responsiveness, and makes linux more suitable for real-time applications.

The approach of implementing tRTOS is shown in Fig. 1. By using Preempt-rt, the original Linux kernel turns into a fully pre-emptible kernel, which could meet the requirements of RTOS. Therefore, the real-time performance of the system is guaranteed.

The upper layer of Linux kernel is SW-TPM which implements 100% TPM commands, is created by Mario Strasser and Heiko Stamer, and it is mainly composed of three parts: tpmd, tddl and tpmd_dev. In this kind of SW-TPM, tpmd is the user space daemon that implements hardware TPM emulation, tddl accesses the emulator as a regular interface, and tpmd_dev is a kernel module that provides character device for low-level compatibility with TPM device drivers [6]. To measure the execution time of the TPM commands in test suits, this paper implements program instrumentation in SW-TPM source code. The details of program instrumentation will be presented in Sect. 3.2.

Trousers is the open-source TCG Software Stack (TSS) launched by IBM.

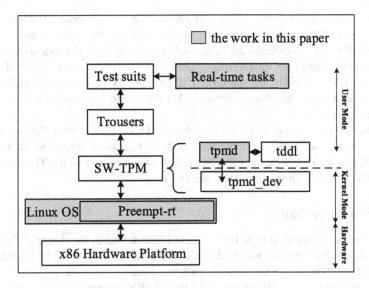

Fig. 1. Trusted computing call flow.

Trousers provides API to interact with TPM, which makes programming more convenient. TSS is an API between user programs and TPM (see Fig. 2). It is composed of several stacked components, TSS Service Provider (TSP), TSS Core Services (TCS) and TPM Device Driver Library (TDDL).

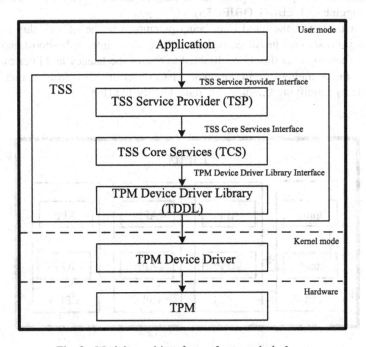

Fig. 2. Modules and interfaces of a trusted platform.

TDDL provides a low-level API and can only run some basic TPM functions. Different from TDDL, TCS works almost like a software implementation of the hardware TPM, it even extends the functionality of TPM [14]. For example, user can run only one command per time through TDDL, but the system can prioritize the TPM commands by TCS. Finally, the top layer TSP provides TCG services for applications. It also provides some additional functions that do not be implemented, such as signature verification.

Test suits provides test cases that exercise the TSS. In user mode, the information flow of general cases is shown in the user mode of Fig. 1, the operations in Testsuite are transferred to TrouSerS, and the latter then communicates with TPM emulator, where TPM corresponding commands are executed.

3.2   Performance Testing

The only necessary configuration for real-time Linux kernel is the choice of the "Fully Preemptible Kernel" preemption model (CONFIG_PREEMPT_RT_FULL). All other kernel configuration parameters depend on system requirements [17].

All kernel debugging options should be turned off when measuring system latency. They require a lot of overhead and can distort the measurement results. Examples of these debugging mechanisms are as follows: DEBUG_PREEMPT, Lock Debugging (spinlocks, mutex, etc.) and DEBUG_OBJECTS [18, 19].

Some of these debugging mechanisms (such as lock debugging) generate random overhead in the range of a few seconds to a few milliseconds, depending on the kernel configuration and compilation options (DEBUG_PREEMPT has a lower overhead than Lock Debugging or DEBUG_OBJECTS).

In order to protect the tpmd from being preempted in the tRTOS, this paper has changed several settings in BIOS, such as CPU C-state, intel turbo-boost and hyper-threading. These options should be disabled to reduce the latency and jitter caused by CPU. After the operating system startup, this paper prevents CPU from getting into the sleep mode by modifying the /dev/cpu_dma_latency file (Fig. 3).

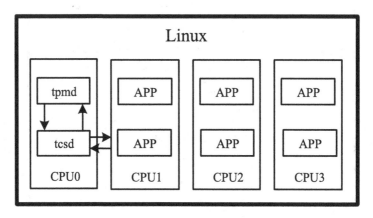

Fig. 3. Main call diagram of tRTOS.

As the resource of the processors is redundant, this paper resolves one of four physical cores in intel core i7-6700 by tuna, which is a diagnostic facility provided by the red hat enterprise for real-time kernel. Besides tpmd, most of the processes and interrupts on CPU0 have been migrated to other CPU cores. The tpmd, working as the SW-TPM daemon, ran in the reserved CPU0. As the processor resource is redundant, we reserve one of four physical cores in Intel I7-6700 CPU by Tuna, which is a diagnostic facility provided with the Red Hat Enterprise Linux for Real Time kernel. By using Tuna, most of the processes and interrupt handle on CPU0 are migrated to other CPUs, only the tpmd and tscd are assigned to CPU0, while the system services as well as user applications are assign to CPU1–CPU3.

The scheduling policy configuration of threads is important. In order to enhance the real-time performance of tpmd, the scheduling policy of tpmd should be tuned into SCHED_FIFO. In addition, the scheduling priority of tpmd has been raised to 91. The priority of all the processes and interrupts have been set between 0 and 99. As the value raises, the priority of process increases. To prevent the tpmd from system preemption, the priority of the other irrelevant threads and interrupts should be reduced below 90.

To evaluate the real-time performance of SW-TPM in the tRTOS, this paper measures the execution time of the TPM commands, including authentication, cryptographic, ownership, storage and key management. These tests are conducted on a DELL OptiPlex 7040, equipped with intel core i7-6700 and 16G RAM. The operating system is CentOS-6.9, and the kernel version is Linux-3.10.0, which is patched with corresponding Preempt-rt.

By using clock function, the precision of measuring execution time has reached to nanoseconds. Program instrumentation is built in SW-TPM source code. In order to reduce data jitter, info function between two time stamps has been deleted. The code is set as follows:

```
struct timespec requestStart, requestEnd;
clock_gettime(CLOCK_REALTIME, &requestStart);
TPM_Command_call();
clock_gettime(CLOCK_REALTIME, &requestEnd);
// Calculate time it took
double accum = ( requestEnd.tv_sec - requestStart.tv_sec )*1000000
  + ( requestEnd.tv_nsec - requestStart.tv_nsec )/1000
```

As comparison, this paper builds a contrast system. The contrast system is based on the same CentOS-6.9 as the tRTOS. The only difference is that the contrast system has not been patched with Preempt-rt. The contrast system can be regarded as a non-real-time system.

In the first test, the tRTOS and the contrast system run in an environment without interference. In the second test, a interference is created to simulate the complexity of the actual environment. During the tests, the TPM commands have been conducted 106 times. The results will be shown in Sect. 4.

4 Data Analysis

Cyclictest accurately and repeatedly measures the difference between the expected wake-up time of the thread and the actual wake-up time to provide statistics on system latency. It measures the latency of real-time systems caused by hardware, firmware and operating systems.

To measure latency, Cyclictest runs a non-real-time main thread (scheduling class SCHED_OTHER) that starts a defined number of measurement threads with a defined real-time priority (scheduling class SCHED_FIFO). The measurement thread is periodically woken up at a prescribed interval by an expiration timer (cyclic alarm). Subsequently, the difference between the programming and the effective wake-up time is calculated and switched to the main thread through the shared memory. The main thread tracks the delay value and prints the minimum, maximum and average delays.

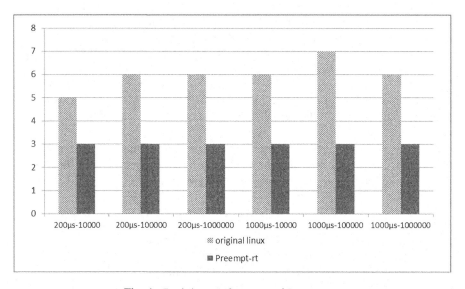

Fig. 4. Real-time performance of Preempt-rt.

To confirm the real-time performance of Preempt-rt, we choose anoriginal linux kernel as a comparison. The new platform also uses SW-TPM to meet the demand of trustworthy, but its kernel has not been patched with Preempt-rt.

Here is an example of what the Cyclictest results could look like.

```
T: 0 (821)  P: 80  I: 200  C: 518063  Min: 1  Act: 1  Avg: 1  Max: 15
T: 1 (822)  P: 80  I: 200  C: 518050  Min: 1  Act: 2  Avg: 1  Max: 23
```

The principle of Cyclictest is to compute delays by constantly making a thread sleep and waking the threads. In Fig. 4, the interval is set as 200 µs and 1000 µs, loops is set as 10^4, 10^5, 10^6. We can see that the average rate of time saving by Preempt-rt is visible.

The non-voluntary context switching number of times in both systems is measured. The non-voluntary context switching times stand for the frequency of tpmd preemption during the test. Table 2 shows that, in the tRTOS, the non-voluntary context switching times of tpmd has reduced rapidly compared to the times in the contrast system. This result shows that this method can protect the tpmd from preemption.

Table 2. Non-voluntary context switching times in tRTOS and contrast system.

Thread	Non-voluntary context switching times (contrast system)	Non-voluntary context switching times (tRTOS)
tpmd	15438	43

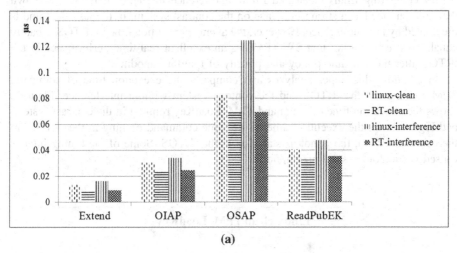

(a)

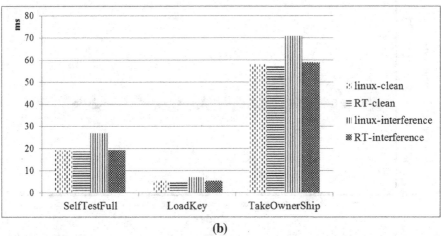

(b)

Fig. 5. Average execution time of TPM commands in tRTOS and contrast system.

Figure 5 shows the average execution time of several TPM commands in the tRTOS and the contrast system.

Linux-clean stands for the average execution time of the TPM commands in the contrast system without interference. RT-clean stands for the average execution time of the TPM commands in the tRTOS without interference, Linux-interference stands for the average execution time of the TPM commands in the contrast system with interference, RT-interference stands for the average execution time of the TPM commands in the tRTOS with interference.

Without interference, the average execution time of the TPM commands is nearly equal. The average execution time of TPM commands in the tRTOS is 15.3% less than that in the contrast system. With interference, the distinction between tRTOS and the contrast system is huge. The average execution time of the TPM commands in the tRTOS is reduced by 32.7% compared to that in the contrast system.

By comparing Linux-clean and Linux-interference in Fig. 5, it is clearly shown that, interference has a strong influence on the contrast system. In the test, the tpmd is preempted by the interference. However, the average execution time in tRTOS is barely equal. This result shows that SW-TPM has an excellent real-time performance in the tRTOS after the schedule policy and priority of tpmd are modified.

In addition, this paper analyzes and compares the execution time of command TPM_Loadkey in the tRTOS and the contrast system without interference. Figure 6 shows the execution time of command TPM_LoadKey running in the contrast system, and Fig. 7 shows the execution time of the same command running in the tRTOS. In the contrast system, the is not as stable as in the tRTOS. Some of the timing jitter is caused by random system preemption.

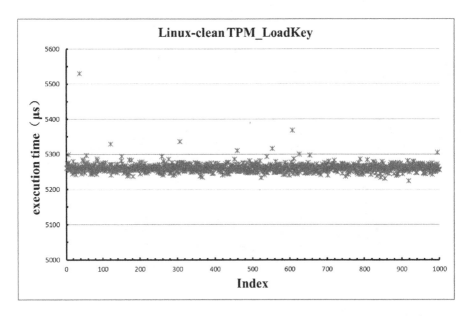

Fig. 6. Execution time of command TPM_LoadKey in contrast system without interference.

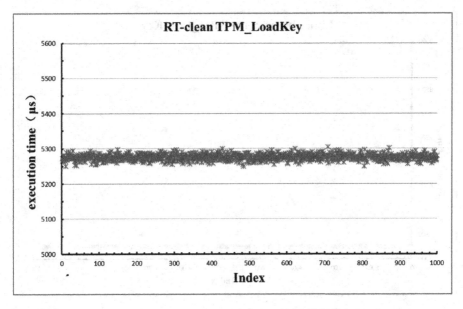

Fig. 7. Execution time of command TPM_LoadKey in tRTOS without interference.

In the tRTOS, the execution time of command TPM_LoadKey is more stable. During the test, few interruptions has occurred on tpmd in the tRTOS. When the system sends out security requests, SW-TPM can provide services at real-time.

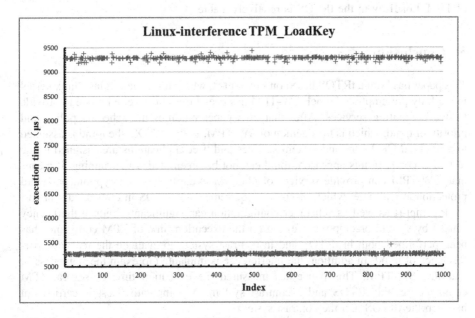

Fig. 8. Execution time of command TPM_LoadKey in contrast system with interference.

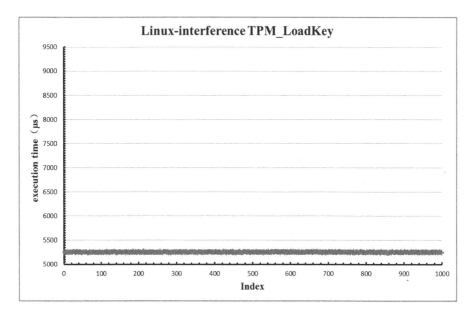

Fig. 9. Execution time of command TPM_LoadKey in tRTOS with interference.

Figures 8 and 9 have shown the execution time of the same TPM command in two systems with interference. As the interference is caused by a kind of latency, which lasts for 100 µs or the multiplier of 100 µs, the latency of TPM_LoadKey in contrast system is more obvious than the one without interference. However, the execution time of TPM_LoadKey in the tRTOS is relatively stable.

5   Conclusion

This paper has built a tRTOS based on Preempt-rt, which turns the original linux kernel into a fully pre-emptible kernel. SW-TPM has been built in the kernel mode to provide trusted computing services. After that, this paper modifies the schedule policy and priority of tpmd, which is the daemon of SW-TPM. In the tRTOS, the tpmd is assigned to a reserved CPU core and system services and user applications are assigned to the rest CPU cores. In this approach, tpmd can not be preempted while running. It means that, SW-TPM can provide services of platform integrity, disk encryption, password protection at real-time, which meets the requirements of RTOS in embedded systems.

Preempt-rt as well as scheduler configuration can significantly reduce the latency caused by system preemption. Testing on the execution time of TPM commands has been performed both in tRTOS and in contrast system to evaluate the real-time performance of tpmd. In addition, the interference is implanted to exam the stableness of real-time SW-TPM. This paper has measured the execution time of several TPM commands in the tRTOS and a contrast system. A comparative test is carried out between the tRTOS and the contrast system.

The result shows that, the average execution time of TPM commands in the tRTOS is reduced by 15.3% without system interference, and 32.7% with system interference. With system interference, the distinction between the two systems is more obvious. With preempt-rt as well as scheduler configuration, the execution time of TPM commands in SW-TPM might be reduced, especially in the case of heavy workload.

Acknowledgments. This work was supported by National Nature Science Foundation of China under grant 61502438, 61272452 and 61403350.

References

1. Mattei, T.A.: Privacy, confidentiality, and security of health care information: lessons from the recent WannaCry cyber attack. World Neurosurg. **104**, 972–974 (2017)
2. Wang, Y., Wang, Y., Zhang, L.: Analysis and defense of the BlackEnergy malware in the Ukrainian electric power system. Chin. J. Netw. Inf. Secur. **1**, 46–53 (2017)
3. Sun, Y., Jing, K., Wang, Y.: A network security protection research for industrial control system. J. Inf. Secur. Res. **3**(2), 171–176 (2017)
4. Strasser, M., Stamer, H.: A software-based trusted platform module emulator. In: Lipp, P., Sadeghi, A.-R., Koch, K.-M. (eds.) Trust 2008. LNCS, vol. 4968, pp. 33–47. Springer, Heidelberg (2008). https://doi.org/10.1007/978-3-540-68979-9_3
5. Khalid, O., Rolfes, C., Ibing, A.: On implementing trusted boot for embedded systems. In: IEEE International Symposium on Hardware-Oriented Security and Trust, pp. 75–80 (2013)
6. Trusted Computing Group.: Secure Embedded Platform with Trusted Computing: Automotive and Other Systems in the Internet of Things Must Be Protected, 10 June 2012. https://www.trustedcomputing-group.org/resources/secure_embedded_platforms_with_trusted_computing_automotive_and_other_systems_in_the_internet_of_things_must_be_protected
7. Johannes, W.: Trusted computing building blocks for embedded linux-based ARM trustzone platforms. In: Proceedings of the 3rd ACM Workshop on Scalable Trusted Computing. ACM Press, Fairfax (2008)
8. Lucas, D., Alexandra, D., Christoph, K.: Trusted virtual domains on OKL4: secure information sharing on smartphones. In: Proceedings of the 6th ACM Workshop on Scalable Trusted Computing. ACM Press, Chicago (2011)
9. Aaraj, N., Raghunathan, A., Jha, N.K.: Analysis and design of a hardware/software trusted platform module for embedded systems. ACM Trans. Embed. Comput. Syst. **8**(1), 1–31 (2008)
10. Xu, M., Yang, L.: Research on trusted computing technology in embedded real-time operation system. Comput. Eng. **40**(1), 130–133 (2014)
11. Litayem, N., Ben Saoud, S.: Impact of the linux real-time enhancements on the system performances for multi-core intel architectures. Int. J. Comput. Appl. **17**(3), 17–23 (2011)
12. Fayyad-Kazan, H., Perneel, L., Timmerman, M.: Linux Preempt-rt v2.6.33 versus v3.6.6: better or worse for real-time applications? ACM SIGBED Rev. **11**(1), 26–31 (2014)
13. Berger, S., Caceres, R.A., Goldman, K.: vTPM: virtualizing the trusted platform module. In: Conference on USENIX Security Symposium BC Canada, pp. 305–320. USENIX Association, Berkeley (2006)
14. Gleixner, T., Niehaus, D.: Hrtimers and beyond: transforming the linux time subsystems. In: Proceeding of the Linux Symposium, Ottawa, Ontario (2006)

15. Trusted Computing Group.: TCG Software Stack (TSS) Specification, Version 1.2, Errata A [EB/OL], 21 April 2011. http://www.trustedcomputinggroup.org/resource/tcg_software_stack_tss_specifacation

16. Koolwal, K.: Myths and realities of real-time linux software systems. In: Proceedings of Eleventh Real-Time Linux Workshop, pp. 13–18 (2009)

17. Hall, C.E.J.: A real-time linux system for autonomous navigation and flight attitude control of an uninhabited aerial vehicle. In: Digital Avionics Systems, DASC Conference, vol. 1, pp. 1A1/1–1A1/9 (2001)

18. Srinivasan, B., Hill, R., Pather, S.: KURT-linux support for synchronous fine-grain distributed computations. In: IEEE Real-Time Technology & Applications Symposium, pp. 78–81 (2000)

19. Lin, K.J., Wang, Y.C.: The design and implementation of real-time schedulers in RED-linux. Proc. IEEE **91**(7), 1114–1130 (2003)

A Multilevel Trusted Clustering Mechanism for the Awareness Layer of the Internet of Things

Jianli Liu[✉], Chunzi Chen, and Yang Cao

Faculty of Information Technology,
Beijing University of Technology, Beijing 100124, China
bjutljl@163.com

Abstract. In order to solve the data transmission security problem of the sensing network, this paper proposes a multi-level trusted clustering mechanism. The proposed mechanism combines multi-level clustering, identity authentication, and trusted computing to solve network expansion problems, reduce energy consumption when ordinary nodes transmit data to aggregation nodes, and ensure that the identity of IOT nodes and the messages are trusted. According to the routing protocol, each sensor node uses a multi-level clustering algorithm to divide each node into multiple levels of clusters. Then it transmits two-way identity authentication and platform integrity authentication to ensure the identity of nodes is trusted. Finally, it adopts a key distribution management method based on vector space to manage keys. Logic analysis and experimental results show that the proposed scheme has a high malicious attack resistance rate and a small amount of computation, which reduces the energy consumption of the IOT nodes during transmission and ensures the security of the transmitted messages.

Keywords: Internet of Things · Multi-level clustering · Identity authentication
Key distribution

1 Introduction

With the development of sensor technology and wireless communication technology, the application of sensing networks has become more widespread. The Internet of Things sensing layer network usually consists of multiple sensing nodes. The sensing nodes collect data by observing the surrounding environment and report the information to one or more reliable links. The data transmission distance from the sensor node to the target node in the monitoring area is generally not the same. Therefore, it is difficult to ensure the security of broadcast data transmitted from a single wireless sensing node to a sink node. Due to the special nature of the network such as limited resources, how to ensure the security and reliability of data transmission has become the most concerned issue in the sensing networks.

In order to solve the security problem of the sensing network, many scholars have conducted relevant researches on the multi-level trusted clustering mechanism of the sensing network. In [9], the authors proposed a stable and energy-saving multi-level clustering (SEEC) protocol based on heterogeneous wireless sensing networks.

H. Zhang et al. (Eds.): CTCIS 2018, CCIS 960, pp. 113–129, 2019.
https://doi.org/10.1007/978-981-13-5913-2_8

This protocol provides multiple layers of scalability for wireless sensing networks, provides higher throughput for the network, extends the network's settling time and has a lower energy cost. In [10], the authors proposed a multi-level energy-saving hybrid clustering protocol (MHEEHCP) based on wireless sensing networks. This protocol mainly uses a hybrid clustering method that combines static and dynamic clustering to extend the network life cycle, reduce network energy consumption, and outperform LEACH and SEEC in FND and network life cycle. In [11], the authors proposed an original multi-level clustering protocol based on a partitioned binary search tree (PBST*). The protocol uses the sensing network as a root balanced tree at the convergence node (BS) and allows more balanced energy consumption among different cluster head nodes. This protocol can prolong the network lifetime and increase the data packet transmission rate.

Although the above studies solve the overhead problem of traditional clustering protocols and improve the sensing network lifetime, it only considers the stability and energy consumption of wireless sensing networks and does not consider the credibility of the sensing nodes and the credibility of the cluster network. The communication data in the network is not protected and is easily stolen by attackers. At the same time, no authentication mechanism is set up between the sensing nodes, and the network is vulnerable to internal attacks.

In addition, there are some studies on key distribution management. The classic key distribution management schemes mainly include: the SH-GKDS [12] scheme which expands point-to-point key exchanges to multi-party key exchanges in group communication for achieving multi-party secret sharing, the GSAKMP scheme which directly expands from unicast to multicast, the CRT-KM protocol [54] which based on Chinese remainder theorem, the TJET scheme [15] which based on tree structure.

Unfortunately, many scholars have conducted many researches on multi-level security clustering of sensing networks and have proposed many solutions, but none of them have truly addressed the trusted issues of sensing nodes and sensing networks. Therefore, this paper proposes a multi-level trusted clustering mechanism based on the sensing layer network of the Internet of Things. In the scheme, each sensor node firstly uses a multi-level clustering algorithm to divide each node into clusters according to the applicable routing protocol. Then, it adopts the trusted authentication mechanism and key space distribution management method based on vector space to improve the efficiency of shared key distribution and reduce the amount of calculation, so as to solve the problem of transmission energy consumption among the nodes of the sensing networks and guarantee the credibility of nodes and the transmission messages.

The remaining sections of this paper are structured as follows: Sect. 2 provides a brief frame design to illustrate the proposed scheme. Sections 3, 4 and 5 detail the proposed scheme. Section 6 illustrates the experimental evaluations. Finally, Sect. 7 concludes this paper.

2 Frame Design

The multi-level trusted clustering mechanism of the sensor network is composed of a multi-level clustering algorithm, a trusted authentication, and a key management mechanism. These three mechanisms jointly guarantee the security and credibility of the sensor network.

(1) Multi-level clustering algorithm: is responsible for the construction of the original cluster, and complete the clustering structure;
(2) Trusted authentication: is responsible for identity authentication and platform integrity authentication between ordinary nodes and cluster head nodes;
(3) Key management mechanism: is responsible for managing keys used interactively between nodes to improve key distribution efficiency.

The relationship between these three mechanisms is as Fig. 1.

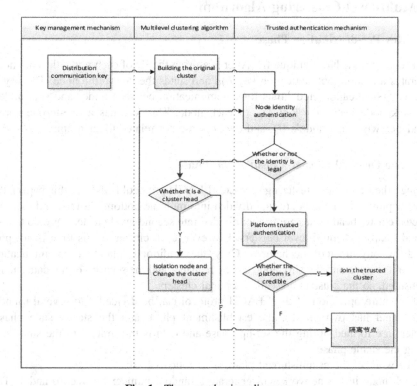

Fig. 1. Three mechanism diagrams

Based on the clustering structure, this paper adopts a multi-level clustering structure. We divide the cluster head node of each cluster which is the first-level cluster head node into multiple clusters again, and select again a new cluster head node named secondary cluster head node. We do that so on until eventually meet the sink node.

By implementing multi-level clustering on the sensing network, the transmission energy consumption problem of the interaction between the cluster head node and the sink node is effectively solved. At the same time, the scalability of the sensing network can also be increased.

In order to ensure the security and credibility of data transmission on the sensor network, this paper further performs trusted authentication on the sensor node based on the multi-level clustering network topology, and isolates the uncertified node from the network. If the cluster head node fails the authentication, a multi-level clustering algorithm is implemented to re-cluster the network, and then the new cluster heads elected are authenticated again. At the same time, in order to manage the keys needed during the communication between the sensing nodes, a key space management and distribution mechanism based on vector space is adopted to ensure the smooth transmission of data and guarantee the credibility of the data.

3 Multi-level Clustering Algorithm

3.1 Key Pre-distribution Phase

Each sensing node has a unique ID. After acquiring the ID of each node, the sink node generates a random authentication key K_{ID} and sends the key to the node. The key is used as authentication credentials for communication between nodes and sink nodes. The sink node keeps the key K_{ID} of each node. This key has a one-to-one correspondence with each node's ID, and the keys are not related to each other.

3.2 The Original Cluster Construction Phase

Through the traditional clustering protocol (LEACH protocol is used in this paper), the nodes deployed in the area are first divided into multiple bottom clusters, and then the selected cluster head nodes are further divided into second level clusters. We do that so on and finally get multi-level clusters. However, each cluster at this time is not protected by any trusted mechanism. Only the traditional plaintext communication between the node and the sink node can be realized, and the security of the data cannot be ensured, so the clusters are called original clusters.

The entire operation of the LEACH protocol can be divided into several rounds. Each round has two phases: the establishment phase and the steady state phase. Clusters are formed during the set-up phase and data is transmitted to the sink node during the stable phase.

The work of the establishment phase is as follows [16]:

Each node in the network will generate a random number between 0 and 1. The value of the generated random number will be compared with the threshold $T(n)$. If the number is less than $T(n)$, the node is selected as the cluster head. The value of the threshold $T(n)$ is calculated as follows:

$$T(n) = \begin{cases} \frac{P}{1-P*(r \bmod \frac{1}{p})} & \text{if } n \in G \\ 0 & \text{otherwise} \end{cases}$$

Where n is the ID of the node in the current Internet of Things sensing layer network, P is the predefined percentage of cluster heads, r is the current number of rounds, and G is the set of nodes that have not been selected as cluster heads since the last $1/P$ round.

By using this function, the cluster heads are randomly selected, so the same node does not continuously consume energy to death. After the cluster head is determined, all cluster head nodes will send broadcast messages in the network to other nodes. All common nodes will decide which cluster to join based on the distance from the cluster head node. It then sends the request message to the corresponding cluster head. After receiving a request message from a node, the cluster head acknowledges them as members of that particular cluster, adds them to the routing table, assigns a TDMA time slot table to the cluster members, and tells each member what time slot can transmit data.

After the establishment of the clustering phase is completed, the stable phase is entered. At this phase, all cluster member nodes send their data to their sink cluster head nodes via single-hop communications according to the time slots allocated by the TDMA time slot table. After the cluster head node receives data from each cluster member node, the cluster head fuses it into a single signal and sends it to the sink node. After the data transmission is completed, the entire network enters the next round.

3.3   Trusted Cluster Construction Phase

Based on the normal communication of the original cluster, each cluster sensing node of the underlying cluster sends its own authentication request to the first level cluster head node, and then the first level cluster head node sends the collected authentication request and its own authentication request to the second level cluster head node. Ordinary sensing nodes and cluster head nodes obtain two-party authentication keys K_{ID} by using the other party's identity ID to perform two-way identity authentication. The trusted root TCM of an ordinary node sends its own platform integrity signature certificate to the cluster head node. Then, the cluster head node sends the node's signature certificate together with its own platform integrity signature certificate to the IOT trusted authentication center (TC-IOT). TC-IOT verifies the validity of the certificate, encrypts the platform integrity verification keys of both parties, and sends them to the cluster head node and the common node. The trusted root TCM of an ordinary node sends its integrity information to the trusted root of the cluster head node. The trusted root TCM of the cluster head node determines whether the node is trusted by comparing the integrity measure value of the ordinary node. If the node is not trusted, the node will not be added to its own cluster; similarly, the root of the cluster head node also needs to send its own integrity information to the root of the ordinary node. The trust root of the cluster head node also needs to send its integrity information to the root of the ordinary node. The common node TCM determines whether the cluster head node is trusted by comparing the integrity measure value of the cluster head node. If the cluster head node is not trusted, ordinary nodes will not join this cluster.

4 Sensing Network Trusted Authentication Mechanism

4.1 Two-Way Identity Authentication When a Sensing Node Joins a Cluster Network

When the sensing node joins the cluster network, the cluster head node C needs to perform identity authentication and platform integrity authentication on the sensing node N. Identity authentication uses a two-pass authentication based on symmetric ciphers.

When the sensing node N wants to join a cluster C, the nodes C and N first authenticate each other:

(1) The sensing node N sends personal information to the cluster head node C. The information includes: node identity ID_N, node type, and the request Req to join the cluster network.

(2) The cluster head node C checks whether the type of the sensing node satisfies the intra-cluster policy. If the requirements are satisfied, the cluster head node C obtains the authentication keys K_{CN} of both parties according to the identity of the sensing node N.

(3) The cluster head node C encrypts the random number r_C and the sequence number T_C to obtain $\{r_C \| T_C \| ID_N\}_{K_{CN}}$ using the authentication key K_{CN}, and the cluster head node C sends r_C and $\{r_C \| T_C \| ID_N\}_{K_{CN}}$ to the sensing node N.

(4) The sensing node N obtains the two authentication keys K_{CN} according to the identity ID_C of the cluster head node C, decrypts the $\{r_C \| T_C \| ID_N\}_{K_{CN}}$, and verifies the correctness of the signature.

(5) The sensing node N uses the authentication key K_{CN} to encrypt its own sequence number T_N and the random number r_N to obtain $\{r_N \| T_N \| ID_N\}_{K_{CN}}$, and sends $\{r_N \| T_N \| ID_N\}_{K_{CN}}$ and r_N to the cluster head node C.

(6) The cluster head node C decrypts $\{r_N \| T_N \| ID_N\}_{K_{CN}}$ and verifies the correctness of the signature.

The shared key of the communication between the cluster head node C and the sensing node N is $\hat{k}_{CN} = \{r_C, r_N\}_{K_{CN}}$.

4.2 Platform Integrity Certification

Before performing platform integrity authentication, nodes N and C need to obtain the platform integrity authentication key first:

(1) The trusted root TCM N of the sensing node N encrypts its own identity ID_N and anti-replay random number $\hat{r}_N$ with its own platform integrity signature certificate AIK_N to obtain $\{ID_N, \hat{r}_N\}_{AIK_N}$, and sends $\{ID_N, \hat{r}_N\}_{AIK_N}$ and AIK_N to the cluster head node C together.

(2) The trusted root TCM C of the cluster head node C also encrypts ID_C and anti-replay random number $\hat{r}_C$ to obtain $\{ID_C, \hat{r}_C\}_{AIK_C}$ using AIK_C.

(3) TCM C sends AIK_C, $\{ID_C, \hat{r}_C\}_{AIK_C}$, AIK_N and $\{ID_N, \hat{r}_N\}_{AIK_N}$ to the TC-IOT.

(4) TC-IOT determines whether AIK_C and AIK_N are legal and decrypts $\{ID_C, \hat{r}_C\}_{AIK_C}$ and $\{ID_N, \hat{r}_N\}_{AIK_N}$ to verify the correctness of the signature.

(5) The TC-IOT uses its shared communication keys K_C, K_N of $TCM\ C$ and $TCM\ N$ to calculate $\{\hat{r}_C + 1, k_{CN}\}_{K_C}$ and $\{\hat{r}_N + 1, k_{CN}\}_{K_N}$, and sends them to $TCM\ C$ and $TCM\ N$ respectively.

(6) $TCM\ C$ and $TCM\ N$ respectively decrypt $\{\hat{r}_C + 1, k_{CN}\}_{K_C}$ and $\{\hat{r}_N + 1, k_{CN}\}_{K_N}$ to obtain platform integrity authentication key k_{CN}.

After nodes N and C obtain the platform integrity authentication key, they begin mutual authentication:

(1) $TCM\ C$ sends a request verification message $Req\{i_1, \ldots, i_r\}$ to $TCM\ N$, where $\{i_1, \ldots, i_r\}$ is the PCR integrity identifier corresponding to the sensing node N.

(2) After receiving the request information, $TCM\ N$ will send $TCM\ C$ its own integrity information $\{nPCR_1, \ldots, nPCR_r\}_{k_{CN}}$.

(3) $TCM\ N$ sends a platform integrity verification request message $Req\{j_1, \ldots, j_s\}$ to $TCM\ C$, where $\{j_1, \ldots, j_s\}$ is the PCR integrity identifier corresponding to the cluster head node.

(4) $TCM\ C$ verifies the platform integrity information $\{nPCR_1, \ldots, nPCR_r\}_{k_{CN}}$ sent by $TCM\ N$ to determine whether the sensing node N is trusted. If the sensing node N is not trusted, the cluster head node will not add node N to its own cluster.

(5) After receiving the platform integrity verification request message from $TCM\ N$, $TCM\ C$ sends its integrity information $\{cPCR_1, \ldots, cPCR_r\}_{k_{CN}}$ to $TCM\ N$.

(6) $TCM\ N$ verifies $\{cPCR_1, \ldots, cPCR_r\}_{k_{CN}}$ and determines whether C is trusted. If cluster head node C is not trusted, then sensing node N will not join C's cluster.

4.3 Security Analysis

The protocol is described as follows:

$N \to TCN$ $\quad\quad\quad\quad\quad$ $Req, ID_N, type$

$TCN \to N$ $\quad\quad\quad\quad\quad$ $\{r_C \| T_C \| ID_C\}_{K_{CN}}, r_C$

$N \to TCN$ $\quad\quad\quad\quad\quad$ $\{r_N \| T_N \| ID_N\}_{K_{CN}}, r_N$

$TCM\ N \to TCN$ $\quad\quad\quad$ $AIK_N, \{ID_N, \hat{r}_N\}_{AIK_N}$

$TCM\ C \to TC\text{-}IOT$ $\quad$ $AIK_C, \{ID_C, \hat{r}_C\}_{AIK_C}, AIK_N, \{ID_N, \hat{r}_N\}_{AIK_N}$

$TC\text{-}IOT \to TCM\ C$ $\quad$ $\{\hat{r}_C + 1, k_{CN}\}_{K_C}$

$TC\text{-}IOT \to TCM\ N$ $\quad$ $\{\hat{r}_N + 1, k_{CN}\}_{K_N}$

$TCM\ C \to TCM\ N$ $\quad$ $Req\{i_1, \ldots, i_r\}$

$TCM\ N \to TCM\ C$ $\quad$ $\{nPCR_1, \ldots, nPCR_r\}_{k_{CN}}, Req\{j_1, \ldots, j_s\}$

$TCM\ C \to TCM\ N$ $\quad$ $\{cPCR_1, \ldots, cPCR_r\}_{k_{CN}}$

In the protocol:

$TCN, N, TCM\ C, TCM\ N$: Main certification body.

K_{CN}: $\quad\quad\quad\quad$ Authentication key between TCN, N

AIK_C, AIK_N: $\quad$ Platform integrity certificate.

k_{CN}:	Integrity authentication shared key between *TCM C* and *TCM N*.
K_C, K_N:	The Fixed shared key of trusted certification center and *TCM C*, *TCM N*.
PCR:	The node's integrity identifier.

Use the BAN logic to define the following assumptions:

(1) $TCN \mid\equiv TCN \overset{K_{CN}}{\leftrightarrow} N$

(2) $N \mid\equiv TCN \overset{K_{CN}}{\leftrightarrow} N$

(3) $TCM\ C \mid\equiv TCMC \overset{K_C}{\leftrightarrow} TC - IOT$

(4) $TCM\ N \mid\equiv TCMN \overset{K_N}{\leftrightarrow} TC - IOT$

(5) $TCN \mid\equiv \#(r_C)$

(6) $N \mid\equiv \#(r_N)$

(7) $TCM\ C \mid\equiv \#(\hat{r}_C)$

(8) $TCM\ N \mid\equiv \#(\hat{r}_N)$

(9) $TCM\ C \mid\equiv TC - IOT \mid\Rightarrow TCM\ C$

(10) $TCM\ N \mid\equiv TC - IOT \mid\Rightarrow TCM\ N$

The formula of the BEN logic applied to this article is as follows:

(1) $\dfrac{P \mid\equiv Q \overset{K}{\leftrightarrow} P, P \lhd \{X\}K}{P \mid\equiv Q \sim X}$

(2) $\dfrac{P \mid\equiv \#(X), P \mid\equiv Q \mid \sim X}{P \mid\equiv Q \mid\equiv X}$

(3) $\dfrac{P \mid\equiv Q \mid\Rightarrow P, P \mid\equiv Q \mid\equiv X}{P \mid\equiv X}$

(4) $\dfrac{P \mid\equiv Q \mid \sim (X, Y)}{P \mid\equiv Q \mid \sim X}$

The proof hypothesis is as follows:

(1) Proof: $TCN \mid\equiv TCN \overset{K_{CN}}{\leftrightarrow} N$

$$TCN \lhd \{r_C \| r_N \| ID_N\}_{K_{CN}}$$

According to the hypothesis (1) and the formula (1), we can get:

$$TCN \mid\equiv N \sim \{r_C \| r_N \| ID_N\}$$

According to the hypothesis (5) and the formula (4), we can get:

$$TCN \mid\equiv \#\{r_C \| r_N \| ID_N\}$$

According to the formula (2), we can get:

$$TCN \mid\equiv N \mid\equiv \{r_C \| r_N \| ID_N\}$$

Therefore,

$$TCN \mathrel{|\!\equiv} N \mathrel{|\!\equiv} TCN \stackrel{\hat{k}_{CN}}{\leftrightarrow} N$$

(2) Proof: $N \mathrel{|\!\equiv} TCN \mathrel{|\!\equiv} TCN \stackrel{\hat{k}_{CN}}{\leftrightarrow} N$

$$N \triangleleft \{r_N \| ID_C\}_{K_{CN}}$$

According to the hypothesis (2) and the formula (1), we can get:

$$N \mathrel{|\!\equiv} TCN \sim \{r_N \| ID_C\}$$

According to the hypothesis (6) and the formula (4), we can get:

$$TCN \mathrel{|\!\equiv} \#\{r_N \| ID_C\}$$

According to the formula (2), we can get:

$$N \mathrel{|\!\equiv} TCN \mathrel{|\!\equiv} \{r_N \| ID_C\}$$

Therefore,

$$N \mathrel{|\!\equiv} TCN \mathrel{|\!\equiv} TCN \stackrel{\hat{k}_{CN}}{\leftrightarrow} N$$

(3) Proof: $TCM\ C \mathrel{|\!\equiv} TCMC \stackrel{k_{CN}}{\leftrightarrow} TCM\ N$

$$TCM\ C \triangleleft \{AIK_N, \hat{r}_C, k_{CN}\}_{K_C}$$

According to the hypothesis (3) and the formula (1), we can get:

$$TCM\ C \mathrel{|\!\equiv} TC - IOT \sim \{AIK_N, \hat{r}_C, k_{CN}\}$$

According to the hypothesis (7) and the formula (4), we can get:

$$TCM\ C \mathrel{|\!\equiv} \#\{AIK_N, \hat{r}_C, k_{CN}\}$$

According to the formula (2), we can get:

$$TCM\ C \mathrel{|\!\equiv} TC - IOT \mathrel{|\!\equiv} \{AIK_N, \hat{r}_C, k_{CN}\}$$

Therefore,

$$TCM\ C \mid\equiv TC - IOT \mid\equiv TCMC \overset{k_{CN}}{\leftrightarrow} TCM\ N$$

According to the hypothesis (9) and the formula (3), we can get:

$$TCM\ C \mid\equiv TCM\ C \overset{k_{CN}}{\leftrightarrow} TCM\ N$$

(4) Proof: $TCM\ N \mid\equiv TCM\ C \overset{k_{CN}}{\leftrightarrow} TCM\ N$

$$TCM\ N \triangleleft \{AIK_C, \hat{r}_N, k_{CN}\}_{K_N}$$

According to the hypothesis (4) and the formula (1), we can get:

$$TCM\ N \mid\equiv TC - IOT \sim \{AIK_C, \hat{r}_N, k_{CN}\}$$

According to the hypothesis (8) and the formula (4), we can get:

$$TCM\ N \mid\equiv \#\{AIK_C, \hat{r}_N, k_{CN}\}$$

According to the formula (2), we can get:

$$TCM\ N \mid\equiv TC - IOT \mid\equiv \{AIK_C, \hat{r}_N, k_{CN}\}$$

Therefore,

$$TCM\ N \mid\equiv TC - IOT \mid\equiv TCM\ C \overset{k_{CN}}{\leftrightarrow} TCM\ N$$

According to the hypothesis (9) and the formula (3), we can get:

$$TCM\ N \mid\equiv TCM\ C \overset{k_{CN}}{\leftrightarrow} TCM\ N$$

If $TCM\ C$ and $TCM\ N$ communicate again, we know that:

$$TCM\ C \mid\equiv TCM\ N \mid\equiv TCM\ C \overset{k_{CN}}{\leftrightarrow} TCM\ N$$

$$TCM\ N \mid\equiv TCM\ C \mid\equiv TCM\ C \overset{k_{CN}}{\leftrightarrow} TCM\ N$$

5   Sensing Network Key Distribution Management Mechanism Based on Vector Space

After completing the above work, we use the key space distribution method based on vector space to manage the shared key used in the authentication process.

5.1   Kramer's Law

If there is a system of equations consisting of n unknown numbers $a_1, a_2, \ldots, a_n$, n constant terms and n equations:

$$\begin{cases} x_{11}a_1 + x_{12}a_2 + \ldots + x_{1n}a_n = b_1 \\ x_{21}a_1 + x_{22}a_2 + \ldots + x_{2n}a_n = b_2 \\ \ldots \\ x_{n1}a_1 + x_{n2}a_2 + \ldots + x_{nn}a_n = b_n \end{cases}$$

Where the coefficient matrix of the equations is:

$$X = \begin{bmatrix} x_{1,1} \ x_{1,2} \ \cdots \\ x_{2,1} \ x_{2,2} \ \cdots \\ \ldots \\ x_{n,1} \ x_{n,2} \ \cdots \end{bmatrix}$$

When the determinant of the coefficient matrix is satisfied $|X| \neq 0$, then the equations have unique solutions:

$$A = (a_1, a_2, \ldots, a_n)$$

This law is called the Cramer law.

Assume that the constant term $b_1, b_2, \ldots, b_n$ of the system of equations is equal to k, and when we know any set of row vectors $X_i = (x_{i,1}, x_{i,2}, \ldots, x_{i,3})$ in coefficient matrix X, we can calculate k by A and X_i.

$$k = X_i \times A^T$$

However, it is impossible to derive another set of row vectors X_j in the coefficient matrix by using a certain set of row vectors X_i, A, and k in the coefficient matrix X, where $i \neq j$.

5.2   Key Distribution

(1) Firstly, we assume that there are n sensing nodes in the sensing network G and the sensing node number is u_i. The sensing network is managed by the sensing network administrator GM. The sensing network administrator GM shares a fixed encryption key with each sensing node in the sensing network. At the same time,

the GM allocates an $n + 1$ dimensional key vector $X_i = (x_{i,0}, \ldots\ldots, x_{i,n})$ for each sensing node u_i, which must be sent over the secure channel.

(2) In order to ensure the scalability of the sensing network G, the sensing network controller allocates a vector $X_i = (x_{i,1}, 0, \ldots, 0, x_{i,i+1}, 0, \ldots\ldots, 0)$ to the sensing network sensing node u_i. The vector X_i is composed of a plurality of zero elements and two non-zero-elements, and its determinant is expressed as:

$$X = \begin{pmatrix} x_{0,0} & 0 & \cdots & \cdots & 0 \\ x_{1,0} & x_{1,1} & 0 & \cdots & 0 \\ x_{2,0} & 0 & x_{2,2} & \cdots & 0 \\ \cdots & \cdots & \cdots & \cdots & \cdots \\ x_{n,0} & 0 & \cdots & 0 & x_{n,n} \end{pmatrix}$$

Then we know the determinant of X is not zero, that is

$$|X| = \prod_{i=0}^{n} x_{i,i} \neq 0.$$

We assume that $X = (X_0, X_1, \ldots\ldots, X_n)^T$, and then X is an invertible matrix, so X is a non-singular matrix.

(3) The sensing network controller GM selects the random number $k_1, \ldots\ldots, k_m$, sets

$$K = (k_1, \ldots\ldots, k_m)^T$$
$$A = (a_1, a_2, \ldots, a_n)$$

Where $a_1, a_2, \ldots, a_n$ is an unknown variable. Since step (2) has proved that X is a non-singular matrix, $A \times X = K$ has a unique solution $A = X^{-1}K = (a_0, \ldots\ldots, a_n)^T$. The sensing network controller GM sets the sensing network private key to k, and calculates $R = (k_1 \oplus k, \ldots, k_m \oplus k)^T$. The sensing network controller GM broadcasts A and R to all sensing network sensing nodes u_i. After the sensing network sensing node u_i receives the A and R, it calculates the perceived network key

$$k = X_i A \oplus (k_i \oplus k).$$

This completes the process in which the sensing network controller GM distributes keys for sensing network-aware nodes.

5.3   Key Management

(1) If a new sensing node u_t wants to join the sensing network G, the sensing network controller GM firstly allocates an n-dimensional key vector X_t for the new sensing

node u_t, and then sends the vectors X_t and k to the new sensing node u_t through the secure channel.

$$X_t = (x_{t.1}, \ldots \ldots, x_{t.n})^T$$

(2) If there is a sensing node u_t wanting to exit the sensing network G, the sensing network controller GM selects an n-dimensional vector $K' = (k'_1, \ldots \ldots, k'_m)^T$ and a sensing network private key k, sets:

$$A = X^{-1}K = (a_0, \ldots \ldots, a_n)^T$$

GM calculates:

$$R = (k_1 \oplus k, \ldots \ldots, k_m \oplus k)^T$$

GM broadcasts A and R to all sensing network-aware node u_t. If the number of exiting sensing nodes is greater than the threshold, the GM reassigns the key vector X_i to all sensing nodes u_t in the sensing network.

5.4 Security Analysis

In this mechanism, since k_i is selected randomly, the attacker cannot infer the key k of the sensing node based on $k_i \oplus k$. Even if the key k of the sensing node leaks within a certain time, the attacker could not infer from the key k at this time that the GM is the key for realizing the redistribution of the network. Therefore, the scheme has forward secrecy and backward secrecy.

In this mechanism, since the perceiving network administrator GM shares a fixed private key with each sensing node in the sensing network, and the private keys are transmitted using the secure channel, each sensing node cannot infer other nodes according to its own private key. The calculation method of the scheme key k is $k = X_i A \oplus (k_i \oplus k)$, so the valid node in the non-sensing network cannot calculate the key k, and the captured node cannot attack other nodes in the network.

6 Experimental Evaluation

6.1 Efficiency Analysis

We analyze the efficiency of key distribution management mechanism, and first assume that each member only saves its own two-dimensional private vector;

L: The maximum possible length of the element
n: The number of node members
M: The average cost of multiplication of two elements (Table 1).

Table 1. Sensing Network Controller GM Table

	Storage capacity	Amount of calculation
Key distribution	$O(nL)$	$O(nM)$
Membership	$O(L)$	$O(M)$
Withdrawal of Membership	$O(nL)$	$O(nM)$

In this scheme, the amount of storage and computation of each sensing node and the sensing network controller GM are fixed, and will only increase linearly because of the membership and exit of the member nodes (Table 2).

Table 2. Member Node Table

	Storage capacity	Amount of calculation
Key distribution	$O(nL)$	$O(nM)$
Membership	$O(L)$	$O(M)$
Withdrawal of Membership	$O(nL)$	$O(nM)$

The following table compares this solution with some typical key distribution management schemes.

From the above table, we can see that the scheme used in this paper has advantages in all aspects over the other three schemes. By comparing with ours, we can know that the basic knowledge used in this paper and the other three typical key distribution schemes are different. GSAKMP and TJET are vulnerable to attacks based on traditional cryptography, and this solution can avoid this type of attack. Although CRT-KM is not based on a cryptographic scheme, it does not have good scalability, and this scheme can provide good scalability, forward secrecy and backward secrecy. At the same time, in terms of the computational complexity of member nodes and GM, the schemes used in this paper are also lower than the other three schemes (Table 3).

Table 3. Comparison of Key Distribution Management Schemes

	GSAKMP	TJET	CRT-KM	The scheme of this paper
Theoretical basis	encrypt and decode	encrypt and decode	Chinese remainder theorem	vector space
Forward confidentiality	F	Y	Y	Y
Backward confidentiality	Y	Y	Y	Y
Extensibility	F	Y	F	Y
The number of private keys saved by a member	$O(1)$	$O(\log_2 n)$	$O(1)$	$O(1)$
Member calculation	$O(1)$ for Decryption	$O(\log_2 n)$ for Decryption	$O(1)$ for Decryption and Modular operation	$O(1)$ for Multiplication operation
GM calculation	$O(n)$ for Encryption	$O(\log_2 n)$ for encryption	$O(n)$ for Encryption and Modular operation	$O(n)$ for Multiplication operation

6.2   Scheme Comparison

The multi-level trusted clustering mechanism proposed in this paper has greatly improved the scalability, security, and key distribution efficiency compared with the existing secure clustering schemes. The following Table 4 shows the solution and classic cluster routing comparison of LEACH and existing secure clustering schemes.

Table 4. Comparison of Schemes

	The scheme of this paper	LEACH	The scheme [17]
Extensibility	Good	Not good	Expansion requires higher costs
Certification stage	Dual authentication mechanism with identity and platform integrity, with good security	No authentication mechanism, no security	Only have an authentication mechanism
Key distribution	Using a vector-space-based key distribution scheme, key distribution efficiency and computational efficiency are high	No key mechanism	Using a point-to-point key distribution mechanism, the aggregation node saves the keys of all nodes, and the key distribution efficiency is low
Calculation amount	The calculation is small and fixed	Huge	Huge

7   Conclusion

This paper proposes a multi-level trusted clustering mechanism based on the IOT sensing layer network. This trusted mechanism combines a multi-level clustering algorithm and trusted computing to design a new trusted authentication scheme. According to the applicable routing protocol, each sensor node first uses multi-level clustering algorithm to divide each node into multiple levels of clusters, so as to solve the problem of network expansion, and reduce the energy consumption when the node transfers data to the sink node. On this basis, the two-transmission identity authentication method and platform integrity authentication based on symmetric ciphers are adopted for the sensing node. The key distribution management method based on the vector space is used to manage the key and improve the distribution efficiency of the shared key. To reduce the amount of node computations, the problem of transmission energy consumption between nodes in the sensing network is improved, and the purpose of ensuring node identity credibility and guaranteeing transmission message credibility is achieved. In the future, we will carry out specific experimental tests on scalability and computational efficiency of the proposed scheme to further optimize the proposed scheme.

Acknowledgments. This work was supported by the National Natural Science Foundation of China (Grant No. 61501007).

References

1. Potsubay, J., Duduk, V.: Security for the internet of things: a survey of existing protocols and open research issues. IEEE Commun. Surv. Tutor. **17**(3), 1294–1312 (2015)
2. Yassen, M.B., Aljawaerneh, S., Abdulraziq, R.: Secure low energy adaptive clustering hierarchal based on internet of things for wireless sensor network (WSN): survey. In: 2016 International Conference on Engineering & MIS (ICEMIS), Agadir, pp. 1–9 (2016)
3. Bhandary, V., Malik, A., Kumar, S.: Routing in wireless multimedia sensor networks: a survey of existing protocols and open research issues. J. Eng. **2016**(7), 1–27 (2016)
4. Mpanti, A., Nikolopoulos, S.D., Polenakis, I.: Defending hardware-based attacks on trusted computing using a hardware-integrity attestation protocol. In: International Conference on Computer Systems and Technologies, pp. 155–162. ACM (2017)
5. Shen, H., Bai, G.: Routing in wireless multimedia sensor networks: a survey and challenges ahead. J. Netw. Comput. Appl. **71**(3), 30–49 (2016)
6. Ukani, V., Thakkar, P., Parikh, V.: Routing protocols for wireless multimedia sensor networks: challenges and research issues. In: Satapathy, S.C., Joshi, A. (eds.) ICTIS 2017. SIST, vol. 84, pp. 157–164. Springer, Cham (2018). https://doi.org/10.1007/978-3-319-63645-0_17
7. Shaikh, R., Sasikumar, M.: Trust model for measuring security strength of cloud computing service. Procedia Comput. Sci. **45**, 380–389 (2015)
8. Bhuiyan, M.Z.A., Zaman, M., Wang, G., Wang, T., Wu, J.: Privacy-protected data collection in wireless medical sensor networks. In: 2017 International Conference on Networking, Architecture, and Storage (NAS), Shenzhen, pp. 1–2 (2017)
9. Farouk, F., Rizk, R., Zaki, F.W.: Multi-level stable and energy-efficient clustering protocol in heterogeneous wireless sensor networks. IET Wirel. Sens. Syst. **4**(4), 159–169 (2014)
10. Vandana, A.K., Mohan, C.: Multi-level heterogeneous energy efficient hybrid clustering protocol for wireless sensor network. In: 2015 2nd International Conference on Recent Advances in Engineering & Computational Sciences (RAECS), Chandigarh, pp. 1–6 (2015)
11. Merabtine, N., Zegour, D.E., Djenouri, D., Boumessaidia, B.: New PBST-based multi-level clustering protocol for Wireless Sensors Networks. In: 2016 4th International Conference on Control Engineering & Information Technology (CEIT), Hammamet, pp. 1–5 (2016)
12. Rams, T., Pacyna, P.: Self-healing group key distribution with extended revocation capability. In: 2013 International Conference on Computing, Networking and Communications (ICNC), San Diego, CA, pp. 347–353 (2013)
13. Rafiq, J.I., Abdullah-Al-Omar, Chakraborty, A., Yusuf, A.: Adaptive secured multicast key management with re-keying process. In: 2016 IEEE Conference on Systems, Process and Control (ICSPC), Bandar Hilir, pp. 181–185 (2016)
14. Janani, V.S., Manikandan, M.S.K.: CRT-KM: Chinese remainder theorem based key management scheme for securing ad-hoc networks. In: 2015 IEEE International Conference on Signal Processing, Informatics, Communication and Energy Systems (SPICES), Kozhikode, pp. 1–5 (2015)
15. Xu, C., Lu, R., Wang, H., Zhu, L., Huang, C.: TJET: ternary join-exit-tree based dynamic key management for vehicle platooning. IEEE Access **5**, 26973–26989 (2017)
16. Singh, S.K., Kumar, P., Singh, J.P.: A survey on successors of LEACH protocol. IEEE Access **5**(99), 4298–4328 (2017)

17. El-hajj, M., Chamoun, M., Fadlallah, A., Serhrouchni, A.: Analysis of authentication techniques in Internet of Things (IoT). In: 2017 1st Cyber Security in Networking Conference (CSNet), Rio de Janeiro, Brazil, pp. 1–3 (2017)
18. Vardhan, A., Hussain, M., Garimella, R.M.: Simple and secure node authentication in Wireless Sensor Networks. International Conference on Recent Advances and Innovations in Engineering, pp. 1–5. IEEE (2017)
19. Peng, Q., Enqing, D., Juan, X., Xing, L., Wei, L., Wentao, C.: Multipath routing protocol based on congestion control mechanism implemented by cross-layer design concept for WSN. In: 2014 IEEE 17th International Conference on Computational Science and Engineering, Chengdu, pp. 378–384 (2014)
20. Ming-hao, T., Ren-lai, Y., Shu-jiang, L., Xiang-dong, W.: Multipath routing protocol with load balancing in WSN considering interference. In: 2011 6th IEEE Conference on Industrial Electronics and Applications, Beijing, pp. 1062–1067 (2011)
21. Gupta, S.K., Kuila, P., Jana, P.K.: Energy efficient multipath routing for wireless sensor networks: a genetic algorithm approach. In: 2016 International Conference on Advances in Computing, Communications and Informatics (ICACCI), Jaipur, pp. 1735–1740 (2016)
22. Yuvaraju, M., Rani, K.S.S.: Secure energy efficient load balancing multipath routing protocol with power management for wireless sensor networks. In: 2014 International Conference on Control, Instrumentation, Communication and Computational Technologies (ICCICCT), Kanyakumari, pp. 331–335 (2014)
23. Mao, Y., Wei, G.: A secure routing mechanism for wireless sensor network based on multiple feedback-paths. Chin. J. Sens. Actuators 23(10), 1486–1493 (2010)
24. Mao, Y.X.: Secure data collection approach for wireless sensor networks based on multipath routing and feedback. J. Commun. (2010)

A Multi-layer Virtual Network Isolation Detection Method for Cloud Platform

Bo Zhao[1], Rui Guo[1(✉)], Peiru Fan[1], and Zhijun Wu[2]

[1] Key Laboratory of Aerospace Information Security and Trusted Computing,
Ministry of Education, School of Cyber Science and Engineering,
Wuhan University, Wuhan 430072, China
ruiguo@whu.edu.cn
[2] Staff Room of Information Operation,
Rocket Force Command College, Wuhan, China

Abstract. In the trusted testing of cloud platforms, isolation testing of virtual networks is one of the important tasks. The traditional isolation detection method only extracts network configuration information from the database and reconstructs the network structure. However, these data do not necessarily reflect the current status of the virtual network and may affect the test results. To solve the above problems, this paper proposes a multi-layer virtual network isolation detection method based on trusted third party for distributed cloud platform environment. Firstly, The basic idea of the method is to extract the correct test input data from the database and each agent node, and then compare these data with the reference value, and then conduct a multi-layer evaluation of the isolation of the virtual network based on the comparison result. Then, a formal method is used to verify the effectiveness of the proposed scheme in detecting network isolation under both the policy updating and post-update scenarios. Finally, build a simulation experiment environment based on CloudSim4.0 to evaluate the performance of the multi-layer detection method, including the comparison with the traditional detection methods, and test the performance overhead of the test method on the test-end system. The experimental results show that the multi-layer detection method has less impact on the test-end system's performance, and as the test scale increases, the gap with the traditional program's overhead will gradually decrease.

Keywords: Cloud computing · Distributed system
Network isolation · Trusted test · Trusted third party

1 Introduction

The cloud platform provides users with unified management, and can dynamically expand and calculate storage services that are flexibly allocated on-demand, and the use of virtualization technology can significantly reduce the cost of user hardware deployment and resource management. In a multi-tenant cloud environment, network virtualization technology allows tenants to create their own

H. Zhang et al. (Eds.): CTCIS 2018, CCIS 960, pp. 130–148, 2019.
https://doi.org/10.1007/978-981-13-5913-2_9

virtual networks and multi-tenant share network resources. However, due to the lack of visibility and controllability of users within the cloud management platform, the security of virtual networks depends on the security measures [1] deployed by the CPP (cloud platform provider). Moreover, the specific configuration of cloud nodes and the transparency of security information are low, which makes users question their own virtual network isolation. That is, while sharing network resources, it is unable to determine whether there is an illegal network resource access.

In a multi-tenant cloud environment, unintentional misconfigurations or malicious attacks against vulnerabilities may compromise the isolation of the virtual network. It is an effective method to enhance the credibility of virtual networks by making virtual network isolation tests for cloud platforms and assessing whether the actual virtual network isolation status is consistent with pre-configured security policies. At present, research work on virtual network detection is mainly divided into two directions. On the one hand, some security indicators are extracted to test the credibility of the network. However, due to the lack of integrated and unified trusted cloud standards [2,3], people still have different understanding of the trust of the cloud platform [4–6], so the limited test indicators cannot fully characterize the trusted state of current virtual networks. Another test idea is to obtain the network configuration information from the cloud database, reconstruct the virtual network structure to different degrees, and then compare it with the user's preset security policy. The second method is more representative and has higher credibility. However, in the actual distributed cloud platform, in order to avoid the problem of data access bottlenecks caused by node centralization, the database access adopts a hierarchical management structure, and therefore may be causes the following problems in the actual test scenario:

Due to the complexity and dynamic nature of the cloud environment, the data in the cloud platform database does not necessarily reflect the real state of the current virtual network in real time. The focus of the existing virtual network isolation test is how to verify or reconstruct the virtual network model, and compare the reconstruction results with the preset benchmarks, but during the network configuration data collection phase of the virtual network isolation test, a single collection of data from a cloud platform database does not effectively ensure the authenticity and integrity of the data: (1) Unintentional misconfiguration of the administrator or malicious attack against the database by the attacker may damage the authenticity of the database's own data or collected data, making the virtual network security policy and configuration used for testing inconsistent with the actual situation, thereby affecting the accuracy of network isolation testing; (2) If there is a loophole in the cloud management platform, for example, the network and address management module cannot perform legal verification on the underlying network topology, the tenant may set up an illegal bridge to access other tenants on the routing port. Some similar problems indicate that the virtual network isolation status may not be reflected in the cloud platform database due to system vulnerabilities, thus affecting the test evaluation of virtual network isolation.

To solve the above problems, the main contribution of this paper is to propose a multi-layer virtual network isolation detection method for cloud platform. In the test model [7–9] based on trusted third party TTP (Trusted Third Party), the tasks of virtual network isolation detection are completed by a test agent jointly deployed on the cloud node by the CPP and the TTP. The method collects the virtual network configuration information from the control node database and the data storage space of the proxy node of the cloud platform, and uses the above data to reconstruct the network structure of the test domain. Firstly, match the reconstruction network structure of the cloud database layer with the reconstruction network structure of the proxy layer, and then the reconstruction network structure of cloud database layer is matched with the preset security policy to achieve multi-layer verification of the network isolation of the cloud platform.

The remainder of the paper is organized as follows: Sect. 2 describes the current work related to virtual network detection; Sect. 3 describes the attack model; Sect. 4 describes the architecture and key methods of a multi-layer network isolation detection method for cloud platform. Section 5 analyzes the effectiveness of the proposed detection method. Section 6 conducts an experimental evaluation of the proposed detection method and analyzes the performance of the mechanism. Section 7 summarizes the content of this paper.

2 Related Works

2.1 Index-Based Detection Method

Literature [10] proposed an isolation testing system for cloud computing infrastructure-as-a-service (IaaS) layer, which mainly tests a number of important attributes including virtual network isolation. Literature [11] proposed a monitoring mechanism for the change of virtualized infrastructure and established an automated security analysis of the virtualized infrastructure. Similar to the virtual network detection mechanism, literature [12] proposed a TTP-based security attribute evaluation mechanism for cloud service provider. This method quantitatively evaluates the security attributes of the cloud platform from DDoS attacks, side-channel attacks, and password security. Literature [13] proposed an extensible online security compliance verification method for large-scale cloud platforms. Feature extraction was performed on multiple system security attribute data. Once the potential violations of the system are detected, the system begins to actively prepare for the verification of high time loss, it effectively reducing the response time of compliance verification to an acceptable layer in the actual application scenario. However, regardless of the length of the detection cycle, limited detection indicators cannot fully characterize the current virtual network state.

2.2   Compliance-Based Detection Methods

Literature [14] proposed a verification tool NOD for dynamic virtual networks and used a specification language to check the security status of the current dynamic network model. Literature [15] proposed an automatic security analysis method for network access control on the cloud platform IaaS layer, combining static analysis and dynamic analysis methods to detect accessibility and unpredictable misconfiguration in the virtual network infrastructure. Literature [16] proposed a dynamic virtual network isolation detection model for medium-to-large-scale cloud platforms. The RadixTree data structure was used to optimize the detection efficiency of virtual network structures and to effectively process network configuration information such as routers tables, subnets and security groups. The above work focuses on how to verify or reconstruct the virtual network model, and compare the reconstruction results with the preset benchmarks, but during the network configuration data collection phase of the virtual network isolation test, a single collection of data from a cloud platform database does not enough to prove that the structure of the virtual network has not been destroyed.

3   Threat Model and Problem Description

3.1   Threat Model

The isolation detection method proposed in this paper focuses on verifying the state of the network within a specified test domain rather than detecting specific attacks or vulnerabilities. The latter is mainly the work of intrusion detection system (IDS). In addition, extracting the correct test input data from the database and each agent node is the basis for the correct detection result. Therefore, in this solution, the data preprocessing stage only verifies the authenticity of the test data. When an illegal input is detected, only the current input is determined to be invalid, and the measures such as evidence protection and channel security detection are beyond the scope of this article. Then, we assume that the detection scheme will not cause privacy leakage problems. For example, the detection process will involve the connectivity of the VM under the tenant, and the potential privacy protection in the test is one of the future work directions.

In this detection method, we assume that each cloud tenant has defined its own network isolation security policy for the connectivity between virtual machines based on its own needs. At the same time, the agent node proxy is logically located between the computing node and the cloud management node. Because the proxy node is closer to the computing node, it not only can effectively reduce the network load, but also can focus on simple and efficient security measures such as identity authentication, firewall, and access control, so it is difficult to attack the agent node proxy. Therefore, this article assumes that the proxy is safe and reliable, that is, the original data from the proxy server is authentic and trustworthy. How to ensure the authenticity of the data read from the proxy belongs to the work of evidence protection. This article only discusses the basic protection ideas, and the specific technical details are not the focus of this paper.

3.2   Problem Description

In the actual distributed cloud platform environment, in order to avoid the data access bottleneck caused by node centralization, database access adopts a layered management structure. A single extraction of network configuration information from a cloud database and comparison of the reconstructed network structure with a predetermined baseline is not sufficient to prove that the isolation of the virtual network is not compromised. Based on the mainstream open source cloud platform OpenStack, the following describes a security scenario for this test scenario.

Assuming there are currently tenants Alice and Bob, and the VM_A^1 under the tenant Alice is connected to the VM_B^2 under the tenant Bob. The simplified node distribution is as shown in Fig. 1.

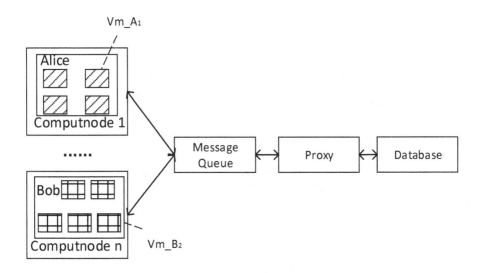

Fig. 1. OpenStack node distribution model

The Nova module of OpenStack deployed on the control node is an important module for storing and executing virtual network policies. The nova-network module provides network operation services for virtual machine and the nova-conductor module provides database connection services. Suppose now that Alice wants to change the network connectivity structure so that VM_A^1 and VM_B^2 cannot be connected. Therefore, it is necessary to send the network policy change command nova sec_group_add_rule to the high-level node and update the high-level network policy library (Database). However, a security vulnerability of OpenStack was exposed in 2015 [17], that is, the changes of nova security policy will not be implemented on the running virtual machines, and the nova $secgroup - add - rule$ command does not affect the running VM_A^1 and VM_B^2. Therefore, there are inconsistencies in the process of sending policies from the database to the cloud nodes. In addition, OpenStack exposed another security vulnerability [18] in 2014. Tenants can set up bridges on the routers port to access other tenants, but the network and address management module Neutron in OpenStack cannot verify the underlying network topology, so that Neutron cannot detect the illegal network connections between VM_A^1 and VM_B^2. In summary, even if the policy in database has been updated to disable the connection between VM_A^1 and VM_B^2, but in actual situations, VM_A^1 and VM_B^2 may still be connected. Therefore, it is not sufficient to collect the configuration information from database alone to reconstruct the real network structure.

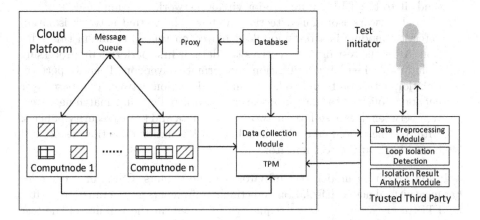

Fig. 2. OpenStack node distribution model

4   A Multi-layer Cloud Platform Virtual Network Isolation Detection Method

4.1   System Model

This paper presents a multi-layer cloud platform virtual network isolation detection method. The overall architecture is shown in Fig. 2. Our detection model mainly involves two entities:

(1) Test data collection node Agent. In the TTP-based cloud platform virtual network isolation detection model, the agent is essentially a test data collection program that is deployed by both the CSP and the TTP at the cloud node virtualization software stack (hypervisor). In the actual distributed cloud platform environment, in order to avoid the data access bottleneck caused by node centralization, the database access adopts a hierarchical management structure. Data access or modification requests need to be processed by multi-layer data proxy nodes before data can be obtained and returned. In fact, when the policy is distributed and executed, in the process

of processing the request, if the channel or the data packet itself is subjected to some strong attack, the data in the node may be inconsistent with the data in the database, resulting in a difference between the policy decision point (PDP) and the policy enforcement point (PEP). Therefore, comparing the network structure reconstructed from the network configuration information in a single database with a preset benchmark is not sufficient to reconstruct the correct network structure, and thus the correctness of the virtual network isolation detection result cannot be guaranteed. The agent collects data required for detection from both the cloud database and proxy nodes, and sends a series of cryptographic signatures to the data and then sends it to the TTP to prepare for virtual network isolation detection.

(2) Virtual network isolation detection module. The virtual network isolation detection module is a test module deployed on the TTP side in this solution. After the test module receives the data, it first performs preprocessing including authenticity verification and format conversion. Then we perform isolation detection from two layers: match detection between database-layer network policy data and proxy-layer network policy, and matching detection between database-layer network policy data and preset security policies. After testing is complete, the virtual network isolation detection results will be fed back to the test initiator.

In our detection model, test initiators can be tenants, CSPs, or other roles that have virtual network isolation detection requirements and permissions. After the TTP receives the detection request, it will confirm the validity of the test initiator's identity. If it is detected that the test initiator does not have the right to initiate isolation detection, the test request is rejected; if the test initiator identity is determined, TTP will send the cloud platform virtual network isolation detection command to the agent deployed in the cloud node. After the agent receives the test command, it collects the data required for testing from the cloud platform at multiple layers and sends the data packet to the TTP. After the TTP receives the data and carries out preprocessing including credibility verification and format conversion, it will perform loop isolation detection and multi-layer matching detection. Finally, the test results will be fed back to the test initiator.

The following describes the virtual network isolation detection method in this test model from three steps: multi-layer data preprocessing mechanism, loop isolation detection, and isolation matching detection.

4.2   Multi-layer Data Preprocessing Mechanism

When TTP receives the data required for testing from the cloud database and the proxy node, TTP needs to perform preprocessing operations such as authenticity verification and format conversion on the received test data. The pre-processing mechanism is used to determine the authenticity of the data and convert the original format from which the source data is read in the database to a format that the test program can parse to facilitate subsequent loop isolation testing.

Before describing the data preprocessing mechanism, we need to introduce some cryptographic and format conversion primitives used in the paper. Firstly, we use the following notations for cryptographic and format conversion operations throughout the paper:

Definition 1. *The set of all binary strings of length n is denoted by $\{0,1\}^n$, and the set of all finite binary strings as $\{0,1\}^*$.*

Definition 2. *For an arbitrary message $m \in \{0,1\}^*$, we denote by $c = Enc(K, m)$, a symmetric encryption of using the observed key $K \in \{0,1\}^*$. The corresponding symmetric decryption operation is denoted by $m = Dev(K, c) = Dec(K, Enc(K, m))$.*

Definition 3. *A digital signature over a message is denoted by $\sigma = Sign_{sk}(m)$. The corresponding verification operation for a digital signature is denoted by $b = Verify_{pk}(m, \sigma)$, where $b = 1$ if the signature is valid and $b = 0$ while the signature is illegal.*

Definition 4. *We denote by $m^* = Convert(m)$ a data processing, which converts raw data m to another form m^*. The processed data m^* can be resolved by the following detection programme.*

We now present our construction for the data preprocessing mechanism. The message flow in the data preprocessing mechanism is shown in Fig. 3. In the following, we show the data preprocessing process.

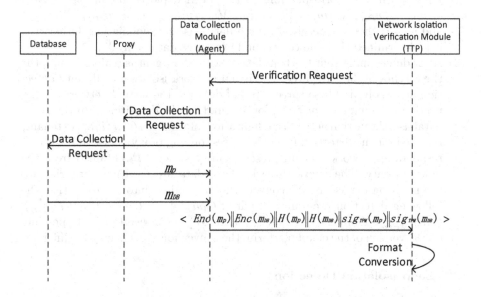

Fig. 3. The message flow of the data preprocessing mechanism

(1) After receiving the virtual network isolation detection request, the TTP
    sends an authentication request to the agent deployed on the cloud plat-
    form. After determining that the request is valid, the agent sends a data
    collection request to both the cloud database and proxy nodes. When receiv-
    ing the data sent from cloud database and proxy, Agent encrypts valid
    data with pre-negotiated symmetric key first, and generate cipher text
    $c_{p1} = Enc(K_p, m_p)$ and $c_{p2} = Enc(K_p, m_{DB})$. Then we do hash operations
    on the database layer valid network configuration data mDB and proxy
    nodes valid network configuration data mp respectively, generate digest
    $H_{P1} = Hash(m_p)$ and $H_{P2} = Hash(m_{DB})$, and attach the abstract to
    the cipher text. Then we use the signature private key SK_{sign} generated by
    the TPM deployed on the agent side to sign the above digest to generate
    a digital signature, and generate signature $\sigma^1_{TPM} = Sign_{SK_{sign}}(H_{P1})$ and
    $\sigma^2_{TPM} = Sign_{SK_{sign}}(H_{P2})$. Finally, agent sends the following data to TTP:
    $Enc(K_p, m_p) \| Enc(K_p, m_{DB}) \| H_{p1} \| H_{p2} \| \sigma^1_{TPM} \| \sigma^2_{TPM}$.
(2) After the TTP receives the data packet, it first decrypts the cipher text part
    of the data packet with a pre-negotiated symmetric key K_p to generate the
    plaintext $m'_p = Dec(K_1, c_1)$ and $m'_{DB} = Dec(K_2, c_2)$. Then we perform Hash
    operations on the generated plaintext data separately to generate a digest
    $H'_{p1} = Hash(m'_p)$ and $H'_{p2} = Hash(m'_{DB})$. We compare the digest values H'_{p1}
    and H'_{p2} with H_{p1} and H_{p2} in the data packet respectively. If $H_{p1} = H_{p1}$ and
    $H_{p2} = H_{p2}$, it means that the integrity of the test data from the agent is not
    destroyed, otherwise it is determined that the data sent by the corresponding
    node is invalid. Then verify the signature with the signature public key
    PK_{sign} which is corresponding to the TPM deployed on the agent side:
    $b_1 = Verify_{PKsign}(m_p, \sigma^1_{TPM})$, $b_2 = Verify_{PKsign}(m_p, \sigma^2_{TPM})$. If $b_1 = 1$
    and $b_2 = 1$, then the received source data has non-repudiation. Otherwise,
    it is determined that the corresponding source data is invalid.
(3) After determining that the test data sent by the Agent is real and valid, the
    three types of data required for virtual network isolation credibility detec-
    tion are resolved. These three types of data are the virtual network config-
    uration information $Config^i_{DB}$ of required for the detection from the cloud
    database, the virtual network configuration information $Config^i_{Pro}$ of tenant$_i$
    required for the detection from the corresponding proxy nodes, and the cor-
    responding network domain preset security policy SP_i obtained from the
    policy library. The above three kinds of data are used as a criterion for
    the isolation detection. We convert the above data into a format that the
    following detection program can parse: $Config^{i^*}_{DB} = Convert(Config^i_{DB})$,
    $Config^{i^*}_{Pro} = Convert(Config^{i^*}_{Pro})$, and $SP^*_i = Convert(SP_i)$. Depending
    on the version of the cloud platform, the conversion process may be different.

4.3 Loop Isolation Detection

After completing the data preprocessing operation, in order to reconstruct the
network structure in the test domain, we input the test data, which contains the
virtual network configuration information $Config^i_{DB}$ of *tenant$_i$* from the cloud

database and the virtual network configuration information $Config^i_{Pro}$ of $tenant_i$ from the corresponding proxy nodes, to the loop isolation detection program.

We employ an efficient RadixTree data structure to store network configuration information such as routing rules and firewall rules. In the RadixTree data structure, each tree node holds one bit in the IP address. The left subtree of each node represents 0 and the right subtree represents 1, and the corresponding jump address of the current prefix in the routing table is stored in the node. So that we can save the forwarding relationship between all IP addresses. Figure 4 shows an example of converting the routing rules in Route R into Radix Tree structure storage.

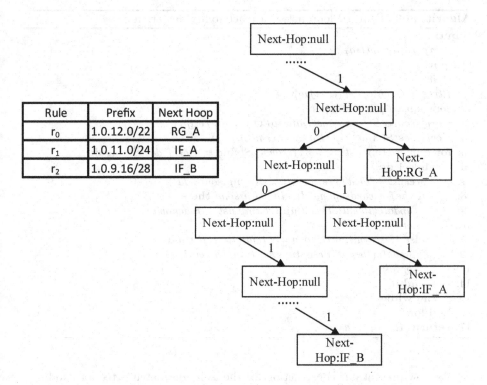

Rule	Prefix	Next Hoop
r_0	1.0.12.0/22	RG_A
r_1	1.0.11.0/24	IF_A
r_2	1.0.9.16/28	IF_B

Fig. 4. An example of routing table rule in RadixTree structure

We used the RadixTree longest match algorithm to test the connectivity of each pair of VMs in the test network domain based on the start and end IP addresses of the test domain and the routing rules stored by the RadixTree. Algorithm 1 describes the loop isolation detection method to verify whether there is a forwarding path between the IP ports of each pair of VMs. If there is, that is, the corresponding IP can be reached; if not, the corresponding IP is unreachable. At the same time, the connectivity status is updated in the corresponding leaf node in Result_Tree where the detection result is stored.

4.4　Isolation Match Detection

Before describing the isolation match detection module, we need to introduce some process primitives used in the paper firstly. We use the following notations for process operations throughout the paper:

Definition 5. *We denote by* $\gamma = VN\_Verify(m_1^*,\ m_2^*)$, *as network structure matching program, where* γ *stands for the consistency proportion between object* m_1^* *and* m_2^*.

Algorithm 1. IP-to-IP loop network reachability detection

Input:
　　$Config_{DB}^{i*}$, $Config_{Pro}^{i*}$;
Output:
　　btrie.
1: $Rtree = CreateTree(Config_{Pro}^{i*})$
2: $source_i p, dst_i p = GetInput()$
3: $Verif\_sourceString = getData.ipTOint(source\_ip)$
4: $Verif\_destString = getData.ipTOint(dst\_ip)$
5: **for** $tmp\_src, tmp\_dsti = Verif\_sourceString$ to $Verif\_destString$ **do**
6: 　　**while** 1 **do**
7: 　　　　$sresult = TestTree.search\_best(temp\_sourceIP)$
8: 　　　　**if** $the forwarding and filtering path is end$ **then**
9: 　　　　　　$update(Result\_Tree, tmp\_src, tmp\_dst, unreachable)$
10: 　　　　　　$break$
11: 　　　　**else if** $sresult.next\_hoop == temp\_destIP$ **then**
12: 　　　　　　$update(Result\_Tree,\ tmp\_src, tmp\_dst, reachable)$
13: 　　　　　　$break$
14: 　　　　**end if**
15: 　　**end while**
16: **end for**
17: **return** $Result_T ree$

We now present our construction for the isolation match detection module.

In the above loop isolation detection process, we input the test data, which contains the virtual network configuration information $Config_{DB}^i$ of $tenant_i$ from the cloud database, and the virtual network configuration information $Config_{Pro}^i$ of $tenant_i$ required from the corresponding proxy nodes. We input above test data to the loop isolation detection program, in order to reconstruct the network structure $Result\_Tree(DB)$ stored in the cloud database and the network structure $Result\_Tree(P)$ stored in the proxy nodes of the test domain. After the loop isolation detection is completed, network structure matching detection will be performed from two layers respectively: match detection of database layer network structure and proxy layer network structure, and match detection of database layer network structure and preset security policies, thus we can analyze the results of the isolation results for the results of the loop isolation detection program. Algorithm 2 describes the matching detection process of the database layer network structure and the proxy layer network structure, which separately traverses the leaf nodes of $Result\_Tree(DB)$ and $Result\_Tree(P)$. We verify the consistency of the network structure stored in the leaf node and updates the consistency matching ratio γ_1. Algorithm 3 describes the matching detection process of the database layer network structure and the preset security policy, which traverses the security policy preset in SP_i^* one by one, and perform matching search on the corresponding content in the leaf node of $Result\_Tree(DB)$. At the same time, the consistency matching ratio γ_2 will be updated.

Algorithm 2. Match detection between DB and Proxy

Input:
   $Result\_Tree(DB)$, $Result\_Tree(P)$;
Output:
   γ_1.
1: $\gamma_1 = 1$
2: **for** $leave\_node1, leave\_node2$ in $Result\_Tree(DB), Result\_Tree(P)$ **do**
3:    $tmp\_r = VN\_Verify(leave\_node1, leave\_node2)$
4:    $update(\gamma_1, tmp\_r)$
5: **end for**
6: **return** γ_1

Algorithm 3. Match detection between DB and Proxy

Input:
   $Result\_Tree(DB)$, SP_i^*;
Output:
   γ_2.
1: $\gamma_2 = 1$
2: **for** $line$ in SP_i^* **do**
3:    $src\_ip = getData.ipTOint(line[0])$
4:    $dst\_ip = getData.ipTOint(line[1])$
5:    $tmp\_node = Result\_Tree(DB).getNode(src\_ip)$
6:    $tmp\_r = VN\_Verify(tmp\_node, dsp\_ip)$
7:    $update(\gamma_2, tmp\_r)$
8: **end for**
9: **return** γ_2

In the above isolation match detection algorithm, γ_1 and γ_2 respectively represent the consistency ratio between the database layer network policy and the proxy layer network policy, and the consistency ratio between the database layer network policy data and the preset security policy. If $\gamma_1 = 1$ and $\gamma_2 = 1$, the virtual network in the test domain is well isolated; If $\gamma_1 < 1$, it indicates that the database layer network policy data and the Proxy layer network policy are inconsistent. That is, when the network policy is distributed and executed, the channel or the data packet itself has been subjected to some kind of strong attack during the processing of the request, and the virtual network isolation is destroyed. If $\gamma_2 < 1$, it indicates that the database layer network policy data is inconsistent with the preset security policy. That is, during the setting and execution of network policies, virtual network isolation is disrupted due to unintentional configuration errors or packet hijacking by malicious tenants. After the detection is complete, we send the virtual network isolation detection results γ_1 and γ_2 back to the test initiator.

5   Effectivity Analysis

For the cloud platform virtual network isolation detection scheme proposed in this paper, this section through theoretical analysis shows that the program is effective against the attack mentioned in the problem description.

Proposition 1. *(The effectiveness of multi-layer network isolation detection schemes). The multi-layer network isolation detection scheme can effectively generate specific feedback information for the attacks of the data collection strategy and provide a basis for evaluating the credibility of the network isolation detection results.*

Proof. Assume that the attacker ADV attempts to exploit the vulnerabilities of the cloud management platform to tamper with the isolation strategy of the virtual network. The attack may affect the agent's collection of virtual network configuration information $Config^{i^*}_{DB}$ of tenanti from the cloud database of the CSP, and virtual network configuration information $Config^{i^*}_{Pro}$ of tenanti from the proxy nodes. These collected data may be inconsistent with the actual virtual network state under the influence of the attack. Below we analyze the situation in two ways.

Section 1. After the virtual network isolation policy is updated, the attacker tampers with or destroys the network configuration data of the cloud database. According to actual needs, changes the connectivity between the virtual machines VM^1_i and VM^2_i belonging to the change to isolation. That is, $connection(VM^1_i, VM^2_i) = 0$. Then, under normal conditions, the virtual network configuration information $Config^{i(t)}_{DB}$ of the $tenant_i$ is updated to be $Config^{i(t1)}_{DB}$, and $Config^{i(t)}_{DB} \neq Config^{i(t1)}_{DB}$. Suppose that the attacker exploits the vulnerabilities of the cloud management platform so that the virtual network configuration information $Config^{i(t1)}_{DB}$ is tampered with. So in practice, $connection(VM^1_i, VM^2_i) = 0$. However, $Config^{i(t1)}_{DB}$ may reflect that VM^1_i and VM^2_i are still connected, which leads to the $Config^{i(t1)}_{DB}$ collected by the agent to be different from the actual virtual network status.

Section 2. In the strategy virtual network isolation policy update process, the attacker tampers with or destroys the network configuration data of the cloud database and the proxy nodes. According to actual needs, changes the connectivity between the virtual machines VM_i^1 and VM_i^2 belonging to the change to isolation. That is, $connection(VM_i^1, VM_i^2) = 0$. If the proxy nodes were attacked before it was feed back to the cloud management platform, the virtual isolation of the virtual machine did not change. That is, when $Config_{DB}^{i(t)} \rightarrow Config_{DB}^{i(t1)}$ and $Config_{Pro}^{i(t)} \rightarrow Config_{Pro}^{i(t1)}$, $connection(VM_i^1, VM_i^2) = 1$. This will cause $Config_{DB}^{i(t1)}$ and $Config_{Pro}^{i(t1)}$ collected by the agent to be different from the actual virtual network status.

In Sect. 1 above, the attacker tampers with the network configuration data of the cloud database, and the configuration data of the data agent node Proxy can still reflect the true state of the virtual network configuration. Therefore, the final result in the TTP isolation detection will be $\gamma_1 < 1$ and $\gamma_2 = 1$, indicating that the database layer network policy data and the proxy layer network policy are inconsistent. This shows that in the process of network policy distribution and execution, the channel or packet itself has been subjected to some kind of strong attack during the processing of the request, and the virtual network isolation may be damaged. In Sect. 2, since the proxy nodes were attacked, the configuration information of both the Proxy and the cloud management terminal was updated, but the actual network isolation instructions did not produce results. Therefore, the isolation test will result in $\gamma_1 < 1$ and $\gamma_2 < 1$, indicating that the database layer network policy data and the proxy layer network policy are inconsistent, and the database layer network policy data is inconsistent with the preset security policy. This shows that during the process of setting and executing sub-network policies, the virtual network isolation is disrupted due to inadvertent configuration errors or packet hijacking by malicious tenants. In summary, the method we proposed not only can effectively determine whether the network isolation is correct, but also can locate the components that are attacked to some extent, and provide data support for the system repair.

6 Experiments

6.1 Experimental Settings

In our test, we build a multi-node cloud platform environment based on CloudSim4.0 to simulate the IaaS cloud environment to be tested. The simulated cloud platform runs in ubuntu16.04.02 VM, with Intel(R) Core(TM) i7-8550U processor, 1.80 GHz CPU frequency and 16.00 GB RAM. There are one control node and 10 computing nodes in the IaaS cloud environment. One of the nodes is deployed as an agent, and the remaining nodes are bound to a data proxy node every 3 groups. The agent is responsible for communicating with the TTP side, collecting the configuration information of test network domain from the IaaS cloud database (DataCenterBroke in the simulation environment) and the data proxy node (DataCenterBroke in the simulation environment) according to the instruction sent from the TTP, and then return the collected data to the TTP. There is another computer served as TTP, which sends test requests to the IaaS cloud, and performs specific network isolation detection work based on the acquired data. The simulated TTP runs in ubuntu16.04LTS VM, with Intel(R) Core(TM) i5-2400 CPU @3.10 GHz processor and 8.00 GB RAM.

6.2 Result and Analysis

This section compares the performance of our detection method with the traditional network isolation detection method, and analyses the performance overhead our detection method bring to the test-end system. Therefore, we evaluate our performance of multi-layer cloud platform virtual network isolation detection method from the above two aspects.

(1) Comparison with the traditional network isolation detection method performance.

For the two inputs of network isolation detection, we take two independent experimental variables, the amount of strategy and the size of the detection domain. In order to improve the accuracy and scientificity of the time measurement results, 1000 testing procedures were repeated at each independent variable value, and the average value of 1000 execution results was taken. We also calculate delay ratio of our multi-layer virtual network isolation detection method compared to the traditional detection method. We define this ratio as $1-T$, where $T = $ (Traditional method detection time/Multi-layer method detection time).

Table 1. Performance comparison with traditional detection method about the sum of rules.

Sum of rules	128	256	512	1024	2048
Traditional detection method(s)	0.259754	0.262402	0.263218	0.282071	0.293977
Multi-layer detection method(s)	0.286647	0.300598	0.310489	0.315551	0.335284
Delay overhead(s)	0.026893	0.038196	0.047271	0.03348	0.041307
Delay ratio	10.35%	14.56%	17.96%	11.87%	14.05%

Table 2. Performance comparison with traditional detection method about the sum of IPs.

Sum of IPs	50	100	150	200	250
Traditional detection method(s)	0.259754	2.809346	13.318271	40.818756	99.408507
Multi-layer detection method(s)	0.286647	2.986119	13.778629	41.954479	101.003907
Delay overhead(s)	0.026893	0.176773	0.460358	1.135723	1.5954
Delay ratio	10.35%	6.29%	3.46%	2.78%	1.60%

Tables 1, 2 and Figs. 5, 6 show that, detection time of multi-layer detection method increased compared with the traditional detection method. Table 1 indicated that, when we change strategies amounts, the maximum increase of multi-layer detection method is 17.96%, the minimum increase is 10.35%, and the maximum difference is below 0.047271 s. It can be seen that the increase is more stable. Combined with Table 2, it can be seen that when the size of the test domain is gradually increased, the delay ratios of the above two detection methods are getting smaller and smaller, decreasing from 10.35% to 1.60%. Therefore, when the scale of testing is gradually increased, the gap between the detection delay of the multi-layer cloud platform network isolation detection method and the traditional detection method is narrowing.

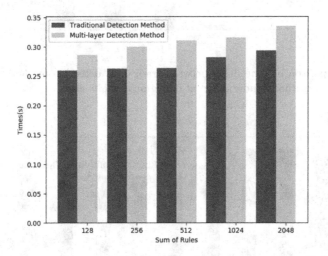

Fig. 5. Comparison of time delay between traditional detection methods and multi-layer detection methods under different strategies amounts.

(1) Performance overhead that multi-layer detection method bring to test-end system.

Our multi-layered cloud platform virtual network isolation detection method is deployed in the TTP-side test module. Therefore, it is necessary to consider the performance overhead our isolation detection method bring to the test-end system. In this section, nbench2.2.3 was run when only the test program was run and the program was not run. The score given by nbench was used as the benchmark value when the test program was not run. Figure 7 shows that the overhead caused by the multi-layer detection method on the system memory is negligible. That is to say, the performance overhead of the multi-layer detection method proposed in this paper does not affect the normal operation of other functions of the TTP end test module.

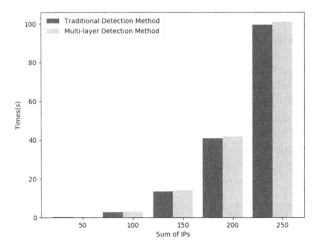

Fig. 6. Comparison of time delay between traditional detection methods and multi-layer detection methods under different detection domain size.

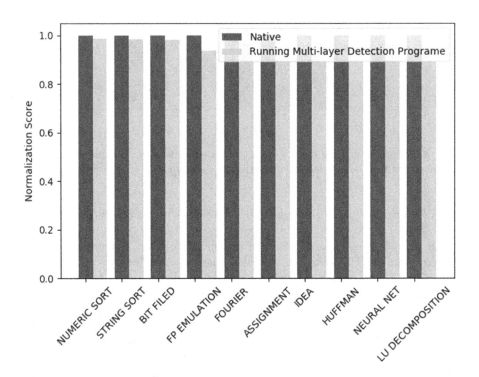

Fig. 7. Result of performance overhead that multi-layer detection method bring to test-end system

7 Conclusions and Future Work

In the actual distributed cloud platform, in order to avoid the problem of data access bottlenecks caused by node centralization, the database access adopts a hierarchical management structure. The focus of the existing virtual network isolation test is how to verify or reconstruct the virtual network model, and compare the reconstruction results with the preset benchmarks, but during the network configuration data collection phase of the virtual network isolation test, a single collection of data from a cloud platform database does not effectively ensure the authenticity and integrity of the data. In response to the above problems, this paper proposes a multi-layer virtual network isolation detection method for cloud platform. Combining with the distributed cloud platform environment, firstly propose the architecture of multi-layer virtual network isolation detection method, and introduce the entity and main flow included in this test method, and give the technical basis of this paper. Then, from the three stages of data preprocessing, loop isolation testing, and isolation matching detection, the detection method is further described. And then, a formal method is used to verify the effectiveness of the proposed scheme in detecting network isolation under both the policy updating and post-update scenarios. Finally, through the experiments and analysis, it can be seen that the multi-layer detection method has less impact on the test-end system's performance, and as the test scale increases, the gap with the traditional program's overhead will gradually decrease.

Although the scheme of this paper can detect network isolation at multiple layers, the correctness of the detection results depends on extracting the correct test input data from the database and each agent node. Although the data preprocessing stage verifies the authenticity of the test data, however, there are still some problems. Therefore, as an extension of system protection, evidence protection and channel security detection are the main directions for future research. Then, during the detection process, the solution may involve the connectivity of the VM under the tenant, which may cause privacy leakage during the data transmission or detection process. Therefore, the privacy protection is also a challenge to improve the solution in the future.

Acknowledgments. This work was supported in part by the National Key Basic Research Program of China (973 Program) under Grant 2014CB340600 and in part by the Wuhan FRONTIER Program of Application Foundation under Grant 2018010401011295.

References

1. Riddle, A.R., Chung, S.M.: A survey on the security of hypervisors in cloud computing. In: IEEE International Conference on Distributed Computing Systems Workshops, pp. 100–104. IEEE (2015)
2. Shahzad, F.: State-of-the-art survey on cloud computing security challenges, approaches and solutions. Procedia Comput. Sci. **37**, 357–362 (2014)

3. Saravanakumar, C., Arun, C.: Survey on interoperability, security, trust, privacy standardization of cloud computing. In: International Conference on Contemporary Computing and Informatics, pp. 977–982. IEEE (2015)
4. Common Criteria Project Sponsoring Organisations: Common Criteria for Information Technology Security Evaluation. ISO/IEC International Standard (IS) Version 2.1 1–3 (15408)
5. Trusted Computing Group (TCG), TCPA Main Specification, Version 1.1
6. IEEE Computer Society Technical Committee on Dependable Computing and Fault Tolerance. http://www.dependability.org/
7. Zech, P.: Risk-based security testing in cloud computing environments. In: IEEE International Conference on Software Testing, pp. 411–414. IEEE Computer Society (2011)
8. Khan, I., Rehman, H., Anwar, Z.: Design and deployment of a trusted eucalyptus cloud. In: 2011 IEEE International Conference on Cloud Computing (CLOUD), Washington, DC, USA, pp. 380–387, 4–9 July 2011
9. Pham, C., Chen, D., Kalbarczyk, Z., et al.: CloudVal: a framework for validation of virtualization environment in cloud
10. Zhao, Y., Cheng, S.Y., Jiang, F.: Testing system for cloud computing IaaS isolation properties. Comput. Syst. Appl. **26**(1), 44–49 (2017)
11. Bleikertz, S., Vogel, C.: Cloud radar: near real-time detection of security failures in dynamic virtualized infrastructures. In: Computer Security Applications Conference, pp. 26–35. ACM (2014)
12. Whaiduzzaman, M., Gani, A.: Measuring security for cloud service provider: a third party approach. In: International Conference on Electrical Information and Communication Technology, pp. 1–6. IEEE (2014)
13. Majumdar, S., et al.: Proactive verification of security compliance for clouds through pre-computation: application to OpenStack. In: Askoxylakis, I., Ioannidis, S., Katsikas, S., Meadows, C. (eds.) ESORICS 2016, Part I. LNCS, vol. 9878, pp. 47–66. Springer, Cham (2016). https://doi.org/10.1007/978-3-319-45744-4_3
14. Lopes, N.P., Godefroid, P., Jayaraman, K., et al.: Checking beliefs in dynamic networks. In: USENIX Conference on Networked Systems Design and Implementation, pp. 499–512. USENIX Association (2015)
15. Probst, T., Alata, E., Kaâniche, M., Nicomette, V.: An approach for the automated analysis of network access controls in cloud computing infrastructures. In: Au, M.H., Carminati, B., Kuo, C.-C.J. (eds.) NSS 2014. LNCS, vol. 8792, pp. 1–14. Springer, Cham (2014). https://doi.org/10.1007/978-3-319-11698-3_1
16. Majumdar, S., Wang, Y., Madi, T., et al.: TenantGuard: scalable runtime verification of cloud-wide VM-level network isolation. In: The Network and Distributed System Security Symposium (2017)
17. OpenStack: Nova network security group changes are not applied to running instances (2015). https://security.openstack.org/ossa/OSSA-2015-021.html. Accessed May 2016
18. OpenStack: Routers can be cross plugged by other tenants (2014). https://security.openstack.org/ossa/OSSA-2014-008.html. Accessed May 2016

A Behavioral Measurement Model Suitable for the Sensing Nodes of Internet of Things

Yubo Wang, Mowei Gong[✉], and Bei Gong

Beijing University of Technology, Beijing 100124, China
love.haier@163.com

Abstract. The Internet of Things connects a large number of real objects with the Internet through a variety of sensing technologies and it is a network that implements the concept of connected objects. However, as a new concept of network, because of its large number and variety of terminals, wide range of distribution, the traditional security mechanisms are not adapted to the Internet of Things (IoT) architecture, and the existed researches use the static information of sensing nodes to measure and judge the trust of sensing nodes. It results the real-time trust of Internet of Things hard to be judged. Therefore, this paper purposes a behavioral measurement model suitable for the sensing nodes of Internet of Things to make up the insufficient of existed sensing nodes measurement mechanism of Internet of Things. This model is designed for the Internet of Things, and bases on the identity authentication and the static measurement to measure the behavior of sensing nodes. It through designs different behavior measurement functions to assess and calculate the behavior of sensing nodes synthetically. According to divide the trusted level of sensing nodes, this model can defense the attacks, such as the node hijacking attack, the physical capture attacks and the denial of service attacks.

Keywords: Internet of Things · Security of sensing layer
Behavioral measurement · Trusted computing

1 Introduction

With the development of information technology in the 21st century, the Internet of things has become another hot topic after the computer and the Internet application. It is a network which bases on the Internet and uses a communication technology to realize the concept of connected objects. On the basis of traditional Internet technology, the Internet of things uses a large number of sensing equipment to combine the real environment with human application, and realizes the exchange between human to object, and object to object [1].

Generally speaking, the Internet of things is classified as the sensing layer, the transport layer and the application layer [2]. In this three layers architecture, the sensing layer composed of a variety of hardware equipment is responsible for the data gathering as the bottom. The transport layer is responsible for processing and transmitting the massive data collected by the sensing layer, which is composed of a large number of data processing node groups. The application layer is used for information and

H. Zhang et al. (Eds.): CTCIS 2018, CCIS 960, pp. 149–166, 2019.
https://doi.org/10.1007/978-981-13-5913-2_10

feedback control of the transmission layer, which is composed of many applications [3]. However, in the actual implementation process, the transmitting and gathering of sensing nodes is limited by its storage space, calculate ability and energy supply. It results many complex encryption techniques and authentication methods are difficult to implement.

In the current Internet of things, the security mechanisms used in the Internet of things are mostly based on the traditional networks and it lacks a security research applicable to the sensing layer of the Internet of Things. However, the Internet of Things will fail to gain the data information when the sensing nodes which is used as the peripheral nerves of the architecture of Internet of Things is attacked. To the Internet of things, the trusted operation of the sensing nodes is the foundation of the trusted running and construction of Internet of things and it plays a vital role in the wide application of the Internet of things [4]. It is necessary to measure the trust of sensing nodes for guaranteeing the trusted running of Internet of things, but the existed trusted measurement technologies mostly do the static measurement around the status information of the sensing nodes. It lacks the dynamic measurement of sensing nodes behaviors during the Internet of things running, and it results the real-time trust of sensing nodes can not be guaranteed.

In view of the above problems, this paper proposes a behavior measurement model applicable to the sensing nodes of Internet of things. This model can do the trusted measurement of the behavior of sensing nodes based on the status measurement. According to the different characteristics of each node, it can guarantee the trusted gathering and transmitting of data information and realize the trusted running of sensing layer of Internet of Things.

2 Research Status

According to the description in the previous section, it can be found that the trusted measurement of sensing nodes of the Internet of things is the key of the trusted running of Internet of things. In the current research, the trusted measurement can be divide into two parts which are static measurement and dynamic measurement [5]. The static measurement means when the sensing nodes is started, it will do the status measurement through its static information, such as the hardware information of nodes, the information of trusted platform control module, the data status information and the environment information of nodes. And the dynamic measurement means when the system is running, it do the behavior measurement through the various behaviors of the sensing nodes [6]. In order to ensure the trusted operation of the Internet of things, it is necessary to measure the sensing nodes from static and dynamic.

The literature [7] points out that the dynamic trusted value of the system can only focus on the behaviors associated with trust, but how to judge and measure if the behaviors is associated with trust has not be explicitly written. The literature [8] researches the connection between the value of trust and the expected behaviors based on the UCON model, but the limitation of the UCON model leads the trusted measurement can not be used well. The literature [9, 10] introduces a dynamic integrity model based on software behavior, which can obtain expected behavior by analyzing the API call relation of executable file or source code and compare the software behavior with the expected behavior to determine whether the behavior is trusted. However, to the sensing nodes of Internet of Things, the measuring granularity of this method will produce a status space explosion. As can be seen from the above researches, in terms of behavior measurement, most researches still revolve around the traditional computer system and it has poor adaptability in the architecture of Internet of Things.

However, with the integration of the software and hardware of Internet of things, the trusted measurement is gradually being studied by researchers because of using trusted measurement technology in sensing nodes can improve the overall security of the Internet of things, real-time monitoring of the Internet of things and decrease the cost of computation. The literature [11] proposes a trusted measurement model based on the role description of sensing nodes. Although this model realizes the trusted measurement of nodes according to the identity elements, its result can not depict the process of the trusted change of nodes and its measurement value just can be a reference. The literature [12] proposes a measurement model of malicious behaviors of nodes based on the Kalman filter calculation. This model can resist the malicious attack behavior, but the model has high false alarm rate and poor operational stability. The literature [13] combines the trusted value smoothing integral and the gaussian distribution to propose a trusted measurement model based on the subjective trust. This model is smooth in trust calculation and stable in operation, but it lacks the consideration of recommendation trust. The literature [14] combines the theory of trusted computing and the theory of the decay of trust relationship with time in sociology to propose a trusted measurement model of sensing nodes based on the change of trust. This model fully considers the decay of behavior and status with time, but its space complexity and time complexity are too high for the sensing node. At the same time, the model is mainly calculated based on subjective trust, so the trust smoothness and practical are poor. The literature [15] designs a trusted measurement model based on the location information. It can detect and eliminate malicious nodes in real time, but the key information of the sensing node is easy to leak.

In summary, the theoretical research in the trusted measurement field is more than the actual development research. And most of the theoretical research is around the static measurement and poor in the dynamic measurement researches, especially in the sensing layer of Internet o Things. It is because the status space of model will become extremely large when the complication of node behavior and the refinement of the granularity of measurement in the process of the behaviors trusted measurement, and finally the status space explodes. It is a seriously problem to the sensing nodes of Internet of Things which is limitation of the computation ability. Therefore, it is necessary to design a behavior measurement model which is suitable for the sensing layer of Internet of Things, and this model needs to satisfy the trusted running of sensing layer of Internet of Things based on the computation ability and energy cost of sensing nodes.

3   The Description of the Behavior Measurement Model of Sensing Nodes

As it is mentioned in the previous section, to solve the problems in sensing node of the Internet of Things, this paper do the trusted measurement of behaviors of nodes based on existed status measurement methods of nodes. It ensures the trust of sensing nodes in data collection and transmission and realizes the trusted running of sensing nodes of Internet of Things. The Fig. 1 describes the process of the trusted measurement of behaviors of sensing nodes of Internet of Things logically.

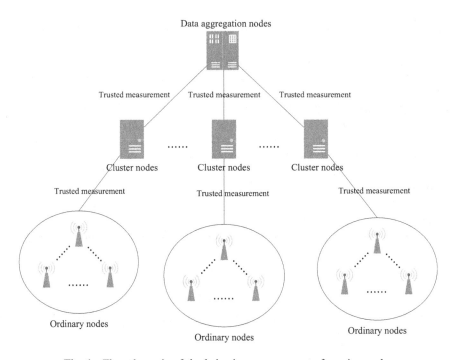

Fig. 1. The schematic of the behavior measurement of sensing nodes

As shown in the Fig. 1, sensing nodes can be divided into three types. There are ordinary nodes, cluster nodes and data aggregation nodes. The ordinary node consists of a large number of sensors, which is responsible for the collection and transmission of mass information. The cluster node is the superior node of ordinary nodes. It does the two-way identity authentication and the trusted measurement to ordinary nodes before it forwards the data which is transmitted by ordinary nodes. The data aggregation node is the superior node of cluster nodes. It does the two-way identity authentication and the trusted measurement to cluster nodes before it sends the data which is forwarded by cluster nodes to the application layer via the Internet.

The trusted measurement of nodes bases the identity authentication of nodes. It includes the status measurement and the behavior measurement. The status measurement refers the superior node measuring the static status information of the lower node and the behavior measurement refers the superior node measuring the dynamic behavior information of the lower node. The superior node does the status measurement on the lower node accessing. After the identity authentication, it finishes the static measurement with the initial status of nodes, the computing environment of nodes and the status information of data. And the superior node does the behavior measurement with the addressing behavior of nodes, the computing behavior and the transmitting behavior of network on the lower node running. In this section, a behavior measurement model of the cluster node to ordinary nodes and the data aggregation node to cluster nodes will be built. The logical diagram of the measurement model is as follows:

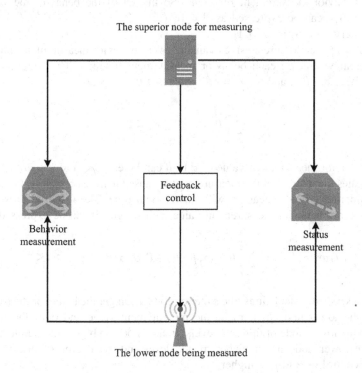

The superior node for measuring

Feedback control

Behavior measurement

Status measurement

The lower node being measured

Fig. 2. The logical diagram of the trusted measurement model

According to the Fig. 2, the node does the trusted measurement after it finishes the identity authentication. First of all, the superior node does the status measurement to the lower node with its computing environment and the status information of data. Then the superior node does the behavior measurement to the lower node with its addressing behavior, computing behavior and the transmitting behavior of network. Finally, through the comprehensiveness of the results of the status measurement and the behavior measurement of nodes, the trusted value of nodes can be judged. And according to the judgment result, the superior node feedback-controls the lower node.

In this model, the level of nodes is divided with its computation ability and energy. It means the data aggregation node is the superior node of cluster nodes which aggregate to this data aggregation node and the cluster node is the superior node of all ordinary nodes in this cluster.

4 The Model of the Behavior Measurement

4.1 The Establishment of This Model

The α is set as the superior node which does measure and the β is set as the lower node which is measured. The behavior measurement value of α to β is assessed by integrating i behavior measurement functions. So the set of the behavior measurement value of α to β can be expressed as $\partial = \{\partial_1(\alpha, \beta), \partial_2(\alpha, \beta), \ldots\ldots, \partial_i(\alpha, \beta)\}$ and the value of every $\partial_i(\alpha, \beta)$ is in $[0, 1]$.

When this paper comprehensive evaluates every behavior measurement function, it puts different weight on each behavior measurement function. The weight is set as $\theta = \{\theta_1, \theta_2, \ldots\ldots, \theta_i\}$, and the $\theta = \{\theta_1, \theta_2, \ldots\ldots, \theta_i\}$ satisfies:

$$\sum_{n=1}^{i} \theta_n = 1, 0 \le \theta_n \le 1 \tag{1}$$

The behavior measurement value of α to β can be expressed as $Trust(\alpha, \beta, \varepsilon)$, and the ε indicates the interval of the measurement because the measurement value of nodes has the timeliness which means it will change with time. The value of $Trust(\alpha, \beta, \varepsilon)$ integrates every behavior measurement value with weight. It can be expressed as:

$$Trust(\alpha, \beta, \varepsilon) = \sum_{s=1}^{i} \theta_s \partial_s(\alpha, \beta), \theta_s \in \theta, \partial_s(\alpha, \beta) \in \partial, 0 \le s \le i \tag{2}$$

After a series of calculations, the superior node α can get the behavior measurement value of the lower node β. It ranks the measurement value and does the feedback control to the lower node of different levels. In this model, a bigger measurement value means the lower node has a higher trusted level and the degree of priority of the feedback control of α to β is higher.

In this paper, the trusted level λ of nodes can be divided into k parts which means $\lambda = \{\lambda_1, \lambda_2, \ldots\ldots, \lambda_k\}, 0 \le \lambda_k \le 1$. When $\lambda_k = 0$, this node is completed untrusted and when $\lambda_k = 1$, this node is completed trusted. In this set, if it assumes $\lambda_u, \lambda_v \in \lambda$ and $u < v$, the $\lambda_u < \lambda_v$.

In this paper, the degree of priority φ of the feedback control of the superior node α to the lower node β can be divided into k parts which means $\varphi = \{\varphi_1, \varphi_2, \ldots\ldots, \varphi_k\}$. Therefore, the correspondence between φ and the trusted level of α and the behavior measurement value of β is as follows:

$$\Omega(Trust(\alpha, \beta, \varepsilon), \lambda, \varphi) = \begin{cases} \varphi_1, \lambda_1 \leq Trust(\alpha, \beta, \varepsilon) \leq \lambda_2 \\ \varphi_2, \lambda_2 < Trust(\alpha, \beta, \varepsilon) \leq \lambda_3 \\ \ldots \ldots \\ \varphi_{k-1}, \lambda_{k-1} < Trust(\alpha, \beta, \varepsilon) \leq \lambda_k \\ \varphi_k, \lambda_k < Trust(\alpha, \beta, \varepsilon) \leq 1 \end{cases} \quad (3)$$

In this model, the degree of priority of the feedback control of the superior node α to the lower node β is got after finish the behavior measurement of nodes. According to the behavior measurement, it can get the trusted value of different and divided the degree of priority of the feedback control efficiently. This model reduces the risk when transmitting the data in the Internet of Things.

4.2   The Actual Description of the Behavior Measurement Model

According to the established behavior measurement model, this paper applies it to the actual environment of Internet of Things. And it divides the trust level into four parts which are completely trusted, general trusted, critical trusted and untrusted. Therefore, there are also four kinds of priority of the feedback response corresponding to the trust level which are priority receiving data, acceptable data, non-acceptable data, and refusal to accept data. The description of the trust level is shown as Table 1 and the priority of the feedback response can be described as Table 2:

Table 1. The description of the trust level

λ	Trust level	Definition
λ_1	Untrusted	The node can not be trusted
λ_2	Critical trusted	The node can be trusted or untrusted
λ_3	General trusted	The node has a certain degree of trust
λ_4	Completely trusted	The node can be trusted

Table 2. The description of the priority of the feedback response

φ	The priority of the feedback response	The actual operation
φ_1	Refusal to accept data	The superior node α refuses to accept the data sent from the lower node β
φ_2	Non-acceptable data	The superior node α can don't accept the data sent from the lower node β according to its status
φ_3	Acceptable data	The superior node α can accept the data sent from the lower node β according to its status
φ_4	Priority receiving data	The superior node α accepts the data sent from the lower node β priority

If the trust level of the node is in the $\lambda = \{\lambda_1, \lambda_2, \lambda_3, \lambda_4\}$, the $\lambda_1, \lambda_2, \lambda_3, \lambda_4$ can be set as $\lambda_1 = 0, \lambda_2 = 0.3, \lambda_3 = 0.5, \lambda_4 = 0.8$ and the correspondence between the priority of feedback response and the value of the behavior measurement can be expressed as:

$$\Omega(Trust(\alpha, \beta, \varepsilon), \lambda, \varphi) = \begin{cases} \varphi_1, 0 \leq Trust(\alpha, \beta, \varepsilon) \leq 0.3 \\ \varphi_2, 0.3 < Trust(\alpha, \beta, \varepsilon) \leq 0.5 \\ \varphi_3, 0.5 < Trust(\alpha, \beta, \varepsilon) \leq 0.8 \\ \varphi_4, 0.8 < Trust(\alpha, \beta, \varepsilon) \leq 1 \end{cases} \tag{4}$$

The above relationship can be interpreted as when the value of the behavior measurement $Trust(\alpha, \beta, \varepsilon)$ of the lower node β is 0.2, the superior node α will refuse to accept the data sent from the lower node β. When the value of the behavior measurement $Trust(\alpha, \beta, \varepsilon)$ of the lower node β is 0.4, the superior node α can don't accept the data sent from the lower node β according to its status. When the value of the behavior measurement $Trust(\alpha, \beta, \varepsilon)$ of the lower node β is 0.6, the superior node α can accept the data sent from the lower node β according to its status. When the value of the behavior measurement $Trust(\alpha, \beta, \varepsilon)$ of the lower node β is 0.9, the superior node α accepts the data sent from the lower node β priority.

5   The Calculation of the Behavior Measurement Functions

To the behavior measurement of sensing node of Internet of Things, the accurate calculation of the measurement value is directly related to the feedback control of the superior nodes to the lower nodes. Therefore, in order to measure the behavior of nodes more accurately, this paper does the dynamic trusted measurement to the lower node through the addressing behavior, the computational behavior, the network transmission behavior of nodes. In this paper, the superior node uses the addressing behavior function, the computational ability evaluation function, the network transmission behavior function, the social trust evaluation function, the effectiveness evaluation function, and the activity evaluation function get the different value of measurement of the lower node. And with the concept of information entropy, the multiple values of measurement can be balanced and the final behavior measurement function of sensing nodes can be obtained.

5.1   The Addressing Behavior Function of Nodes

The addressing behavior function of nodes includes the source address of the sender and the destination address of the receiver. In the sending process of data, each node has a physical address. Meanwhile, to the data sending behavior, the address of the lower node β is the source address and the address of the superior node α is the destination address. The addressing behavior function of nodes compares the destination address of data sending behavior with the physical address of the superior node α and the source address of data sending behavior with the physical address of the lower node β. The specific function is expressed as follows:

$$\partial_1(\alpha, \beta) = (add_\alpha \wedge da) \wedge (add_\beta \wedge sa) \tag{5}$$

This function performs the logical AND operation on the physical address add_α of the superior node α and the destination address of data sending behavior da. Then this function performs the logical AND operation on the physical address add_β of the lower node β and the destination address of data sending behavior sa. When the result of this function is 1 which means the physical address of nodes is same as the destination or the source address of data sending behavior and the addressing behavior is normally. When the result of this function is 0 which means the addressing behavior is abnormally and it needs to be isolated or access control.

5.2 The Computational Ability Evaluation Function of Nodes

The computational ability evaluation function of nodes refers the superior node α evaluates the computational ability of the lower node β when the data needs to be calculated. When the memory size om of the lower node β is fixed, the data computational ability of nodes decreases with the existing memory occupied by a running program on the node increasing. And specific function is expressed as follows:

$$\partial_2(\alpha, \beta) = \begin{cases} 1 - \dfrac{\sum\limits_{i=1}^{n} O(ap_i)}{om}, \sum\limits_{i=1}^{n} O(ap_i) < om \\ 0, \sum\limits_{i=1}^{n} O(ap_i) \geq om \end{cases} \tag{6}$$

In this function, $O(ap_i)$ refers the existing memory size occupied by the running program ap_i. And in the formula (6), if the existing memory occupied by a running program on the node less than the actual memory size of the node, it evaluates the data computational ability by the proportion of the remaining memory size. And if the existing memory occupied by a running program on the node more than the actual memory size of the node, it indicates that the node has abnormal behavior and assumes that the node does not have computational ability and the result is 0.

5.3 The Network Transmission Behavior Function of Nodes

The network transmission behavior function of nodes refers the superior node α evaluates the trust of the lower node β by the size of the transmitted data traffic in the process of fata transmission and it follows a normal distribution. The specific function is expressed as follows:

$$\partial_3(\alpha, \beta) = \frac{1}{\sqrt{2\pi}} e^{\left[-\frac{(dt-\gamma)^2}{2}\right]} \tag{7}$$

In this formula, $Y = \sqrt{-\ln(2\pi T_s^2)}$ and the T_s is the initial measurement value of the node initialization. When the transmitted data traffic is 0, the trust of nodes is its initial measurement value and with the increasing of the transmitted data traffic, the trust of nodes becomes higher. But if the transmitted data traffic reaches the critical point, the trust of nodes will decreases quickly. The critical point is set according to the specific application environment of the node.

5.4   The Social Trust Evaluation Function of Nodes

According to the Simerian classic trust theory in sociology, the trust value of individual is not only determined by its own behavior, state, and information, but also needs to refer to the trust values of other individuals that it communicates with. Therefore, in the behavior measurement model of Internet of Things, the social trust evaluation function of nodes refers the superior node α needs to consider the trust value of other nodes which communicate with the lower node β when it does the trusted measurement to β. For the same node, the effect of a frequent interaction with the node which has a higher trust value is different from the effect of a frequent interaction with the node which has a lower trust value. The specific function is expressed as follows:

$$\partial_4(\alpha, \beta) = \sum_{j=1}^{n} \varpi(\gamma_j) \cdot \partial_1(\alpha, \beta) \cdot [\partial_3(\alpha, \beta) + \partial_2(\alpha, \beta)] \tag{8}$$

In the formula (8), the node which communicates with the lower node β is expressed by γ and $\gamma = \{\gamma_1, \gamma_2, \ldots, \gamma_n\}$, $\gamma_j \in \gamma, j \in [1, n]$. The $\varpi(\gamma_j)$ is the weight of the trust value of nodes who communicate with β and the specific description can be expressed as follows:

$$\varpi(\gamma_j) = \begin{cases} \partial_1(\alpha, \gamma_j) \cdot [\partial_3(\alpha, \gamma_j) + \partial_2(\alpha, \gamma_j)], & t = 1 \\ \prod_{t=1}^{m} [\partial_1(\alpha_t, \gamma_j) \cdot (\partial_3(\alpha_t, \gamma_j) + \partial_2(\alpha_t, \gamma_j))], & t > 1 \end{cases} \tag{9}$$

Because of the node γ_j that interact with β may have different superior nodes, and according to the sociological principles, with the interaction distance between two entities getting shorter, the influence of their trust value gets greater. Therefore, in the formula (9), t refers the number of superior nodes passed when the γ_j communicates with β. When $t = 1$, it means the γ_j and the β belong to the same superior node and the weight is determined by the addressing behavior function, the computational ability evaluation function and the network transmission behavior function that the superior node α does to the lower node γ_j. When $t > 1$, it means the γ_j and the β belong to the different superior node and it will pass m superior nodes when the γ_j communicates with the β. The α_t refers superior nodes passed by and the weight is determined by the addressing behavior function, the computational ability evaluation function and the network transmission behavior function that m superior nodes do to the lower node γ_j.

5.5   The Effectiveness Evaluation Function of Nodes

The effectiveness evaluation function of nodes refers to the possibility of task failure when the lower node do the addressing behaviors, network transmission behaviors, and calculation behaviors, and this failure will affect the trust value of this node. The specific function is expressed as follows:

$$\partial_5(\alpha, \beta) = 1 - \frac{\sum\limits_{v=1}^{n} F_v(\alpha, \beta)}{\sum\limits_{u=1}^{n} L_u(\alpha, \beta)} \tag{10}$$

In this formula, $L_u(\alpha, \beta)$ refers the total number of tasks that the superior node α requires the lower node β to complete. And the $F_v(\alpha, \beta)$ refers the number of failed tasks of the lower node β. To the superior node α with the same total number of tasks, the more failed tasks of the lower node β, the lower trust value of the behavior of β.

5.6   The Activity Evaluation Function of Nodes

The activity evaluation function of nodes refers the activity degree of the lower node β. In the sensing layer of Internet of Things, the higher activity degree of the lower node β is, the superior node α thinks the higher trust value of the lower node β is. The activity degree of nodes can be mainly reflected in three aspects. There are the number of successful interactions of the lower node β, the number of interacted nodes, and the number of superior nodes which are passed during this interaction. The specific function is expressed as follows:

$$\partial_6(\alpha, \beta) = \frac{J(N) \cdot J(S) \cdot J(G)}{J(N) + J(S) + J(G)} \tag{11}$$

In this formula, N refers the number of interacted nodes, S refers the number of successful interactions of the lower node β, and G refers the number of superior nodes which are passed during the interaction. $J(x) = 1 - \frac{1}{x+\tau}$ is a function to synthesize N, S and G. And in this function, τ is an adjustment constant. When $\tau > 0$, it can adjust the value of $J(x)$. According to the formula (5–7), when the x is fixed, the $J(x)$ gradually approaches 1 with the increase of τ. Therefore, when $\tau \to \infty$, the $J(x)$ will infinity approach 1.

5.7   The Behavior Measurement Value of Sensing Nodes

The behavior measurement of the nodes are synthesized based on the results of the above different angles of the behavior measurement functions. It puts different weight to the addressing behavior function, the computing capability evaluation function, the network transmission behavior function, the social trust evaluation function, the effectiveness evaluation function and the activity evaluation function of sensing nodes for getting a final behavior measurement value. However, due to the lack of certain objectivity that the superior node directly assign weight to each function, this section introduces the concept of information entropy [17] and uses it to smooth the values of each measurement function so that the final calculation results are as consistent as possible with the objective facts.

The concept of entropy was first introduced by Boltzmann in thermodynamics, and Shannon cites it in information theory, resulting in the concept of information entropy. Information entropy is a measurement of the uncertainty of random variables in information theory. It has monotonicity, non-surname and accumulativeness [18]. The information entropy formula for a discrete random variable X is defined as follows:

$$H(X) = -\sum_{x \in \chi} p(x) \log_2 p(x) \tag{12}$$

This section uses this definition in the calculation of behavior measurement for sensing nodes of the Internet of Things. Event X is the trusted value of the lower node β under the behavior measurement function $\partial_i(\alpha, \beta)$ and $X = \partial_i(\alpha, \beta)$. The specific formula is expressed as follows:

$$H(\partial_i(\alpha, \beta)) = -\partial_i(\alpha, \beta) \log_2 \partial_i(\alpha, \beta) \tag{13}$$

For different behavior measurement functions, when $H(\partial_u(\alpha, \beta)) < H(\partial_v(\alpha, \beta))$ and $u, v \in \{1, 2, 3, 4, 5, 6\}$, it means the trusted value calculated by this behavior measurement function has a small information entropy, so the uncertainty of the value is small, and it can not reflect the change of the credibility of the node well. Therefore, the superior node should give a smaller weight to this function. The formula (14) can only sort the weight of each behavior measurement function, so the specific weight value is calculated by the following formula:

$$\theta_i = \begin{cases} \dfrac{1 - \dfrac{H(\partial_i(\alpha,\beta))}{\log_2 k}}{n - \sum\limits_{i=1}^{n} \dfrac{H(\partial_i(\alpha,\beta))}{\log_2 k}} & , H(\partial_i(\alpha, \beta)) > \xi \\ 0, H(\partial_i(\alpha, \beta)) < \xi \end{cases} \tag{14}$$

In this formula, k is the number of trusted levels of sensing nodes of the Internet of Things, i is the number of behavior measurement functions, and ξ is the critical value of information entropy. When the value of the information entropy of the behavior measurement function obtained by the formula (14) is smaller than the critical value, it means the uncertainty of the lower node that obtains the trusted value under the behavior measurement function is determined to be too small. And the credibility of the lower nodes can not be well reflected, so the weight of the function is directly set to 0. In this paper, $k = 4, i = 6, \xi = 0.1$. According to the above formula, the calculation formula for the behavior measurement of the sensing nodes of the Internet of Things in this paper can be obtained as:

$$Trust(\alpha, \beta, \varepsilon) = \sum_{i=1}^{6} \theta_i \partial_i(\alpha, \beta) \qquad (15)$$

6   The Analysis of the Behavior Measurement Model

This paper proposes a trusted behavior measurement model applicable to the sensor nodes of the Internet of Things. This model divides the behavior of nodes into addressing behaviors, computational behaviors and network transmission behaviors. It calculates the trusted value of those behaviors from different angles and balances those different trusted values with the concept of information entropy to obtain the real-time trusted value of the nodes. This section uses NS2 to simulate the behavior measurement model of the node of the Internet of Things to check the correctness and effectiveness of the model. In addition, the model of this paper is qualitatively compared with other trusted models of the Internet of Things proposed in literature [19], literature [20], literature [21], literature [21], literature [22], literature [23], and literature [24] for analyzing the characteristics of this model.

6.1   Parameter Setting

In this section of the simulation experiment is based on Ubuntu14.04 platform and the simulation tool is NS2. The relevant experimental parameter settings are shown in Table 3:

Table 3. Simulation experiment parameter table

Parameter content	Parameter setting letter	Parameter setting value
Wireless propagation model	$prop$	FreeSpace
Sender antenna gain	G_t	1
Receiver antenna gain	G_r	1
System loss	L	1
Energy model	en	EnergyModel
The initial energy of data aggregation nodes	$initialEnergy_{nh}$	100 J
The initial energy of cluster nodes	$initialEnergy_{nc}$	60 J
The initial energy of ordinary nodes	$initialEnergy_{no}$	30 J
The initial energy of malicious nodes	$initialEnergy_{ne}$	30 J
Number of data aggregation nodes	nh	1
Number of cluster nodes	nc	4
Number of ordinary nodes	no	36
Number of malicious nodes	ne	9
Energy consumed in sending data	$txPower$	4
Energy consumed in receiving data	$rxPower$	2
The threshold of trusted measurement	t	0.8

The nodes in this simulation experiment have four kinds of roles: data aggregation nodes, cluster nodes, ordinary nodes, and malicious nodes. And in this experiment, the ordinary node only can communicate with the node in the same cluster.

The threshold of trusted measurement is set as 0.8 which means if the measurement value of a node is less than 0.8, this node is judged to be an untrusted node. Since the main purpose of this experiment is to verify the correctness and effectiveness of this behavioral measurement model, it is assumed that there are 9 malicious nodes. Through the experimental results, we can observe whether and when these malicious nodes can be discovered to prove the correctness and validity of this model.

6.2 The Distribution of Nodes

A total of 50 nodes were established in this simulation experiment, and their positions were randomly distributed in the 500*500 grid. The specific distribution is shown in Fig. 3:

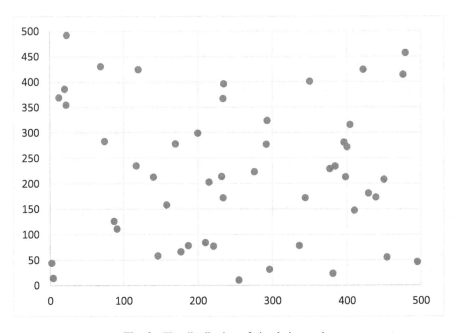

Fig. 3. The distribution of simulation nodes

Among all the 50 nodes, there are one data aggregation node, four cluster head nodes, thirty-six ordinary nodes, and nine malicious nodes. The logical link diagram is shown in Fig. 4:

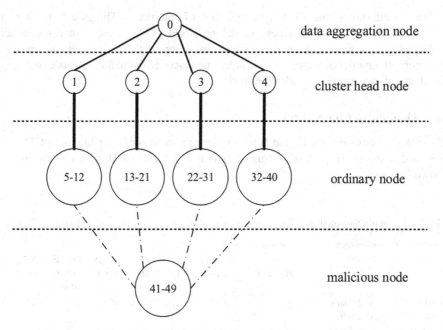

Fig. 4. The logical link diagram of simulation nodes

6.3 The Analysis of the Simulation Result

According to the behavior measurement model established in this paper, the simulation result of this experiment is shown in Fig. 5:

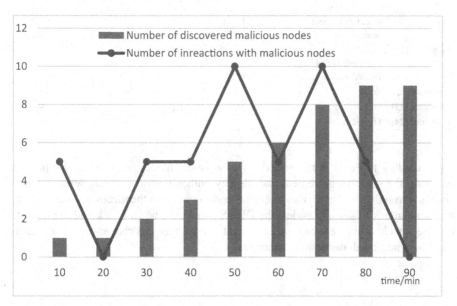

Fig. 5. The diagram of the malicious node discovered

The result shows that when sensing nodes of Internet of Things are running in 90 min, the behavior measurement model proposed in this paper can discover all malicious nodes and stop normal nodes interacting with those malicious nodes. Therefore, the model proposed in this paper can discover the malicious node and stop the attack of the malicious node effectively.

6.4   Qualitative Comparison

This section compares the trusted behavior measurement model of Internet of Things proposed in this paper with other trusted models of Internet of Things. The results are shown in Table 4:

Table 4. Qualitative analysis of measurement models of sensing layer of Internet of Things

Model name	Measurement content	Comparison point					
		Static measurement	Dynamic measurement	Node hijacking attack	DDOS attack	Physical capture attack	Witch attack
Model proposed in this paper	Addressing behavior, Computing behavior, Network transmission behavior	√	√	√	√	√	√
Literature [19]	Trusted value	√	–	–	–	–	√
Literature [20]	Activity, reliability, QoS trust, Component permissions	√	√	–	–	–	√
Literature [21]	Security overhead, Delay, Trusted value	√	–	–	√	–	–
Literature [22]	None	√	–	–	–	–	–
Literature [23]	None	√	–	√	–	–	–
Literature [24]	Trusted level	√	–	–	–	–	–

According to Table 4, the behavior measurement model proposed in this paper is based on the static measurement and identity authentication and can detect kinds of attacks through the static measurement and identity authentication, such as: the hijacking attack of sensing nodes, the DDOS attack, the witch attack and the physical capture attack. This behavior measurement model has the characteristics of active measurement and dynamic measurement.

7   Conclusion

The Internet of Things develops rapidly in this world and more areas are introducing the Internet of Things into their production and life, such as, the environmental monitoring, the traffic management, the agriculture and the military. However, the security mechanism of Internet of Things develops slowly and it limits the development of Internet of Things. For keep the Internet of Things safe, it needs to guarantee the safety running of Internet of Things which determined by the trusted running of sensing nodes Internet of Things.

Therefore, this paper analyzes the existing security mechanisms in the sensing layer of the Internet of Things. According to those studies and the characteristics of sensing nodes, this paper proposed a behavior measurement model which measures the behaviors of sensing nodes dynamically based on the static measurement and identity authentication. This model divided sensing nodes into three parts, there are ordinary nodes, cluster head nodes which are the superior node of ordinary nodes and data aggregation nodes which are the superior node of cluster head nodes. In this model, the superior node of sensing layer measures behaviors of the lower node and divides its trusted level with its trusted value for feedback control different nodes. The correctness and validity of this model are verified by the simulating experiment in NS2 and the qualitative comparing with other trusted measurement model proposed in some literatures.

Acknowledgments. This work was supported by the Postdoctoral Fundation of Beijing (Grant No. 2018-22-025).

References

1. Zhang, Y., Zhou, W., Peng, A.: Safety review of the Internet of things. Comput. Res. Dev. **54**(10), 2130–2143 (2015)
2. Zhang, Y.-J., Liu, I., Feng, L.: Internet information security and privacy protection and research review. J. Logist. Technol. **40**(01), 69 (2017)
3. Ma, Z.: Trusted access wireless network theory and its application research. Xi 'an University of Electronic Science and Technology (2010)
4. Wang, Y.: Key technology research on the trusted operation of the node of the IoT sensor. Beijing University of Technology (2017)
5. Zhuang, L., Shen, C.-X., Cai, M.: Based on the behavior of the trusted dynamic measurement of the state space reduction research. J. Comput. **5**(5), 1071 (2014)
6. Li, X., Zuo, X.D., Shen, C.-X.: Based on the behavior of the system computing platform reliable proof. J. Electron. J. **7**, 1234–1239 (2007)
7. Li, W., Zhang, T., Lin, W., Deng, S., Wang, C.: Security audit based on the reliability measurement of dynamic network behavior. Comput. Technol. Dev. **22**(5), 250–253 (2012)
8. Zhang, J., Zhang, G., Zhang, X.: Network access control model based on real-time behavior trusted measurement. Comput. Appl. Softw. **7**, 32–38 (2017)
9. Yan, L., Jia, X., Chen, P.: Software dynamic reliability measurement based on behavior trajectory. Comput. Appl. Res. **34**(02), 539–542 (2013)

10. Liu, G., Zhou, Z., Zhou, R.: A static and trusted measurement model of software behavior. J. Naval Aviat. Eng. **27**(04), 459–463 (2012)
11. Letian, S., et al.: Methods of sensitive information protection under the Internet of things. Sichuan Univ. J. Eng. Sci. Edn. **01**, 132–138 (2016)
12. Chien, H., Chen, C.: Mutual authentication protocol for RFID conforming to EPC Class 1 Generation 2 standards. Computers and Standards (2007)
13. Zhou, Z., Li, J., Zhang, J.: A credible measurement model of principal behavior. Comput. Eng. **07**, 35–37 (2008)
14. Yan, Z.: A Conceptual architecture of a trusted mobile environment. In: Proceedings of the Second International Workshop on Security, Privacy and Trust in Pervasive and Ubiquitous Computing (SecPerU 2006)
15. Balfe, H., Chen, L.: Pervasive trusted computing. In: Proceedings of the Second International Workshop on Security, Privacy and Trust in Pervasive and Ubiquitous Computing (SecPerU 2006) (2006)
16. Liang, L.: Sociological study on the behavior of dishonesty. Wuhan University (2014)
17. Sun, C.: Characteristics of super-high dimensional classification data based on conditional information entropy. Nanjing Information Engineering University (2017)
18. Peng, C., Ding, H., Zhu, Y., Tian, Y., Fu, Z.: Information entropy model of privacy protection and its measurement method. Softw. Sci. **27**(8), 2016-1903 (2016)
19. Ge, H., Tate, S.R.: A direct anonymous attestation scheme for embedded devices. In: Okamoto, T., Wang, X. (eds.) PKC 2007. LNCS, vol. 4450, pp. 16–30. Springer, Heidelberg (2007). https://doi.org/10.1007/978-3-540-71677-8_2
20. Schryen, G., Volkamer, M., Ries, S., Habib, S.M..: A formal approach towards measuring trust in distributed systems, pp. 1739–1745 (2011)
21. Chen, I.-R., Guo, J.: Dynamic hierarchical trust management of mobile groups and its application to misbehaving node detection. In: 2014 IEEE 28th International Conference on Advanced Information Networking and Applications, pp. 49–56 (2014)
22. Mana, A., Koshutanski, H., Perez, E.J.: A trust negotiation based security framework for service provisioning in load-balancing clusters. Comput. Secur. **1**, 4–25 (2011)
23. Wu, Q.-X.: Secure solution of trusted Internet of things base on TCM. J. China Univ. Posts Telecommun. **20**, 47–53 (2013)
24. Xu, X., Bessis, N., Cao, J.: An autonomic agent trust model for IoT systems. **21**, 107–113 (2013)

An Efficient and Revocable Decentralizing Attribute-Based Encryption for Mobile Cloud Computing

Lei Sun, Yumeng Fu$^{(\boxtimes)}$, and Zuohui Li

Zhengzhou Information Science and Technology Institute,
Zhengzhou 450001, China
fym25jessica@qq.com

Abstract. Mobile cloud computing (MCC) is becoming an important way of data sharing. It is of great value for people to store and retrieve personal data at anytime and anywhere. Attribute-based encryption (ABE) can solve the problem of flexible sharing among multiple users in traditional encryption, but it cannot apply to mobile clients directly because of its low efficiency. How to meet the people's practical application needs and to control and manage the personal data safely and flexibly is a concrete embodiment of the security problem after the cloud computing is mobile. In this paper, an efficient and revocable decentralizing attribute-based encryption scheme for mobile cloud environment is proposed. In the scheme, it does not have the upper limit of the total attribute, and without the central authority (CA), each attribute authority generates private key independently with the users. In addition, the linear secret-sharing scheme (LSSS) is used to construct the access structure with a high flexibility. The method of precomputing and outsourcing can reduce the computation cost of the user side. Besides, the scheme is proved to be static secure and support revocation under the random oracle model. Compared to the existing related schemes, the proposed scheme is more practical and effective in mobile cloud environment.

Keywords: Mobile cloud computing · Attribute-based encryption · Outsourcing · Revocation · Decentralizing

1 Introduction

For some sensitive data sharing issues (including their personal files, health records, e-mails, etc.) that users store in the cloud, since cloud server loyalty cannot be ensured, access control is generally stored and implemented in encrypted form. Traditional cryptographic algorithms are difficult to implement flexible sharing with multiple users. The attribute-based encryption (ABE) system can solve this problem better. It is an important technical means for data security sharing in cloud computing.

With the popularity of mobile devices and the rapid development of 5G networks, the mobile cloud computing model has been recognized and appreciated by more and more people. Mobile Cloud Computing (MCC) is the combination of cloud computing, mobile computing and wireless networks to bring rich computational resources to

© Springer Nature Singapore Pte Ltd. 2019
H. Zhang et al. (Eds.): CTCIS 2018, CCIS 960, pp. 167–183, 2019.
https://doi.org/10.1007/978-981-13-5913-2_11

mobile users, net-work operators, as well as cloud computing providers [1]. The combination of mobile network and cloud computing gives people the freedom to the greatest extent. It enables cloud computing to be greatly expanded in application scope. Users can get rid of the limitations of time and space and enjoy cloud-based powerful computing, storage, and software service capabilities more conveniently. At present, well-known domestic and foreign enterprises have successively provided mobile cloud computing services, such as Ali "Apsara Mobile" weighs in 2017, Apple's "MobileMe" service, and Microsoft "Live Mesh".

The typical ABE scheme cannot apply to the actual application of mobile cloud directly, mainly because of efficiency. Most of the proposed schemes are based on the bilinear mapping. The overhead of large bilinear pairings and group power operations is very high, and the amount of computing in the encryption and decryption phases is proportional to the size of the attribute set or the size of the access structure. Secondly, in the actual application scenario, different authorities manage the different attributes of the user, so the ABE scheme expanded from a single authority to a multi-authority has higher computational complexity and management complexity. In addition, in order to improve the security of the scheme, scholars have improved the scheme that can achieve selective security by using the composite order bilinear group and the dual system encryption technology. The improved scheme proves that the adaptive security is satisfied, but the same group operation in the new method is 1–2 orders of magnitude slower than the prime group in the number order group, and it does not meet the actual security requirements. Therefore, research on flexible and practical attribute-based encryption schemes based on the improvement of security performance has important application value for data security sharing in mobile cloud environment.

In this paper, a decentralized multi-authority architecture is adopted. To make use of the semi-trusted features of the cloud server, we divide the encryption and decryption into two phases. The cloud server participates in the partial encryption, decryption, and revocation, and reduces the computational overhead of the user. We use the mapping idea to map attributes and group elements in a one-to-one mapping. Any string can be added as an attribute into the system, which is more in line with the actual application scenario. Finally, it is proved that the proposed scheme is static secure under the random oracle model and is suitable for data security sharing in mobile cloud environment.

2 Related Work

In 2005, Sahai and Waters [5] expanded the concept of IBE, and they put forward the concept of attribute encryption for the first time. Since then, Goyal et al. [6] defines two forms of ABE based on the location of the access strategy in the scheme: key policy attribute-based encryption (KP-ABE) and ciphertext policy attribute-based encryption (CP-ABE). We put forward a CP-ABE scheme that is more suitable for solving the problem of data security sharing in cloud environment, in which access policies can be defined simultaneously when data owners encrypt plaintext.

Cheung et al. [7] proposed a CP-ABE scheme based on the AND access structure. Then, Goyal et al. [8] proposed a CP-ABE scheme based on the access tree structure. Waters [9] has published a CP-ABE scheme based on the linear secret sharing schemes (LSSS) access structure to achieve stronger expressive and higher efficiency. But the essence of the ABE efficiency problem is that when using bilinear mapping technology to build a scheme, the complex function is realized by some modular exponentiation or bilinear pairing, so it is difficult to achieve a breakthrough in the calculation efficiency in the construction of the scheme. Therefore, scholars naturally think of outsourcing complex computing and use powerful computing power to solve the problem. Early research on outsourcing computing is mainly around a single type of computing, until 2011, Green et al. [10] introduced the outsourcing idea into the ABE, greatly alleviated the decryption burden of the end users, and also provided a new possibility for the development of the attribute-based encryption in the mobile cloud computing.

Since the mobile cloud computing is proposed in 2010, the problem of attribute-based data security sharing has been paid much attention by scholars, but the attribute-based encryption schemes for mobile cloud environment are still very few. Until 2014, Hohenberger et al. [11] introduced a method of reducing the computational complexity of encryption operations in ABE schemes by precomputing and proposed an online/offline ABE scheme. It can be used to solve the problem of data sharing in the cloud computing environment due to the above method that reduce the computing overhead of users online effectively, so it is especially suitable for the setting of user low end equipment in mobile cloud.

In order to solve the problem that the property can not only be managed by a single authority in the actual environment, the scholars have deeply studied the multi-authority attribute-based encryption (MA-ABE) scheme, which mainly focuses on how to reduce the security threats brought by the corruption of the central authority and how to ensure that the authorities do not affect the independent operation of each other. In 2011, Lewko and Waters et al. [12] proposed a MA-ABE scheme that did not need a CA and each authority even not knowing each other and implemented a decentralizing attribute-based encryption (DABE). In 2015, Vijay et al. [13] proposed a CP-ABE scheme in the mobile cloud environment with attribute revocation. This scheme takes into account that the ABE scheme of a single authority cannot solve the different attribute issues of the multi-authority management user in the real application scenario and supports multiple attribute authority to work simultaneously. In 2016, Li et al. [14] proposed a lightweight data sharing scheme in the mobile cloud environment. By changing the access control tree structure, most of the computation was handed over to the external proxy server and the revocation function was realized. In 2017, Lyu et al. [15] adopted an anonymous key release protocol to achieve privacy protection, in addition to online/offline technology and outsourced decryption. Zhao et al. [16] proposed a mobile cloud CP-ABE scheme that verifiable outsourced computing, verified by two kinds of hash functions, and De [17] proposed a scheme for fast encryption and decryption in mobile cloud environment, which could realize the decentralization of attributes. Li et al. [18] uses dual factor identity authentication mechanism to realize anonymous authentication to users and proposes a multi authority CP-ABE scheme without CA in mobile cloud environment.

In terms of security, in 2010, Lewko et al. [19] improved the CP-ABE structure by using multiple order bilinear groups and dual system encryption technology to make the scheme change from the security based on the selection attribute set attack model to the higher security level of adaptive security from the same period, but the performance of the scheme was greatly sacrificed. In 2015, the Rouselakis of the Waters team proposed a static security [20] model to adapt to the setting of multi authority institutions, which would be more consistent with data sharing in the multi authority scenario, and a considerable degree of recognition in the industry.

In summarizing the above work, the paper finds that the design (composite order and prime order) of the adaptive security solution needs to sacrifice the performance of the solution to a certain extent, and it is not suitable for data sharing under the mobile cloud environment. Since the attributes of the user in the CP-ABE are associated with the decryption key, and the attributes are distributed in a fragmented manner, each attribute should correspond to a different permission (in a single organization scenario, the private key request is independent and complete). In this paper, the static security model proposed by Rouselakis and Waters is applied to the setting of multi-authority. At the same time, for the computational complexity caused by the multi-authority setting, this paper uses the pre-computing of the encryption phase and partial outsourcing in the decryption phase, making the scheme more suitable for mobile devices, so that users can get better application experience.

3 Preliminaries

This section will introduce the relevant basic knowledge and data sharing model of the proposed mobile cloud environment attribute-based encryption scheme and give the complexity assumption and the security model based on the scheme.

A. Linear Secret Sharing Schemes (LSSS)

Let p be a prime and U the attribute universe.

A secret-sharing scheme Π with domain of secrets $\mathbb{Z}_p$ realizing access structures on U is linear over $\mathbb{Z}_p$ if

(1) The shares for each party form a vector over $\mathbb{Z}_p$
(2) There exists a matrix A with rows ℓ and n columns called the share-generating matrix for Π. For all $i = 1, \ldots, \ell$, the row of A is labeled by a party $\rho(i)$ ($\rho(i)$ represents the participants marked by the A line i). When we consider the column vector $v = (s, y_2, \ldots, y_n) \in \mathbb{Z}_p$, where $s \in \mathbb{Z}_p$ is the secret to be shared, and $y_2, \ldots, y_n \in \mathbb{Z}_p$ are randomly chosen, then Av is the vector of ℓ shares of the secret s according to Π. The ith share $(Av)_i$ belongs to party $\rho(i)$.

It is shown in [21] that every linear secret-sharing scheme according to the above definition also enjoys the linear reconstruction property, defined as follows. Suppose that Π is an LSSS for the access structure. Let $S \in A$ be any authorized set and let $I \subseteq \{1, 2, \ldots, l\}$ be defined as $I = \{i : \rho(i) \in S\}$. Then there exist constants $\{\omega_i \in \mathbb{Z}_p\}_{i \in I}$ such that, if $\{\lambda_i\}$ are valid shares of any secret s according to Π, then $\sum_{i \in I} \omega_i \lambda_i = s$. There is no such constant for unauthorized sets.

B. Complexity Assumption

For our security proof we will use a q-type assumption on prime order bilinear groups. It is a slightly modified version of the q-Decisional Parallel Bilinear Diffie-Hellman Exponent Assumption [20]. We will be referring to our assumption as q-DPBDHE2 for short. The assumption is defined as follows:

Choose a bilinear group G of order p according to the security parameter κ, which admits a non-degenerate bilinear mapping $e : G \times G \to G_T$. Pick $a, s, b_1, b_2, \ldots,$ $b_q \in \mathbb{Z}_p^*$. Let

$$D = \begin{pmatrix} p, g, G, e, g^s, \{g^{a^i}\}_{i \in [2q], i \neq q+1}, \{g^{b_j a^i}\}_{(i,j) \in [2q,q], i \neq q+1}, \\ \{g^{s/b_i}\}_{i \in [q]}, \{g^{sa^i b_j / b_{j'}}\}_{(i,j,j') \in [q+1,q,q], j \neq j'} \end{pmatrix} \tag{1}$$

The assumption states that no polynomial-time distinguisher can distinguish the distribution $e(g, g)^{sa^{q+1}}$ from the distribution R (R is randomly chosen from G)with more than negligible advantage.

C. Security Model

(1) The static security model we define is a security game between the challenger and the attacker, and the difference between the adaptive model is that the attacker must specify the attack object and the query content immediately after receiving the public parameters, then send it to the challenger and change it after the game is over. In the same way as the adaptive model, the static security model allows an attacker to ask the user's private key and some decryption ciphertext stored in the cloud many times, that is to say, the attacker can decrypt the ciphertext by asking the outsourced decryption key to get some decryption ciphertext. In addition, we allow an attacker to participate in encryption by generating some authoritative authority to generate authoritative public key. On the basis of resisting the cloud server attack, the model increases the conspiracy attack against multiple legitimate users through the inquiry of the private key and can be described by the Games in the following stages. The symbolic correspondence is shown in Table 1.

Global Setup: The global initialization algorithm in the challenger's operation plan and send the public parameters GP to the attacker.

Attacker's Queries: The attacker first came from the authority V select a part of the authority $C(C \subseteq V)$, then generate and send $\{PK_\beta\}_{\beta \in C}$ to the challenger, Then the attacker responds with:

- Select authorized m users $\{GID_i\}_{i=1}^m$ to inquire about their public and private key.
- Select some non-corrupt authorities $N(N \subseteq V)$ to ask their public key.
- Select n users $\{S_i, GID_i\}_{i=1}^n$ to ask its outsourcing decryption key. $S_i \subseteq U$ is the attribute set of user i. Required $T(S_i) \cap C = \varnothing$ means the attributes owned by the users are authorized by the uncorrupted authority. In addition, requiring $n > m$ is that the attacker can not only query the user's outsourcing decryption key in the m authorized users, but also ask other users for the corresponding outsourced decryption key.

Table 1. Symbol corresponding list

Symbol	Meaning
GP	The global parameter
U/V	Space of attribute/authority
S	Attribute set of user
GID_i	The ith user global identities
PK_β/SK_β	AA_β's public/private key
$userPK_i/key$	User's public/private key
SK_{Out}	CSP's private key
TK	The temporary key
IC	Intermediate ciphertext
Klist	CSP's key list
CT	Ciphertext

- Two messages m_0, m_1 of equal length, and a challenge access structure (A, ρ) encoded in a suitable form. We require that for every $i(1 \le i \le n)$ the set $S_i \cup S_C$ is an unauthorized set of the access structure (A, ρ).

Challenger's Replies: The challenger flips a random coin $b \in \{0, 1\}$ and replies with:

- The secret keys of users $\{GID_i\}_{i=1}^m$: $\{userPK_{GID_i}, key\}_{i=1}^m$
- The public keys of authorities $N \subseteq V$: $\{PK_\beta\}_{\beta \in N}$
- The secret keys of cloud serve provider: $\{SK_{Out}\}_{i=1}^n$
- The challenge ciphertext CT*

Guess: The attacker outputs a guess $b' \in \{0, 1\}$.

Definition 1. We say that an attacker statically breaks the scheme if it has a non-negligible advantage in correctly guessing the bit b in the above security game.

When the game does not contain a class queries, the security model is converted to attack only against cloud servers.

(2) We propose a revocable security model for collusion attacks of multiple revocation users, regardless of whether their attributes satisfy the access policy. Therefore, an opponent can ask multiple private keys to revoke the user. In this article, it is assumed that the revocation user cannot conspire with the cloud server and the authority, so the enemy cannot ask for the private key of the cloud server corresponding to the cancellation of the user, nor the public key of the authority. At the same time, in order to ensure that the enemy can obtain partial decryption ciphertext from the unrevoked user, the model allows the enemy to access the private key of the cloud server that corresponds to the unrevoked user. The game description between the adversary and the challenger is basically the same as the static security model. During the enquiry phase, the opponent inquired the challenger as follows:

- Select a part of the revocation of the users $\{GID_i\}_{i=1}^m$ to inquire about their public and private key.
- Select some non-corrupt authorities $N(N \subseteq V)$ to ask their public key.
- Select n users $\{S_i, GID_i\}_{i=m}^n$ to ask its outsourcing decryption key.
- Two messages m_0, m_1 of equal length, and a challenge access structure (A, ρ) encoded in a suitable form. Ask them the challenge ciphertext.

Definition 2. We say that the scheme is revocable if the attacker has a non-negligible advantage in correctly guessing the bit b in the above security game.

D. Data Sharing Model

The data sharing model in the mobile cloud environment contains four entities: the data owner (DO), the cloud service provider (CSP), the data user i.e. mobile user (DU), and attribute authority (AA). Among them, the data owner DO draws up the access structure according to the security policy, then encrypts the data according to the access structure, and then uploads the encrypted result, that is, the ciphertext associated with the access policy to the cloud end; any user can freely access and obtain the ciphertext files on the cloud service, when and only as the user DU The attributes that are available can only be decrypted when they satisfy the access policy of ciphertext. The attribute authority AA generates a private key for the cloud service provider according to the user's permissions, and the user DU generates the private key for himself. Only when the cloud server decrypts the original ciphertext with its own private key, can the user decrypt the ciphertext. When the user is revoked, the cloud server simply removes the user's corresponding private key of the cloud server. The shared framework is shown in Fig. 1.

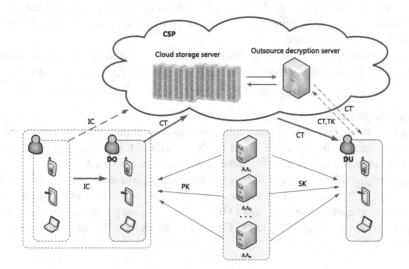

Fig. 1. Data sharing model in MCC

Cloud service provider CSP is generally considered honest and curious, with powerful storage and computing power, but only used for storing ciphertext, partially deciphering, and assisting revocation, and cannot get any information about the data or key from it; DU does not need to over consider its own hardware and software conditions and can be configured by different configurations. The device can access the CSP to obtain its authorized resources.

The DO and DU here mainly refer to users of low-end devices, such as mobile phones, vehicle systems, and high-end devices such as PC.

4 Our Scheme

Taking into account the actual application requirements and cloud data sharing mechanism research, we use functions T mapping attributes $i \in U$ to i's authority $\beta \in V$. That is, the existence of a full shot δ can correspond to the row x of a matrix and an authority β $(\delta(x) = T(\rho(x)) \rightarrow \beta)$. In addition, we introduce pre-computing outsourcing operation before the scheme encryption, and divide the mobile cloud attribute-based security sharing into four aspects, namely, initialization, user registration, data encryption and data access. Our scheme is constructed as follows:

A. Initialization
GlobalSetup(λ) $\rightarrow$ GP. The global setup algorithm takes as input the security parameter λ, chooses a suitable bilinear group G of prime order p with generator g. It also chooses a function H mapping GID, GID $\in G$. Another function F mapping strings, interpreted as attributes, to elements of G. Both of these functions will be modeled as random oracles in the security proof. Finally, it defines U, V, and T. The global parameters are GP $= \{p, G, g, H, F, U, V, T\}$. GP as the common input parameter of the remaining seven algorithms, for the sake of conciseness, the following algorithms will no longer be mentioned.

AuthoritySetup(GID$_\beta$) $\rightarrow$ {PK$_\beta$, SK$_\beta$} The authority run setup algorithm independently, input GID$_\beta(\beta \in V)$ chooses two random exponents $\alpha_\beta, y_\beta \in \mathbb{Z}_p^*$ and publishes PK$_\beta = \{e(g, g)^{\alpha_\beta}, g^{y_\beta}\}$ as its public key. It keeps SK$_\beta = \{\alpha_\beta, y_\beta\}$ as its secret key.

B. User Registration
When new users access the system, users need to request private keys to the attribute authority. The private key is generated by the execution KeyGen$_{Out}$ algorithm by the authority corresponding to each attribute of the user attribute set S.

KeyGen$_{user}$(GID$_i$) $\rightarrow$ {userPK$_i$, key} First, this algorithm is run on the mobile device, that is, the user part of the key generation algorithm in the classic scheme, which is completed by the user, input GID$_i(i \in U)$, and output the public and private key pairs of the user {userPK$_i$, key}. Chooses a random $z \in \mathbb{Z}_p^*$, using its own GID$_i$

computing the user's public key $\text{userPK}_{\text{GID}_i} = \{g^z, H(\text{GID}_i)^z\}$ and publish it. The relevant authority operates the outsourcing decryption server key generation algorithm for cloud service provider CSP:

$$\text{KeyGen}_{\text{Out}}(\text{GID}_i, \text{userPK}_i, S, \{\text{SK}_j\}) \rightarrow \text{SK}_{\text{Out}}$$

For example, user GID_i input userPK_i, S and the private key set $\{\text{SK}_\beta\}$ of the relevant authority (i.e. $\forall i \in S, T(i) = \beta$), output the decryption key for the user GID_i, and add the attribute based data sharing system.

For $\forall i \in S$, if $T(i) = \beta$, Then the authorized β mechanism chooses the random element $t_i \in \mathbb{Z}_p^*$ and calculation: $K_{i,1} = g^{z\alpha_i}H(\text{GID})^{zy_i}F(i)^{t_i}$, $K_{i,2} = g^{t_i}$, outputs the secret key: $\text{SK}_S = \{S, K_{i,1}, K_{i,2}\}_{i \in S}$. The user secrecy the private key key $= 1/z$ and calculate: $K'_{i,1} = K_{i,1}^{1/z}$, $K'_{i,2} = K_{i,2}^{1/z}$, output cloud server decryption key: $\text{SK}_{\text{Out}} = \{S, K'_{i,1}, K'_{i,2}\}_{i \in S}$, added $\{\text{GID}, \text{SK}_{\text{Out}}\}$ to the cloud server key list Klist.

C. Data Encryption

When the mobile device is idle, run the algorithm $\text{Pre}_{\text{Enc}}(\{\text{PK}_\beta\}) \rightarrow \text{IC}$, enter a public key set $\{\text{PK}_\beta\}$ of authoritative authorities based on user-defined access policies. Output the intermediate ciphertext IC, it can be uploaded to the cloud storage server. Mainly in the formal encryption before, for each attribute i in U, complete pre-calculation at first, for the encryption provides the calculation results. The attribute i, random selection $\lambda'_i, \omega'_i, r_i \in \mathbb{Z}_p^*$, and calculation: $\text{IC}_{i,1} = e(g,g)^{\lambda'_i}e(g,g)^{\alpha_i r_i}$, $\text{IC}_{i,2} = g^{-r_i}$, $\text{IC}_{i,3} = g^{y_i r_i}g^{\omega'_i}$, $\text{IC}_{i,4} = F(i)^{r_i}$. The encrypted person can choose to upload the middle ciphertext $\text{IC} = \{\text{IC}_{i,1}, \text{IC}_{i,2}, \text{IC}_{i,3}, \text{IC}_{i,4}\}_{i \in U}$ to the CSP outsourced storage server to save the storage resources of the device.

The temporary key $\text{TK} = \{\lambda'_i, \omega'_i\}_{i \in U}$ is stored locally.

When mobile users need to share secret data, run $\text{Encrypt}(\text{IC}, M, (A, \rho)) \rightarrow \text{CT}$. This algorithm can also skip precomputation and encrypt plaintext directly. Input messages, access policies, intermediate ciphertext and temporary keys in turn. Then random selection $s, y_2, \ldots, y_n, z_2, \ldots, z_n \in \mathbb{Z}_p^*$, order vector $v = (s, y_2, \ldots, y_n)^T$, $w = (0, z_2, \ldots, z_n)^T$, for all $x \in [\ell]$ calculations $\lambda_x = (Av)_x$, $\omega_x = (Aw)_x$. Due to $\delta(x) = T(\rho(x)) \rightarrow \beta$, it can be mapped $x \in [\ell]$ to authority β.

Computing ciphertext: $C_0 = Me(g,g)^s$, among them $C_{x,j} = \text{IC}_{\rho(x),j} \big| j \in \{\mathbb{Z}_p^* \big| 1 \le j \le 4\}$, $C_{x,5} = \lambda_x - \lambda'_{\rho(x)}$, $C_{x,6} = \omega_x - \omega'_{\rho(x)}$, Output ciphertext: $\text{CT} = ((A, \rho), C_0, \{C_{x,j}\}_{x \in [\ell], j \in \{\mathbb{Z}_p^* \big| 1 \le j \le 6\}})$. The above operations can also be precomputed by the data owner when the official data is encrypted, and then the encryption is completed. This design draws on the idea of online/offline, making full use of the idle time and cloud storage capacity of the user side, providing some calculation results for the formal encryption phase and alleviating the encryption pressure to a certain extent.

D. Data Access

DU downloads ciphertext from CSP. If the ciphertext is legal, the mobile terminal uses the private key to complete the decryption.

When the cloud server receives the access request, it first depends userPK$_{\text{GID}}$ on the terminal. Find the corresponding cloud server decryption key SK$_{\text{Out}} = \{S, K'_{i,1}, K'_{i,2}\}_{i \in S}$ in the cloud server key list Klist.Then run Out$_{\text{Dec}}$(SK$_{\text{Out}}$, userPK$_i$, CT) $\rightarrow$ CT$'$ to partial decryption. When the end user's associated attribute set S in the key of the outsourcing decryption server does not satisfy the access policy (A, ρ) in the ciphertext, decryption fails. Otherwise, for $I = \{x : \rho(x) \in S\} \subseteq \{1, 2, \ldots, \ell\}$, the decryption server compute $\{c_x \in \mathbb{Z}_p\}$ to satisfied $\sum\limits_{x \in I} c_x A_x = (1, 0, \ldots, 0)$, and finally sent the partially decrypted ciphertext CT$' = (C_0, C_{\text{part1}}, C_{\text{part2}})$ to DU. Among them:

$$C_{part1} = \prod_{x \in I} \{C_{x,1} \cdot e(g, g)^{C_{x,5}} e(K'_{\delta(x),1}, C_{x,2}) e(K'_{\delta(x),2}, C_{x,4})\}^{c_x} \tag{2}$$

$$C_{part2} = \prod_{x \in I} \{e(H(\text{GID})^z, C_{x,3} \cdot g^{C_{x,6}})\}^{c_x} \tag{3}$$

After receiving the encrypted ciphertext from the cloud server part, the end user runs the algorithm Decrypt(), uses the reserved user's private key key $= 1/z$ to complete the remaining decryption operation, calculates $C_{\text{part1}} \cdot C_{\text{part2}}^{1/z} = e(g, g)^s$ and finally returns: $M = \dfrac{C_0}{C_{\text{part1}} \cdot C_{\text{part2}}^{1/z}}$.

Revoke(GID,KT) The user revoked. Enter the user identity and key list, find and delete the array in the list $\{$GID,SK$_{\text{Out}})$, update the list KT $=$ KT$\backslash\{$GID,SK$_{\text{Out}})$.

5 Analysis

A. Correctness

(1) Outsourcing decryption process: when the attribute set S satisfies the access policy (A, ρ), $I = \{x : \rho(x) \in S\} \subseteq \{1, 2, \ldots, \ell\}$, there is the constant $\{c_x \in \mathbb{Z}_p\}$ satisfies $\sum\limits_{x \in I} \lambda_x c_x = s$ and $\sum\limits_{x \in I} \omega_x c_x = 0$. The following results are as follows:

C_{part1}

$$= \prod_{x \in I} \{C_{x,1} \cdot e(g,g)^{C_{x,5}} e(K'_{\delta(x),1}, C_{x,2}) e(K'_{\delta(x),2}, C_{x,4})\}^{c_x}$$

$$= \prod_{x \in I} \{e(g,g)^{\lambda'_{\rho(x)}} e(g,g)^{\alpha_{\rho(x)} r_{\rho(x)}} e(g,g)^{(\lambda_x - \lambda'_{\rho(x)})} e((g^{z\alpha_{\rho(x)}} H(GID)^{zy_{\rho(x)}} F(\rho(x))^{t_{\rho(x)}})^{1/z},$$
$$g^{-r_{\rho(x)}}) e((g^{t_{\rho(x)}})^{1/z}, F(\rho(x))^{r_{\rho(x)}})\}^{c_x}$$

$$= \prod_{x \in I} \{e(g,g)^{\alpha_{\rho(x)} r_{\rho(x)}} e(g,g)^{\lambda_x} e((g,g)^{-\alpha_{\rho(x)} r_{\rho(x)}} e(H(GID),$$
$$g)^{-y_{\rho(x)} r_{\rho(x)}} e(F(\rho(x)), g)^{-r_{\rho(x)} t_{\rho(x)}/z} e((g, F(\rho(x)))^{r_{\rho(x)} t_{\rho(x)}/z}\}^{c_x}$$

$$= \prod_{x \in I} \{e(g,g)^{\lambda_x} e(H(GID), g)^{-y_{\rho(x)} r_{\rho(x)}}\}^{c_x}$$

$$= e(g,g)^{\sum_{x \in I} \lambda_x c_x} e(H(GID), g)^{-\sum_{x \in I} y_{\rho(x)} r_{\rho(x)} c_x}$$

$$= e(g,g)^{s} e(H(GID), g)^{-\sum_{x \in I} y_{\rho(x)} r_{\rho(x)} c_x}$$

$$(4)$$

C_{part2}

$$= \prod_{x \in I} \{e(H(GID)^z, C_{x,3} \cdot g^{C_{x,6}})\}^{c_x}$$

$$= \prod_{x \in I} \{e(H(GID)^z, g^{y_{\rho(x)} r_{\rho(x)}} g^{\omega'_{\rho(x)}} \cdot g^{(\omega_x - \omega'_{\rho(x)})})\}^{c_x}$$

$$= \prod_{x \in I} \{e(H(GID)^z, g^{y_{\rho(x)} r_{\rho(x)}} g^{\omega_x})\}^{c_x} \qquad (5)$$

$$= \prod_{x \in I} \{e(H(GID), g)^{z \cdot y_{\rho(x)} r_{\rho(x)}} e(H(GID), g)^{z \cdot \omega_x}\}^{c_x}$$

$$= e(H(GID), g)^{z \sum_{x \in I} y_{\rho(x)} r_{\rho(x)} c_x} e(H(GID), g)^{z \sum_{x \in I} \omega_x c_x}$$

$$= e(H(GID), g)^{z \sum_{x \in I} y_{\rho(x)} r_{\rho(x)} c_x}$$

(2) The mobile device completes the final decryption:

$$C_{part1} \cdot C_{part2}^{1/z}$$

$$= \{e(g,g)^{s} e(H(GID), g)^{-\sum_{x \in I} y_{\rho(x)} r_{\rho(x)} c_x}\} (e(H(GID), g)^{z \sum_{x \in I} y_{\rho(x)} r_{\rho(x)} c_x})^{1/z} \qquad (6)$$

$$= e(g,g)^{s} \frac{C_0}{C_{part1} \cdot C_{part2}^{1/z}} = \frac{Me(g,g)^{s}}{e(g,g)^{s}} = M$$

B. Security

(1) Static Security

Lemma 1. assumes that the Rouselakis-Waters (RW) scheme [20] is static security, then the decentralizing multi authority CP-ABE scheme for the mobile cloud computing is also static security.

Proof. Assuming that the attacker cannot ignore the advantage of the probability polynomial time breaking this scheme, it is proved that we can construct a probability polynomial time algorithm Φ to break the RW scheme,
    Φ runs algorithm of Global Setup: output and send the public parameters GP to the attacker.
Attacker's Queries: The attacker first came from the authority V select a part of the agency $C(C \subseteq V)$, then generate and send its public key $\{PK_\beta\}_{\beta \in C}$ to the Φ, Then ask Φ as follows:

- Select m authorized users $\{GID_i\}_{i=1}^m$ to inquire about their public and private key.
- Select some non-corrupt authorities $N(N \subseteq V)$ to ask their public key.
- Select n users $\{S_i, GID_i\}_{i=1}^n$ to ask its outsourcing decryption key. $S_i \subseteq U$ is the attribute set of the user i. Required $T(S_i) \cap C = \varnothing$ means the attributes owned by the users are authorized by the uncorrupted authority. In addition, the requirement $n > m$ is that the attacker can not only query the user's outsourcing decryption key in the m authorized users, but also ask other users for the corresponding outsourced decryption key.
- Two messages m_0, m_1 of equal length, and a challenge access structure (A, ρ) encoded in a suitable form. We require that for every $i(1 \leq i \leq n)$ the set $S_i \cup S_C$ is an unauthorized set of the access structure (A, ρ).

Challenger's Replies: Φ send $\{PK_\beta\}_{\beta \in C}$ to the challenger and inquire about the corresponding public key of $N \subseteq V$ in the RW scheme, also do the corresponding private key and the challenge ciphertext of $\{S_i, GID_i\}_{i=1}^m$. The challenger turns back $\{SK_{S_i, GID_i} = (g^{\alpha_\beta} H(GID_i)^{y_\beta} F(j)^{t_j}, g^{t_j})_{j \in S_i}\}_{i=1}^m$, The public keys $\{PK_\beta\}_{\beta \in N}$ of authorities $N \subseteq V$ and the challenge ciphertext CT*. First, Φ calculate the user's private key in this scheme: for $1 \leq i \leq m$, chooses the random element $z \in \mathbb{Z}_p^*$, calculate userPK$_{GID_i} = \{g^z, H(GID_i)^z\}$ and key$_{GID_i} = \{1/z\}_i$, then discuss the corresponding outsourced decryption key for $\{S_i, GID_i\}_{i=1}^n$, as shown below:

- for $1 \leq i \leq m, j \in S_i$,

$$K_{j,1,GID_i} = (g^{\alpha_\beta} H(GID_i)^{y_\beta} F(j)^{t_j})^{z_i} = g^{\alpha_\beta z_i} H(GID_i)^{y_\beta z_i} F(j)^{t_j z_i} \tag{7}$$

$$K_{j,2,GID_i} = (F(j)^{t_j})^{z_i} = F(j)^{t_j z_i} \tag{8}$$

Order

$$\text{SK}_{\text{Out,GID}_i} = \{S_i, K^{z_i}_{i,1,\text{GID}_i}, K^{z_i}_{i,2,\text{GID}_i}\}_{j \in S_i} \tag{9}$$

- for $m \leq i \leq n$, chooses the random element $g_j \in G$, $k_j \in \mathbb{Z}^*_p$, calculate $K_{j,1,\text{GID}_i} = g_j F(j)^{k_j} g_j$, $K_{j,2,\text{GID}_i} = F(j)^{k_j}$, order $\text{SK}_{\text{Out,GID}_i} = \{S_i, K^{z_i}_{i,1,\text{GID}_i}, K^{z_i}_{i,2,\text{GID}_i}\}_{j \in S_i}$. Notice the $g^{\alpha\beta} H(\text{GID}_i)^{y_\beta}$ is an element of group G, and G is a cyclic group, and there is an unknown element $z_i \in \mathbb{Z}^*_p$, s. t. $g_j = (g^{\alpha\beta} H(\text{GID}_i)^{y_\beta})^{z_i} = g^{\alpha\beta z_i} H(\text{GID}_i)^{y_\beta z_i}$. So, $K_{j,1,\text{GID}_i} = g_j F(j)^{k_j} = g^{\alpha\beta z_i} H(\text{GID}_i)^{y_\beta z_i} F(j)^{k_j}$, $K_{j,2,\text{GID}_i} = F(j)^{k_j}$, is a uniform distribution of the outsourced decryption key.
- Φ send the above results to attacker.

Guess: The attacker outputs a guess $b' \in \{0, 1\}$ with Φ at the same time.

The above distribution is truly indistinguishable from the attacker. Therefore, if the attacker can break this scheme with non-negligible advantage, he can also break the RW scheme with non-negligible advantage.

Lemma 2. Given that the q-DPBDHE2 assumption holds, the RW scheme is statically safe under the random oracle model.

Proof: The document [20] has given a detailed proof. For reasons of space, it will not be repeated here.

Theorem 1. Assuming that the q-DPBDHE2 assumption holds, the scheme in this paper is statically secure under the random oracle model.

Proof: Lemmas 1 and 2 can be obtained directly.

(2) Revocable Security Certificate

The idea of this section is similar to that of Lemma 1. First of all, the following lemmas are proved.

Lemma 3. Assuming that the Rouselakis-Waters (RW) scheme [20] is static and secure, the no-centric multi-agency CP-ABE scheme proposed in this paper supports user revocation.

Proof: Assumptions For the proposed scheme of this paper, there is a polynomial-time opponent A who can win the revocable game in Sect. 3 with the advantage ε, then a simulator B can be constructed to defeat the RW scheme with the advantage ε. Let C be the challenger to interact with B in the RW scheme.

Same as static security certificate, Challenger C sends the public parameter GP in the RW scheme to simulator B. B sends the GP as an open parameter of the scheme to adversary A.

Adversary A asks B about the uncorrupted authority's public key, part of the user's public/private key pair, and the corresponding cloud server private key and challenge cipher text.

Challenger's Replies: Simulator B queries the public key and challenge ciphertext of the noncorrupted institution in the RW solution. C returns to B, then B performs the following operations.

– for $1 \leq i \leq m$, chooses the random element $z \in S_i$,

$$K_{j,1,\text{GID}_i} = (g^{\alpha_\beta} H(\text{GID}_i)^{y_\beta} F(j)^{t_j})^{z_i} = g^{\alpha_\beta z_i} H(\text{GID}_i)^{y_\beta z_i} F(j)^{t_j z_i} \tag{10}$$

$$K_{j,2,\text{GID}_i} = (F(j)^{t_j})^{z_i} = F(j)^{t_j z_i} \tag{11}$$

order

$$\text{SK}_{\text{Out,GID}_{i'}} = \{S_i, K_{i,1,\text{GID}_i}^{z_i}, K_{i,2,\text{GID}_i}^{z_i}\}_{j \in S_i} \tag{12}$$

– for $1 \leq i \leq m$, chooses the random element $z \in \mathbb{Z}_p^*$, calculate $\text{userPK}_{\text{GID}_i} = \{g^z, H(\text{GID}_i)^z\}$ and $\text{key}_{\text{GID}_i} = \{1/z\}_i$.
– for $m \leq i \leq n, j \in S_i$ chooses the random element $g_j \in G$, $k_j \in \mathbb{Z}_p^*$, calculate $K_{j,1,\text{GID}_i} = g_j F(j)^{k_j} g_j$, $K_{j,2,\text{GID}_i} = F(j)^{k_j}$, order

$$\text{SK}_{\text{Out,GID}_i} = \{S_i, K_{i,1,\text{GID}_i}^{z_i}, K_{i,2,\text{GID}_i}^{z_i}\}_{j \in S_i}. \tag{13}$$

Notice the $g^{\alpha_\beta} H(\text{GID}_i)^{y_\beta}$ is an element of group G, and G is a cyclic group, there is an unknown element $z_i \in \mathbb{Z}_p^*$, s. t.

$$g_j = (g^{\alpha_\beta} H(\text{GID}_i)^{y_\beta})^{z_i} = g^{\alpha_\beta z_i} H(\text{GID}_i)^{y_\beta z_i}. \tag{14}$$

So, $K_{j,1,\text{GID}_i} = g_j F(j)^{k_j} = g^{\alpha_\beta z_i} H(\text{GID}_i)^{y_\beta z_i} F(j)^{k_j}$, $K_{j,2,\text{GID}_i} = F(j)^{k_j}$, is a uniform distribution of the outsourced decryption key.
– B send the above results to A.

Guess: A outputs a guess $b' \in \{0, 1\}$ with B at the same time.

Theorem 2. Assuming that the q-DPBDHE2 hypothesis holds, the scheme in this paper supports user revocation under the random oracle model.

Proof can be obtained directly from Lemmas 2 and 3.

C. Performance Comparison Analysis

This section mainly compares and analyzes the performance of the proposed scheme and related schemes, Table 2 shows the performance comparison results for each scheme. We mainly performed functional analysis and comparison with the current attribute-based encryption schemes proposed for mobile cloud environments.

Except that the scheme [16] is a single authority establishment, other programs are multi-authority institutions. By comparison, it can be seen that scholars choose the bilinear group of prime number order to construct the scheme because the same group operation is 1–2 orders of magnitude faster than the order group in the prime order group, which is more suitable for the mobile cloud environment.

Table 2. Performance comparison of attribute-based encryption schemes proposed in this paper and mobile cloud environment

	AA	CA	Prime order	Pre-calculation	Outsource decryption	Access structure	Safety	Large universe
Vijay [13]	Multi-authority	×	√	×	×	Not mentioned		×
Li [14]	Multi-authority	×	√	×	√	Access Tree	CPA	×
Lyu [15]	Multi-authority	√	√	√	√	LSSS	CPA	×
Zhao [16]	Single	−	√	√	√	Access Tree	CPA	×
De [17]	Multi-authority	√	√	√	√	LSSS	CPA	×
Li [18]	Multi-authority	√	√	√	√	LSSS	CPA	×
Our scheme	Multi-authority	√	√	√	√	LSSS	Static Security	√

Since the biggest difference between a mobile cloud environment and an ordinary cloud environment is the device performance of a user terminal, most schemes consider adopting technical means at the encryption and decryption stages to migrate the amount of computation that should have been completed by the user terminal to a third party and encrypt the information. Files are securely stored to the cloud. Schemes [13, 14] all require a central authority to certify their identities. This does not prevent the central organization from corrupting the entire encryption process. The central authority must interact with each authority to exchange information. The communication costs brought about by this cannot be ignored either. The [15, 17, 18] are similar to the schemes proposed in this paper, but our scheme is static secure and is superior to the plaintext security of the above scheme.

Our scheme draws on the mapping idea in [22] and uses functions $F : U \rightarrow G$ to map the attribute space to group G. [22] was proposed in cloud computing environment and did not consider precomputing, Table 3 gives the performance comparison results of our scheme and the scheme proposed by [22]. The advantage of this is that the number of attributes in the system is not limited, and any string in group G can be used as a new one in the later period. That is, our scheme is to support large attribute universe. There is no need to specify the number of attributes to be used when the system is established. In addition, this scheme maps the user identifier GID to G through the function H, so that the user and organization that have the unique identifier can achieve complete decentralization, thereby resisting the collusion attack between the user and the organization.

In addition, the solution of this paper is also superior to the multi-authority scheme proposed in the current cloud environment in terms of user costs and is more suitable for the requirements of the user's low-end and configuration equipment.

Table 3. Performance comparison of our scheme and [22]

	Environment	Pre-calculation	Outsource	Encryption of users	Decryption of users
Ref [22]	Cloud computing	×	√	$(6\ell + 1)E$	E
Our scheme	MCC	√	√	E	E

6 Conclusion

At present, the research of mobile cloud data security sharing mechanism is still at the initial stage, and there is no secure, effective and thorough trusted deletion scheme.

The scheme proposed in this paper adopts attribute-based encryption technology, which utilizes pre-computation and outsourcing decryption, effectively reduces the computational overhead of the client, satisfies the large attribute domain, supports revocation, and has no central setting, which is more in line with practical application requirements. Finally, the security of the scheme is proved under the random oracle model. Compared with related schemes, our method can effectively reduce the overhead of mobile devices and is suitable for data security sharing in mobile cloud environments.

Acknowledgments. This work was supported by the National Key Research Program of China "Collaborative Precision Positioning Project" (Grant No.2016YFB0501900)

References

1. Wikipedia: The definition of Mobile Cloud Computing. https://en.wikipedia.org/wiki/Mobile_cloud_computing
2. White Paper: Mobile Cloud Computing Solution Brief. Aepona (2010)
3. Cui, Y., Song, J., Miao, C., et al.: Mobile cloud computing research progress and trends. Chin. J. Comput. **40**(2), 273–295 (2017)
4. Gartner: Five trends in cybersecurity for 2017 and 2018. https://www.gartner.com/smarterwithgartner/5-trends-in-cybersecurity-for-2017-and-2018/
5. Sahai, A., Waters, B.: Fuzzy identity-based encryption. In: Cramer, R. (ed.) EUROCRYPT 2005. LNCS, vol. 3494, pp. 457–473. Springer, Heidelberg (2005). https://doi.org/10.1007/11426639_27
6. Goyal, V., Pandey, O., Sahai, A., et al.: Attribute-based encryption for fine-grained access control of encrypted data. In: Proceedings of the ACM Conference on Computer and Communications Security, pp. 89–98 (2006)
7. Cheung, L., Newport, C.: Provably secure ciphertext policy ABE. In: Proceedings of the ACM Conference on Computer and Communications Security, pp. 456–465. ACM (2007)
8. Goyal, V., Jain, A., Pandey, O., Sahai, A.: Bounded ciphertext policy attribute based encryption. In: Aceto, L., Damgård, I., Goldberg, L.A., Halldórsson, M.M., Ingólfsdóttir, A., Walukiewicz, I. (eds.) ICALP 2008. LNCS, vol. 5126, pp. 579–591. Springer, Heidelberg (2008). https://doi.org/10.1007/978-3-540-70583-3_47

9. Waters, B.: Ciphertext-policy attribute-based encryption: an expressive, efficient, and provably secure realization. In: Catalano, D., Fazio, N., Gennaro, R., Nicolosi, A. (eds.) PKC 2011. LNCS, vol. 6571, pp. 53–70. Springer, Heidelberg (2011). https://doi.org/10.1007/978-3-642-19379-8_4

10. Green, M., Hohenberger, S., Waters, B.: Outsourcing the decryption of ABE ciphertexts. In: Usenix Conference on Security, p. 34. USENIX Association (2011)

11. Hohenberger, S., Waters, B.: Online/offline attribute-based encryption. In: Krawczyk, H. (ed.) PKC 2014. LNCS, vol. 8383, pp. 293–310. Springer, Heidelberg (2014). https://doi.org/10.1007/978-3-642-54631-0_17

12. Lewko, A., Waters, B.: Decentralizing attribute-based encryption. In: Paterson, K.G. (ed.) EUROCRYPT 2011. LNCS, vol. 6632, pp. 568–588. Springer, Heidelberg (2011). https://doi.org/10.1007/978-3-642-20465-4_31

13. Vijay, H., Goyal, D., Singla, S.: An efficient and secure solution for attribute revocation problem utilizing CP-ABE scheme in mobile cloud computing. Int. J. Comput. Appl. **129**(1), 16–21 (2015)

14. Li, R., Shen, C., He, H., et al.: A lightweight secure data sharing scheme for mobile cloud computing. IEEE Trans. Cloud Comput. **6**(2), 344–357 (2017)

15. Lyu, M., Li, X., Li, H.: Efficient, verifiable and privacy preserving decentralized attribute-based encryption for mobile cloud computing. In: IEEE Second International Conference on Data Science in Cyberspace, pp. 195–204. IEEE Computer Society (2017)

16. Zhao, Z., Wang, J.: Verifiable outsourced ciphertext-policy attribute-based encryption for mobile cloud computing. Ksii Trans. Internet Inf. Syst. **11**(6), 3254–3272 (2017)

17. De, S.J., Ruj, S.: Efficient decentralized attribute based access control for mobile clouds. IEEE Trans. Cloud Comput. (2017)

18. Li, X., Lyu, M.: Multi-authority attribute-based encryption scheme in mobile cloud environment. Appl. Res. Comput. **35**(05), 1–9 (2018)

19. http://www.arocmag.com/article/02-2018-05-006.html

20. Lewko, A., Okamoto, T., Sahai, A., Takashima, K., Waters, B.: Fully secure functional encryption: attribute-based encryption and (hierarchical) inner product encryption. In: Gilbert, H. (ed.) EUROCRYPT 2010. LNCS, vol. 6110, pp. 62–91. Springer, Heidelberg (2010). https://doi.org/10.1007/978-3-642-13190-5_4

21. Rouselakis, Y., Waters, B.: Efficient statically-secure large-universe multi-authority attribute-based encryption. In: Böhme, R., Okamoto, T. (eds.) FC 2015. LNCS, vol. 8975, pp. 315–332. Springer, Heidelberg (2015). https://doi.org/10.1007/978-3-662-47854-7_19

22. Beimel, A.: Secure schemes for secret sharing and key distribution. Int. J. Pure Appl. Math. (1996)

23. Zhang, K., Ma, J., Li, H., et al.: Multi-authority attribute-based encryption with efficient revocation. J. Commun. **38**(3), 83–91 (2017)

A Voting Scheme in Blockchain Based on Threshold Group Signature

Lipeng Wang[✉], Mingsheng Hu, Zijuan Jia, Bei Gong[✉],
Yanyan Yang, Xinxin Liu, and Wenjun Cui

School of Information Science and Technology, Zhengzhou Normal University,
Zhengzhou 450044, China
wlpscu@126.com, tekkman_blade@126.com

Abstract. Traditional voting schemes are used for the credit evaluation and authentication. During the voting process, the contents need to be verified through the signature algorithms. Traditional signature schemes for voting scenes exist several drawbacks such as distrust of central nodes for the group signature and inefficiency for the ring signature. A trusted center selection scheme is proposed based on Dynamic Bayesian Network, which can be adapted in the isomerized blockchain. By introducing the historical interaction window, the aging factor, and the penalty factor, the adaptive trusted metrics can be obtained through aggregating the direct credibility and the indirect credibility. A new threshold group signature scheme is introduced through collaboration between users and the trusted centers. In order to protect the user identities, the blinding process is proposed. In case of compromising, the trusted centers create redundant backup, and can be updated with the proposed selection scheme. Security analysis shows that the proposed signature, whose difficulty is equivalent to the discrete logarithm of the elliptic curve, achieves a high level of anonymity and can resist impersonation attacks. Computational complexity analysis shows that the new method with low computational cost and transmission efficiency can be effectively adapted to the isomerized blockchain scene.

Keywords: Blockchain · Confidential computation
Threshold group signature · Dynamic Bayesian Network

1 Introduction

Blockchain is a distributed database technology which can record transaction. The characteristics of blockchain are "decentralization", "anonymization" and "de-trusted" [1]. It handles distrust among nodes and has been widely applied in the fields of e-money, financial investment, internet of things, medical care, and energy network [2]. The blockchain falls into three categories: public chain, permissioned chain, and private chain. At present blockchain-based voting schemes existing on permissioned chain and private chain have been used in credit assessment and decision making. The paper is devoted to develop a safe and transparent online voting mechanism on the blockchain: coordinating participants to ensure the fairness, allowing the voting manager to check the voting result and cancel illegal ballots [3]. Compared with existing voting

© Springer Nature Singapore Pte Ltd. 2019
H. Zhang et al. (Eds.): CTCIS 2018, CCIS 960, pp. 184–202, 2019.
https://doi.org/10.1007/978-981-13-5913-2_12

schemes, blockchain-based voting methods have the ability of being irrevocable and non-repudiation, and the process can be automated in accordance with the statute, without human interference. Applications based on the blockchain with neutrality and security have shown the wide prospects.

The identities in the blockchain node, similar to the bankcard account number, are the pseudonym information used by the user to participate in the voting process. The temporary identify labels are generated by the participants using the public key encryption algorithm with anonymity. Recent studies [4, 5] have shown that the blockchain has the risk of identity leakage. The attackers exploit the message propagation vulnerabilities and trace out the initiator identities. It means that the native blockchain architecture cannot guarantee the anonymity. How to design a highly anonymous and non-repudiation blockchain architecture is the focus of this study.

To implement the voting scheme based on the group signature in blockchain, the native blockchain architecture needs to be redesigned to pick out the trusted centers. However, once the trusted centers are breached, the user secrets will be stolen. What's more, attackers can tamper with the voting results. How to guarantee the security of the trusted centers in the isomerized blockchain is the prerequisite for the voting scheme.

To select the trusted centers on the blockchain, the metrics must be updated in order to feed back the credibility to other nodes in time. When initiating, all nodes need to generate their own private keys to calculate the share signatures which will be passed to the trusted centers. The trusted centers will accumulate the share signatures to composite the group signature. To trace the abnormal behaviors, the trusted centers must be allowed to open the signature and locate the corresponding user identities. When some nodes are unavailable, their signatures are allowed to revoke. How to design such a revocable and traceable threshold group signature scheme is the main contribution of this study.

2   Related Researches

In 1994, Marsh firstly proposed the concept of trusted computing and elaborated on the canonical representation of trust metrics [6]. The key of implementing the signature scheme in blockchain is selection of the trusted centers.

To solve the problems that the user identities on general devices are unsafe, [7] builds a mathematical model based on the D-S evidence theory and proposes the trustworthiness metrics in Ad-hoc and P2P networks. [8] proposes a dynamic trusted model based on Bayesian Network. The credibility metrics depend on the neighbors with the dynamic objective variables. However, the model still needs to be optimized in terms of prediction accuracy and time continuity. [9] quantifies the credibility based on the information theory and measures the trust propagation path in the Ad-hoc network. Since the degree of trust is regarded as the uncertainty, the entropy is introduced to quantify it. [10] proposes the trusted security discovery model TSSD in pervasive circumstances. The model is a composite architecture that supports discovery functions in both secure and insecure scenarios. [11] proposes a penalty-based incentive mechanism based on the repeated game, which can adjust the penalty according to the reputation.

Due to heterogeneity and complexity of the blockchain, the trusted metrics need to meet the requirements of dynamic adaptability, high efficiency, and strong timeliness. When adapting the traditional measurements to the blockchain, existing schemes mainly include several drawbacks [12]:

1. Assumptions made by those methods limit their applications.
2. The computing power of blockchain nodes is uneven, which leads existing methods to be inferior in terms of interaction timeliness and adaptability.
3. Autonomy of blockchain makes the node behaviors unpredictable. Protection methods without cooperation among nodes make them vulnerable when facing up to the attacks.
4. Existing researches lack robustness whose accuracy will be declined when adapting to the blockchain.

The threshold group signature schemes, according to the way of key distribution, are mainly divided into the ones with the trusted center and the ones without the trusted center. For the group signature scheme without the trusted center, each node has a high degree of autonomy, which enhances the security level with the cost of increasing computation. The trusted center for the threshold group signature scheme is considered as the management node and can trace user identities which is promising for the blockchain based voting scenes.

Traditional signature schemes based on the large number decomposition and discrete logarithm problems cannot meet the requirements of low computation and bandwidth required in the blockchain. The group signatures scheme based on the elliptic curve with lower resource consumption are more suitable for the blockchain scenarios [13].

In 2004, Tzer-Shyong et al. [14] integrated the short key feature with a threshold method and proposed a signature scheme (YC scheme) based on the elliptic curve encryption algorithm. However, it lacks the operations of tracking and cancellation of the signatures. [15] points out that arbitrary member conspiracy in the YC scheme can be able to obtain the private keys. Therefore, [16] proposes an ECC threshold signature scheme with the elliptic curve discrete logarithm difficulty, which could track the signer identity with the help of the trusted center and can effectively resist the members conspiring to forge the signature. The above threshold group signatures are based on the Shamir secret sharing scheme. Some other secret sharing methods will be discussed later.

In [17], a threshold group signature scheme is proposed based on the bilinear mapping and secret sharing. The keys are distributed in the members of the signature set. In [18], the threshold group signature scheme with the elliptic curve discrete logarithm difficulty is proposed, including signature verification, thresholds modification, etc. [19] proposes a threshold group signature scheme based on ECC scheme, which has a shorter key length, lower computation and bandwidth requirement. [20] and [21] propose the ECDSA threshold signature schemes, whose participants can reconstruct keys. Goldfeder et al. proposes a threshold signature scheme to realize the multi-party control functions on bitcoin [22], which applies the threshold cryptography for key management. However, when to recover the keys, multiple parties must be present.

To address the above problems, the paper redesigns the native blockchain, and selects the trusted centers based on Dynamic Bayesian Network, which correlates the time factor to perform the dynamic trusted metrics. In addition, this paper proposes a threshold group signature scheme. Through cooperation between users and the trusted centers, the share signatures will be synthesized to form the group signature. In order to protect the user identities, the proposed method will blind the user identities. In case of the trusted centers unavailable, the new scheme will back up the user signatures and update the trusted centers dynamically.

3 Background

3.1 Digital Signature

Digital signature is a password protection scheme, which utilizes cryptography to confirm source and integrity of the data. It is mainly used in asymmetric key encryption and digital summarization. The sender first signs the message, then others verify it. The signature is temporally valid for a single process. The steps are as follows [23]:

1. $G(p) \overset{generate-keys}{\longrightarrow} (sk, pk)$, where sk is the private key and pk is the public key.

2. $S(sk, m) \overset{generate-signatures}{\longrightarrow} sig$, where m is the plaintext, and sig is the result signature.

3. $Verify(pk, m, sig) \overset{verrify-signatures}{\longrightarrow} \{True, False\}$, which verifies integrity of the data through the public key, the plaintext, and the signature.

The typical signature schemes mainly include the elliptic curve digital signature [24] and the partial blind signature [25]. The elliptic curve digital signature will be the focus in the paper.

The elliptic curve digital signature algorithm is mainly designed based on the elliptic curve discrete logarithm. The elliptic curve E on the finite field F_q is expressed as [24]:

$$y^2 = x^3 + ax + b \pmod{q},$$

where $a, b, x, y \in F_q$. Assuming $E(F_q)$ represents the point set of the elliptic curve, and the base point is $G \in E(F_q)$, $|G| = n$. The parameters are (F_q, a, b, G, n). The steps of the elliptic curve algorithm are as follows:

1. d is a randomly selected value, where $\{d | d \in Z, d \in [1, n-1]\}$. $Q = dG$, where the public key is Q, and the private key is d.
2. Randomly select $k \in [1, n-1]$ to obtain $kG = (x, y)$.
3. $r = x \bmod n$, and verify $r = 0$. If it holds, return to step 2.
4. $e = H(m)$, where $H(\cdot)$ is a custom hash function.
5. $s = k^{-1}(e + dr) \bmod n$, if $s = 0$, go back to the step 2 to continue, otherwise return the result (r, s).

6. The formula to verify the signature (r, s) with the plaintext m and the public key G is $s^{-1}(eG + Qr) = k(e + dr)^{-1}(eG + dGr) = kG$. If it does not hold, it means that the message may be tampered.

3.2 Secret Sharing Scheme

The concept of secret sharing was first proposed by Shamir [26] and Blackey [27]. The idea is to split the secret into N copies and send each copy to different participants for management. When to recover the secret, it needs to involve a certain number of participants, whose number must be greater than or equal to the specified threshold.

The classic secret sharing scheme is the Shamir sharing scheme. The scheme firstly divides the secret S into n copies. Any k copies can recover S, and $k - 1$ ones could not. The whole process is divided into three steps:

1. Initialization: Assuming n participants $(P_1....P_n)$ with the threshold k, let p be a prime number, the trusted center coding range be the finite field GF(p), and each participant be $x_i \in \text{GF(p)}(i = 1, 2, ... n)$.
2. Encryption: The trusted center selects a $k - 1$ order polynomial $f(x) = a_0 + a_1 x + a_2 x^2 + ... + a_{k-1} x^{k-1}$, where $a_i \in \text{GF}(P)(i = 1, 2, ..., k - 1)$, $a_0 = S$. Put $x_i \in \text{GF(p)}(i = 1, 2, ... n)$ into the above equation to obtain $(x_1, f(x_1)), ..., (x_n, f(x_n))$ which will be sent to each participant.
3. Decryption: k pairs of $(x, f(x))$ will be optionally collected from n participants to reconstruct the polynomial $f(x)$, from which we can obtain $f(0) = a_0 = S$ with Lagrange interpolation.

3.3 Threshold Signature Scheme

The (t, n) threshold signature algorithm mainly includes three steps, which are key generation, signing and verification. For n members, the threshold key generation step returns the public key pk and the private key $sk_i\{1 \leq i \leq n\}$ with the system parameter I. The threshold signature process takes on the input m and I with the private key sk_i, and outputs the signature σ [28]. The threshold verification process can be able to verify the signature σ with the public key pk.

The threshold signature algorithm is considered as safe when meeting two requirements [29]:

1. Unforgeability: Given the system parameter I, an attacker can destroy up to a maximum of $t - 1$ nodes through issuing at most k questions, where k is generally equal to 2^n times the length of the message.
2. Robustness: When the attacker breaks through up to $t - 1$ nodes, the correct signature can still be generated.

4 Trusted Center Selection Criterion

The threshold group signature scheme needs the trusted center to trace user identities. Its corresponding measurements must obey several principles which will be discussed later. This paper proposes a trusted center selection scheme based on Dynamic Bayesian Network. The new scheme introduces the historical interaction window, the aging factor, the penalty factor, and aggregates the direct and indirect credibility to form a set of dynamic and adaptive trusted metrics. When the reliability for the current centers is declined to a certain level, they will be re-selected as soon as possible. This paper adopts the selection scheme to the blockchain as shown in Table 1, which reduces the computational complexity and is proved to be equivalent to [12].

Table 1. Diagram of trusted centers construction

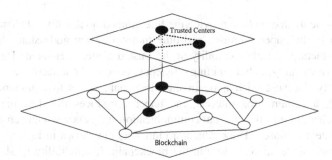

4.1 Definitions

Definition 1: Assuming $C = \{c_i | i \in N^*, 1 \leq i \leq n\}$ represents a set of network nodes. For the current node c, if $\forall c_i \in C$, $c \neq c_i$, the interactive factor r_i exists to make $r_i(c, c_i)$ not empty, and the set $R = \{r_1, r_2, \ldots, r_n\}$ is the local relational database.

Definition 2: For the local relational database $R = \{r_1, r_2, \ldots, r_n\}$, if a relational window w exists to make $R_w = \{r_{n-w}, r_{n-w-1}, \ldots, r_n\}$ be the trusted metrics for the target entity, w is said to be valid.

Definition 3: For the valid relationship window w, at time t, the corresponding context is denoted as $W(w, t)$.

Definition 4: With n trust levels, the credibility set of the current network is denoted as $L = \{l_1, l_2, \ldots, l_n\}$ where $i < j$, $l_i < l_j$. The greater l, the higher the credibility.

Definition 5: Assuming $X = \{x_1[t], x_2[t], \ldots x_n[t]\}$ denotes the attribute set at time t, and $x[t]$ denotes a serial of values for the random variable $x_i[t]$. Assuming continuous events occur at discrete time and the attribute evolving process satisfies the Markov chain model, that is $P(x[t+1]|x[0], \ldots x[t]) = P(x[t+1]|x[t])$, the resulting network is called Dynamic Bayesian Network.

Definition 6: Let the priori network be N_0 and the transfer network be N. N_0 is the distribution of $x[0]$, and N represents the transition probability $P(x[t+1]|x[t])$.

4.2   Trusted Metrics

For the credibility measurement, this paper adopts a strategy combining the static and dynamic behaviors to perform the trusted authentication, which considers the objective and subjective factors to make the comprehensive measurement. The proposed method tries to minimize the resource requirements when applied to the blockchain.

The static trusted metrics are the basis which includes the operating system integrity, additional protection, and hardware performance. The nodes in the blockchain who own more computing resources are able to carry out more tasks, so a high credibility will be assigned to them. The static measurement of this paper does not adopt the traditional identity authentication metric because of anonymity of the blockchain.

The dynamic trusted metrics provide the fine-grained quantitative standards for the measurement in the paper. Through real-time monitoring the node status and timely feedback to others, real-time credibility of the trusted center is ensured. The dynamic behavior metrics mainly include mining efficiency, abnormal connection attempts, and node reliability. Because each node in the blockchain needs to communicate with others during a certain time interval, the paper introduces the dynamic behavior assessment scheduling to the original communication frequency which can effectively utilize the system resource. The evaluation indicators are shown in Fig. 1.

When a new node attempts to join the blockchain, its credibility needs measurement. This paper considers the trustworthiness as a measure of the satisfaction degree for the task. The measurement relies on the correlation among nodes with a combination of subjective and objective factors. The proposed method first initializes the measurement module, calculates the direct credibility (Dc) and the indirect credibility (Ic), then obtains the comprehensive credibility Sc based on Dc and Ic.

Definition 7: Assuming $\delta'(t)$ is the aging factor, which represents the attenuation factor of the credibility with time. The formula is:

$$\delta'(t) = 1 - \frac{\Delta t \times \zeta'}{t - t_0},$$

where $\zeta' \in (0, 1)$, $\delta'(t) \in (0, 1)$, t_0 denotes the start time, and t represents the current time. ζ' is used to adjust the decay rate. As the value increases, the decay rate will become faster. Δt is the interval between two operations.

Theorem 1: In the blockchain scenario, $\delta'(t)$ is equivalent to $\delta(t)$, and $\delta(t)$ is:

$$\delta(t) = 1 - \frac{\zeta}{t - t_0},$$

where $\zeta \in (0, 1)$, $\delta(t) \in (0, 1)$.

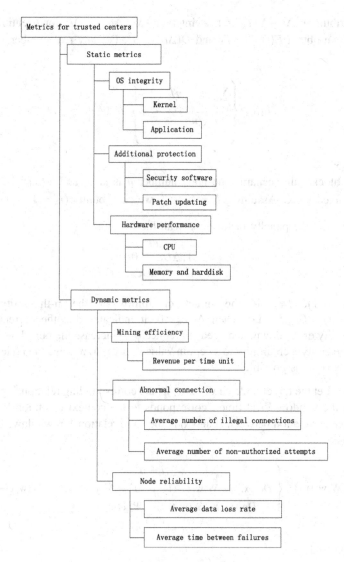

Fig. 1. Metrics for selection of the trusted centers

Proof: In the blockchain scenario, nodes in the network send heartbeat packets at a certain interval T_h. In order to make full use of resources, the time interval to update the aging factor can be set as $\Delta t = T_h$. Due to the fluctuation of the network, there is a certain disturbance during the process of message transmission. Assuming Δt obeys the normal distribution: $\Delta t \sim N(T_h, \sigma^2)$, at intervals $\Delta t_1, \Delta t_2, \ldots \Delta t_n$ for n entities in the blockchain, we obtain $E(\Delta t_i) = T_h$ and $D(\Delta t_i) = \sigma^2$. For any real number x, we can obtain

$$\lim_{n \to \infty} P \left\{ \frac{\sum\limits_{i=1}^{n} \Delta t_i - nT_h}{\sqrt{n}\sigma} \leq x \right\} = \Phi(x),$$

where $E(\Phi(x)) = 1$.

For the blockchain scenario, the node number n is large and Δt can be approximated as a fixed value. Assuming $\zeta = \Delta t \times \zeta'$, we can obtain $\delta(t) = 1 - \frac{\zeta}{t - t_0}$.

Definition 8: Let the penalty factor be ψ with the formula:

$$\psi = \begin{cases} 1, \Delta Dc_n \geq 0 \\ 0 < \psi < 1, \Delta Dc_n < 0 \end{cases},$$

where $\psi \in (0, 1)$. Dc_n is the direct credibility of the n-th entity, where $\Delta Dc_n = Dc_n(t) - Dc_n(t-1)$. When $\Delta Dc_n < 0$, it indicates that the current entity's direct credibility drops down, and needs to reduce ψ to increase the punishment, which can lower the entity's credibility to a certain value in order to remove the node from the trusted set as soon as possible.

Definition 9: Let the target node be x_j. $\forall x_i \in X$, the corresponding relationship between x_i and x_j in the window W at time t corresponds to the context condition $W(w, t)$. w represents the correlation between x_i and x_j in the valid relationship window. The direct credibility is:

$$Dc_n(x_i, x_j, W(w, t), t) = \begin{cases} \left(\frac{1}{n}, \frac{1}{n}, \ldots, \frac{1}{n}\right), t = 0 \\ Dc_n(x_i, x_j, W(w, t-1), t-1) \times \delta(t), W(w, t) - W(w, t-1) = \Phi, \\ Dc_n(x_i, x_j, W(w, t), t) \times \Psi, else \end{cases}$$

where $\sum\limits_{i=1}^{n} Dc_i = 1$.

When initializing the direct credibility, the credibility for target node's neighbors are set to be the same value. If there is no change at a certain interval, the node's credibility decays with time. When the increment of the direct credibility is positive, the penalty factor $\psi = 1$, and the direct credibility remains unchanged. Otherwise, the direct credibility needs to be punished.

Definition 10: $\forall x_i \in X$, let the target node be x_j, and the context condition at time t for the node x_i and x_j within the valid window w be $W(w, t)$. We can obtain the indirect credibility for the target node with the formula:

$$Ic_n\big(x_i,\, x_j,\, W(w,t),t\big)=\begin{cases} \left(\frac{1}{n},\frac{1}{n},\ldots,\frac{1}{n}\right), t=0 \\ Ic_n(x_i,\, x_j,\, W(w,t-1),\, t-1) \times \delta(t),\, W(w,t)\text{ - }W(w,t-1)=\Phi \\ \dfrac{\sum_{z\in X} Dc_n(x_i,x_k,W(w,t-1),t-1)\times Sc_n(x_k,x_j,W(w,t-1),t-1)}{\sum_{z\in X} Dc_n(x_i,x_k,W(w,t-1),t-1)} \times \Psi,\, else \end{cases},$$

where Z represents neighbors of the target node. The indirect credibility of its neighbors is initialized as $\frac{1}{n}$. For the subsequent process, if the target node does not generate a new context condition, the indirect credibility decays over time. Conversely, we can obtain the target node credibility combining the direct credibility and the comprehensive credibility of the target node and its neighbors. When the increment of the indirect credibility is positive, the penalty factor $\psi = 1$, and the indirect credibility remains unchanged. Otherwise, the indirect credibility of the target node needs to be punished.

Definition 11: Let μ be the weight factor for the direct credibility with the formula:

$$\mu = 0.5 + \frac{w}{2\Omega},$$

where Ω is the length of the valid relationship window, $\mu \in (0.5, 1]$. μ is used to adjust the weight between the direct credibility and the indirect credibility when calculating the comprehensive credibility. Since its value is always greater than 0.5, it means the priority will be assigned to the direct credibility.

Definition 12: $\forall x_i \in X$, let the target node be x_j, the corresponding context condition of x_i and x_j is $W(w, t)$. The comprehensive credibility is:

$$Sc_n\big(x_i,\, x_j,\, W(w,t),t\big) = \begin{cases} Ic_n(x_i, x_j, W(w,t),t),\, W(w,t) = \Phi \\ Dc_n(x_i,\, x_j,\, W(w,t),t),\, W(w,t) = W(\Omega, t) \\ Sc_n(x_i,\, x_j,\, W(w,t-1),t-1) \times \delta(t),\, W(w,t) - W(w,t-1) = \Phi \\ [\mu \times Dc_n(x_i,\, x_j,\, W(w,t),t) + (1-\mu)Ic_n(x_i,\, x_j,\, W(w,t),t)] \times \Psi,\, else \end{cases}$$

The comprehensive credibility is considered as the ultimate credibility of the target node. If no change of context condition between the time $t-1$ and t, the comprehensive credibility decays. Otherwise the priority will be given to the direct credibility compared with the indirect credibility. If the increment is negative, the comprehensive credibility will be punished.

5   Blockchain Based Threshold Group Signature Scheme

The participants for the proposed scheme mainly include the blockchain nodes (*US*), the trusted centers (*TC*), and the backup node (*BK*), where the trusted centers are retrieved through Dynamic Bayesian Network as above. The proposed threshold group signature scheme adapts the signature to the blockchain scenario, which blinds user identities, and improves the effectiveness with security guarantees. In addition, the new scheme adds the backup operation to avoid the corruption of the trusted centers.

As shown in Fig. 2, the blockchain based threshold group signature is divided to eight steps which comprise selecting the trusted centers, registration, generation of the share signature, synthesizing the group signature, signature verification, signature backup, signature openness, and signature revoking. They will be discussed later.

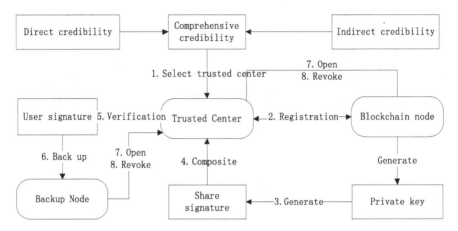

Fig. 2. Architecture diagram of the proposed scheme

For the convenience, the symbols are defined as Table 2.

Table 2. Symbols of the proposed scheme

Symbol	Description	Symbol	Description
TC	trusted centers	Id_i	identity of i th node
N_i	i th node	u_s	private key for users
c_s	private group key	u_p	public key for users
c_p	public group key	P	set comprising t members
TC_s	private key of trusted center	Id	set comprising t member identities
TC_p	public key of trusted center	UL	the user signatures
ID_i	blinded identity of i th node		

1. Select the trusted centers
   When the blockchain is initializing, the trusted center is selected based on Dynamic Bayesian Network as above.
2. Registration
   The parameters of the proposed threshold group signature scheme need to be set to generate the corresponding keys and hash functions. When a node attempts to join the blockchain, it needs to interact with the trusted center, blind the identities, and verify the keys.

First, select the appropriate parameters to generate the elliptic curve. p is a large prime number and F_p is a finite field. Select a and b at random, where $a, b \in F_p$, to construct the non-singular elliptic curve: $y^2 = x^3 + ax + b$, $4a^3 + 27b^2 \neq 0 \pmod{p}$, where G represents generators, $ord(G) = \Upsilon$, and Υ represents a large prime.

If the private key of the trusted center $TC_s = s$ has been decided, its public key is $TC_p = sG$. The signature is based on the Shamir secret sharing scheme with the polynomial: $f(x) = a_0 + a_1 x + a_2 x^2 + \ldots + a_{t-1} x^{t-1}$, where $a_i \in GF(p)(i = 1, 2, \ldots, t-1)$. Set the private group key as $c_s = a_0 = f(0)$ and the public group key as $c_p = c_s G = f(0)G = a_0 G$. Select a one-way hash function $h(x)$ to blind the user identities.

$<a, b, G, c_p, p, h(x)>$ are denoted as the public information with global accessibility in the proposed scheme. $<c_s, f(x)>$ serves as the confidential information, which is stored on the trusted center and backed up to prevent the central node from malfunctioning or being offline to affect the availability of the blockchain.

When a certain node i attempts to join the blockchain, it needs to apply to the trusted centers, including identities of verification and blinding. The trusted centers then issue the partial key which will be sent to the corresponding user node after being encrypted. The specific process is as follows:

- The node sends the randomly generated partial key $u \in Z_p^*$ and its own identity Id_i to the trusted center. The trusted center then obtains $X_i = uG$ according to the value u of the node i. The trusted center searches the user signatures database to determine whether the node has joined the blockchain or not. If it does, the trusted center rejects its application, otherwise the trusted center obtains $U = uG = (x_u, y_u)$, $ID_i = (x_u + s)h(Id_i) + u \bmod p$ where ID_i is the blinded user identity and $<U, ID_i>$ will be sent to the node i.
- After the node i receives $<U, ID_i>$, it needs to verify $ID_i G = (x_u G + TC_p)h(Id_i) + U$. If it holds, the node is required to resend its application. Otherwise its private key will be set as $x_i = u$, $X_i = x_i G$, and $<X_i, U, ID_i, Id_i>$ will be sent to the trusted center.
- When receiving $<X_i, U, ID_i, Id_i>$, the trusted center verifies $ID_i G = (x_u G + TC_p)h(Id_i) + X_i$. If it does not hold, the node will be refused to join the blockchain, otherwise it can allow to enter the network and add itself to UL.
- The trusted center obtains another part of the private key for the node $i : y_i = f(ID_i)$, and y_i will be sent to the corresponding node via a secret channel. $a_i G$ will be broadcasted in the network by the trust centers. After the user receives y_i, it needs to verify $y_i G = Gf(ID_i) = \sum_{i=0}^{t-1} a_i G ID_i^i$. If it does not hold, the trusted center needs to re-execute this step.
- The private key for node i is $u_s = x_i + y_i$ and the public key is $u_p = u_s G$. Blinded identity ID_i of the node i and the public key u_p are broadcasted to the blockchain.

1. Generate the share signature
   Assuming the set of participants as $\Lambda = \{N_1, N_2, \ldots, N_t\}$, with corresponding blinded identities as $ID = \{ID_1, ID_2, \ldots, ID_t\}$. First, the node i randomly selects $k_i \in Z_p^*$, then obtains $r_i = k_i G = (x_{ri}, y_{ri})$ and the hash value $z = h(m)$ of the

message m. The node can obtain its share signature $s_i = k_i x_{ri} - z u_s I_i \bmod p$ where $I_i = \prod_{i \neq j} \frac{ID_i}{ID_i - ID_j}$. It means that the share signature of the node i is (r_i, s_i), which will be sent to the trusted center through a secret channel.

2. Synthesize the group signature

   After the trusted center receives the share signature (r_i, s_i), it should be verified. Calculate $I_i = \prod_{i \neq j} \frac{ID_i}{ID_i - ID_j}$ and z with the member set Λ and its corresponding identities $ID = \{ID_1, ID_2, \ldots, ID_t\}$. Verify $s_i G + z u_p I_i = r_i x_{ri}$. If it holds, it shows that the share signature is legal, otherwise return to the step 3 to continue.

   The way to generate the threshold group signature is as follows: First we can obtain $R = \sum_{i=1}^{t} r_i x_{ri} \bmod p$, and then merge the share signatures with $S = \sum_{i=1}^{t} s_i$ to get $W = \sum_{i=1}^{t} I_i X_i$. (R, S) is the final threshold group signature. Add the signature $<r_i, s_i, ID_i>$ to UL which can allow to open the signatures.

3. Verify the signature

   The trusted center obtains (R, S) which needs to be verified. The verification steps are as follows: First, calculate $z = h(m)$ and verify $SG + z(c_p + W) = R$. If it does not hold, reject the signature; otherwise, perform the backup operation.

4. Signature backup

   In order to prevent the user signatures from tampering, it needs to select the sub-optimal node as backup which can be obtained with the above scheme based on Dynamic Bayesian Network to duplicate the user signatures.

5. Open the signature

   It needs to connect the trusted centers to perform the open operation. For the signature (R, S), the trusted centers first searches $<r_i, s_i, ID_i>$, then locates the target identity from $<X_i, Id_i, ID_i>$ indexed by ID_i.

6. Revoke the signature

   When a node in the blockchain leaves the network, the trusted center is required to delete its information. First, reinitialize $f(x) = a_0 + \alpha_1 x + a_2 x^2 + \ldots + a_{t-1} x^{t-1}$, where a_0 remains unchanged. Then we can obtain the partial key $y_i = f(ID_i)$, re-execute from step 2 to determine whether it needs to receive y_i.

6 Security Analysis

6.1 Correctness Analysis

Theorem 2: When the node i is being registered to the trusted center, two authentication equations $ID_i G = (x_u G + TC_p)h(Id_i) + U$ and $ID_i G = (x_u G + TC_p)h(Id_i) + X_i$ hold.
Proof: Since $U = uG = (x_u, y_u)$, $ID_i = (x_u + s)h(Id_i) + u$ and $TC_p = sG$, we can obtain $ID_i G = ((x_u + s)h(Id_i) + u)G = (x_u G + sG)h(Id_i) + uG = (x_u G + TC_p)h(Id_i) + U$.

Since $x_i = u$, $X_i = x_i G$, we can obtain $ID_i G = ((x_u + s)h(Id_i) + u)G = (x_u G + TC_p)h(Id_i) + X_i$.

Theorem 3: The equation $y_i G = Gf(ID_i) = \sum_{i=0}^{t-1} a_i GID_i^i$ holds which is used to verify the key of the trusted center by node i.

Proof: Since $y_i = f(ID_i)$, $f(x) = a_0 + a_1 x + a_2 x^2 + \ldots + a_{t-1}x^{t-1}$, we can obtain $y_i G = Gf(ID_i) = a_0 G + a_1 GID_i + \ldots + a_{t-1}GID_i^{t-1} = \sum_{i=0}^{t-1} a_i GID_i^i$.

Theorem 4: When synthesizing the group signature, the verification formula $s_i G + z u_p I_i = r_i x_{ri}$ holds.

Proof: Since $s_i = k_i x_{ri} - z u_s I_i$, $u_p = u_s G$, $r_i = k_i G = (x_{ri}, y_{ri})$, we can obtain $s_i G = k_i x_{ri} G - z u_s I_i G = r_i x_{ri} - z u_p I_i$ and $s_i G + z u_p I_i = r_i x_{ri}$.

Theorem 5: When the trusted center obtains the signature (R, S), the verification equation $SG + z(c_p + W) = R$ holds.

Proof: Since $S = \sum_{i=1}^{t} s_i$, $s_i = k_i x_{ri} - z u_s I_i$, we obtain $SG = \sum_{i=1}^{t} s_i G = \sum_{i=1}^{t} (k_i x_{ri}G - z u_s I_i G)$. As $r_i = k_i G$, $u_s = x_i + y_i$, $y_i = f(ID_i)$, $R = \sum_{i=1}^{t} r_i x_{ri}$, we infer $SG = \sum_{i=1}^{t} s_i G$

$= \sum_{i=1}^{t} (r_i x_{ri}) - \sum_{i=1}^{t} \{z(x_i + f(ID_i))I_i G\} = R - \sum_{i=1}^{t} (z x_i I_i G + z f(ID_i)I_i G)$. Since $X_i = x_i G$,

we get $SG = R - \sum_{i=1}^{t} (z X_i I_i + z f(ID_i)I_i G)$. According to the Lagrange's theorem,

$I_i = \prod_{i \neq j} \frac{ID_i}{ID_i - ID_j}$, we deduce $\sum_{i=1}^{t} (f(ID_i)I_i G) = \sum_{i=1}^{t} ((a_0 + a_1 ID_i + a_2 ID_i^2 + \ldots + a_{t-1}$

$ID_i^{t-1})I_i G) = f(0)G = c_p$. Since $W = \sum_{i=1}^{t} I_i X_i$, $SG = R - \sum_{i=1}^{t} (z X_i I_i) - z c_p = R -$

$zW - z c_p$, we obtain $SG + z(c_p + W) = R$.

6.2   Security Analysis

6.2.1   Threshold Safety Analysis

The threshold group signature scheme is adapted to the blockchain. For the blockchain with n nodes, at least t nodes must cooperate to obtain the resulting signature. For a well-designed threshold group signature, if an attacker breaks through a certain number of nodes, as long as the number of valid nodes is greater than or equal to t, the voting result still be correct.

For n participants, when generating the share signatures, each node in the blockchain utilizes its own private key u_s to sign the message and generate the share signature with the formula $s_i = k_i x_{ri} - z u_s I_i \bmod p$. After the trusted center receives the share signature (r_i, s_i) for each participant, the trusted centers synthesize them with the

formula $S = \sum_{i=1}^{t} s_i = \sum_{i=1}^{t} (k_i x_{ri} - z u_s I_i)$, and need to verify the result with the formula $SG + z(c_p + W) = R$.

At least t nodes are required to synthesize the share signatures. If the number of available signatures is less than t, the synthesis will fail. After obtaining the group signature, it is necessary to verify $SG + z(c_p + W) = R$. According to the Lagrange's theorem, we can obtain $\sum_{i=1}^{t} (f(ID_i)I_iG) = f(0)G = c_p$, which needs at least t identities to pass the verification. In practice, because the public key c_p and G is well-known, the attacker can obtain them. When we want to obtain the private group key $f(0)$, the difficulty is equivalent to the discrete logarithm problem of the elliptic curve which has been proved hard, it shows that the proposed scheme is safe.

6.2.2 Anonymity Analysis

For the blockchain applications, recent studies [4, 5] exploit the vulnerabilities of propagation and transaction mechanism of the blockchain, and successfully obtain the address of the targeted transaction to infer user identities, which shows the native blockchain cannot guarantee anonymity.

The proposed scheme blinds the user identities with $ID_i = (x_u + s)h(Id_i) + u \bmod p$, which relies on the partial key x_u of the current node i and the private key s of the trusted center. The values are respectively grasped by the users and the trusted center, other unauthorized nodes are not able to access them. Even the attacker obtains x_u and s, it is still difficult for him to retrieve the user identities through the one-way hash function $h(x)$.

6.2.3 Unforgeability Analysis

Unforgeability means that the node in the blockchain cannot impersonate others to generate the signature. In the blockchain scenario, the trusted center and the users may impersonate other identities to sign the messages. For the convenience, the current node is defined as i, and one of other nodes is defined as j. Unforgeability of the trusted center and other nodes will be analyzed separately.

For the first case, the trusted center impersonates one user identity to sign. Since the trusted center is updated based on Dynamic Bayesian Network, the metrics of the trusted center depends on feedback from other nodes. If the attacker breaks through the trusted center, it will inevitably show some abnormal behavior characters, such as multiple re-entry, unauthorized access, etc. The credibility of the trusted center will be adjusted, which may strip the trusted center out of the blockchain. Because of $Sc_n(x_i, x_j, W(w, t), t) = Sc_n(x_i, x_j, W(w, t-1), t-1) \times \delta(t), W(w, t) - W(w, t-1) = \Phi \times \delta(t), W(w, t) - W(w, t-1) = \Phi$, it means that the credibility of the trusted center will decline without other positive incentive. The rigorous measurement ensures the security of the trusted center.

If the trusted center personally conducts the attack, and impersonate the user node i, he can obtain some related information such as $<c_s, f(x)>$ and UL. The trusted center TC randomly selects $u_i' \in Z_p^*$, and because of $x_i' = u_i'$, he can obtain the private key $u_s' = x_i' + y_i'$, and $X_i' = u_i'G$. After that, he can obtain the public key $u_p' = u_s'G$. $<r_i, s_i, ID_i>$ and $<X_i, Id_i, ID_i>$ for UL have been backed up, which need to check the integrity. However, the prerequisite to pass the verification must satisfy $X_i' = X_i$, which denotes that the trusted center TC must obtain $X_i = X'_i = u'_i G$ and u'_i. The difficulty is equivalent to the discrete logarithm of the elliptic curve which is computationally hard.

For the second scenario, the node j poses as the node i for signature. At this time, the node j only knows ID_i of the node i. The node j randomly selects $u'_i \in Z^*_p$, and generates the private key $u'_s = x'_i + y'_i$, $X'_i = u'_i G$, and the public key $u'_p = u'_s G$. However, the trusted center has backed up the information whose integrity will be checked. It shows that the process is computationally hard.

7   Performance Analysis

The difficulty of the blockchain threshold group signature scheme proposed in the paper is equivalent to the discrete logarithm of the elliptic curve. Compared with those schemes based on the large number decomposition and discrete logarithm, the proposed scheme can obtain the higher security level with the shorter key length. In order to compare with existing signature schemes, the following symbols are defined (Table 3).

Table 3. Symbols of operations in the proposed scheme

Symbols	Description
C_m	Modular multiplication
C_{ec_m}	Elliptic curve scalar multiplication
C_{ec_a}	Elliptic curve addition
C_i	Modular inverse
C_h	Hash

Due to low overhead of modular addition and modular subtraction, those operations will not be considered in the paper. According to [14], $C_{ec\_m} \approx 29C_m$, $C_{ec\_a} \approx 0.12C_m$, the following parts will compare the proposed scheme with other schemes uniformly.

The paper will conduct the performance analysis from three aspects that are registration, generation and verification of the signature. In addition, when calculating the complexity of the hash function, it counts only once for the same tasks. The computational complexity is shown in Table 4.

Table 4. Computational complexity of the proposed scheme

Steps	Computational complexity	Total
Register	$(3+t)C_{ec\_m} + tC_{ec\_a} + C_h$	$(87 + 29.12t)C_m + C_h$
Signature generation	$4tC_{ec\_m} + 2(t-1)C_{ec\_a} + 3tC_m + (t+1)C_h$	$(119.24t - 0.24)C_m + (t+1)C_h$
Signature verification	$C_{ec\_m} + C_{ec\_a} + C_h$	$29.12C_m + C_h$

When comparing with existing threshold signature methods, two aspects that are generation and verification of the signature will be considered. The paper utilizes the comparison method presented in [13]. It should be noted that only the cryptographic schemes based on the elliptic curve are considered.

Table 5 is the comparison result of the computational complexity. From the table, we can infer that for the signature generation, [15] is superior to the proposed scheme, and for the signature verification, it is inferior. In the blockchain, the trusted center must undertake most of the computation. The proposed metrics consider the computing power, which makes the selected one own the abundant resource to increase the system throughout. On the other hand, the latter one does not realize the cancellation operation, which is not suitable for the blockchain.

Table 5. Comparison of computational complexity

Algorithms	Signature generation	Signature verification
Proposed	$(119.24t - 0.24)C_m + (t+1)C_h$	$29.12C_m + C_h$
Algorithm in [30]	$(209.36t - 87.88)C_m + C_h + tC_i$	$145.36C_m + C_h$
Algorithm in [14]	$(90.24t - 0.24)C_m + (t+1)C_h + tC_i$	$(58.12 + t)C_m + C_h$
Algorithm in [16]	$(235.12t - 0.12)C_m + (t+1)C_h$	$87.24C_m + C_h$
Algorithm in [15]	$(88.24t - 0.24)C_m + (t+1)C_h$	$58.12C_m + C_h$
Algorithm in [13]	$(119.24t - 0.24)C_m + (t+1)C_h$	$58.24C_m + C_h$

Compared with [13], the proposed scheme introduces the strategy based on Dynamic Bayesian Network to construct the trusted centers to enhance the security. For uneven distribution of computing resource in the blockchain, the proposed scheme is able to assign those tasks with high complexity to the trusted center, which can reduce the overhead of communication and effectively increase the system throughput. In addition, the identities have been blinded in the proposed design to achieve anonymity.

The signature generation process in [14, 30] contains the modular inverse operation, which has the high computational complexity, and [30] does not have the revoking operation. The proposed scheme can achieve the better result than [16] in the process of signature generation and signature verification.

In summary, the proposed method has the higher degree of anonymity and unforgeability that involves opening and revoking signatures. Compared with existing threshold group signature schemes, the proposed one has the lower computational complexity.

8 Conclusion

When applying the threshold group signature scheme to the blockchain to achieve the voting function, we will face up to the untrustworthy of the trusted center and the leakage of the user signatures. The paper proposes a trusted center selection scheme based on Dynamic Bayesian Network, which considers the time factor to perform the trusted metrics. The paper introduces the history interaction window, the aging factor and the penalty factor, and aggregates the direct and indirect credibility to form the dynamic metrics.

The voting scheme based on the threshold group signature for the isomerized blockchain is proposed. Through cooperation of users and the trusted centers to generate the group signature, the computational difficulty is equivalent to the discrete logarithms of the elliptic curve. The new design blinds and backs up the user identities. Security analysis shows that the proposed scheme can achieve the higher level of anonymity and effectively resist the impersonation attack. Computational complexity analysis shows that the cost of this scheme is low when adapting to the blockchain.

Acknowledgments. This work was supported by the National Natural Science Funds (U1304614, U1204703), the construct program of the key discipline in Zhengzhou Normal University, aid program for Science and Technology Innovative Research Team of Zhengzhou Normal University, Henan Province Education Science Plan General Topic "Research on Trusted Degree Certification Based on Blockchain" ((2018)-JKGHYB-0279).

References

1. Liehuang, Z., et al.: Survey on privacy preserving techniques for blockchain technology. J. Comput. Res. Dev. **54**(10), 2170–2186 (2017)
2. Miers, I., Garman, C., Green, M., Rubin, A.D.: Zerocoin: anonymous distributed E-Cash from Bitcoin. In: IEEE Symposium on Security and Privacy, San Francisco, pp. 397–411 (2013)
3. Baohua, Y., Chang, C.: Principle. Design and Application of Blockchain. China Machine Press, Beijing (2017)
4. Biryukov, A., Khovratovich, D., Pustogarov, I.: Deanonymisation of Clients in Bitcoin P2P Network. Eprint Arxiv, 15–29 (2014)
5. Koshy, P., Koshy, D., Mcdaniel, P.: An analysis of anonymity in Bitcoin using P2P network traffic. In: International Conference on Financial Cryptography and Data Security, Barbados, pp. 469–485 (2014)
6. Marsh, S.P.: Formalising trust as computational concept (1994)
7. Almenarez, F., Marin, A., Diaz, D., Sanchez, J.: Developing a model for trust management in pervasive devices. In: IEEE International Conference on Pervasive Computing and Communications Workshops, p. 267 (2006)
8. Melaye, D., Demazeau, Y.: Bayesian dynamic trust model. In: International Central and Eastern European Conference on Multi-Agent Systems, Budapest 2005, pp. 480–489 (2005)
9. Sun, Y.L., Yu, W., Han, Z., Liu, K.J.R.: Information theoretic framework of trust modeling and evaluation for ad hoc networks. IEEE J. Sel. Areas Commun. **24**(2), 305–317 (2006)
10. Ahamed, S.I., Sharmin, M.: A trust-based secure service discovery (TSSD) model for pervasive computing. Comput. Commun. **31**(18), 4281–4293 (2008)
11. Chun-Mei, G., Qiang, J., Huai-Min, W., Quan-Yuan, W.: Repeated game theory based penalty-incentive mechanism in internet-based virtual computing environment. J. Softw. **21** (12), 3042–3055 (2010)
12. Liang, H., Wu, W.: Research of trust evaluation model based on dynamic Bayesian network. J. Commun. **34**(9), 68–76 (2013)

13. Liquan, C., Zheng, Z., Muyang, W., Xiaoyan, S.: A threadhold group signature scheme for mobile internet application. Chin. J. Comput. **41**(5), 1–18 (2018)
14. Chen, T.S., Hsiao, T.C., Chen, T.L.: An efficient threshold group signature scheme. In: TENCON 2004, pp. 13–16 (2004)
15. Ya, P.: Research on Threshold Digital Signature Theory and Application. Zhongshan University, China (2010)
16. Dong, X., Jiajia, L., Zhonghua, S.: A new threshold signature scheme based on elliptic curve cryptosystem. J. Hangzhou Norm. Univ. (Nat. Sci. Ed.) **12**(1), 57–60 (2013)
17. Liu, H.W., Xie, W.X., Jian-Ping, Y.U., Peng, Z.: Efficiency identity-based threshold group signature scheme. J. Commun. **30**(5), 122–127 (2009)
18. Jie, Y., Xuri, Y., Wujun, Z.: Research on group signature with threshold value based on elliptic curve. J. Southeast Univ. (Nat. Sci. Ed.) **38**, 43–46 (2008)
19. Chung, Y.F., Chen, T.L., Chen, T.S., Chen, C.S.: A study on efficient group-oriented signature schemes for realistic application environment. Int. J. Innov. Comput. Inf. Control. Ijicic **8**(4), 2713–2727 (2012)
20. Gennaro, R., Jarecki, S., Krawczyk, H., Rabin, T.: Robust threshold DSS signatures. In: Maurer, U. (ed.) EUROCRYPT 1996. LNCS, vol. 1070, pp. 354–371. Springer, Heidelberg (1996). https://doi.org/10.1007/3-540-68339-9_31
21. Gennaro, R., Jarecki, S., Krawczyk, H., Rabin, T.: Secure distributed key generation for discrete-log based cryptosystems. In: International Conference on Theory and Application of Cryptographic Techniques, pp. 295–310 (1999)
22. Bonneau, J., et al.: Securing Bitcoin wallets via a new DSA/ECDSA threshold signature scheme (2015). https://www.cs.princeton.edu/~stevenag/threshold_sigs.pdf
23. Si, C.: Research on Anonymity and Key Management of Bitcoin. Xidian University, Xi'an (2017)
24. Stinson, D.R., Dengguo, F.: Cryptography Theory and Practice. Publishing House of Electronics Industry, Beijing (2016)
25. Abe, M., Fujisaki, E.: How to date blind signatures. In: Kim, K., Matsumoto, T. (eds.) ASIACRYPT 1996. LNCS, vol. 1163, pp. 244–251. Springer, Heidelberg (1996). https://doi.org/10.1007/BFb0034851
26. Shamir, A.: How to Share a Secret. Commun. ACM **22**(11), 612–613 (1979)
27. Blakley, G.R.: Safeguarding cryptographic keys. In: AFIPS, p. 313 (1979)
28. Boldyreva, A.: Threshold signatures, multisignatures and blind signatures based on the Gap-Diffie-Hellman-Group Signature Scheme. In: International Workshop on Public Key Cryptography, pp. 31–46 (2003)
29. Cai, Y., Zhang, X., Jiang, N.: A novel identity-based threshold signature. Acta Electron. Sin. **37**(4A), 102–105 (2009)
30. Dahshan, H., Kamal, A., Rohiem, A.: A threshold blind digital signature scheme using elliptic curve dlog-based cryptosystem. In: Vehicular Technology Conference, Glasgow, pp. 1–5 (2015)

HABKS: Hierarchical Attribute-Based Keyword Search on Outsourcing Data

Jingyang Yu[1,2], Wenchang Shi[1], Bo Qin[1(✉)], and Bin Liang[1]

[1] School of Information, Renmin University of China, Beijing 100190, China
boqin@ruc.edu.cn
[2] School of Computer and Information Engineering,
Henan University, Kaifeng 475004, China

Abstract. Searching over encrypted data is a critical operation to enforce the encryption-before-outsourcing mechanism, which is a fundamental solution to protect data privacy in the untrusted cloud environment. However, most of the existing searchable encryption solutions suffer from the problem of key management and the problem of flexible and fine-grained access control in multi-data owners and multi-data users environment.

Therefore, we propose a hierarchical attribute-based keyword search (HABKS) scheme. Our scheme not only realizes the order management of the key because of its hierarchical structure, but also implements a flexible and fine-grained access control depending on CP-ABE for encrypting keywords indexes and data files. We formally prove the security of HABKS, and then analyze the performance of HABKS. Finally, we implement HABKS scheme with comprehensive experiments. Experiment results show that it is efficient and flexible for searching encrypted data in cloud.

Keywords: Cloud computing · Outsourcing data · Searchable encryption
Hierarchical authorization · Attribute-Based Encryption

1 Introduction

In nowadays ages of big data, enterprises and users who own mass data often choose to outsource their data to cloud facilities [1]. Data outsourcing can help data owners obtain the high-quality on-demand services. It also reduces the cost of computing and storage. However, outsourcing also implies that the owners will lose the absolute control over the data. Therefore, the security and privacy problem of outsourcing data is becoming more and more prominent.

Encryption-before-outsourcing has been considered a basic solution to protect data privacy from the cloud server [2]. The use of encrypted data in cloud, such as searching, is a challenging task. Recently, researchers have proposed many ciphertext search solutions [3–9], through different encryption technologies. However, some new challenges for searchable encryption have been proposed in a complex cloud environment and a big data scenario. For example, how to effectively manage the private key of a good deal of users in complex cloud? How to handle flexible and fine-grained access control in a big data scenario? The above solutions cannot solve these problems.

© Springer Nature Singapore Pte Ltd. 2019
H. Zhang et al. (Eds.): CTCIS 2018, CCIS 960, pp. 203–219, 2019.
https://doi.org/10.1007/978-981-13-5913-2_13

Attribute-based encryption (ABE) is a popular encryption method [10–13]. Because of the fine-grained access control property of ABE, it has been introduced into SE, e.g. [7, 8]. Zheng et al. put forword a keyword search algorithm ABKS based on ABE [7]. However, specific attribute expression and access control aren't given, and user revocation isn't involved in [7]. Sun et al. implemented the access control on file level [8], but its access structure of encryption index is composed of a series of properties connected by AND. The search authority way is a coarse-grained user list, and flexible access control and search authorization of sensitive data cann't be implemented. User revocation is implemented by the proxy heavy encryption and lazy encryption technology in [8]. Because of the large amount of computing, user revocation is delegated to cloud servers, which will bring potential safety hazard.

So we propose a hierarchical attribute-based keyword search (HABKS) scheme. HABKS scheme introduces a hierarchical structure to generate the keys. Moreover, HABKS scheme adopts CP-ABE [11] to encrypt keywords indexes and data files to achieve a fast search and a fine-grained access control.

Our contribution is as follows:

We propose HABKS based on CP-ABE. The scheme extends CP-ABE algorithm with a searchable encrypted index to implement fast search for encrypted data files and with a hierarchical structure to manage the keys of users. Meanwhile HABKS possesses the characteristic of fine-grained access control for CP-ABE.

We show an integrated search system over encrypted data in cloud based on HABKS scheme. The system gives support to hierarchical user grant, keyword and file encryption, trapdoor generation, encrypted index search, and file decryption in cloud computing.

We formally prove the security of HABKS based on the security of CP-ABE, and then analyze the theoretic computation complexity of HABKS.

Finally, comprehensive experiments of HABKS are implemented and performance evaluation is given.

The paper is organized as follows. In Sect. 2, we introduce some basic techniques which will be used later. In Sect. 3, we present our system model, security assumptions and design goals. In Sect. 4, we describe the construction of HABKS in details. After analyzing the security and performance of HABKS in Sect. 5, we give the conclusion in Sect. 6.

2   Preliminaries

The following is an introduction to the relevant knowledge used in our HABKS scheme.

2.1   Bilinear Maps

Suppose that G_0 and G_1 are two multiplicative cyclic groups of prime order p. Let g be a generator of G_0. The bilinear map e is defined as e: $G_0 \times G_0 \to G_1$. The bilinear map e satisfies the following properties:

- Bilinearity: for any u, v $\in G_0$ and a, b $\in Z_p$, we have $e(u^a, v^b) = e(u, v)^{ab}$.
- Non-degeneracy: $e(g, g) \neq 1$.

If both the group operation in G_0 and the bilinear map e: $G_0 \times G_0 \rightarrow G_1$ are efficiently computable, G_0 is considered as a bilinear group. Especially the map e is symmetric due to $e(g^a, g^b) = e(g, g)^{ab} = e(g^b, g^a)$.

2.2 Attribute-Based Encryption (ABE)

The concept of ABE was first introduced by Sahai and Waters [10]. In recent years, ABE is a popular encryption method for its fine-grained access control property. According to how to execute the access control policy, ABE are divided into two categories. One is key-policy attribute-based encryption (KP-ABE) [12]. Another is ciphertext-policy attribute-based encryption (CP-ABE) [11]. In CP-ABE schemes, the ciphertext is encrypted with an access control tree designed by an cipherer, and the corresponding decryption key is generated for an attribute set. The decryption key can decrypt the ciphertext only if the relevant attribute set satisfies the access control tree. Many works about ABE have been proposed for various feature, such as more flexible version of this technique [13].

We construct a new search solution called HABKS on the outsourced encrypted data based on CP-ABE. Among the scheme, keywords and data files are encrypted depending on different access policies. Only if the attributes of data users satisfy access policies, they can search and access over the outsourced encrypted data.

2.3 Access Control Tree

We use access control trees [11] to describe access control policies in our scheme. Setting T be a tree describing an access structure. Each leaf of T is associated with an attribute. Each non-leaf node of T is a threshold gate. Every threshold gate is composed of its children and a threshold value. Let num_x be the children's number of node x, and k_x be its threshold value, then $0 < k_x \leq num_x$. When $k_x = 1$, the threshold gate represents OR. When $k_x = num_x$, it represents AND. Each leaf node of T represents an attribute. Its threshold value is equal to one, i.e. $k_x = 1$.

Let parent(x) denote the parent of node x. Let att(x) denote the attribute associated to leaf node x. Let lvs(T) denote the set of leaves of access tree T. T_x denote the subtree of T rooted at node x.

The parent of node x is expressed as parent(x). The label of node x is expressed as ind(x). The attribute of leaf node x is expressed as att(x). The set of leaves of access tree T is expressed as lvs(T). The subtree of T rooted at node x is expressed as T_x (e.g., $T_{root} = T$).

In the access tree T, the children of a node are numbered starting from 1. The number corresponding to node x is returned by the function index(x).

3   Problem Formulation

3.1   System Model

The cloud storage system has five characters. They are the trusted authority, domain authorities, data owners, data users, and cloud servers. These characters besides cloud servers are construct to a hierarchical structure. Figure 1 shows that.

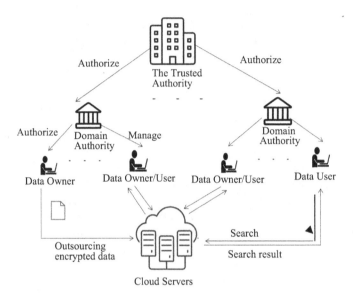

Fig. 1. System structure.

The trusted authority is in the top of the hierarchy. By it the keys is distributed to the lower domain authorities. Moreover, the trusted authority is the root authority and the manager of top-level domain authorities. A top-level domain authority is correspondence to a top-level organization, such as a local health bureau or a subcompany in a group company, meanwhile a lower-level domain authority is correspondence to a lower-level organization, such as a local hospital or a department of a subcompany. Data owners or users are administrated by the corresponding domain authority. For example, doctors are data owners or users under the authority domain of a hospital.

The cloud server provides data storage and search services. Data files are encrypted by data owners, and then uploaded to the cloud for storage. The encrypted data files in cloud can be shared among data users. Data users firstly search the encrypted index by keywords of their interest. Then if there are the encrypted data files of matching the searching in the cloud, the encrypted data files will be downloaded. Finally data users decrypt these files.

In the system, data owners and data users will be not always online. While the cloud servers, the trusted authority, and domain authorities are always online. We assume that storage and computing resources in the cloud are sufficient, and that the data files are read-only to data users.

3.2 Security Model

Suppose the cloud server (CS) is honest-but-curious. That is, the CS is honest about its compliance with the specified protocol, but is curious about the data privacy information available.

In the hierarchical structure, each party has a pair of keys. The trusted authority is the trust root. Domain authorities are authorized by the trusted authority. A domain authority is trusted by its users, but it may attempt to obtain the secret keys of out-of-scope users maliciously. It is possible for each user to attempt to access data both within and outside their access rights. Even some malicious users may collude with each other to try to access sensitive data outside their access rights.

In addition, the assumption is that the CS doesn't collude with the revoked malicious users to help them get unauthorized access. Moreover, all communication channels between the parties are protected by standard security protocols.

3.3 Design Goals

The following functions and security goals is achieved in our HABKS scheme:

Hierarchical Key Management: In a complex cloud data owners and data users are enormous commonly. How we manage the private key of enormous users is a very difficult problem in the cloud. In reality, a tree structure is a common form of organizational structure. Therefore, a tree structure for hierarchical key management is used in hierarchical key management.

Fine-Grained Access Control: In the big data environment, different access control policies is required by different data. How we meet the fine-grained access control is another very important issue facing enormous data. Only users who meet the access policy of owner-defined, can query on encrypted indexes and access encrypted search results. CP-ABE is an acknowledged fine-grained access control scheme. Here we use CP-ABE.

Security Goals: We expect that HABKS has the same security as CP-ABE. Directly, security means that the cloud gets nothing but the search results.

4 HABKS Construction

The HABKS scheme is presented in this section. HABKS implements hierarchical searchable encryption with hierarchical user grant. And we show how hierarchical user grant, file encryption, index encryption, encryption index search, and ciphertext decryption is implemented in HABKS scheme.

4.1   Algorithm Definition

The main algorithms of HABKS are as follows.

Setup(1^l) -> (PK, MK): The inputs of the Setup algorithm are the implicit security parameter l. The outputs are a public key PK and a master key MK.

KeyGen(PK, MK, S) -> SK: The inputs of the key generation algorithm are PK, MK and a attributes set S which describes the key. The outputs are the private key SK which is for a domain authority DA.

Delegate(SK, u, S_i) -> SK_i: For a lower domain authority DA_i or a new user u, the inputs of the delegate algorithm are SK and a subset S_i of S. The outputs are the private key SK_i for the lower domain authority DA_i or the user u.

EnIndex(PK, K, T_k) -> CK: A keyword $K(K \in KG)$ is encrypted with access control tree T_k.

EnFile(PK, F, T) -> CF: F is encrypted with access control tree T. Then the encrypted file CF and the encrypted keywords group CK are uploaded to the cloud by data owners.

Trapdoor(SK, w) -> TK: The inputs of the trapdoor algorithm are SK and searched keyword w. The output is a search token TK for w.

SearchIndex(CIndex, TK) -> RS: According to TK, the cloud servers search all encrypted keyword group indexes CIndex, and return a search result set RS to users.

Decrypt(CT, SK) -> F: Data user descrypts the ciphertext CT among RS using his key SK, and then get the original data file F.

4.2   Construction of HABKS Scheme

The main operations of HABKS consist of System Setup, Granting Top-Level Domain Authority, Granting New Domain Authority/User, Generating User Credential, Encrypting Data File and Index Record, Generating Trapdoor, Searching Index, and Decrypting Ciphertext. The concrete functions of different components is described as below.

System Setup: The algorithm of Setup(1^l) is called by the trusted authority to generate PK and MK. PK is public to other parties. MK is secret.

The algorithm of Setup(1^l) sets PK and MK as follows. Let G_0 and G_1 be cyclic groups of prime order p, and let g be a generator of G_0. Here p is an l-bits prime. A security parameter l will determine the size of the groups. Let e: $G_0 \times G_0 \rightarrow G_1$ denote the bilinear map. The bilinear map is represented by e: $G_0 \times G_0 \rightarrow G_1$. In addition, for modelling a random oracle, a hash function H_1: $\{0, 1\}^* \rightarrow G_0$ is adopted. H_1 will map any attribute to a random group element. Let H_2 be an one-way hash function. H_2 is represented as H_2: $\{0, 1\}^* \rightarrow Z_p$. We can randomly select a, b, c $\in Z_p$, and set

$$PM = \left(G_0, G_1, H_1, H_2, g, g^c, h = g^b, f = g^{1/b}, e(g,g)^a \right) \tag{1}$$

$$MK = (c, b, g^a) \tag{2}$$

Granting Top-Level Domain Authority: Whenever a new top-level DA need join the system, the validity of the DA must be verified by the trusted authority firstly. If it is valid, KeyGen(PK, MK, S) will be called to generate the key SK of DA. Here S is a set of attributes. The set is used to describe the key structure of DA. After getting the key SK, the DA can give authority to the next level domain authorities or users of its domain.

This algorithm firstly selects a random $r \in Z_p$ for the DA, which is also for the set S, and then selects random $r_i \in Z_p$, for each attribute $j \in S$. Finally, the key is computed for DA as follows.

$$SK = (S, D = g^{(a-r)/b}, D' = g^{(c-r)/b}, \forall j \in S : D_j = g^r \cdot H_1(j)^{r_j}, D'_j = g^{r_j}) \qquad (3)$$

Granting Lower Domain Authority or User: Whenever a new user u need join the system, the validity of the new entity must be verified by the administrating DA firstly. If it is true, the new attribute set Si with its role and a unique ID will be assigned. Take notice of that Si is a subset of S, i.e. $S_i \subseteq S$. DA calls Delegate (SK, u, S_i) to generate the SK_i of the new user u. The new SK_i is a secret key of S_i.

Similarly, if a new DA_i joins the system, the DA_i can give authority to the lower domain authorities/users of its domain, and then generates the corresponding secret keys.

This algorithm Delegate() randomly chooses $\tilde{r}$ and $\tilde{r}_k$, $\forall k \in S_i$. Here $SK = (S, D, \forall j \in S : D_j, D'_j)$. Then it creates a new SK as follows.

$$SK_i = (S_i, \widetilde{D} = D \cdot f^{(-\tilde{r})}, \widetilde{D'} = D' \cdot f^{(-\tilde{r})},$$
$$\forall k \in S_i : \widetilde{D}_k = D_k \cdot g^{\tilde{r}} \cdot H_1(k)^{\tilde{r}_k}, \widetilde{D'}_k = D'_k \cdot g^{\tilde{r}_k}) \qquad (4)$$

Encrypting Keywords Group and Data File: Before uploading, Data files and corresponding keywords group must be encrypted by the data owner. The process is as follows:

Pick a unique ID of a data file F.

Choose the keywords group KG of this data file F, then generate corresponding index record IR = (ID, KG).

Define a access tree T_k for the file index record IR, call the algorithm EnIndex(PK, K, Tk), encrypt each keyword $K(K \in KG)$ using T_k to return the ciphertext CK, and then get the encrypted keywords group CKG. The encrypted index record is denoted as CIR = (ID, CKG).

Define an access tree T for a data file F, call the algorithm EnFile (PK, F, T), encrypt data file F with the symmetric key DK to return CD, then encrypt DK with T to return the ciphetext CT, and finally get the encrypted file CF = (ID, CT, CD).

Upload the encrypted data files and corresponding index records to the cloud. Then the cloud build the encrypted index CIndex with the encrypted index records.

In the above process, EnFile() firstly chooses a polynomial q_x for each node x in T. These polynomials start from the root node R in a top-down manner. For each node x in T, we denote d_x as the degree of q_x, and $d_x = k_x - 1$.

Starting from R, select randomly $s \in Z_p$ and sets $q_R(0) = s$. Then, select d_R random numbers to define the polynomial q_R. Similarly, set $q_x(0) = q_{parent}(x)(index(x))$ and select d_x random numbers to define q_x for other node x.

Let Y be the leaf node set in T. Input the access tree T. Then the ciphertext CT is builded. The computing process is as follows.

$$CT = (T, \widetilde{C} = F \cdot e(g, g)^{a \cdot s}, C = h^s,$$
$$\forall y \in Y : C_y = g^{q_y(0)}, C'_y = H_1(att(y))^{q_y(0)}) \tag{5}$$

The algorithm EnIndex() chooses polynomials for access control tree T_k and deals with the polynomials parameters similar to the algorithm EnFile(). Let Y' be the leaf node set in T_k, R' be the root node of T_k, choose a random $d \in Z_p$. Input the access tree T_k. Then the ciphertext CK is constructed. The computing process is as follows.

$$CK = (T_k, \widetilde{M} = \left(g^c \cdot g^{b \cdot H_2(K)}\right)^d, M = g^{b \cdot s}, M' = g^d,$$
$$\forall y \in Y' : M_y = g^{q_y(0)}, M'_y = H_1att(y))^{q_y(0)}) \tag{6}$$

Generating Trapdoor: An authorized data user calls this algorithm Trapdoor(SK, w) to generate a TK of keyword w. Here S is the attribute set in SK. Select a random $t \in Z_p$, a search token TK is computed as follows.

$$TK = (S, tok_1 = \left(g^{b \cdot H_2(w)}\right)^t, tok_2 = D^t = g^{\frac{(c-r)}{b} \cdot t}, tok_3 = g^t,$$
$$\forall k \in S : A_k = D_k^t, B_k = D_k'^t) \tag{7}$$

According to the actual situation, the input SK can be replaced by SK_i. At the same time, S is also replaced by S_i. At this point, a search token TK is computed as follows.

$$TK_i = (S_i, \widetilde{tok}_1 = \left(g^{b \cdot H_2(w)}\right)^t, \widetilde{tok}_2 = \widetilde{D}'^t = g^{\frac{(c-r-\widetilde{r})}{b} \cdot t}, \widetilde{tok}_3 = g^t,$$
$$\forall k \in S_i : \widetilde{A}_k = \widetilde{D}_k^t, \widetilde{B}_k = \widetilde{D}_k'^t) \tag{8}$$

Searching Encrypted Index: Assuming that the result set RS is an empty set, the cloud server calls the algorithm SearchIndex(Cindex,TK), and searches respectively every encrypted index record CIR in encrypted index CIndex.

Given attribute set S as specified in TK, choose $S' \subseteq S$. S' meets T_k which is specified in CK.

If S' is null, return 0; or else, for each $i \in S'$, we compute E_v or $\widetilde{E}_v$:

$$E_v = e(A_i, M_i)/e(B_i, M'_i) = e(g, g)^{r \cdot t \cdot q_v(0)} \tag{9}$$

$$\tilde{E}_v = e\left(\tilde{A}_i, M_i\right)/e\left(\tilde{B}_i, M_j'\right) = e(g, g)^{(r+\tilde{r})\cdot t\cdot q_v(0)} \tag{10}$$

Where att(v) = i for v ∈ lvs(T). Compute $E_R = e(g, g)^{r\cdot d\cdot t}$ or $\tilde{E}_R = e(g, g)^{(r+\tilde{r})\cdot d\cdot t}$ using the following decryption method, where R is the root of T_k.

$$e\left(\tilde{M}, tok_3\right) = e(M', tok_1) \cdot E_R \cdot e(M, tok_2) \tag{11}$$

$$e\left(\tilde{M}, \widetilde{tok}_3\right) = e\left(M', \widetilde{tok}_1\right) \cdot \tilde{E}_R \cdot e\left(M, \widetilde{tok}_2\right) \tag{12}$$

If the above formula (11) or (12) is satisfied, it means that the index record CK satisfy the search criteria, the corresponding encryption file is added to the result set RS. Otherwise, continue to the next index record. Finally the search result set RS is returned to the user.

Decrypting Ciphertext: According to the result set RS of searching index, the data users get the ID set of all files related with search keyword w, and then find the ciphertext CF corresponding to each ID. Next, the data user calls the algorithm Decrypt(CF, SK) to first decrypt the ciphertext CT using SK to get the decrypted DEK, and then decrypt the CD using DEK to get the original data file F.

Firstly DecryptNode(CT, SK, x) is defined as a recursive algorithm. The inputs of the algorithm are a ciphertext $CT = \left(T, \tilde{C}, C, \forall y \in Y : C_y, C_y'\right)$, a private key SK, and a node x in T.

If x is a leaf node, let i = att(x), and compute as below:
If i ∈ S, then

$$\begin{aligned} \text{DecryptNode(CT, SK, x)} &= \frac{e(A_i, C_x)}{e(B_i, C_x')} \\ &= \frac{e\left(g^r \cdot H_1(i)^{r_i}, g^{q_x(0)}\right)}{e\left(g^{r_i}, H_1(i)^{q_x(0)}\right)} \\ &= e(g, g)^{r\cdot q_x(0)} \end{aligned} \tag{13}$$

If i ∉ S, then DecryptNode(CT, SK, x) = ⊥.

The recursive case must be considered when x is a non-leaf node. DecryptNode (CT, SK, x) is processed as follows: Let z be a children of x. For each z, DecryptNode (CT, SK, z) is called, and the output is denoted as F_z. Let S_x be an arbitrary k_x-sized set of child nodes z such that $F_z \neq \perp$. If no such set exists, the node was not satisfied and ⊥ is returned.

If such set exists, we compute using the Lagrange coefficient as follows.

$$
\begin{aligned}
F_x &= \prod_{z \hat{l} S_x} F_z^{\Delta_{i,s'_x(0)}}, \text{ where } \frac{i = \text{index}(z)}{S'_x = \{\text{index}(z) : z \in S_x\}} \\
&= \prod_{z \in S_x} \left(e(g,g)^{r \cdot q_z(0)} \right)^{\Delta_{i,s'_x(0)}} \\
&= \prod_{z \in S_x} \left(e(g,g)^{r \cdot q_{parent(z)}(index(z))} \right)^{\Delta_{i,s'_x(0)}} \text{ (by construction)} \qquad (14) \\
&= \prod_{z \in S_x} \left(e(g,g)^{r \cdot q_x(i)} \right)^{\Delta_{i,s'_x(0)}} \\
&= e(g,g)^{r \cdot q_z(0)} \text{ (using polynomial interpolation)}
\end{aligned}
$$

Then the result is returned.

After our function DecryptNode is defined, the decryption algorithm can be defined. Firstly the decryption algorithm simply calls the function on R of T. Then, if S satisfies T, we set $A = \text{DecryptNode}(CT, SK, r) = e(g,g)^{rqR(0)} = e(g,g)^{rt}$. Finally, the algorithm can decrypt by computing as follows.

$$
\frac{\tilde{C}}{A \cdot e(C,D)} = \frac{\tilde{C}}{e(g,g)^{r \cdot t} \cdot e(h^t, g^{(a-r) \cdot b})} = F \qquad (15)
$$

5   Performance Evaluation

Firstly we analyze the security of HABKS. Then we discuss theoretic computation complexity of each step in HABKS. Finally, we give the result of the experimental implementation.

5.1   Security Analysis

Because data file encryption and index encryption in HABKS are based on CP-ABE, the security analysis of HABKS is carried out on the basis of CP-ABE's security.

We have the following conclusion about the safety of our scheme.

Theorem 1: If no polytime adversary can break the security of CP-ABE with non-negligible advantage, then no polytime adversary can break the security of HABKS with nonnegligible advantage.

Proof: Assume that adversary A has a nonnegligible advantage against HABKS scheme. Next, Let's demonstrate how to construct adversary B. B can break CP-ABE scheme with nonnegligible advantage.

Initialization. The adversary B gets the public key of CP-ABE $PK' = (G_0, G_1, H_1, H_2,$
$g, g^c, h = g^b, f = g^{1/b}, e(g, g)^a)$, but B doesn't know the corresponding private key
(c, b, g^a).

Setup. B selects randomly $t \in Z_p$, and calculates the public key of HABKS from PK' as
$PK = (G_0, G_1, H_1, H_2, g, g^c, h_1 = g^b, h_2 = g^{tb}, f_1 = g^{1/b}, f_2 = g^{1/tb}, e(g, g)^a)$.
That is, the adversary B sets $b_1 = b$ and $b_2 = tb$. Then the adversary B get the PK.

Phase 1. B answers private key queries. Assume a set S doesn't satisfy T*. The private
key query associated with S is sent to B. To answer the query, B sends two private key
queries to the CP-ABE challenger for S. Then B gets two different private keys:

$$SK = (S, D = g^{(a-r)/b}, D' = g^{(c-r)/b},$$
$$\forall j \in S : D_j = g^r \cdot H_1(j)^{r_j}, D'_j = g^{r_j}) \tag{16}$$

$$SK' = (S, D = g^{(a-r')/b}, D' = g^{(c-r')/b},$$
$$\forall j \in S : D_j = g^{r'} \cdot H_1(j)^{r'_j}, D'_j = g^{r'_j}) \tag{17}$$

According to SK and SK', B can obtain $D = g^{(r'-r)/b}$. B randomly selects
$t, t_j \in Z_p$. Let $r^* = t - r'$ and $r'' = t_j - r'_j$. In this way, B can export the private key
requested by A below.

$$SK^* = (D = g^{(a-r)/b}, D' = g^{(c-r)/b},$$
$$\forall j \in S : D_j = g^{r^*} \cdot H_1(j)^{r''}, D'_j = g^{r''}) \tag{18}$$

So, the adversary A gets the private key.

Challenge. When Phase 1 ends, A outputs an access tree T and two challenge messages $M_0, M_1 \in G$. B sends the two messages to CP-ABE challenger. The challenge
ciphertext CT sent to B is as follows.

$$CT = (T, \tilde{C} = M_b \cdot e(g, g)^{a \cdot s}, C = h^s,$$
$$\forall y \in Y : C_y = g^{q_y(0)}, C'_y = H(att(y))^{q_y(0)}) \tag{19}$$

According to CT, B calculates the challenge ciphertext CT* for A as follows:

$$CT^* = (T, \tilde{C} = M_b \cdot e(g, g)^{a \cdot s}, C = h_1^s, \overline{C} = h_2^s,$$
$$\forall y \in Y : C_y = g^{q_y(0)}, C'_y = H(att(y))^{q_y(0)}) \tag{20}$$

So, A gets CT*.

Phase 2. The adversary A sends unsent queries in Phase 1. Then the response of the adversary B is similar to Phase 1.

Guess. At the end, A outputs a guess $b' \in \{0, 1\}$. Next B outputs b' and ends the game. On the grounds of the security model, B has the following advantages against HABKS.

$$Adv_B = |Pr[b = b'] - 1/2| = Adv_A \qquad (21)$$

The above result shows that B has nonnegligible advantage against CP-ABE. The above process has realized the proof.

Theorem 2: If CP-ABE is secure against chosen-plaintext attack, HABKS is selectively secure against chosen-keyword attack.

The proof of Theorem 2 is similar to [7].

5.2   Performance Analysis

The computation complexity of main algorithms in HABKS scheme is discussed below.

System Setup. When the system starts, several exponentiation operations are used in the process of generating PK and MK. So the computation complexity of this step is O(1).

Granting Top-Level Domain Authority. The main purpose of this step is to calculate the master key SK. $SK = (S, D, D', \forall j \in S : D_j, D'_j)$, where S is a attributes set associated with a domain authority. Let N be the number of attributes in S, $1 \le j \le N$. Then the calculation of SK mainly includes two exponentiations for each attribute of S. The computation complexity of this step is O(2N).

Granting Lower Domain Authority/User. The purpose of this step is also to calculate the secret key SK_i. The secret key SK_i is in the form of $SK_i = \left(S_i, \widetilde{D}, \widetilde{D}', \forall k \in S_i : \widetilde{D}_k, \widetilde{D}'_k\right)$, where S_i is the attribute set of a new user or domain authority, and $S_i \subseteq S$. Similar to the previous step, the computation complexity of this step is O(2n), where n is the attribute number of S_i.

Encrypting Keywords and Data File. Since a data file is encrypted with a symmetric key, its computational complexity depends on the file size and the selected symmetric encryption algorithm. The symmetric key is encrypted with an access tree T to obtain the ciphertext CT. The calculation process of CT includes two exponentiations for each leaf node in T. Let Y be the leaf nodes set of T. So the computation complexity of encrypting a file is O(2|Y|).

The complexity of encrypting an index depends on the number of keywords in each index entry and the number of index entries. Similarly, Encrypting an index entry with an access tree T_k also includes two exponentiations per leaf node in T_k. Let Y' be the leaf nodes of T_k. So the computation complexity of encrypting an index entry is O(2|Y'|).

Generating Trapdoor. The trapdoor TK is in the form of $TK = (S, tok_1, tok_2, tok_3, \forall k \in S : A_k, B_k)$, where S is the attributes set of a data user. Let N be the attribute number of S, $1 \leq k \leq N$. Then the computation of TK includes two exponentiations for each attribute in S. So the computation complexity of this step is O(2N).

Searching Encrypted Index. The complexity of searching on encrypted index CIndex depends on the number of index entries, the structure of the index and search method.

5.3 Implementation

A multilevel HABKS has been implemented that is based on the CP-ABE toolkit [14]. The CP-ABE toolkit was developed using the Pairing-Based Cryptography library [15]. Then we carried out comprehensive experiments on a computer which is dual core 3.20 GHz CPU and 4 GB RAM. The experimental data are analyzed and the statistical data are given.

Private key generation operation is associated with the attribute number of the attribute set. The key is generated by function KeyGen or function Delegate. Figure 2 shows the time required by function KeyGen to generate a private key for different number of attributes. Figure 3 shows the time required by function Delegate to generate a private key for different number of attributes. The cost of private key generation operation increases linearly with the number of attributes in the attributes set.

When the attribute number is identical, the time of generating a private key are roughly the same for function KeyGen and function Delegate as Fig. 4 show.

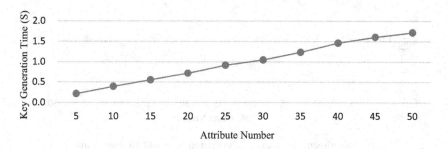

Fig. 2. Experiments on key generation.

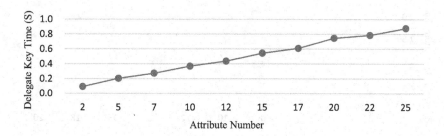

Fig. 3. Experiments on delegate key generation.

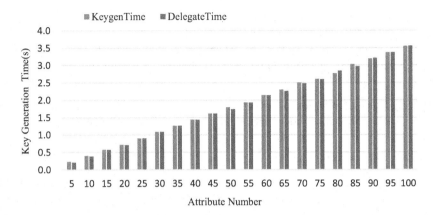

Fig. 4. KeygenTime VS DelegateTime.

Trapdoor generation operation is associated with the number of searched keywords and the number of attributes set for a data user who searches the encrypted index. The operation time is determined by the number of the above keywords and attributes. When the number of searched keywords is fixed to be 2, the trapdoor generation time grows linearly with the number of attribute set for a data user as Fig. 5 shows. When the number of the attribute set is fixed to be 10, the trapdoor generation time grows linearly with the number of searched keywords as Fig. 6 shows.

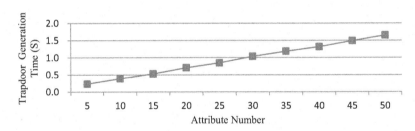

Fig. 5. Experiments on trapdoor generation time and attribute number.

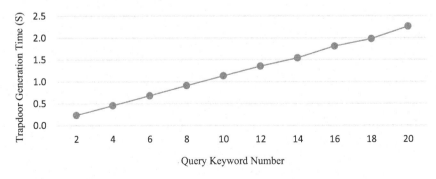

Fig. 6. Experiments on trapdoor generation time and query keyword number.

Encrypted index search operation is associated with the number of searched keywords, the number of keywords in each encrypted file, and the number of leaf nodes in the access tree of the index. Note that the keywords for each encrypted file form an index entry. In addition, the operation is related to the index structure and the number of encrypted files. In our experiment, we assumed that there was only one encrypted file, used a linear structure to store the encrypted keywords group of each file, and the attribute number was fixed to 10. Figure 7 shows that the query time increases linearly with the number of searched keywords. The cost also increases linearly with the number of keywords in each index entry as shown in Fig. 8.

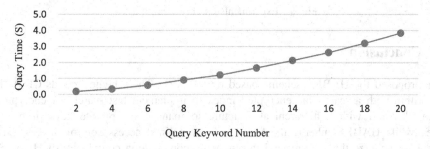

Fig. 7. Experiments on query operation.

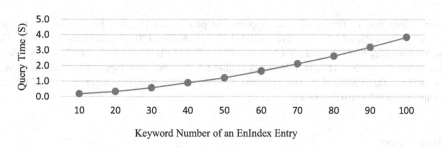

Fig. 8. Experiments on query operation.

Index encryption operation is completed by the data owner on the client side. The data owner encrypts the keyword group of a file, and uploads to the cloud with the corresponding encrypted file. The cloud puts the encrypted keyword group in an index and creates a pointer to it and the corresponding encrypted file to form an index term. The time for this encrypting every index entry depends on the keyword number in every index entry and the leaf node number in the access tree of the index. According to the keywords and leaf nodes number, the time required to encrypt the index is shown in Fig. 9. We can see the cost increases with the leaf node number and the keyword number.

Results of the above figures conform to the preceding theoretic analysis.

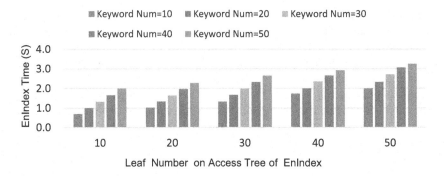

Fig. 9. Experiments on encrypting index

6 Conclusion

We proposed the HABKS scheme based on CP-ABE. The scheme extends CP-ABE algorithm with a searchable encrypted index to implement fast search for encrypted data files and with a hierarchical structure to manage the private keys of users. Meanwhile HABKS inherits the feature of fine-grained access control of CP-ABE. Then we analyze the security and the theoretic computation complexity of HABKS. Finally, We implement comprehensive experiments of HABKS. Experiment results show that it is efficient and flexible for searching encrypted data in cloud.

Acknowledgments. This work was supported in part by the National Nature Science Foundation of China (Grant NO. 61472429, 61070192, 91018008, 61303074, 61170240, 61772538), the National Key R&D Program of China (Grant No. 2017YFB1400700), Beijing Nature Science Foundation (Grant No. 4122041), National High-Tech Research Development Program of China (Grant No. 2007AA01Z414), and National Science and Technology Major Project of China (Grant No. 2012ZX01039-004).

References

1. Shan, Z., Ren, K., Blanton, M.: Practical secure computation outsourcing: a survey. ACM Comput. Surv. **51**(2), 31 (2017)
2. Kamara, S., Lauter, K.: Cryptographic cloud storage. In: Sion, R., et al. (eds.) FC 2010. LNCS, vol. 6054, pp. 136–149. Springer, Heidelberg (2010). https://doi.org/10.1007/978-3-642-14992-4_13
3. Song, D.X., Wagner, D., Perrig, A.: Practical techniques for searches on encrypted data. In: Proceeding 2000 IEEE Symposium on Security and Privacy, pp. 44–55. IEEE, Berkeley (2000)
4. Boneh, D., Di Crescenzo, G., Ostrovsky, R., Persiano, G.: Public key encryption with keyword search. In: Cachin, C., Camenisch, J.L. (eds.) EUROCRYPT 2004. LNCS, vol. 3027, pp. 506–522. Springer, Heidelberg (2004). https://doi.org/10.1007/978-3-540-24676-3_30

5. Yu, S., Wang, C., Ren, K., Lou, W.: Achieving secure, scalable, and fine-grained data access control in cloud computing. In: 2010 Proceedings IEEE INFOCOM, pp. 1–9. IEEE, San Diego (2010)

6. Li, M., Yu, S., Zheng, Y., Ren, K., Lou, W.: Scalable and secure sharing of personal health records in cloud computing using attribute-based encryption. IEEE Trans. Parallel Distrib. Syst. **24**(1), 131–143 (2013)

7. Zheng, Q., Xu, S., Ateniese, G.: VABKS: verifiable attribute-based keyword search over outsourced encrypted data. In: IEEE INFOCOM 2014-IEEE Conference on Computer Communications, pp. 522–530. IEEE, Toronto (2014)

8. Sun, W., et al.: Protecting your right: attribute-based keyword search with fine-grained owner-enforced search authorization in the cloud. In: IEEE INFOCOM 2014-IEEE Conference on Computer Communications, pp. 226–234. IEEE, Toronto (2014)

9. Fu, Z., et al.: Privacy-preserving smart semantic search based on conceptual graphs over encrypted outsourced data. IEEE Trans. Inf. Forensics Secur. **12**(8), 1874–1884 (2017)

10. Sahai, A., Waters, B.: Fuzzy identity based encryption. In: Cramer, R. (ed.) Advances in Cryptology – EUROCRYPT 2005, LNCS, vol. 3494, pp. 457–473. Springer, Berlin, Heidelberg (2005). https://doi.org/10.1007/11426639_27

11. Bethencourt, J., Sahai, A., Waters, B.: Ciphertext-policy attribute-based encryption. In: 2007 IEEE Symposium on Security and Privacy, pp. 321–334. IEEE, Berkeley (2007)

12. Goyal, V., Pandey, O., Sahai, A., Waters, B.: Attribute-based encryption for fine-grained access control of encrypted data. In: Proceedings of the 13th ACM Conference on Computer and Communications Security, pp. 89–98. ACM, New York (2006)

13. Wan, Z., Liu, J., Deng, R.H.: HASBE: a hierarchical attribute-based solution for flexible and scalable access control in cloud computing. IEEE Trans. Inf. Forensics Secur. **7**(2), 743–754 (2012)

14. CP-ABE toolkit. http://acsc.csl.sri.com/cpabe/

15. Pairing-Based Cryptography library. http://crypto.stanford.edu/pbc/

A Trusted Measurement Model
for Mobile Internet

Yong Wang[1], Jiantao Song[2(✉)], and Jia Lou[3]

[1] Information Technology Department,
Beijing Capital International Airport Co., Ltd., Beijing, China
[2] Faculty of Information Technology, Beijing University of Technology,
Beijing 100124, China
volltekka@126.com
[3] China International Data System Co., Ltd., Beijing, China
loujia@ec.com.cn

Abstract. With the explosive development of the mobile Internet, the security threats faced by the mobile Internet have grown rapidly in recent years. Since the normal operation of the mobile Internet depends on the trust between nodes, the existing trusted measurement model cannot fully and dynamically evaluate mobile Internet computing nodes, and the trust transmission has a great deal of energy consumption. Aiming at above problems, this paper proposes a trusted measurement model combining static measurement and node behavior measurement. The model is based on the computing environment measurement of the mobile Internet computing node, and is also based on node behavior measurement, combining direct and recommended trust values to complete the measurement of nodes. It can more objectively reflect the trust degree of nodes, effectively detecting malicious nodes, and ensuring the normal operation of mobile Internet services. The simulation experiment results show that this method can effectively balance the subjectivity and objectivity of trust assessment, and can quickly avoid malicious nodes and reduce the energy consumption of the trust transmission.

Keywords: Mobile Internet · Trusted measurement · Behavior measurement
Direct trust · Recommendation trust

1 Introduction

Mobile Internet can access the Internet through wireless access devices, which can realize the data exchange between mobile terminals. It is the fifth technology development cycle in the computer field after mainframe, minicomputer, personal computer and desktop Internet [1–3]. As an organic fusion of mobile communication and traditional Internet technologies, mobile Internet is regarded as the core and one of the most important trends of the future network development. Despite the rapid development of mobile Internet services, Morgan Stanley's survey report [4] pointed out that: at present, it is still in the initial stage of mobile Internet development. The large-scale development and application of mobile Internet still need to solve many technical problems, such as wireless access, handover and routing, resource management, quality

© Springer Nature Singapore Pte Ltd. 2019
H. Zhang et al. (Eds.): CTCIS 2018, CCIS 960, pp. 220–238, 2019.
https://doi.org/10.1007/978-981-13-5913-2_14

of service assurance, network security and so on. At present, the technical problems in the field of mobile Internet, especially the security issues, have attracted wide attention, and a large number of related solutions have been put forward.

As an integral part of the Internet, mobile Internet has no essential difference in system architecture except access technology. It also faces various security threats and challenges of the traditional Internet. First of all, the root cause of mobile Internet security problem is that its open IP architecture based on the traditional Internet. The IP architecture makes it easy for attackers to obtain network topology and the IP address of any important node in the network. It is possible to initiate vulnerability scanning and attack on a node in the network, intercept and modify the data transmitted in the network, resulting in insecure network data security. In addition, the user can access the network with opaque networks, non-strict authentication, and authentication mechanisms that are not strictly authenticated by the terminal. The network has no knowledge or control over the security capabilities and security condition of the terminal. User addresses can also be forged and cannot be traced.

From the point of view of the existing Internet, after the fusion of traditional mobile communication networks, a large number of IP-based mobile communication devices (such as WAP gateways, IMS devices, etc.) with security vulnerabilities or security holes have been introduced, and wireless air interfaces have been added at the same time, resulting in new security threats. For example, an attacker can crack an air interface access protocol and then access the network illegally, can intercept and steal the information transmitted by air interface, and can also make service abuse attacks on wireless resources and devices [6]. Therefore, the mechanism of information dissemination and control in traditional Internet services cannot smooth transition to mobile Internet to a large extent, so it has become a consensus in the international research community to think about how to ensure the security of mobile Internet. Since the normal operation of the mobile Internet depends on the mutual trust of computing nodes in the mobile Internet, the trust relationship between mobile terminals and terminals, terminals and service terminals has become a hot research topic.

However, existing trusted measurement methods for computing nodes in the mobile Internet are still one-sided evaluation of a specific service, and lack comprehensive and dynamic assessments of mobile Internet computing nodes. Existing methods of trust assessment are based on the past behavior characteristics of nodes and different application scenarios. They do not consider the combination of subjective judgment and objective evaluation. In addition, the trust value is represented by a floating-point number rather than a single-byte integer value, which leads to excessive energy consumption in the transfer of recommendation trust between nodes and is not suitable for mobile Internet environments. Therefore, this paper proposes a trust assessment model that combines supervisor and objective, based on static measurement, and measures the behavior of nodes as the core. It can quickly judge whether the network node is a trusted node while reducing the energy consumption of the trust transfer, and can also effectively discover and eliminate malicious nodes to ensure the normal operation of mobile Internet services.

2   Related Work

The research on behavioral trustworthiness of mobile Internet computing nodes not only can improve the security of the network, but also simplify the overhead of monitoring and prevention brought by distrust. At present, the trust evaluation of node behavior is mainly based on the behavioral evidence of past interactions, and establishes a trusted behavior model. Zhu et al. proposed a trust authentication model for periodic node behavior [5], which evaluated the behavior of nodes by collecting routing evidence and random sampling. Li et al. proposed a role-based trust assessment model [6], in which the identity of nodes in wireless sensor networks is taken as the basis for the evaluation of trust. Bao et al. proposed a trust assessment model based on intrusion detection [5], which realized the dynamic detection of node behavior. He et al. studied the behavior of nodes in medical sensor networks and established a distributed behavior trust assessment model [7]. Bo et al. proposed a node abnormal behavior detection model based on Kalman filter calculation method [8].

Xiao et al. proposed a network reputation model based on Gaussian distribution and reputation distribution fitting [9]. Hani et al. performed a comprehensive analysis and summary of the vulnerabilities in the existing trust model [10]. Zhang adopted the method of rounding the trust value, calculated the direct trust through the interaction success rate, and proposed a hierarchical structure trust evaluation model [11]. The trust model achieved good results, but it failed to consider the real-time performance of the node behavior trust evaluation. Lin Xi and others proposed behavioral trusted measurement model based on sliding windows from multiple perspectives such as information security, trusted systems, and trusted computing [12]. Crosby et al. proposed a trust model based on location detection [13], which can effectively detect and isolate the nodes that have been attacked. Based on the analysis of data packet ID, Hu et al. proposed a low-cost, lightweight node selective forwarding attack detection algorithm [14]. Zhan et al. studied the relationship between node behavioral trust assessment and routing, and presented a trusted routing scheme [15], which took into account both node behavior trust evaluation and transmission energy consumption, but this scheme placed too much emphasis on the energy consumption of routing and weakens the role of trust.

The research of trust-based recommendation method in social network environment has achieved certain results, mainly including link prediction and matrix decomposition. For example, in reference [16], a reputation management algorithm for point-to-point networks is proposed. Literature [17] proposed that the algorithm made reference to all the neighbors trusted by the source node in predicting the score of the item. Literature [18, 19] proposed that the algorithm was based on TidalTrust improvement, mainly relying on experience, so the accuracy was greatly affected by the value, the model was not stable enough, and the TrustWalker was a recommended strategy proposed in [20], with the increase of roaming steps, the algorithm can calculate the reliability in the prediction process. In the social network environment, the research on trust-based recommendation also included system level, semantic level [21, 22], but the model was slightly different from our Trust-PMF hybrid recommendation algorithm in the research level, which was worthy of reference. Literature [23] proposed another trust-based recommendation algorithm, which made up for the deficiency of Trust-PMF. Literature [24] proposed that the user's trust relationship and interest preference model through the shared feature space modeling, proposed a socialized recommendation algorithm, but the algorithm simply used similarity between users to replace trust, the whole calculation process only used scoring information, and relationships were not really exploited.

Literature [25] mainly discusses the trust measurement mechanism of the nodes in the medical and health field. The trusted measurement mechanism mainly realizes the real-time monitoring of the node based on the identity authentication and the access control mechanism, but the mechanism is too dependent on the hardware of the equipment and the application prospect is too narrow. Document [26] achieves a trusted measure of wearable devices based on the user's biometrics, but the mechanism is only applicable to the field of wearable equipment. Literature [27] in Internet video monitoring application field puts forward a trusted measurement model which is suitable for video surveillance equipment. This mechanism can be applied to the intelligent camera, but this calculation process is too complicated, energy consumption is too high, resulting in a significant reduction in the credibility of the node measurement results.

Literature [28] puts forward the multidimensional awareness mobile node trust metric model, and the trust values of the measured nodes in this model contain three parts: supervisor trust, recommendation trust, and associated trust. The higher-level node that measures the node will query the node's trusted recommendation to its neighbor node, and calculate the direct trust value of the node according to the node's own state at the same time. Finally, the node trust value is calculated according to the association degree of the node. The model can effectively find malicious nodes, but the calculation process is too cumbersome, energy consumption is too high. Based on the cloud model, a trusted measurement model of the mobile node is proposed in the literature [29], the model can construct the measurement model according to the communication radius and the computational feature of the sensing node, which can effectively reflect the change characteristics of the node's trusted degree, but the model needs to occupy a large number of communication channels and could significantly affect the normal data transmission. Literature [30] proposes a trust evaluation model based on mobile node reputation, which is based on the Bayesian full probability model. However, the Bayesian full probability trust assessment process requires sufficient prior probabilities event, and the collection of the evidence is a very difficult process. In the literature [31], the trust metric model of mobile nodes is put forward from the perspective of game theory. The relationship between the interaction and trust between nodes is discussed from the countermeasure income model. However, the model is too concerned with the trust income and neglects the data transmission task of the sensing node, which leads to the disconnection from the practical application.

3   The Trusted Measurement Model

In the mobile Internet, computing nodes can be divided into two types: ordinary mobile Internet terminals and service terminals. When a mobile Internet terminal needs to access the network, the server firstly needs to confirm that the computing environment of the terminal is trusted. At the same time, interactions between different mobile nodes also need to confirm each other's trusted computing environment. After completing the trusted measurement of the computing environment, it is necessary to measure the behavior of the mobile Internet computing nodes. Due to the diversity of the node behavior, there must be differences in transmission speed, packet loss rate or transmission delay. It is not good to judge whether the node behavior is trusted, and it is very possible to judge the normal behavior of the node as abnormal behavior by only judging the behavior characteristics or statistics of the node behavior to distinguish the normal behavior from the abnormal behavior. Therefore, the model of this paper will calculate the trust value of the behavior by comprehensively evaluating the recommended trust value, historical statistical trust value and subjective judgement direct trust value and, then the anomaly of the node behavior is detected. Then the trust queue of the node is updated by combining the results of the trusted measurement, and the feedback control strategy is adopted, and the penalty response mechanism is executed if the behavior is abnormal. The trusted measurement process is shown in Fig. 1.

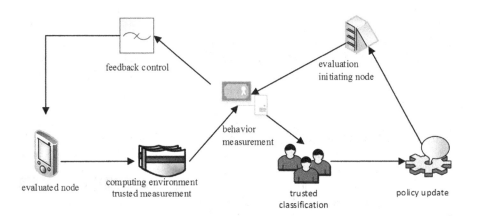

Fig. 1. Trusted measurement process

3.1   Computing Environment Trusted Measurement

When the mobile internet computing node needs to access the network, the server needs to determine whether the computing environment of the node is trusted. The server node located in an area is S_t, and the terminal that applies for access to the area is M_i. For any mobile terminal, the computing environment information includes the software and hardware information of the node, network information and security policies. Therefore, the computing environment attribute of M_i can be formally described as a triple $C_e = (H_s, N_e)$, where H_s represents the hardware information of the terminal and S_h represents the software attributes. In $H_s = (h_{s0}, h_{s1}, h_{s2}, \ldots, h_{sn})$, h_{s0} represents the terminal hardware feature value, and h_i represents the feature value of other software (memory, motherboard and network devices, etc.). In $S_h = (s_1, s_2, \ldots, s_n)$, s_i represents the feature value of the software running on the sensing node (including OS bootstrap, operating system kernel, and key application programs).

According to the security requirements, the management node uses $C = (H_i, S_i, N_i, S_p)$ as input and determines whether the computing environment of M_i is trusted by the trusted assessment function $M_{ce}(C)$, so the security evaluation function of each component is described as follows:

Definition 3-1. Hardware attribute component trusted measurement function $J_{ce}(H_s)$
In the function $J_{ce}(H_s)$, both h_0' and h_i' are the hardware information submitted when the terminal registers with an upper node at the initial time. The calculation process of the function $J_{ce}(H_s)$ indicates that the data acquisition and processing module of the sensing node is not allowed to be changed, but the mobile terminal may need to replace hardware such as battery and memory card during operation, so other hardware can be allowed to replace, the degree of hardware replacement depends on the security policy of the upper node.

$$J_{ce}(H_s) = (h_{s0} \wedge h_{s0}') \wedge \frac{1}{n} \sum_{i=1}^{n} h_{si} \wedge h_{si}' \tag{1}$$

Definition 3-2. Software attribute component trusted Measurement function $J_{se}(S_h)$
In $S_h = (s_1, s_2, \ldots, s_n)$, s_1 to s_k represent the operating system boot program, operating system kernel, and key data acquisition and transmission programs, s_k to s_n represent other programs. Then $J_{se}(S_h)$ can be described as:

$$J_{se}(S_h) = \prod_{i=1}^{k} (s_i \wedge s_i') \wedge \frac{1}{n} \sum_{i=k+1}^{n} s_i \wedge s_i' \tag{2}$$

s_i' is the software information submitted by the sensing node when it registers with the upper node at the initial time.

Definition 3-3. Computing environment assessment function $J_{me}(C)$
Given $J_{ce}(H_s)$, $J_{se}(S_h)$, $J_{me}(C)$ can be described as:

$$J_{me}(C) = \alpha_1 J_{ce}(H_s) + \alpha_2 J_{se}(S_h), \text{where} \quad \alpha_1 + \alpha_2 = 1. \tag{3}$$

α_1, α_2 are weight factors, the value of which are determined according to the network, and the value of α_1, α_2 is usually 1/2. The server node may set a threshold mt. If $J_{me}(C) < mt$, it indicates that the mobile terminal is not trusted, otherwise the terminal behavior should be measured.

3.2   Behavioral Trusted Measurement

With the development of the mobile Internet, information in the mobile Internet is vulnerable to eavesdropping, tampering, counterfeiting and other threats. Although lightweight authentication protocols and encryption technologies can prevent malicious attacks from outside the network, it cannot solve the internal attacks such as denial of service, information interception, injection of a large number of redundant data packets and other abnormal behaviors in legitimate network nodes. The main target of the internal malicious attack is to destroy network devices and tamper with the data, which will lead to the abnormal behavior of the attacking node different from other nodes, such as deleting, modifying, injecting and repeatedly transmitting data. Therefore, trust assessment based on node behavior detection is of great significance to network security. In this paper, data packet forwarding, data packet repetition rate and transmission delay are selected as node behavior characteristics to detect node's direct trust value.

3.2.1   Behavioral Direct Trusted Measurement

The trust assessment model of this paper divides mobile Internet computing nodes into three types: mobile terminal, relay and server. In the process of node behavior trust assessment, only relay nodes generate the recommended trust value among each other. The mobile terminal is directly evaluated the behavior trust value by the relay node in its communication range, and the recommended trust value is not transferred between the adjacent mobile terminals. This paper assumes that the server is completely trusted.

(1)   Direct trusted measurement of mobile internet computing nodes

The malicious attacks on mobile Internet computing nodes mainly include stealing, tampering with perceptive information, and injecting a large amount of error information. Therefore, the amount of data packet forwarding becomes one of the important indicators to detect the abnormal behavior of nodes directly.

When the mobile internet computing node M_1 requests d data packets to node M_2, the node M_2 sends $m(m \leq d)$ data packets, the trusted measurement value of M_1 to M_2 in data transmission behavior can be calculated by data packet forwarding. Therefore, the data transmission behavior of the M_1 to the M_2 can be expressed as a logarithmic function:

$$T_b = \frac{m}{d+1} \tag{4}$$

The repetition rate of the data packet transmitted by the node can effectively judge whether the node has abnormal behavior. When the repetition rate K^l of the data packets transmitted by the node is smaller, the direct trust value of the forwarded data packet behavior will gradually decrease as Rr increases. As Rr gradually tends to be larger than the critical value of the repetition rate, the node is likely to be a malicious node. This trend is consistent with an exponential function curve whose base is greater than one.

Therefore, the trust value T_r based on the repetition rate of the packet forwarding data in the node is expressed as

$$T_b^l = \begin{cases} 2 - \beta^{K^l} & K^l < \chi \\ 0 & other \end{cases}, \tag{5}$$

where $\beta > 1$, $\beta^\chi = 2$, and the value of χ is determined by the mobile Internet network environment.

In the mobile Internet, the data transmitted by nodes may cause transmission delay due to signal interference and other factors, but the transmission delay of the network must fluctuate within the range that users can tolerate.

The mobile terminal M_1 transmits data to the mobile terminal M_2. If the transmission delay t_d is less than the threshold γ, the mobile terminal M_1 fully believes in the mobile terminal M_2. As the transmission delay t_d exceeds a threshold and becomes larger, the possibility of malicious attack by the mobile terminal M_2 is becoming more and more, and the corresponding direct trusted measurement value is declining rapidly.

The direct trusted measurement value T_d of the node in the characteristics of transmission delay behavior is represented as

$$T_d = \begin{cases} \alpha^{\frac{td-\gamma}{\gamma}}, & td \geq \gamma \\ 1, & other \end{cases}, \tag{6}$$

where $\alpha = 0.1$, and the critical value γ is related to the mobile Internet computing environment.

Definition 3-4. Direct trusted measurement of data transmission behavior. The trusted measurement function of the data transmission behavior of the mobile Internet node M_1 to the M_2 is calculated by a weighted method. Three weight coefficients are η_d, η_r, η_f. Each weight coefficient may take different values. The actual size of the value is determined by the actual network requirements for node behavior. So T_M can be described as:

$$T_M = \eta_d T_b + \eta_r T_b^l + \eta_f T_d, \tag{7}$$

where $0 \leq \eta_d, \eta_r, \eta_f \leq 1, \eta_d + \eta_r + \eta_f = 1$.

(2) Recommended trust

When multiple mobile computing nodes push trust values to a single terminal at the same time, it is possible to bring opportunities to malicious nodes. The malicious node intentionally raises or lowers the trust of a node by sending false, conflicting recommended trust values. Therefore, it is necessary to solve multiple recommended trust issues by trust-merging rules. In this paper, the similarity between each trust value and the average trust value is used as the weight, and the smaller the weight from the expected value, the greater the possibility of its maliciousness.

First, the average trust value of all recommended trust is calculated, and the sequence of all recommended trust values for mobile terminal M_i is set to $m_{r1}, m_{r2}, \ldots, m_{rk}$, then the mathematical expectation of recommendation trust is:

$$E(mr) = \frac{1}{k} \sum_{i=1}^{k} m_{ri} \tag{8}$$

The weight of each recommendation trust can be calculated by the Euclidean space distance similarity discrimination method. The specific calculation method is as follows:

$$\lambda_i = \frac{m_{ri}}{\sqrt{\sum_{i=1}^{k} (E(m_r) - m_{ri})^2}} \tag{9}$$

Therefore, according to the weights of the recommendation trust and the recommendation trust, the recommendation trust calculation for the mobile terminal M_i can be described as follows:

$$T_r = \sum_{i=1}^{k} \lambda_i \cdot m_{ri} \tag{10}$$

(3) **Statistical trust value of historical behavior**

The behavioral trust of mobile computing nodes is a concept borrowed from social sciences, and excessive subjectivity can affect the trust value of trust assessment. Therefore, the trust evaluation of node behavior must take into account the subjectivity and objectivity of trust. Long-term and large-scale node behavior statistics can be evaluated objectively with stability and representativeness. Therefore, this paper evaluates nodes from the perspective of node historical behavior. Historical records include data forwarding trust value, data packet repetition rate trust value, time delay trust value, time, and abnormal labels. There are z interactions between the mobile computing node M_1 and the mobile computing node M_2, wherein the node M_2 is evaluated by the node M_1 as having x normal behaviors and y abnormal behaviors. Then, the distribution probability of the statistical trust value θ of the mobile computing node M_1 to the mobile computing node M_2 can be described as:

$$\Pr(\theta|x, y) = \frac{\Pr(\theta, x, y)}{\Pr(x, y)}, \tag{11}$$

where $\Pr(\theta,x,y) = \dfrac{\binom{z}{x}\theta^x(1-\theta)^y}{\int_0^1 \binom{z}{x}\theta^x(1-\theta)^y d\theta} = \dfrac{\theta^x(1-\theta)^y}{\int_0^1 \theta^x(1-\theta)^y d\theta}$, So give $\int_0^1 \theta^{x-1}(1-\theta)^{y-1}d\theta$, So

$$\Pr(\theta|x,y) = \frac{\theta^x(1-\theta)}{\int_0^1 \theta^{x-1}(1-\theta)^{y-1}d\theta} \tag{12}$$

Thus, the behavioral trust values of the mobile computing node M_1 and the mobile computing node M_2 obey the beta distribution with parameters $x+1$ and $y+1$:

$$f(\theta|x+1,y+1) = \begin{cases} \dfrac{\theta^x(1-\theta)^y}{\int_0^1 \theta^x(1-\theta)^y d\theta}, & 0<\theta<1 \\ 0 & , \ others \end{cases} \tag{13}$$

So the final historical statistical trust value T_h can be calculated based on the probability density function:

$$T_h = E(\theta) = \frac{x+1}{x+y+2} \tag{14}$$

3.2.2 Integrated Trusted Measurement for Nodes

The main task of node behavior modeling is to establish a node behavior comprehensive trust profile. This paper has given the direct observation trust T_M, recommendation trust T_r and historical behavior statistical trust value of the evaluated node T_h. The trust of the evaluated node B should base on the direct trust value. The recommended trust value and statistical trust value are auxiliary references, so the overall trust value of the node can be described as:

$$T_x = \mu_1 T_M + \mu_2 T_r + \mu_3 T_h \tag{15}$$

$0<\mu_3<\mu_2<\mu_1<1, \mu_3+\mu_2+\mu_1 = 1$, In the process of integrated trust calculation, the same value can be used in μ_3, μ_2, and the specific selection of each weight depends on the actual network application requirements. The node behavior analysis module first generates node behavior data by interacting with the occurrence and periodicity of interaction events, and then uses the node behavior data as the input for the direct trust value calculation, and combines the historical trust statistics with the trust value to obtain the current behavior of the node as a whole. Trust value.

Finally, according to the time decay formula, the comprehensive trust value of the node is calculated and compared with the system's preset minimum trust threshold to evaluate the authenticity of the node's current behavior and measure the value of the behavior.

According to the social characteristics of trust, the greater the proportion of recent trust values in the overall trust assessment, assume that within a window of time T_w, the trust measurement of the node is set to the metric that is the oldest one now. The value T_{xn}, which is the measurement of the data sending behavior at the current moment, can be defined as:

$$T = \begin{cases} \sum_{i=1}^{dn} T_{xi}h(i)/i & i \neq 0 \\ 0 & i = 0 \end{cases} \tag{16}$$

Among them, $h(i) \in [0, 1]$ is the attenuation function and can reasonably weight trusted measurement at different times. According to the law that the data transmission behavior decays with time, the newly generated data transmission behavior should have more weights, so the attenuation function can be specified as follows:

$$h(i) = \begin{cases} 1 & i = n \\ h(i-1) = h(i) - \frac{1}{n}, & 1 \leq i \leq n \end{cases} \tag{17}$$

Attenuation function and time window show that the trust value of node's data transmission behavior is attenuated according to the change of time. The attenuation function and time window increase the accuracy of trust quantification. In addition to evaluating the node's trust value, it is also necessary to prevent malicious nodes from using a small number of low-value visits in exchange for high-trust fraud, and to punish the fraud that has occurred. Usually, the fraud is greatly reduced by using the trust value. When some of the behaviors of the evaluated node are evaluated as untrusted, it indicates that the behavior of the node has been abnormal. This behavior may be an abnormal behavior due to a weak communication signal or signal interference, or it may be one attack tentatively initiated by a malicious node. Therefore, the behavior of this node needs to be further observed and its trust value reduced according to the number of times of its untrusted behavior δ.

3.3   Behavior Detection Algorithm

The behavioral algorithm obtains its communication behavior characteristic data through the node behavior feature selection and evidence collection module, calculates the direct trust value of the node behavior, and then takes the direct trust value, the recommendation trust value and the historical statistical trust value as the input data of the behavior abnormality detection. Through weighted calculations, the node's behavior comprehensive trust value is obtained, and compared with the trust threshold set by the system to determine whether the node behavior is abnormal. Once the behavior of the node is found to be abnormal, a penalty response operation is immediately executed and the malicious node is isolated. The algorithm steps are as follows:

Input: direct trust value T_M, recommended trust value T_r, historical trust value T_h, current node behavior sequence B

Node malicious behavior flag: δ

Node malicious behavior flag threshold: υ

Normal behavior trust threshold: T_u

Malicious node trust value threshold: T_a

Array: array of malicious node records

Output: node record sequence, behavior exception flag

1) If the current record is empty, a trust record file is started to be created, and the trust value of all the initial test trust values is uncertain; ;

2) Calculate overall trust based on $T_x = \mu_1 T_M + \mu_2 T_r + \mu_3 T_h$;

3) Calculate current behavior comprehensive trust value T based on

$$T = \begin{cases} \sum_{i=1}^{dn} T_{xi} h(i) / i & i \neq 0 \\ 0 & i = 0 \end{cases}$$

4) if $(T > T_u)$
5) return false

6) if $(T_u > T_a > T)$

7) while(B)

8) if $(\delta > \upsilon)$

9) Node is not trusted
10) End while
11) Return true
  12) End if
13) Add node Node to array Array

---

4 Simulation

In this paper, a network environment is simulated by NetLogo simulation software to analyze the performance of the proposed trusted model and its algorithm, so as to verify the effectiveness, efficiency and environmental adaptability of the proposed user behavior prediction model. Table 1 is the experimental parameters of this article:

Table 1. Simulation parameters

Parameters	Parameter description	Parameter value
r	Total number of nodes in the experimental environment	50
k	The average number of node interactions	200
n	Number of clusters	5
log1	Maximum number of history interactions in mobile terminal interactions	15
log2	The maximum number of records of historical behavior on the server	20
t1	Trusted measurement threshold	0.8
tw	Trusted Measurement Time Window	1000 s

Simulation experiments consider three types of malicious nodes: Type 1 malicious nodes discard data packets during the transmission of data, and Type 2 malicious nodes forward a large number of erroneous duplicate data packets. Type 3 malicious nodes both discard data packets and send a large number of duplicate and useless data packets.

There are three types of entities in the simulation experiment, as described below:

(1) The entities in the experiment have three types of roles: ordinary mobile terminal, relay node, and server. The nodes are independent of each other.

(2) In the experiment, the trust threshold is set to 0.8, and all nodes whose trust metrics are less than 0.8 are untrusted nodes.

(3) The weight parameters in the node's trust measurement evaluation model are adjusted according to the computing environment.

In order to verify the validity of the model proposed in this paper, three performance indicators were introduced, namely malicious behavior detection rate, false alarm rate, and false negative rate. Assume that the total number of trusted behaviors f_h, malicious behaviors f_m, and actual trusted behaviors f_{hm} but the trusted model misjudges as malicious behavior in one cycle is the total number of malicious behaviors but the mistrusted model is trusted by trusted models f_{mh}. The ratio of actual malicious evaluation behavior is ε: the detection rate of malicious behavior $\xi = \frac{f_m - f_{hm}}{\varepsilon(f_h + f_m)}$, false alarm rate $\rho = \frac{f_{hm}}{f_m}$, and false negative rate $\tau = \frac{f_{mh}}{f_m}$. Figures 2, 3 and 4 show the detection rate of malicious behavior of the three types of malicious nodes described in this paper respectively. The report rate and the missing report rate were simulated.

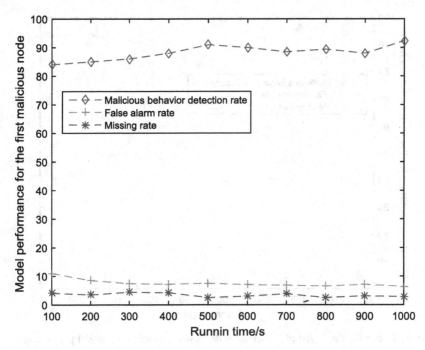

Fig. 2. For the first type of malicious node trusted measurement model performance

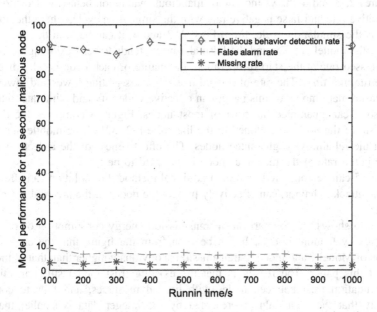

Fig. 3. For the second type of malicious node trusted measurement model performance

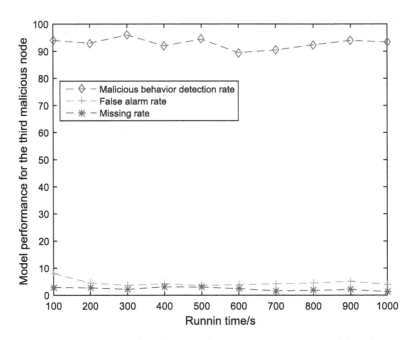

Fig. 4. For the third type of malicious node trusted measurement model performance

Figures 2, 3 and 4 shows the law of malicious evaluation behavior detection rate, false positive rate and false negative rate with the simulation cycle, where the abscissa represents the simulation cycle. From Figs. 2, 3 and 4, it can be seen that the performance of the model is good and the false alarm rate tends to zero. Although there is a certain missed rate at the start of operation, the nature of each node is fully displayed with the running time. The rate of missed inspections is getting lower and lower. The trust measurement model of this paper can effectively identify and eliminate untrusted nodes, so it can guarantee the trust of most nodes. Figure 5 compares the defense mechanism of the nodes mentioned in the literature [32, 33] of the mobile internet in terms of the reliability of guarantee nodes. The effectiveness of the aspect, in which case the initial rate of the malicious node is assumed to be 5%.

Figure 5 can be compared with the traditional method, this solution can effectively detect the attack behavior, can effectively protect the nodes in the area did not receive the attack.

Figure 6 shows the comparison of transmission energy consumption of three different trust evaluation models. It can be seen from the figure that the energy consumption of Model 1 and model 2 transmission is obviously higher than that of the trust model of this paper. The reason is that the existing trust model still transmits the recommendation trust between nodes with limited resources, and fails to consider effectively that the trust value represented by the integer data is smaller than the floating-point trust value, and the transmission energy consumption is low.

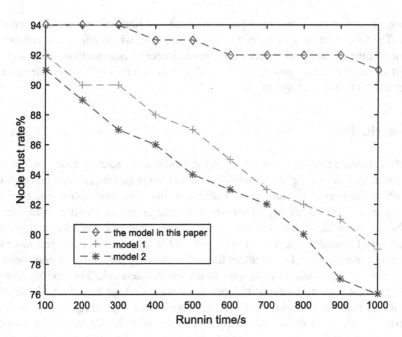

Fig. 5. Comparison of node trustworthiness under the premise of 5% of initial malicious node

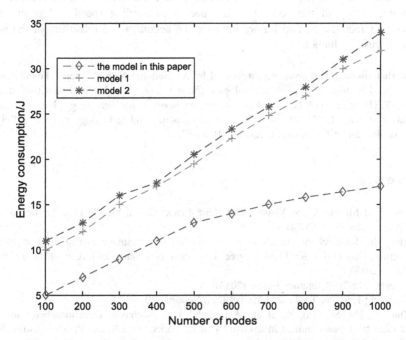

Fig. 6. Comparison of energy consumption of three different trust models

The trust model in this paper only passes recommendation trust values between relay nodes. The trust value is an integer between 0 and 100, which effectively reduces the amount of trust storage and reduces transmission energy consumption. Therefore, the number of recommended trust should be reduced as much as possible while ensuring the accuracy of trust assessment.

5 Conclusion

This dissertation proposes a trust assessment model and anomaly based on the node behavior detection, aiming at the problem that IoT node behavioral trust research fails to combine the energy consumption of different trust recommendation numbers with the subjectivity and objectivity of trust and the energy consumption of trust transfer. For the detection algorithm, the model uses event-triggered detection and periodic detection, and considers the direct trust value, statistical trust value and recommended trust value comprehensively, calculates the comprehensive trust value of node behavior and judges whether there is malicious attack on the network. This model adopts a rounding method of trust values, reduces the storage of trust records, and can effectively detect malicious attacks and mark malicious nodes. Simulation results show that this method can avoid malicious nodes with abnormal behavior in a short period of time, improve network security, and effectively reduce the transmission energy of recommended trust. The next step will be to expand the model, taking into account the remaining energy of the node, the data packet forwarding speed and other more behavior characteristics, and further improve the accuracy and reliability of the node behavior trust evaluation.

Acknowledgments. This work was supported by the National Natural Science Foundation of China The key trusted running technologies for the sensing nodes in Internet of things: 61501007, The research of the trusted and security environment for high energy physics scientific computing system: 11675199. General Project of science and technology project of Beijing Municipal Education Commission: KM201610005023.

References

1. CiscoVNI Mobile: Cisco Visual Networking Index: Global Mobile Data Traffic Forecast Update 2013–2018 (2014)
2. Chen, F.: Research on quality of experience oriented resource management in Mobile Internet. Dissertation for Ph.D. Degree. University of Science and Technology of China, Hefei (2013)
3. Meeker, M.: 2014 Internet Trends (2014)
4. Ericsson.: Ericsson Traffic and Market Data Reports (2013)
5. Zhu, H., Du, S., Gao, Z., et al.: A probabilistic misbehavior detectionscheme towards efficient trust establishment in delay-tolerant networks. IEEE Trans. Parallel Distrib. Syst. **99**, 1–6 (2013)
6. Li, X.Y., Zhou, F., Du, J., et al.: LDTS: a lightweight and dependable trust system for clustered wireless sensor networks. IEEE Trans. Inf. Forensics Secur. (2012)

7. Chang, M.J., et al.: Trust-based intrusion detection in wireless sensor networks. In: 2011 IEEE International Conference on Communications (ICC), Kyoto, Japan, 6 Jan 2011

8. He, D., Chen, C., Chan, S., et al.: A distributed trust evaluation model and its application scenarios for medical sensor networks. IEEE Trans. Inf Technol. Biomed. **16**(6), 1164–1175 (2012)

9. Sun, B., Shan, X.M., Wu, K., et al.: Anomaly detection based secure in-network aggregation for wireless sensor networks. IEEE Syst. J. **7**(1), 13–25 (2013)

10. Xiao, D.Q., Feng, J.Z., Zhou, Q., et al.: Gauss reputation framework for sensor networks. J. Commun. **29**(3), 47–53 (2008)

11. Crosby, G.V., Hester, L., Pission, N.: Location-aware, trust-based detection and isolation of compromised nodes in wireless sensor networks. Int. J. Netw. Secur. **12**(2), 107–117 (2011)

12. Zhang, J., Shankaran, R., Orgun, M.A., et al.: A dynamic trust establishment and management framework for wireless sensor networks. In: 2010 IEEE/IFIP 8th International Conference on Embedded and Ubiquitous Computing (EUC), Hong Kong, China, pp. 484–491 (2010)

13. Lin, C., Tian, L.Q., Wang, Y.Z.: Research on user behavior trust in trustworthy network. J. Comput. Res. Dev. **45**(12), 2033–2043 (2008)

14. Hu, X.D., Yu, P.Q., Wei, Q.F.: Detection of selective forwarding attacks in the Internet of Things. J. Chongqing Univ. Posts Telecommun. **24**(2), 148–152 (2012)

15. Zhan, G., Shi, W., Deng, J.: Design and implementation of TARF: a trust-aware routing framework for WSNs. IEEE Trans. Dependable Secur. Comput. **9**(2), 184–197 (2012)

16. Kamvar, S.D., Schlosser, M.T., Garcia-Molina, H.: The eigentrust algorithm for reputation management in P2P networks. In: Proceedings of the 12th International Conference on World Wide Web, pp. 640–651. ACM Press (2003)

17. Golbeck, J.: Computing and Applying Trust in Web-Based Social NetWorks. University of Maryland, Maryland (2005)

18. Avesani, P., Massa, P., Tiella, R.: A trust-enhanced recommender system application: Moleskiing. In: Proceedings of the 2005 ACM Symposium on Applied Computing, pp. 1589–1593 (2005)

19. Massa, P., Avesani, P.: Trust-aware recommender systems. In: Proceedings of the 2007 ACM Conference on Recommender Systems, Minneapolis, pp. 17–24 (2007)

20. Jamali, M., Ester, M.: Trustwalker: a random walk model for combining trust-based and item-based recommendation. In: Proceedings of the 15th ACM SIGKDD International Conference on Knowledge Discovery and Data Mining, Paris, pp. 397–406 (2009)

21. Walter, F.E., Battiston, S., Schweitzer, F.: A model of a trust-based recommendation system on a social network. Auton. Agents Multi-Agent Syst. **16**(1), 57–74 (2008)

22. Bedi, P., Kaur, H., Marwaha, S.: Trust based recommender system for the semantic Web. In: Proceedings of the IJCAI 2007 (2007)

23. Ma, H., Yang, H., Lyu, M.R., King, I.: SoRec: social recommendation using probabilistic matrix factorization. In: Proceedings of the International Conference on Information and Knowledge Management, pp. 931–940. ACM Press (2008)

24. Ma, H., King, I., Lyu, M.R.: Learning to recommend with social trust ensemble. In: Proceedings of the 32nd Annual International ACM SIGIR Conference on Research and Development in Information Retrieval, pp. 203–210. ACM Press (2009)

25. Rghioui, A., L'aarje, A., Elouaai, F., Bouhorma, M.: The Internet of Things for healthcare monitoring: security review and proposed solution. In: Proceedings of the 2014 Third IEEE International Colloquium in Information Science and Technology (CIST), pp. 384–389 (2014)

26. Sarvabhatla, M., Giri, M., Vorugunti, C.S.: Cryptanalysis of a biometric-based user authentication mechanism for heterogeneous wireless sensor networks. In: Proceedings of the 2014 Seventh International Conference on Contemporary Computing (IC3), pp. 312–317 (2014)

27. Ntalianis, K., Tsapatsoulis, N.: Remote authentication via biometrics: a robust video-object steganographic mechanism over wireless networks. IEEE Trans. Emerg. Top. Comput. **4**, 156–174 (2016)

28. Ren, Y., Bonkerche, A.: Performance analysis of trust-based node evaluation mechanisms in wireless and mobile ad hoc networks. In: Proceedings of the 2009 IEEE International Conference on Communications (ICC 2009), pp. 5535–5539 (2009)

29. Cai, S.B., Han, Q.L., Gao, Z.G., Yang, D.S., Zhao, J.: Research on cloud trust model for malicious node detection in wireless sensor network. J. Electron. **40**(11), 2232–2238 (2012)

30. Ganeriwal, S., Balzano, L.K., Srivastava, M.B.: Reputation-based framework for high integrity sensor networks. ACM Trans. Sens. Netw. (TOSN), 15–19 (2016)

31. Kamhoua, C., Pissinou, N., Maldd, K.: Game theoretic modeling and evolution of trust in autonomous multi-hop networks: application to network security and privacy. In: Proceedings of the 2011 IEEE International Conference on Communications (ICC 2011), pp. 1–6 (2011)

32. Jamali, M., Ester, M.: A matrix factorization technique with trust propagation for recommendation in social networks. In: Proceedings of the 4th ACM Conference on Recommender Systems, pp. 135–142 (2010)

33. Wang, D., Ma, J., Lian, T., Guo, L.: Recommendation based on weighted social trusts and item relationships. In: Proceedings of the 29th Annual ACM Symposium on Applied Computing, pp. 254–259. ACM Press (2014)

A Fast Identity Authentication Solution for the Sensing Layer in Internet of Things

Yong Wang[1], Yang Du[2(✉)], Jia Lou[3], and Bei Gong[2]

[1] Information Technology Department,
Beijing Capital International Airport Co., Ltd., Beijing, China
[2] Faculty of Information Technology, Beijing University of Technology,
Beijing 100124, China
volltekka@126.com
[3] China International Data System Co., Ltd., Beijing, China
loujia@ec.com.cn

Abstract. Trusted access to the Internet of Things sensing layer node is the precondition for the trusted operation of the Internet of Things. How to quickly and accurately implement identity authentication of a sensing node is currently a research hotspot. After comprehensive consideration of the security requirements and functional requirements of the sensing Node Identity Authentication, this paper proposes a fast identity authentication scheme for sensing nodes. In the identification process of sensing nodes, the data aggregation node is responsible for the selection of system parameters and the registration of sensing nodes. It does not directly participate in the authentication process and simplifies the authentication process. The computational efficiency is high, and the security analysis shows that the scheme has forward security and can resist malicious attacks such as replay attacks, key information disclosure attacks, and forgery attacks. Also, the solution supports key updates. Computational complexity analysis shows that this protocol uses only a small amount of computational complexity in exchange for higher security and more features.

Keywords: Internet of Things · Trusted access · The sensing layer
Authentication

1 Introduction

The sensing layer of the Internet of Things is composed of a large number of heterogeneous sensing networks. After the sensing nodes are deployed in the corresponding environment, the tasks that they undertake in the sensing network, the service content they carry, and the data transmission content are carried out. All of these will change with time, and this change will bring unpredictable security risks to the sensing network. Therefore, these nodes faced with a variety of security threats and attacks related to identity authentication such as witch attacks, unauthorized accesses, wormhole attacks, and replay attacks due to high security vulnerabilities of sensing nodes [1–3]. Designing an identity authentication method for the sensing nodes of the Internet of Things has a fundamental role in the security of the Internet of Things and is an important attribute for the Internet of Things to operate reliably.

© Springer Nature Singapore Pte Ltd. 2019
H. Zhang et al. (Eds.): CTCIS 2018, CCIS 960, pp. 239–254, 2019.
https://doi.org/10.1007/978-981-13-5913-2_15

The main purpose of identity authentication for the Internet of Things sensing node is to ensure that the key attributes of the sensing node are not forged, falsified, impersonated, thus ensuring the authenticity of the node, and on this basis to ensure the authenticity and completeness of data transmission, on-repudiation. At present, domestic and foreign scholars have put forward many research proposals for the identity authentication methods of the Internet of Things sensing nodes. However, the authentication process of these solutions is rather complicated. Although the corresponding security goals are achieved, they can still be a relatively heavy burden for sensing nodes with limited computing capabilities [4]. At the same time, the existing identity authentication mechanism is mainly based on the traditional cryptographic mechanism design, and often only for a specific application scenario design, it is difficult to meet a wide variety of application scenarios, service types and diversity of security strengths of the Internet of Things [1, 5]. The sensing computing layer of the Internet of things is composed of multi-source heterogeneous complex sensing networks. The requirements for identification of different sensing nodes are complex and diverse. For example, in the military field, especially in battlefield situation awareness, the identity of the sensing node must be real. The information passed must also be true, otherwise it will bring great hidden dangers to combat; in the field of air pollution monitoring, the requirements are relatively low, the transmitted atmospheric data can be true and correct, and usually it does not care which one node returns; in the medical wearable area, not only the node identity is correct, but also the delay and correctness of data transmission are strictly required.

With the popularity of the Internet of Things, the data collected and processed by sensing nodes often contains a large amount of high-value and sensitive data. Therefore, for the sensing layer of the Internet of Things, the authenticity of the sensing node identity and the trust of the computing environment are its safe and trusted basis. In view of the different types of sensing node's computing, storage, and communication resources, the requirements for the security of identity authentication are also different. To solve this problem, this paper proposes a fast identity authentication scheme for sensing nodes. In this solution, the data aggregation node does not directly participate in the authentication process and simplifies the authentication process. The protocol has forward security and can resist replay attacks, key information disclosure attacks, forgery attacks, and parallel session attacks. The scheme is user-friendly and supports self-renewal of the key. Finally, from the analysis of the protocol, it can be seen that this protocol uses only a small amount of computational complexity to obtain higher security and more features. This protocol is more practical and available.

2   Related Work and Formal Description of Sensing Nodes

2.1   Related Work

At present, most Internet technologies and communication protocols are not designed to support the Internet of Things. Studying the network security connection model is essential to ensure the security and trustworthiness of the IoT-sensing computing layer. Literature [6] discusses three IoT reference models, and defines the security of their respective models, discusses the security challenges faced by different applications, and proposes security strategies for different attacks, but the above network model is from specific security. The threat starts and the ability to deal with unknown security threats is poor. The emergence of social networks and proximity services is driving the Internet of Things to a model that uses location-aware information to connect to society. Peer-Aware Communications (PAC) is widely used in location awareness, and computing power and energy are based on lightweight PAC devices. Level, the literature [7] proposed a lightweight network connection authentication model for PAC equipment, fully considering the computing resources and energy characteristics of different devices, supporting fast authentication and session key negotiation, and Security level is divided, but the model can only be used for specific application scenarios and lacks versatility.

The basic function of the sensing node of the Internet of Things is to perceive information and transmit information. In this process, the trusted node's trusted access is the basis for the trusted operation of the Internet of Things. Literature [8] proposes a method for centralized updating of certificates. The node authentication center periodically issues temporary certificates. This updating method is centralized and non-real-time. There is a problem that the authentication center has a single point of failure. Literature [9] discusses the anonymous PKI system, which overcomes the need for centralized certificate updating. In the process of offline defects and single-point failures, the user can communicate with the authentication center in real time to obtain the current certificate. The mechanism iteratively solves anonymity, non-connectivity and traceability, and maintains anonymity with external attackers, attackers with certain information, and third-party authentication centers. However, the computing resources required for certificate authentication and revocation are huge, and computing resources are huge. The limited IoT node is a heavy burden; literature [10] proposes a method for presetting a set of certificates. This method presets a set of a large number of certificates and can dynamically select a certificate as the identity of the current moment. This method for terminals has low computing power, but a large number of certificates are added to the CRL after revocation, how to ensure that the certification covers the latest CRL is a huge challenge; literature [11–13] proposes the method from the perspective of encryption, according to the initial vector and privacy preservation certification Algorithms. However, the computational model of temporary identity is usually implemented based on symmetric or asymmetric encryption algorithms, which requires high time overhead. Literature [14] adopts a dynamic control strategy to dynamically determine the level of privacy based on policies of services, users, and regulations at run time based on different levels of data and identities.

Literature [15] proposes an identification and trust-based identity authentication mechanism based on identity verification, this mechanism integrates trust-fuzzy computing to achieve access control for sensing nodes, with good scalability and low energy consumption. This mechanism has a low degree of abstraction of node attributes and does not fully reflect the operating characteristics of the node, and it lacks the protection of key information. Because IPv6 can provide enough public addresses, Machine-to-Machine communication protocol is considered to be the core protocol of the future Internet of Things [16]. Literature [17] proposes a distribution based on the integration of IPv6 and M2M communication. The access control architecture improves the overall performance of the sensing network and enables dynamic network management and load balancing. However, this architecture overemphasizes network performance, lacks comprehensive assessment of the security posture of the sensing node, and lacks the ability to respond to security threats. Literature [18] refers to human relations in sociology and proposes an adaptive sensing node access control mechanism. Through an adaptive access control protocol, a sensing node can adaptively select optimal parameter settings to cope with changing application environments. However, the subjective nature of this mechanism is too strong and the actual operation is subject to too much fluctuation.

2.2 Formal Description of Sensing Nodes

The Internet of Things sensing layer is mainly composed of various heterogeneous sensing networks. The current sensing network mainly exists in the form of a cognitive network. Figure 1 logically shows the layout of a sensing network element in the Internet of Things. The Internet of Things sensing layer uses the sensing node as the main device to complete the information acquisition. The sensing node generally consists of four parts: wireless communication module, processor module, energy supply module and sensor module. In the actual implementation of the Internet of Things, nodes of different composition structures need to be selected according to different detection tasks and application scenarios, and renewable energy components, mobile devices and positioning systems may be included in these nodes.

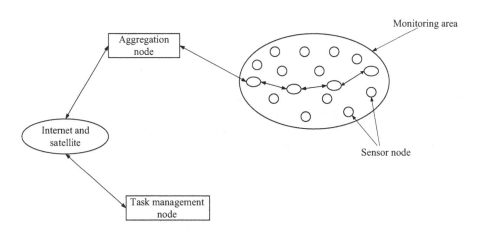

Fig. 1. The layout of a sensor network of Internet of Things

According to the node computing power and energy, nodes can be divided into ordinary nodes, cluster head nodes, and data aggregation nodes. The tasks undertaken by different types of nodes are different. Ordinary nodes only need to collect and send data. Cluster head nodes need to authenticate ordinary nodes and complete the collection and forwarding of some ordinary node data. Data aggregation nodes send the data from the monitoring area to the application layer node via the Internet. According to the different tasks of the nodes, different nodes are separately described in a formal way. Ordinary nodes should contain identity information, computing environment, and data transmission status.

The formal description is as follows:

(1) The identity of the node

Ordinary nodes include two elements: the identity information of the node *id* (the identity information includes network identification number *ni*, identity verification key *k* and attached authority information *pm*), and the actual physical address of the node in the wireless sensing network *pa*. Therefore, the identity of the node can be described with a two tuple of $ID = (id, pa)$.

(2) Node computing environment

The node computing environment includes the basic information of software and hardware, the program running on the node itself and the communication protocol. Therefore, the node computing environment can be described as a four-tuple: $NE = (hw, ho, ap, cp)$, where *hw* is the node hardware information (mainly replaced by the summary value of the hardware), *ho* is the summary value of the node operating system and key processes, $ap = (p_1, p_2 \ldots \ldots p_n)$ is the current running program collection of the node, and $cp = \{cp_1, cp_2 \ldots \ldots cp_n\}$ is the current communication protocol of the node.

(3) Data transmission state

The core task of the sensing layer node is to collect and transmit data. The data transmission should include the amount of data requested, the amount of data actually transmitted and the time point of data transmission, which can be described in sequence $Da = (dr, ds, t_b, ad)$. *dr* is the requested data, *ds* is the actual transmitted data, t_b is the time of data transmission and *ad* is the destination address for data transmission. Therefore, ordinary nodes can be described by the triple (ID, NE, Da).

For cluster head node and data aggregation node, the description of identity and computing environment is similar to that of ordinary node, but the description of the data transmission state is different. In addition, the cluster head node has an ordinary node list, and the data aggregation node has a list of cluster head nodes. It shows that ordinary nodes are managed and measured by cluster head nodes, and cluster head nodes are managed and measured by data aggregation nodes.

For cluster head node and data aggregation node, the description of identity and computing environment is similar to that of ordinary node, but the description of the data transmission state is different. In addition, the cluster head node has an ordinary node list, and the data aggregation node has a list of cluster head nodes. It shows that ordinary nodes are managed and measured by cluster head nodes, and cluster head nodes are managed and measured by data aggregation nodes. The two attributes of the data transmission status and list of the cluster head node and the data aggregation node are separately described here:

The data transmission state of cluster head node/data aggregation node: the data transmission state of cluster head node and data aggregation node is similar, besides receiving data, it also needs to forward data, so it can be described by sequence

$Ds = (D, T, dr, ds, t_b)$. $D = \{d_1, d_2 \ldots .d_n\}$ indicates that the data sent by each ordinary node/cluster head node is requested by the cluster head/data aggregation node, $T = \{t_1, t_2 \ldots .t_n\}$ indicates the time of sending the data from each ordinary node/cluster head node to the cluster head node/data aggregation node. There is no difference in the definition of dr, ds, t_b and ad.

List of nodes maintained by cluster head nodes/data aggregation: cluster head nodes/data aggregation nodes perform trusted measurement on ordinary nodes/cluster head nodes, and each node maintains a list of ordinary node/cluster head nodes. The list can be described by sequence $L = (N, T)$, where $N = (w_1, w_2 \ldots .w_n)$ stands for ordinary node/cluster head node (w_i saves the basic hardware information of the node and the digest value of the operating system and key processes), and $T = (t_1, t_2 \ldots .t_n)$ represents the trusted measurement value of each node. Therefore, the cluster head node and the data aggregation node can be represented by the following quadruple (ID, NE, Ds, L).

3   Description of Identity Authentication Mechanism

In the sensing network, different nodes have different computing power, communication bandwidth and energy. According to the resources owned by the node itself, the nodes can be divided into ordinary nodes, cluster head nodes and data aggregation nodes. The ordinary nodes are only responsible for collecting and transmitting data, the cluster head node manages ordinary nodes within its communication radius. The data aggregation node is responsible for collecting and sending data in a certain area to the Internet. At the same time, the data aggregation node is responsible for managing the cluster head nodes in a certain area. Therefore, in the identity authentication protocol designed in this paper, the data aggregation node dominates the two-way identity authentication with the cluster head node, and the cluster head node acts as the master to complete the bidirectional identity authentication for ordinary nodes. Although the authentication process of ordinary nodes is similar to that of cluster head authentication, but in this scheme, each level of authentication is a two-level authentication, that is, there are only two participants involved in identity authentication, and the data aggregation node does not participate in the identification of ordinary nodes. The ordinary node will not also participate in the identity authentication process of the cluster head node. Figure 2 logically describes the secondary identity authentication process of the sensing nodes:

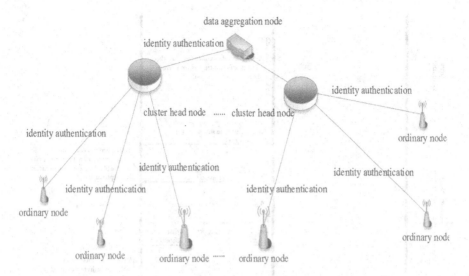

Fig. 2. Secondary identity authentication mechanism for sensing nodes

3.1 Process Description of Identity Authentication

The authentication protocol designed in this section mainly consists of two parts: the cluster head node authenticates the ordinary node and the data aggregation node authenticates the cluster head node. And in the process of identifying the ordinary nodes, the data aggregation node is only responsible for providing relevant parameters, and does not directly participate in the process of identification. At the same time, since the authentication process of the cluster head node by the data aggregation node is similar to the identity authentication process of the ordinary node by the cluster head node, this section mainly discusses the identity authentication process of an ordinary node by a cluster head node. There are three participants during the implementation of this protocol, which are ordinary node GN_i, cluster head node CN_i, and data aggregation node AN_i. It is assumed that each node includes a trusted platform control module TPCM and a trusted cryptographic module TCM. The identity authentication process of this protocol is divided into four phases, namely node registration phase, node trusted self-test phase, identity authentication phase and key update phase. The authentication process is shown in Fig. 3.

The main parameters of the protocol are as follows:

$h()$: A collision-free safe hash function
mk: The protocol master key
sk: The ordinary node authentication key
$||$: String connection symbol
$\oplus$: XOR

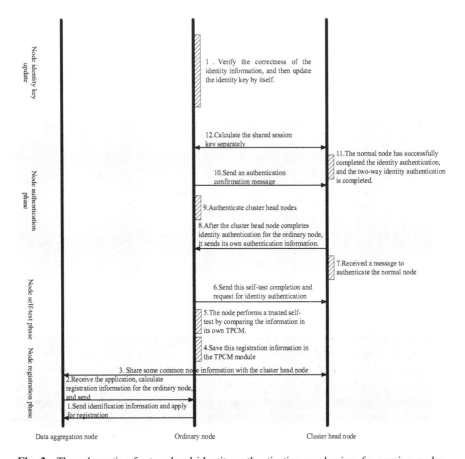

Fig. 3. The schematic of a two-level identity authentication mechanism for sensing nodes

3.2 The Node Registration Phase

Since the sensing node may not only face one sensing network service, any ordinary sensing node GN_i may need to register with multiple data aggregation nodes without losing its generality. This section describes the registration process for ordinary nodes GN_i, cluster head CN_i, and data aggregation node AN_i:

(1) The ordinary node GN_i extracts its own identity GID and identity proof key k, then selects a random number r, GN_i calculates $E_i = h(r \oplus k)$. The ordinary node GN_i then sends the E_i and identity GID to the data aggregation node AN_i over the secure channel.

(2) The data aggregation node does the calculation after receiving E_i and identity GID: $L_i = h(r||mk)$, $M_i = h(GID||h(sk)||E_i)$, $N_i = h(L_i||h(mk||sk))$, $O_i = L_i \oplus h(mk||sk)$, $h(mk \parallel sk)$, $h(CID \parallel h(sk))$.

(3) The data aggregation node shares $h(mk \parallel sk)$ and $h(CID \parallel h(sk))$ to the cluster head node under the data aggregation node.

(4) The data aggregation node sends the $(M_i, N_i, O_i, h(), h(sk))$ to the trusted platform control module of the ordinary node GN_i through the secure channel, and the trusted platform control module of the ordinary node GN_i saves the $(M_i, N_i, O_i, h(), h(sk))$ respectively.

(5) After the ordinary node GN_i receives $(M_i, N_i, O_i, h(), h(sk))$, the random number r is saved in the trusted platform control module. At this time, the information contained in the trusted platform control module is $(M_i, N_i, O_i, h(), h(sk), r)$.

3.3 The Node Trusted Self-detection Phase

Before the sensing node is authenticated by the cluster head node, it needs to perform a trusted self-detection of its identity, and speaks to the ordinary sensing node GN_i. The specific steps are as follows:

(1) The trusted platform module of the ordinary node GN_i extracts the identity information GN_i and the identity authentication key k of the node GN_i, and the trusted platform control module calculates $E_i = h(r \oplus k)$ and $M_i^* = h(GID||h(sk)||E_i)$. The trusted platform control module then compares whether M_i^* and M_i are equal, if they are equal, they continue to perform trusted self-detection, if they are not equal, the process of trusted self-detection is terminated.

(2) The trusted platform control module of ordinary node GN_i generates a random number r', and then calculates $R_i = O_i \oplus h(h(CID||h(sk))||r')$ separately, in which R_i in CID is the public identification of cluster head node CN_i, $S_i = E_i \oplus h(N_i||CID||r')$, $T_1 = h(R_i||S_i||E_i||r')$, $T_2 = h(CID||h(sk)) \oplus r'$.

(3) The ordinary node GN_i transmits (R_i, S_i, T_1, T_2) to cluster head node CN_i through a secure communication channel.

3.4 The Node Identity Authentication Phase

After the cluster head node CN_i receives the message (R_i, S_i, T_1, T_2), the cluster head node CN_i will perform bidirectional authentication with the ordinary node GN_i. The specific process is as follows:

(1) The cluster head node CN_i calculates: $r' = h(CID||h(sk)) \oplus T_2$, $O_i = R_i \oplus h(h(CID|| h(sk))||r')$, $L_i = O_i \oplus h(mk||sk)$, $N_i = h(L_i||h(mk||sk))$ and $E_i = S_i \oplus h(N_i||CID||r')$ based on (R_i, S_i, T_1, T_2).

(2) The cluster head node CN_i calculates $h(R_i||S_i||E_i||r')$ and determines whether the $h(R_i||S_i||E_i||r')$ is equal to the T_1. If $h(R_i||S_i||E_i||r')$ does not equal T_1, the cluster head node terminates the bidirectional identity authentication process. If both are equal, the cluster head node CN_i is considered to have successfully authenticated the ordinary node GN_i. After completing the authentication of the node GN_i, the cluster head node CN_i generates a random number r'', then calculates $T_3 = h(N_i||E_i||r''||CID)$ and $T_4 = E_i \oplus r' \oplus r''$, and then the cluster head node CN_i sends (T_3, T_4) to the ordinary node GN_i.

(3) The ordinary node GN_i calculates $r'' = E_i \oplus r' \oplus T_4$ and $h(N_i||E_i||r''||CID)$ after receiving the (T_3, T_4), and then determines whether $h(N_i||E_i||r''||CID)$ and T_3 are equal. If they are not equal, the ordinary node GN_i considers that the cluster head node CN_i is not trusted and terminates the authentication process. Otherwise, the ordinary node GN_i completes the identity authentication for the cluster head node CN_i, and then the ordinary node GN_i calculates $T_5 = h(N_i||E_i||r'||CID)$, and then sends the $T_5 = h(N_i||E_i||r'||CID)$ to the cluster head node CN_i.

(4) The cluster head node CN_i calculates whether the $T_5 = h(N_i||E_i||r'||CID)$ is correct after receiving the T_5. If it is correct, the bidirectional identity authentication process between the ordinary node GN_i and the cluster head node CN_i is completed.

(5) Finally, the ordinary node GN_i and the cluster head node CN_i respectively calculate $PK = h(N_i||E_i||r'||r''||CID)$, as the transmission of messages between them sharing the session key.

3.5   Node Identity Key Update

According to the formal description of the sensing node, it can be found that if the identity authentication key of the sensing node is not updated, a man-in-the-middle attack or a replay attack is likely to occur. Therefore, the identity authentication key of the sensing node needs a certain update period. Taking the update of the identity attestation key of the common node as an example, assume that the key update period of the ordinary node is T, that is, the identity authentication key k of the ordinary node GN_i needs to be updated after time T. In the process of updating the identity attestation key of an ordinary node GN_i, no participation of the data aggregation node AN_i is required, and the entire process of updating the identity attestation key can be described as follows:

(1) The trusted platform control module of the ordinary node GN_i extracts the identification GID of GN_i and the current identity attestation key k;

(2) The trusted platform control module calculates $E_i = h(r \oplus k)$ and $M_i^* = h(GID||h(sk)||E_i)$, and determines if M_i^* is equal to M_i. If equal, then the ordinary node GN_i will generate a new identity attestation key k' and a new random number rx;

(3) The trusted platform control module calculates $E_i' = h(rx \oplus k')$ and $M_i = h(GID||h(sk)||E_i')$;

(4) The ordinary nodes GN_i updates the original identity attestation key to k', and the trusted platform control module updates E_i and M_i, at this time, the update of the identity attestation key is completed.

4   Security Analysis of Identity Authentication Mechanism

This section will analyze the security of the secondary identity authentication mechanism applicable to sensing nodes. This analysis will focus on whether the mechanism can resist identity forgery attacks, replay attacks, pseudo-registration attack, etc., and analyze the computational complexity of the identity authentication mechanism on this basis.

4.1 Analysis of the Correctness of the Identity Authentication Mechanism

Before the security analysis of the identity authentication mechanism, it is necessary to prove the correctness of the secondary identity authentication mechanism proposed in this paper. In the process of the authentication protocol mechanism, taken an ordinary node GN_i as an example, the GN_i sends (R_i, S_i, T_1, T_2) to the cluster head node CN_i. Then, CN_i calculates r', O_i, L_i, N_i, E_i and judges whether $h(R_i||S_i||N_i||r')$ is equal to T_1. If equal, then the cluster node CN_i's authentication to the common node GN_i is completed. Otherwise, the authentication process is terminated. Since $h(R_i||S_i||E_i||r')$'s computational security depends on the security of the hash function, any forged message (R_i', S_i', T_1', T_2') cannot pass the cluster head node authentication unless the hash function $h()$ is breached.

After receiving (R_i, S_i, T_1, T_2), the cluster head node CN_i calculates (T_3, T_4) and then sends (T_3, T_4) to the ordinary node GN_i. After GN_i received (T_3, T_4), it calculates $r'' = E_i \oplus r' \oplus T_4$ and then verify whether $r'' = E_i \oplus r' \oplus T_4$ is equal to T_3. If equal, the ordinary node GN_i successfully completes the authentication of the cluster head node CN_i, otherwise the authentication process terminates. Since $h(R_i||S_i||E_i||r')$'s computational security depends on the security of the hash function, any forged message (R_i', S_i', T_1', T_2') cannot pass the cluster head node authentication unless the hash function $h()$ is breached. Likewise, any falsified message T_5' cannot be authenticated by the cluster head node CN_i, so the authentication protocol proposed in this section is correct.

4.2 Anti-replay Attack Security Analysis

The principle of the replay attack is that the attacker intercepts the authentication information between the nodes on the communication channel, disguises as an honest sensing node according to the authentication information, and completes the identity authentication of the sensing node by replaying the intercepted information.

In the implementation process of the second-level identity authentication mechanism proposed in this section, taken an ordinary node as an example, the ordinary node GN_i and the cluster head node CN_i respectively select two random numbers r' and r'' complete the bi-directional identity authentication process, which makes that the authentication and interaction messages are valid only for this authentication process in all two-way authentication processes.

Therefore, even if an attacker intercepts the authentication information (R_i, S_i, T_1, T_2) of an ordinary node GN_i and disguises as an honest ordinary node GN_i to imitate the authentication process, however, in this process, the attacker receives the bidirectional authentication message (T_3, T_4) from the cluster head node CN_i, but the attacker does not obtain M_i, E_i, r. This makes it impossible for the attacker to obtain $T_5 = h(N_i||E_i||r'||CID)$ according to the existing information at this time, and thus the attacker cannot complete the next authentication.

On the other hand, if the attacker masquerades as an honest cluster head node and sends intercepted the information (T_3, T_4) to ordinary nodes, but because of the different choice of random numbers during the two interactions, and the r'' calculated by ordinary nodes is different from the random number in this interaction process, so $h(N_i||E_i||r''||CID)$ is not equal to T_3, which causes the authentication process to fail.

So the attacker cannot use the intercepted information to successfully implement the replay attack. Therefore, the two-level identity authentication mechanism proposed in this section can resist replay attacks.

4.3   Anti-identity Forgery Attack Security Analysis

Identity forgery attack is that the attacker imitates an honest common node to deceive the cluster head node to complete identity authentication. For this purpose, the attacker must be able to forge a legal message (R_i, S_i, T_1, T_2), that is, the attacker needs to obtain information (O_i, M_i, E_i, r_i) first to forge and Send a message.

Firstly, it is assumed that the attacker is a legal ordinary node GN_j that was once registered, but this ordinary node does not know the mk, sk, r, k of the ordinary node GN_i, so the ordinary node GN_j cannot calculate M_i, E_i according to itself and its eavesdropping message (R_i, S_i, T_1, T_2), So even if a legitimately registered sensing node GN_j is compromised, it cannot fake the key information of GN_i.

Secondly, suppose that the attacker successfully obtains the key information $(M_i, N_i, O_i, r, h(), h(sk))$ in the ordinary node GN_i. At this time, if the attacker wants to fake the authentication request message of the ordinary node GN_i, it should have the E_i of ordinary node GN_i and its identity attestation key k, but these information are already processed by a hash function $h()$. Therefore, unless the attacker break the hash function $h()$, he cannot obtain E_i and its identity attestation key k.

Therefore, in summary, the two-level identity authentication mechanism proposed in this section can resist forgery attacks.

4.4   Forgery Security Analysis of Anti-cluster Head Nodes and Data Aggregation Nodes

First, it is assumed that the attacker is a registered legitimate sensing node in the sensing network. It is disguised as a cluster head node or data aggregation node to implement attacks on the sensing network. Then the attacker must be able to correctly calculate the valid (T_3, T_4) to send to the common node GN_i. But for the attacker, it doesn't know about $h(mk||sk)$, so it cannot calculate (T_3, T_4) based on $(M_i, N_i, E_i, r, h(), h(sk))$ and its intercepted message (R_i, GID, T_1, T_2). This fact proves that even legitimate users who are aware of the network cannot effectively attack the cluster head node.

Secondly, assuming that the attacker is a legitimate cluster head node in the network, the attacker cannot know the key information $h(CID||h(sk))$ of other cluster head nodes. Therefore, an attacker cannot verify the authentication information of ordinary nodes under the jurisdiction of other cluster head nodes, that is, it is difficult to effectively calculate (T_3, T_4). This means that in the sensing network, even a legitimate cluster head node is difficult to simulate other cluster head nodes to deceive users, so the two-level identity authentication mechanism proposed in this paper can effectively resist cluster head node forgery attacks.

Finally, for a data aggregation node, even a legitimate data aggregation node cannot compute the mk, sk selected by other cluster head nodes. Therefore, other data aggregation nodes cannot be forged to deceive the cluster head node. In summary, the two-level identity authentication mechanism proposed in this section can effectively defend against counterfeit attacks from cluster head nodes and data nodes.

4.5   Anti-critical Information Disclosure Attacks

If the $(M_i, N_i, E_i, r, h(), h(sk))$ saved in common node GN_i's trusted platform control module leaks, the attacker obtains these messages and tries to change the identity certificate key of the normal node GN_i to complete the authentication. However, in this process, the attacker must obtain the identity authentication key k of the ordinary node, and the above information has been calculated by the hash function. Given the strong unidirectionality of the function $h()$, it is not possible to restore the identity GID and its identity proof key k from the $(M_i, N_i, E_i, r, h(), h(sk))$ without knowing the master key mk. So this mechanism can resist critical information disclosure attacks.

4.6   Security Analysis of Session Keys

After the common node GN_i and the cluster head node CN_i complete the bidirectional authentication, they need to transmit data. In this case, the session key is needed to ensure the security of data transmission. In the two-level identity authentication mechanism proposed in this section, the session key $PK = h(N_i||E_i||r'||r''||CID)$ needs to be obtained by computing N_i, E_i, r', r''. Even if the attacker obtains the previous session key PK', it still needs to break the hash function $h()$, since N_i, E_i cannot be obtained directly. Because of the strong unidirectionality of $h()$, the attacker cannot obtain any information about N_i, E_i from the PK' and cannot obtain the final session key. Therefore, the information for subsequent communication cannot be obtained, so the authentication mechanism proposed in this section can guarantee the security of the session key.

On the other hand, if the attacker gets the master key mk. Since the attacker does not know the r, k, sk of the sensing node GN_i, Therefore, the attacker could not calculate the session key before sensing the node GN_i and the cluster head node CN_i. Therefore, the identity authentication mechanism proposed in this section satisfies forward security.

5   Analysis of the Computational Complexity of the Authentication Protocol

This section compares the computational complexity, protocol performance, and security features of the proposed two-level identity authentication mechanism with other identity authentication mechanisms. Table 1 gives a comparison of the two-level identity authentication mechanism and other identity authentication mechanisms proposed in this section. From the table, we can see that the node's two-level identity authentication mechanism proposed in this section satisfies the correctness, two-way trusted authentication, forward security, support for session key generation, and can resist multiple attacks against the sensing node.

Table 1. The comparison between the mechanism in this paper and others

Protocol	Anti-forgery	Replay	Key update	Key agreement	Bidirectional authentication	Cluster header camouflage	Anonymity attack	Forward security
[19]	No	Yes	Yes	Yes	No	No	No	No
[20]	No	Yes	Yes	Yes	No	No	No	No
[21]	No	Yes	Yes	Yes	No	No	No	No
The scheme	Yes	Yes	Yes	Yes	Yes	Yes	Yes	No
Yes in this paper								

The two-level identity authentication mechanism proposed in this section, the highest computational complexity is hashing. Therefore, it is defined that the time taken to complete a hash operation is H_t, and E_t indicates the time of one-module exponentiation operation. Because of the computational complexity, the computational complexity of E_t far exceeds the computational complexity of H_t. Therefore, for the two-level identity authentication mechanism proposed in this section, the computational complexity of string connection operations and XOR operations is negligible except for hash operations in performance evaluation. Table 2 compares the three classical identification mechanisms proposed in documents [17–19] with the two-level identity authentication mechanism proposed in this section in terms of computational complexity. The specific results are as follows:

Table 2. The performance comparison between the mechanism in this paper and others

Protocol	Registration	Trust self-test	Identification	Total calculation
[19]	E_t	E_t	$2H_t+6E_t$	$2H_t+8H_t$
[20]	E_t+H_t	$2H_t$	$3H_t+6E_t$	$6H_t+8H_t$
[21]	E_t+2H_t	$2H_t$	$3H_t+6E_t$	$7H_t+8H_t$
The scheme	$4H_t$	$5H_t$	$8H_t$	$17H_t$
In this paper				

Therefore, from the perspective of Tables 2 and 3, the two-level identity authentication mechanism proposed in this section for sensing nodes is superior to the traditional identity authentication mechanism in terms of security and computational complexity.

6   Conclusion

Based on the trusted access requirements of the sensing node, this paper proposes a two-level identity authentication mechanism for sensing nodes and a three-level identity authentication mechanism for sensing nodes. In the two-level identity authentication mechanisms for sensing nodes, the data aggregation node only provides related parameters and does not directly participate in the identity authentication process. The two-level identity authentication mechanism satisfies correctness, two-way trusted authentication, forward security, support for generation of session key, and can defend against multiple types of attacks for sensing nodes. Compared with several traditional identity authentication mechanisms, the proposed two-level identity authentication mechanism has better security and computational efficiency.

Acknowledgments. This work was supported by the National Natural Science Foundation of China The key trusted running technologies for the sensing nodes in Internet of things: 61501007, The research of the trusted and security environment for high energy physics scientific computing system: 11675199. General Project of science and technology project of Beijing Municipal Education Commission: KM201610005023.

References

1. Georgakopoulos, D., Jayaraman, P.P.: Internet of Things: from internet scale sensing to smart services. Computing **98**(10), 1041–1058 (2016)
2. Venkatesh, J., Aksanli, B., Chan, C.S., Akyurek, A.S., Rosing, T.S.: Scalable-application design for the IoT. IEEE Softw. **34**(1), 62–70 (2017)
3. Al-Fuqaha, A., Guizani, M., Mohammadi, M., Aledhari, M., 'Ayyash, M.: Internet of Things: a survey on enabling technologies, protocols, and applications. IEEE Commun. Surv. Tutor. **17**(4), 2347–2376 (2015)
4. Romana, R., Zhoua, J., Lopezb, J.: On the features and challenges of security & privacy in distributed Internet of Things. Comput. Netw. **57**(10), 2266–2279 (2013)
5. Ntalianis, K., Tsapatsoulis, N.: Remote authentication via biometrics: a robust video-object steganographic mechanism over wireless networks. IEEE Trans. Emerg. Top. Comput. **4**(1), 156–174 (2016)
6. Mosenia, A., Jha, N.K.: A comprehensive study of security of Internet-of-Things. Emerg. Top. Comput. **5**(4), 586–602 (2017)
7. Dao, N.-N., Kim, Y., Jeong, S., Park, M., Cho, S.: Achievable multi-security levels for lightweight IoT-enabled devices in infrastructure less peer-aware communications. IEEE Access **5**(3), 26743–26753 (2017)
8. Hummen, R., Ziegeldorf, J.H., Shafagh, H., Raza, S., Wehrle, K.: Towards viable certificate-based authentication for the Internet of Things. In: Proceedings of the 2nd ACM Workshop on Hot Topics on Wireless Network Security and Privacy, HotWiSec 2013, pp. 37–42 (2013)
9. Crescenzo, G., Zhang, T., Pietrowicz, S.: Anonymity notions for public-key infrastructures in mobile vehicular networks. In: IEEE International Conference on Mobile Adhoc and Sensor Systems, pp. 1–6 (2007)
10. Raya, M., Papadimitratos, P., Hubaux, J.: Securing vehicular ad hoc networks. J. Comput. Secur. **15**(1), 39–68 (2007)
11. Buttyán, L., Holczer, T., Vajda, I.: On the effectiveness of changing pseudonyms to provide location privacy in VANETs. In: Stajano, F., Meadows, C., Capkun, S., Moore, T. (eds.) ESAS 2007. LNCS, vol. 4572, pp. 129–141. Springer, Heidelberg (2007). https://doi.org/10.1007/978-3-540-73275-4_10
12. Fonseca, E., Festag, A., Baldessari, R., Aguiar, R.L.: Support of anonymity in VANETs-putting pseudonymity into practice. In: IEEE Wireless Communications and Networking Conference, pp. 3400–3405 (2007)

13. Sampigethaya, K., Li, M., Huang, L., Poovendran, R.: AMOEBA: robust location privacy scheme for VANET. IEEE J. Sel. Areas Commun. **25**(8), 1569–1589 (2007)

14. Juels, A., Rivest, R.: The blocker tag: selective blocking of RFID tags for consumer privacy. In: Proceedings of the 10th ACM Conference on Computer and Communications Security, pp. 103–111 (2003)

15. Mahalle, P.N., Thakre, P.A., Prasad, N.R., Prasad, R.: A fuzzy approach to trust based access control in Internet of Things. In: Wireless VITAE 2013, pp. 1–5 (2013)

16. Abbas, R., Shirvanimoghaddam, M., Li, Y., Vucetic, B.: Random access for M2M communications with QoS guarantees. IEEE Trans. Commun **65**(7), 2889–2903 (2017)

17. Li, Y., Chai, K., Chen, Y., Loo, J.: Distributed access control framework for IPv6-based hierarchical Internet of Things. IEEE Wirel. Commun. **16**(10), 17–23 (2016)

18. Chen, I.-R., Bao, F., Guo, J.: Trust-based service management for social Internet of Things systems. IEEE Trans. Dependable Secure Comput. **13**(6), 684–696 (2016)

19. Yu, J., Wang, G., Mu, Y., Gao, W.: An efficient generic framework for three-factor authentication with provably secure instantiation. IEEE Trans. Inf. Forensics Secur. **9**(12), 2302–2313 (2014)

20. Gasti, P., Šeděnka, J., Yang, Q., Zhou, G., Balagani, K.S.: Secure, fast, and energy-efficient outsourced authentication for smartphones. IEEE Trans. Inf. Forensics Secur. **11**(11), 2556–2571 (2016)

21. Liang, T., Chen, J.: Remote attestation project of the running environment of the trusted terminal. J. Softw. **25**(6), 1273–1290 (2014)

Cryptanalysis of an ElGamal-Like Cryptosystem Based on Matrices Over Group Rings

Jianwei Jia[1], Houzhen Wang[2,3], Huanguo Zhang[2,3], Shijia Wang[4], and Jinhui Liu[5(✉)]

[1] Huawei Technologies Co., Ltd., Xi'an 710075, China
[2] School of Cyber Science and Engineering, Wuhan 430072, Hubei, China
[3] Key Laboratory of Aerospace Information Security and Trusted Computing Ministry of Education, Wuhan 430072, Hubei, China
[4] Department of Statistics and Actuarial Science, Simon Fraser University, Burnaby, Canada
[5] School of Computer Science, Shaanxi Normal University, Xi'an 710062, China
jh.liu@snnu.edu.cn

Abstract. ElGamal cryptography is one of the most important Public Key Cryptography (PKC) since Diffie-Hellman exchanges was proposed, however these PKCs which are based on the hard problems that discrete logarithm problem and integer factorization problem are weak with advances in quantum computers. So some alternatives should be proposed. Majid Khan et al. proposed two ElGamal-like public-key encryption schemes based on large abelian subgroup of general linear group over a residue ring, however the two schemes were not long before it was proved unsafe by us. Then, Saba Inam and Rashid (2016) proposed an improved cryptosystem which can resist my attack on "NEURAL COMPUTING & APPLICATIONS". By analyzing the security of the public key cryptography, we propose an improved method of algebraic key-recovery attack in the polynomial computational complexity despiteing the designers' claim the cryptosystem is optimal security. Besides, we provide corresponding practical attack example to illustrate the attack method in our cryptanalysis, which breaks instances claiming 80 bits of security less than one minute on a single desktop computer.

Keywords: Cryptography
Post-quantum computational cryptography · Cryptanalysis
Conjugator search problem · Computational complexity

1 Introduction

Whitfield Diffie and Martin Hellman proposed the first public key cryptography in 1976 [1], which make it is possible that two or more participants communicate to obtain a common key on a unbelievable channel by which everyone can

H. Zhang et al. (Eds.): CTCIS 2018, CCIS 960, pp. 255–269, 2019.
https://doi.org/10.1007/978-981-13-5913-2_16

intercept and capture the information. Then many PKCs have been proposed and broken henceforth. ElGamal is one of the most important PKCs since Diffie-Hellman exchanges was proposed, however these PKCs which are widely used these decades (such as RSA, ECC, and ElGamal) are vulnerable with advances in quantum computers. The reason is that these PKCs are based on hardness of discrete logarithm problem and integer factorization problem [2–6]. In order to resist the attack of quantum computer, Many cryptography use algebraic cryptography that resists the potential of quantum computers to replace the number theoretic cryptosystem [7–10,14]. The classical ElGamal cryptosystem is closely related to the Diffie-Hellman key exchange protocol and ElGamal cryptosystem was introduced by Taher ElGamal in 1984. In retro-spect, it is somewhat surprising that this scheme was not discovered before the RSA cryptosystem.

The original ElGamal encryption scheme goes as follows. The standard ElGamal encryption scheme over a cyclic group G of prime order p works as follows. The public key consists of a generator g of G and $X = g^x$, where $x \in Z_p$ is the secret key. Encryption defines the ciphertext as $C = g^r$ and uses the symmetric key X^r to blind the message, i.e., $C_1 = X^r m$. Decryption defines the message $m = C_1/C^x$ by using the private key x.

Breaking the above scheme and the Diffie-Hellman key exchange protocol are equally difficult. Using modern terminology, ElGamal showed that his cryptosystem is one-way against chosen-plaintext attacks (OW-CPA) under the computational Diffie-Hellman (CDH) assumption. The CDH assumption says that given two random elements $A = g^a$ and $B = g^b$ in F_p^*, the value of $g^{ab} \in F_p^*$ cannot be recovered. It is now easy to see that an attacker against the one-wayness of the ElGamal cryptosystem can be used to solve a CDH problem in F_p^*. Namely, obtaining $g^{ab} \bmod p$ from (p, g, g^a, g^b). One gives the attacker the public key $pk = g, g^a, p$ and the challenge ciphertext $c = (g^b, c_2)$ for some random value $c_2 \in F_p^*$. The attacker answer with the corresponding message $m = c_2(g^b)^a$ (mod p), which yields the value of g^{ab} as c_2/m (mod p). The other direction is immediate.

The security of ElGamal encryption scheme depends on the difficulty of the discrete logarithm problem. The standard security notion for ElGamal encryption scheme is indistinguishability under a chosen plaintext attack (IND-CPA) and it is not the stronger notion of indistinguishability under a chosen ciphertext attack (IND-CCA). The difference between IND-CPA and IND-CCA security is that the latter notion allows the adversary to see decryptions of ciphertexts via a decryption oracle. Informally, "encrypt-then-prove" schemes require an adversary to prove knowledge of a plaintext as part of a valid ciphertext. But then a decryption oracle which the adversary can only call for ciphertexts on messages that she already knows is, intuitively, redundant. Hence, the encrypt-then-prove should reduce CCA-security to IND-CPA of the basic scheme. Interestingly, this intuition appears to be hard to turn into a formal proof, as we discuss for the case of the Signed ElGamal encryption scheme.

Cryptography is essential for the security of online communication, cars and implanted medical devices. However, many commonly used cryptosystems will be completely broken once large quantum computers exist. Post-quantum cryptography is cryptography under the assumption that the attacker has a large quantum computer; post-quantum cryptosystems strive to remain secure even in this scenario. The central challenge in post-quantum cryptography is to meet demands for cryptographic usability and flexibility without sacrificing confidence [15–25].

There has also been some interest in constructing ElGamal encryption scheme via group ring [26–35]. One of the best possible ways is to replace the digital theoretical cryptosystem which will has the potential to resistant to by quantum computers attacks. Extend the discrete logarithm problem to an arbitrary group using the difficulty of so-called conjugation Search for questions [36–40]. See references [11–14,41]. In this context, Majid Khan et al. proposed two new ElGamal public key encryption schemes based on the large commutative subgroups of general linear groups on the residual ring. They claim that they can choose a session key in an Abel subgroup that can effectively perform encryption in an easy way and reduce the index. It is disappointing that two public key cryptosystems based on general linear groups can be destroyed using structural attacks respectively [42].

In 2016, Inam and Ali [43] improve it and propose a new ElGamal-like cryptosystem based on matrices over group ring, which can resist the attack of [42]. The authors claim that the cryptosystem is safe against known plaintext attacks and has the potential to resist quantum computing. The proposed cryptosystem is based on the group of circulant matrices over a group ring, These solutions ultimately lead to a simple and efficient construction of fast calculations based on non-Abel algebraic structure-based circulatory systems.

The rest of this article is organized as follows. The second section reviews some necessary knowledge background for this work. The third part describes the ElGamal-like cryptosystem proposed by Saba Inam and Rashid. Part 4 introduces our main attack and gives a corresponding description and performance analysis. In Sect. 5, the computational complexity and actual attacks of the scheme are presented. Finally, Sect. 6 provides some conclusions and discusses the operability of future work.

2   Preliminaries

In this section, this manuscript recall some background information on the cryptosystem with noncommutative platform groups, mainly focusing on materials related to our subsequent cryptographic applications.

In this article, we use the following symbols.

q is a power of prime.

$\mathbf{F}_q$ is a finite field of order q.

k is an integer and $k \geq 1$, $\mathbf{GL}_k(\mathbf{F}_q)$ is a set of invertible matrices which are $k \times k$ of $\mathbf{F}_q$-entries.

$\mathbf{M}_k(\mathbf{F}_q)$is a set of matrices which are $k \times k$ of $\mathbf{F}_q$-entries.

$\mathbf{I}_k \in \mathbf{GL}_k(\mathbf{F}_q)$ is the identity matrix.

$\mathbf{A}$ and $\mathbf{T}$ are two matrices, $\mathbf{A}^{\mathbf{T}} = \mathbf{T}^{-1}\mathbf{A}\mathbf{T}$.

Definition 1 (Discrete Log Problem, DLP). Suppose that G is a finite cyclic group which is generated by g. g and $h = g^k$ in G are known,

$$\text{to find an integer } k \text{ satisfying } h = g^k$$

is called **discrete log problem**.

Definition 2 (Conjugator Search Problem, CSP). Suppose that G is a finite cyclic group.

$$g, h \in G \text{ and } h = g^x = x^{-1}gx$$

are given in G, x is unknown. To determine the conjugator $x \in G$ satisfying

$$h = g^x = x^{-1}gx$$

is called **conjugator search problem**.

Definition 3 (Group ring). $\mathbf{G} = \{g_i : i \in I\}$ is a finite group. $\mathbf{R}$ is a commutative ring without zero unity. Defined $\mathbf{GR}$ is a group ring which is defined to be the set of all formal sums.

$$\sum_{g_i \in G} r_i g_i,$$

where $r_i \in R$, and all but a finite number of r_i are zero.

Define the sum of two elements in $\mathbf{GR}$ by

$$\sum_{g_i \in G} a_i g_i + \sum_{g_i \in G} b_i g_i = \sum_{g_i \in G} (a_i + b_i)g_i,$$

where $a_i, b_i \in R$.

Note that $(a_i + b_i) = 0$ for all but a finite number of i, hence the above sum is in $\mathbf{GR}$. Thus $(\mathbf{GR}, +)$ is an abelian group.

Multiplication of two elements of $\mathbf{GR}$ is defined by the use of the multiplications in G and R as follows:

$$\left(\sum_{g_i \in G} a_i g_i\right)\left(\sum_{g_i \in G} b_i g_i\right) = \sum_{g_i \in G} \sum_{g_j g_k = g_i \in G} (a_j b_k)g_i$$

Example 1. As an example of a group ring, we use the symmetric group S_5 and the ring Z_7 and form the group ring $Z_7[S_5]$. Let the identity element of S_m be e. Sample elements and operations are given as follows:

$$a = 5(123) + 2(15)(24) + (153)$$
$$b = 3(123) + 4(1453)$$
$$a + b = (123) + 2(15)(24) + (153) + 4(1453)$$
$$ab = (5(123) + 2(15)(24) + (153))(3(123) + 4(1453))$$
$$= 15(132) + 20(145)(23) + 6(14235) + 8(124)(35) + 3(12)(35) + 4(1435)$$
$$= (132) + 6(145)(23) + 6(14235) + (124)(35) + 3(12)(35) + 4(1435)$$
$$ba = (3(123) + 4(1453))(5(123) + 2(15)(24) + (153))$$
$$= 15(132) + 6(15243) + 3(15)(23) + 20(12)(345) + 8(13)(254) + 4(1345)$$
$$= (132) + 6(15243) + 3(15)(23) + 6(12)(345) + (13)(254) + 4(1345)$$

Example 2. Now that a group ring have been defined, then we provide how to define $M_2(Z_n[S_m])$, the ring of 2×2 matrices over the group ring $Z_n[S_m]$. Now we are only going to be concerned with matrices multiplication in this ring; using the same a and b defined above as an example, Define

$$M_1 = \begin{pmatrix} a & e \\ e & b \end{pmatrix}$$

and

$$M_2 = \begin{pmatrix} b & e \\ 0 & a \end{pmatrix}$$

Then

$$M_1 M_2 = \begin{pmatrix} ab & 2a \\ be & ba \end{pmatrix}$$

$$= \begin{pmatrix} ab & 3(123) + 4(15)(24) + 2(153) \\ 3(123) + 4(1453) & e + ba \end{pmatrix}.$$

The detail of addition and multiplication is refered to [43–45]

Definition 4 (circulant matrix). An $n \times n$ matrix over a field R is called circulant matrix, if it is a special kind of Toeplitz matrix where each row vector is rotated one element to the right relative to the preceding row vector. So a circulant matrix $\mathbf{K}$ is defined by its first row

$$\begin{pmatrix} t_0 & t_{n-1} & \cdots & t_2 & t_1 \\ t_1 & t_0 & t_{n-1} & \cdots & t_2 \\ \vdots & \vdots & \vdots & \vdots & \vdots \\ t_{n-2} & t_{n-3} & \cdots & t_0 & t_{n-1} \\ t_{n-1} & t_{n-2} & \cdots & t_1 & t_0 \end{pmatrix}$$

Definition 5 (Basic circulant matrix). $\mathbf{D}$ is a circulant matrix, $\mathbf{D}$ can be defined a basic circulant matrix which is given as follows:

$$\mathbf{D} = \begin{pmatrix} 0 & 1 & 0 & \cdots & 0 \\ 0 & 0 & 1 & \cdots & 0 \\ \vdots & \vdots & \vdots & \vdots & \vdots \\ 0 & 0 & 0 & \cdots & 1 \\ 1 & 0 & 0 & \cdots & 0 \end{pmatrix}$$

Definition 6 (circulant matrix basic column). Let $\mathbf{T}$ be a circulant matrix, Let

$$\mathbf{J}_i = \mathbf{D}^i (i = 1, 2, ..., n).$$

$$\mathbf{J}, \mathbf{J}_1, \mathbf{J}_2, ..., \mathbf{J}_{n-1}$$

is defined as circulant matrix basic column, where

$$\mathbf{J} = \mathbf{D}^n = \mathbf{I}_n$$

is a $n \times n$ unit matrix.

Property 1: Arbitrary nth-order cyclic matrix $\mathbf{A}$ can be linearly represented by the basic matrix of the circulant matrix. that is,

$$\mathbf{A} = a_0 \mathbf{I} + a_1 \mathbf{I}_1 + ... + a_{n-1} \mathbf{I}_{n-1}$$

Property 2: $\mathbf{A}$ is a $n \times n$ circulant matrix. $\mathbf{B}$ is a $n \times n$ circulant matrix. Then the product of A and b is also a $n \times n$ circulant matrix. That $\mathbf{AB}$ is a circulant matrix.

Property 3: $\mathbf{A}$ is a $n \times n$ circulant matrix. $\mathbf{B}$ is a $n \times n$ circulant matrix. then the matrix $\mathbf{A}$ and $\mathbf{B}$ is Commutative. That is

$$\mathbf{BA} = \mathbf{AB}.$$

Property 4: If a matrix $\mathbf{A}$ can be denoted by

$$\mathbf{A} = a_0 \mathbf{I} + a_1 \mathbf{I}_1 + ... + a_{n-1} \mathbf{I}_{n-1},$$

where $\mathbf{I}, \mathbf{I}_1, \mathbf{I}_2, ..., \mathbf{I}_{n-1}$ are circulant matrix basic column. Then matrix $\mathbf{A}$ is a circulant matrix.

3   Description of the Public Key Cryptosystem

We will describe the new ElGamal-like cryptosystem proposed by Saba Inam and Rashid. Mainly introduce that how to generate the key, how to encrypt the plaintext and decrypt the ciphertext in detail.

$\mathbf{M}(n, \mathbf{GR})$ is the set of all $n \times n$ matrices on the group ring $\mathbf{GR}$. $\mathbf{H} \subseteq \mathbf{M}(n, \mathbf{GR})$ is the subgroup of $n \times n$ circulant matrices on the group ring $\mathbf{GR}$. Bob and Alice communicate in the following steps.

KeyGen:

1. Randomly selected $\mathbf{A}, \mathbf{B} \in \mathbf{H}$ and do matrix product operation

$$\mathbf{M}_1 = \mathbf{A}\mathbf{B}^2, \mathbf{M}_2 = \mathbf{B}\mathbf{A}^2.$$

2. Then select a matrix $\mathbf{N} \in \mathbf{GL}(n, \mathbf{GR})$ randomly and do conjugate operation of $\mathbf{N}$ by $\mathbf{M}_1$ and $\mathbf{M}_2$.
3. The public key is the pair

$$\mathbf{pk} = (\mathbf{P}_1, \mathbf{P}_2) = (\mathbf{N}^{\mathbf{M}_1}, (\mathbf{N}^{-1})^{\mathbf{M}_2}).$$

At the same time
$$\mathbf{sk} = (\mathbf{A}, \mathbf{B})$$

is the secret key.

Enc(m, pk):

In order to send the message $m \in \mathbf{M}(n, \mathbf{GR})$ to Alice, Bob get the knowledge of the public key **pk** and plaintext m. Bob selects $\mathbf{X} \in \mathbf{H}$ and computes conjugates

$$\mathbf{P}_1^{\mathbf{X}} \text{ and } \mathbf{P}_2^{\mathbf{X}}.$$

After that picks group ring $\mathbf{GR}'s$ unit element η at random and computes the ciphertext pair
$$\mathbf{C} = (\mathbf{C}_1, \mathbf{C}_2),$$

where

$$\mathbf{C}_1 = \eta^{-1}\mathbf{P}_2^{\mathbf{X}} \text{ and } \mathbf{C}_2 = \eta m \mathbf{P}_1^{\mathbf{X}}.$$

Dec(C, sk):

Alice gets the information including the ciphertext $\mathbf{C}$ and the private key **sk**. Then computes
$$\mathbf{S} = (\mathbf{C}_1^{\mathbf{B}})^{\mathbf{A}^{-1}}$$

and
$$m = \mathbf{C}_2 \mathbf{S}.$$

The Correctness of Cryptosystem

According to
$$(\mathbf{C}_1^{\mathbf{B}})^{\mathbf{A}^{-1}} = \mathbf{A}\mathbf{C}_1^{\mathbf{B}}\mathbf{A}^{-1}$$

and
$$\mathbf{C}_2 = \eta m \mathbf{P}_1^{\mathbf{X}} = \eta m \mathbf{X}^{-1}\mathbf{P}\mathbf{X}$$

It is easily to prove that:

$$
\begin{aligned}
\mathbf{C}_2 \mathbf{S} & \\
&= \eta m \mathbf{P}_1^{\mathbf{X}}(\mathbf{C}_1^{\mathbf{B}})^{\mathbf{A}^{-1}} \\
&= \eta m \mathbf{X}^{-1}\mathbf{P}\mathbf{X}\mathbf{A}\mathbf{C}_1^{\mathbf{B}}\mathbf{A}^{-1} \\
&= \eta m \mathbf{X}^{-1}\mathbf{M}_1^{-1}\mathbf{N}\mathbf{M}_1\mathbf{X}\mathbf{A}\mathbf{B}^{-1}\mathbf{C}_1\mathbf{B}\mathbf{A}^{-1}
\end{aligned}
$$

Because of $\mathbf{C}_1 = \eta^{-1}\mathbf{P}_2 X$,

$\mathbf{C}_2\mathbf{S}$

$= \eta m\mathbf{X}^{-1}\mathbf{B}^{-2}\mathbf{A}^{-1}\mathbf{N}\mathbf{A}\mathbf{B}^2\mathbf{X}\mathbf{A}\mathbf{B}^{-1}\eta^{-1}\mathbf{P}_2^\mathbf{X}\mathbf{B}\mathbf{A}^{-1}$

$= \eta m\mathbf{X}^{-1}\mathbf{B}^{-2}\mathbf{A}^{-1}\mathbf{N}\mathbf{A}\mathbf{B}^2\mathbf{X}\mathbf{A}\mathbf{B}^{-1}\eta^{-1}\mathbf{X}^{-1}\mathbf{P}_2\mathbf{X}\mathbf{B}\mathbf{A}^{-1}$

$= \eta m\mathbf{X}^{-1}\mathbf{B}^{-2}\mathbf{A}^{-1}\mathbf{N}\mathbf{A}\mathbf{B}^2\mathbf{X}\mathbf{A}\mathbf{B}^{-1}\eta^{-1}\mathbf{X}^{-1}\mathbf{M}_2^{-1}\mathbf{N}^{-1}\mathbf{M}_2\mathbf{X}\mathbf{B}\mathbf{A}^{-1}$

$= \eta m\mathbf{X}^{-1}\mathbf{B}^{-2}\mathbf{A}^{-1}\mathbf{N}\mathbf{A}\mathbf{B}^2\mathbf{X}\mathbf{A}\mathbf{B}^{-1}\eta^{-1}\mathbf{X}^{-1}\mathbf{B}^{-1}\mathbf{A}^{-2}\mathbf{N}^{-1}\mathbf{A}^2\mathbf{B}\mathbf{X}\mathbf{B}\mathbf{A}^{-1}$

$= \eta m\mathbf{X}^{-1}\mathbf{B}^{-2}\mathbf{A}^{-1}\mathbf{N}\mathbf{A}\mathbf{B}^2\mathbf{X}\eta^{-1}\mathbf{A}^{-1}\mathbf{B}^{-2}\mathbf{X}^-\mathbf{N}^{-1}\mathbf{A}^2\mathbf{A}\mathbf{B}^2\mathbf{X}$

$= \eta\eta^{-1}m\mathbf{X}^{-1}\mathbf{B}^{-2}\mathbf{A}^{-1}\mathbf{N}\mathbf{X}\mathbf{A}\mathbf{B}^2\mathbf{A}^{-1}\mathbf{B}^{-2}\mathbf{X}^-\mathbf{N}^{-1}\mathbf{A}\mathbf{B}^2\mathbf{X}$

$= m\mathbf{X}^{-1}\mathbf{B}^{-2}\mathbf{A}^{-1}\mathbf{N}\mathbf{X}\mathbf{X}^{-1}(\mathbf{B}^2\mathbf{B}^{-2})\mathbf{N}^{-1}\mathbf{A}\mathbf{B}^2\mathbf{X}$

$= m\mathbf{X}^{-1}\mathbf{B}^{-2}\mathbf{A}^{-1}\mathbf{N}\mathbf{N}^{-1}\mathbf{A}\mathbf{B}^2\mathbf{X}$

$= m\mathbf{X}^{-1}\mathbf{B}^{-2}\mathbf{A}^{-1}\mathbf{A}\mathbf{B}^2\mathbf{X}$

$= m\mathbf{X}^{-1}\mathbf{X}\mathbf{B}^{-2}\mathbf{B}^2\mathbf{A}^{-1}\mathbf{A}$

$= m$

In the Sects. 4 and 5, we will show that the ElGamal-like cryptosystem proposed is broken by linear algebra attacks.

4   Key Recovery Attack

According to the description of the third section, a adversary $\mathcal{A}$'s ability to get the public key

$$\mathbf{Pk} = (\mathbf{GR}, P_1, P_2) \text{ and the ciphertext } (C_1, C_2)$$

which communicates over a public channel.

Because

$$\mathbf{P}_1 = \mathbf{N}^{\mathbf{M}_1}$$
$$= \mathbf{M}_1^{-1}\mathbf{N}\mathbf{M}_1$$
$$= \mathbf{M}_1^{-1}\mathbf{N}\mathbf{A}\mathbf{B}^2$$

and

$$\mathbf{P}_2 = (\mathbf{N}^{-1})^{\mathbf{M}_2}$$
$$= \mathbf{M}_2^{-1}\mathbf{N}^{-1}\mathbf{M}_2$$
$$= \mathbf{A}^{-2}\mathbf{B}^{-1}\mathbf{N}^{-1}\mathbf{M}_2$$

By the reason that A, B are circulant matrix, AB is a circulant matrix and $BA = AB$ according of Properties 2 and 3 and $\mathbf{AB} = \mathbf{BA}$ (the reason is that A and B are circulant matrices)

The attacker can get the following equality:

$$\mathbf{P_1AB^{-1}P_2}$$
$$= \mathbf{M_1^{-1}NA^2B^2A^{-2}B^{-2}N^{-1}M_2}$$
$$= \mathbf{M_1^{-1}M_2}$$
$$= \mathbf{AB^{-1}}$$

$\mathbf{AB^{-1}}$ can be denoted as $\mathbf{T}$. Obviously, $\mathbf{T}$ is a circulant matrix. So there exits a series of $a_i \in \mathbf{GR}$, $i \in [0, n-1]$ such as

$$\mathbf{T} = \Sigma_{i=0}^{i=n-1} a_i \mathbf{I}_i.$$

$\mathcal{A}$ solves $\mathbf{T}$ satisfying the following system:

$$\begin{cases} \mathbf{T} = \displaystyle\sum_{i=0}^{n-1} a_i \mathbf{I}_i \\[2ex] \mathbf{P_1 T P_2} = \mathbf{T} \end{cases} \tag{1}$$

The information $(\mathbf{P_1}, \mathbf{P_2}, \mathbf{I}_i)$ is known, so $\mathcal{A}$ gets a series of $a_i \in \mathbf{GR}$, $i \in [0, n-1]$ from Eq. (3).

Let

$$\mathbf{T} = \Sigma_{i=0}^{i=n-1} a_i \mathbf{I}_i.$$

So

$$\mathbf{P_1 T P_2} = \mathbf{T} \text{ and } \mathbf{T}$$

is a circulant matrix.

Property 5: If an adversary can find a $\mathbf{T}$ such as Eq. (1), then the ElGamal-like cryptosystem proposed by Saba Inam and Rashid can be broken.

Proof: Due to

$$\hat{\mathbf{S}}$$
$$= \mathbf{C_1^{T^{-1}}}$$
$$= \mathbf{T C_1 T^{-1}}$$
$$= \mathbf{T}\eta^{-1}\mathbf{X^- P_2 X T^{-1}}$$

and

$$\mathbf{C_2 \hat{S}}$$
$$= \eta m \mathbf{X^{-1} P_1 X T}\eta^{-1}\mathbf{X^{-1} P_2 X T^{-1}}$$
$$= \eta\eta^{-1}m\mathbf{X^{-1} P_1 X T X^{-1} P_2 X T^{-1}}$$
$$= m\mathbf{X^{-1} P_1 T P_2 X T^{-1}}$$
$$= m\mathbf{X^{-1} T X T^{-1}}$$
$$= m$$

So the legal message can be obtained. The ElGamal-like cryptosystem proposed by Saba Inam and Rashid is not secure.

From the Property 5, we can see that $\mathbf{T}$ is an equivalent secret key.

5 Computational Complexity and Practical Attack the ElGamal-Like Cryptosystems

5.1 Computational Complexity of Attack Methods

Though the description of the Sect. 4, the main work to recover the plaintext m is to solve the Eq. (1).

The Eq. (1) can be converted to

$$\sum_{i=0}^{n-1}(a_i\mathbf{P}_1\mathbf{I}_i) = \sum_{i=0}^{n-1}(a_i\mathbf{I}_i\mathbf{P}_2^{-1}) \tag{2}$$

The information

$$(a_i\mathbf{P}_1\mathbf{I}_i, a_i\mathbf{I}_i\mathbf{P}_2^{-1})$$

are known matrix. It doesn't matter that let

$$\mathbf{M}_i = a_i\mathbf{P}_1\mathbf{I}_i$$

and

$$\mathbf{N}_i = a_i\mathbf{I}_i\mathbf{P}_2^{-1}$$

So Eq. (2) can be transformed to the Eq. (3) and it is equivalent to Eq. (3):

$$\sum_{i=0}^{n-1}(a_i\mathbf{M}_i) = \sum_{i=0}^{n-1}(a_i\mathbf{N}_i) \tag{3}$$

$\mathbf{M}_i, \mathbf{N}_i$ are known.

$\mathcal{A}$ solves a_i satisfying the Eq. (3).

In [43], No parameter recommendations are given, may as well suppose that the rank of group $\mathbf{G}$ is k. Then a_i can be denoted

$$a_i = \sum_{j=1}^{k} k_i^j g_j.$$

Thus the task is to solve Eq. (3) which is an nonhomogeneous n^2 linear equations with nq entries.

Formally, the attack can be described by Algorithm 1. It takes as input Matrices

$$(\mathbf{P}_1, \mathbf{P}_2, \mathbf{C}_1, \mathbf{C}_2)$$

and out put the plaintext m.

Algorithm 1.   Getting the message m

1:    Input known information $(\mathbf{P}_1, \mathbf{P}_2, \mathbf{C}_1, \mathbf{C}_2)$ and plaintext m;

2:    Solve nonhomogeneous linear equations in the nq entries of a_i respectively

   $\sum_{i=0}^{n-1}(a_i\mathbf{M}_i) = \sum_{i=0}^{n-1}(a_i\mathbf{N}_i)$;

3:    Compute $\mathbf{T} = \Sigma_{i=0}^{i=n-1} a_i\mathbf{I}_i$;

4:    Compute $m = \mathbf{C}_2\mathbf{C}_1^{\mathbf{T}^{-1}}$;

5:    Return m.

Then, the complexity of Algorithm 1 is analyzed and the conclusions are as follows:

Since the classical techniques for matrix multiplication/inversion takes about $m^\omega (logn)^2$ bit operations [46–49]. Then, the complexity for Algorithm 1 can be mainly concluded as follows. In Step 2, Solve nonhomogeneous n^2 linear equations in nq variables and then its complexity is about $O(n^2(nq)^{\omega-1})$. Step 4 is for computing 3 times $n \times n$ matrix multiplications and 1 times matrix inversions. It is roughly estimated by $O(4(2^\omega))$. Now, if we neglect small constant factors, then the structural attack against cryptosystem 1 can be finished with the bit complexity of $O(n^{\omega+1}q^{\omega-1}(logn)^2)$.

5.2 A Toy Example

In [43], The author give a toy example which illustrate their proposed cryptosystem. Here we illustrate our Algorithm 1 with the toy example give in [43]. Let ring $\mathbf{R} = \mathbf{Z}_2 = \{0,1\}$ and group

$$\mathbf{G} = \mathbf{C}_2 = \{1, y\} = <y : y^2 = 1>.$$

Then we can define

$$\mathbf{Z}_2[\mathbf{C}_2] = \{\sum_{g \in \mathbf{C}_2} a_g g : a_g \in \mathbf{R}\} \text{ and}$$

$$\mathbf{GR} = \mathbf{Z}_2[\mathbf{C}_2] = \{0, 1, y, 1+y\}.$$

Let $\mathbf{H}$ be the subgroup of general linear group of matrices of order 2.

Public key:

$$\mathbf{P}_1 = \begin{pmatrix} 1 & 0 \\ 1+y & y \end{pmatrix} \in H$$

and

$$\mathbf{P}_2 = \begin{pmatrix} 1 & 0 \\ 1+y & 1 \end{pmatrix} \in H.$$

Private key:

$$\mathbf{A} = \begin{pmatrix} y & 1+y \\ 1+y & y \end{pmatrix} \in \mathbf{H}$$

and

$$\mathbf{B} = \begin{pmatrix} 1 & 1+y \\ 1+y & 1 \end{pmatrix} \in \mathbf{H}$$

Known information:
Ciphertext $\mathbf{C} = (\mathbf{C}_1, \mathbf{C}_2)$, where

$$\mathbf{C}_1 = \begin{pmatrix} 1 & 0 \\ 1+y & y \end{pmatrix} \in \mathbf{H} \text{ and } \mathbf{C}_2 = \begin{pmatrix} y & 1 \\ 1 & y \end{pmatrix} \in \mathbf{H}.$$

According to the known information $\mathbf{C}_1, \mathbf{C}_2, \mathbf{P}_1, \mathbf{P}_2$ and the Eq. (3), we have

$$\mathbf{T} = \begin{pmatrix} 0 & a_1 \\ a_1 & 0 \end{pmatrix},$$

then we compute

$$m = \mathbf{C}_2 \mathbf{T} \mathbf{C}_1 \mathbf{T}^{-1} = \begin{pmatrix} y & 1 \\ 1 & y \end{pmatrix}$$

which is the encrypted message in [43].

5.3   Experiments

Using the software Magma, we carry out our experiments with different parameters for Algorithm 1 on a 3.30 GHz Intel processor PC. Besides, we collect the results of our analysis in Table 1, where the notation "s" denotes seconds. Experiments show that Algorithm 1 is efficient and the computation complexity of Algorithm 1 is low of some small constant factors. We collect our analysis in Table 1 as follows.

Table 1. Complexity of the Algorithm 1

q	n	k	Design security	Memory complexity	Data complexity	Attack time
2^{16}	5	15	2^{160}	$2^{12.80}$	$2^{14.80}$	0.094 s
2^{18}	5	18	2^{180}	$2^{12.97}$	$2^{15.22}$	0.156 s
2^{20}	5	21	2^{200}	$2^{13.12}$	$2^{15.58}$	0.167 s
2^{25}	5	24	2^{250}	$2^{13.25}$	$2^{16.16}$	0.750 s
2^{20}	6	27	2^{240}	$2^{14.08}$	$2^{16.70}$	0.344 s
2^{20}	10	30	2^{400}	$2^{16.22}$	$2^{19.23}$	4.297 s
2^{20}	20	33	2^{800}	$2^{19.08}$	$2^{22.62}$	213.672 s
2^{20}	40	36	2^{1600}	$2^{21.94}$	$2^{26.00}$	11742.50 s

Through Table 1, we can see that computation cost of Algorithm 1 is not high with only with several seconds.

Finally, we note that the basic construction described in this paper can be adopted, with some simple modifications, in other algebraic systems, e.g. associative rings or Lie rings, and key exchange protocols similar to ours can be built on those.

6   Conclusion

We have presented a cryptanalysis of a new ElGamal-like cryptosystem based on matrices over group ring with less computation. Though the author claim His cryptographic scheme seems to be resistant to known plaintext attacks, we found a linear algebraic attack which required polynomial time to compute all the equivalent keys of all given public keys. The cryptosystem is designed base on circulant matrix, which are faster because they use less memory. However the circulant matrix also have many algebraic properties such as Properties 1–4, with which the cryptosystem may be broken if the cryptosystem is not designed well. If a abelian structure circulant is chosen instead of circulant matrix, I don't think our algorithm can work. Whether there are another method to broke the improved cryptosystem is a an open question.

Acknowledgements. The author would like to thank the anonymous reviewers for their constructive comments and suggestions. This work was supported by National Key R&D Program of China (2017YFB0802000), National Natural Science Foundation of China (61772326, 61572303, 61872229, 61802239), NSFC Research Fund for International Young Scientists (61750110528), National Cryptography Development Fund during the 13th Five-year Plan Period (MMJJ20170216, MMJJ201701304), Foundation of State Key Laboratory of Information Security (2017-MS-03), Fundamental Research Funds for the Central Universities (GK201702004, GK201803061) and China Postdoctoral Science Foundation (2018M631121).

References

1. Diffie, W., Hellman, M.E.: New directions in cryptography. IEEE Trans. Inf. Theor. **22**(6), 644–654 (1976)
2. Grover, L.K.: A fast quantum mechanical algorithm for database search. In: Annual ACM Symposium on Theory of Computing, pp. 212–219 (1996)
3. Shor, P.W.: Polynomial-time algorithms for prime factorization and discrete logarithms on a quantum computer. SIAM review **41**(2), 303–332 (1999)
4. Zhang, H.G., Han, W.B., Lai, X.J., et al.: Survey on cyberspace security. Sci. China Inf. Sci. **58**(11), 1–43 (2015)
5. Buchmann, J.A., Butin, D., Göpfert, F., Petzoldt, A.: Post-quantum cryptography: state of the art. IEEE Security & Privacy **15**(4), 12–13 (2017)
6. Bernstein, D.J., Lange, T.: Post-quantum cryptography. Nature **549**(7671), 188 (2017)
7. Regev, O.: On lattices, learning with errors, random linear codes, and cryptography. J. ACM (JACM) **56**(6), 34 (2009)
8. Ding, J., Petzoldt, A.: Current state of multivariate cryptography. IEEE Secur. Priv. **15**(4), 28–36 (2017)
9. Sendrier, N.: Code-based cryptography: state of the art and perspectives. IEEE Secur. Priv. **15**(4), 44–50 (2017)
10. Wu, W., Zhang, H.G., Wang, H.Z., et al.: A public key cryptosystem based on data complexity under quantum environment. Sci. China Inf. Sci. **58**(11), 1–11 (2015)
11. Anshel, I., Anshel, M., Goldfeld, D.: An algebraic method for public-key cryptography. Math. Res. Lett. **6**(3), 287–292 (1999)

12. Dehornoy, P.: Braid-based cryptography. Contemp. Math. **7**, 5–33 (2004)
13. Myasnikov, A.G., Shpilrain, V.: Group theory, statistics, and cryptography, vol. 360 (2004)
14. Hurley, B., Hurley, T.: Group ring cryptography. Mathematics **69**(1), 67–86 (2012)
15. Shor, P.W.: Algorithms for quantum computation: discrete logarithms and factoring. In: Proceedings of the 35th Annual Symposium on Foundations of Computer Science (FOCS 1994), pp. 124–134. IEEE (1994)
16. McEliece, R.J.: A public-key cryptosystem based on algebraic coding theory. Deep space network progress report 42-44 (1978). http://ipnpr.jpl.nasa.gov/progress-report2/42-44/44N.PDF
17. Lyubashevsky, V., Peikert, C., Regev, O.: On ideal lattices and learning with errors over rings. J. ACM **60**, 43:1–43:35 (2013)
18. Patarin, J.: Hidden fields equations (HFE) and isomorphisms of polynomials (IP): two new families of asymmetric algorithms. In: Maurer, U. (ed.) EUROCRYPT 1996. LNCS, vol. 1070, pp. 33–48. Springer, Heidelberg (1996). https://doi.org/10.1007/3-540-68339-9_4
19. Petzoldt, A., Chen, M.S., Yang, B.Y., Tao, C., Ding, J.: Design principles for HFEv-based multivariate signature schemes. In: Iwata, T., Cheon, J. (eds.) ASIACRYPT 2015. LNCS, vol. 9452, pp. 311–334. Springer, Heidelberg (2015). https://doi.org/10.1007/978-3-662-48797-6_14
20. Bernstein, D.J., et al.: SPHINCS: practical stateless hash-based signatures. In: Oswald, E., Fischlin, M. (eds.) EUROCRYPT 2015. LNCS, vol. 9056, pp. 368–397. Springer, Heidelberg (2015). https://doi.org/10.1007/978-3-662-46800-5_15
21. Alkim, E., Ducas, L., Pöppelmann, T., Schwabe, P.: Post-quantum key exchange a new hope. In: Holz, T., Savage, S. (eds.) 25th USENIX Security Symposium, USENIX Security 2016, pp. 327–343. USENIX Association (2016)
22. PQCRYPTO Project: Initial recommendations of long-term secure post-quantum systems (2015). https://pqcrypto.eu.org/docs/initial-recommendations.pdf
23. Braithwaite, M.: Experimenting with post-quantum cryptography. Google Security Blog (2016). https://security.googleblog.com/2016/07/experimenting-with-post-quantum.html
24. NIST Information Technology Laboratory: Secure Hash Standard (SHS). Federal Information Processing Standards Publication 180-4. NIST (2012). http://nvlpubs.nist.gov/nistpubs/FIPS/NIST.FIPS.180C4.pdf
25. Bernstein, D.J., Lange, T.: Post-quantum cryptography. Nature **549**(14), 188–195 (2018)
26. Jia, J., Liu, J., Wu, S., et al.: Break R.S. Bhalerao's public key encryption scheme. J. Wuhan Univ. **62**(5), 425–428 (2016)
27. Wu, W.Q., Zhang, H.G., Wang, H.Z., et al.: A public key cryptosystem based on data complexity under quantum environment. Sci. China Inf. Sci. **58**(11), 110102 (2015)
28. Liu, J., Fan, A., Jia, J., et al.: Cryptanalysis of public key cryptosystems based on non-abelian factorization problems. Tsinghua Sci. Technol. **21**(3), 344–351 (2016)
29. Mao, S., Zhang, H., Wu, W., et al.: A resistant quantum key exchange protocol and its corresponding encryption scheme. China Commun. **11**(9), 124–134 (2014)
30. Liu, J., Zhang, H., Jia, J.: A linear algebra attack on the non-commuting cryptography class based on matrix power function. In: Chen, K., Lin, D., Yung, M. (eds.) Inscrypt 2016. LNCS, vol. 10143, pp. 343–354. Springer, Cham (2017). https://doi.org/10.1007/978-3-319-54705-3_21
31. Liu, J., Zhang, H., Jia, J.: Cryptanalysis of schemes based on polynomial symmetrical decomposition. Chin. J. Electron. **26**(6), 1139–1146 (2017)

32. Liu, J., Jia, J., Zhang, H., et al.: Cryptanalysis of a cryptosystem with non-commutative platform groups. China Commun. **15**(2), 67–73 (2018)
33. Jia, J., Liu, J., Zhang, H.: Cryptanalysis of a key exchange protocol based on commuting matrices. Chin. J. Electron. **26**(5), 947–951 (2017)
34. Liu, J., Zhang, H., Jia, J., et al.: Cryptanalysis of an asymmetric cipher protocol using a matrix decomposition problem. Sci. China Inf. Sci. **59**(5), 1–11 (2016)
35. Mao, S., Zhang, H., Wanqing, W.U., et al.: Key exchange protocol based on tensor decomposition problem. China Commun. **13**(3), 174–183 (2016)
36. Habeeb, M., Kahrobaei, D., Koupparis, C., Shpilrain, V.: Public key exchange using semidirect product of (semi)groups. In: Jacobson, M., Locasto, M., Mohassel, P., Safavi-Naini, R. (eds.) ACNS 2013. LNCS, vol. 7954, pp. 475–486. Springer, Heidelberg (2013). https://doi.org/10.1007/978-3-642-38980-1_30
37. Kahrobaei, D., Koupparis, C., Shpilrain, V.: A CCA secure cryptosystem using matrices over group rings. http://www.sci.ccny.cuny.edu/~shpil/res.html. (preprint)
38. Kahrobaei, D., Koupparis, C., Shpilrain, V.: Public key exchange using matrices over group rings. Groups Complex. Cryptol. **5**, 97–115 (2013)
39. Miasnikov, A.G., Shpilrain, V., Ushakov, A.: Non-commutative cryptography and complexity of group-theoretic problems. In: Mathematical Surveys and Monographs. AMS (2011)
40. Myasnikov, A.D., Ushakov, A.: Quantum algorithm for discrete logarithm problem for matrices over finite group rings. http://eprint.iacr.org/2012/574 (preprint)
41. Shpilrain, V., Zapata, G.: Combinatorial group theory and public key cryptography. Appl. Algebra Eng. Commun. Comput. **17**(3–4), 291–302 (2006)
42. Jia, J., Liu, J., Zhang, H.: Cryptanalysis of cryptosystems based on general linear group. China Commun. **13**(6), 217–224 (2016)
43. Inam, S., Ali, R.: A new ElGamal-like cryptosystem based on matrices over group ring. Neural Comput. Appl. **29**(11), 1279–1283 (2018)
44. Roseblade, J.E.: The algebraic structure of group rings. Bull. Lond. Math. Soc. **11**, 1–100 (2011)
45. Kusmus, O., Hanoymak, T.: On construction of cryptographic systems over units of group rings. Electron. J. Pure and Appl. Math. **9**(1), 37–43 (2015)
46. Gu, L., Zheng, S.: Conjugacy systems based on nonabelian factorization problems and their applications in cryptography. J. Appl. Math. **2014**(2), 1–10 (2014)
47. Khan, M., Shah, T.: A novel cryptosystem based on general linear group. 3D Res. **6**(1), 1–8 (2015)
48. Storjohann, A., Mulders, T.: Fast algorithms for linear algebra modulo N. In: Bilardi, G., Italiano, G.F., Pietracaprina, A., Pucci, G. (eds.) ESA 1998. LNCS, vol. 1461, pp. 139–150. Springer, Heidelberg (1998). https://doi.org/10.1007/3-540-68530-8_12
49. Gashkov, S.B., Sergeev, I.S.: Complexity of computation in finite fields. J. Math. Sci. **191**(5), 661–685 (2013)

An Analysis About the Defects of Windows UAC Mechanism

Zejin Zhu[1,2] and Guojun Peng[1,2(✉)]

[1] Key Laboratory of Aerospace Information Security and Trusted Computing,
Ministry of Education, Wuhan University, Wuhan, China
guojpeng@whu.edu.cn
[2] School of Cyber Science and Engineering, Wuhan University, Wuhan, China

Abstract. In order to deeply understand Windows security and explore the flaws of Windows UAC mechanism, the origin of UAC mechanism is firstly introduced, and then its implementation principles are analyzed. After that, various current UAC bypass methods are classified and different types of UAC bypass methods are elaborated on. Based on the understanding of the existing bypassing methods, the defects of the current UAC mechanism are discussed in depth, and the improvement scheme of the UAC mechanism is proposed.

Keywords: Windows · User Account Control · Vulnerabilities
Privilege

1 Introduction

The Windows operating system from Microsoft is one of the most widely used operating systems. In the meantime, a large number of security vulnerabilities have been discovered on this platform. In 2017, there are more than 1000 vulnerabilities on the Windows platform recorded by the CVE organization [19]. To alleviate the security problems caused by software vulnerabilities, Microsoft has launched a series of vulnerability mitigation measures, including the User Account Control (UAC) mechanism which was introduced from the Windows Vista version [14].

In a nutshell, the UAC mechanism protects computers from malwares from a privilege perspective. Under the influence of UAC mechanism, when a user logs in to Windows as an administrator, the process he created is still running with standard user rights. If a process needs administrator privileges to execute, the operating system will pop up a warning window to the user, listing the details of the process to be executed, and wait for the user to confirm it. Under the protection of UAC mechanism, if a malware wants to get administrator privileges it must trigger the alarming window; therefore, the user will have a chance to stop it from running.

Although the concept of restricting the privileges of running processes is commendable, the implementation of UAC mechanism is not consummated. It is easy for malwares to bypass the UAC mechanism and obtain administrator privileges without user's knowledge [28]. Back in 2009, Leo Davidson released a method to bypass the UAC mechanism on Windows 7 [16]. After years of development, there are a large number of programs which can bypass UAC on Windows 7, 8 and 10, and these technologies have been widely adopted by malwares.

© Springer Nature Singapore Pte Ltd. 2019
H. Zhang et al. (Eds.): CTCIS 2018, CCIS 960, pp. 270–285, 2019.
https://doi.org/10.1007/978-981-13-5913-2_17

This paper will first introduce the UAC mechanism in detail and analyze how it is implemented. Subsequently, this it will synthesize the existing UAC research, collect various UAC bypass methods and classify them. Then the paper will delve into the defects of current UAC mechanism and make improvements to it. The remaining parts of the paper are organized as follows: in Sect. 2 we will introduce the implementation of UAC in detail. Current UAC bypass methods are classified in Sect. 3 and they are analyzed in detail in Sect. 4. In Sect. 5, we analyze the defects of current UAC mechanism and in Sect. 6 we make improvements to it. Finally, we conclude the full paper in Sect. 7.

2   User Account Control (UAC)

2.1   Least Privilege Principle

The User Account Control mechanism is an implementation of the "Least Privilege Principle [24]". It was originally proposed by Saltzer and Schroeder to protect information in computer systems from disclosure. They point out that users and processes in a computer system should only be given the minimum permissions needed to complete their tasks [22]. The principle of least privilege can effectively reduce the loss caused by security incidents, and minimize the possibility that permissions are incorrectly used. In a Windows operating system on which the UAC mechanism is enabled, processes will run under standard user rights by default instead of administrator privileges, thus limiting the capabilities of malicious software, reducing its harmfulness.

2.2   The Implementation of UAC Mechanism

Starting with Windows Vista, the Windows operating system introduced the concept of Integrity Level (IL) as a part of the Mandatory Access Control. The integrity level is divided into four levels: low, medium, high and system. An attempt to access a higher integrity level will fail. When a process attempts to access other objects, in addition to the standard access control checks, operating system will also check the integrity level of the process and the object to be accessed. Therefore, even if this access is granted by the corresponding DACL (Discretionary Access Control List), it will fail if the integrity levels of both sides do not meet the requirements.

On Windows platform, an administrator account has more privileges than a standard user account [5], such as *SeSystemtimePrivilege*. After the UAC mechanism is introduced, when a user with administrator rights logs in to Windows, the operating system generates two tokens. One of them is a token with full administrator privileges and its integrity level is set to high. The other token is called "Filtered Token", and all the high level privileges, such as *SeSystemtimePrivilege* mentioned above, are removed from the token. The integrity level of the filtered token is set to medium. User will use the filtered token by default. For example, explorer.exe will be launched with this token, which is used to show the desktop. Since all processes launched by the user will be the child process of explorer.exe, user's daily operations are then limited to the medium integrity level [14].

Users with administrator privileges can use the filtered token to complete most of their daily tasks. When a user needs to perform a specific task which requires administrator privileges, the operating system will use the Admin Approval Model (AAM) for privilege escalation. A process named "consent.exe" will be launched by the Application Information Service (AIS), showing a dialog box which display information about the process to be elevated. User will be asked whether to approve this elevation. If the user approves it, AIS service will use function *CreateProcessAsUser* to create the target process with administrator privileges. The parent process of the new process is set to the process which initiates this privilege escalation request; therefore, the entire privilege escalation procedure is transparent. The concept map of the privilege escalation procedure is shown in Fig. 1.

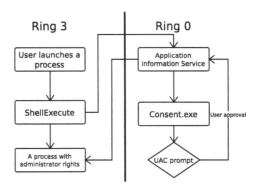

Fig. 1. Privilege escalation process of UAC

2.3 Auto Elevation Mechanism

Since the UAC mechanism in Windows Vista pops up dialog boxes far too frequently, which seriously reduces the user experience, Microsoft introduced a mechanism similar to "whitelisting" on Windows 7. Some trusted Windows executables can be executed under full administrative rights without user's confirmation, and this is called the auto elevation mechanism.

Auto Elevation of .exe File. Some specific programs can get administrator rights directly without popping up a confirmation box. In the paper we call these specific programs "whitelisted programs". A whitelisted program must meet the following requirements:

a. The executable has a valid digital signature signed by Microsoft Windows.
b. The executable declares an auto-elevate property in its manifest.
c. The executable is located in a secure directory that a standard user cannot modify, which includes %SystemRoot%\system32 and most of its subdirectories.

Since a very small part of whitelisted programs cannot declare theirs auto-elevate properties in their manifests due to compatibility reasons, they do not need to satisfy the condition b. Instead, they are hardcoded by Windows. These programs include Migwiz.exe, Pkgmgr.exe and Spinstall.exe [21].

Auto Elevation of COM Objects. In addition to executable programs, there are also some COM objects that have the auto-elevate property. For a COM object to be auto elevated, the following requirements must be met:

a. There is a key indicating the COM object's auto-elevate property in registry.
b. The DLL where the COM object is implemented should have the signature of Microsoft Windows and is located in secure directory.
c. The COM object is instantiated by a Windows executable. A Windows executable is an executable which is signed by Microsoft Windows and located in secure directory.

The auto elevation mechanism has effectively reduced the frequency of UAC prompts, improving the user experience; however, such a design has also become a hidden danger to UAC mechanism, and there are a large number of UAC bypass methods which abuse the auto elevation mechanism.

2.4 UAC Levels

Starting with Windows 7, UAC can be set to four different levels. When UAC is set to the lowest level, processes can obtain administrator rights directly without user's confirmation. At the second level, UAC's confirmation dialog is not protected by the "safe desktop" technique, which allows malwares to confirm the dialog by simulating a mouse click [27]. At the third level the dialog is protected by safe desktop technique, and this is the default level of UAC. When UAC is set to the highest level, the auto elevation mechanism is disabled and UAC will prompt every time a process wants to obtain administrator privileges.

In this paper, we assume the UAC level is set to the third level for the following reasons:

a. When UAC level is set below the third level, the UAC mechanism can be easily bypassed.
b. When UAC level is set to the highest level, UAC's performance will return to Windows Vista period, which is not widely accepted by users.
c. Most of users will not modify the UAC level, so their UAC levels are maintained at the third.

3 Classification of UAC Bypass Methods

Since the introduction of UAC, there has been an endless stream of research on how to break through it. The main goal of this attack is to gain administrator privileges without user's confirmation. There have been many ways to bypass UAC. Based on

Ernesto Fernandez's work on UAC bypass [7], the open source project "UACMe" [13] and some other technical articles, we summarize 49 known UAC bypass methods and classify them as follows.

3.1   UAC Bypass Using DLL Hijacking

When a process runs under administrator rights, the code in its DLL modules is also executed under administrator rights. Therefore, if a malware can trick an elevated process to load a malicious DLL, then the code within that DLL will gain administrator rights. The DLL hijacking methods for UAC bypass can be classified into following types.

DLL Hijacking Inside Secure Directory. As executables with auto-elevate property can gain administrator privileges silently, it becomes a good target for DLL hijacking. By abusing DLL search order, malwares can place a malicious DLL in a path with higher priority so a whitelisted program will load the malicious DLL rather than the legitimate one.

Windows's "Side by Side (SxS)" mechanism is often abused by malwares to achieve DLL hijacking [15]. With SxS mechanism, there are multiple versions of a DLL with the same name storing in Windows, and they can be loaded by different processes. By abusing the SxS mechanism, malwares can prevent its malicious DLL from affecting other programs in the system and also avoid the possible failure caused by the original DLL being occupied.

However, no matter which kind of hijacking methods is used, the malicious DLL has to be placed in safe directory which a process with medium integrity level cannot modify. To solve this challenge, many solutions have been proposed.

Abusing Wusa.exe. Wusa.exe is an executable shipped with Windows which has auto-elevate property. Malwares can abuse it to write arbitrary files to any directories using its */extract* parameter. An attack can use *wusa.exe* to write a malicious DLL to safe directory and then trigger the DLL hijacking to bypass UAC. It was introduced by Joe Schmoe in his blog in 2016 [25]. The */extract* parameter of *wusa.exe* has been deprecated since 10147 version of Windows 10, but this method is still valid in the latest Windows 7 and 8.

Abusing IFileOperation COM Interface. It was originally proposed by Leo Davidson [16]. By abusing the *IFileOperation* interface of a whitelisted COM object named "Copy/Move/Rename/Delete/Link Object", malwares can place a malicious DLL to safe directory. In order to have the COM object auto elevated, malwares need to instantiate this object in a trusted process context. Specifically, malwares can obtain the trusted context in the following two ways.

a. Process injection. Malwares only need to inject a Windows executable and instantiate the COM object in it. As a Windows executable is considered trusted by the operating system, the COM object instantiated in it will be auto elevated to administrator privileges. Then malwares can use the COM object to copy the malicious DLL to safe directory, performing a DLL hijacking.

b. Masquerade-PEB. Since it is easy for anti-virus software to detect process injection, Ruben Boonen proposed a method call "Masquerade-PEB" to counterfeit a trusted context in his blog [2]. The operating system uses Process Status API (PSAPI) to identify which process instantiates the COM object and PSAPI will use the process's Process Environment Block (PEB) structure to get this information; however, a process's PEB structure can be modified by malwares easily. Therefore, a malware can modify its own PEB to disguise itself as a Windows executable and then instantiate a whitelisted COM object. With this method, a process injection is not needed to obtain a COM object with administrator privileges. Trojan *Dridex*, which spreads by Word macros, adopts this method to bypass UAC [1].

Most of the current UAC bypass methods will abuse the IFileOperation COM interface to achieve DLL hijacking, and the difference between them is that they use different whitelisted executables and hijack different DLLs. The general flowchart of these bypass methods is presented in Fig. 2.

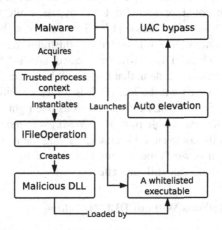

Fig. 2. The flowchart of bypass method abusing IFileOperation

DLL Hijacking Outside Secure Directory. There are some other bypass methods which do not need to place the malicious DLL inside secure directory. The detail of these methods are presented below.

Registry Manipulation. In Windows operating system, when a program is to use a COM object, it will look up the registry to find the corresponding DLL and load it. A whitelisted executable will not look for the corresponding record in HKEY_-CURRENT_USER as it can easily be modified by malwares. Instead, it will look for the record in HKEY_LOCAL_MACHINE; however, the runtime environment of .Net process does not take this into account and will look up for HKCU to load certain DLLs [4]. In this case malwares can make a whitelisted .Net process to load a malicious DLL by controlling the value of key "*CodeBase*" in HKCU\Software\Classes\CLSID \{*COM_CLSID*}\InprocServer32 in the registry. A malicious DLL will be loaded when the whitelisted .Net process starts and the code in the DLL will be executed under administrator privileges.

Environment Variable Manipulation. Some whitelisted executables will locate their dependent DLLs by environment variables. By tempering with related environment variables malwares can trick a whitelisted executable to load a malicious DLL, making the code within it executed under administrator rights silently [7]. For example, by specifying the following three environment variables a .Net program can load any DLLs.

```
%COR_ENABLE_PROFILING%=1
%COR_PROFILER%={COM_GUID}
%COR_PROFILER_PATH%=D:\path\payload.dll
```

A malware can bypass UAC by modifying these three environment variables and then launch a whitelisted .Net process. Then, the malicious DLL specified in environment variable %COR_PROFILER_PATH% will be loaded and the malicious code will be granted administrator privileges.

Race Condition. Matt Nelson and Matt Graeber discovered a schedule task named "*SilentCleanup*" which could be used for UAC bypass while they were examining Windows 10's built-in schedule tasks [17]. This task can be started by a non-administrator account and it will run under administrator rights. When started, an executable and some related DLLs will be created under "*AppData\Local\Temp*" folder. After creation, the executable in that folder will be launched under administrator privileges and all these DLLs will be loaded. It is a race condition where an attacker can replace one of the created DLLs with a malicious one right after the related DLLs are created and before the executable runs. By a WMI event monitor, Matt Nelson and Matt Greaber successfully completed this attack, making the newly-created executable load a malicious DLL. It is worth mentioning that even if the UAC level is set to the highest, this bypass method can still take effect.

3.2   UAC Bypass Methods Without DLL Hijacking

There are always processes running under administrator privileges in the operating system. Without DLL hijacking, malwares can still control the startup and execution procedure of high privilege processes in some other ways. Therefore, there are ways to bypass UAC without DLL hijacking.

Registry Manipulation. This approach takes advantage of the whitelisted executables which can be elevated to administrator privileges automatically. By manipulating the Windows Registry, a malware can cause a certain whitelisted program to create arbitrary child processes. As the child process inherits the token of its parent process, it will be granted administrator privileges without UAC prompt. For example, there is a UAC bypass method which abuses the built-in executable "eventvwr.exe" which is a whitelisted executable [18]. *Eventvwr.exe* uses shell API and will start a child process according to a value specified in the registry. By manipulating the registry, an attacker can control *eventvwr.exe* to create a malicious child process. As *eventvwr.exe* is a whitelisted executable and runs under administrator rights, the malicious child process will bypass the UAC mechanism and acquire administrator privileges silently. The whole flowchart of this bypass method is presented in Fig. 3.

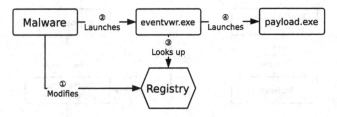

Fig. 3. The UAC bypass method by manipulating the registry.

In the first step, the malware writes the path of a malicious executable to HKCU \Software\Classes\mscfile\shell\open\command in the registry. The malware will then launch *eventvwr.exe*. After looking up in the registry, *eventvwr.exe* will launch the malicious executable mentioned above. Since *eventvwr.exe* runs under administrator privileges, the malicious child process will also be granted administrator rights. In 2016, the malware *Fareit* was found to adopt this method to bypass UAC [23].

Environment Variable Manipulation. This bypass method is primarily aimed at the high-privilege processes launched by the operating system automatically. For example, a schedule task might launch a high-privilege process at some point. James Forshaw finds that, some schedule tasks will launch a process at high privileges, and the path to the process to be launched contains environment variables [8]. In this case, an attacker can trick the schedule task to launch any processes by modifying the related environment variables, then the launched process will be executed at administrator privileges. It is also worth mentioning that, if a suitable schedule task can be found, this bypass method can still take effect even if the UAC level is set to the highest.

Abusing Whitelisted COM Objects. The *IFileOperation* interface of a whitelisted COM object is often abused to bypass UAC by DLL hijacking; therefore, we classified it into DLL hijacking. Apart from DLL hijacking, whitelisted COM objects can also be abused to achieve UAC bypass in some other ways. For example, the *ARP UninstallString Launcher* COM object is used to launched a specific uninstaller at administrator privileges. A Malware can firstly register the corresponding uninstaller in the registry, specifying a malicious executable as the uninstaller. Then the malware instantiates this COM object by either DLL injection or PEB forgery, and then use the *IARPUninstallStringLauncher* interface to start the uninstaller, namely the malicious process [6]. In this case the malicious process will be executed under administrator privileges so UAC bypass is achieved. The entire flowchart of this bypass method is presented in Fig. 4.

Other Types of UAC Bypass Methods. In addition to the types mentioned above, there are some other types of UAC bypass methods which are hard to be classified. They exploit the operating system's design flaws and can be fixed by Windows easily.

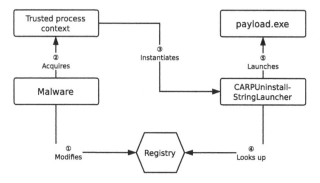

Fig. 4. The UAC bypass method abusing whitelisted COM object.

Abusing AppCompact. *AppCompact* is a compatibility framework developed by Microsoft to make the applications running on older version of Windows compatible with the latest Windows. There is a database storing all the compatibility settings of various applications in this framework and malwares can add records to this database [20]. The *AppCompact* framework provides a compatibility method called "RedirectExe" and applications that have this method will be replaced with another program during startup. By specifying the *RedirectExe* method for a whitelisted executable, a malicious process can be created under administrator privileges when the whitelisted executable is launched [12].

This bypass method has been assigned CVE-2015-0002 and has been fixed in the latest version of Windows [26].

Token Impersonation. Under the effect of UAC mechanism, different tokens are assigned to medium integrity level processes and high integrity level ones; however, in order for a process at medium integrity level to obtain some specific information for a higher integrity level process, the token assigned to the process at medium integrity level will have a special privilege, *QueryLimitedInformation*. As this privilege is not well-designed, malwares can abuse this privilege to get a copy of a high integrity level process's token. Then malwares can use this token to create a new process with administrator privileges. James Forshaw explained this bypass method in his blog in 2017 [9–11].

4   A Comprehensive Analysis of UAC Bypass Methods

Based on the classification of known UAC bypass methods in Sect. 3, this paper calculates the number and proportion of UAC bypass methods for each type. The result is shown in Table 1.

Table 1. The number and proportion of various types of UAC bypass methods.

UAC bypass methods	Number	Specific methods	Number	Proportion
With DLL hijacking	29	DLL hijacking inside secure directory	23	55.1%
		DLL hijacking outside secure directory	6	
Without DLL hijacking	20	Hijacking high privilege process	9	44.9%
		Abusing whitelisted COM objects	6	
		Others	5	

Compared with the UAC bypass methods without DLL hijacking, the bypass methods using DLL hijacking are more extensible: that is, a variety of bypass methods can be derived from a single example. The reason is that there are a great number of whitelisted executables shipped with Windows and the vast majority of them are threatened by DLL hijacking. As can be seen from Table 1, the bypass methods using DLL hijacking account for more than a half of all the bypass methods, so the majority of UAC bypass methods are based on DLL hijacking technique.

After that, this paper counts the proportion of each subtype in each type of UAC bypass methods. The result is presented in Fig. 5.

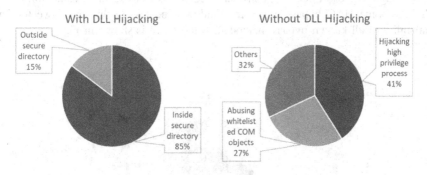

Fig. 5. The proportion of each subtype in each type of UAC bypass methods.

As is shown in Fig. 5, most of the DLL hijacking takes place in secure directory, and the DLL hijacking happening outside secure directory only accounts for 15%. Among the bypass methods without DLL hijacking, 68% of them will either abuse the whitelisted COM objects or hijack the high privilege processes, and more bypasses of these types may be discovered in the future. There are some bypass methods hard to be categorized and are classified into "others", which accounts for 32% of the bypass methods without DLL hijacking. These bypass methods exploit operating system's design flaws and most of them are fixed by Windows.

The "whitelisting" mechanism provides malwares with great opportunities to bypass UAC. For UAC bypass methods abusing "whitelisting" mechanism, their proportion in all the bypasses is presented in Fig. 6.

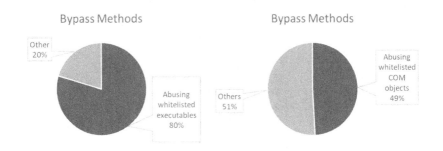

Fig. 6. The proportion of bypasses abusing whitelisting mechanism.

As can be seen from Fig. 6, more than three quarters of the bypasses abuse the auto elevation mechanism of a .exe file. For the whitelisted COM objects, although there are only eight COM objects used for UAC bypass (their related interfaces are *ISecurityEditor, IARPUninstallStringLauncher, ICMLuaUtil, IFwCplLua, IColorDataProxy, ICMLuaUtil, ISPPLUAObject* and *IFileOperation*), but as the *IFileOperation* interface can be used in most DLL hijacking attacks, the methods using whitelisted COM objects still make almost half of all the bypasses.

Although Microsoft does not consider UAC bypasses as security vulnerabilities, it still fixes some UAC bypass issues in Windows updates. In this paper we test the availability of all known bypass methods and the result is shown in Fig. 7.

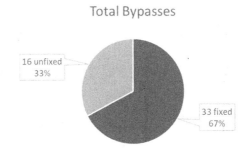

Fig. 7. The availability of all known bypass methods.

As can be seen from Fig. 7, nearly one-third of UAC bypass methods are still available. They pose a significant security risk to the operating system.

For the methods still available, we find that all of them abuse the system's auto elevation mechanism. Combining this observation with Fig. 6, we believe that the whitelisting mechanism has become a major breakthrough for malwares to bypass UAC.

5 The Defects of UAC Mechanism

Since the introduction of Windows UAC mechanism, various ways of UAC bypass methods have sprung up. The UAC mechanism is becoming ineffective, and some researchers even believe that to set the UAC level to the default level equals to have it disabled [3].

The main reason that the UAC mechanism can be easily bypasses is the "whitelisting" mechanism introduced since Windows 7. In order to solve the problem that UAC's prompting was far too annoying in Windows Vista version, some Windows executables and COM objects were granted an "auto-elevate" property to allow them to run at administrator privileges without prompting. Although Windows has imposed some restrictions on the whitelisting mechanism to prevent it from being abused, these restrictions are not well considered. Therefore, when Microsoft decided to make a compromise for convenience, the security of UAC was greatly threatened.

Based on the analysis of current UAC bypass methods, this paper highlights several defects of UAC mechanism, and they are presented as follows.

5.1 Insufficient Validation of the Caller of a COM Object

A COM object with administrator rights does not necessarily mean a bypass of UAC, as what a particular COM object can do is limited; however, considering the fact that there is a variety of COM objects in Windows, they pose a great threat to the UAC mechanism. There have already been eight COM objects known to be harmful to UAC currently, so the operating system must prevent the whitelisted COM objects from being abused to bypass UAC.

However, malwares can easily obtain an elevated COM object currently. By querying the process context, the operating system limits the process which instantiates the COM object to the programs with valid Windows signature when the auto elevation happens, but this restriction can easily be bypassed. As COM objects rely on PEB to identify the process they are running in, malwares can forge a trusted caller of the COM object by modifying its own PEB. The Trojan *Dridex* adopts this method to obtain a high privilege COM object and bypass UAC [1]. Even without PEB Masquerade, malwares still have the opportunity to obtain a high privilege COM object. As there is a great number of Windows executables running in the operating system, and their integrity levels are mostly set to medium, malwares can instantiate a COM object within these processes by process injection. Windows cannot identify the real process which instantiates the COM object, and therefore the whitelisted COM objects can be easily abused currently.

5.2 Insufficient Validation of Modules Loaded by Whitelisted Process

When Windows silently elevates a whitelisted process to administrator privileges, it must ensure the process to be elevated is trusted. Currently, Windows only protects the integrity of the .exe module of a process by verifying its signature and checking whether it is located in secure directory, but there are no restrictions on the DLL modules loaded by the process. A DLL without a valid signature can still be loaded by an elevated process and the code within the DLL will be granted administrator privileges. For example, bypass method [25] hides its malicious code in a DLL without signature and achieve UAC bypass through DLL hijacking.

The path of a DLL loaded by whitelisted process is not restricted either. The reason why there are many UAC bypass methods requiring a malicious DLL stored in secure directory is that they need to place the malicious DLL in a path with higher search order, and the UAC mechanism does not require a DLL loaded by a whitelisted process to be stored in secure directory. In some bypass methods a whitelisted program can load a DLL outside secure directory, such as the malware *Fareit* which achieves UAC bypass by controlling the registry.

5.3   Insufficient Validation of the Parent Process of a Whitelisted Process

When a whitelisted executable is abused to bypass UAC, the parent process of the process will mostly be a third-party executable rather than a legitimate Windows executable. If not being abused, a whitelisted executable will most likely be launched through Windows UI, or started by other Windows executables, so their parent processes will be Windows executables. Currently, Windows does not impose any restrictions on the parent process of a whitelisted process when it is to be auto elevated. The operating system should verify the parent process of a whitelisted process, and if the parent process is a third-party program instead of a Windows executable, the auto elevation procedure should be aborted.

5.4   Inappropriate Privilege Inheritance for the Whitelisted Process

An auto-elevated process only means the process itself is trusted, and does not mean that all the child processes created by it are trusted. Currently, if a process is elevated to administrator rights silently, all its child processes will also be granted administrator rights without prompting. If not being abused, a whitelisted process will not create any child processes in general, or the created process will also be a Windows executable. However, when it is abused to bypass UAC, the whitelisted process will often create a malicious child process without a valid Windows signature. Therefore, the operating system should redesign the privilege inheritance of a whitelisted process: if the child process is not a Windows executable, it should be granted standard user rights instead of administrator privileges.

5.5   Incompatible Whitelisted Executables

Most of the whitelisted executables existed before UAC mechanism appears. When the "whitelisting" mechanism of UAC was designed, Windows did not adapt these executables to UAC, but added all of them directly to the whitelist. Therefore, some functions of the whitelisted executables contradict to the UAC mechanism. For example, the */extract* parameter of a whitelisted program, *wusa.exe*, can be used to write arbitrary files anywhere without triggering UAC prompts. Although the */extract* parameter of *wusa.exe* has been removed in the latest version of Windows 10, the remaining whitelisted executables still pose a great threat to the UAC mechanism.

6 UAC Improvement Proposal

Based on the analysis of the defects of UAC, we believe the UAC mechanism can be improved in the following ways.

1. Improve the verification of COM object auto elevation procedure. The operating system should take a more reliable way to identify the process the COM object running in. Currently, the verification of the process which instantiates the COM object is not reliable, and malwares can obtain high privilege COM objects easily.
2. Verify the DLL modules loaded by whitelisted programs. The operating system should prevent the auto elevated process from loading untrusted modules by checking the DLL's signature and its file path. If an executable to be auto elevated has a DLL module without Windows signature or stored outside secure directory, the elevation should be aborted.
3. Verify the parent process of a whitelisted process. When being abused to bypass UAC, a whitelisted process's parent process is mostly a third-party process rather than a Windows executable. Therefore, if the parent process of a whitelisted process to be elevated is not a Windows executable, the auto elevation procedure should be aborted.
4. Improve the privilege inheritance mechanism of whitelisted processes. Currently the operating system will grant every child process of an elevated whitelisted process administrator rights. The operating system should check if the child process created by the whitelisted program is a Windows executable, and the child process without a valid Windows signature should be granted standard user rights rather than administrator privileges.
5. Make the whitelisted executables compatible with UAC. The operating system should inspect every executable in the whitelist and adapt them to UAC. For example, functions like the */extract* parameter of *wusa.exe* should be removed. The operating system should ensure that programs in the whitelist will not compromise the UAC mechanism.

7 Conclusion

The whitelisting mechanism was introduced in Windows 7 to improve the user experience of UAC, and it serves its purpose quiet successfully; however, it also poses a great threat to the security of UAC. By analyzing the known bypass methods of UAC, this paper makes a classification of all the bypass methods. Then the paper makes an in-depth analysis of the defects of UAC, and provides some improvement proposals in the end.

References

1. 360 Security Report. http://bobao.360.cn/learning/detail/420.html. Accessed 20 Aug 2018
2. Boonen, R.: Anatomy of UAC attacks, Fuzzysecurity. https://www.fuzzysecurity.com/tutorials/27.html. Accessed 20 Aug 2018
3. Chen, R.: There are really only two effectively distinct settings for the UAC slider. https://blogs.msdn.microsoft.com/oldnewthing/20160816-00/?p=94105. Accessed 23 Aug 2018
4. Clavoillotte, UAC bypass via elevated .NET applications. https://offsec.provadys.com/UAC-bypass-dotnet.html. Accessed 20 Aug 2018
5. Conover, M.: Symantec Corporation, Analysis of the Windows Vista security model. http://www.symantec.com/avcenter/reference/Windows_Vista_Security_Model_Analysis.pdf. Accessed 13 Aug 2018
6. ExpLife, Abusing COM Interface IARP Uninstall String Launcher to Bypass UAC (in Chinese), Freebuf. http://www.freebuf.com/articles/system/116611.html. Accessed 21 Aug 2018
7. Fernández, E.: Testing User Account Control (UAC) on Windows 10
8. Forshaw, J.: Exploiting Environment Variables in Scheduled Tasks for UAC Bypass. https://tyranidslair.blogspot.com/2017/05/exploiting-environment-variables-in.html. Accessed 20 Aug 2018
9. Forshaw, J.: Reading you way around UAC (Part 1). https://tyranidslair.blogspot.com.es/2017/05/reading-your-way-arounduac-part-1.html. Accessed 21 Aug 2018
10. Forshaw, J.: Reading you way around UAC (Part 2). https://tyranidslair.blogspot.com.es/2017/05/reading-your-way-arounduac-part-2.html. Accessed 21 Aug 2018
11. Forshaw, J.: Reading you way around UAC (Part 3). https://tyranidslair.blogspot.com.es/2017/05/reading-your-way-arounduac-part-3.html. Accessed 21 Aug 2018
12. Graham, C.: Using Application Compatibility fixes to bypass UAC, Digital Defense. https://www.digitaldefense.com/ddi-labs/using-application-compatibility-fixes-to-bypass-user-account-control/. Accessed 21 Aug 2018
13. hfiref0x, UACME, Github. https://github.com/hfiref0x/UACME. Accessed 17 Aug 2018
14. Licht, B.: How User Account Control works, Microsoft. https://technet.microsoft.com/eses/itpro/windows/keep-secure/how-user-account-control-works. Accessed 12 Aug 2018
15. LM Security. DLL hijacking attacks revisited, InfoSec Institute. http://resources.infosecinstitute.com/dll-hijackingattacks-revisited/. Accessed 15 Aug 2018
16. Mudge, R.: User Account Control – What penetration testers should know, Cobalt Strike. https://blog.cobaltstrike.com/2014/03/20/user-account-control-what-penetration-testers-should-know/. Accessed 14 Aug 2018
17. Nelson, M.: Bypassing UAC on Windows 10 using Disk Cleanup. https://enigma0x3.net/2016/07/22/bypassing-uac-on-windows-10-using-disk-cleanup/. Accessed 20 Aug 2018
18. Nelson, M.: Fileless UAC Bypass using eventvwr.exe and registry hijacking. https://enigma0x3.net/2016/08/15/fileless-uac-bypass-using-eventvwrexe-and-registry-hijacking/. Accessed 20 Aug 2018
19. Özkan, S.: Top 50 products by total number of 'distinct' vulnerabilities in 2016, CVE Details. https://www.cvedetails.com/top-50-products.php?year=2016. Accessed 10 Aug 2018
20. Pierce, S.: Malicious Application Compatibility shims, Black Hat. https://www.blackhat.com/docs/eu-15/materials/eu-15-Pierce-Defending-Against-Malicious-Application-Compatibility-Shims-wp.pdf. Accessed 21 Aug 2018

21. Russinovich, M.: User account control inside Windows 7 user account control. http://technet.microsoft.com/en-us/magazine/2009.07.uac.aspx?rss_fdn=TNTopNewInfo. Accessed 15 Aug 2018

22. Saltzer, J., Schroeder, M.: The protection of information in computer systems. Proc. IEEE **63** (9), 1278–1308 (1975)

23. Salvio, J., Joven, R.: Malicious Macro Bypasses UAC to Elevate Privilege for Fareit Malware. https://www.fortinet.com/blog/threat-research/malicious-macro-bypasses-uac-to-elevate-privilege-for-fareit-malware.html. Accessed 20 Aug 2018

24. Sara, M., Hawkey, K., Beznosov, K.: Do windows users follow the principle of least privilege?: Investigating user account control practices. In: Proceedings of the Sixth Symposium on Usable Privacy and Security. ACM (2010)

25. Schmoe, J.: Bypass UAC using DLL hijacking. https://nullbyte.wonderhowto.com/how-to/bypass-uac-using-dll-hijacking-0168600/. Accessed 21 Aug 2018

26. Security TechCenter. Microsoft Security Bulletin MS15-001, Microsoft. https://technet.microsoft.com/en-us/library/security/ms15-001.aspx. Accessed 21 Aug 2018

27. Vista UAC secure desktop explained. http://cybernetnews.com/vista-uac-secure-desktop-explained/. Accessed 15 Aug 2018

28. Zheng, L.: UAC in Windows 7 still broken, Microsoft won't/can't fix code-injection vulnerability. http://www.istartedsomething.com/20090611/uac-in-Windows-7-still-broken-microsoft-wont-fix-code-injection-vulnerability/. Accessed 13 Aug 2018

A Privacy Protection Scheme in VANETs Based on Group Signature

Xinxin Liu$^{(\boxtimes)}$, Zhijuan Jia, Erfeng Xu, Bei Gong$^{(\boxtimes)}$,
and Lipeng Wang

School of Information Science and Technology, Zhengzhou Normal University,
Zhengzhou 450044, China
liuxinxin325@163.com, tekkman_blade@126.com

Abstract. At present, Vehicular Ad-Hoc Networks (VANETs) has been a hot research topic for researchers in the intelligent transportation. It can not only provide real-time traffic information for managers, but also provide effective safety protection for drivers. However, in practical applications, the communication between vehicles is in a real-time changing network environment, which may be eavesdropping, locating and tracking. Therefore, it is essential to preserve the privacy in VANETs. Based on the Chinese remainder theorem and DSA signature algorithm, this paper proposes an efficient revocable group signature privacy protection scheme for VANETs. It can not only protect the anonymity of the vehicles, but also provide traceability for the Trusted Authority (TA) when traffics escape. At the same time, it can provide revocable functions for the vehicles when they send malicious messages or are in dispute. From the proofs of correctness and security, we know that they can not only have the properties of traceability and anonymity, but also can resist against framed attacks. According to the performance verification, we obtain it can improve the efficiency of signatures and meet the demand for real-time and efficient for VANETs.

Keywords: Vehicular Ad-Hoc Networks (VANETs) · Group signature
Chinese remainder theorem · DSA signature algorithm

1 Introduction

Vehicular Ad-Hoc Networks (VANETs) is a self-organizing network that integrates various wireless communication technologies and Internet technologies [1]. Because of much safer, more efficient, and more comfortable driving experience, VANETs have received extensive attention. However, due to the openness and high-speed mobility of the VANETs, vehicle nodes are facing the general network attacks and security threats such as illegal information injection and communication information tampered. At the same time, malicious nodes may be able to track and locate other vehicles by eavesdropping on communication messages, causing safety hazards to drivers.

With the expansion of VANETs scale and the traffic flow, and the openness of the communication channel, various attacks constantly updated [2]. VANETs put higher requirements on security protection. Therefore, researchers must combine the characteristics of the VANETs to design a suitable security strategy to provide a nice safety environment for VANETs.

© Springer Nature Singapore Pte Ltd. 2019
H. Zhang et al. (Eds.): CTCIS 2018, CCIS 960, pp. 286–300, 2019.
https://doi.org/10.1007/978-981-13-5913-2_18

The research on VANETs security environment is mainly concentrated on the following aspects [3]:

(1) The legality of identity. It aims to provide legal authentication and certificates generation for users, and it stipulates that only authorized legal users can use the system resources.
(2) Privacy protection and confidentiality. Due to the openness of the VANETs environment, some applications may require the vehicles to send their own identity information for authentication, which will reveal vehicles privacy. Therefore, user identity privacy, data privacy, and location privacy in the VANETs Environment have gradually become the focus of researchers.
(3) Traceability. Traffic management departments should be able to track down malicious vehicles that abuse the network system and recall the OBU of the vehicle in time to prevent the vehicle from continuing to endanger the entire network system.
(4) Real-time performance. Due to the large scale of the VANETs and rapid information flow, some information related to life safety must be quickly resolved. Therefore, efficient signature algorithms must be proposed to ensure the security of information.

2 Related Researches

In this section, we will introduce the research progress about the privacy protection of the VANETs. There were many schemes proposed to solve the problem, such as pseudonym authorization, ring signature, and group signature.

The pseudonym authorization was widely used early for the VANETs. In the research of identity privacy protection, Vijayalakshmi proposed an identity-based pseudonym authentication scheme for VANETs, which protected the privacy of the user identity, but the authentication efficiency is low [4]. In order to improve the authentication efficiency, Jiang proposed a batch pseudonym authentication algorithm, which reduced the authentication overhead through the calculation of Hash-based Message Authentication Code (HMAC) [5]. In addition, Forster proposed a complete anonymity scheme for the honest users [6]. In the scheme, periodic n-show anonymous certificate was used to authenticate the PCA identity to remain complete anonymity. However, there was the restriction on the number of users requested, so it only remained a certain number of anonymous users. In the research of location privacy protection, Based on pseudonyms and anonymous authentication, Rabieh proposed a privacy protection scheme against collusion attacks, which further prevented rivals from obtaining driving routes [7]. According to the lack of infrastructure in the harsh environment, Sucasas proposed a pseudonym authentication scheme that did not require real-time connection to the TA (Trusted Authority) to protect the privacy protection for VANETs in the special environment [8].

In summary, Although the pseudonym authorization scheme protects the privacy of vehicle location and user identity, improves the efficiency of authentication and reduces the cost of authentication, the real-time replacement strategy of the pseudonym may cause some schemes to be invalid, and gradually becomes the bottleneck of the development of vehicle networking, and restricts the development of the pseudonym authorization scheme.

Another scheme is the ring signature scheme for VANETs. Zeng proposed an anonymous authentication scheme for VANETs, which solved the problem of over reliance on traffic management institutions [9]. Cui adopted conditional ring signature technology on lattice-based to achieve unconditional anonymity and conditional traceability and anti-quantum attacks for the VANETs [10]. However, there is a problem with all ring signatures that is the traceability of signers can not be realized.

In the past several decades, many efforts have been devoted to consider the group signature to achieve the privacy protection for VANETs. [11–14] proposed many group signature authentication protocols to achieve the privacy protection for VANETs. However, in practical applications, due to the high openness of the VANETs, group users can join or quit at any time. Therefore, there is a problem that the keys of the users must be regenerated when a user wants to join or quit, which will increase the computational overhead.

Peters proposed an extensible revocation scheme that solved the keys regeneration problem, but the certificate occupied a large amount of storage space, increased the operational burden, and reduced revocation efficiency [15]. Zhong proposed a revocable group signature scheme based on the complete subtree method to reduce the storage cost of the certificate [16]. Due to the high-speed mobility and large-scale for VANETs, these two solutions are not suitable for VANETs. Chen firstly proposed the application of the Chinese remainder theorem to the design group signature to achieve efficient revocable scheme [17]. Based on the above researches, Huang proposed a group signature scheme based on the Chinese remainder theorem and the complete subtree method, which not only realized the non-correlation but also didn't need to change the private key of other users, and it could resist against framed attacks [18].

To summarize, the group signature technology based on the Chinese remainder theorem can protect the identities privacy, can realize the efficient revocable mechanism without changing the private key of other users, can resist against framed attacks and suitable for VANETs.

With the further attention of the VANETs, some privacy protection schemes such as elliptic curve cryptography and identity-based cryptography had been proposed. For example, Liu proposed a blind signature scheme to protect identity privacy [19]. Guo proposed an elliptic curve-based anonymous authentication scheme that not only protected identity privacy, but also had traceability [20]. In addition, based on the above researches, some hybrid schemes had also been gradually proposed, such as Buttner proposed a key agreement protocol based on elliptic curves and ring signatures to ensure user safety while implementing privacy protection and conditionality tracking [21].

Based on the above researches, this paper proposes an efficient revocable group signature privacy protection scheme for VANETs which based on the Chinese remainder theorem and DSA signature technology. While protecting the unconditional anonymity of users, and authorities can open the group signatures to track the malicious users and ensure the safety of the users. In the research of group users joining and revocation, Due to the Chinese remainder theorem, the scheme don't need to change the keys and certificates of other users, and only need to regenerate the group public key, which improves efficiency of joining and revocation. Furthermore, a more efficient DSA signature algorithm is proposed to the signature and verification, which improves the efficiency of signatures and is suitable for real-time requirements of the VANETs.

3 System Model and Preliminaries

In this section, we will review some basic knowledge related to our privacy protection scheme, including the system model, group signature, Chinese remainder theorem, hash function, DSA signature algorithm.

3.1 System Model

In this paper, the system model of VANETs consists of a TA (Trusted Authority), fixed RSUs (Road Side Units) at the road side, and mobile OBUs (On-Board Units) equipped in vehicles, as shown in Fig. 1.

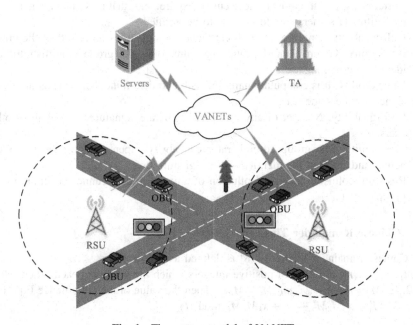

Fig. 1. The system model of VANETs.

OBUs accesses the VANETs through the roadside deployment infrastructure RSUs, and periodically broadcasts its own vehicle information to other vehicles, including safety information such as the location, speed, direction, acceleration, road conditions, traffic events, and time stamps, so that other OBUs can quickly obtain useful information on the road. RSUs can broadcast and receive some signature information in the group, provide various services for the OBUs, broadcast the identification information of revoked vehicles and assist the TA to reveal the real identification of some illegal vehicles. Each RSU has its own storage space and computing capabilities [22].

3.2 Group Signature

Group signature is a special kind of digital signature technology. It allows any group users to perform anonymous signature on behalf of the group [23].

The group manager has some responsibilities of generating and distributing keys and protecting the identity privacy of group users. The group users can sign the message to ensure the security of the messages, and then join or quit the group at any time. In addition, the group manager can reveal the real identity of the signers. It is infeasible to distinguish whether two different group signatures are from the same signer.

A group signature scheme is composed of the following eight algorithms: initialization, registration, group establishment, signature, verification, joining, revocation and opening.

The group signature defines many of the security properties as follows:

(1) Correctness: It is the most basic security requirement, that is, signatures generated by legitimate signers should be able to be verified.
(2) Unforgeability: Only group users can generate signatures on behalf of the group.
(3) Anonymity: Given a valid group signature, only the group administrator can identify the real signer.
(4) Unlinkability: It is computationally infeasible to determine that two signatures are signed by the same user.
(5) Unforgeability: No user of any group can generate signatures on behalf of other users.
(6) Traceability: The group administrator can always open a legitimate group signature and find out the identity of the signature user.
(7) Resisting collusion attacks: Collusion of any group user cannot generate a legal group signature.

3.3 Chinese Remainder Theorem

The Chinese remainder theorem [18] is defined as follows:

$m_1, m_2, \ldots, m_k$ are a set of positive integers which are primes to each other, where $k \geq 2$, set $M = m_1, m_2, \ldots, m_k, M = M_i m_i$. Then the value of the congruence Eq. (1) is

$$c \equiv x_1 M_1 M_1' + x_2 M_2 M_2' + \ldots + x_k M_k M_k' (\mod M)$$

Where $M_i M_i' \equiv 1 (\text{mod } m_i), i = 1, 2, \ldots, k$

$$
\begin{cases}
c \equiv x_1 (\text{mod } m_1) \\
c \equiv x_2 (\text{mod } m_2) \\
\quad \cdots\cdots \\
c \equiv x_i (\text{mod } m_i)
\end{cases}
\tag{1}
$$

3.4 Hash Function

Hash function is defined as $h : \{0, 1\}^* \to \{0, 1\}^n$, where $\{0, 1\}^*$ denotes a bit string of arbitrary length, $\{0, 1\}^n$ indicates a string of length with n. A one-way hash function is considered to be secure if it satisfies the following properties.

(1) Given m, it is easy to calculate $H(m) = y$. While conversely, given $y = H(m)$, it is infeasible to compute m.
(2) Given m and m', it is infeasible to compute $H(m) = H(m')$.

3.5 DSA Signature Algorithm

DSA signature algorithm is a short signature algorithm based on ELGamal signature algorithm and Schnorr signature algorithm [24]. The DSA signature algorithm is defined as follows:

First, TA chooses randomly primes b and c, such that $c|(b - 1), b \geq 2^{512}, c \geq 2^{160}$. If let $x \in z_c^*, x^c \equiv 1 (\text{mod } b)$, and $d \in z_c^*$, computing $d \in [0, c - 1]$ as its private key and $D \equiv x^d (\text{mod } b)$ as the public key.

Then choose randomly one prime $k \in z_c^*$, and compute $f \equiv (x^k \bmod b) \bmod c$, $l \equiv k^{-1} (h(M) + df) \bmod c$.

Finally, (f, l) is the signature on the massage M. The verification of the signature is done by the following calculation:

$$
e_1 \equiv \left(h(M) l^{-1} \right) \bmod c, \ e_2 \equiv f l^{-1} \bmod c, \ l' \equiv (x^{e_1} D^{e_2} \bmod b) \bmod c
$$

If the equation $l' = l$ holds, the verification passes.

4 Proposed Scheme

In this section, we propose our new privacy protection scheme based on group signature for VANETs. In the scheme, TA manages the registration of OBUs and RSUs, identity authentication, certificate issuance and revocation. We assume that the TA is fully trusted, whereas RSUs are honest but curious. The scheme as shown in Fig. 2.

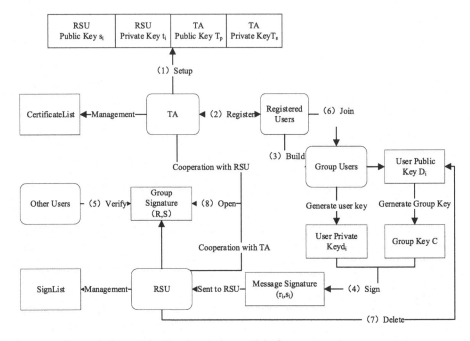

Fig. 2. The system model of VANETs.

The group signature process includes eight parts as follows:

(1) Initialization: TA chooses the system parameters and generates its own keys and RSU keys.

(2) Registration: TA generates certificates *UID* of the group users.

(3) group establishment: RSU verifies the identity certificates of joining users, and generates a users keys based on the DSA algorithm, and updates the group public key based on the Chinese remainder theorem.

(4) signature: The group user U_i performs the signature on messages M based on the DSA signature algorithm.

(5) verification: The group user first verifies its own public key, and then performs signature verification to confirm that the signature is signed by the group user.

(6) joining: When one user join to the group, The new user becomes the user of the group according to (3), generates its own keys and update the group public key.

(7) revocation: When one user quit to the group, RSU updates the user public key D_i into D_i', so the equation $D' \equiv D_i (\mod b_i)$ unholds and then updates the group public key.

(8) opening: When RSU finds malicious message or there is a disputed user in the group, the signature is opened by RSU and TA to reveal the user real identity.

4.1   Initialization

TA generates its own public/private key pair making use of the algorithm as follows:

TA chooses randomly primes p and q, such that $p \geq 2^{512}, q \geq 2^{512}$ and $n = pq$. Then choose randomly one prime $T_p \in \varphi(n)$ as its own public key, where $\varphi(n) = (p - 1)(q - 1)$, and $\gcd(T_p, \varphi(n)) = 1$. Then TA computes d as its private key, which satisfies $T_p T_s \equiv 1 (\text{mod } \varphi(n))$. Finally, publish public parameters (T_p, n) and preserve (p, q, T_s) secretly.

TA generates the public/private key pair for RSUs making use of the algorithm as follows:

TA chooses randomly primes c_i and $v_i (1 \leq i \leq I)$, such that $c_i \geq 2^{512}, v_i \geq 2^{512}$ and $m_i = c_i v_i$. Then choose randomly one prime $s_i \in \varphi(m_i)$ as its own public key, where $\varphi(m_i) = (c_i - 1)(v_i - 1)$, and $\gcd(s_i, \varphi(m_i)) = 1$. Then TA computes d as its private key, which satisfies $s_i t_i \equiv 1 (\text{mod } \varphi(m_i))$. Finally, publish public parameters $(s_i, m_i, h())$ and preserve (c_i, v_i, t_i) secretly.

4.2   Registration

In this paper, vehicle users and RSUs need to register at the TA when they want to join to the VANETs and TA generates a certificate for each user. Then TA will send all the certificates to RSU so that it can verify the validity of the new group users. Finally, RSU will broadcast the identity of the legal users so that other users are aware of the new legal users. TA generates certificates for each user making use of the algorithm as follows:

If G is a additive cyclic group of prime order q, G_T is a multiplicative cyclic group of prime order q, where $R_1, R_2 \in G$ are generators of G and $e : G \times G \rightarrow G_T$ is a computable bilinear map.

TA chooses randomly one prime $\mu \in z_q^*$, and then generates user certificates, public parameters and time stamps making use of the algorithm as follows:

$$U = \mu R_1 + R_2 = (x_\mu, y_\mu), \ UID = (x_\mu + T_s)h(ID_i) + \mu \text{ mod } q.$$

4.3   Group Establishment

RSU establishes a group consisting of r users in their corresponding area. When RSU receives a request from the vehicle user, it first verifies the validity and timeliness of the vehicle user certificate. When the verification is successful, the vehicle user is allowed to join to the group under the jurisdiction of RSU. After the Initialization is completed, RSU will generate the group key pair and the group user key pairs to facilitate the group users to generate the signature message.

In this paper, the Chinese remainder theorem is used to generate group public key and the DSA algorithm is used to the group user key pairs.

(1) User certificate concurrency verification

User U_i submits its request, ID_i and time stamps T' to RSU. RSU verifies the validity of the ID_i with $U(x_\mu, y_\mu)$ and makes use of the algorithm as follows: $UIDR_1 + R_2 = (x_\mu R_1 + R_2 + T_p)h(ID_i) + U$.

When the equation holds, and $T' - T \le \Delta T$ (ΔT is the validity period), that is the certificate is valid and unexpired, the verification is successful. Therefore, RSU allows U_i to join the group and store its certificate into the database.

(2) Generation of user signature key pairs and group public key

Because of the Initialization, we know that RSU's public key is s and the private key is t.

 a. RSU chooses randomly primes b_i and $c_i (i \in [2, r])$, such that $c_i | b_i - 1$ and $b_i \ge 2^{512}, c_i \ge 2^{160}$, where $c_i \ge g, g$ is the identity code of RSU. And then RSU sends the tuple $(g, b_i, c_i, b_i^t, c_i^t)$ to U_i in a secure environment. The user verifies the validity of public tuple by RSU's public/private key pair and the Eq. (2).

$$\begin{cases} (b_i^t)^s \equiv b_i \pmod m \\ (c_i^t)^s \equiv c_i \pmod m \end{cases} \tag{2}$$

 b. U_i chooses randomly one prime $d^i \in Z_{b_i}^*$ as its private key, and computes $D_i \equiv g^{d_i} \pmod{b_i}$ as its public key. Then, U_i sends D_i to RSU through a secure channel and RSU saves the public key and its certificate into the database.

 c. RSU generates the group public key by the received public keys of r users. RSU computes the group key according to the congruence Eq. (3).

$$\begin{cases} C \equiv D_1 \pmod{b_1} \\ C \equiv D_2 \pmod{b_2} \\ \quad\quad \ldots\ldots \\ C \equiv D_r \pmod{b_r} \end{cases} \tag{3}$$

The value to the Eq. (3) is $C \equiv x_1 B_1 B_1' + x_2 B_2 B_2' + \ldots + x_k B_k B_k' \pmod B$.

Where $B_i B_i' \equiv 1 \pmod{b_i}, i = 1, 2, \ldots, r$. RSU chooses a secure hash function $h()$, and publishes $(g, m, s, C, h())$.

4.4 Signature

In order to ensure the security of message propagation and the authentication efficiency, this paper used DSA algorithm to sign messages. If U_i wants to sign a message M, U_i will sign it making use of the algorithm as follows:

 U_i chooses randomly one prime $k \in z_c^*$, and computes $f \equiv (g^k \bmod b)$ $\bmod c, l \equiv k^{-1}(h(M) + df) \bmod c$, where g is the identity code of RSU, b_i, c_i are the primes chosen by RSU for U_i, d_i is the private key of U_i. So, (f, l, b_i) is the signature of U_i on M.

4.5 Verification

In this paper, Anyone else can verify the signed message with the signature (f, l, b_i) and the group public key $(g, m, s, C, h())$.

Anyone else can obtain the public key D_i of the U_i by computing $C \equiv D_i(\mathrm{mod}\, b_i)$. Check whether the D_i is in the database. Compute the equations $e_1 \equiv (h(M)l^{-1})\,\mathrm{mod}\, c_i$, $e_2 \equiv fl^{-1}\,\mathrm{mod}\, c_i$, and $l' \equiv (g^{e_1}D_i^{e_2}\,\mathrm{mod}\, b_i)\,\mathrm{mod}\, c_i$ if it is true. If the equation $l'=l$ holds, it can be confirmed that the message is signed by U_i.

4.6 Joining

In this paper, it is supported that vehicle user U_{r+1} wants to join to the group of RSU, which includes r users. U_{r+1} joins to the group according to Sect. (4.3). When RSU receives a request from the vehicle user, it first verifies the validity and timeliness of the vehicle user certificate. When the verification is successful, the vehicle user is allowed to join to the group. And then the new user generates its own signature key pairs making use of the DSA algorithm. Finally, the public key and the user certificates are saved into the database. RSU computes the new group key according to the congruence Eq. (4).

$$\begin{cases} C_w \equiv D_1(\mathrm{mod}\, b_1) \\ \quad\cdots\cdots \\ C_w \equiv D_r(\mathrm{mod}\, b_r) \\ C_w \equiv D_{r+1}(\mathrm{mod}\, b_{r+1}) \end{cases} \tag{4}$$

The value of the congruence Eq. (4) is $C \equiv x_1B_1B_1' + x_2B_2B_2' + \ldots + x_kB_kB_k'(\mathrm{mod}\, B)$, where $B_iB_i' \equiv 1(\mathrm{mod}\, b_i), i = 1, 2, \ldots, r$ and the equation $C \equiv C_w(\mathrm{mod}\, B_w)$ unholds.

To summarize, the user joining strategy based on the Chinese remainder theorem only needs to update the group public key, and does not affect the key pairs of other users, which improves the joining efficiency.

4.7 Revocation

Assume that there are r members in the group for VANETs. When RSU receives an quit request from the vehicle user U_i, RSU changes the public key D_i to D_i' in the database, and then computes the new group key C_{new} according to the congruence Eq. (5).

$$\begin{cases} C_{new} \equiv D_1(\mathrm{mod}\, b_1) \\ \quad\cdots\cdots \\ C_{new} \equiv D_i'(\mathrm{mod}\, b_i) \\ \quad\cdots\cdots \\ C_{new} \equiv D_r(\mathrm{mod}\, b_r) \end{cases} \tag{5}$$

The value of the congruence Eq. (5) is $C_{new} \equiv x_1 B_1 B_1' + x_2 B_2 B_2' + \ldots + x_k B_k B_k' (\mod B)$

Where $B_i B_i' \equiv 1 (\mod b_i), i = 1, 2, \ldots, r$.

4.8 Opening

When RSU finds that malicious message or there is a disputed vehicle user in the group, the signature is opened by RSU and TA, which reveal the real identity of the vehicle user. RSU can obtain the public key of the malicious user by calculating the known group public key C and congruence equation $C \equiv D_i (\mod b_i)$, and then obtain the certificate of the malicious user from the public key list. TA can obtain the identity ID_i by computing the equation $UID = (x_\mu + T_s) h(ID_i) + \mu \mod q$ with UID $h()$, $U(x_\mu, y_\mu)$, and its private key T_s. That reveals the real identity of malicious vehicle user.

5 Security and Performance Analysis

5.1 Correctness Analysis

The correctness analysis of this paper involves the correctness of identity information, the correctness of RSU public parameters and the correctness of signatures.

(1) Correctness of identity information

RSU receives the vehicle user U_i identity information ID_i and generates time stamps T'. RSU computes $UIDR_1 + R_2 = (x_\mu R_1 + R_2 + T_p) h(ID_i) + U$ with $U(x_\mu, y_\mu)$ and verifies the validity of the identity, the certificate is valid and unexpired. So it proves that the identity information is correct.

(2) Correctness of RSU public parameters

When the vehicle user U_i receives the public parameter $(g, b_i, c_i, b_i^t, c_i^t)$, from RSU, where t is the private key of RSU and s is the public key of RSU. U_i computes the equation $(b_i^t)^s \equiv b_i (\mod m), (c_i^t)^s \equiv c_i (\mod m)$. When the equation holds, and it proves that the public parameters are legal and the key pairs of the user U_i are correct.

(3) Correctness of the signatures

RSU computes the equations $e_1 \equiv (h(M)l^{-1}) \mod c_i, e_2 \equiv fl^{-1} \mod c_i, l \equiv (g^{e_1} D_i^{e_2} \mod b_i) \mod c_i$. When the equations holds, it proves that the signature is correct.

5.2 Security Analysis

(1) Anonymity

Since the certificate signature technology and periodic update strategy are used in this paper, attackers cannot deduce the real identity of OBUs from the certificate. In addition, the key pairs of group users are not related to their real identity. So, it is impossible for attackers to obtain the identity information of users.

(2) Traceability

There is a disputed user in the group, RSU and TA can obtain the public key D_i of the disputed user by calculating the known group public key C and congruence equation $C \equiv D_i(\mod b_i)$. Then we can obtain the certificate from the public key list. TA can decrypt the certificate to obtain the real identity of the disputed user by its own private key.

(3) Unforgeability

Unforgeability means that no user of the group can generate signatures on behalf of other users. In our scheme, if an attacker attends to forge a signature (f', l', b_i, M') of the user U_i on the message M, and he will choose randomly one prime $k' \in z_c^*$ and compute $f' \equiv \left(g^{k'} \mod b_i\right) \mod c_i'$, $l' \equiv k'^{-1}\left(h(M) + d_i' f'\right) \mod c_i'$, where $c_i' | b_i - 1$, d_i' is the private key of the user U_i, and $D_i \equiv g^{d_i}(\mod b_i)$. So, it is impossible to obtain the private key d_i' according to the discrete logarithm problem. Therefore, it is considered that the message signature cannot be forged and framed.

Moreover, the public key D_i is unique according to the equation $C \equiv D_i(\mod b_i)$, and it is proved that the user of the signed message cannot deny the signature.

(4) Forward security

Forward security means that it is illegal for a new group user to use the old group public key to sign message.

A new user U_{r+1} joins to the group, which must generate its own public/private key pair (D_{r+1}, d_{r+1}) with the public parameters, and RSU computes the new group key C_w according to the congruence Eq. (6).

$$
\begin{cases}
C \equiv D_1(\mod b_1) \\
C \equiv D_2(\mod b_2) \\
\cdots\cdots \\
C \equiv D_r(\mod b_r)
\end{cases}
\rightarrow
\begin{cases}
C_w \equiv D_1(\mod b_1) \\
\cdots\cdots \\
C_w \equiv D_r(\mod b_r) \\
C_w \equiv D_{r+1}(\mod b_{r+1})
\end{cases}
\tag{6}
$$

If the messages are verified to be valid, the congruence equation $C \equiv C_w(\mod B_w)$ should hold. But $C \equiv C_w(\mod B_w)$ should not be established. It is illegal for the signature using the old public key. So, the algorithm of the joining has the forward security.

(5) Backward security

Backward security means that it is illegal to use a new group public key for signatures of the revoked users.

We assume that U_i is one of the revocation user in the group, we need to update the public key D_i to D_i', and the equation $D' \equiv D_i(\mod b_i)$ should not be established. And RSU computes the new group key C_{new} according to the congruence Eq. (7).

$$\begin{cases} C \equiv D_1(\bmod b_1) \\ C \equiv D_2(\bmod b_2) \\ \cdots\cdots \\ C \equiv D_r(\bmod b_r) \end{cases} \rightarrow \begin{cases} C_{new} \equiv D_1(\bmod b_1) \\ \cdots\cdots \\ C_{new} \equiv D_i'(\bmod b_i) \\ \cdots\cdots \\ C_{new} \equiv D_r(\bmod b_r) \end{cases} \qquad (7)$$

If a revocation user U_i can sign the message with its own private key, the equations $C_{new} \equiv D_i(\bmod b_i)$ and $D' \equiv D_i(\bmod b_i)$ hold. But the algorithm of the revocation required by $D' \equiv D_i(\bmod b_i)$ should not be established. So it proves that a revocation user U_i can not sign the message with its own private key and the algorithm of the revocation has the backward security.

5.3   Performance Analysis

(1) Here, we have a function comparison between our proposed scheme and some other schemes in VANETs is made as Table 1.

Table 1. Function comparison

Function	Ours scheme	Literature 14 scheme	Literature 25 scheme
Member joining	✔	✔	✔
Member revocation	✔	✔	✔
Anonymity	✔	✔	✔
Traceability	✔	✔	✔
Unforgeability	✔	✔	
Forward security	✔		
Backward security	✔		

(2) Here, we have a computational cost comparison between our proposed scheme with others. First, we have a simulate in a modern personal computer, which is conducted with Intel i7-7700-3.6 GHz CPU and 8-GB RAM. The operation time of the scheme is made as Table 2.

Table 2. Operation time

Code	Denotation	Time (ms)
T_{EX}	An exponentiation in z_c^*	0.12
T_{ADD}	An addition in z_c^*	0.001
T_{MUL}	A multiplication in z_c^*	0.001
T_{INV}	An inverse operation in z_c^*	0.003
T_H	A hash operation in z_c^*	0.0001
T_P	A pairing operation in z_c^*	12.055

The computational cost of the scheme mainly includes revocation, signature and verification. We assume that there are r users in the group. And based on the bilinear logarithm calculations, the inverse operation is equivalent to a 10 power operation, and the multiplication and addition calculations have minimal time.

In [14], the total computational load of this scheme is $15T_{ADD} + 6T_{MUL} + 10T_P$. In [25], the total computational load of this scheme is $T_{ADD}(r-1) + T_{MUL}(r+9) + T_P(r+7) + 28T_{EX}$. A computational cost comparison between our proposed scheme and others is made as Table 3.

Table 3. Computational cost comparison

Function	Ours scheme	Literature 14 scheme	Literature 25 scheme
RSU cost	$2T_{ADD} + 4T_{MUL}$	$3T_{ADD} + T_{MUL} + 2T_P$	$(T_{ADD} + 2T_{MUL} + 2T_{EX})(r-1)$
Revocation cost	0	T_{MUL}	$T_{MUL} + 2T_{EX} + T_P$
Signature Cost	$3T_{MUL} + 2T_{EX}$	$8T_{ADD} + 4T_{MUL}$	$14rT_{EX} + 4T_P$
Verification cost	$5T_{MUL} + 2T_{EX} + T_{INV}$	$10T_P + 4T_{ADD}$	$10T_{MUL} + 14rT_{EX} + 4T_P$
Total cost	$12T_{MUL} + 2T_{ADD}$ $+ 4T_{EX} + T_{INV}$	$15T_{ADD} + 6T_{MUL} + 10T_P$	$T_{ADD}(r-1) + T_{MUL}(r+9)$ $+ T_P(r+7) + 28T_{EX}$

6 Conclusion

In this paper, an efficient revocable group signature privacy protection scheme for VANETs is proposed, which includes initialization, registration, group establishment, signature, verification, joining, revocation and opening. This not only protects the anonymity of the group users of the VANETs, but also can track the real identity of the group users by opening the signature when there is a disputed user in the group. when the users join or quit, the joining and the revocation strategy based on the Chinese remainder theorem only needs to update the group public key, and does not affect the key pairs of other users, which improves the joining and revocation efficiency. Furthermore, Efficient DSA signature algorithm has a higher message validation efficiency and lower computing time. Therefore, this scheme is suitable for the dynamic VANETs.

Acknowledgments. This work was supported by the National Natural Science Funds (U1304614, U1204703), the construct program of the key discipline in Zhengzhou Normal University, aid program for Science and Technology Innovative Research Team of Zhengzhou Normal University, Henan Province Education Science Plan General Topic "Research on Trusted Degree Certification Based on Blockchain" ((2018)-JKGHYB-0279).

References

1. Ren, K., Li, J., et al.: Development status and tendency of IoV communication technology. Commun. Technol. **48**(5), 507–513 (2015)
2. Chen, C., Han, W., Wang, X.: Survey on security in vehicular ad hoc networks. J. Chin. Comput. Syst. **32**(5), 896–904 (2011)

3. Liu, H.: A Study of Message Authentication and Privacy Preservation in Vehicular Ad Hoc Networks. Xidian University (2012)
4. Vijayalakshmi, N.F., Sasikumar, R.S.: An ID-based privacy preservation for VANET. In: Computing and Communications Technologies, pp. 164–167 (2015)
5. Jiang, S., Zhu, X., Wang, L.: An efficient anonymous batch authentication scheme based on HMAC for VANETs. IEEE Trans. Intell. Transp. Syst. **17**(8), 2193–2204 (2016)
6. Förster, D., Kargl, F., Löhr, H.: PUCA: a pseudonym scheme with strong privacy guarantees for vehicular ad-hoc networks. Ad Hoc Netw. **37**, 122–132 (2016)
7. Rabieh, K., Mahmoud, M.M.E.A., Younis, M.: Privacy-preserving route reporting scheme for traffic management in VANETs. IEEE Trans. Veh. Technol. **66**, 2703–2713 (2017)
8. Sucasas, V., Saghezchi, F.B., Radwan, A., et al.: Efficient privacy preserving security protocol for VANETs with sparse infrastructure deployment. In: IEEE International Conference on Communications, pp. 7047–7052 (2015)
9. Zeng, S., Huang, Y., Liu, X.: Privacy-preserving communication for VANETs with conditionally anonymous ring signature. Int. J. Netw. Secur. **17**(2), 135–141 (2015)
10. Cui, Y., Cao, L., et al.: Ring signature based on lattice and VANET privacy preservation. Chin. J. Comput., 1–14 (2017)
11. Enganti, P., Velagalet, S.B.: VANET based secure and privacy preserving navigation. IEEE Trans. Comput. **2**(63), 510–524 (2014)
12. Mamun, M.S.I., Miyaji, A., Takada, H.: A multi-purpose group signature for vehicular network security. In: International Conference on Network-Based Information Systems, pp. 511–516 (2014)
13. Fan, C.I., Sun, W.Z., Huang, S.W., et al.: Strongly privacy-preserving communication protocol for VANETs. In: Information Security, pp. 119–126 (2015)
14. Shao, J., Lin, X., Lu, R., et al.: A threshold anonymous authentication protocol for VANETs. IEEE Trans. Veh. Technol. **65**(3), 1711–1720 (2016)
15. Peters, T., Yung, M.: Scalable group signatures with revocation. In: International Conference on Theory and Applications of Cryptographic Techniques, pp. 609–627 (2012)
16. Zong, H., Huang, C., et al.: Efficient group signature scheme with revocation. J. Commun. **37**(10), 18–24 (2016)
17. Chen, Z., Zhang, L., et al.: A group signature scheme based on Chinese remainder theorem. Acta Electronica Sinica **32**(12), 140–142 (2008)
18. Huang, C., Zhong, H., Wang, Y.: Improved group signature scheme based on Chinese remainder theorem. Comput. Sci. **43**(3), 174–178 (2016)
19. Liu, Z., Liu, J.: A study of privacy improvement using a randomized blind signature scheme in vehicular networks. In: IEEE International Conference on Ubiquitous Intelligence and Computing and 2015 IEEE International Conference on Autonomic and Trusted Computing and 2015 IEEE International Conference on Scalable Computing and Communications and ITS Associated Workshops, pp. 1631–1637 (2015)
20. Guo, S., Zeng, D., Xiang, Y.: Chameleon hashing for secure and privacy-preserving vehicular communications. IEEE Trans. Parallel Distrib. Syst. **25**(11), 2794–2803 (2014)
21. Büttner, C., Huss, S.A.: A novel anonymous authenticated key agreement protocol for vehicular ad hoc networks. In: International Conference on Information Systems Security and Privacy, pp. 259–269 (2016)
22. Mei, Y.: Research on the privacy preservation for VANETS. Huazhong University (2014)
23. Xie, R.: Research on Group Signatures and Their Applications. University of Electronic (2016)
24. Zhao, Z.: Research on efficient group signatures schemes in VANET. Xidian University (2015)
25. Mamun, M.S.I., Miyaji, A.: Secure VANET applications with a refined group signature. In: 2014 Twelfth Annual International Conference on Privacy, Security and Trust (PST), pp. 199–206. IEEE (2014)

Analysis of Wireless Sensor Networks Behavior for Trustworthiness Evaluation

Ying Zhang[1(✉)], Peisong Li[1], Jun Wang[2], Mingxing Wang[1], and Dengpan Ye[3]

[1] Shanghai Maritime University, Shanghai 201306, China
yingzhang@shmtu.edu.cn
[2] University of Central Florida, Orlando, FL 32816, USA
[3] Wuhan University, Wuhan 430072, China

Abstract. Wireless sensor networks (WSNs) face many security challenges in their applications. In order to improve the security of WSNs, a trust security algorithm based on nodes behavior analysis and cloud model is proposed. According to the behavior characteristics of the conventional attacks, three kinds of trust factors are defined and introduced to the trust security algorithm: the transmission rate factor, the spatial correlation factor and the replay attack factor. The cloud model is used to judge the security status of the nodes according to these three trust factors. In the comprehensive calculation of the trust value, the time attenuation factor and the strategy for excluding the impersonation factor by historical evaluations are introduced. Moreover, the influence of the impersonation factor is further excluded by considering the acceptance domain of the trust distribution, and the defamatory nodes could get punished finally. Simulation experiments show that the proposed algorithm can detect the malicious nodes, identify the impersonation nodes, and resist on impersonation attacks effectively.

Keywords: Wireless sensor networks · Trust security · Malicious nodes Cloud model · Trust factors

1 Introduction

Wireless sensor networks (WSNs) have been getting more attentions in various industry applications. Their autonomous field computing function and flexible networking capabilities have brought a wide application prospect in many dedicated fields. WSNs can be widely used in industrial control system, environmental monitoring, data acquisition, border detections, disaster preventions, national defenses, and so on [1–5]. However, WSNs are usually deployed in unattended harsh areas, and they are Ad hoc dynamic networks, which do not rely on any network infrastructures. Since the network node does not have a unique identification code, the nodes are easy to be captured and are subject to various attacks by adversaries and hence the security of the network often faces various threats. With its popularity of being used in Internet of things, industrial internets, it becomes a great challenge to improve the safety performance of WSNs which makes it one of the hot topics to study in this research field.

© Springer Nature Singapore Pte Ltd. 2019
H. Zhang et al. (Eds.): CTCIS 2018, CCIS 960, pp. 301–317, 2019.
https://doi.org/10.1007/978-981-13-5913-2_19

Compared with the nodes in the conventional computer networks, the WSN node is cheaper, and has the characteristics of lower computing power, smaller storage space and difficulty to supplement energy. Therefore, the traditional security mechanisms are not applicable to be used in WSNs directly. The features of WSNs should be considered while designing defense attacks schemes. There are many attacks occurring in WSNs, such as the Replay, Tampering, HELLO attacks, Impersonation attacks, and the Denial of Service (DoS) [6–13]. However, we can find that, with these attacks, there are often some different behavioral characteristics from the normal nodes. For example, data tampering attacks can cause the data submitted by the node to be quite different from the data submitted by the other nodes, the correlation between the data packages of the Replay attacks will be higher, and the nodes of Denial of Service attack will send fewer packets. Feature analysis of the malicious behavior of these attacks can greatly improve the sensitivity of intrusion detection.

This paper fully analyzes the characteristics of attack behaviors, and proposes a behavior-cloud-model based trust security algorithm (BCMT), which can effectively resist on the conventional network attacks and the impersonation attacks in WSNs. At first, three trust factors: the transmission rate factor, the spatial correlation factor and the repetition factor are defined according to the network transmission rate, data spatial consistency, and time correlation of the nodes. However, these three kinds of trust factors are not directly used to participate in weighted calculation. Instead, the three factors will be judged separately, and the output state of each judgment is one of the three states: normal, pending and malicious. If the states determined by the three factors are all normal, that node state is normal. If the state determined by any one factor is malicious, that node is considered as a malicious node. Except to these two situations above, the status of the node will be defined as pending. When calculating the trust value comprehensively, the time attenuation factor and the recommended trust value weighting factor will be taken into account synchronously, which can further improve the sensitivity of the detection. Additionally, we introduce a strategy to exclude the impersonation factor through historical evaluations and negative records. To treat evaluation records in the same time period for single trust factor, the impersonation evaluation could be excluded and the masquerade node could get punished by considering the acceptance domain of the trust distribution. Simulation experiments indicate that the proposed algorithm can detect malicious nodes and resist on impersonation attacks effectively.

2 Related Work

Most common security algorithms of WSNs are based on the secret keys or trust mechanisms, and there are some key-based security algorithms with high recognition [14–16]. These algorithms show excellent performance against external attacks of the network, but they are not ideal to resist the internal attacks within the network. Also, these algorithms have higher requirements in terms of node computing and storage capacity. In addition, because the key-based security algorithms' certification process is more cumbersome, the communication energy consumption will be larger, and their applicability to the application scenarios of WSNs is not better than the security algorithms with the trust-based mechanism. The trust-based mechanism caters to the features of lower computing power and poorer storage capacities of network nodes, and it can resist on the external and internal attacks from the network. Trust based mechanisms have been extensively studied in recent years, and we will discuss some of it below.

Pirzada et al. proposed a DSR routing protocol based on trust value [17]. In this algorithm, each node evaluates the surrounding neighbor nodes, each time a node sends a packet, and waits for a trust update interval. During this interval, it monitors whether the node has forwarded this packet after it receives the packet. However, this model cannot prevent the data integrity attacks from malicious nodes, and its complex trust value exchange mechanism will cause a larger quantity of communication overhead. In [18], a novel trust building algorithm was proposed. This algorithm is based on a novel watchdog mechanism, which not only considers the forwarding behavior of the nodes, but also considers the link quality between them. But this scheme requires the node's geographic location information dynamically. In [19], an improved TEEN_TQ (TEEN based Trust QoS routing algorithm) based on trust value was proposed, which is a dynamic trust management model. The algorithm determines the security status of the nodes through a periodic data collection mechanism. Thereby, it can improve the cluster head selection strategy and routing strategy of TEEN. However, this scheme cannot prevent impersonation attacks. The authors in [20] studied the security threats and energy consumption problems when deploying the WSN nodes, and proposed a trust-based security and energy preserving routing protocol (TEPP) in multi-hop WSNs. By monitoring the trust value of the node and maintaining the interaction history between the nodes, it can determine a safe and reliable path of routing. However, this method has higher requirements on nodes' storage capacity and computing power. Chen et al. proposed a TLES algorithm based on trust value [21], which takes into account the direct trust value and the indirect trust value, and uses the historical evaluation to calculate the comprehensive trust value, but TLES is insensitive to on-off type attacks, it does not have the punishment mechanism, and it is not good enough to resist on the impersonation attacks from the network.

3   Model and Definitions

3.1   Definition of the Cloud Model

The cloud model was formally presented by Professor Li in 2009 [22], and then it has been used in a large number of applications on the need for qualitative and quantitative conversions to deal with some uncertainty problems. The uncertainty of trust relationship is mainly manifested in the randomness and fuzziness, it is difficult to quantitatively give an accurate evaluation of trust, and the trust evaluation has a lot of randomness. We would like to give a detailed definition of the cloud model in this paper as follows.

Definition 1 (Cloud and cloud droplets): Assuming that $U = \{x_i \mid i = 1, 2, \cdots, N\}$ is a quantitative domain, the elements in U are all the exact values. T is defined as a qualitative concept on U, and the degree of determination that T describes the concept is called the membership $\mu(x) \in [0, 1]$, which is a random number with stable tendency. That can be described as $\mu(x) : U \to [0, 1]$, $\forall x \in U$, $x \to \mu(x)$, the distribution of the membership in U is called the cloud. Each x_i and its corresponding membership form a sequence as $(x_i, \mu(x_i))$, which is called as the cloud droplets. If U is an n dimensional domain, the cloud model can also be extended to n dimensions.

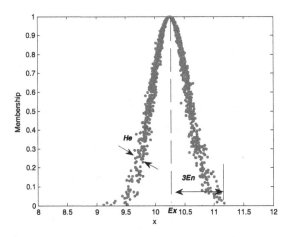

Fig. 1. Cloud model graph and its digital features

Cloud models have multiple distribution types, and the type with highest universality is the normal distribution, which can represent the majority of the natural science in the field of uncertainty. The cloud model uses the three digital features of expectation (*Ex*), entropy (*En*), and super entropy (*He*) to reflect the distribution characteristics. As shown in Fig. 1: the expectation (*Ex*) can represent the overall level of the data; entropy (*En*) can characterize the degree of the data discretization. According to the triple standard deviation principle, the probability that the cloud droplets are distributed outside the interval $[Ex - 3En, Ex + 3En]$ is less than 3%. The super entropy (*He*) can characterize the uncertainty and the change speed of the data. The distribution type used in this paper is a one-dimensional normal distribution, and the definition of the one-dimensional normal cloud can be made as follows:

Definition 2 (One-dimensional normal cloud): On the basis of Definition 1, if $x_i \sim N(Ex, En_i'^2)$, $En_i' \sim N(En, He^2)$, and the membership degree satisfies the condition:

$$\mu(x_i) = e^{-\frac{(x_i - Ex)^2}{2(En_i')^2}} \tag{1}$$

That is called as a one-dimensional normal cloud.

3.2   Definition of the Trust Factors

Considering the characteristics of the WSN node, in order to reduce the occupied storage and the transmission loss, the trust factors defined in this paper are non-uniformly quantized to 16 levels, and the quantization value can be represented by a 4-bits binary number.

According to the research on nodes attack behaviors in WSNs, when the malicious nodes perform HELLO diffusion, Denial of Service (DoS), and so on, the number of packets sent by malicious nodes is different from that of normal nodes. In accordance with this feature, we can make the definition as follows:

Definition 3 (Transmission rate factor):

$$SR(i) = \begin{cases} 1 & sn_i/sd \le Sl \\ floor(\frac{16sn_i}{(Sh-Sl)*sd}) & Sl < sn_i/sd \le Sh \\ 16 & sn_i/sd > Sh \end{cases} \tag{2}$$

where sn_i is the total number of the packets sent by the evaluation node n_i in the time slice t, sd is the expected value in the setting time slice t, Sl is the minimum threshold of the setting ratio of sn_i to sd, and Sh is the maximum threshold of the setting ratio of sn_i to sd.

According to the characteristics of nodes distribution, the collected data from the node will have higher spatial dependencies with the data from its neighboring nodes. If the data submitted by the node is tampered, the data of this node will be very different from that of the surrounding neighbor nodes, and it will show a lower correlation between them. So the spatial dependencies can be defined as follows:

Definition 4 (Spatial dependency factor):

$$CR(i) = \begin{cases} 1 & c_i/c_j \le Rl \\ floor(\frac{16c_i}{(Rh-Rl)*c_j}) & Rl < c_i/c_j \le Rh \\ 16 & c_i/c_j > Rh \end{cases} \tag{3}$$

where c_i is the data submitted by node i, c_j is the data collected by cluster head j of node i, Rl is the minimum threshold of the setting ratio of c_i to c_j, and Rh is the maximum threshold of the setting ratio of c_i to c_j.

According to the correlation of the packets sent by the node before and after, it is possible to judge whether the node is performing a Replay attack. The replay attack factor can be defined as follows:

Definition 5 (Replay attack factor):

$$DR(i) = \begin{cases} 1 & d_i/dT_i \le Dl \\ floor(\frac{16d_i}{(Dh-Dl)*dT_i}) & Rl < d_i/dT_i \le Dh \\ 16 & d_i/dT_i > Dh \end{cases} \tag{4}$$

where dT_i is the total number of packets sent by node i in time slice t; d_i is the number of the same packets sent by node i in time slice t; Dl is the minimum threshold of the setting ratio of d_i to dT_i; and Dh is the maximum threshold of the setting ratio of d_i to dT_i. The value of the node trust factor is given by the other nodes that have interacted with the evaluated node, and it can be calculated by the formulas (1)–(3). The calculated trust factor will be sent to the base station in a time interval after setting up the time slice t, and will participate in the calculation of the comprehensive trust value.

4 Security Algorithm of WSNs Based on the Trust Mechanism

4.1 Removal of Impersonation Evaluation

The trust data set needs to be calculated before the calculation of the comprehensive trust value, and the trust data set will include the evaluations from all the nodes that have ever interacted with the evaluated node. Among these evaluations, there may be malicious evaluations, so it is necessary to first exclude the malicious evaluations from the trust data set. The process of eliminating the influence of impersonation attacks is shown as Fig. 2.

First, the trust factor with impersonation behavior given by different evaluation nodes at the same time slice will be excluded. The sizes of the trust factor given by each node can be regarded as a normal distribution. Then the impersonation attack can be distinguished by setting the appropriate acceptance domain. For example, suppose that the evaluation set for node i is $T = \{x_{i,j} \ j = 1, 2, \cdots, n\}$, if we want to discuss whether the evaluation given by a node k $(x_{i,k} \in T)$ is a malicious evaluation, according to the distribution of $x'_{i,j}$ $(j = 1, 2, \cdots, n \ , \ j \neq k)$, when the probability that $x_{i,k}$ is fallen into the acceptance domain is greater than P_α (95.4% is set in this paper as an example), that means this evaluation is normal, otherwise it is considered as a possible defamatory evaluation. According to the knowledge of probability theory, we can get this accep-

tance domain as $[\overline{x'_{i,j}} - 2 \times \sqrt{\frac{1}{n}\sum_{i=1}^{n}(x'_{i,j} - \overline{x'_{i,j}})^2}, \overline{x'_{i,j}} + 2 \times \sqrt{\frac{1}{n}\sum_{i=1}^{n}(x'_{i,j} - \overline{x'_{i,j}})^2}]$. Based on

this way, we can distinguish and exclude a defamatory evaluation from the acceptance domain, and the trust level of node k will be reduced by one level.

This paper sets two kinds of history records for each node.

(1) The evaluation of the record: that is the history record regarding this node evaluating the other nodes, and the last n items of the records will be reserved all the way.
(2) Record of the bad reviews: that is the history record that this node has got a malicious evaluations by the other nodes, and the last n items of the records will be reserved all the way.

When the evaluation is too low, the history evaluation records will be inquired, the authenticity of the evaluation will be judged, and a decision should be chosen whether to discard it. Finally, the new result set will be regarded as a new trusted data set after removing the possible effect of the impersonation attacks.

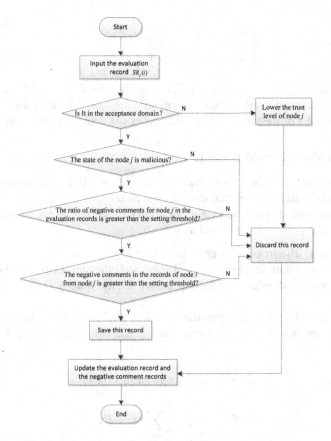

Fig. 2. The process of excluding the impersonation attacks

4.2 Introduction of the Time Attenuation Factor

For some attacks, such as the on-off attack, the malicious nodes will accumulate the trust value of the good performance through a certain period of time. However, when the trust value of the malicious node is accumulated and high enough, the malicious node will launch its attack to the other nodes. Unfortunately, the other nodes will continue to think that the malicious node is a normal node because of its good records in the history, thus they will suffer from the attacks by this malicious node. In order to reduce this effect, the time attenuation factor is defined in this paper. In the use of cloud model to determine the safety status of the nodes, the historical evaluations will be weighted, so that the latest records could have greater impacts on the judgment of the outcome. This mechanism could improve the sensitivity of detecting malicious nodes to a certain extent. The definition of the time attenuation factor can be made as follows:

Definition 6 (Time attenuation factor): Suppose that we need to consider the latest n records: $t_1, t_2, \cdots, t_n$, the weighting coefficient of the ith record for the trust evaluation is ω_i, then ω_i needs to meet the following constraints:

$$\begin{cases} \sum_{i=1}^{n} \omega_i = 1 \\ \omega_{i+1} > \omega_i \quad i = 1, 2, \cdots, n-1 \end{cases} \tag{5}$$

In the mapping of $i \rightarrow \omega_i \quad i = 1, 2, \cdots, n$, the lower the ω_i is, the lower the dependence on the historical evaluations will be. That means the later the record is, the greater the impact of the record is, and the higher the detection sensitivity will be.

4.3 Generation of Cloud Droplets

After the impersonation factor is excluded, a new trusted data set is generated. In this case, the trusted data set is inputted into the trust cloud generator to obtain the specified number of the cloud droplets, and the expectation Ex, the entropy En, the super entropy He as well. The process is described as follows:

Algorithm 1: The trust cloud generator algorithm:
Input: the trust data set $X = \{x_i \mid i = 1, 2, \cdots, n\}$, the number of cloud droplets N.
Output: N cloud droplets, and the expectation Ex, the entropy En, the super entropy He.

Step1: According to the input data set $X = \{x_i \mid i = 1, 2, \cdots, n\}$, calculate the expected Ex, entropy En and the super entropy He, the corresponding formulas are defined as follows:

$$Ex = \overline{X}, X = \{x_i | i = 1, 2, \cdots, n\} \tag{6}$$

$$En = \sqrt{\frac{\pi}{2}} \times \frac{1}{n} \sum_{i=1}^{n} |X_i - Ex| \tag{7}$$

$$He = \sqrt{\frac{1}{n-1} \sum_{i=1}^{n} (X_i - Ex)^2 - E^2 n} \tag{8}$$

Step2: Generates a normal random number En'_i with the expectation En and variance $H^2 e$.

Step3: Generates a normal random number x_i with the expectation Ex and variance En'^2_i.

Step4: Calculate the membership $\mu(x_i) = e^{-\frac{(x_i - Ex)^2}{2(En'_i)^2}}$, get a cloud droplet $(x_i, \mu(x_i))$;

Step5: Repeat the above steps to get N cloud droplets finally.

4.4 Determine the Node Status with the Single Factor

In this paper, the trust factors will be separated to consider when the status determination of the node is made. That is because an attacking behavior of a node often conforms to only one of the most obvious features, such as Tampering with Data Attacks, the other factors may all be normal except the factor of data relevance, and only this factor is not quite normal. If we use the common weighting algorithm, the calculated trust value may only have a small change, which may not be lower than the judgment threshold, and it is not easily to be recognized. So here we use the trust cloud model to judge each factor separately. The result of each output of the discriminant is one of the three states: normal, pending, or malicious. Taking the transmission rate factor SR as an example, the algorithm for determining the state of a node with the single factor is as follows:

Algorithm: 2: The node state is determined by the transmission rate factor SR.

Input: The trust value data set $SR(i)$ $i = 1, 2, \cdots, n$.

Output: The state of the node: normal, to be determined, malicious.

Step 1: Preprocess the data, and exclude the impersonation evaluations from the trust value data set (the process is shown as Fig. 2).

Step 2: Weight the trust evaluations for the data after preprocessing. Assuming that $x_{i,j}$ is the trust evaluation of node j to node i, and S_j is the state of node j, which can be one of the states: normal, to be determined, or malicious, these states are denoted by 2, 1, and 0 respectively. In addition, when the state of node j is to be determined, there is an auxiliary value $A_j \in [1, 2]$, and the corresponding weighting factor is w_j. The calculation method of w_j can be given by formula (9).

$$w_j = \begin{cases} 1 & S_j = 2 \\ \frac{A_j}{m} & S_j = 1 \\ 0 & S_j = 0 \end{cases} \tag{9}$$

Step 3: Weight the preprocessed data according to the time attenuation factor in Definition 6.

Step 4: Generate the cloud droplets by using the trust cloud generator in Algorithm 1, and get the expectation Ex, the entropy En, and the super entropy He.

Step 5: Use the cloud similarity algorithm in [23] to get the output state.

4.5   Application of the Algorithm

As a kind of trust mechanism for node security judgment, the proposed algorithm can be added to the topology control algorithm to detect the malicious nodes and improve the network security of WSNs. As an example of the application in the representative SEP (Stable Election Protocol) algorithm, the cluster head node has a great influence on the security of the network because they are the backbone of the whole WSNs. Therefore, the security of the cluster head node has more significance. The security state of the node can be judged by using the proposed algorithm, and the outcome can be regarded as an important evidence to select the cluster head nodes. The nodes with the normal state have the greatest probability to become the cluster head nodes, the nodes to be determined have a slightly lower probability to be the cluster head than the nodes with the normal state, and the nodes with malicious state cannot become the cluster head nodes, and the data submitted from the malicious nodes will be ignored in the data fusion. This process is described as follows:

(1) The clustering stage: Each node selects its cluster head node to form the cluster structure according to the trust value and other factors, and the initial trust value will be set to the highest level.

(2) The stable working stage:

(i) The node monitors the communication behavior of its surrounding nodes, calculates the specific values of the three trust factors, and passes them to the base station.

(ii) For each trust factor and each node, the base station determines the state of the node by using the method in Sect. 4.

(iii) All the state values judged out from the second step need to be multiplied each other. If the result of the multiplication is 0, the final state of the node is 0 (that means malicious); if the result is 8, the final state of the node is 2 (that means normal); if the result is the others, the node state will be 1 (that means to be determined).

(iv) The base station saves the results of the judgment and updates the trust table to each node at the end of the current round.

In addition, considering the situation in an impersonation attack, the malicious node can continually disguise itself as the other node, reduce the trust value of the node, and after a while, it may disguise itself as another node. In some trusted security modes, the trust value of a node is always considered to be a malicious node once it falls below the threshold. So when the network encounters an impersonation attack, it may lead to paralysis of the entire network. In order to avoid this phenomenon, the proposed security algorithm in this paper performs the monitoring and evaluating to the malicious nodes as usual. However, it permits that the nodes with malicious state can convert to other states depending on its subsequent performances.

5   Simulation Analysis

The proposed algorithm, designed to enhance terms of security for the general topology control of WSNs, can be applied to most of the topology control algorithms of WSNs. The performances, such as energy consumption and life cycle of the networks, shall not be considered in the simulation [24]. In order to test the performance of the algorithm in trust security, the algorithm development platform MATLAB (R2010b) is used to carry out the simulation experiments. 100 wireless sensor nodes are distributed in an area of 100 m × 100 m randomly, and the base station is located at the coordinate (50, 50). A topology control protocol SEP (Stable Election Protocol) is adopted in the network. On the basis of the SEP protocol, the proposed trust security mechanism is introduced. The specific parameters are set up as follows (Table 1):

Table 1. Simulation parameters setting table

Simulation parameters	The value of the parameter
Number of nodes N	100
Distribution area	100 m * 100 m
Base station location	(50 m, 50 m)
Packet length	4000 bit
Maximum communication radius	50 m
Node capture rate	10%
Attack type	On-off, Replay, HELLO attack, Data tampering
P_α	95.4%
Time slice	3.6 s

5.1 The Changes of the Trust Cloud Before and After the Node Is Attacked

In order to observe the changes of the trust cloud before and after the attacks, in these experiments, we set the node's capture probability as 0.1. The captured node will have the capacity to perform one of the attacks: Replay attack, HELLO attack, and Tampering with data attack. The cloud images and its digital features of the three kinds of trust factors before and after suffering from the attacks can be observed in the following experiments.

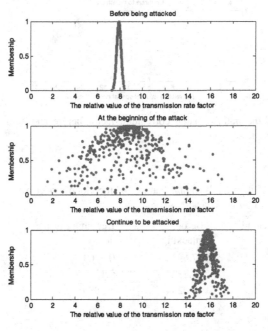

Fig. 3. Changes of the transmission rate of the node before and after suffering from the HELLO attacks

Table 2. Changes of the node's digital features of the cloud model before and after suffering from the HELLO attacks

Digital features of the cloud model	Before attacking	Beginning of the attack	Continuous attack
Expectation Ex	7.8699	0.1943	0.0673
Entropy En	8.7732	2.0128	1.5967
Super entropy He	15.7500	0.5069	0.2247

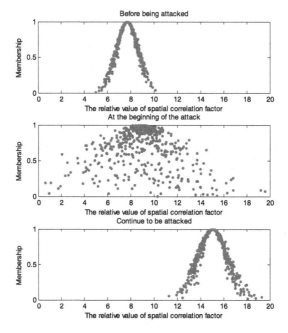

Fig. 4. Changes of the node's spatial correlation factor before and after suffering from the tampering with data attacks

Table 3. Changes of the node's digital features of the cloud model before and after suffering from the tampering with data attacks

Digital features of cloud model	Before attacking	Beginning of the attack	Continuous attack
Expectation Ex	7.6912	0.9264	0.0928
Entropy En	8.8824	2.1380	1.6308
Super entropy He	15.0294	1.2880	0.1704

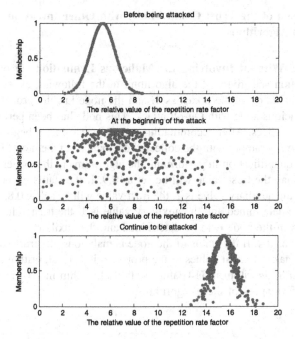

Fig. 5. Changes of the node's repetitive factor before and after suffering from the replay attacks

Table 4. Changes of the node's digital features of the cloud model before and after suffering from the replay attacks

Digital features of cloud model	Before attacking	Beginning of the attack	Continuous attack
Expectation Ex	5.3015	1.0171	0.2280
Entropy En	6.5809	2.7777	2.2369
Super entropy He	15.4412	0.9270	0.1616

As shown in Figs. 3, 4, 5 and Tables 2, 3, 4 at the beginning of the attacks, the unconventional behavior of the nodes will cause big changes in the trust cloud image. As shown in Fig. 4 and Table 3, although the change of expectation Ex is not obvious, the entropy En and the super entropy He are greatly changed. At this time, the true state of the node can be easily identified by the proposed algorithm, and it has higher detection sensitivity. The node that suffers from the sustained attacks will have a significant change in its expectation Ex compared with that before the attacks, which makes it easy to set the judgment threshold to distinguish the state of the nodes.

5.2 Comparison of the Trust Cloud Model with Other Intrusion Detection Algorithms

On-Off Attacks Without Involving the Malicious Evaluation. In order to further verify the detection sensitivity of the algorithm, in the following experiments, we set the initial trust value of all the nodes as 1, and the node has the probability of 0.1 to become the malicious node with On-off attack. This node has been performing well in the initial 20 time slices. After accumulating higher trust value, it begins to launch the attack, and randomly tamper with the collected data and send them out. In addition, we make a specific quantification in performing the algorithms in this paper. If the state of the node is normal, the trust value will be set as 0.9. If the status of the node is to be determined and the auxiliary value is 2, the trust value will be set as 0.8. If the status of the node is to be determined and the auxiliary value is 1, the trust value will be set as 0.6. If the status of the node is to be determined and the auxiliary value is 0, the trust value will be set as 0.4. If the status of the node is malicious, the trust value will be set as 0.2. We can make the trust values in the proposed BCMT algorithm compared with those in the TLES algorithm in [14] and the IDS algorithm in [16] respectively, and analyze the performances of these algorithms.

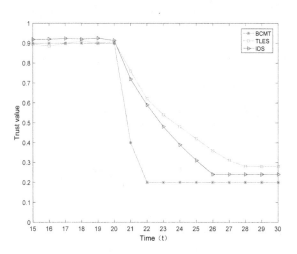

Fig. 6. Comparison of the trust values for the three algorithms

As seen from Fig. 6, the proposed BCMT algorithm can detect the malicious behavior of the node after about two time slices, while IDS needs about 6 time slices and TLES needs about 8 time slices. We could find that the BCMT algorithm has better detection sensitivity than the other two algorithms, and it could detect the nodes with malicious attacks earlier.

On-Off Attacks with Malicious Evaluation Capabilities. In the case of keeping other conditions unchanged in last subsection, the On-off attack node has the ability to launch the impersonation attack after 20 time slices. The node with impersonation attack gives the evaluation of trust factor as a rounding up normal random number with the expectation of 2 and the variance of 0.8. At this time, we just focus on analyzing the changes of the trust values of these two kind of nodes between the proposed BCMT algorithm and the TLES algorithm in [14] when a node continues to maliciously evaluate another node.

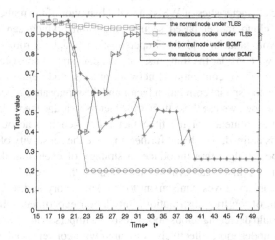

Fig. 7. Changes of the trust values of the defamatory node and the normal node under the two algorithms

Figure 7 shows the changes of the trust values of the impersonation attack nodes and the slandered nodes. From observing the trust value of the slandered node under TLES algorithm, we can find that the slandered node is mistakenly regarded as the malicious node after suffering from the attacks for about 20 time slices. Compared with the conventional algorithm that does not consider the indirect trust values, this algorithm can resist on the impersonation attacks to a certain extent. However, after many experiments, we can find that the trust value of the slandered node has a large probability to fall below the threshold of 0.3, which could cause it to be wrongly judged as a malicious node after several continuous recommended evaluations become less. In addition, by observing the trust value of the malicious node in the TLES algorithm, we can find that the TLES algorithm does not have any detection and penalty mechanisms for the nodes which are performing the impersonation attacks. By observing the trust value of the slandered node in the proposed algorithm, we can find that, although the trust value of the node is affected by the impersonation attack in the beginning of encountering the impersonation attacks, eventually it can effectively resist on the impact of the impersonation attacks by the proposed exclusion strategy for impersonation attack with the punishment mechanism. After about 9 time slices, the trust value of the slandered node is restored to its normal level, the trust value of the node which initiates the impersonation attack will drop to a minimum level after about 3 time slices, and it will be judged as the malicious node. Therefore, by comparing with some representative algorithms, we can find that the proposed algorithm has the abilities to resist on the impersonation attacks and identify the defamatory nodes in the networks more effectively.

6 Conclusions

On the basis of the characteristics of WSNs and the behavior of the malicious attacks, this paper proposes a cloud model based security algorithm, which can effectively resist conventional network attacks and the impersonation attacks. From the behaviors of malicious attacks, we consider the transmission rate, data spatial consistency and the time correlation of the nodes in conventional network attacks, and define three trust factors: transmission rate factor, spatial correlation factor and the replay attack factor. Furthermore, through the cloud model, we use these three trust factors to judge the nodes security. In the states judgment, the influence of the time factor is taken into account, and the time attenuation factor is defined, which can further improve the sensitivity of the detection. In addition, the proposed algorithm introduces a strategy of excluding the impersonation influence through the historical evaluations. This further excludes the influence of impersonation factors and gives punishment to the defamatory nodes by considering the acceptance domain of the trust distribution. Simulation experiments show that the proposed algorithm could detect malicious nodes, resist on impersonation attacks, and identify the impersonation nodes more effectively compared with conventional algorithms.

Acknowledgments. This work was supported by the National Natural Science Foundation of China (no. 61673259, U1636101, U1636219, U1736211); International Exchanges and Cooperation Projects of Shanghai Science and Technology Committee (No. 15220721800); partially supported by the National Key Research Development Program of China (2016QY01W0200), also supported in part by the US National Science Foundation Grant CCF-1337244.

References

1. Rao, W., Hu, Y., Hu, Z., Xiong, S.: Towed vector fiber optic sensor used in ocean seismic exploration. In: Proceedings of SPIE - The International Society for Optical Engineering, pp. 4–16 (2012)
2. Luque-Nieto, M.A., Moreno-Roldán, J.M., Poncela, J., Otero, P.: Optimal fair scheduling in S-TDMA sensor networks for monitoring river plumes. J. Sens. **2016**(5), 1–6 (2016)
3. Mythrehee, H., Julian, A.: A cross layer UWSN architecture for marine environment monitoring. In: 2015 Global Conference on Communication Technologies, Communication Technologies (GCCT), Thuckalay, India, pp. 211–216 (2015)
4. Jin, Y., Kwak, K.S., Sengoku, M., Shinoda, S.: Wide area sensor network for disaster prevention and monitoring: concept and service coverage. In: 2014 IEEE Asia Pacific Conference on Circuits and Systems, Circuits and Systems (APCCAS), Ishigaki, Japan, pp. 391–394 (2014)
5. Lee, S.H., Lee, S., Song, H., Lee, H.S.: Wireless sensor network design for tactical military applications: remote large-scale environments. In: 2009 Military Communications Conference, Boston, MA, USA, pp. 911–917 (2009)

6. Sharma, V., Hussain, M.: Mitigating replay attack in wireless sensor network through assortment of packets. In: Satapathy, S.C., Prasad, V.K., Rani, B.P., Udgata, S.K., Raju, K. Srujan (eds.) Proceedings of the First International Conference on Computational Intelligence and Informatics. AISC, vol. 507, pp. 221–230. Springer, Singapore (2017). https://doi.org/10.1007/978-981-10-2471-9_22

7. Azam, S., Manzoor, R., Rehman, M.: Secure solution to data transfer from sensor node to sink against aggregator compromises. In: 2011 Frontiers of Information Technology (FIT), Islamabad, Pakistan, pp. 247–252 (2011)

8. Bysani, L.K., Turuk, A.K.: A survey on selective forwarding attack in wireless sensor networks. In: 2011 International Conference on Devices and Communications (ICDeCom), Devices and Communications, Mesra, India, pp. 24–25 (2011)

9. Mahajan, M., Reddy, K.T.V., Rajput, M.: Design and simulation of a blacklisting technique for detection of hello flood attack on LEACH protocol. Procedia Comput. Sci. **79**, 675–682 (2016)

10. Pongaliur, K., Xiao, L., Liu, A.X.: Dynamic camouflage event based malicious node detection architecture. J. Supercomput. **64**(3), 717–743 (2013)

11. Tian, B., Yao, Y., Shi, L., Shao, S., Liu, Z., Xu, C.: A novel sybil attack detection scheme for wireless sensor network. In: 5th IEEE International Conference on Broadband Network & Multimedia Technology, Broadband Network and Multimedia Technology (IC-BNMT), Guilin, China, pp. 294–297 (2013)

12. Yang, G., Ying, S., Yang, W.: Reputation model based on behaviors of sensor nodes in WSN. J. Commun. **30**(12), 18–26 (2009)

13. Upadhyay, R., Bhatt, U.R., Tripathi, H.: DDOS attack aware DSR routing protocol in WSN. Procedia Comput. Sci. **78**, 68–74 (2016)

14. Fakhrey, H., Tiwari, R., Johnston, M., Al-Mathehaji, Y.A.: The optimum design of location-dependent key management protocol for a WSN with a random selected cell reporter. IEEE Sens. J. **16**(19), 7217–7226 (2016)

15. Tufail, A., Khan, A.M., Kim, K.H.: A reliable and secure hybrid key management scheme for WSNs. J. Int. Technol. **16**(4), 629–642 (2015)

16. Baburaj, E.: Polynomial and multivariate mapping-based triple-key approach for secure key distribution in wireless sensor networks, **59**, 274–290 (2017)

17. Pirzada, A.A., McDonald, C., Datta, A.: Performance comparison of trust-based reactive routing protocols, **5**(6), 695–710 (2006)

18. Salehi, M., Boukerche, A., Darehshoorzadeh, A.: Towards a novel trust-based opportunistic routing protocol for wireless networks, **22**(3), 1–17 (2016)

19. Junwei, W., Xiaoyi, F.: Improved TEEN based trust routing algorithm in WSNs. In: 27th Chinese Control and Decision Conference (CCDC), Qingdao, China, pp. 4379–4382 (2015)

20. Raza, S., Haider, W., Durrani, N.M., Khan, N.K., Abbasi, M.A.: Trust based energy preserving routing protocol in multi-hop WSN. In: Bouajjani, A., Fauconnier, H. (eds.) NETYS 2015. LNCS, vol. 9466, pp. 518–523. Springer, Cham (2015). https://doi.org/10.1007/978-3-319-26850-7_42

21. Chen, Z., He, M., Liang, W., Chen, K.: Trust-aware and low energy consumption security topology protocol of wireless sensor network, **2015**(1), 1–10 (2015)

22. Li, D., Liu, C., Gan, W.: A new cognitive model: cloud model, **24**(3), 357–375 (2009)

23. Lu, H., Pi, E., Peng, Q., Wang, L., Zhang, C.: A particle swarm optimization-aided fuzzy cloud classifier applied for plant numerical taxonomy based on attribute similarity, **36**(5), 9388–9397 (2009)

24. Sajjad, S.M., Bouk, S.H., Yousaf, M.: Neighbor node trust based intrusion detection system for WSN, **63**, 183–188 (2015)

Digging Evidence for Violation of Cloud Security Compliance with Knowledge Learned from Logs

Yue Yuan, Anuhan Torgonshar, Wenchang Shi[✉], Bin Liang, and Bo Qin

School of Information, Renmin university of China, Beijing, China
{yuanyue,anuhan,wenchang,liangb,bo.qin}@ruc.edu.cn

Abstract. Security compliance auditing against standards, regulations or requirements in cloud environments is of increasing importance to boost trust between stakeholders. Many automatic security compliance auditing tools have been developed to facilitate accountability and transparency of a cloud provider to its tenants in a large scale and complex cloud. User operations in clouds that may cause security compliance violations have attracted attention, including some management operations conducted by insider attackers. System changes induced by the operations concerning security policies are captured for auditing. However, existing cloud security compliance auditing tools mainly concentrate on verification rather than on evidence provision. In this paper, we propose an automatic approach to digging evidence for security compliance violations of user operations, by mining the insights of system execution for the operations from system execution traces. Both known and potentially unknown suspicious user operation re-quests that may cause security compliance violations, or suspect system execution behavior changes, are automatically recognized. More importantly, evidences related to the detected suspicious requests are presented for further auditing, where the abnormal and expected snippets are marked in the relevant extracted execution traces. We have evaluated our method in OpenStack, a popular open source cloud operating system. The experimental results demonstrate the capability of our approach to detecting user opera-tion requests causing security compliance violations and presenting relevant evidences.

Keywords: Security compliance · Cloud security · Auditing · IaaS
User operations · OpenStack

1 Introduction

An IaaS cloud enables convenient on-demand access to shared cloud resources via various user operations like VM creation. On the other hand, the multi-tenancy and self-service nature in clouds implies significant operational complexity, which may prepare the floor for misconfigurations and vulnerabilities leading to violations of security compliance [1]. For example, frequent concurrent operation

© Springer Nature Singapore Pte Ltd. 2019
H. Zhang et al. (Eds.): CTCIS 2018, CCIS 960, pp. 318–337, 2019.
https://doi.org/10.1007/978-981-13-5913-2_20

requests are issued and large numbers of VMs are created, deleted and reconfigured, which leads to server sprawls and potential security breaches. The cloud provider and customers are exposed at great risk to potential loss of reputation and the breach of confidential data.

Security compliance, in IT systems, is the state of conformance with external imposed functional security requirements and of providing evidence therefrom. Security compliance auditing provides proofs regarding the compliance, and assures the accountability and transparency of a cloud provider to its tenants. Security compliance auditing is demanded by both cloud providers and customers. For cloud providers, some cloud users including cloud operators maybe malicious. For cloud customers, cloud providers and other users maybe malicious. To verify security compliance, recent researches have focused on analysis of the impacts of cloud user operations on the system to tell whether com-pliance violation is caused after the operations. Although Cloud Security Alliance (CSA) [2] has developed the framework of CloudAudit [3] and guidelines of Cloud Control Matrix (CCM) [4] to provide high-level security compliance auditing approaches, how to generate the low-level security compliance related information is still under research.

To generate the low-level compliance related information for security compliance auditing in clouds is challenging. Extraction of required data from cloud system for security control verification is sophisticated. Firstly, identification of relevant data on the right server node can be increasingly difficult as the cloud scales up. Secondly, massive cloud user operation requests are handled in parallel. It is difficult to filter and correlate the retrieved data for verification. Moreover, it is not easy to determine a proper processing method on the extracted data to automatically detect compliance violations and provide the evidences thereof.

Recently, many researchers(e.g. [1, 5–7]) have been working hard to verify the compliance of each user operation request in clouds. The user operation requests causing compliance violations can be detected by verification of the operation request against the desired security property. However, the existing approaches mainly focus on verification of compliance rather than evidence provision once the suspicious violation is detected after an operation request is issued. A case in point is confidential data breach from violation of secure VM disposal after the deletion operation. The customer tries to delete the VM. The cloud deletes the resource record in the central database but does not destroy underlying relevant resources. We seek the answer to the question of how to detect this scenario of a cloud handling numerous various concurrent user operation requests and provide evidence for it.

To this end, an automatic approach is proposed in this paper to recognize the cloud operation requests that may potentially breach security properties, and more importantly, to provide relevant evidence once the suspicious operation request is recognized. The execution traces to represent the cloud execution behaviors related to each user request of target operation are extracted from cloud system logs. Execution insights of user operations are mined from both normal and abnormal cloud behaviors based on system execution traces under predefined and historical scenarios. The mined low-level execution patterns can denote the high-level security properties. In this way, based on the mined knowledge, suspicious user operation requests with suspect system execution behavior changes can be recognized. Relevant evidences are presented for auditors. Additionally, there is still potential in the cloud logging mechanisms to simplify and improve the extraction of system execution traces related to user operations, which has not been fully exploited. We furthermore demonstrate the capability of our approach to detect security compliance violations and present relevant evidences with experimental evaluation results on OpenStack [8]. To be more specific, our work helps in security compliance auditing for OpenStack in the following way.

- Extracting source data for auditing with consideration of the underlying principle in OpenStack, in which way traces related to each user operation request can be identified and extracted from corresponding distributed log files automatically.
- Classifying execution traces related to user operations for automated compliance violation detection of user requests, with N-gram based method as well as TF-IDF technique for feature representation and machine learning technique for execution pattern recognition.
- Detecting potential suspicious operation requests that have not met before where the relevant execution traces deviate from the execution patterns under known scenarios especially known normal scenarios.
- Presenting relevant evidences of each suspicious operation request by automated marking and presentation of abnormal and expected snippets in the extracted execution traces.

The remainder of the paper is organized as follows. Section 2 discusses related work. Section 3 describes the preliminaries. Section 4 introduces our approach. Section 5 presents experiment and evaluation. Finally, Sect. 6 concludes.

2   Related Work

Many tools have been designed to troubleshoot the cloud. CloudWatch [9] and Ceilometer [10] provide metrics of cloud resources such as CPU usage of VMs. Vitrage [11] provides root cause analysis service based on cloud metric information. Congress [7] offers a policy framework for cloud services to enforce user policies and then to check the cloud compliance. CloudTrail [12] enables cloud users to track their history operations. Moreover, [13] builds the correlation between cloud metrics and logs for operation anomaly detection in AWS cloud. Many recent studies have focused on problems related to user operations in OpenStack. [14] detects bugs with logs using intrusive failure injection framework targeting service communications during the processing of external operation requests. [15] analyzes relevant network messages and distributed system state for fault location and root cause analysis in OpenStack operations. [16] diagnoses failures with tracing tools and combines failure injection with data analytics. [1] proposes to proactively verify security compliance for clouds by analysis of potential operations causing violations. LeaPS [5] adopts Bayesian Network for proactive security auditing of cloud operations. [17] verifies user-level security properties including common access control and authentication mechanisms for a large cloud. Furthermore, some work have targeted on inconstancy problems in OpenStack. CloudSight [18] allows cloud users system-wide visibility through a transparency-as-a-service abstraction. [19] proposes network inconsistency checking based on the comparison of metadata from cloud controller and the actual state of network resources on edge nodes. Additionally, some work target on software-defined network (SDN) environments. For example, Sphinx [20] detects both known and potentially unknown attacks where the actual network operations are modeled to enable incremental validation of all network updates and constrains. Libra [21] verifies forwarding tables in very large networks.

Compared with above work, we focus on identification of both known and unknown potential suspicious cloud user operation requests based on OpenStack logs for security compliance auditing. Our work provide as a complementary fine-grained approach to present relevant low-level evidences for auditors once the compliance violation is detected.

While many existing tools [22–24] are able to get insights into distributed systems with intrusive approaches, many log mining tools have been deployed for problem diagnosis purely with system logs. Some [25,26] aim to detect anomalies in cloud, where a model is learned from logs by correct system runs and the model is then applied on logs in production. Many tools use system logs for problem identification. For example, [27] provides a lightweight approach for cloud deployment failures identification. CSight [28] mines logs of a system's executions to a model of that system's behavior in the form of a finite state machine to provide developers with more insight into concurrent systems. LogCluster [29] proposes a log clustering based problem identification approach for online service systems. [30,31] recognize system issues with relevant transaction logs and produce healing suggestions by adapting the healing actions of similar historical issues for online service systems. CAM [32] uses supervised machine learning technique for test alarm cause analysis based on test logs. [33] makes full use of recent Natural Language Processing (NLP) tool to process system logs to train classifiers for system problem analysis. Moreover, some work specifically focus on attack detection. DeepLog [34] detects system anomalies for system security assurance using deep learning technique. [35] finds early-stage enterprise infections with logs using belief propagation. LAEPS [36] mines control flow graph from logs and trains binary classifier for attack detection.

Our work target on detecting user operations causing compliance violations in the cloud. We identify target user operations, obtain the insights into known suspicious operation requests and detect unknown suspicious operation requests. Furthermore, we present relevant execution traces as the evidence where abnormal snippets are marked and relevant expected snippets are shown for auditors.

Additionally, usually as the first step for automated log analysis, log parsing is to abstract log messages to structured events. Many recent work have concentrated on automated log parsing. [37] proposes to extract log events from log statement in source code, while many other work focus on data-driven approaches using data mining techniques. As a represent of data-driven approaches, [38] provides implementations for several representative log parsers. We provide a simplified method for log parsing in OpenStack considering the characters of its logging mechanism, whereas the mentioned work can be applied in our framework for situations where logging configurations are not allowed.

3   Preliminaries

3.1   Threat Model

In our work, patterns are learned from logged traces generated by execution paths under predefined and historical scenarios for cloud security compliance auditing. Thus, we assume (1) no unauthorized modifications of the cloud source code or configuration to change its logging behavior, and (2) the integrity of cloud logs can not be attacked. Existing techniques can be used to protect these data in cloud, such as hashchain schema [39] or techniques on trusted computing to establish a chain of trust from TPM chips embedded inside the cloud hardware [40]. Moreover, cloud users including cloud operator may also be malicious.

Our approach can assist to detect violations of specified security properties. Instead of detecting specific attacks and intrusions, we focus on detecting suspicious cloud user operations causing security compliance violations. A comprehensive list of critical user operations and several attack scenarios are assumed to be provided. The guideline on provision of critical operations and attack scenarios can be inferred in [1].

Motivating Examples. In addition to the insecure resource disposal example in Sect. 1, two more examples are illustrated in the following for concrete discussions. The first one is violations of the security property of cloud resource abuses. CCM [4] has emphasized no abuse of cloud resources since anonymous users can be affordable to rent thousands of servers from a cloud provider. This can lead to criminal and malicious activities such as to crack an encryption key or to stage a DDos attack. In this case, a malicious user may issue suspicious VM creation requests causing the abuse of VM resources. Another example is the bypassing firewall rules. A vulnerability [41] in OpenStack can be exploited. Once the port with no security property enabled is attached to a VM though update port operation, no firewall rules will be attached to the VM for spoofing protection and bypassing of firewall rules is caused.

3.2   User Operations in OpenStack

OpenStack is an open source cloud operating system controlling large pools of compute, storage, and network resources throughout a data center. Cloud users can perform various operations on cloud resources in need. OpenStack contains multiple service components managing different resources in the cloud. For example, the core component Nova provides an interface to manage VMs, and supports various virtualization technologies for underlying implementation. Cloud users can submit operation requests through command line interface, e.g., 'nova boot' and 'nova delete' to create and delete VMs.

The execution of a user operation often involves coordination between service components as well as between several distributed service processes within one service component. For example, to create a VM, Keystone for authentication, Nova to prepare the VM, Glance to provide image, and Neutron to allocate networks are typically involved. Furthermore, nova-api, nova-scheduler, and nova-conductor as service processes of Nova on controller node collaborate to handle user request data and to choose a target host. After RPC messages are sent to nova-compute on the target host by Advanced Message Queuing Protocol (AMQP), image and network resources are obtained asynchronously from service components of Glance and Neutron. Finally, the hypervisor takes the request from nova-compute to launch the VM. More to the point, as each service process executes, critical events are recorded in relevant log files of each service process. When a user operation fails, one can check theses log files for insights into system executions of the operation.

(a) Some default configurations.   (b) Modified configurations.

Fig. 1. Configurations for logging format in OpenStack.

3.3   Logging in OpenStack

As a Python-based system, OpenStack encapsulates logging functions into a shared module based on standard logging packages in Python. What and how to log can be configured in every component as needed. Some important default configurations for logging format in OpenStack are shown in Fig. 1a. Typically, a log would record timestamp, the process producing this log, logging level, the module producing this log, context information, the related resource identifier if exists, and the logged message. Additionally, the exception logs, which are important for root cause analysis, contain no context information.

Moreover, the message part in a log corresponds to the formatted string in a log statement in the source code. Thus, logs generated by the same logging call are formatted by a common template and share similarity in text. Log parsing is to abstract the log event from the logs generated by the same log statement. In other words, a log event can correspond to a log statement. We adopt the modified configurations in Fig. 1b for log parsing. The modified part in the configuration denotes the function containing the logging call. We can later leverage this modified part to denote the log event of each log. Note that we refer log entries to logs and log content to the message part of a log in this paper.

4   Approach

4.1   Overview

Figure 2 presents the overall working process of our approach, which consists of two stages: training stage and production stage. At the training stage, logs are grouped, extracted and parsed into *log event sequences* to represent cloud behaviors related to user operations. In this way, execution traces can be recovered and labeled after monitoring a cloud which is experiencing normal and various abnormal behaviors under predefined and historical scenarios. After that, the recovered execution traces are vectorized for feature representation using N-gram based method and TF-IDF (Term Frequency - Inverse Document Frequency) technique. Classifiers can then be trained with the labeled vectors for automatic recognition of suspicious operation requests. Meanwhile, traces related to system executions of user operations under normal scenarios are collected for further unknown failure diagnosis. At the production stage, when user operations are to be verified, log files are collected and relevant execution traces representing relevant cloud behaviors are extracted. Each trace is then recognized by the classifier after vectorization. Typically, if some traces are recognized as suspicious operation requests, the normal, abnormal and predicted log events would be marked in these traces as evidences of compliance violations for auditors.

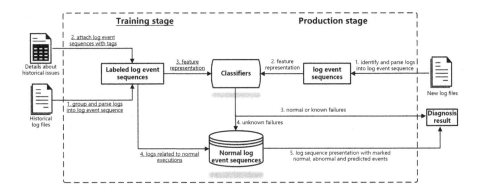

Fig. 2. Overview of the approach.

Note that the normal scenario refers to the baseline expected system execution of the user operation. Moreover, the suspicious scenarios refer to system executions of user operations causing security compliance violations. Conversely, non-suspicious scenarios refer to executions of user operations without violations including normal scenarios and some failure scenarios.

4.2 Data Extraction to Separate Traces from Logs

As shown in Fig. 1a, a log entry contains context information and resource information identified by request identifier and instance (namely VM) identifier respectively, except that exception logs contain no context information. Logs generated by system tasks related to user operations mostly contain either of these identifiers. We first merge each exception log with its previous log entry. Then we use the combination of request and instance identifiers to group logs.

Given n log entries after exception logs are handled $F_{log} = < l_1, l_2, ..., l_n >$, we use regulation expressions to extract identifiers in each log entry l_i. Specifically, $(req\text{-}[\backslash w\backslash\text{-}]*)$ is used for request identifiers and $\backslash [instance : ([\backslash w\backslash\text{-}]*)\backslash]$ is used for instance identifiers. Then F_{log} is transformed to a sequence of three-tuples :

$$T_{log} = < (r(l_1), v(l_1), l_1), (r(l_2), v(l_2), l_2), ..., (r(l_n), v(l_n), l_n) >$$

where l_i is the log entry, $r(l_i)$ is the request identifier, $v(l_i)$ is the instance identifier, and either $r(l_i)$ or $v(l_i)$ can be *None*. All request and instance identifiers are denoted as $Q = \{q_1, q_2, ..., q_k, q_{k+1}\}$ and $S = \{s_1, s_2, ..., s_m, s_{m+1}\}$ respectively, where q_{k+1} and s_{m+1} are *None*.

Moreover, any request identifier q_i is associated with the instance identifier s_j if q_i appears in the same tuple with s_j, and any log entry l_p is associated with the instance identifier s_j if s_j appears in l_p. We group the three-tuples following two rules:

1. Tuples with the same request identifier q_i are grouped together.
2. If any request identifier q_i is associated with multiple instance identifiers, tuples with the same q_i and having the log entry associated with the same instance identifier s_j are extracted and grouped together.

In this way, we can get a dataset extracted from T_{log}:

$$D_{log} = \{((q_i, s_{ij}), < l_{ij_1}, l_{ij_2}, ..., l_{ij_{end}} >)|1 \le i \le k, 1 \le j \le a(q_i)\}$$

where $q_i \in Q$ is the request identifier, $s_{ij} \in S$ is the instance identifier, $l_{ij_p} \in F_{log}$ is the log entry, q_i is associated with s_{ij} and $a(q_i)$ is the number of instance identifiers associated with q_i. Any element in D_{log} is identified by (q_i, s_{ij}) and the element corresponds to the trace generated by the cloud execution task. There are some additional explanations of D_{log}.

– q_i is not *None*. This means the context information is identified in each log entry:
  - q_i is associated with multiple instances. This represents concurrent bulk operations in one request (e.g., create multiple VMs in one user request). In this case, log entries without instance identifiers associated can be confusing, and thus are dropped. If log entries identified by q_i are analyzed as a whole in this situation, it could be intricate because different instances may correlated with different failures.
  - q_i is associated with unique or no instance. This means such tasks as network creation where instance identifier is *None* and VM migration with unique instance identifier.
– q_i is *None*. Related log entries are mostly generated by some internal sub-tasks.

A simple data extraction example can be seen in Fig. 3. Firstly, logs are grouped by request identifiers according to rule (1). Then, logs with the request identifier *req-d*81 are further grouped by instance identifiers, and the fifth and the last log entry is dropped, according to rule (2). The two rules are defined to gather as more accurate and typical logs as possible for a task related to the cloud resource.

The objective is to gain insights into the executions about a certain type of user operations like VM creation. In a cloud operating system like OpenStack, different types of user operation requests are related to different APIs. Since the first log entry related to a user request records the entry point of the service program, we can use the content of the first log entry related to each user request to identify the operation type. The log content to identify each known operation is also stored so that we can extract log event sequences related to any targeted operation type. Moreover, note that although one user operation request may trigger multiple sub-requests, we take a first step to analyze the logs related to each original request in this paper. In the experiment, it actually proves effective.

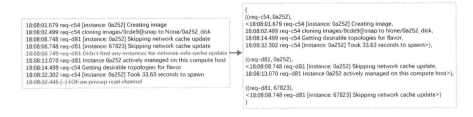

Fig. 3. A simplified example for data extraction from logs.

4.3   Log Parsing

Log parsing is to abstract log events from log entries. Recording event ID in logs may greatly facilitate log parsing process [38]. To this end, for each log entry, we use the logging level part and the modified part as shown in Fig. 1b as the event ID to identify a log event. The modified part records the function name containing the logging call and the module containing the function. Additionally, the log entries with ERROR logging level are handled differently, where the log content part are kept and the variables in the log content are eliminated. After this step, take D_{log} in Sect. 4.2 as input, we can get:

$$D'_{log} = \{(O_{ij}, < e_{ij_1}, e_{ij_2}, ...e_{ij_{end}} >)|O_{ij} = (q_i, s_{ij}), q_i \in P_{op}\}$$

where q_i is the request identifier directly associated with user operation request, P_{op} is the set of user operation requests related to a common type of operation identified by the first log entry, j is the number of instance identifiers associated with q_i, and e_{ij_p} is the log event parsed from the log entry l_{ij_p}.

Note that P_{op} represents a type of cloud user operation such as VM creation, and each type corresponds to a dataset of D'_{log}. Moreover, each element in D'_{log} represents a log event sequence corresponding to an execution trace.

4.4   Classification of Execution Traces for Compliance Violation Detection

The objective in this step is to classify the recovered execution traces like the log event sequences in D'_{log}. There could be concurrently running threads and redundant sub tasks for a cloud to accomplish a user operation, leading to uncertainty in the permutation and combination of log events corresponding to one operation. Henceforth, to automatically recognize the execution traces, or log event sequences, we make use of standard classification algorithms to learn the patterns of log event sequences related to the operations from limited predefined and historical cloud issues.

Feature Representation. Any log event sequence corresponding to an execution trace identified by O_{ij} in D'_{log} can represent a sequence of function calls related to an execution of the operation. We combine a N-gram based method with a term weighting technique in information retrieval TF-IDF (Term Frequency-Inverse Document Frequency) [42] to model a log event sequence as a natural language sequence. Each log event sequence can be treated as a natural language sequence and each log event in the log event sequence can be treated as a word.

An n-gram is a contiguous sequence of n items (log events in this paper) from a given sample of text or speech (log event sequence in this paper). By converting a sequence of log events to a set of n-grams, the sequence can be embedded in a vector space for feature representation, thus allowing the comparison between log event sequences. In this way, with N-gram based method, features related to event sequences can be constructed with their sequential information maintained. Typically, when $N = 1$, it becomes the BOW (bag of words) representation.

Given D'_{log}, a train set consisting of log event sequences, we extract n-grams of all sequences as features. Each feature consists of n log events, and denotes a dimension of the vector space. Moreover, for any object O_{ij} from either train set or test set, its feature values represent the occurrence value of the respective feature in the corresponding event sequence of O_{ij}. The feature value is calculated using TF-IDF technique as follows:

$$TF\text{-}IDF(t, O_{ij}) = f(t, O_{ij}) \times \log \frac{|D'_{log}|}{c(t)}$$

where t is an n-gram feature consisting of n log events extracted from the train set, $f(t, O_{ij})$ is the frequency of the feature t appearing in the object O_{ij} and $c(t)$ is the number of objects containing t in the train set. By this means, the log event sequence denoted by O_{ij} is transformed to a feature vector. Then a dataset can be constructed from D'_{log}:

$$D_{fin} = \{(O_{ij}, \mathbf{x}_{ij}) | O_{ij} = (q_i, s_{ij}), q_i \in P_{op}\}$$

where $\mathbf{x}_{ij}$ is the vector of feature representation of the log event sequence identified by O_{ij}.

Classification. We attach each object in D_{fin} with labels of corresponding scenarios including both normal as well as suspicious system executions of the operation. After that, we train the labeled dataset by leveraging Multinomial Logistic Regression model where One-vs-the-Rest (OvR) multiclass strategy is adopted. This model is a supervised learning algorithm, and there are more than two categories of the dependent variables (the scenarios of the operation or the failure types in our case) in question.

For any known scenario c of the user operation, a decision function f_c is learned from D_{fin} where this scenario c is treated as positive and any scenario which is not c is treated as negative:

$$f_c(\mathbf{x}) = sigmoid(\boldsymbol{\omega}^T \mathbf{x} + b)$$

where $\mathbf{x}$ is the feature vector converted from the log event sequence, and $\boldsymbol{\omega}$ as well as b are learned values. Then given a new vector converted from a newly recovered event sequence, each function f_c is evaluated on the vector. The vector, and thus the corresponding event sequence, will be assigned to the scenario of the function that returns the highest value pr. The normalized value pr represent the probability that the sequence is categorized to a specific known scenario. We set the threshold for pr to a common value 0.5 so that we can identify 'unknown' suspicious scenarios if the value pr is below the threshold.

The resulting classifier can be used to recognize new recovered execution traces for suspicious scenario recognition of the operation. In this way, the suspicious operation requests causing security security violations can also be recognized, since each execution of the operation is categorized to a expected normal execution, or an execution under a specific abnormal scenario.

4.5   Evidence Presentation for Compliance Auditing

If any recovered execution trace related to a user operation request is categorized as a suspicious scenario by the trained classifier at the production stage, we present the evidences for auditing in the execution trace by comparing the trace with the traces labeled as the normal system executions of the operation in train set.

At the training stage, with N-gram based method, we get all subsequences of N events from the normal traces in train set like D'_{log} in Sect. 4.3. At the production stage, new extracted traces with the same event sequence are first grouped together. Then for each trace corresponding to each group, we can tag each event e_i in the trace as normal or abnormal by comparing e_i with the last event of each normal subsequence starting with the $N-1$ events previous to e_i. If an event is tagged as abnormal, we would present the predicted events that should occur after the previous $N-1$ events. To be more specific, these predicted events are provided by collecting the last events of the normal subsequences starting with the $N-1$ events previous to the abnormal event. Moreover, these predicted events are ordered by calculating the confidence of each predicted event. The confidence is calculated as follows: $cf(e_h=e_{pr}|e_{h-N},...,e_{h-1}) = count(e_{h-N},...,e_{h-1},e_h=e_{pr})/count(e_{h-N},...,e_{h-1})$ where e_{pr} is the predicted event, $count(s)$ represents the frequency of sub event sequence s appearing in the normal traces in train set.

By this means, the normal, abnormal and predicted log events are automatically marked in the extracted execution trace of each suspicious user request, to provide as the evidence of security compliance violation to auditors. In addition, the D_{log} in Sect. 4.2 can provide raw logs related to the suspicious user operation request as additional evidences for auditing where the user identity information as shown in Fig. 1a can also be extracted.

5   Experiment and Evaluation

5.1   Experimental Settings

We deploy OpenStack version Ocata as the test bed, including one controller node, two networking nodes, three nodes as Ceph-cluster for storage backend, and up to fifty compute nodes. Logging level for OpenStack is set to DEBUG and logging format is set as shown in Fig. 1b. As a result, all service daemons of OpenStack would generate all level logs providing rich information for cloud security auditing. These logs from all server nodes are collected as the data source.

Concurrent user operation requests are submitted through command line interface. Two typical VM related operations and two typical port related operations are analyzed in the experiment including VM creation, VM deletion, port creation and port update. We inject anomalies to simulate real world scenarios. All scenarios, or injected anomalies, are described in Table 1. For each scenario, operation requests are submitted randomly, where the corresponding anomaly is injected, the target operation is replayed and the requests of other operations are also submitted as noises. In addition, multiple VM instances are created in one request while the creation requests are submitted concurrently.

Table 1. All scenarios for the experiment. (*: Security compliance violation)

Operation	Scenario	Type	Security property
VM creation	Quota exceeded	*	No abuse of cloud resource[43]
	Timeout waiting for vNIC becoming available.	Execution failure	–
	Scheduling timeout	Execution failure	–
	Ceph connection error	Execution failure	–
	Success	Normal scenario	–
VM deletion	Disability of nova-compute on the host	*	Secure disposal of cloud resources[44]
	Success	Normal scenario	–
Port creation	IP resource exhaustion	*	No cloud resource exhaustion[45]
	Success	Normal scenario	–
Port update	Disabled port security property the network	*	Bypassing of firewall rules[41]
	Success	Normal scenario	–

After log files are collected, logs related to the respective execution of the targeted operation in each scenario are extracted as described in Sect. 4.2, and then parsed into log event sequences to represent execution traces as described in Sect. 4.3. The recovered execution traces are then labeled according to the respective scenario. In this way, data sets of labeled execution traces are constructed. Each operation and each execution correspond to a data set and a user request respectively.

5.2   Evaluation

In what follows, we first evaluate the trace recognition ability of our approach, by checking the performance of the model to give accurate compliance violation detection results for each user request related to the target operation. Then we present the results of suspicious traces to show that evidences can be provided for compliance violation verification.

Trace Recognition Capability for Compliance Violation Detection.
Two aspects are considered: the ability to detect unknown scenarios and the ability to recognize known scenarios. As mentioned before, a scenario is denoted as a system execution of the cloud to complete a user operation request, which is described by a recovered trace related to the execution. An execution trace is described by a log event sequence. A known scenario has execution traces labeled as that scenario in the train set. Contrariwise, an unknown scenario does not

have any execution traces labeled as that scenario in the train set. Moreover, an unknown scenario is likely be a potential suspicious scenario where the security compliance violation is caused, since the unknown deviates from the execution patterns of known scenarios where the normal expected scenarios are included. To evaluate the ability to detect unknown scenarios, we randomly select one scenario in the data set, and separate related execution traces from the data set as an unknown set and the traces are labeled as unknown.

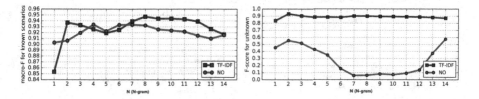

Fig. 4. F-score of N-gram with different N and with or without TF-IDF.

5-fold cross-validation is used to evaluate the model. After unknowns are separated, the remaining data set is randomly divided into 5 equal sized portions. Of the 5 portions, a single portion is retained with the unknown set as the test set for validation. The cross-validation process is repeated 5 times, where each of the 5 portions are used once. The 5 results from the folds are then averaged to produce a estimation. We use $macro$-F_β of all known scenarios and F_β-$score$ for the unknown scenario to evaluate each result. Firstly, precision and recall are calculated for each scenario: $precision = \frac{\#correctly\ recognized\ as\ this\ scenario}{\#recognized\ as\ this scenario}$, $recall = \frac{\#correctly\ recognized\ as\ this scenario}{\#this\ senario\ actually\ in\ the\ test\ set}$. Then, for unknown scenario, its F-$score$ is calculated with its $precision$ and $recall$: F-$score = \frac{2\times precision\times recall}{prescision+recall}$. Moreover, the mean $precision$ of all known scenarios $macro$-P and the mean $recall$ of all known scenarios $macro$-R are calculated. In this way, $macro$-F of all known scenarios can be calculated: $macro$-$F = \frac{2\times macro\text{-}P\times macro\text{-}R}{macro\text{-}P+macro\text{-}R}$.

We specifically take the popular VM creation operation as a case to evaluate the trace recognition capability of our approach. Totally 500 VM creation requests are submitted in all 4 scenarios of VM creation as described in Table 1. We precisely recover every execution trace related to each request. After the 500 recovered traces are labeled according to each scenario, these labeled traces form a data set of VM creation. We randomly select a scenario as an unknown scenario.

The 'quota exceeded' ccan be precisely detect with perfect precision and recall. Moreover, Fig. 4 shows the results of classifiers with different n-grams and with or without TF-IDF technique for VM creation. The result for each classifier is obtained from 5-fold cross-validations. The trace would be categorized as an unknown scenario if the returned value of the classifier is under the threshold 0.5 as described in Sect. 4.4. As mentioned before, the unknown scenario is not included for calculation of macro-F. The higher macro-F indicates the better

(a) VM creation.

(b) Port update.

(c) VM deletion.

(d) Port creation.

Fig. 5. The simplified evidence presentation results for suspicious user operation requests where dotted boxes are predicted events, boxes with face color are unexpected events and the rest boxes are normal events

performance of the model to recognize the known scenarios and provide accurate auditing results for each VM creation request of users. As for unknown scenario, the higher F-score indicates the better performance to detect the unknown scenario. It can be observed that after improvement from 1-gram by 2-gram, higher n-gram at most yields slight improvements. Furthermore, all results with TF-IDF turn out better than those without TF-IDF except for 1-gram. Above all, 2-gram with TF-IDF works well and provides satisfactory results of our model for trace recognition.

The above results show that our approach can recognize previously met scenarios especially the suspicious ones where security compliance violation is caused. Moreover, unknown scenarios where are likely to be suspicious ones can also be detected.

Evidence Presentation for Suspicious Scenarios. For the detected suspicious scenarios, we provide relevant evidence for security compliance verification. VM creation, VM Deletion, port creation, and port update operations are analyzed in this section. The execution traces generated by system executions of user operations under normal expected scenarios are used as the knowledge base. The parameter n of n-gram as mentioned in Sect. 4.5 is set to 5.

For VM creation as shown in Fig. 5a, the security property of no abuse of cloud resources is violated. We can observe that Nova failed to provision instances since provision_instance event is absent. Accidents occur when checking instance quota, because the user attempts to create a huge amount of VMs exceeding the predefined quota. As for VM deletion presented in Fig. 5c, the expected event handle_one_response does not occur right after event compute.api.delete but occurs at end of the trace. We can infer from the trace that Nova does a local delete for the VM. This insecure disposal of the VM can cause inconsistency among cloud layers and security compliance violation.

Evidence for a suspicious port creation request is presented in Fig. 5d. It can be observed that the event to handle security group is absent. After this port update operation, the related VM is attached with a port of no spoofing filtering. We can spot the abnormal event and determine that the absent of spoofing protection is caused by the suspicious port update operation. As for port creation shown in Fig. 5b, the IP resource of the related network is exhausted. The expected store_ip_location event did not occur. Cloud resource exhaustion is caused.

Above all, we can get insights into the system execution of each operation. Our method provides essential evidence for compliance violation of suspicious user operation requests.

5.3 Experiment Summary and Discussions

The experimental results demonstrate the capability of our approach to detect security compliance violations by automatically recognize both known and unknown potential suspicious user requests. Moreover, relevant evidences are presented for further auditing.

Table 2. Comparison with existing most related approaches. The column title F1, F2, F3, and F4 mean user operation oriented analysis, unknown suspicious scenario detection, system execution level analysis and evidence provision respectively.

Proposal	Objective	F1	F2	F3	F4
LogCluste [29]	Problem identification	No	No	Yes	No
DeepLog [34]	Anomaly detection	No	Yes	Yes	Yes
Weatherman [6]	Compliance auditing	Yes	No	No	No
LeaPS [5]	Compliance auditing	Yes	No	No	No
Our work	Compliance auditing	Yes	Yes	Yes	Yes

Table 2 shows comparison between four most related approaches and our work. Four features are mainly considered: user operation oriented analysis (F1), unknown suspicious scenario detection (F2), system execution level (F3) and evidence provision (F4). In what follows, we discuss our work with consideration of detailed comparison with the most related approaches.

LogCluster groups logs into system execution sequences and identify cloud problems by comparing new execution sequences with those met before. To extract and correlate data for auditing, we group logs into execution traces similar to LogCluster. But differently, we take a step further to mine system execution insights of user operations from the extracted traces, so that the mined low-level execution patterns can be mapped to the high-level security properties.

DeepLog uses deep learning to model a system log from normal system executions so that anomalies can be detected when the log patterns deviate from the model. Once an anomaly is detected, workflows are furthermore constructed from the log to provide evidences for further analysis. Attacks can be detected in the complex computer systems including clouds. However, the major limit is to handle the cloud scenario where various concurrent user operation requests are submitted. In such cases, log patterns are extremely uncertain since how users issue operation requests are unclear, and false anomalies can be detected. To solve this problem, we extract and separate execution traces from logs first to separate target user operations instead of building model directly on the raw log sequence like DeepLog. Moreover, we build a model to automatically recognize different scenarios rather than just to distinguish whether abnormal or not. This allows us to recognize security compliance violations of user operations for auditing.

Weatherman focuses on analysis of changes introduced by user operations with respect to security properties in the cloud. How operations change the infrastructure's topology and configuration is captured using a graph-based model. The dependency model is established through manual efforts by expertise. We target on the underlying cloud system dynamic execution behavior changes of user operations regarding security properties, and use an automatic log-based approach to recognize the changes.

LeaPS detects critical operations from logs, and verify security compliance of these operations with cloud data of event notifications and database records. Predefined attack scenarios with respect to security compliance are detected in clouds. We build a learning model to recognize different scenarios related to critical operations, so that unknown potential suspicious scenarios are also detected. Moreover, relevant evidences extracted from underlying system logs are provided for auditors.

6   Conclusions

In this paper, we propose an automatic security compliance auditing method to detect suspicious user operation requests causing security compliance violations and present relevant evidence based on underlying cloud system execution logs. Cloud behavior changes related to suspicious user operation requests violating security properties can be automatically captured by utilizing machine learning techniques. The extracted execution trace related to each suspicious user request of each targeted critical operation is presented with normal, abnormal and predicted log events being tagged as the evidence. The evidence we presented can assist to prove whether a specific user operation request accounts for the compliance violation. In addition, we can detect unknown suspicious scenarios related to user operation requests, where the security compliance is likely to be violated. As cloud services are going on, these unknown scenarios can in turn be used as training data to update the learning model for future auditing. Furthermore, once an execution of an operation is recognized to be a known abnormal scenario, a corresponding solution can also be recommended for treating the anomaly. The experimental results on OpenStack results demonstrate the effectiveness of our approach to detect suspicious cloud user operation requests and present relevant evidences. In the future, we will take a step further to clarify the accountability so as to determine the responsibility of the compliance violations based on this work.

Acknowledgments. This work was supported in part by the National Nature Science Foundation of China under grant NO. (61472429, 61070192, 91018008, 61303074, 61170240), Beijing Nature Science Foundation under grant No. 4122041, National High-Tech Research Development Program of China under grant No. 2007AA01Z414, and National Science and Technology Major Project of China under grant No. 2012ZX01039-004.

References

1. Majumdar, S., et al.: Proactive verification of security compliance for clouds through pre-computation: application to OpenStack. In: Askoxylakis, I., Ioannidis, S., Katsikas, S., Meadows, C. (eds.) ESORICS 2016, Part I. LNCS, vol. 9878, pp. 47–66. Springer, Cham (2016). https://doi.org/10.1007/978-3-319-45744-4_3
2. Alliance, C.S.: Cloud Security Alliance (2012). https://cloudsecurityalliance.org/
3. CloudAudit: Cloudaudit (2014). https://cloudsecurityalliance.org/research/cloudaudit/
4. Matrix, C.C.: Ccm (2014). https://cloudsecurityalliance.org/research/ccm/
5. Majumdar, S., et al.: LeaPS: learning-based proactive security auditing for clouds. In: Foley, S.N., Gollmann, D., Snekkenes, E. (eds.) ESORICS 2017. LNCS, vol. 10493, pp. 265–285. Springer, Cham (2017). https://doi.org/10.1007/978-3-319-66399-9_15
6. Bleikertz, S., Vogel, C., Groß, T., Mödersheim, S.: Proactive security analysis of changes in virtualized infrastructures. In: ACSAC 2015, pp. 51–60 (2015)
7. Congress: Openstack policy as a service (2017). https://wiki.openstack.org/wiki/Vitrage
8. OpenStack: Open source software for creating private and public clouds (2010). http://www.openstack.org
9. CloudWatch, A.: Cloud and network monitoring services (2009). http://aws.amazon.com/cloudwatch
10. Ceilometer: Openstack telemetry service (2013). https://wiki.openstack.org/wiki/Ceilometer
11. Vitrage: Openstack rca (root cause analysis) service (2017). https://wiki.openstack.org/wiki/Vitrage
12. CloudTrail, A.: Track user activity and API usage (2014). http://aws.amazon.com/cloudtrail/

13. Farshchi, M., Schneider, J.G., Weber, I., Grundy, J.: Metric selection and anomaly detection for cloud operations using log and metric correlation analysis. J. Syst. Softw. **137**, 531–549 (2017)

14. Ju, X., Soares, L., Shin, K.G., Ryu, K.D., Da Silva, D.: On fault resilience of openstack. In: SOCC 2013 (2013)

15. Goel, A., Kalra, S., Dhawan, M.: Gretel: Lightweight fault localization for openstack. In: CoNEXT 2016 (2016)

16. Pham, C., et al.: Failure diagnosis for distributed systems using targeted fault injection. IEEE Trans. Parallel Distrib. Syst. **28**(2), 503–516 (2017)

17. Majumdar, S., et al.: User-level runtime security auditing for the cloud. IEEE Trans. Inf. Forensics Secur. **13**(5), 1185–1199 (2018)

18. Baek, H., Srivastava, A., Van der Merwe, J.: Cloudsight: a tenant-oriented transparency framework for cross-layer cloud troubleshooting. In: CCGrid 2017 (2017)

19. Xu, Y., Liu, Y., Singh, R., Tao, S.: Identifying SDN state inconsistency in openstack. In: SOSR 2015 (2015)

20. Dhawan, M., Poddar, R., Mahajan, K., Mann, V.: Sphinx: detecting security attacks in software-defined networks. In: NDSS 2015 (2015)

21. Zeng, H., et al.: Libra: divide and conquer to verify forwarding tables in huge networks. In: NSDI 2014 (2014)

22. Curtsinger, C., Berger, E.D.: Coz: finding code that counts with causal profiling. In: SOSP 2015 (2015)

23. Mace, J., Roelke, R., Fonseca, R.: Pivot tracing: dynamic causal monitoring for distributed systems. In: SOSP 2015 (2015)

24. Chow, M., Meisner, D., Flinn, J., Peek, D., Wenisch, T.F.: The mystery machine: end-to-end performance analysis of large-scale internet services. In: OSDI 2014 (2014)

25. Yu, X., Joshi, P., Xu, J., Jin, G., Zhang, H., Jiang, G.: Cloudseer: workflow monitoring of cloud infrastructures via interleaved logs. In: ASPLOS 2016 (2016)

26. Nandi, A., Mandal, A., Atreja, S., Dasgupta, G.B., Bhattacharya, S.: Anomaly detection using program control flow graph mining from execution logs. In: KDD 2016 (2016)

27. Shang, W., Jiang, Z.M., Hemmati, H., Adams, B., Hassan, A.E., Martin, P.: Assisting developers of big data analytics applications when deploying on hadoop clouds. In: ICSE 2013 (2013)

28. Beschastnikh, I., Brun, Y., Ernst, M.D., Krishnamurthy, A.: Inferring models of concurrent systems from logs of their behavior with CSight. In: ICSE 2014 (2014)

29. Lin, Q., Zhang, H., Lou, J.G., Zhang, Y., Chen, X.: Log clustering based problem identification for online service systems. In: ICSE 2016 (2016)

30. Ding, R., et al.: Healing online service systems via mining historical issue repositories. In: ASE 2012 (2012)

31. Ding, R., Fu, Q., Lou, J.G., Lin, Q., Zhang, D., Xie, T.: Mining historical issue repositories to heal large-scale online service systems. In: DSN 2014 (2014)

32. Jiang, H., Li, X., Yang, Z., Xuan, J.: What causes my test alarm?: automatic cause analysis for test alarms in system and integration testing. In: ICSE 2017 (2017)

33. Bertero, C., Roy, M., Sauvanaud, C., Tredan, G.: Experience report: log mining using natural language processing and application to anomaly detection. In: ISSRE 2017 (2017)

34. Du, M., Li, F., Zheng, G., Srikumar, V.: Deeplog: anomaly detection and diagnosis from system logs through deep learning. In: CCS 2017 (2017)

35. Oprea, A., Li, Z., Yen, T.F., Chin, S.H., Alrwais, S.: Detection of early-stage enterprise infection by mining large-scale log data. In: 45th Annual IEEE/IFIP International Conference on Dependable Systems and Networks (DSN), pp. 45–56 (2015)

36. Gu, Z., Pei, K., Wang, Q., Si, L., Zhang, X., Xu, D.: Leaps: Detecting camouflaged attacks with statistical learning guided by program analysis. In: 45th Annual IEEE/IFIP International Conference on Dependable Systems and Networks (DSN), pp. 57–68 (2015)

37. Xu, W., Huang, L., Fox, A., Patterson, D., Jordan, M.I.: Detecting large-scale system problems by mining console logs. In: SOSP 2009 (2009)

38. He, P., Zhu, J., He, S., Li, J., Lyu, M.R.: Towards automated log parsing for large-scale log data analysis. IEEE Trans. Dependable Secure Comput. **15**(6), 931–944 (2017)

39. Zawoad, S., Dutta, A.K., Hasan, R.: Towards building forensics enabled cloud through secure logging-as-a-service. IEEE Trans. Dependable Secure Comput. **13**(2), 148–162 (2016)

40. Li, M., Zang, W., Bai, K., Yu, M., Liu, P.: Mycloud: supporting user-configured privacy protection in cloud computing. In: ACSAC 2013, pp. 59–68 (2013)

41. OpenStack: Neutron iptables firewall anti-spoof protection bypass (2016). https://security.openstack.org/ossa/OSSA-2016-009.html/

42. Manning, C.D., Raghavan, P.: Introduction to Information Retrieval. Cambridge University Press, Cambridge (2008)

43. Alliance, C.S.: The Notorious Nine Cloud Computing Top Threats in 2013 (2013)

44. ISO/IEC: ISO/IEC 27017:2015: Information technology - security techniques - code of practice for information security controls based on ISO/IEC 27002 for cloud services (2015). https://www.iso.org/standard/43757.html/

45. European Network and Information Security Agency (ENISA): Cloud computing: benefits, risks and recommendations for information security (2012). https://resilience.enisa.europa.eu/cloud-security-and-resilience/publications/cloud-computing-benefits-risks-and-recommendations-for-information-security

Two Anti-quantum Attack Protocols for Secure Multiparty Computation

Lichao Chen, Zhanli Li[✉], Zhenhua Chen, and Yaru Liu

School of Computer Science and Technology,
Xi'an University of Science and Technology, Xi'an 710054, China
lizl@xust.edu.cn

Abstract. Millionaire problem and private set intersection problem are not only the basic issues in the secure multiparty computation, but also the building block for privacy-preserving cooperative computation. However, so far the existing solutions to the two problems cannot resist the quantum attack, and in the meanwhile are inefficient enough. Aiming at these drawbacks, in this paper we first construct two new 0–1 encoding. Subsequently, using the designed 0–1 encoding, we transform Millionaire problem into the summation problem, and further transform the set intersection problem into the product problem. Lastly, taking advantage of NTRU homomorphic encryption, we propose Protocol 1 for Millionaire problem and Protocol 2 for the secure set intersection problem, respectively. The final analyses indicate that the two protocols designed in this paper are not only secure against the quantum attack but also more efficient compared with the previous schemes, In addition, Protocol 1 has more fine-grained comparing result for any two elements in total order set than the previous; Protocol 2 has a two-fold functionality in that it is not only secure against quantum attacks but also applicable for cloud computing environment.

Keywords: Millionaire problem · Private set intersection · Cloud computing
Multi-key NTRU

1 Introduction

The concept of Secure Multiparty Computation (SMC), first introduced by Yao [1], refers to the fact that multiple parties jointly compute a common function over their own private inputs without the help of an untrusted third party, such as a cloud server (CS) [2], where no information about individual inputs can be disclosed. Afterwards, Goldreich et al. [3, 4] further systematically studied on the security of SMC and extended the secure two-party computation to multi-party as well as. In the meanwhile, a formal definition of security about SMC was presented. Actually, all the privacy-preserving cooperative computation can be classified into in the research field of SMC, such as privacy-preserving data mining [5–8], privacy-preserving electronic auction and electronic voting [9], secure credit card payment inquiry [10], privacy-preserving scientific computing [11], and secure cloud computing [9, 12, 13]. Among the above problems, Millionaire problem and private set-intersection problem are two most basic problems in the field of SMC. Millionaire problem means that two millionaires Alice

© Springer Nature Singapore Pte Ltd. 2019
H. Zhang et al. (Eds.): CTCIS 2018, CCIS 960, pp. 338–359, 2019.
https://doi.org/10.1007/978-981-13-5913-2_21

and Bob want to know who is richer, but unwilling to disclose their wealth value to each other. In fact, it can be viewed as the privacy-preserving comparison with two secret numbers. Private set intersection problem means that multiple parties want to find out the set intersection, while each participant not obtaining any information about the others. The two problems are often encountered with by people in real world, such as the scenarios as follows.

Scenario 1: Two countries want to compare the range of a certain missile. Since such occasion is a strategic secret about their countries, they can not reveal the distance to each other except obtaining which country has a longer range. This scenario can be viewed as Millionaire problem.

Scenario 2: Different military factories want to compare the quality of a certain precision instrument with the same type. To achieve this goal, they first find out such precision instrument from different military factories, however there is no military factory which is willing to expose their own private data to others. This scenario can be viewed as privacy-preserving set intersection problem.

Since the construction of many SMC protocols heavily depends on the two above problems, the study on these two problems has an important significance in theory and practice.

1.1 Related Work

Aiming at Millionaire problem, Yao [14] first proposed the general approach known as the garbled circuit, which has exponential time complexity with regard to inputs. Taking advantage of the oblivious transfer and the conversion table of output, Goldreich et al. [3, 4] also provided a garbled circuit method, which required to encrypt twice for both parties' inputs, respectively. Since these general approaches are inefficient and impractical, for the sake of efficiency, Goldreich [3] declared that the specific and efficient protocols should be constructed. Motivated by Goldreich declaration, therefore, many researchers have contributed specific protocols on particular problems about SMC to improve the performance. Among them, Tuyls et al. [15] designed a threshold scheme for Millionaire problem through threshold homomorphic encryption, in which there are $2m$ intermediate calculation results generated and each requires 6 modulus exponential operations, i.e., the total cost of modulus exponential operations is $12m$ (where m is the size of the integer held by the participants). The computational cost increases linearly with m. Ioannidis and Grama et al. [16] solved Millionaire problem by utilizing the oblivious transfer protocol as a sub-protocol. Nonetheless, both computational and communication complexity are still $O(m^2)$. Tzeng et al. [17] transformed Millionaire problem into the set intersection problem using the technique of 0–1 coding. Likewise, Li et al. [18] also encoded a private data into a vector using the technique of 0–1 encoding to handle this problem. Despite the non-trivial encoding technique in the literature [17, 18], they have a common limitation that they can only handle whether $x \geq y$ or $x \leq y$, but not further distinguish $x = y$ from $x \geq y$ or $x \leq y$. In order to solve this problem, Zuo et al. [19] employed Paillier homomorphic encryption and constructed a protocol for Millionaire problem, which can distinguish three cases: $x > y$, $x = y$ or $x < y$. In their scheme, the protocol requires m encryption operations,

1 decryption operation, and $l + 3$ homomorphic operations (where m is the elements number of the total order set, and l is the rank of data held by Bob in the set). However, Paillier encryption is less efficient than NTRU encryption (showed in Fig. 1). Thus, their scheme is not efficient enough.

Aiming another problem, private set intersection (PIS) [20–23], many researchers provide some solutions. Nevertheless, the cost of users in these schemes is considerably high. In order to save the cost of users, most of the computing tasks can be outsourced to the cloud through the pay-on-demand pattern. Dong et al. [24] proposed the protocol for private set intersection with the help of the cloud computing. They make full use of the properties of polynomial and transform the set intersection problem into the greatest common factor problem of two polynomials. The transformation technique in this scheme is very ingenious, and the authors further extend two parties situation to multiple parties. The solution does save the cost for users by virtue of cloud outsourcing technology. Despite this advantage, since it requires $2(Nm + 1) \log n (\bmod n^2)$ modular multiplication operation (where N is the number of participants, m is the number of elements in the total order set, and n is the public key of Paillier encryption), the computational cost of users is still high. In addition, the scheme can not resist the collusion between the cloud server and the participant who owns the private key. Recently Zhou [25] combined the encoding method with ElGamal homomorphic encryption and then solved the private set intersection problem in cloud environment. However, the protocol requires $(2N + 1)m \log p (\bmod p)$ modular multiplication operations (where N is the number of participants, and p is the public key of the ElGamal encryption), which makes the computational cost expensive. In addition, the protocol is the same as Dong's protocol, which can not fully resist collusion attack. That is, if the private key holder P_N colludes with any other $N - 2$ participants, they will learn the encoding of the rest's secret set, and further obtain all information about other participants by decoding.

More generally, the common drawback in both schemes mentioned above is not secure against quantum attack since their security is based on the assumptions of mathematical hard problems, such as large integer factorization and discrete logarithm problem, which will be solved in the future with the development of quantum computers although these solutions are secure currently. Thus, these protocols relied on such mathematical hard assumptions will become insecure. In 1996, Hoffstein et al. [26] proposed an NTRU (Number Theory Research Unit) encryption, which is a public-key cryptosystem based on polynomial rings. Essentially, its security depends on the shortest vector problem (SVP) in the lattice and its security is equivalent to solving the hard problem at lattice in the worst-case. Thus it is considered to be secure against quantum attacks. For the shortest vector problem in lattice, the Shor's attack algorithm is invalid, and there is no other fast algorithm to solve it in quantum computer, therefore, NTRU can resist the Shor's attack under quantum computing. This public key cryptosystem about NTRU has the characteristics of being fast to generate public and private keys, and easy to execute with parallel computation [27–29].

In addition to the above works, Xia et al. [30] make use of the improved LWE (Learning With Error) encryption version proposed by Gentry et al. [31] to construct a protocol for set intersection problem which can resist quantum attack. However, the protocol is only suitable for two parties, which is unable to be extend to multiple parties. Moreover, since this scheme does not deploy in cloud environment and thus the capability of cloud computing will be useless for users, the cost of users are higher than that in other schemes [24, 25].

1.2 Our Contributions

In order to overcome the drawbacks above, in this paper we design two protocols employing encoding method and multi-key NTRU fully homomorphic encryption (NTRU FHE). The main contributions are listed as follows.

(1) Two new 0–1 encoding method were proposed: Millionaire problem and private set intersection problem were resolved by combining this 0–1 encoding and the NTRU FHE, respectively.
(2) It is the first time that a new anti-quantum attack solution to Millionaire problem were presented: Protocol 1 designed in this paper not only can resist quantum attacks but also is more efficient than the existing protocols as well as the comparison results in Protocol 1 is more fine-grained than that in others.
(3) It is the first time that a new anti-quantum attack solution suitable for the cloud computing environment to the private set intersection problem: Protocol 2 in cloud computing environment designed in this paper not only can resist quantum attack but also is more efficient than the existing protocols.

1.3 Organization

For clarity, we present a roadmap about this paper. The preliminaries is introduced in Sect. 2, The concreted protocols are described in Sect. 4. While in Sect. 5, we provide the security analysis about our protocols in detail. In Sect. 6, we make a performance analysis and an comparison of ours and the existing Finally, we conclude this paper and point out the open issues and the future research in Sect. 7.

2 Preliminaries

2.1 Multi-key NTRU FHE [32]

The concept of homomorphic encryption was introduced in [33], which allows us to directly operate on ciphertext to achieve the purpose of plaintext calculating. Initially, only the semi-homomorphic encryption (SME) is presented, such as ElGamal encryption and Paillier encryption, all of which merely have one type of homomorphic operation. Subsequently, FHE has emerged gradually, which can carry out two types of operations simultaneously. The NTRU FHE is the famous one of all FHE, which is described as follows.

(1) **Single-key NTRU FHE** [32]

Setup: Given a security parameter κ, a large prime $q = q(\kappa)$, and a B-bounded error distribution χ (discrete Gaussian distribution) over the ring $R \equiv z[x]/\langle x^n + 1 \rangle$, the parameters (κ, n, q) are published, The operations in each of the following algorithms are performed on the ring $R \equiv R/(qR)$.

KeyGen.: Given a bounded polynomial $f', g \in \chi$, suppose $f = 2f' + 1$ such that $f \equiv 1 \pmod{2}$. Let the public key $h = 2gf^{-1} \in R_q$ and f as the private key (where if the inverse of f in the ring does not exist, resample f').

Enc.: Sample bounded polynomials $s, e \in \chi$ $m \in M = \{0, 1\}$ (i.e., the plaintext message m is encoded as a polynomial whose coefficients are set 0 or 1). Output ciphertext $c = hs + 2e + m \in R_q$.

Dec.: Calculate $u = fc \in R_q$, outputting $u \pmod{2}$ as the message m, where the coefficients of u is required in the range $\{-\lfloor q/2 \rfloor, \cdots, \lfloor q/2 \rfloor\}$, and the necessary condition to decrypt correctly is subject to $q > 72nB^2$ according to [32].

Eval.: Suppose that there are t ciphertexts $c_1, \cdots, c_t$ generated by one public key pk. Given a Boolean circuit C, a new ciphertext, denoted by $c^* = Eval(C, c_1, \cdots, c_t)$, was generated by homomorphic operation with t ciphertext.

Based on the above, the multi-key NTRU FHE is improved as follows [32], which consists of four algorithms for all circuit families C.

(2) **Multi-key NTRU FHE** [32]

KeyGen.: Given a security parameter κ, the algorithm generates (pk_i, sk_i, ek) $(i \in [t])$, where (pk_i, sk_i) is a public/private key pair for each user, and ek is a public evaluation key.

Enc.: Given the public key pk_i and the message m_i, the algorithm generates a ciphertext $c_i = (pk_i, m_i)(i \in [t])$.

Dec.: Given t private keys sk_i from different users and a ciphertext c^{**}, where the ciphertext c^{**} results from homomorphic operations of multi-key FHE, the algorithm generates the corresponding plaintext by virtue of $Dec(sk_1, \cdots, sk_t, c^{**}) = C(m_1, m_2, \cdots, m_t)$.

Eval.: For Boolean circuit C, outputs the result of t ciphertext homomorphic operation as the following: $c^{**} = Eval(C, (c_1, pk_1, ek_1), \cdots, (c_t, pk_t, ek_t))$.

Actually, the fully homomorphic operation in the above algorithm Eval. can be considered as the sum or product of two new ciphertexts c_1' and c_2', where c_1' results from some of t ciphertexts, and c_2' from the others. In the meanwhile, each new ciphertext corresponds to a set of public keys, denoted by K_1 and K_2, respectively. Now, we specify the Eval. operation in the following.

(1) Additive homomorphism: directly calculates $c_{add} = c^{**} = c_1' + c_2'$;
(2) Multiplicative homomorphism: if $K_1 \cap K_2 = \phi$, then $c_{mult} = c^{**} = c_1' \times c_2'$; otherwise, let $K_1 \cap K_2 = \{pk_{i_1}, \cdots, pk_{i_r}\}$, and outputs $c_{nult} = c_r^{**}$ by means of the following method.

Taking as input $s_\tau, e_\tau \in \chi$ for all $\tau \in \{0, 1, \cdots, \lfloor \log q \rfloor\}$, outputs $\gamma_\tau = h s_\tau + 2 e_\tau + 2^\tau f$. Let $ek = (\gamma_0, \cdots, \gamma_{\lfloor \log q \rfloor}) \in R_q^{\lfloor \log q \rfloor}$. The equation $c_{j-1}^{**} = \sum_{\tau=0}^{\lfloor \log q \rfloor} c_{j-1,\tau}^{**} 2^\tau$ can be represented as a binary format for $j \in [r]$, where r is the cardinality of the intersection for K_1 and K_2. Let $c_j^{**} = \sum_{\tau=0}^{\lfloor \log q \rfloor} c_{j-1,\tau}^{**} \gamma_{j,\tau} . c_j^{**}$ iterate to the end, and there must be $c_{nult} = c_r^{**}$ being outputted.

Generally speaking, the above t ciphertexts are encrypted by $|K_1 \cup K_2|$ public keys. Then, the corresponding decryption key for c_{add} and c_{nult} are from private keys: $(f_{K_1} f_{K_2})(\prod_{j \in (K_1 \cap K_1)} f_j)^{-1}$, where f_{K_i} denotes the private keys in K_i for $i = 1, 2$. For more detail, please refer to the literature [32].

To clarify the decryption process of multi-key NTRU FHE, we present a practical example for $N = 2$. Then the decryption process can be simplified as follows.

(I) the decryption process of additive homomorphism:

$$f_1 f_2(c_{add}) = f_1 f_2(c_1 + c_2) = 2(f_1 f_2(e_1 + e_2) + f_2 g_1 s_1 + f_1 g_2 s_2) + f_1 f_2(m_1 + m_2)(\bmod 2)$$
$$= m_1 + m_2(\bmod 2)$$

(II) the decryption process of multiplicative homomorphism:

$$f_1 f_2(c_{mult}) = f_1 f_2(c_1 c_2) = 2(2 g_1 g_2 s_1 s_2 + g_1 s_1 f_2(2e_2 + m_2) + g_2 s_2 f_1(2e_1 + m_1)$$
$$+ f_1 f_2(e_1 m_2 + e_2 m_1 + 2e_1 e_2)) + f_1 f_2(m_1 m_2)$$
$$= m_1 m_2(\bmod 2)$$

For $N \geq 3$, the decryption process is similar to that for $N = 2$.

2.2 Security Model

Goldreich [3] proved that, given a protocol that privately computes functionality f in a semi-honest model, a protocol that can privately compute functionality f in a malicious model can be constructed by introducing bit commitment and zero-knowledge proof that forces each party to either behave in a semi-honest manner or to be detected. The semi-honest model is not merely an important methodological tool but may also provide a good model in many settings. It suffices to prove that a protocol is secure in a semi-honest setting. Therefore, our work focuses on solutions in semi-honest settings and assumes that all parties are semi-honest.

(1) Semi-honest participants

We assume that all parties are semi-honest. Roughly speaking, a semi-honest party is one who follows the protocol properly with the exception that it keeps a record of all its intermediate computations and might derive the other parties' inputs from the record.

(2) **Security model in a semi-honest setting**

Assuming $f(f_1, f_2)$ is a probabilistic polynomial time functionality, and π is a two-party protocol computing f, Alice and Bob hold secret data x and y, respectively. Alice and Bob compute $f(f_1, f_2)$ collaboratively where $f_i = f(x, y)$, $i = 1, 2$ in such way that Alice and Bob can obtain $f_1(x, y)$ and $f_2(x, y)$ without disclosing any information about x, y, respectively. The intermediate view during the execution of π Alice obtained denoted by $view_1(x, y)$. Similarly, the intermediate view Bob obtained denoted by $view_2(x, y)$, and the output obtained by Alice and by Bob denoted by $output_1(x, y)$, and, $output_2(x, y)$, respectively,

Definition 1 [4]. For a functionality f, we say the protocol π securely computes $f(x_1, \cdots, x_N)$ in the presence of semi-honest participants, if there exist polynomial-time algorithms (simulators) S_1 and S_2 such that

$$\{(S_1(x, f_1(x, y)), f_2(x, y))\} \underset{c}{\subseteq} \{(view_1(x, y), output_2(x, y))\}; \tag{1}$$

$$\{(f_1(x, y), S_2(y, f_2(x, y)))\} \underset{c}{\subseteq} \{(output_1(x, y), view_2(x, y))\}. \tag{2}$$

where $\underset{c}{}$ denotes computational indistinguishability. Thus, to prove that a multi-party computation protocol is secure, we must show the simulator S_1 and S_2 subject to Eqs. (1) and (2) hold, respectively.

(3) **Security model in a cloud computing environment**

SMC in a cloud computing environment is different from that in a traditional environment since there exists an additional participant as a semi-honest cloud sever (CS) besides original participants. Therefore, the security simulation paradigm in a cloud computing environment is more complicated than that in the traditional. Here, we assume that all parties including CS are honest-but-curious.

Suppose each participant P_i holds secret data x_i for $i = 1, 2, \cdots, N$. $f(x_1, \cdots, x_N) = (f_1(x_1, \cdots, x_N), \cdots, f_N(x_1, \cdots, x_N))$ is a probabilistic polynomial time function. The total $N + 1$ parties including CS jointly compute $f(x_1, \cdots, x_N)$ in such way that each participant P_i obtains $f_i(x_1, x_2, \cdots, x_N)$ without revealing any information about data x_i. During the process, we must ensure that no information about secret input x_i is disclosed to others, even in the presence of collusion.

Similarly, the view obtained by each participant P_i denoted by $view_i(x_1, \cdots, x_N)$ and the view by CS denoted by $view_0(x_1, \cdots, x_N)$ during the execution of the protocol π. There exist two types of collusion in this setting. One is that at most $N - 1$ participants collude to compromise the privacy of the others; the other is that the CS collude with some participants for the same sake and in the worst case, the CS will conspire with at most $N - 1$ participants. We denoted the view in the former by $view_I(x_1, \cdots, x_N)$ where $I \subseteq [N]$, $2 \le |I| \le N - 1$ and the view in the latter by $view_{I'}(x_1, \cdots, x_N)$ where $I' \subseteq [N] \cup \{CS\}$, $2 \le |I'| \le N$. Each user P_i sends his encrypted data $E(x_i)$ to CS. $E(x_1, \cdots, x_N)$ is defined as the intermediate result computed by CS, who forwards them to each participant (i.e., the output generated by CS).

Table 1. Security model in cloud computing environment

	Secure acquirement	Simulator
Non-collusion	Privacy of each participant $P_j (j \in [N])$ (for P_i, $i \neq j$)	$S_i(x_i, f_i(x_1, \cdots, x_N))$ $\underset{c}{\equiv} view_i(x_1, \cdots, x_N)$
	Privacy of N participants $P_1, P_2, \ldots, P_N$ (for CS)	$S_0(E(x_1), \cdots, E(x_N), E(x_1, \cdots, x_N))$ $\underset{c}{\equiv} view_0(x_1, \cdots, x_N)$
Collusion	Privacy of each P_j (for the collusion among I participants $P_1, P_2, \ldots, P_{|I|}$, where $j \notin I, |I| \leq N - 1$	$S_I(\{x_i\}^I, \{f_i(x_1, \cdots, x_N)\}^I)$ $\underset{c}{\equiv} view_I(x_1, \cdots, x_N)$
	Privacy of $P_j (j \in [N])$ for the collusion between CS and I' participants $P_1, P_2, \ldots, P_{|I'|}$, where, $j \notin I' |I'| \leq N$	$S_{I'}(\{x_i\}^{I'}, \{E(x_i)\}^{I'}, \{f_i(x_1, \cdots, x_N)\}^{I'}, E(x_1, \cdots, x_N))$ $\underset{c}{\equiv} view_{I'}(x_1, \cdots, x_N)$

Note: The notation $\underset{c}{\equiv}$ represents that the calculation is computational indistinguishability.

Notation $\{f_i(x_1, \cdots, x_N)\}^I$ and $\{x_i\}^I$ present $\{f_i(x_1, \cdots, x_N)\}^I = \{f_i(x_1, \cdots, x_N) | f_i(x_1, \cdots, x_N) \in \{f_1(x_1, \cdots, x_N), \ldots, f_{N-1}(x_1, \ldots, x_N)\}$ and $\{x_i | x_i \in \{x_1, x_2, \cdots, x_{N-1}\}, i \in I\}$, respectively. others similarly. When the four formulas hold simultaneously in the Table 1 above, we can guarantee that any participants do learn nothing about the private information of any other participants in the entire process of running the protocol π, regardless of there exist collusion or not. Therefore, to prove that in the cloud computing environment MPC is secure, we must construct a simulator that makes all the equations in Table 1 hold simultaneously.

Definition 2. In a cloud computing environment, we say the protocol π computes $f(x_1, \cdots, x_N)$ securely, if there exist polynomial-time algorithms (simulators) S_i, S_0, S_I and $S_{I'}$ such that all the equalities in the following Table 1 hold simultaneously.

3   Millionaire Problem

3.1   Description of the Problem

Alice has the secret data x, and Bob has the secret data y. Both of them want to decide whether $x < y, x = y$ or $x > y$ without disclosing the privacy of each other's data.

3.2   Transformation of the Problem

In this paper, we first encode the secret data of either party into a 0–1 vector according to 0–1 encoding method, and then solve Millionaire problem with the single-key NTRU FHE. Now, we describe the 0–1 encoding as follows.

0–1 Encoding: Define a total order set $U = \{v_1, v_2, \cdots, v_m\}$, where the elements are satisfied with $v_1 < v_2 < \cdots < v_m$. Assume $x = v_k, y = v_l$. Alice encodes the secret data $x = v_k$ into an m dimensional 0–1 vector $a = (\alpha_1, \alpha_2, \cdots, \alpha_6)$ where each component α_i is set 1 or 0 according to the following rule:

$$\alpha_i = \begin{cases} 1, & i = k, k+1 \\ 0, & others \end{cases}. \tag{3}$$

Furthermore, Bob calculates the sum $\sum_{i=1}^{l} \alpha_i = w$ according to the position of $y = v_l$ in the set U. The resulting value w can be divided into three cases: if $w = 0$, then $k > l$, i.e., $x > y$; if $w = 1$, then $k = l$, i.e., $x = y$; otherwise $k < l$, i.e., $x < y$.

Using the above encoding method, Millionaire problem is transformed into a summation problem. To clarify our encoding method, the specific Example 1 is given as follows.

Example 1. Define a total order set $U = \{1, 2, 3, 4, 5, 6\}$. Alice holds the secret integer $x = 3$, and Bob holds three different integers $y = 2, 3, 4$ which will be ready to compare with Alice's data. The process of comparison between both is shown in Table 2.

Table 2. Comparison of two integers

Alice's data	0–1 encoding	Bob's data	Summation	Comparison result
3	$a = (a_1, a_2, a_3, a_4, a_5, a_6)$ $= (0, 0, 1, 1, 0, 0)$	2	$w = \sum_{i=1}^{2} \alpha_i = 0$	$x > y$
		3	$w = \sum_{i=1}^{3} \alpha_i = 1$	$x = y$
		4	$w = \sum_{i=1}^{4} \alpha_i = 2$	$x < y$

3.3 Concreted Protocol

Protocol 1. Efficient solution to Millionaire problem.

   Input: Define a total order set $U = \{v_1, v_2, \cdots, v_m\}$. Alice's input is the secret data x, and Bob's input is the secret data y, such that $x, y \in U$, and $x = v_k$, $y = v_l$.

   Output: Alice and both want to decide whether $x > y$, $x = y$, or $x < y$ without learning any other information.

(1) Alice encodes her own secret data x into an m-dim. 0–1 vector $a = (\alpha_1, \cdots, \alpha_m)$ according to Eq. (3).

(2) Taking as input a security parameter κ. The KeyGen. algorithm of single-key NTRU FHE generates a pair of public and private keys for Alice and publishes the public key. Subsequently, Alice encrypts each component of vector a with the public key, and sends the encrypted vector to Bob.

(3) Upon receiving the encrypted vector $E(a) = (E(\alpha_1), \cdots, E(\alpha_m))$, Bob randomly chooses two polynomials $r_1, r_2 \in \chi$, and computes $\sum_{i=1}^{l} E(\alpha_i) + h r_1 + 2 r_2 = E(\sum_{i=1}^{l} \alpha_i) = E(w)$ by using the property of NTRU additive homomorphism. Later, Bob returns $E(w)$ to Alice.

(4) Upon receiving $E(w)$, Alice obtains $w = \sum_{i=1}^{l} \alpha_i$ with his own private key. Then Alice can determine whether $x > y, x = y$, or $x < y$ according to the value w.

(5) Alice tells Bob the result.

Sketch. On one hand, the encrypted vector a are not able to disclose the privacy of data x since only Alice holds the private key. Therefore, this guarantees on the privacy of the data x. On the other hand, upon receiving $E(a)$ from Alice, Bob chooses two random polynomials $r_1, r_2 \in \chi$ to mask $E(a)$ and calculates $E(w) = \sum_{i=1}^{l} E(\alpha_i) + (h r_1 + 2 r_2) = E(\sum_{i=1}^{l} \alpha_i)$ by using the property of additive homomorphism. Here, the random polynomial $h r_1 + 2 r_2$ plays a crucial role in protecting the privacy of data y while not affecting the result of decryption due to the self-blind property of NTRU FHE. In contrast, if Bob calculates the value $E(w') = \sum_{i=1}^{l'} E(\alpha_i) = \sum_{i=1}^{l} E(\alpha_i)$ directly without blinding, then Alice will obtain l' through a brute force attack, and further learn $l = l'$. This will reveal the privacy of data y. Therefore, there is no way to obtain the privacy of each other's data in our protocol. For more detail, we will give the informal version of security analysis in Sect. 5.

4 Private Set Intersection in Cloud Environment

4.1 Description of the Problem

We say the private set intersection (PSI) that N clients want to find out the intersection of their sets with the help of cloud sever and also want to prevent the other parties including the cloud sever from finding out anything more about their own set than the elements of the intersection.

4.2 Transformation of the Problem

As mentioned in the introduction, our contribution focuses on resisting quantum attacks and save the cost of clients. For the sake, we first present another new 0–1 encoding method to encode each set into an m-dimensional 0–1 vector, and further solve PSI problem with the help of CS by using the multi-key NTRU. Significantly, it is the first time in cloud environment that we design a protocol for PSI resisting quantum attack. Now, we present another 0–1 encoding as follows.

0–1 Encoding: Given N clients $P_1, \cdots, P_N$, each has a private set, respectively, $S_1, \cdots, S_N \subseteq U = \{v_1, v_2, \cdots, v_m\}$, where U is defined a total order set and its elements are satisfied with $v_1 < v_2 < \cdots < v_m$. Each client P_i encodes his own private set S_i into an m-dim. 0–1 vector $a_i = (\alpha_{i1}, \alpha_{i2}, \cdots, \alpha_{im})$ for $i = 1, 2, \cdots, N$, where each component α_{ij} is set 1 or 0 for $j = 1, 2, \cdots, m$ according to the following rule:

$$\alpha_{ij} = \begin{cases} 1, v_j \in S_i \\ 0, v_j \notin S_i \end{cases}, (i = 1, 2, \cdots, N, \quad j = 1, 2, \cdots, m). \tag{4}$$

Next, the product of the j-th component in all vector can be calculated and finally result in an m-dim. vector, each component of which denoted by w_j, i.e., $w_j = \prod_{i=1}^{N} \alpha_{ij}, j = 1, 2, \cdots, m$. The resulting value w_j can be divided into two cases: if $w_j = 1$, it means that there is a common element v_j will be appeared in the intersection S; otherwise, the element v_j will not be appeared.

From the above encoding method, PSI problem is transformed into a product problem. To clarify our new encoding method, the specific Example 2 is given as follows.

Example 2. Define a total order set $U = \{1, 2, 3, 4, 5, 6, 7\}$. Given clients P_1, P_2, P_3, each has a private set, respectively, $S_1 = \{1, 3, 6, 7\}, S_2 = \{2, 3, 6, 7\}, S_2 = \{3, 4, 6\}$. The process of computation on the intersection about S_1, S_2, S_3 is shown in Table 3.

Table 3. Computation on intersection

Participants	Secret sets	Corresponding 0–1 encoding	Calculate product	Non-zero elements	Set intersection
P_1	$S_1 = \{1, 3, 6, 7\}$	$a_1 = (a_{11}, a_{12}, a_{13}, a_{14}, a_{15}, a_{16}, a_{17})$ $= (1, 0, 1, 0, 0, 1, 1)$	$w_j = \prod_{i=1}^{3} \alpha_{ij}$	$w_3 = 1,$ $w_6 = 1$	$S = \{3, 6\}$
P_2	$S_2 = \{2, 3, 6, 7\}$	$a_2 = (a_{21}, a_{22}, a_{23}, a_{24}, a_{25}, a_{26}, a_{27})$ $= (0, 1, 1, 0, 0, 1, 1)$	$= (0, 0, 1, 0, 0, 1, 0)$ $j = 1, 2, \cdots, 7$		
P_3	$S_3 = \{3, 4, 6\}$	$a_3 = (a_{31}, a_{32}, a_{33}, a_{34}, a_{35}, a_{36}, a_{37})$ $= (0, 0, 1, 1, 0, 1, 0)$			

4.3 Concreted Protocol

Protocol 2. PSI in cloud computing environment.

Input: Define a total order set $U = \{v_1, v_2, \cdots, v_m\}$. Given number of N clients $P_1, \cdots, P_N$, each has a private set, $S_1, \cdots, S_N \subseteq U$, respectively.

Output: With the help of CS, each client wants to find out the intersection $S = S_1 \cap S_2 \cap \cdots \cap S_N$ without learning any other information.

(1) Each client P_i encodes their own secret sets S_i into an m-dim. 0–1 vector $a_i = (\alpha_{i1}, \alpha_{i2}, \cdots, \alpha_{im})$ according to Eq. (4).

(2) Taking as input a secure parameter κ, the KenGen. algorithm of multi-key NTRU FHE generates a public/private key pair $(pk_i = h_i, sk_i = f_i)$ for each client P_i. Next, each client encrypts vector a_i with his own public key $pk_i = h_i$ and further obtains $E(a_i) = (E(\alpha_{i1}), E(\alpha_{i2}), \cdots, E(\alpha_{im}))$. Lastly, all encrypted vectors are sent to CS.

(3) Upon receiving encrypted vectors, CS computes the product of the j-th component in all vector by using the homomorphic property of the multi-key NTRU FHE, i.e., $E(w_j) = \prod_{i=1}^{N} E(\alpha_{ij})$, $j = 1, 2, \cdots, m$. Lastly, CS returns $E(w) = (E(w_1), \cdots, E(w_m))$ to any client. For simplicity, here we assume $E(w)$ will be sent to the first client P_1.

(4) After receiving $E(w)$, client P_1 calculates $u_1 = f_1 E(w) = (f_1 E(w_1), \cdots, f_1 E(w_m))$ with his private key f_1. Then client P_1 sends u_1 to client P_2.

(5) For $i = 1, 2, \cdots N$, each client P_i in turn calculates $u_i = f_i u_{i-1} = \prod_{i=1}^{i} f_i E(w)$ upon receiving u_{i-1} from client P_{i-1}. Eventually, the last client P_N obtains $w = u_N = f_N u_{N-1} = \prod_{i=1}^{N} f_i E(w)$ and finds out the intersection $S = S_1 \cap S_2 \cap \cdots \cap S_N$ according to the value w.

(6) P_N publishes the result S to other clients.

Sketch: In the non-collusive setting, any client can not learn any information except the encrypted vectors since each client encrypts the private data with his own public key. In the collusive setting, the collusion is divided into two types: one is that at most $N - 1$ clients conspire to compromise the privacy of the rest; the other is at most $N - 1$ clients collude with CS to compromise the privacy of the rest. First, we analyze the latter. Without loss of generality, assume that clients $P_1, \cdots, P_{N-1}$ collude with CS to compromise the privacy of client P_N. On one hand, any party directly learns nothing about the privacy of client P_N from the encrypted vector $E(a_N) = (E(\alpha_{N1}), \cdots, E(\alpha_{Nm}))$ without the private key of client P_N when receiving the encrypted vectors $E(a_i) = (E(\alpha_{i1}), E(\alpha_{i2}), \cdots, E(\alpha_{im}))$ from each participant. On the other hand, CS computes $E(w) = (E(w_1), \cdots, E(w_m))$ by the homomorphic operation, and $N - 1$ clients obtain directly the intersection S by their sets. The intersection S is the subset of the result from the $N - 1$ collusive participants. In such case, they still learn nothing information about non-intersection elements for P_N. Next, we analyze the former. When CS does not participate in collusion, the worst case is that there are at most $N - 1$ participants to collude. In general, suppose that $N - 1$ participants $P_1, \cdots, P_{N-1}$ conspire to obtain the privacy of participant P_N. The analysis of this case is similar to that without CS participating. For more detail, we will give the informal version of security analysis in Sect. 5.

5 Security Analysis

Theorem 1. Protocol 1 securely computes Millionaires problem in the semi-honest setting.

Proof: We will prove this theorem by showing two simulators, S_1, S_2, such that Eqs. (1) and (2) hold simultaneously. We will first show the simulators S_1. Assume $f_1(x, y) = f_2(x, y) = w$. Randomly choosing $y' = v_l \in U$ so that $f_1(x, y') = f_1(x, y)$ and taking (x, y') as input, S_1 proceeds as follows.

(1) Constructs a vector $a = (\alpha_1, \alpha_2, \cdots, \alpha_m)$ according to protocol 1.
(2) Encrypts the vector a by using the single-key NTRU FHE, and obtains the encrypted vector $E(a) = (E(\alpha_1), E(\alpha_2), \cdots, E(\alpha_m))$.
(3) Chooses two random polynomials $r_1', r_2' \in \chi$, and further calculates

$$E(w') = \sum_{i=1}^{l} E(\alpha_i) + 2gf^{-1}r_1' + 2r_1' = E(\sum_{i=1}^{l} \alpha_i).$$

(4) Decrypts $E(w')$, and obtain w'.

In Protocol 1, $S_1(x, f_1(x, y)) = \{a, E(a), E(w'), f_1(x, y')\}$, $view_1(x, y) = \{a, E(a), E(w), f_1(x, y)\}$. Obviously, the equality $w' = w$ holds since $f_1(x, y) = f_1(x, y')$. Therefore, the equality $E(w') \underline{c} E(w)$ holds. Consequently, we have

$$\{S_1(x, f_1(x, y)), f_2(x, y)\} \underline{c} \{view_1(x, y), output_2(x, y)\}.$$

Likewise, we can further show the other simulator S_2 in a same way such that

$$\{f_1(x, y), S_2(y, f_2(x, y))\} \underline{c} \{output_1(x, y), view_2(x, y)\}.$$

For simplicity, we have omitted the detailed process of constructing simulator S_2. Combining the above, we conclude Protocol 1 is secure and complete our proof.

Theorem 2. In cloud computing environment, Protocol 2 securely computes the intersection of multiple sets in the semi-honest setting.

Proof: To prove Theorem 2, we must construct simulates $S_i, S_0, S_I, S_{I'}$ so that all equalities in Table 1 hold simultaneously. For simplicity, here we only give the construction method about $S_i, S_{I'}$. The construction process for S_0, S_I is omitted.

Case 1. Construct the simulator S_i.
On this occasion, there is no collusion between participants and CS. In Protocol 2, $f_i(a_1, \cdots, a_N) = f_j(a_1, \cdots, a_N) = w(i \neq j)$,   or $f_i(a_1, \cdots, a_N) = f_j(a_1, \cdots, a_N) \neq w(i \neq j)$, suppose $f_i(a_1, \cdots, a_N) = f_j(a_1, \cdots, a_N) = w(i \neq j)$, and we construct the simulator S_i. S_i randomly chooses $a_1', \cdots, a_{i-1}', a_{i+1}', \cdots, a_N'$ so that $f_i(a_1', \cdots, a_{i-1}', a_i, a_{i+1}', \cdots, a_N') = f_i(a_1, \cdots, a_i, \cdots, a_N)$, and takes a_i and $f_i(a_1, \cdots, a_i, \cdots, a_N)$ as input to proceed the following steps.

(1) Constructs $N-1$ vectors as the following according to Protocol 2:

$$a'_1 = (\alpha'_{11}, \cdots, \alpha'_{1m}), \cdots, a'_{i-1} = (\alpha'_{i-1,1}, \cdots, \alpha'_{i-1,m}),$$
$$a'_{i+1} = (\alpha'_{i+1,1}, \cdots, \alpha'_{i+1,m}), \cdots, a'_N = (\alpha'_{N1}, \cdots, \alpha'_{Nm}).$$

(2) Encrypts $a'_1, \cdots, a'_{i-1}, a_i, a'_{i+1}, \cdots, a'_N$ by using the multi-key NTRU FHE, and obtains $E(a'_1), \cdots, E(a'_{i-1}), E(a_i), E(a'_{i+1}), \cdots, E(a'_N)$.

(3) After receiving $E(a'_1), \cdots, E(a'_{i-1}), E(a_i), E(a'_{i+1}), \cdots, E(a'_N)$, $S_{I'}$ calculate

$$E(w^*) = \prod_{k=1, k\neq i}^{N} E(a'_k)E(a_i).$$

(4) Decrypts $E(w^*)$, and obtain w^*.

In Protocol 2,

$$S_i(x_i, f_i(x_1, \cdots x_N)) = \{a_i, f_i(a'_1, \cdots a'_{i-1}, a_i, a'_{i+1}, \cdots, a'_N), E(w^*), w^*\},$$

$$view_i(x_1, \cdots, x_N) = \{a_i, f_j(a_1, \cdots, a_N), E(w), w\}(j \in [N], j \neq i).$$

Since $w^* = f_i(a'_1, \cdots, a'_{i-1}, a_i, a'_{i+1}, \cdots, a'_N)$, and $f_i(a'_1, \cdots, a'_{i-1}, a_i, a'_{i+1}, \cdots, a'_N) = f_i(a_1, \cdots, a_N) = w$, equality $w^* = w$ holds, further, $E(w^*) \underline{c} E(w)$ holds as well. Therefore, we have

$$S_i(x_i, f_i(x_1, \cdots, x)) \underline{c} \, view_i(x_1, \cdots, x_N).$$

Likewise, we can construct anther simulator S_0 such that

$$S_0(E(x_1), \cdots, E(x_N), E(x_1, \cdots, x_N)) \underline{c} \, view_0(x_1, \cdots, x_N).$$

Case 2. Construct the simulator $S_{I'}$.

Without loss of generality, suppose CS colludes with $N-1$ participants $P_1, \cdots, P_{N-1}$, they want to obtain the information about the non-intersection elements of P_N. In Protocol 2, $f_i(a_1, \cdots, a_N) = f_j(a_1, \cdots, a_N) = w(i \neq j)$, or $f_i(a_1, \cdots, a_N) = f_j(a_1, \cdots, a_N) \neq w(i \neq j)$, suppose $f_i(a_1, \cdots, a_N) = f_j(a_1, \cdots, a_N) = w(i \neq j)$, and construct the simulator $S_{I'}(I' = \{P_1, \cdots, P_{N-1}, CS\})$. Let $\{E(a_i)\}^{[N]}$ and $E(w) = \prod_{i=1}^{N} E(a_i)$ as the input and output generated by CS, respectively. Let $\{a_i\}^{[N-1]}$ and $\{f_i(a_1, \cdots, a_N)\}^{[N-1]}$ as the input and the output of participants $P_1, \cdots, P_{N-1}$. Simulator $S_{I'}$ takes $\{a_i\}^{I'}, \{E(a_i)\}^{[N]}, \{f_i(a_1, \cdots, a_N)\}^{I'}$ as input, and proceeds the following steps.

(1) Randomly chooses a vector $a'_N = (\alpha'_{N1}, \cdots, \alpha'_{Nm})$, so that

$$f_i(a_1, \cdots, a_{N-1}, a_N) = f_i(a_1, \cdots, a_{N-1}, a'_N) \ (i \in [N-1]).$$

(2) Encrypts the vectors $a_1, \cdots, a_{N-1}, a'_N$ by using the multi-key NRTU FHE, and obtains $E(a_1), \cdots, E(a_{N-1}), E(a'_N)$.

(3) After receiving $E(a_1), \cdots, E(a_{N-1}), E(a'_N)$, $S_{I'}$ calculate $E(w'') = \prod_{i=1}^{N-1} E(a_i)E(a'_N)$.

(4) Decrypt $E(w'')$, and obtain w''.

In Protocol 2,

$$\begin{aligned}
&S_{I'}(\{x_i\}^{I'}, \{E(x_i)\}^{[N]}, \{f_i(x_1, \cdots, x_N)\}^{I'}, E(x_1, \cdots, x_N)) \\
&= \{\{a_i\}^{[N-1]}, \{E(a_i)\}^{[N]}, E(w''), w''\},
\end{aligned}$$

$$view_{I'}(x_1, \cdots, x_N) = \{\{a_i\}^{[N-1]}, \{E(a_i)\}^{[N]}, E(w), w\}.$$

Since $w'' = f_i(a_1, \cdots, a_{N-1}, a'_N)$ and $f_i(a_1, \cdots, a_{N-1}, a_N) = f_i(a_1, \cdots, a_{N-1}, a'_N)$, $w = w''$ holds, and further $E(w) \underline{c} E(w'')$ holds. Therefore, we have

$$S_{I'}(\{x_i\}^{I'}, \{E(x_i)\}^{[N]}, \{f_i(x_1, \cdots, x_N)\}^{I'}, E(x_1, \cdots, x_N)) \underline{c} \ view_{I'}(x_1, \cdots, x_N).$$

The above process proves that privacy of participant P_N can be protected even if CS and $P_1, \cdots, P_{N-1}$ are collusive. The reason is that $view_{I'}(x_1, \cdots, x_N)$ is derived only from $\{E(a_i)\}^{[N]}, \{a_i\}^{[N-1]}, \{f_i(a_1, \cdots, a_N)\}^{[N-1]}$, and $E(w)$, which contains nothing information about participant P_N where $\{E(a_i)\}^{[N]}$, and $\{a_i\}^{[N-1]}$ are the input about the CS and $P_1, \cdots, P_{N-1}$.

In contrast, if CS does not participate in collusion, i.e., there are just some participants $P_1, \cdots, P_N$ collude, we can also construct another simulator S_I in a similar way as simulator $S_{I'}$ such that

$$S_I(\{x_i\}^I, \{f_i(x_1, \cdots, x_N)\}^I) \underline{c} \ view_I(x_1, \cdots, x_N).$$

6 Performance Analysis

6.1 Analysis of Protocol 1

(1) Theoretical analysis

For Millionaire problem, the technique in the literature [17–19] mentioned in Introduction is similar to ours. Therefore, we make a performance comparison between the literature [17–19] and our protocol 1 in this section. The operation mainly included in the literature [17–19] and ours is encryption and decryption operations. For the computational cost, we only consider the "costly computation". As the computational overhead of modular multiplication operation dominate those of the others, we evaluate the computational overhead of each protocol by counting the number of encryption, decryption, and modular multiplication operations included in all phases except the preparing phase. For comparison, we assume that the encoding size m in all protocols is identical.

Computational Cost: Let U be the total order set, and $|U| = m$. There are m encryption operations and 1 decryption operations required in Protocol 1, and m encryption operations, m decryption operations, and $2m \log p + 4m - 6$ modular multiplication operations required in [17]. While in [18], there are m encryption, 1 decryption, and $3l$ modular multiplication operations required, and in [19], m encryption operations, 1 decryption operation, and $l + 3$ modular multiplication operations required where l represents the position of Bob's data in the set U.

Communication Overhead: There are two types of measurements to evaluate the communication overhead: one is the number of exchanged bits in the protocol; the other is the number of communication rounds. Generally, in SMC field the latter is used to measure the communication overhead. There is a three-round communication required in [17–19] and our protocol 1, respectively.

Properties: Here, we refer the more fine-grained result and the better resistance to quantum attack as a measurement evaluating the properties in [17–19] and our protocol 1, where $\times$ means no this property, otherwise $\sqrt{}$. The detailed comparison of our protocol 1 and those in [17–19] in terms of computational cost and communication overhead are shown in Table 4, and the properties comparison of our protocol 1 and [17–19] is shown in Table 5, where E and D denote encryption and decryption, respectively.

Table 4. Efficiency Comparison of Protocol 1 and Those in [17–19]

	Computational cost		Communication overhead
	Encryption and decryption time	Module multiplication	
Protocol 1	$mE + D$		3
Literature [17]	$mE + mD$	$2m \log p + 4m - 6$	3
Literature [18]	$mE + D$	$3l$	3
Literature [19]	$mE + D$	$l + 3$	3

Table 5. Properties Comparison of Protocol 1 and Those in [17–19]

	Anti-quantum attack	Fine-grained
Protocol 1	$\sqrt{}$	$\sqrt{}$
Literature [17]	$\times$	$\times$
Literature [18]	$\times$	$\times$
Literature [19]	$\times$	$\sqrt{}$

From Table 4, we can observe that though the communication overhead in the literature [17–19] is the same as our protocol 1, the computational cost in them is higher than that in ours. In addition, as shown in Table 5, our protocol 1 can obtain the more fine-grained result than others because our protocol 1 can determine two numbers equal or not whereas the others not even though all protocols can determine which number is larger. More importantly, None of protocols in [17–19] can resist quantum attack except ours. Therefore, our solution to the Millionaire problem is not only resistant to quantum attacks but also more efficient than the existing protocols, as well as the comparison results is more fine-grained than others as well.

(2) **Experiment simulation**

From the theoretical analysis, we can observe the efficiency of the protocols in [17, 18] is lower than that in [19]. Therefore, here we can merely compare the efficiency between our protocol 1 and that in [19]. For clarity, we provide experiment simulation to evaluate the consuming time of Paillier encryption in [19] and NTRU encryption in our protocol 1, The whole experimental setting is implemented in JAVA on a PC with the following configurations: Intel(R), Windows 7 Ultimate, CPU AMD A6-3240M 1.5 GHz, 4.00 GB memory.

During the experiment, the public key n used by Paillier encryption in [19] has the same size as the module n in modular polynomial $\varphi(x) = x^n + 1$ used by NTRU encryption in protocol 1. Fix q equal to 1024 bits in the equality $\varphi(x) = x^n + 1$. Let n equal to 128 bits, 192 bits, 256 bits, 384 bits, and 512 bits, respectively. We can obtain the sum of the consuming time of encryption and decryption operations corresponding to different n in Paillier encryption and NTRU encryption, respectively. Further, the average time is evaluated by seven experimental data chosen randomly from the results Finally, A comparison of the average time consumed by NTRU encryption and Paillier encryption is showed as Fig. 1.

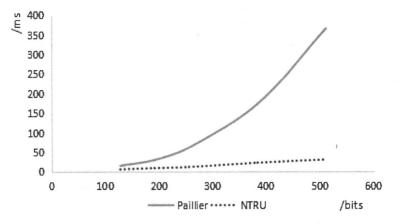

Fig. 1. Comparison of average time consumed between two algorithm

According to Fig. 1, we observe that the consuming time of NTRU encryption is fewer than Paillier encryption. Especially with n increasing, this advantage is more prominent than before. Therefore, the efficiency of protocol 1 is higher than that in [19], and obviously, it is higher than that in [17, 18].

6.2 Analysis of Protocol 2

(1) Theoretical analysis

For PSI problem, we make a performance comparison between the literature [24, 25] and our protocol 2 in this section. These three schemes are all based on homomorphic encryption. As the modular multiplication operation dominates those of the others, we evaluate the computational overhead of each protocol by counting the number of modular multiplication operation. In [24] and [25], Paillier and ElGamal encryption systems are employed and the corresponding modulus n^2 and p denoted by M_{n^2} and M_p, respectively. q and 2 are the modulus of our protocol 2, denoted by $M_{\varphi,q,2}$. For comparison, we assume that the encoding size m in all protocols is identical and N denotes the number of participants.

Computational Cost: Let each client P_i holds a set $S_i \subseteq U$ for $i = 1, 2, \ldots, N$, respectively. Each parties P_i in Protocol 2 requires $2m$ modular multiplication operations, and all clients require a total of $2Nm$ modular multiplication operations. In [24], all the participants require $Nm + 1$ modular exponentiation operations, each of which can account for $2 \log n$ multiplication operations in [17]. Therefore, $2(Nm + 1) \log n$ modular multiplications are required in [24]. In [25], there are mN encryption operations and m decryption operations required. Each encryption requires $2 \log p(\mathrm{mod}\, p)$ modular multiplications and each decryption requires $\log p$ modular multiplication operations. Thus, the protocol in [25] requires a total of $(2N + 1)m \log p$ modular multiplication operations.

Communication Overhead: There are $4N - 2$ and $(2 + k)N - k - 2$ communication rounds required in the literature [24, 25], respectively (where k is the number of share about segmentation ciphertext for each participant, $2 \leq k \leq N$). The protocol 2 requires $3N - 1$ rounds communication.

Properties: Here, we refer whether the protocol is suitable for a cloud computing environment, whether can resist quantum attack, and whether can resist collusion attack as a measurement evaluating the properties in [24, 25] and our protocol 2. where $\times$ means no this property, and $\not\prec$ means having part of property, otherwise $\sqrt{}$.

The comparison of our protocol 2 and those in [24, 25] in terms of computational cost and communication overhead are shown in Table 6, and the properties comparison is shown in Table 7.

Table 6. Efficiency Comparison of Protocol 2 and Those in [24, 25]

	Computational cost	Communication overhead
Literature [24]	$2(Nm+1)\log nM_{n^2}$	$4N-2$
Literature [25]	$(2N+1)m\log pM_p$	$(2+k)N-k-2\ (2\leq k\leq N)$
Our protocol 2	$2NmM_{\varphi,q,2}$	$3N-1$

Table 7. Performance Comparison of Protocol 2 and Those in [24, 25]

	Cloud computing environment	Anti-quantum attack	Anti-collusion attack
Literature [24]	√	×	×
Literature [25]	√	×	⊀
Our protocol 2	√	√	√

From Table 6, we can observe that the efficiency in Protocol 2 in this paper is higher than those in [24, 25]. From Table 7, though Protocol 2 and those in [24, 25] all make use of cloud computing technology, Protocol 2 can not only resist quantum attacks but also fully resist collusive attack, while [24] cannot resist collusion, and [25] can not fully resist collusion. Therefore, Protocol 2 designed in this paper achieves a better performance than others.

(2) **Experiment simulation**

For clarity, we provide experiment simulation to evaluate the consuming time of $\log n(M_{n^2})$ in [24], $\log p(M_p)$ in [25] and $M_{\varphi,q,2}$ in our protocol 1, respectively. The whole experimental setting is the same to the Subsect. 6.1.

During the experiment, the public key n used by Paillier encryption in [24] and public key p used by ElGamal encryption have the same size as the module n in modular polynomial $\varphi(x) = x^n + 1$ used by NTRU encryption in protocol 2. Fix q equal to 1024 bits. Let n equal to 128 bits, 256 bits, 380 bits, and 512 bits respectively, We calculate the time consumed by the modular multiplication operation $M_{n^2}M_p$ and $M_{\varphi,q,2}$, respectively. For each group of parameters, we randomly take 7 experimental results from the total to come up with each modular multiplication operation. Then the average time consumed by each modular multiplication is obtained eventually, a total of time consumed by $\log n(M_{n^2})$, $\log p(M_p)$, and $M_{\varphi,q,2}$ are further calculated, respectively. As showed in Table 8.

Table 8. Average time consumed by one modular multiplication under different modulus

n (p) (bits)	$\log nM_{n^2}$	$\log pM_p$	$M_{\varphi,q,2}$
128	2.179	1.741	0.456
256	7.910	6.424	0.561
380	14.027	12.545	0.713
512	25.424	19.581	1.035

From Table 8, the trend graphs about them are plotted as shown in following Fig. 2.

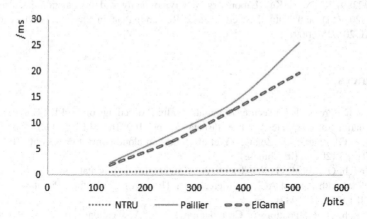

Fig. 2. Comparison of average time consumed among the three algorithms

According to Fig. 2, the average time consumed of $\log n(M_{n^2})$ in Paillier encryption and that of $\log p(M_p)$ in ElGamal encryption are more than that of $M_{\varphi,q,2}$ in NTRU encryption. That is, $\log n(M_{n^2}) > M_{\varphi,q,2}$ and $\log p(M_p) > M_{\varphi,q,2}$, and the gap of consuming time among them become larger as the modulus increasing. Thus, from the theoretical analysis and the experiment simulation, we can conclude the efficiency of protocol 2 in this paper is higher than that in [24, 25].

7 Conclusion and Open Problems

Millionaire problem and private set intersection problem are two basic problems in SMC, which have can be applied to many scenarios. To our knowledge, however, the security of the most existing solutions guaranteed by traditionally hard problem will be collapsed if the quantum computers are built. To deal with it, in this paper we design two new protocols, combining 0–1 encoding with NTRU FHE, to solve Millionaire problem and private set intersection problem. It is the first time that both our protocols can resist quantum attack. Especially, our protocol 2 can be conducted in cloud environment, and our protocol 1 can obtain the fine-grained result. The final performance analysis indicate that the two protocols in this paper can achieve a higher efficiency than others.

With the rapid development of cloud computing, outsourced computing is becoming indispensable technology. In the meanwhile, it is desirable that to solve real-time online problems will become increasing by virtue of cloud computing. Therefore, we will explore the real-time online solution to SMC problems in the cloud environment in the future work.

Acknowledgments. This work was supported by the National Natural Science Foundation of China (Grant No. U1261114), the National Natural Science Foundation of China (Grant No. 61872289), Guangxi Key Laboratory of Cryptography and Information Security (Grant No. GCIS201714), and Natural Science Basic Research Plan in Shaanxi Province of China (Grant No. 2017JM6069).

References

1. Yao, A.C.: Protocols for secure computations. In: Proceedings of 23rd IEEE Symposium on Foundations of Computer Science, Piscataway, pp. 160–164. IEEE (1982)
2. Feng, D.G., Zhang, M., Zhang, Y., et al.: Study on cloud computing security. J. Softw. **22** (1), 71–83 (2011). (in Chinese)
3. Goldreich, O., Micali, S., Wigderson, A.: How to play any mental game. In: Proceedings of the Nineteenth Annual ACM Conference on Theory of Computing, Piscataway, pp. 218–229. IEEE Press (1987)
4. Goldreich, O.: Foundations of Cryptography: Basic Applications, pp. 599–729. Cambridge University Press, London (2004)
5. Li, Y.P., Chen, M.H., Li, Q.W., et al.: Enabling multilevel trust in privacy preserving data mining. IEEE Trans. Knowl. Data Eng. Inst. Electr. Electron. Eng. **24**(9), 1598–1612 (2012)
6. Agrawal, R., Srikant, R.: Privacy-preserving data mining. In: Proceedings of ACM International Conference oil Management of Data and Symposium on Principles of Database Systems, pp. 439–450. ACM Press, New York (2000)
7. Lindell, Y., Pinkas, B.: Secure multiparty computation for privacy-preserving data mining. J. Priv. Confid. **25**(2), 761–766 (2009)
8. Clifton, C., Marks, D.: Security and privacy implications of data mining. In: Proceedings of the ACM SIGMOD Workshop on Research Issues on Data Mining and Knowledge Discovery, pp. 15–19. ACM Press, New York (1996)
9. Loftus, J., Smart, N.P.: Secure outsourced computation. In: Nitaj, A., Pointcheval, D. (eds.) AFRICACRYPT 2011. LNCS, vol. 6737, pp. 1–20. Springer, Heidelberg (2011). https://doi.org/10.1007/978-3-642-21969-6_1
10. Boneh, D., Waters, B.: Conjunctive, subset, and range queries on encrypted data. In: Vadhan, S.P. (ed.) TCC 2007. LNCS, vol. 4392, pp. 535–554. Springer, Heidelberg (2007). https://doi.org/10.1007/978-3-540-70936-7_29
11. Du, W.L., Atallah, M.J.: Privacy-preserving cooperative scientific computations. In: Proceedings of 14th IEEE Computer Security Foundations Workshop Lecture, Piscataway, pp. 273–282. IEEE Press (2001)
12. Chen, Z.H., Li, S.D., Huang, Q., et al.: Privacy-preserving determination of spatial location relation in cloud computing. Chin. J. Comput. **40**(2), 351–363 (2017). (in Chinese)
13. Hohenberger, S., Lysyanskaya, A.: How to securely outsource cryptographic computations. In: Kilian, J. (ed.) TCC 2005. LNCS, vol. 3378, pp. 264–282. Springer, Heidelberg (2005). https://doi.org/10.1007/978-3-540-30576-7_15
14. Yao, A.C.: How to generate and exchange secrets. In: Proceedings of 27th Annual Symposium on Foundations of Computer Science (FOCS 1986), pp. 162–167. Institute of Electrical and Electronics Engineers (1986)
15. Schoenmakers, B., Tuyls, P.: Practical two-party computation based on the conditional gate. In: Lee, P.J. (ed.) ASIACRYPT 2004. LNCS, vol. 3329, pp. 119–136. Springer, Heidelberg (2004). https://doi.org/10.1007/978-3-540-30539-2_10

16. Ioannidis, I., Grama, A.: An efficient protocol for Yao's millionaires' problem. In: Proceedings of the 36th Hawaii International Conference on System Sciences, Hawaii, USA, pp. 6–9 (2003)
17. Lin, H.-Y., Tzeng, W.-G.: An efficient solution to the millionaires' problem based on homomorphic encryption. In: Ioannidis, J., Keromytis, A., Yung, M. (eds.) ACNS 2005. LNCS, vol. 3531, pp. 456–466. Springer, Heidelberg (2005). https://doi.org/10.1007/11496137_31
18. Li, S.D., Wang, D.S.: Efficient secure multiparty computation based on homomorphic encryption. Chin. J. Electron. 41(4), 798–803 (2013). (in Chinese)
19. Zuo, X.J., Li, S.D., Yang, X.L.: An efficient homomorphic encryption based solution to millionaires' problem. J. Chin. Comput. Syst., 455–459 (2017). (in Chinese)
20. Pinkas, B., Schneider, T., Zohner, M.: Faster private set intersection based on OT extension. In: USENIX Security 2014, pp. 797–812. USENIX (2014)
21. Hazay, C.: Oblivious polynomial evaluation and secure set-intersection from algebraic PRFs. In: Dodis, Y., Nielsen, J.B. (eds.) TCC 2015, Part II. LNCS, vol. 9015, pp. 90–120. Springer, Heidelberg (2015). https://doi.org/10.1007/978-3-662-46497-7_4
22. Zhu, G.B., Tan, Y.W., Zhao, Y., et al.: An efficient and secure geometric intersection computation protocol. J. Univ. Electron. Sci. Technol. China 43(5), 781–786 (2014). (in Chinese)
23. Li, S.D., Dou, J.W., Jia, X.L.: Secure two-party computation for set intersection problem. J. Xian Jiaotong Univ. 40(10), 1091–1093 (2006). (in Chinese)
24. Abadi, A., Terzis, S., Dong, C.: O-PSI: delegated private set intersection on outsourced datasets. In: Federrath, H., Gollmann, D. (eds.) SEC 2015. IFIP AICT, vol. 455, pp. 3–17. Springer, Cham (2015). https://doi.org/10.1007/978-3-319-18467-8_1
25. Li, S.D., Zhou, S.F., Guo, Y.M., et al.: Secure set computing in cloud environment. J. Softw. 27(6), 1549–1565 (2016). (in Chinese)
26. Hoffstein, J., Pipher, J., Silverman, J.H.: NTRU: a ring-based public key cryptosystem. In: Buhler, J.P. (ed.) ANTS 1998. LNCS, vol. 1423, pp. 267–288. Springer, Heidelberg (1998). https://doi.org/10.1007/BFb0054868
27. Ducas, L., Durmus, A., Lepoint, T., Lyubashevsky, V.: Lattice signatures and bimodal Gaussians. In: Canetti, R., Garay, J.A. (eds.) CRYPTO 2013, Part I. LNCS, vol. 8042, pp. 40–56. Springer, Heidelberg (2013). https://doi.org/10.1007/978-3-642-40041-4_3
28. Peikert, C.: Lattice cryptography for the internet. In: 6th International Conference on Post-Quantum Cryptograp (PQCrypto 2014), Waterloo, ON, Canada, pp. 197–219 (2014)
29. Duan, R., Gu, C.X., Zhu, Y.F., et al.: Efficient identity-based fully homomorphic encryption over NTRU. J. Commun. 38(1), 66–75 (2017). (in Chinese)
30. Xia, F., Yang, B., Zhang, M.W., et al.: Secure two-party computation for set intersection and set equality problems based on LWE. J. Electron. Inf. Technol. 34(2), 462–467 (2012). (in Chinese)
31. Gentry, C., Peikert, C., Vaikuntanathan, V.: Trapdoors for hard lattices and new cryptographic constructions. In: STOC 2008, Victoria, BC, Canada, pp. 197–206. ACM (2008)
32. López-Alt, A., Tromer, E., Vaikuntanathan, V.: On-the-fly multiparty computation on the cloud via multikey fully homomorphic encryption. In: Proceedings of the Forty-Fourth Annual ACM Symposium on Theory of Computing, pp. 1219–1234. ACM (2012)
33. Rivest, R.L., Adleman, L., Dertouzos, M.L.: On data banks and privacy homomorphisms. Found. Secur. Comput. 4(11), 169–180 (1978)

A Cloud Storage Data Access Control Scheme Based on Attribute-Sets Encryption

Lihua Zhang[1]([✉]), Panpan Jiang[2], Qi Yi[1], Fan Lan[1],
and Tengfei Jiang[2]

[1] School of Software, East China Jiaotong University,
Nanchang 330000, Jiangxi, China
lhzhangbuaa@163.com
[2] School of Electrical and Automation Engineering, East China Jiaotong
University, Nanchang 330013, Jiangxi, China

Abstract. In order to solve the data security problem in cloud storage system, an access control scheme which supports for a finer attribute expression for cloud storage data based on CP-ASBE (Ciphertext-Policy Attribute-Sets Based Encryption) is proposed in this paper, which can solve the problem of attribute confusion based on attribute encryption algorithm. A multi-authorization center is used to address single-point security issues. The digest of plaintext is used to encrypt the plaintext, and then the CP-ASBE encryption key is used to improve the efficiency and save the storage space of the cloud storage. In terms of attribute revocation, access control lists are used to handle coarse-grained privilege revocation. For fine-grained attribute revocation, proxy re-encryption is used and the complex calculations are delegated to the computationally powerful DataNode node. The confidentiality, integrity, non-repudiation, availability and security of the scheme are analyzed and proved. The results show that the cloud storage data access control scheme based on CP-ASBE can effectively improve the security of user data in HDFS (Hadoop Distributed File System) cloud storage system.

Keywords: Access control protocol · Cloud storage
Attribute set based encryption scheme

1 Introduction

With the rapid development of science and technology, the amount of data needed to be processed in the application of the industry is increasing rapidly. At the same time, the amount of data generated by the applications of the industry is also increasing explosively [1]. Traditional data processing technology has been unable to handle data with terabytes [2] or even petabytes [3, 4] magnitude order, the big data technology has solved this problem preferably, but the security problem of big data technology has also caused huge losses to some users. As a part of cloud storage, access control plays a very important role in the whole cloud storage system. With the conditions of access control become more and more, the fine-grained degree of access control becomes finer and finer, the time cost in the access control process increases dramatically, which has gradually become a performance bottleneck of cloud storage system [5].

© Springer Nature Singapore Pte Ltd. 2019
H. Zhang et al. (Eds.): CTCIS 2018, CCIS 960, pp. 360–371, 2019.
https://doi.org/10.1007/978-981-13-5913-2_22

HDFS (Hadoop Distributed File System) cloud storage system is a cloud storage platform studied by many scholars. The existing Kerberos-based access control mechanism in HDFS has some shortcomings, such as load problems, single-point security issues, fine-grained access control, data transported in plaintext and data encryption. Li and Ma et al. proposed an access control scheme on HDFS based on PKI (public key infrastructure) [6, 7], while Yin et al. proposed an access control scheme based on PKI and ECC [8], using ECC to reduce computing and transmission costs. However, all these solutions have some drawbacks, and each user is assigned a pair of public and private keys, which means the key management is difficult and the flexibility and scalability of the system are poor.

Due to the shortcomings of the PKI security scheme, many scholars have begun to study the use of IBE scheme [9, 10] which is based on identity-based cryptosystem to achieve access control. Liu et al. [11] realized the access control of cloud data through IBE, and some symmetrical encryption methods such as 3DES, AES are used to encrypt the data in transit to ensure that files are not snooped. Liu et al. [12] proposed another scheme to achieve access control using IBE. However, in the IBE scheme, the same file may be encrypted into multiple files due to using different keys, which will seriously waste the storage space of the cloud storage cluster.

In order to solve the problem based on the IBE security mechanism, Sahai and Waters proposed an attribute-based security system ABE [13], Chase [14], Ruj [15] and others proposed a distributed ABE scheme, an improved ABE scheme for distributed authorization centers is proposed by Chase et al. [16]. Kim [17] and Muller [18] et al. have developed an ABE system with multiple authorization centers based on shamir threshold sharing mechanism. However, all of the above schemes are based on the study of simple attribute set, which can not achieve the precise definition of users with complex attributes, can not support the cloud storage environment with complex ciphertext rules well, and can not resist the attack of user confusing attributes. The CP-ASBE-based scheme was first proposed by Bobba et al. [19]. The key structure in this algorithm is a set of attributes based on a recursive set. The elements in the set can be either a set of attributes or a single attribute. In this way, the algorithm can not only support complex attribute representation, but also avoid user confusing attribute attack by placing associated attributes in a set of attributes and limiting the way that users can only associate attribute elements in the same subset when decrypting ciphertext. Firstly, this paper analyzes the shortcomings of the security mechanism of HDFS cloud storage system, and then discusses the advantages and disadvantages of various schemes for improving cloud storage access control at home and abroad. Then, based on the shortcomings of the above schemes, a cloud storage data access control scheme based on attribute set encryption algorithm is proposed.

In the first section, the modeling of the scheme is given, and the framework of the scheme is introduced. The second section describes the specific process of the scheme. The third section evaluates the confidentiality, integrity, non-repudiation and availability of the scheme. Finally, the security proof of the scheme is given in the fourth section.

2 Scheme Modeling

2.1 Safety Hypothesis

(1) The cloud storage server is honest and curious. While processing the data according to the protocol, there is the possibility of snooping through the user data.
(2) The central authorization center is trusted, while the general authorization center is semi-trusted.
(3) Communication between authorized centers or between authorization centers and users is performed in full accordance with secure communication protocols.

2.2 Overall Framework

The scheme is made up of three main entities: cloud storage server HDFS, authorization center AA and users. HDFS includes a NameNode and several Data Nodes; the authorization center consists of a central authorization center and several general authorization centers; Each general authorization center has a set of attributes that are not intersected. The user is divided into file uploader Owner and general user. The system frame diagram is shown in Fig. 1.

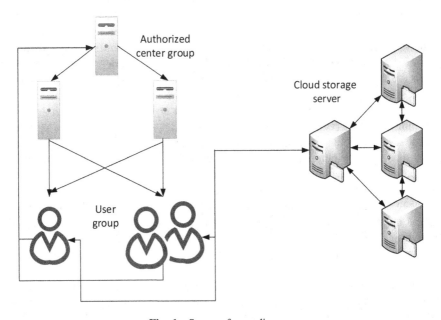

Fig. 1. System frame diagram

Where attribute authorization center is mainly composed of central authorization center and general authorization center, which mainly provides user attribute authorization service. When a user makes a request for attribute validation to the system, the central authorization center validates the attributes submitted by the user first, and then the corresponding set of attributes will be generated. After that, several other general authorization centers generate their own private keys for the attributes according to the set of attributes and distribute the private keys to the users through a secure way.

The file owner is the uploader of the file. He can set the access policy for the file he uploaded. Only the user who satisfies the access policy can decrypt the file. At the same time, for the file that is not uploaded by him, he is just a normal user.

The general user has the attribute private key obtained from the authorization center and can obtain the ciphertext from the cloud storage server. However, the ciphertext can be decrypted only if the attribute private key in his hand satisfies the access policy of the ciphertext.

NameNode is the commander in HDFS. It maintains the file system tree and all directories and files in the tree for the entire cloud storage system. It is also responsible for managing and maintaining the file system namespace, and records the corresponding information of each file block to the DataNode. In addition, it needs to direct all the DataNode.

DataNode is the working node of the cloud storage server and the actual data storage medium. All the data is stored on several DataNodes, which obey the instructions of NameNode. When users request files, they are responsible for transmitting files to users.

3   Specific Process

3.1   System Initialization

(1) The central authorization center (CA) initializes the system using the CP-ASBE scheme proposed in Ref. [19] to generate the system master key MK and the public key PK, where the MK is kept by CA.

(2) The CA verifies the general authorization center AA, and after the verification is passed, it is authorized and assigned the corresponding master key.

(3) The CA responds to the request of the user and verifies its attributes, and the corresponding attribute set is generated after the verification is passed.

(4) The general authorization center AA generates a corresponding attribute private key SK and an attribute certificate for the user according to the attribute set of the user and the attribute possessed by itself, and distributes it to the user. The user's attribute certificate is similar to the PKI's public key certificate, except that it binds the user's identity information to the user's attribute information.

3.2   Writing Files

(1) Before uploading a file to a cloud storage server, a user with write authority needs to establish an access policy P for the file to allow a particular user to access the file first.

(2) The user generates the private keys K_v and public keys K_s, which are used for signing and verifying the file, respectively.

(3) The user generates digest 'a' for files to be uploaded.
(4) The user uses K_s to sign 'a' and generates Signa.
(5) The user encrypts files with 'a' and generates ciphertext CP.
(6) Users use CP-ASBE algorithm and P policy to encrypt 'a', Signa, K_s and K_v to generate ciphertext CK.

The flow chart of user writing files is shown in Fig. 2.

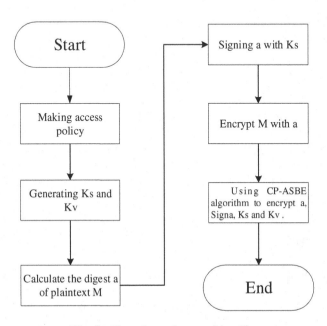

Fig. 2. Flow chart of user writing files

3.3   Reading Files

(1) After the user obtains the file from the cloud server, the user decrypts the CK using the attribute private key. If the attribute private key cannot satisfy the access policy set by the file owner, the file cannot be decrypted.
(2) If the user's attribute private key meets the read access policy set by the file owner, the user can get Signa, a, and K_v from the CK. When the read/write access policy set by the file owner is satisfied, the user can obtain Signa, a, K_v and Ks from CK, where Ks is used for writing file operations.
(3) The user uses a to decrypt the CP and get the plaintext M from it.
(4) The user calculates a digest a' of M, compares a with a' to confirm whether they are the same, and verifies the integrity of M.
(5) The user uses K_v to decrypt the Signa and compares a' with a* obtained from Signa to verify the legitimacy of the data source.

The flow chart of the user reading files is shown in Fig. 3.

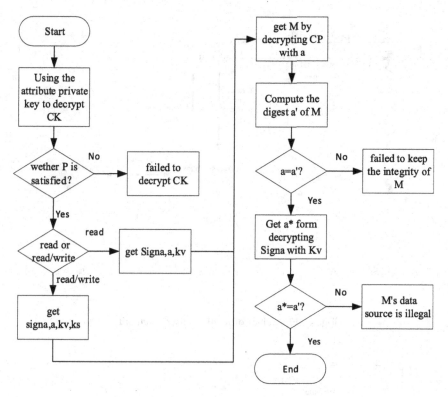

Fig. 3. Flow chart of user reading files

3.4 Attribute Revocation

Attribute revocation is also an important issue affecting the efficiency of the whole scheme. Attribute revocation means that some attributes of the user in the system are invalid or the user is no longer authorized at all.

The access control rights in this scheme are determined by the access control list in NameNode and the attribute private key in the user's hand. In the attribute-based encryption scheme, the steps of attribute revocation are cumbersome and the computational overhead is relatively large. Therefore, for the control of some coarse-grained access rights, we can use the access control list in the NameNode to complete. For example, if you want to revoke a user's authority to read a file, we just need to add control rules to the file's own access control list. The user's attribute private key does not need to be updated through cumbersome operations. The specific steps for revoking the user's authority to read files are shown in Fig. 4.

To revoke an attribute, you need to update the corresponding components in the system public key PK and the system master key MK associated with the attribute, then update the private key for each user who owns the attribute and has not revoked it yet, and finally update all the ciphertext in the cloud whose access policies are related to the attribute.

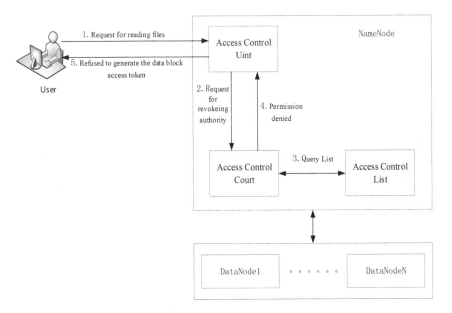

Fig. 4. Flow chart of revoking user's authority

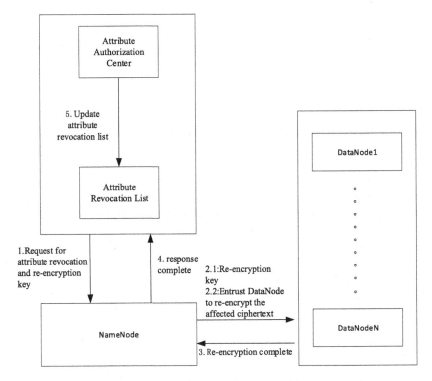

Fig. 5. Diagram of attribute revocation

When ciphertext needs to be re-encrypted, the traditional way is to decrypt the ciphertext first and then re-encrypt it with the new key. If the data is decrypted and then encrypted in the cloud, there is a risk of privacy leakage. Therefore, the scheme uses proxy re-encryption to complete the operation of updating the user private key and updating the ciphertext. The authorization center can delegate to the DataNode for proxy re-encryption to lighten the burden on the authorization center. A diagram of attribute revocation is shown in Fig. 5.

4 Security Analysis

(1) Confidentiality

In this scheme, the encryption of data is based on attribute set. Each ciphertext needs the user to satisfy the access control policy set by the file owner to be decrypted into plaintext. Compared with the schemes [6–8], this scheme does not need to manage a large number of keys. In addition, the encryption of data is based on the end-to-end encryption mode. Because the scheme is designed in an environment where the cloud storage server is not entirely trusted, the encryption of plaintext by the file owner and the decryption of data ciphertext by the user are carried out on the client side. In this way, even if the ciphertext is stolen by a malicious user by a special means during the transmission process or when stored in the cloud storage server, the malicious user does not have the attribute key required to decrypt the ciphertext, so it is impossible to decrypt the ciphertext to snoop on the plaintext.

(2) Integrity

Compared with the schemes [14] and [15], this scheme can verify the integrity of the file after downloading the file. In the stage of reading files, the user downloads the ciphertext together with the digest information from the cloud storage server. The user can verify the integrity of the ciphertext by calculating the digest of the plaintext and then comparing it with the decrypted digest information.

(3) Non-repudiation

In many attribute-based encryption schemes, such as scheme [14–18], non-repudiation is not involved, in this scheme, at the stage of writing a file, by signing the digest of a document, evidence can be left for the modification of the document. Only when a file's signature is verified can its data source be guaranteed to be legitimate.

(4) Availability

The integrity of the data directly affects the availability of the data. In this scheme, the integrity of the data can be detected as early as possible by verifying the digest. In order to prevent the loss of data when the legitimate user uses the data, in HDFS, each piece of data is kept in at least three copies and stored in different places, when a place fails to provide data to the user for some reason, HDFS will send a copy of the data from other places to the user.

(5) Data redundant

Compared with the scheme [9–12], this scheme improves the utilization of cloud storage space. In this scheme, the digest of plaintext is used to encrypt the plaintext. Because the plaintext is the same, the digest should be the same, so the ciphertext encrypted with the digest is the same, finally the same plaintext will generate the same ciphertext. In this way, the cloud storage server can appropriately discard the same ciphertext to save the storage space of the cloud storage server.

(6) Hybrid encryption mechanism

Hybrid encryption mechanisms are used in many CP-ABE based access control schemes, such as scheme [15], using a generated symmetric key to encrypt attribute ciphertext. This scheme uses the digest of plaintext to encrypt the plaintext, and then uses the scheme based on attribute set encryption to encrypt the digest, which not only avoids the inefficiency of directly using the scheme based on attribute set encryption to encrypt the plaintext, but also can verify the integrity of the data.

(7) Anti-attribute confusion

In many access control schemes based on CP-ABE, such as [14–18], it is possible for users to use the method of attribute confusion to form attributes that they should not hold. The CP-ASBE algorithm used in this scheme prevents the possibility of attribute confusion by setting the concept of attribute set.

5 Proof of Safety

Definition (Decisional Bilinear Diffle-Hellsman (DBDH) problem): Let G1, G2 be two groups, g be generator of G1, e be bilinear mapping. Make a random selection in $a, b, c \in Z_q$, distinguish tuple between $(g, g^a, g^b, g^c, e(g, g)^{abc})$ and $(g, g^a, g^b, g^c, e(g, g)^Z)$.

Hypothesis (DBDH Hypothesis): There is no algorithm that can solve DBDH problems with non-negligible advantages in any polynomial time.

(1) Initialization: The attacker picks an access policy T to be attacked.
(2) System establishment phase: The challenger obtains PK and MK through the initialization algorithm and the key generation algorithm, and sends the PK to the attacker.

$$PK = \{G_0, g, h_1 = g^{\beta_1}, f_1 = g^{\frac{1}{\beta_1}}, h_2 = g^{\beta_2}, f_2 = g^{\frac{1}{\beta_2}}, e(A, B) = e(g, g)^{ab}\}$$

$$MK = \{\beta_1, \beta_2, g^{ab}\}$$

(3) Query phase 1: The attacker asks to generate the attribute private keys of attribute A1 ∼ An, where A1 ∼ An cannot satisfy T. The challenger generates the attribute private keys SK1 ∼ SKn which are corresponding to the attributes A1 ∼ An and sends them to the attacker.

(4) Challenge phase: The attacker sends two plaintexts M1 and M2 of equal length to the challenger. The challenger then randomly selects one of them, then encrypts Mb with T to get the CT, and sends the CT to the attacker.

$$CT = \{T, \tilde{C} = M_b \cdot e(g,g)^{abc}, \{C^{(w)} = h_{w,1}^{\theta}, \overline{C}^{(w)} = h_{w,2}^{\theta},$$

$$\forall y^{(w)} \in Y^{(w)} : C_y^{(w)} = g^{q_y(0)}, C_y'^{(w)} = H(attr(y^{(w)}))^{q_y(0)},$$

$$\forall x^{(w)} \in X^{(w)} : \tilde{C}_x^{(w)} = h_{w,2}^{q_x(0)}\}_{w=1}^{W}\}$$

(5) Query phase 2: Repeat the operation of query phase 1.
(6) Output phase: The attacker outputs a guess b' of b. If $b' = b$, the challenger outputs $b' = 0$. Otherwise, the challenger outputs $b' = 1$.

When $b' = 1$, the attacker did not get information related to Mb, so

$$\Pr[b' = b|b = 1] = \frac{1}{2}$$

When $b' = 0$, it means that the attacker got a Mb, and the attacker has a non-negligible advantage to attack the scheme. And

$$\Pr = [b' = b|b = 0] = \frac{1}{2} + \varepsilon$$

The advantage of the challenger in guessing right about $b' = b$:

$$Adv_c = \Pr[b' = b] - \frac{1}{2} = \frac{1}{2}\Pr[b' = b|b = 0] - \frac{1}{2} = \frac{\varepsilon}{2}$$

If the attacker can break the scheme with a non-negligible advantage ε, then there is a polynomial time algorithm that can solve the DBDH problem with a non-negligible advantage. According to the assumption that the DBDH problem is difficult to solve, it means that there is no polynomial time algorithm that can solve the problem with a non-negligible advantage. Therefore the scheme is safe for CPA (Chosen-Plaintext Attack).

6 Conclusion

In this paper, an access control scheme for cloud storage is proposed based on attribute set encryption algorithm of ciphertext strategy to solve the problems of single point security, waste of storage space and complex key management in existing access control schemes for cloud storage. The scheme can achieve a flexible, fine-grained access control, as well as data source authentication and data integrity verification. At the same time, the multi-authorization center is used to solve the security problem of single-point mode, and the encryption of plaintext by using the digest of plaintext solves the problem of waste of storage space. The algorithm of attribute set encryption based on ciphertext strategy avoids the loophole of CPABE attribute confusion and supports more detailed attribute expression, which makes the proposed scheme more suitable for complex cloud storage environment than the scheme based on CPABE.

References

1. Wang, Y.Z., Ji, X.L., Cheng, X.Q.: Network big data: present and future. Chin. J. Comput. **36**(6), 1125–1138 (2013)
2. Liu, Z.H., Zhang, Q.: Research overview of big data technology. J. Zhejiang Univ. (Eng. Sci.) **48**(6), 957–972 (2014)
3. Li, X.L., Gong, H.G.: A survey on big data systems. Sci. Sinica Informationis **45**(1), 1–44 (2015)
4. Xia, J.B., Wei, Z.K., Fu, K.: Review of research and application on Hadoop in cloud computing. Comput. Sci. **43**(11), 6–11 (2016)
5. Li, H., Zhang, M., Feng, D.-G., Hui, Z.: Research on access control of big data. Chin. J. Comput. **1**, 72–91 (2017)
6. Ijaz, I., Aslam, A., Bukhari, B., et al.: Securing cloud infrastructure through PKI. In: International Conference on Computing, Communication and Networking Technologies, pp. 1–6. IEEE (2014)
7. Ma, Y.: Study of security mechanism based on Hadoop. Inf. Secur. Commun. Priv. **6**, 95–98 (2012)
8. Yin, X.C., Liu, Z.G., Lee, H.J.: An efficient and secured data storage scheme in cloud computing using ECC-based PKI. In: International Conference on Advanced Communication Technology, pp. 523–527 IEEE (2014)
9. Shamir, A.: Identity-based cryptosystems and signature schemes. In: Blakley, G.R., Chaum, D. (eds.) CRYPTO 1984. LNCS, vol. 196, pp. 47–53. Springer, Heidelberg (1985). https://doi.org/10.1007/3-540-39568-7_5
10. Boneh, D., Franklin, M.: Identity based encryption from the weil pairing. SIAM J. Comput. **32**(3), 213–229 (2001)
11. Liu, D., Fan, Y.: Design and implementation on cloud document secure storage management system based on IBE mechanism. Netinfo Secur. **12**, 1–7 (2016)
12. Liu, Z.: Research and implementation on cloud computing security based on HDFS. Comput. Model. New Technol. **17**(5B), 41–45 (2013)
13. Sahai, A., Waters, B.: Fuzzy identity-based encryption. In: Cramer, R. (ed.) EUROCRYPT 2005. LNCS, vol. 3494, pp. 457–473. Springer, Heidelberg (2005). https://doi.org/10.1007/11426639_27
14. Chase, M.: Multi-authority attribute based encryption. In: Vadhan, S.P. (ed.) TCC 2007. LNCS, vol. 4392, pp. 515–534. Springer, Heidelberg (2007). https://doi.org/10.1007/978-3-540-70936-7_28
15. Ruj, S., Nayak, A., Stojmenovic, I.: DACC: distributed access control in clouds. In: IEEE, International Conference on Trust, Security and Privacy in Computing and Communications, pp. 91–98. IEEE (2011)

16. Chase, M., Chow, S.S.M.: Improving privacy and security in multi-authority attribute-based encryption. In: ACM Conference on Computer and Communications Security, pp. 121–130. ACM (2009)
17. Kim, S.H., Lee, I.Y.: Study on user authority management for safe data protection in cloud computing environments. Symmetry 7(1), 269–283 (2015)
18. Müller, S., Katzenbeisser, S., Eckert, C.: Distributed attribute-based encryption. In: Lee, P.J., Cheon, J.H. (eds.) ICISC 2008. LNCS, vol. 5461, pp. 20–36. Springer, Heidelberg (2009). https://doi.org/10.1007/978-3-642-00730-9_2
19. Bobba, R., Khurana, H., Prabhakaran, M.: Attribute-sets: a practically motivated enhancement to attribute-based encryption. In: Backes, M., Ning, P. (eds.) ESORICS 2009. LNCS, vol. 5789, pp. 587–604. Springer, Heidelberg (2009). https://doi.org/10.1007/978-3-642-04444-1_36

Detecting Malicious URLs Using a Deep Learning Approach Based on Stacked Denoising Autoencoder

Huaizhi Yan[1,2(✉)], Xin Zhang[1,2], Jiangwei Xie[1,2], and Changzhen Hu[1,2]

[1] School of Computer, Beijing Institute of Technology, Beijing 100081, China
yhzhi@bit.edu.cn
[2] Beijing Key Laboratory of Software Security Engineering Technology (Beijing Institute of Technology), Beijing 100081, China

Abstract. As the source of spamming, phishing, malware and many more such attacks, malicious URL is a chronic and complicated problem on the Internet. Machine learning approaches have taken effect and obtained high accuracy in detecting malicious URL. But the tedious process of extracting features from URL and the high dimension of feature vector makes the implementing time consuming. This paper presents a deep learning method using Stacked denoising autoencoders model to learn and detect intrinsic malicious features. We employ an SdA network to analyze URLs and extract features automatically. Then a logistic regression is implemented to detect malicious and benign URLs, which can generate detection models without a manually feature engineering. We have implemented our network model using Keras, a high-level neural networks API with a Tensor-flow backend, an open source deep learning library. 5 datasets were used and 4 other method were compared with our model. In the result, our architecture achieves an accuracy of 98.25% and a micro-averaged F1 score of 0.98, tested on a mixed dataset containing around 2 million samples.

Keywords: Network security · Malicious URL detection · Deep learning Stacked denoising autoencoder

1 Introduction

Typing an URL is the first and foremost step for a user to surf the Internet, and this simple move could lead to a variety of attacks such as drive-by download, watering hole, phishing and malicious exploiting attempts. The URLs used to implement the attacks are so-called malicious URLs.

To solve these notorious attacks, an efficient way is determining whether an URL is malicious and stifle the attack in the cradle. Several researchers have proposed machine learning techniques, which can learn features from URL samples and distinguish them from benign URLs. Including support vector machines [1], decision trees [1, 2], logistic regression [3] and ensembles learning [4]. These machine learning approaches bring well-known advantages: freedom from collecting blacklist and artificially crafting filter rule, more efficiency by introducing automatic detection, and result in higher accuracy

H. Zhang et al. (Eds.): CTCIS 2018, CCIS 960, pp. 372–388, 2019.
https://doi.org/10.1007/978-981-13-5913-2_23

rate. Although previous work has a good detection rate, malicious URLs detection based on feature engineering and machine learning still suffered a number of shortcomings: up to 800 billion new websites a year make it harder to extract features, and it could not deal with the higher and higher dimension of feature vector and acquire a acceptable training time, and the shortage of malicious training dataset limit the accuracy. Also, classifier based on feature engineering could be circumvented and evaded [6, 7] through hidden feature created by confusion and encoding [1], one case is using short URL to implement attack [8].

To resolve the problems mentioned above, we make the following contributions in our research:

- Freedom from manually crafting features. Compared with static URL analysis, we introduce the deep learning technique to implement an auto feature extraction module, which can generate detection models without a manually feature engineering. Unlike most existing approaches, the deep learning method can learn high level features by deconstructing and reconstructing URL samples.
- Detecting unknown attacks and fighting against URL evade technology. Since the model did not use artificial features, it breaks the wall of human's fixed cognition to shallow malicious features. The generated model is able to extract implicative correlation between features, which could indicate more intrinsic property of malicious URLs. Therefore, our approach has the capability of identifying new malicious URL sample format that previously unknown.
- Experiment and Evaluation. We have implemented our network model using Keras [10], a high-level neural networks API with a Tensorflow [11] backend, an open source deep learning library. 5 datasets were used and 4 other method were compared with our model. The experiment results in a 98.52% accuracy rate with 1.96% false positive rate.

In a word, our approach offers a qualitative promotion in online malicious URL detection and automate the process of feature extracting, similar with teaching the model to learn features themselves. And we also acquire a good detection rate when meet new samples that never show in test data-set. We present the background in Sect. 2. Then Sect. 3 introduces the main idea of our approach and deep learning framework. Section 4 shows the experiment detail and results. Section 5 reviews a great deal of related work. Finally, Sect. 6 provides the conclusions and discussions.

2 Background

Throughout this paper we focus on how to identify whether an URL is malicious or benign on the Internet. This section provides a background on URL resolution, malicious detection and deep learning, the detection method we use in this paper.

2.1 Uniform Resource Locator Resolution

As people locate a building using a real address on a map, uniform resource locators are the global address of individual resources on the Internet. As specified in the

RFC 1738 [27], URL is a human-readable text string which can be parsed by common browser and translated into multi-step process to locate the server and resource. The following is the syntax format of a standard URL:

<protocol>://<hostname>:<port>/<path>?<query>#<fragment>

2.2 Malicious URL Detection

Malicious URL detection is usually treated as a binary classification problem. Previous approaches to detect malicious URL could be broken down into three categories:

(1) Reactive (Black-list): Services like IE SmartScreen and Google Safe Browsing is using black-list, and they have a low overhead and low false-positive rate. But due to the huge amount of newly generated malicious URLs everyday, maintaining an exhaustive increasing list of malicious URLs is impossible. Also, black-list method can never detect a new sample that appeared before.
(2) Retrospective: Retrospective means classifying URLs offline based on the statistical properties such as lexical features and character-level features to learn a prediction function. Lately, machine learning techniques are applied in proactive methods and gained good effects [7, 12, 18, 19]. However, as mentioned in Sect. 1, these methods relied on feature engineering and training data-set the model used. More related work about classification methods using machine learning is surveyed and presented in Sect. 6.
(3) Proactive and online learning (real-time): proactive method usually analyzes URL in real time and render the web-page to extract more contextual features from html content [9, 20]. To make detection method more scalable and efficient, several researchers employ online learning by updating classify model from sequentially newly learned features in real time [21, 25]. Proactive method need more evaluation time because of the rendering and model updating process.

2.3 Classification of URLs Using Machine Learning

Recently, machine learning techniques have been explored with increasing attention and wildly used in classifying malicious URLs [19]. Ma et al. should be the earlier one who apply machine learning in URL classification [18]. They use a number of statistical methods like naive Bayes, support vector machine (SVM) and logistic regression to classify websites. They use lexical and hosted based information to construct the feature vector.

Pao et al. use SVM and adopt a conditional Kolmogorov measure as a single significant feature for detection [22]. As a compression method for its approximation, Kolmogorov measure can also work with other features and achieve good accuracy and efficiency in predicting million URLs.

Thomas et al. present a real-time spam URL filtering service named Monarch [21]. They design a distributed logistic regression with L1-regularization and use stochastic gradient descent to update weight vector within each single shard. In particular, Monarch has a high scalability to handle a could handle the amount of 15 million URLs per day on Twitter.

For URL confusion detection, Wang et al. analyze the click traffic on twitter and extract short URLs' character level features, then use random tree algorithm to achieve a accuracy of 90.81% in detecting short URL spam on twitter [20].

Mohammad et al. propose an intelligent model using artificial neural network (ANN) to predict phishing attacks [12]. They particularly use self-structure cope with the feature significant changing which can determining the type of webpages. The model can automate the process of structuring the network, and achieve a high prediction accuracy of 92.18% and high acceptance for noisy data and high fault tolerance.

2.4 Deep Learning in Related Context

For other malicious detection, Woodbridge et al. leverage character-level Long Short-Term-Memory (LSTM) networks to classify domains generated by domain generation algorithms (DGA) [13]. Their classifier achieve featureless classification and can perform multiclass classification to specific the malware family. Yu et al. further improve the work of Woodbirge et al. by introducing Convolutional Neural Network (CNN) to classifier and deploy a live stream to detect DGA domains [14]. Wang et al. presents stacked denoising auto-encoders to extract high layer features then use logistic regression to classify malicious javascript code [15, 16]. Their work shows that depending on huge training data, deep models can achieve more accurate results. By sparse random projection, Wang et al. reduce vector dimension from 20,000 features to 480 features. Mahmood et al. research the application of autoencoder in cyber security area [23], they show the AE's capability of automatically learning a reasonable notion of semantic similarity among input features, and evaluate their methods in network based anomaly intrusion detection and Malware classification experiments.

3 Detection Approach

We are now ready to describe the key ideas of our detection approach. We employ an SdA network to analyze URLs and extract features automatically. Then a logistic regression is implemented to detect malicious and benign URLs. The whole process of our method is illustrated in Fig. 1.

In our work, URL samples are preprocessed and converted into vectors. A stacked denoising Autoencoders model is built using dA units and receives training data and extract high level features. There are two training stages in our model: unsupervised pre-training stage and supervised fine-tuning and classification stage. Finally, the classification is performed using logistic regression to detect malicious URLs.

The model has the following advantages:

(1) The model can extract features from preprocessed URL samples directly and require no cumbersome feature engineering;
(2) The model is trained in an unsupervised fashion and can provide high level and more discriminative features in contrast to other feature engineering approaches;
(3) The model is capable of automatically learning a reasonable correlation among automatically extracted features;
(4) Deep models have the potential to extract better representations from the raw data to create much better models.

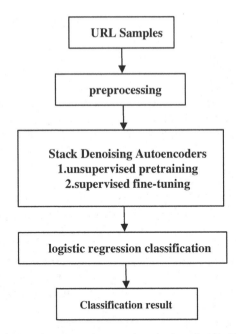

Fig. 1. The whole process of method to classify URL

3.1 Data Preprocessing

As mentioned in Sect. 2.1, many URLs contain URL-Encoded Unicode strings that are not human-readable. And there also exist various meaningless strings. So URL samples cannot be treated as normal text samples and are not suitable for being represented in the form of word vectors, which is usually implemented in many natural language processing models.

Therefore, in data preprocessing stage, we first deal with the URL-Encode encoding and convert Unicode characters into Unicode value. Then we convert other letters into ASCII values. Combined with these two values, a vector represent the URL is generated. To keep all vectors are the same length, a zero padding to the is implemented to extend vector length. An example of data preprocessing is shown in Fig. 2.

3.2 Stacked Denoising Autoencoders

Autoencoders [32] is a feed-forward network, it is unsupervised trained to learn features automatically from unlabeled data and learn a compressed representation of the input.

As Fig. 3 shows, Autoencoders contains input layer, hidden layer and output layer. Input layer firstly deconstruct original feature space vector x into features H using a set of generative weights and activation function f.

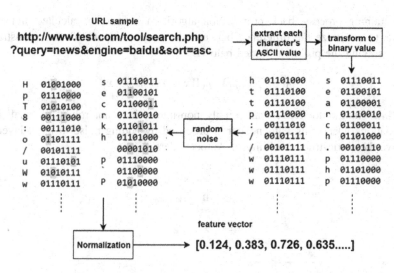

Fig. 2. An example of data preprocessing

$$H = f(Wx + b) \tag{1}$$

Then, in output layer, the features H is reconstructed into $\hat{x}$, an approximate formation of x, using another set of generative weights and same activation function normally

$$W' = WT.$$

$$\hat{x} = f(W'H + b') \tag{2}$$

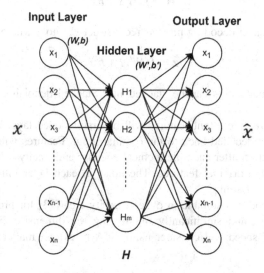

Fig. 3. Model of autoencoders

In training process, back propagation algorithm is used to calculate and adjust weights to minimize the difference between the original input and the reconstructed output, solving the problem formed below:

$$\min_{w,b,w',b'} \|f(W'f(Wx+b)+b') - x\| \tag{3}$$

While since autoencoders are highly non-linear, it is not robust to small input perturbations. Denoising autoencoder is proposed by adding noise in input layer and improve the reconstruction ability of Autoencoders.

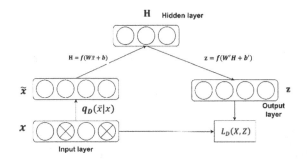

Fig. 4. Structure of dA units.

As Fig. 4 illustrated, x is processed by distribution $q_D(\bar{x}|x)$ and generate $\tilde{x}$, a corrupted version of x. Like Autoencoders described above, denoising autoencoders deconstruct x into H

$$H = f(W\tilde{x}+b) \tag{4}$$

where $H \in R^h$,then in decoding process reconstruct H into z where $z \in R^d z \in R^d$.

$$z = f(W'H+b') \tag{5}$$

Denoising autoencoders can be stacked into Stacked denoising Autoencoders as shown in Fig. 5.

In this deep structure, input features will be first encoded layer by layer and then correspondingly be decoded back to the original input. Features will become a better abstract representation after each hierarchical encoder and finally achieve a high level representation of the original features. The noise in each layer introduce better performance and faster training.

Since Autoencoder is suitable in cyber security area [23] for providing more discriminative features and significantly minimizing the dimensionality of features to improve detecting speed, we consider using SdA to extract malicious features from URLs.

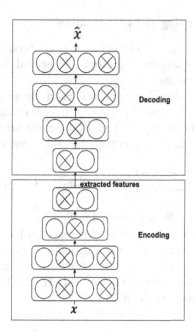

Fig. 5. Structure of stacked denoising autoencoders

3.3 SdA Model Pre-training

In model training process, our target is to form an effective neural network by adjusting parameters and functions in Autoencoders. For each dA unit in encoding and decoding processes, the activation function f is set to be the sigmoid function as follows:

$$f(x) = \frac{1}{1 + e^{-x}} \tag{6}$$

The parameters of each neural units will be calculated using the first-order derivative of sigmoid function, which takes the form below:

$$f'(x) = f(x)(1 - f(x)) \tag{7}$$

We use Gaussian-noise as the denoising method to corrupt the data. The loss take the form below since the loss function is set to be mean squared error function and mini-batch rule updating strategy is taken for a large-scale dataset.

$$L(\mathbf{x}, \mathbf{z}) = -\frac{1}{mn} \sum_{b=1}^{m} \sum_{i=1}^{n} (z_{bi} - x_{bi})^2 \tag{8}$$

where n is the input size and m is the mini-batch size. x_{bi} represents the input value of element i in the b-th minibatch. In a similar way, z_{bi} denotes the reconstruction value of element i in the b-th mini-batch.

Finally, the network is trained by backpropagation using a root mean square propagation optimizer for it's efficiently learning in multi-layer neural networks.

3.4   Supervised Fine-Tuning and Classification

After the pre-training process, a supervised training is operated to tune the parameters and a logistic regression classifier is deployed at the end of the network to finally accomplish the classification task.

Softmax function is used as the output activation function to calculate the probability of each class. Then a supervise mini-batch with optimization of binary cross entropy to achieve fine-tuning stage and adjust the entire network's parameters.

The loss function of binary cross entropy takes the form below:

$$\mathbf{L}(\mathbf{x}, \mathbf{z}) = -\frac{1}{m} \sum_{b=1}^{m} \sum_{n=1}^{d} \left(x_{bn} \log(z_{bn}) + (l - x_{bn}) \log(1 - z_{bn}) \right) \qquad (9)$$

Finally, our SdA-LR model is illustrated in Fig. 6.

The SdA part is like a feature extractor to obtain high-level and comprised abstract features and the logistic regression part is a normal classifier.

The layers number of our SdA model is 4 and dA unit number of each layer are 250, 200, 150 and 100. The corruption level is 0.1. The batch size is 128. Pre-training epochs is 50 and fine-tuning epochs is 25.

4   Experiment

4.1   Dataset Description

A data-set of 2 million benign URL samples and 2 million malicious URL samples was constructed from multiple data source. The legitimate URL samples came from the following data source:

(1) 1 million URLs crawled from Alexa top 1 million domain websites. Since the dataset only contains domains, a crawler was used to crawl URLs from the main page of these websites to fetch path and query information.

   (https://support.alexa.com/hc/en-us/articles/200449834-Does-Alexa-have-a-list-of-its-top-ranked-websites-).

(2) 1 million URLs came from Common Crawl, a public corpus of raw web page data. (http://commoncrawl.org/).

And the malicious URL samples came from three data sources as follows:

(1) 1 million phishing URLs came from Phishtank, a collaborative community site collecting and tracking phishing URLs. (https://www.phishtank.com/).
(2) 0.5 million malicious URLs came from Anti Network-Virus Alliance of china, a organization aiming at virus prevention and safeguarding the Internet security in China. (https://www.anva.org.cn/index).
(3) 0.5 million malicious URLs came from hpHosts, a community maintained various hosts file including a malware sites lists. (https://www.hosts-file.net/).

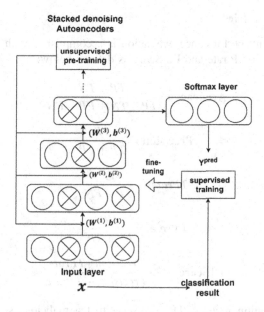

Fig. 6. The SdA-LR model presented in this paper

4.2 Experiment Design

The following experimental design is used to evaluate the proposed technique. A binary classification experiment was designed to test our SdA-LR model's ability of detecting malicious URLs.

To evaluate our featureless SdA-LR model with classifiers based on feature engineering, we compare our model to the following method:

- A native Bayes classifier
- A SVM classifier
- A LSTM network with logistic regression

The first and second model used manually-crafted features of URL proposed in [18]. We also compare our model with a SdA-SVM for strict verification.

Our SdA-LR model is implemented using Keras [10] with Tensorflow [11] backend. And the SVM, random forest and tri-gram model use the implementation of the Scikit-Learn library [31]. All code was deployed and run on a Intel Xeon E5-2686 v4 16 cores computer with a NVIDIA Tesla M60 GPU of 8 GB RAM.

To avoid variance, in training process, this paper used a n-fold cross-validation strategy with 10 folds to run experiment. The data-set was split into 2 parts of a 4:1 partition randomly, which means that four-fifth of the data-set are training and validation set for cross-validation, and one-fifth are testing set.

4.3   Evaluation Metrics

For each experiment, performance evaluation is accomplished with Accuracy, Precision, recall (TP rate), FP rate and F1 Score as defined below:

$$\text{Accuracy} = \frac{TP + TN}{TP + TN + FP + FN}$$

$$\text{Precision} = \frac{TP}{TP + FP}$$

$$\textit{TPrate} = \frac{TP}{TP + FN}$$

$$\text{FPrate} = \frac{FP}{FP + TN}$$

$$F1\text{Score} = 2 \cdot \frac{\textit{Precision} \cdot \textit{TPrate}}{\textit{Precision} + \textit{TPrate}}$$

In these evaluation metrics, TP represents that a malicious sample is correctly identified as malicious. TN means a malicious sample is incorrectly identified as benign. FN indicates a benign URL is correctly labeled as benign and FP denotes a benign sample is incorrectly labeled as malicious.

Receiver Operating Characteristic (ROC) curve is used to evaluate diagnostic ability of the classifier and illustrates Area under the curve (AUC) statistic. Learning curve is illustrated to show the accuracy on the validation set grows with the number of training epochs.

5   Results

5.1   Performance of SdA-LR Model

Results of the experiments are presented in this section.

We tested the accuracy and of our SdA-LR model using the 4 million URLs described above. A confusion matrix is illustrated in Table 1 to show the performance of our SdA-LR model.

Table 1. Confusion matrix result of the best performance fold in 10-fold experiment

	Predicted as malicious	Predicted as benign	Total
Malicious	392408	3936	396344
Benign	7929	395727	403656
Total	400337	399663	800000

In our experiments, the average accuracy of SdA-LR model stands at 98.52%, with a recall of 99.02% and precision of 98.03%. And among different folds, all accuracy results are consistent, having a standard deviation of just 0.06%, indicating a stable performance of our model.

We also evaluated the AUC of our model. The ROC curves are shown in Fig. 8. In average, the models show an AUC statistic of 99.72%.

In Fig. 7 the learning curve of SdA-LR's training process is shown. It is observed that in just 25 epochs, the validation accuracy converges, increasing to over 98% from epoch 20 onward.

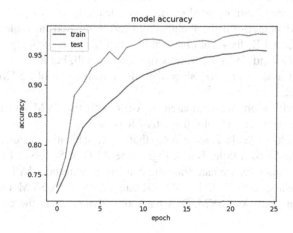

Fig. 7. Learning curve of SdA-LR

5.2 Comparison of the Method

The breakdown of Precision, accuracy, Recall, false positive rate and F1 Score for each model is given in Table 2.

Table 2. Precision, Recall and F1 Score of all models in experiment

Model	Precision	Recall	Accuracy	Fp rate	F1 Score
SdA-LR	0.9803	0.9901	0.9852	0.0198	0.9852
SdA-SVM	0.8416	0.9345	0. 8792	0.1762	0.8856
SVM	0.8359	0.9986	0. 9009	0.1975	0.9099
LSTM	0.9010	0.9960	0.94	0.1093	0.9462
Bayes	0.8271	0.6010	0.7379	0.1255	0.6961

As can be seen, the SdA-LR model significantly outperforms the other models, especially the retrospective SVM model.

We compared the accuracy and F1 Score of all models. In average, the SdA-LR model has an accuracy of 98.52%, much higher than the other deep learning model and feature-engineer model. Similar results were found for the F1 Score and precision.

By comparing the recall rate and false positive rate, we can figure out that our model has the lowest false positive and the third-place recall rate, but the recall rate of 99.01% is higher enough. In comprehensive ways, the SdA-LR model would be the optimal one.

The ROC curves for the SdA-LR, SdA-SVM, LSTM, SVM with manually-crafted features and native Bayes with manually-crafted features are presented in Fig. 8. SdA-LR provides the best performance with an AUC of 0.9972. The second and the third place of AUC are SdA-SVM with 0.9943 and then LSTM with 0.9930.

Considering deep learning method, the deep learning method of SdA-LR, SdA-SVM and LSTM outperform the feature-engineering method in Table 2. Comparing the LSTM and SdA-LR, they both have high recall rate and accuracy. The difference between the LSTM and SVM algorithms may seem small, but in a production system the LSTM could lead more error, since the false positive rate of LSTM is 5 times as much as SdA-LR.

For strict verification, we compared SdA-LR with the SVM and the SdA-SVM models to verify whether and why the SdA-LR is better.

From the results in Table 2, we can see that the classification accuracy of the SdA-SVM exceeds the SVM a little. But in Fig. 8, the AUC of SdA-SVM is much higher then SVM. Consequently, we can draw the conclusion that the SdA helps to improve the accuracy of classification. While SdA-LR outperforms SdA-SVM and SVM, which means that among SdA and SVM, SdA has more advantages in the classification.

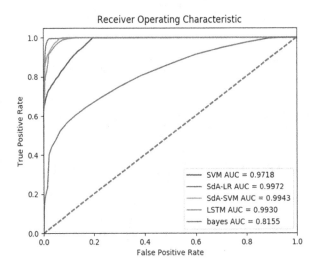

Fig. 8. ROC curve comparison of all experimented method

As Figs. 9 and 10 shows, due to the limitation of SVM on large dataset [34], in the process of fine-tuning, the SdA-LR is much smooth then SdA-SVM.

One thing to notice is that the SVM model perform with the best recall rate, which means that the methods using manually-engineered features are able to detect malicious URL samples with the considered features. But the false positive rate of SVM is high, which in other way indicates that it can't detect new sample with new malicious features.

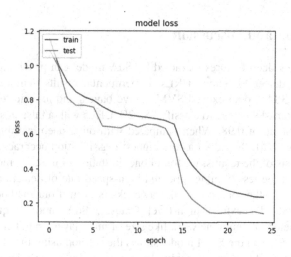

Fig. 9. Loss curve of SdA-SVM

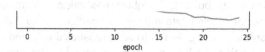

Fig. 10. Loss curve of SdA-LR

Table 3 displays the training time and testing time for all models in experiment. The deep learning model requires significantly more time to train. Even a large dataset was used, the Native Bayes was trained in an average time of less than 10 min. On the other hand, SdA-LR requires 85 min. But the deep model had higher efficient on testing. Comparing the testing time of SVM with 0.27 s per URL, the SdA-LR had a testing time with 0.083 s per URL.

Table 3. Average training-time and testing-time evaluation of each method

Model	Training time (s)	Testing time per URL (s)
SdA-LR	5149	0.083
SdA-SVM	10872	0.52
SVM	7563	0.27
LSTM	5762	0.029
Bayes	563.7	0.18

6 Conclusion and Discussion

We explored how deep features extracted by SdA model can provide a good support for classifier to detect Malicious URLs. Experimental results demonstrated that the performance of SdA model exceed SVM, native bayers and logistic regression based on tri-gram. Our model is able to classify 98.52% URLs with a false positive of 1.96%, and has an F1 Score of 0.98. When compared with other deep learning method such LSTM and SdA-SVM, the SdA has the highest classification accuracy.

In our analysis of the results, we found one limitation of the SdA model is the long training time, but the less training time and high-speed rate of detection makes up for the long period. Another one potential drawbacks is even if our method is featureless and can automatically extract high-level features, SdA model required time for tweaking parameters of neural network like size of inner layers, number of epochs, loss function and so on. And the SVM model shows the method using manually-engineered features were able to detect samples with these features, but it can't detect samples with new malicious features.

In future work there are still potential open problems to be carried for further research. One direction is building a robust prediction system using closed-loop architecture for gathering labeled data and training model. This architecture relies on an efficient real-time online learning design to acquire labeled data and user feedback. To achieve a totally non-artificial label operation, unsupervised learning or reinforcement learning should be considered. The other direction is using cluster analysis algorithm to acquire label tags from unlabeled data to solve the problem of obtaining rare label malicious URL data-set.

Acknowledgments. This work was supported by the National Key R&D Program of China (Grant No. 2016YFB0800700 & No. 2016YFC1000300).

References

1. Ma, J., Saul, L.K., Savage, S., Voelker, G.M.: Beyond blacklists: learning to detect malicious web sites from suspicious URLs. In: Proceedings of the 15th ACM SIGKDD International Conference on Knowledge Discovery and Data Mining, pp. 1245–1254. ACM (2009)
2. Canali, D., Cova, M., Vigna, G., Kruegel, C.: Prophiler: a fast filter for the large-scale detection of malicious web pages. In: Proceedings of the 20th International Conference on World Wide Web, pp. 197–206. ACM (2011)

3. Wang, D., Navathe, S.B., Liu, L., Irani, D., Tamersoy, A., Pu, C.: Click traffic analysis of short URL spam on twitter. In: 2013 9th International Conference on Collaborative Computing: Networking, Applications and Worksharing (Collaboratecom), pp. 250–259. IEEE (2013)
4. Eshete, B., Villafiorita, A., Weldemariam, K.: BINSPECT: holistic analysis and detection of malicious web pages. In: SecureComm, pp. 149–166 (2012)
5. Berners-Lee, T., Masinter, L., McCahill, M.: Uniform resource locators (URL). Technical report (1994)
6. Zhang, H.-L., Zou, W., Han, X.-H.: Drive-by-download mechanisms and defenses. J. Softw. 24(4), 843–858 (2013). (in Chinese)
7. Sha, H.-Z., Zhou, Z., Liu, Q.-Y., Qin, P.: Light-weight self-learning for URL classification. J. Commun. 35(9), 32–39 (2014)
8. Klien, F., Strohmaier, M.: Short links under attack: geographical analysis of spam in a URL shortener network. In: Proceedings of the 23rd ACM Conference on Hypertext and Social Media, pp. 83–88. ACM (2012)
9. Seifert, C., Welch, I., Komisarczuk, P.: Identification of malicious web pages with static heuristics. In: 2008 Australasian Telecommunication Networks and Applications Conference, ATNAC 2008, pp. 91–96. IEEE (2008)
10. Chollet, F.: Keras (2015). https://github.com/fchollet/keras
11. Abadi, M., et al.: Tensorflow: large-scale machine learning on heterogeneous distributed systems. arXiv preprint arXiv:1603.04467 (2016)
12. Mohammad, R.M., Thabtah, F., McCluskey, L.: Predicting phishing websites based on self-structuring neural network. Neural Comput. Appl. 25(2), 443–458 (2014)
13. Woodbridge, J., Anderson, H.S., Ahuja, A., Grant, D.: Predicting domain generation algorithms with long short-term memory networks. arXiv preprint arXiv:1611.00791 (2016)
14. Wang, Y., Cai, W.D., Wei, P.C.: A deep learning approach for detecting malicious JavaScript code. Secur. Commun. Netw. 9(11), 1520–1534 (2016)
15. Bahnsen, A.C., Bohorquez, E.C., Villegas, S., Vargas, J., González, F.A.: Classifying Phishing URLs Using Recurrent Neural Networks (2017)
16. Sha, H.-Z., Liu, Q.-Y., Liu, T.-W.: Survey on malicious webpage detection research. Chin. J. Comput. 39(3), 529–542 (2016)
17. Sahoo, D., Liu, C., Hoi, S.C.: Malicious URL detection using machine learning: a survey. arXiv preprint arXiv:1701.07179 (2017)
18. Wang, D., Navathe, S.B., Liu, L., Irani, D., Tamersoy, A., Pu, C.: Click traffic analysis of short URL spam on Twitter. In: 2013 9th International Conference Conference on Collaborative Computing: Networking, Applications and Worksharing (Collaboratecom), pp. 250–259. IEEE (2013)
19. Thomas, K., Grier, C., Ma, J., Paxson, V., Song, D.: Design and evaluation of a real-time URL spam filtering service. In: 2011 IEEE Symposium on Security and Privacy (SP), pp. 447–462. IEEE (2011)
20. Pao, H.K., Chou, Y.L., Lee, Y.J.: Malicious URL detection based on kolmogorov complexity estimation. In: Proceedings of the 2012 IEEE/WIC/ACM International Joint Conferences on Web Intelligence and Intelligent Agent Technology, vol. 01, pp. 380–387. IEEE Computer Society (2012)
21. Yousefi-Azar, M., Varadharajan, V., Hamey, L., Tupakula, U.: Autoencoder-based feature learning for cyber security applications. In: 2017 International Joint Conference on Neural Networks (IJCNN), pp. 3854–3861. IEEE (2012)
22. Does Alexa have a list of its top-ranked websites? https://support.alexa.com/hc/en-us/articles/200449834-Does-Alexa-have-a-list-of-its-top-ranked-websites. Accessed 06 Apr 2016

23. Zhao, P., Hoi, S.C.H.: Cost-sensitive online active learning with application to malicious URL detection. In: ACM SIGKDD International Conference on Knowledge Discovery and Data Mining, pp. 919–927. ACM (2013)
24. Le Roux, N., Bengio, Y.: Deep belief networks are compact universal approximators. Neural Comput. **22**(8), 2192–2207 (2010)
25. Lipton, Z.C., Berkowitz, J., Elkan, C.: A critical review of recurrent neural networks for sequence learning. arXiv preprint arXiv:1506.00019 (2015)
26. LeCun, Y., Bottou, L., Bengio, Y., Haffner, P.: Gradient-based learning applied to document recognition. Proc. IEEE **86**(11), 2278–2324 (1998)
27. Vincent, P., Larochelle, H., Lajoie, I., Bengio, Y., Manzagol, P.A.: Stacked denoising autoencoders: learning useful representations in a deep network with a local denoising criterion. J. Mach. Learn. Res. **11**, 3371–3408 (2010)
28. Hinton, G.E., Osindero, S., Teh, Y.W.: A fast learning algorithm for deep belief nets. Neural Comput. **18**(7), 1527–1554 (2006)
29. Hinton, G.: A practical guide to training restricted Boltzmann machines. Momentum **9**(1), 926 (2010)
30. Pedregosa, F., et al.: Scikit-learn: machine learning in Python. J. Mach. Learn. Res. **12**, 2825–2830 (2011)
31. Vincent, P., Larochelle, H., Bengio, Y., et al.: Extracting and composing robust features with denoising autoencoders. In: International Conference on Machine Learning, pp. 1096–1103. ACM (2008)
32. Menon, A.K.: Large-Scale Support Vector Machines: Algorithms and Theory. Research Exam (2009)

Predicting Vulnerable Software Components via Bellwethers

Patrick Kwaku Kudjo[1], Jinfu Chen[1(⊠)], Solomon Mensah[2],
and Richard Amankwah[1]

[1] School of Computer Science and Communication Engineering,
Jiangsu University, Zhenjiang 202000, China
jinfuchen@ujs.edu.cn
[2] Department of Computer Science,
City University of Hong Kong, Kowloon Tong, Hong Kong

Abstract. Software vulnerabilities are weakness, flaws or errors introduced during the life cycle of a software system. Although, previous studies have demonstrated the practical significance of using software metrics to predict vulnerable software components, empirical evidence shows that these metrics are plagued with issues pertaining to their effectiveness and robustness. This paper investigates the feasibility of using *Bellwethers* (*i.e.,* exemplary data) for predicting and classifying software vulnerabilities. We introduced a *Bellwether method* using the following operators, *PARTITION, SAMPLE + TRAIN and APPLY*. The *Bellwethers* sampled by the three operators are used to train a learner (*i.e.,* deep neural networks) with the aim of predicting *essential* or *non-essential vulnerabilities*. We evaluate the proposed *Bellwether method* using vulnerability reports extracted from three popular web browsers offered by CVE. Again, the mean absolute error (MAE), Welch's *t-test* and Cliff's δ effect size are used to further evaluate the prediction performance and practical statistical significant difference between the *Bellwethers* and the *growing portfolio*. We found that there exist subsets of vulnerability records (*Bellwethers*) in the studied datasets that can yield improved accuracy for software vulnerability prediction. The result shows that *recall* and *precision* measures from the text mining process were in a range of 73.9%–85.3% and 67.9%–81.8% respectively across the three studied datasets. The findings further show that the use of the *Bellwethers* for predictive modelling is a promising research direction for assisting software engineers and practitioners when seeking to predict instances of vulnerability records that demand much attention prior to software release.

Keywords: Software vulnerability · Bellwethers · Software metrics
Growing portfolio · Web browsers

1 Introduction

Software vulnerabilities are weakness, flaws, faults or errors introduced during the life cycle of a software system [1]. These vulnerabilities normally cause data breaches and have serious security implications when exploited. For example, the National Institute of Standards and Technology estimates that the economic damage of software

© Springer Nature Singapore Pte Ltd. 2019
H. Zhang et al. (Eds.): CTCIS 2018, CCIS 960, pp. 389–407, 2019.
https://doi.org/10.1007/978-981-13-5913-2_24

vulnerabilities is around $60 billion per year [2]. To better protect systems and ameliorate vulnerabilities, several software vulnerability prediction (SVP) models have recently emerged [3–7]. These models are used in predicting vulnerable modules, files in software systems to enable the use of constrained resources for effective detection of vulnerabilities in software systems [8]. Additionally, security managers can prioritize their components and files in order to assess software components that are highly vulnerable [9]. Although many prediction models have been proposed, challenges still exist in obtaining robust and accurate models. For instance, according to Zimmermann et al. [10] and Stuckman et al. [4] sparse vulnerability datasets and vagueness within these datasets account for the low prediction performance. In addition, most prediction models are established and evaluated based on various software code metrics such as code churn, code complexity, vulnerability location, component dependency graphs and SQL hotspot or a combination of code metrics with static code [11]. However, studies by Jiang et al. [12], Graves et al. [13] and Yang et al. [8] suggest that these code metrics exhibit low prediction performance and unable to fully reflect the essential characteristics of software vulnerability sufficiently. Furthermore, Jinkun and Ping [14] raised two main issues in their work to validate the aforementioned claim that the source code metrics are less effective for SVP. According to the authors [14], the rapid change in software application and its source code in the process of release, use, update and repairs makes it difficult for researchers and practitioners to predict vulnerable software systems or the future of software based on just the source code. Lastly, access to source code (i.e. availability of the source code) especially commercial software makes the code-based models less applicable and effective. Aside the code metrics, design metrics are also applied in building effective prediction models [15–17]. Time series-based models such as Rescorla's exponential model [18], Alhazmi's AML model [19] and Poisson Logarithmic [20] have also been considered for predicting the total number of vulnerabilities in software systems. For example, Roumani et al. [21] employed the Autoregressive Integrated Moving Average (ARIMA) and exponential smoothing in their vulnerability prediction model. The evaluated the effectiveness of their model using software vulnerability reports in five open source web browsers namely, Chrome, Mozilla Firefox, Opera and Safari. Per recent research trends, there are other generic vulnerability predictions models based on text mining techniques [9, 22, 23]. Herein, tokens are extracted from a given source code and used as features for their prediction model. Their findings show that the text mining based models have higher recall than the metrics based vulnerability prediction models.

Unfortunately, despite the attempts by the aforementioned studies to improve SVP using these metrics, there are some pitfalls (*i.e., poor prediction accuracy and low cost effectiveness*) [8] between the various models, thus making it difficult for researchers and practitioners in the software engineering community to adopt. One of the key pitfalls is noted by Jinkun and Ping [14]. Thus, it is problematic to use only the aforementioned metrics (*i.e.*, code churn, code complexity, vulnerability location, component dependency graphs) to predict vulnerable modules as they do not accurately define the level of security in software systems. For this reason, Jinkun and Ping [14] proposed a new vulnerability prediction metric named *vulnerability loss*" (VL) based on probit regression.

Their model measures the seriousness of vulnerability by the loss it causes and predicts the accumulative vulnerability loss rather than the number of vulnerabilities. Additionally, the authors [14] argued that it is more plausible to use the accumulative loss caused by vulnerabilities rather than the number of vulnerabilities to reflect the security of a software system. Motivated by the effectiveness of the new techniques presented by Jinkun and Ping [14], Stuckman et al. [4], Pang et al. [24] and Alves et al. [25], we argue that a potential way of improving SVP is to use *Bellwethers* which has been proven reliable by Krishna et al. [26] and Mensah et al. [27, 28] in the domain of software defect prediction and software effort prediction respectively. *Bellwethers* are exemplary data which are obtained based on certain heuristic characteristics referred to as the *Bellwether analysis* [29, 30] or *Bellwether method*. In a study by Mensah et al. [27], a theoretical foundation based on proven postulations has been established that, there exists a set of exemplary project cases from a given dataset that yields improved prediction accuracy against the *growing portfolio* benchmark (i.e., the entire collection of available project cases). Thus, in this paper, we employ the *Bellwether* concept to select a subset of vulnerable records from the textual description of vulnerability reports to yield improved prediction accuracy against the *growing portfolio* benchmark. It is important to reiterate here that the *Bellwether concept* issue raised in this study is in consistent with the assertion made by Stuckman et al. [4], and Pang et al. [9, 24] that the performance of a prediction model heavily depends on how well the features are selected and used in the model setup. For this purpose, we introduce a new approach that substitute the traditional ways of building SVP models using *Bellwethers* to investigate if it will yield improved prediction and classification accuracy in setting up SVP models. Additionally, we trained a deep neural networks (DNN) using the sampled *Bellwethers* (benchmarked against the *growing portfolio*) to enable us classify the extracted vulnerability reports into *essential* or *non-essential*. Note here that, we chose the DNN because it has achieved a state-of-the-art performance in the study of Pang et al. [24]. These exemplary characteristics (i.e. *essential vulnerabilities*) defined as the *Bellwether* in this paper refer to vulnerabilities with high security exploitation or impact [31, 32] in a software system. In other words, they represent a vulnerability instance in a given software system whose security risk or severity is relatively high as compared to other vulnerability instances. For example, Wang et al. [33] showed in their study that vulnerabilities vary in relation to the impact on the quality and security properties of the software product such as confidentiality, integrity, availability, accountability, authorization and non-repudiation. Again, Morrison et al. [34], Munaiah et al. [35] and Jinkun and Ping [14] affirmed this notion that some vulnerabilities may be of a higher value to attackers than others. For instance, according to Munaiah et al. [35], "a vulnerability that allows unauthorized access to the content of a memory may be more valuable to an attacker than a vulnerability that causes a software system to crash when a particular kind of file is opened". The aforementioned cases clearly demonstrate that vulnerabilities are of different threat types (i.e. *unequal amount of loss*) and the threshold of software quality activity will vary between threat types. Hence, the goal of this study is to develop a SVP model that predicts the *essential* vulnerability characteristics (i.e. vulnerabilities with high impact or exploitation) based on the *Bellwether* concept to: (1) Create a better understanding of their exploiting strategies, (2) Assist software engineers to expend more effort on detecting and mitigating the essential vulnerabilities (3) Enable users to design and implement appropriate security policies to mitigate future exploitation (4) Assist security managers to prioritize testing strategies for vulnerabilities with higher risk [36] and lastly (5) Help security managers to prioritize their vulnerability responses, since most security managers are constrained with limited budget and resources for vulnerability management [37]. We therefore formulate the predicting of *essential* vulnerabilities or *non-essential* vulnerabilities as a classification problem as done in previous studies [4, 9, 24].

Using the proposed *Bellwether* concept, we introduce a *Bellwether method* comprising mainly of *PARTITION, SAMPLE + TRAIN* and *APPLY* to help build an effective model that classifies software vulnerability reports as *essential vulnerabilities or non-essential vulnerabilities)* to improve the level of security in software systems. We empirically evaluate the implemented *Bellwether method* using software vulnerability reports obtained from three publicly available vulnerability dataset namely Google Chrome, Internet Explorer and Mozilla Firefox.

The study makes the following contributions:

i. We investigate the existence of *Bellwethers* in the domain of software vulnerability prediction.
ii. We classify software vulnerabilities into *essential* or *non-essential vulnerabilities* based on *Bellwether analysis.*

The remaining sections of the paper are as follows. Section 2 presents the background of the study. Section 3 presents the problem formulation and feasible solution. Section 4 presents the methodology of the study. Section 5 details the experimental results and discussion from the analysis of the study. Section 6 gives a summary of related works in relation to software vulnerability prediction. Section 7 presents the threats to validity. Section 8 summarizes the study and provides future research directions.

2   Background

In this section, we introduce the basic concepts that are vital for understanding this paper.

2.1   Software Vulnerability Prediction

Software vulnerability prediction is an active area of research in the software engineering domain. In most vulnerability prediction models, one is interested in predicting whether a software component or file is vulnerable or non-vulnerable (i.e., *binary classification*). According to Stuckman et al. [4], a software component is vulnerable if it contains one or more vulnerabilities. The non-vulnerable or neutral components are software systems without vulnerabilities. The most widely employed learning algorithms are Deep neural network [24], Logistic regression [25], Random forest [4, 25], Naïve Bayes [25], Support Vector Machine [38] and Bayesian network [25]. Pang et al. [24] outline the procedures for setting up these prediction models as fellows (1) Data collection (2) Feature selection (3) training and (4) evaluating the accuracy of the learning algorithm with a given test data. Thus, in this study, we first mined vulnerability reports from three open source web browsers, namely Google Chrome, Mozilla Firefox and Internet Explorer offered by the Common Vulnerabilities and Exposures (CVE). Secondly, we used the *Bellwether method* to find a feasible subset of vulnerable records (i.e. feature selection) using the textual vulnerability descriptions. Thirdly, we apply a DDN to train and classify the extracted vulnerability reports as *essential and non-essential*. Finally, we evaluate the performance of the learning algorithm via performance indicators such as *recall, precision*, Cliff's delta effect size as done in previous studies [4, 22, 24, 25].

2.2 The Bellwether Concept

The *Bellwether concept* was first considered by Chen et al. [30, 39] in the context of Online Analytical Processing (OLAP) queries. It uses two main approaches namely the *Bellwether effect* and the *Bellwether method*. The *Bellwether effect* defines the existence of exemplary projects within a historical dataset used to build an accurate prediction model [26]. The *Bellwether method* defines the search process used in obtaining the exemplary projects (*Bellwether*) [26, 27]. Krishna et al. [26] used the *Bellwether concept* to find exemplary projects from a set of non-chronological projects to make predictions on the remaining projects. Each project was considered as a potential *Bellwether* in each iteration on the prediction of the remaining projects until the project data with the best prediction accuracy was obtained. In another study, Mensah et al. [27] investigated the existence of *Bellwether* in chronological datasets and defined the notion as a *Bellwether moving window*. In this study, we apply the *Bellwether concept* to find a feasible subset of vulnerable records to yield improved prediction accuracy against the *growing portfolio* benchmark. The *growing portfolio* in this case refers to a set of available vulnerable records that is used to setup SVP models. Thus, the *growing portfolio* has been the state-of-the-art utilized by researchers [6, 7, 40, 41] in training SVP models.

3 Problem Formulation and Feasible Solution

3.1 Problem Formulation

Given a set of N project cases (considered as the *growing portfolio*) from a particular dataset (D), (i.e. security vulnerability reports extracted from the various open source repositories) we seek to obtain a subset of n cases that can be considered as the *Bellwether* to yield improved prediction accuracy against the *growing portfolio* benchmark. Assume each of the cases is labelled with the respective labels or targets (*i.e., the essential or non-essential vulnerability* [42]), then the task is to find such exemplary cases to be considered as the *Bellwether*. As done in previous studies by Mensah et al. [27] and Krishna et al. [26], such exemplary cases (or *Bellwether*) must first exist in D prior to setting up the predictive model. If the *Bellwether* (n) exists in D (i.e., $n \subset D$), then n can yield improved prediction accuracy else, use the *growing portfolio* (N) to set up prediction model.

3.2   Feasible Solution: The Bellwether Method

Based on insights from previous studies [26, 27, 30] we introduce a *Bellwether method* for software Vulnerability (*BellVul*) comprising of three operators, namely *PARTITION, SAMPLE + TRAIN* and *APPLY* to investigate the existence of *Bellwethers* in the studied datasets. In order to support possible replication of this study and possible future work in this domain, we describe the three operators utilized in the *Bellwether method* as follows:

PARTITION
Given a set of N historical vulnerability reports filter out irrelevant cases via data preprocessing and partition remaining reports into q partitions.

1. Preprocess a set of vulnerability reports from D to obtain N cases.
2. Apply *X-means* algorithm [43] to partition N into q partitions.

SAMPLE + TRAIN
For each of the q partitions sampled, consider it as the training set and the remaining q-1 partitions as the validation set.

3. For each sampled partition, use it as the training set.
4. Train a learner with the sampled partition and validate with *q-1* partitions.
5. Evaluate the prediction performance for each iteration.
6. Select the partition with the best performance as the *Bellwether*.

APPLY
Apply the Bellwether to the hold-out or new vulnerability report whose target or label is to be predicted.

7. The *Bellwether* need to have the same feature set as the hold-out or new vulnerability report.
8. Predict the target (*i.e., essential* or *non-essential label*) of the hold-out vulnerability report.

In order to effectively build the *BellVul* model in this study, we first subjected the pre-processed datasets to X-means algorithm [43] to obtain q partitions. In other words, the extracted vulnerability reports obtained from Chrome, Internet Explorer and Mozilla Firefox were stratified into q partitions whereby vulnerability reports with similar characteristics are categorized in the same partition. The X-means algorithm automatically estimate the number of partitions based on the Bayesian Information Criterion or the Akaike Information Criterion [43]. In each iteration, we sample each partition as the training set and the remaining $q-1$ partitions as the validation set. A deep learning approach, namely the deep neural network (DNN) is considered for the training of the sampled partition and validation done with the remaining $q-1$ partitions. This iteration process is done until each partition is considered as the training set. Note that this *Bellwether method* is different from the *k-fold* cross validation approach whereby each partition is considered as the validation set and the $q-1$ partitions as the training set in each iteration. Evaluation performance of the DNN is assessed with the mean absolute error (MAE) and the best partition with the minimum evaluation measure considered as the *Bellwether*. The *Bellwether* is used to make prediction of the hold-out vulnerability reports in each of the studied datasets. Thus, in each dataset, we considered a subset as a hold-out which was not considered for the training and validation needs in setting up the DNN model. Note that all subsets of vulnerability reports from each dataset (*i.e.*, the *Bellwether* and the hold-out) had the same feature sets.

4 Methodology

In attempt to deal with the prediction problem in this study, we introduced a *Bellwether* method in order to build an effective model to detect and predict the essential characteristics of software systems. The first stage defines the various open source vulnerability repositories. The second stage involves data extraction and preprocessing as done in previous studies by Zhang et al. [6] and Movahedi et al. [44]. In stage 3, we mined *N*-gram patterns of vulnerabilities [3]. The extracted *N*-gram patterns of vulnerabilities were classified into *essential and non-essential* vulnerabilities in stage 4. The resulting subset of the classification output is considered as the growing portfolio (GP) (stage 5). We then sample the *Bellwether* from the growing portfolio in stage 6. Furthermore, we train the learning algorithm (DNN) using the *Bellwether,* and the growing portfolio in stage 7. After the training phase, we evaluate the resulting output from the *Bellwether* and the growing portfolio (stage 8). If the *Bellwether* shows improved accuracy, we use the *Bellwether* to classify the test set, else we use the growing portfolio to classify the test set into essential and non-essential vulnerabilities (stage 9). The overall processes are separated into four major steps. Hereafter, we explain these major steps.

4.1   Proposed Framework

Step 1: Data Acquisition (Datasets Description)
In this study, we used software vulnerability reports in three popular open source web browsers (i.e. Google Chrome, Internet Explorer and Firefox) available on the Common Vulnerability and Exposures (CVE) and offered by the National Vulnerability Database (NVD)[1]. CVE is a dictionary of vulnerability reports rather than a vulnerability database; they provide the CVE list to NVD. NVD on the other hand provides more advanced search functions such CVE ID, vendor name, product name, version number, vulnerability type, severity, exploit range and impact level to make the vulnerability records meaningful and useful to researchers and security expert. As indicated earlier, the studied datasets are Google Chrome, Internet Explorer and Firefox. For each of the studied dataset, we first extract (download) vulnerability reports and store the data in our developed database following a similar procedure by Movahedi et al. [44]. The aggregated vulnerability report from the three databases is 2,408. Note here that, the Common Vulnerabilities and Exposures with its agents provides different

---

[1] https://nvd.nist.gov/, www.cvedetails.com.

types of vulnerability feeds such as JSON vulnerability feeds, XML vulnerability feeds, RSS vulnerability feeds, vulnerability translation feeds, etc. However, for the purpose of this study, we extracted the XML format of the stored vulnerability reports. Further details of the aggregated vulnerability reports are presented in Table 1.

Table 1. Description of Open Source Datasets

Metric	Open Source Datasets		
	Google Chrome	Mozilla Firefox	Internet Explorer
No. of Vul.	333	335	1740
Range of years	2014-2017	2004–2017	2008–2017
Operating Systems	Windows and Unix	Windows and Unix	Windows

Step 2: Data Preprocessing

We performed data pre-processing prior to the X-means algorithm [43] to obtain q partitions. We removed all the irrelevant elements such as Punctuations characters in the form of (] [|\~ ! @,.-#$%^*{}? <>) and stop words such as *this, about, above, among, behind, being, but, by, beside, came, certain, come, did, differ, during,* were all removed in the corpus following a similar procedure by Zhang et al. [6] and Sui et al. [45].

Step 3: N-gram Pattern Extraction

In **step 3**, we mine N-grams patterns of vulnerabilities that occur in the studied datasets following a similar procedure by Murtaza et al. [3] and Pang et al. [9, 24]. Thus, patterns of a given length of vulnerabilities are extracted from a sequence of vulnerabilities by sliding a window over vulnerabilities one by one [3]. Thus we use the N-gram pattern extraction algorithm [46, 47] to mine length 2, 3, 4 and 5 N-grams (i.e., 2-grams, 3-grams, 4-grams and 5-grams) vulnerability patterns for each of the studied datasets (i.e. Google Chrome, Mozilla Firefox and Internet Explorer). We limited the extraction of N-gram patterns of vulnerability to 5-grams because, according to Murtaza et al. [3], extracting higher values of N requires exponentially large datasets to identify sequences of vulnerabilities as the number of permutations increases exponentially with N.

Step 3: Grounded Theory Principles

After the N-gram pattern extraction, we used Grounded theory principles as reported by Corbin and Strauss [48] to read through all instances in the studied datasets to detect vulnerabilities forming instances of essential vulnerability characteristics. Vulnerabilities not forming instances of *essential vulnerabilities* were recorded as *non-essential* vulnerabilities. Note that a similar procedure was used by Bavota and Russo [49] and Mensah et al. [50] in the domain of Self-Admitted Technical debt. For example, Bavota and Russo [49] manually analyzed 366 comments reporting SATD to identify the various types of SATD using the Grounded theory principles. Note that, the authors made reference to the vulnerability exploit-database [32] and other annual security reports such as the Cisco ASR or Verizon DBIR to determine instances of security vulnerability forming instances of essential vulnerability characteristics.

Step 4: Sample Bellwether

In **step 4**, we sample a subset of exemplary vulnerability records (*Bellwether*) using the proposed *BellVul* algorithm (Sect. 3) from the *growing portfolio*. We then train the learners (i.e. DNN) using the sampled *Bellwether,* and the *growing portfolio*. Additionally, we evaluate the resulting output between the *Bellwether* and the *growing portfolio* during the training and validation of the constructed SVP models. If the *Bellwether* shows improved prediction accuracy, it is used to classify the test set (or the hold-out vulnerability records); else we used the *growing portfolio* to classify the test set into *essential* or *non-essential vulnerability* classes.

4.2 Research Questions

We design three research questions (*RQ*) for the empirical investigation of this study

> *RQ1:* How can security expert and software engineers distinguish between *essential vulnerabilities* and *non-essential vulnerabilities*?
>
> *RQ2:* How much data is required to find the *Bellwether* in the studied datasets?
>
> *RQ3:* Are there significant differences in using *Bellwether* and *growing portfolio* for predictive modelling for software vulnerabilities?

4.3 Experimental Setup

In this paper, we introduce a *Bellwether method,* namely *BellVul* for improving software vulnerability prediction. We conducted an empirical analysis on three studied datasets (*i.e.,* Google Chrome, Mozilla Firefox and Internet Explorer) using the step-by-step procedures detailed in Sect. 4. We manually categorized the vulnerability records in each dataset into *essential* and *non-essential vulnerabilities*. These labelling was done for each vulnerability record in each studied dataset. This manual labelling process was evaluated using *precision* and *recall* evaluation measures. After sampling the *Bellwether* from each dataset using *BellVul,* we benchmarked it against the *growing portfolio* and evaluated the prediction performances based on MAE, Welch's *t-test* and Cliff's δ effect size.

4.4 Learning Algorithm

In this study, we used deep neural networks on our problem. Deep learning models have been considered in previous studies [24], it is a neural network with multiple hidden layers of units between the input and output layers [51]. Thus, we setup a DNN, which makes use of multiple hidden layers and an output layer with their respective neurons to automatically learn the extracted vulnerability reports (i.e. vulnerability description) to classify them into essential and non-essential vulnerabilities. The Levenberg-Marquardt backpropagation optimization [52] training function is employed to update the weights of the neurons in the hidden and output layers respectively. As indicated earlier, we chose the DNN learning algorithm because it has resulted in the a state-of-the-art performance in the study of Pang et al. [24].

4.5   Performance Measure

We used precision, recall, mean absolute error (MAE), Welch's *t-test* and Cliff's δ effect size to evaluate the performance of the classification and the predictive model. First, we constructed the confusion matrix and computed the *precision* and *recall* measures. That is, we provide evidence of the true positives, false negatives, true negatives and false positives with respect to the classification model and manual exploration process for the three studied datasets. We express the formula for precision and recall in (1) and (2) respectively. Secondly, we used the MAE to measure how close the predictions or forecasts (X_V) are to the actual outcome (X_A) [53]. The formula for the MAE is also presented in (3) where n is the number of vulnerability records under consideration.

$$Precision = \frac{True\ Positive}{True\ Positive + False\ Positive} \tag{1}$$

$$Recall = \frac{True\ Positive}{True\ Positive + False\ Negative} \tag{2}$$

$$MAE = \frac{1}{n}\sum_{i=1}^{n}|X_{vi} - X_{Ai}| \tag{3}$$

We further performed statistical significant tests between the manual and text mining classification approaches employed for obtaining the *essential/non-essential vulnerabilities* prior to setting up the predictive models. For this purpose we used the Welch *t*-test and Cliff's δ effect size as recommended by Kitchenham et al. [54]. The Welch *t*-test [54] is used to test the null hypothesis that the mean of two groups of observations are equal irrespective of the sample size and variances. In our case, the hypothesis for interpreting the statistical differences is considered to be supported when the result from the Welch *t*-test is statistically significant at *p-value* less than 5% asymptotic significance level. We used the Cliff's δ effect size on the other hand to estimate the magnitude of the differences between the manual and text-mining classification approaches. Cliff's δ effect size [55] is a non-parametric effect size measure that makes no assumption of a particular distribution. The rationale behind the use of the Cliff's δ effect size is to determine the overlap between two groups [56]. We adopt the magnitude thresholds proposed by Kampenes et al. [55] and recommended by Kitchenham et al. [54] for interpreting the effect size in this study. We choose an effect size threshold of medium to large since results are misleading when the effect size is relatively small or negligible [57].

5   Results and Discussion

We report our findings to address the study's postulated research questions.

RQ1: How can security expert and software engineers distinguish between *essential vulnerabilities* and *non-essential vulnerabilities*?

We initialized this study with a manual exploration of the three studied datasets to obtain the textual indicators needed for extracting the essential/non-essential characteristics of software vulnerabilities. The statistics of the exemplary characteristics forming instances of *essential* and *non-essential vulnerabilities* are presented in Table 3. We found five textual indicators forming 13.2% of the total (38) textual indicators for extracting *essential vulnerabilities* in the Google chrome dataset. Similarly, eight textual indicators (28.6%) and five textual indicators (25.0%) were obtained for extracting *essential vulnerabilities* in the Firefox and Explorer datasets respectively. In all cases, we found that the textual indicators for obtaining *non-essential vulnerabilities* were higher than that of the *essential vulnerabilities*. We present samples of textual indicator forming instances of essential and non-essential for the three studied datasets in Table 2.

Table 2. Textual indicators forming instances of essential and non-essential vulnerabilities

Essential textual indicators	Non-essential textual indicators
Google Chrome Dataset	
Buffer overflow, Execute Arbitrary Code, Memory Corruption, XSS, Race Condition	Insufficient Policy Enforcement, Inappropriate Implementation of Modal, Insufficient Validation Of Untrusted Input, Lack Of Verification On Extension's Locale Folder
Mozilla Firefox Dataset	
Denial of Service Buffer Error, Execute Arbitrary Code, XSS, Memory Corruption, Cryptographic Issues, Directory Traversal, Race Condition	Insufficient Style-SRC Restrictions, Bad Casting In Bitmap, Incorrect Write Operations, Out-Of-Bounds Array Access, Man-In-The-Middle Attacks, Remote Attacks
Internet Explorer	
Execute Arbitrary Code, Denial of Service, Memory Corruption, Buffer overflow, XSS	Information Disclosure, Bypass, Privileges, CSRF, Http Response Splitting, Spoofing, File Inclusion Improperly Handling Objects In Memory, Scripting Engine Memory

Results from the manual exploration process were used as a benchmark against the text mining process as depicted in Table 5. Thus, after subjecting the textual indicators to the implemented text mining algorithm [42], we provide statistics of the extracted vulnerabilities forming instances of essential vulnerabilities in the three studied datasets. That is, the textual indicators were used as a query in the text mining algorithm [42] and subjected to each corpus of dataset to search for all vulnerability records forming instances of essential vulnerabilities. Note that, we only provided analysis of the essential vulnerabilities in Table 5 since they are of key interests to software engineers, which need to be addressed in order to ameliorate bugs within the systems. On average, we found that vulnerability records forming instances of *Buffer overflow, Denial of service* and *Execute arbitrary code* were prominent across the various versions of Chrome, Firefox and Explorer datasets respectively. Additionally, we observed that memory corruption was also prominent across the studied datasets, for example

Table 3. Statistics of essential and non-essential textual indicators

Project	Essential textual indicators		Non-essential textual indicators	
	Frequency	Percent	Frequency	Percent
Google Chrome	5	13.16	33	86.84
Mozilla Firefox	8	28.57	20	71.43
Internet Explorer	5	25.0	15	75.0

Table 4. Recall and precision of the extracted vulnerabilities from the text mining process

Dataset	Recall	Precision
Google Chrome	0.853	0.792
Mozilla Firefox	0.815	0.818
Internet Explorer	0.739	0.679

recorded 13.68%, 15.45% and 27.76% in Google Chrome, Mozilla Firefox and Internet Explorer respectively. We further provide the *precision* and *recall* measures for the vulnerabilities instances in the three studied datasets in Table 4. On average, we found that the *recall* and *precision* measures from the text mining process are in a range of 73.9%–85.3% and 67.9%–81.8% respectively across the three datasets.

RQ2: How much data is required to find the *Bellwether* in the studied datasets?

We report the results from the empirical analyses after subjecting each of the datasets to *BellVul* as elaborated in Sect. 3. Thus, each version in a given dataset was considered as the *growing portfolio* in which a feasible subset regarded as the *Bellwether* can be sampled. Results in VI denote the respective sizes for the *Bellwethers*; they exist in the various versions across the three studied datasets. On average, we observe that there exist *Bellwether* vulnerability records that can be considered as the training set to yield improved prediction accuracy against the *growing portfolio* benchmark. With regard to the Chrome dataset, we found that *Bellwethers* exist in all versions with the exception of version 4 (*i.e.* V_4). Thus, the size range of vulnerability records that can be considered as the *Bellwether* is 27–41 instances. Results for the Firefox and Explorer datasets are presented in Table 6. On average, we found that the minimum and maximum sizes of the *Bellwether* across all versioning are 27 and 102 respectively.

RQ3: Are there significant differences in using *Bellwether* and *growing portfolio* for predictive modelling for software vulnerabilities?

We subjected the sampled *Bellwethers* in each version to the deep neural network (DNN) model and benchmarked the prediction results against the *growing portfolio*. Note that each version is considered as the *growing portfolio* and the leave-one-out cross validation was used for the training and validation needs of the predictive model. With regard to the *Bellwether* modelling, each sampled *Bellwether* was considered as

Table 5. Statistics of extracted vulnerability records forming instances of essential vulnerabilities

Textual Indicator	Manual Process		Text Mining Process	
	Frequency	Percent	Frequency	Percent
Google Chrome				
Buffer Overflow	53	42.4	49	41.88
Execute Arbitrary Code	27	21.6	25	21.37
Memory Corruption	17	13.6	16	13.68
XSS	18	14.4	19	16.24
Race Condition	10	8.0	8	6.84
Mozilla Firefox				
Denial of Service	157	33.26	161	34.55
Buffer Overflow	69	14.62	64	13.73
Execute Arbitrary Code	140	29.66	138	29.61
XSS	13	2.75	17	3.65
Memory Corruption	80	16.95	72	15.45
Cryptographic Issues	4	0.85	4	0.86
Directory Traversal	5	1.06	6	1.29
Race Condition	4	0.85	4	0.86
Internet Explorer				
Execute Arbitrary Code	1236	29.71	1245	30.0
Denial of Service	913	21.95	901	21.71
Memory Corruption	1161	27.91	1152	27.76
Buffer Overflow	819	19.69	825	19.88
XSS	31	0.75	27	0.65

the training set and the remaining instances that were not sampled considered as the validation set. We used the MAE to evaluate the accuracy in using the *Bellwether* and *growing portfolio* for predictive modelling. We then made use of the Welch's *t-test* and the Cliff's δ effect size to examine the statistical and practical significant differences between the use of the *Bellwether* and *growing portfolio* for predictive modelling. Results are presented in Table 7. As stated earlier, effect size provides a more reliable experimental result irrespective of the *p-value* yielding statistical significance. On average, we found that there exist statistical significant differences between the use of the *Bellwether* and *growing portfolio* for predictive modelling in each of the versions across the studied datasets. Note that V_4 and V_5 in the Chrome and Firefox datasets respectively were null because there was no instance of *Bellwethers* as shown in Table 7. We therefore recommend the use of *Bellwethers* for software vulnerability prediction since it resulted in improved prediction accuracy in the studied datasets.

Table 6. Existence of Bellwethers within versions of studies datasets

Dataset	Version	Existence of Bellwether	Size (# of instances/ training set)	
			Bellwether	*Growing portfolio*
Google Chrome	V_1	Y	27	71
	V_2	Y	41	79
	V_3	Y	38	57
	V_4	N	–	55
	V_5	Y	28	67
Mozilla Firefox	V_1	Y	34	78
	V_2	Y	29	79
	V_3	Y	31	78
	V_4	Y	42	65
	V_5	N	–	51
Internet Explorer	V_1	Y	44	132
	V_2	Y	89	524
	V_3	Y	102	482
	V_4	Y	95	330
	V_5	Y	86	263

Note: 'Y' denotes the existence of Bellwether in a given version ('V') of a dataset and 'N' denotes the absence of Bellwether in a given 'V'

Table 7. Significant differences between Bellwethers and growing portfolios within versions of datasets

Dataset	Version	Welch's *t-test*		Cliff's δ effect size
		t-value	*p-value*	
Google Chrome	V_1	−2.2995	0.0229	0.7898*
	V_2	−3.1470	0.0020	0.2534
	V_3	−3.2309	0.0016	0.3264*
	V_4	–	–	–
	V_5	−3.3354	0.0011	0.3233*
Mozilla Firefox	V_1	−2.3917	0.0190	0.1809
	V_2	−3.1838	0.0019	0.3228*
	V_3	−3.3254	0.0013	0.5018*
	V_4	−3.3434	0.0012	0.5390*
	V_5	–	–	–
Internet Explorer	V_1	−9.8528	1.23E-17	0.1142
	V_2	−8.5403	2.87E-14	0.3018*
	V_3	−8.7479	8.38E-15	0.6354*
	V_4	−7.4441	9.15E-12	0.0236
	V_5	−7.6353	3.52E-12	0.2264

Statistical significance: $p < 0.05$; Practical significance: *δ ≥ 0.276

6 Related Work

Shin and Williams [5] performed an exploratory study using Mozilla Firefox as the case study project. The objective of the study was to determine whether a fault prediction models can be used for vulnerability prediction or a specialized vulnerability prediction model should be develop when using code metrics such as complexity, code churn and fault history. Their model predicted vulnerability with a high recall of over 90% and handful precision of 9%. Han et al. [58] proposed a vulnerability prediction model using deep learning approach, they formulate the prediction problem as multi-class text classification problem based on deep learning approach to predict the severity level of security vulnerabilities using only vulnerability description, which they termed as the *surface level* information. Results showed that the CNN model is effective and can capture the short-term vulnerability description and phrases. Dobrovoljc et al. [31] developed a vulnerability prediction model to evaluate the effectiveness of vulnerability prioritization policies. The proposed model is based on the Common Vulnerability Scoring System vectors and attacker characteristics.

7 Threats to Validity

Threat to *construct validity* evaluates the relation between the theory and the observation. In this study, this threat can be attributed to the three vulnerability datasets used for the analysis. Some errors may have occurred in the selection of the vulnerabilities. However, we mitigated this by selecting datasets from three popular web browsers, namely Chrome, Internet Explorer and Mozilla Firefox to investigate how software vulnerability prediction can be improved. These datasets have been validated and applied in the work of Han et al. [58]. The threat to *External validity*, this threat relate to the datasets used in this study. This study is constraint of a large number of open source datasets for generalization of results obtained. The three selected open source vulnerability datasets might not be a general representative of the sample populations of all open source vulnerability datasets. Additionally, the results from the study of the three datasets to detect *essential* and non-essential cannot be generalized to other systems due partly to the fact that different systems will identify different vulnerabilities that are essential (or non-essential) due to different security requirements. Threat to *Internal validity* examines the factors that may impact the result of our study. In our study, we used the manual process in extracting the textual indicators before subjecting it to the text mining process. This might result in biasness, which can affect the result of our study. Nevertheless, the manual process has done following the Grounded theory principles and validated using the card sorting and labeling technique. The threat to *reliability validity* concerns the possibility of replicating this study. To mitigate this we used open source vulnerability databases that are publicly available to researchers and provided detailed steps of the mining process to assist researchers for possible replication. Again, we introduced a *Bellwether method* for software vulnerability comprising of three operators to investigate the existence of *Bellwethers* in the studied datasets. Lastly, we have made the introduced textual indicators forming instances of the exemplary characteristics publicly available for possible utilization.

8 Conclusion and Future Work

In this study, we investigated the feasibility of using *Bellwethers* for improving the prediction accuracy in the domain of software vulnerability. The goal of using *Bellwethers* in this study is to ameliorate the challenges presented in previous studies [10, 14]. That is, using software metrics which exhibit low prediction performance and unable to fully indicate the essential characteristics of security vulnerability sufficiently. The use of *Bellwethers* in addressing software vulnerabilities will assist software engineers and practitioners to prioritize *essential vulnerabilities, which* require much attention when seeking to improve on the quality of software systems. This study was initialized by first extracting software vulnerability reports from three open source web browsers, namely Google Chrome, Internet Explorer and Mozilla Firefox.

We developed a *Bellwether method* comprising of *PARTITION, SAMPLE + TRAIN* and *APPLY* operators to sample and train a learner (deep neural networks) with the aim of predicting *essential/non-essential vulnerabilities*. Results from the study show that, vulnerability records forming instances of *Buffer overflow, Denial of service* and *Execute arbitrary code* were prominent across the various versions of the studied datasets suggesting that more effort should be expended by software developers in mitigating and fixing these vulnerabilities.

In addition, *recall* and *precision* measures from the text mining process were in a range of 73.9%–85.3% and 67.9%–81.8% respectively across the three studied datasets. To further, validate the results of our study, we used the mean absolute error (MAE) to evaluate the accuracy of the prediction model. We also found that there exists an exemplary subset of vulnerability records (*Bellwether*) that can be considered as the training set to yield improved prediction accuracy against the *growing portfolio* benchmark (*i.e.,* using all available vulnerability records as training set). In future, we plan to extend the scope of the study by investigating the existence of *Bellwethers* in the context of software vulnerability prediction on other open source software projects. We also intend to extend our investigation study on closed systems by conducting industrial case studies to ensure the practicality of our approach.

Acknowledgments. This work is partly supported by National Natural Science Foundation of China (NSFC grant numbers: 61202110 and 61502205), the project of Jiangsu provincial Six Talent Peaks (Grant numbers: XYDXXJS-016), Natural Science Foundation of Jiangsu Province (Grant numbers: BK20170558), University Science Research Project of Jiangsu Province (Grant numbers: 16KJB520008), the Graduate Research Innovation Project of Jiangsu Province (Grant numbers: KYCX17_1807), and the Postdoctoral Science Foundation of China (Grant numbers: 2015M571687 and 2015M581739).

References

1. Longley, D., Shain, M.: The Data and Computer Security Dictionary of Standard. Concepts, and Terms. Macmillan, London (1990)
2. Telang, R., Wattal, S.: An empirical analysis of the impact of software vulnerability announcements on firm stock price. IEEE Trans. Softw. Eng. **33**, 544–557 (2007)

3. Murtaza, S.S., Khreich, W., Hamou-Lhadj, A., Bener, A.B.: Mining trends and patterns of software vulnerabilities. J. Syst. Softw. **117**, 218–228 (2016)
4. Stuckman, J., Walden, J., Scandariato, R.: The effect of dimensionality reduction on software vulnerability prediction models. IEEE Trans. Reliab. **66**(1), 17–37 (2017)
5. Shin, Y., Williams, L.: Can traditional fault prediction models be used for vulnerability prediction? Empir. Softw. Eng. **18**, 25–59 (2013)
6. Zhang, S., Caragea, D., Ou, X.: An empirical study on using the national vulnerability database to predict software vulnerabilities. In: Hameurlain, A., Liddle, Stephen W., Schewe, K.-D., Zhou, X. (eds.) DEXA 2011, Part I. LNCS, vol. 6860, pp. 217–231. Springer, Heidelberg (2011). https://doi.org/10.1007/978-3-642-23088-2_15
7. Neuhaus, S., Zimmermann, T., Holler, C., Zeller, A.: Predicting vulnerable software components. In: Proceedings of the 14th ACM Conference on Computer and Communications Security, pp. 529–540 (2007)
8. Yang, J., Ryu, D., Baik, J.: Improving vulnerability prediction accuracy with Secure Coding Standard violation measures. In: International Conference on Big Data and Smart Computing, BigComp, pp. 115–122 (2016)
9. Pang, Y., Xue, X., Namin, A.S.: Predicting vulnerable software components through n-gram analysis and statistical feature selection. In: Proceedings of the 14th IEEE International Conference in Machine Learning and Applications (ICMLA), pp. 543–548 (2015)
10. Zimmermann, T., Nagappan, N., Williams, L.: Searching for a needle in a haystack: Predicting security vulnerabilities for windows vista. In: Proceedings of the Third IEEE International Conference on Software Testing, Verification and Validation (ICST), pp. 421–428. IEEE (2010)
11. Scandariato, R., Walden, J., Hovsepyan, A., Joosen, W.: Predicting vulnerable software components via text mining. IEEE Trans. Softw. Eng. **40**, 993–1006 (2014)
12. Jiang, Y., Cukic, B., Menzies, T., Bartlow, N.: Comparing design and code metrics for software quality prediction. In: Proceedings of the 4th International Workshop on Predictor Models in Software Engineering, pp. 11–18 (2008)
13. Graves, T.L., Karr, A.F., Marron, J.S., Siy, H.: Software change history. IEEE Trans. Softw. Eng. **26**, 653–661 (2000)
14. Jinkun, G., Ping, L.U.O.: A novel vulnerability prediction model to predict vulnerability loss based on probit regression. Wuhan Univ. J. Nat. Sci. **21**, 214–220 (2016)
15. Subramanyam, R., Krishnan, M.S.: Empirical analysis of CK metrics for object-oriented design complexity: implications for software defects. IEEE Trans. Softw. Eng. **29**, 297–310 (2003)
16. Zimmermann, T., Zeller, A.: Predicting defects for eclipse. In: Proceedings of the Third International Workshop on Predictor Models in Software Engineering, p. 9 (2007)
17. Nagappan, N., Ball, T., Zeller, A.: Mining metrics to predict component failures. In: Proceeding of the 28th International Conference on Software Engineering - ICSE 2006, p. 452 (2006)
18. Rescorla, E.: Is finding security holes a good idea? IEEE Secur. Priv. **3**, 14–19 (2005)
19. Alhazmi, O.H., Malaiya, Y.K.: Prediction capabilities of vulnerability discovery models. In: Annual Reliability and Maintainability Symposium, RAMS 2006, pp. 86–91 (2006)
20. Musa, J.D., Okumoto, K.: A logarithmic Poisson execution time model for software reliability measurement. In: Proceedings of the 7th International Conference on Software Engineering, pp. 230–238 (1984)
21. Roumani, Y., Nwankpa, J.K., Roumani, Y.F.: Time series modeling of vulnerabilities. Comput. Secur. **51**, 32–40 (2015)
22. Scandariato, R., Walden, J., Hovsepyan, A., Joosen, W.: Predicting vulnerable software components via text mining. IEEE Trans. Softw. Eng. **40**(10), 993–1006 (2014)

23. Walden, J., Stuckman, J., Scandariato, R.: Predicting vulnerable components: software metrics vs text mining. In: Proceedings of the 25th IEEE International Symposium on Software Reliability Engineering (ISSRE), pp. 23–33 (2014)

24. Pang, Y., Xue, X., Wang, H.: Predicting vulnerable software components through deep neural network. In: Proceedings of the 2017 International Conference on Deep Learning Technologies, pp. 6–10 (2017)

25. Alves, H., Fonseca, B., Antunes, N.: Experimenting machine learning techniques to predict vulnerabilities. In: Proceedings of the 7th Latin-American Symposium on Dependable Computing, LADC 2016, pp. 151–156 (2016)

26. Krishna, R., Menzies, T., Fu, W.: Too much automation? The bellwether effect and its implications for transfer learning. In: Proceedings of the 31st IEEE/ACM International Conference on Automated Software Engineering, pp. 122–131 (2016)

27. Mensah, S., Keung, J., Macdonell, S.G., Bosu, M.F., Bennin, K.E.: Investigating the significance of bellwether effect to improve software effort estimation. In: IEEE International Conference on Software Quality, Reliability and Security (QRS), pp. 340–351 (2017)

28. Mensah, S., Keung, J., MacDonell, S.G., Bosu, M.F., Bennin, K.E.: Investigating the significance of the Bellwether effect to improve software effort prediction: further empirical study. IEEE Trans. Reliab. 67(3), 1176–1198 (2018)

29. Chen, B., Ramakrishnan, R., Shavlik, J.W., Tamma, P.: Bellwether analysis: searching for cost-effective query-defined predictors in large databases. ACM Trans. Knowl. Discov. Data (TKDD), 3, 5 (2009)

30. Chen, B., Ramakrishnan, R., Shavlik, J.W., Tamma, P.: Bellwether analysis: predicting global aggregates from local regions. In: Proceedings of the 32nd International Conference on Very Large Databases, pp. 655–666 (2006)

31. Dobrovoljc, A., Trcek, D., Likar, B.: Predicting exploitations of information systems vulnerabilities through attackers characteristics. IEEE Access (2017)

32. https://www.exploit-db.com

33. Wang, J.A., Wang, H., Guo, M., Xia, M.: Security metrics for software systems. In: Proceedings of the 47th ACM Annual Southeast Regional Conference, p. 47 (2009)

34. Morrison, P.J., Pandita, R., Xiao, X., Chillarege, R., Williams, L.: Are vulnerabilities discovered and resolved like other defects? Empir. Softw. Eng. 23, 1383–1421 (2018)

35. Munaiah, N., Camilo, F., Wigham, W., Meneely, A., Nagappan, M.: Do bugs foreshadow vulnerabilities? An in-depth study of the chromium project. Empir. Softw. Eng., 22, 1305–1347 (2017)

36. Alhazmi, O.H., Woo, S.-W., Malaiya, Y.K.: Security vulnerability categories in major software systems. Commun. Netw. Inf. Secur., 138–143 (2006)

37. Fruhwirth, T.M.C.: Improving CVSS-based vulnerability prioritization and response with context information. In: Proceedings of the 3rd IEEE International Symposium on Empirical Software Engineering and Measurement, (IEEE Computer Society, 2009), pp. 535–544 (2009)

38. Morrison, P., Herzig, K. , Murphy, B., Williams, L.: Challenges with applying vulnerability prediction models. In: Proceedings of the 2015 Symposium and Bootcamp on the Science of Security, p. 4 (2015)

39. Chen, B.-C., Ramakrishnan, R., Shavlik, J.W., Tamma, P.: Bellwether analysis. ACM Trans. Knowl. Discov. Data 3(1), 1–49 (2009)

40. Rahimi, S., Zargham, M.: Vulnerability scrying method for software vulnerability discovery prediction. IEEE Trans. Reliab. 62, 395–407 (2013)

41. Younis, A.A., Malaiya, Y.K.: Using software structure to predict vulnerability exploitation potential. In: Proceedings of the Eighth IEEE International Conference on Software Security and Reliability-Companion (SERE-C), pp. 13–18 (2014)

42. Li, X., et al.: A mining approach to obtain the software vulnerability characteristics. In: Proceedings of the Fifth IEEE International Conference on Advanced Cloud and Big Data, vol. 1, pp. 2–7 (2017)
43. Pelleg, D., Moore, A.W.: X-means: extending k-means with efficient estimation of the number of clusters. In: Proceedings of the Seventeenth International Conference on Machine Learning, Table Contents, pp. 727–734 (2000)
44. Movahedi, Y., Cukier, M., Andongabo, A., Gashi, I.: Cluster-based vulnerability assessment applied to operating systems. In: Proceedings of the 13th European Dependable Computing Conference (2017)
45. Sui, Y.: Association rule mining and evaluation based on information security vulnerabilities main body. In: Applied Mechanics and Materials, pp. 1282–1285 (20140
46. Kumar, N., Srinathan, K.: Automatic keyphrase extraction from scientific documents using N-gram filtration technique. In: Proceedings of the Eighth ACM Symposium on Document Engineering, pp. 199–208 (2008)
47. N-gram and Fast Pattern Extraction Algorithm. https://www.codeproject.com
48. Corbin, J., Strauss, A.: Grounded theory research: procedures, canons and evaluative criteria. Zeitschrift für Soziologie **19**, 418–427 (1990)
49. Bavota, G., Russo, B.: A large-scale empirical study on self-admitted technical debt. In: Proceedings of the 13th IEEE/ACM Working Conference on Mining Software Repositories (MSR), IEEE 2016, pp. 315–326 (2016)
50. Mensah, S., Keung, J., Svajlenko, J., Bennin, K.E., Mi, Q.: On the value of a prioritization scheme for resolving Self-admitted technical debt. J. Syst. Softw. **135**, 37–54 (2018)
51. Deep learning in neural networks: an overview: J. Schmidhuber. Neural Netw. **61**, 85–117 (2015)
52. Zhang, N., Shetty, D.: An effective LS-SVM-based approach for surface roughness prediction in machined surfaces. Neurocomputing **189**, 35–39 (2016)
53. Zhang, S., Ou, X., Caragea, D.: Predicting cyber risks through national vulnerability database. Inf. Secur. J. Glob. Perspect. **24**, 194–206 (2015)
54. Kitchenham, B., et al.: Robust statistical methods for empirical software engineering. Empir. Softw. Eng. **22**, 579–630 (2017)
55. Kampenes, V.B., Dybå, T., Hannay, J.E., Sjøberg, D.I.K.: A systematic review of effect size in software engineering experiments. Inf. Softw. Technol. **49**(11–12), 1073–1086 (2007)
56. Romano, D., Raila, P., Pinzger, M., Khomh, F.: Analyzing the impact of antipatterns on change-proneness using fine-grained source code changes. In: Proceedings - Working Conference on Reverse Engineering, WCRE, pp. 437–446 (2012)
57. Menzies, T., Yang, Y., Mathew, G., Boehm, B., Hihn, J.: Negative results for software effort estimation. Empir. Softw. Eng. **25**(5), 2658–2683 (2017)
58. Han, Z., Li, X., Xing, Z., Liu, H., Feng, Z.: Learning to predict severity of software vulnerability using only vulnerability description. In: IEEE International Conference on Software Maintenance and Evolution (ICSME), pp. 125–136 (2017)

Author Index

Printed in the United States
By Bookmasters